VICTORIA
THE QUEEN

VICTORIA
THE QUEEN

AN INTIMATE BIOGRAPHY
OF THE WOMAN
WHO RULED AN EMPIRE

JULIA BAIRD

BLACKFRIARS

BLACKFRIARS

First published in the United States in 2016 by Random House
First published in Great Britain in 2016 by Blackfriars

1 3 5 7 9 10 8 6 4 2

Book design by Dana Leigh Blanchette
Printed and bound in Great Britain by
Clays Ltd, St Ives plc

Papers used by Blackfriars are from well-managed forests
and other responsible sources.

MIX
Paper from
responsible sources
FSC® C104740

Blackfriars
An imprint of
Little, Brown Book Group
Carmelite House
50 Victoria Embankment
London EC4Y 0DZ

An Hachette UK Company
www.hachette.co.uk

www.littlebrown.co.uk

For Poppy and Sam,
my magical children

[Queen Victoria did not] belong to any conceivable category of monarchs or of women, she bore no resemblance to an aristocratic English lady, she bore no resemblance to a wealthy middle-class Englishwoman, nor to any typical Princess of a German court. . . . She reigned longer than the other three queens put together. Never in her life could she be confused with anyone else, nor will she be in history. Such expressions as "people like Queen Victoria," or "that sort of woman" could not be used about her. . . . For over sixty years she was simply without prefix or suffix "The Queen."

—ARTHUR PONSONBY

We are all on the look-out for signs of *illness* in the Queen; but . . . the vein of iron that runs thro' her most extraordinary character enables her to bear up to the last minute, like nobody else.

—LADY LYTTELTON

Contents

Part 1

PRINCESS VICTORIA: "POOR LITTLE VICTORY"

Part 2

THE TEENAGE QUEEN

Part 3

ALBERT: THE MAN SOME CALLED KING

Part 4

THE WIDOW OF WINDSOR

Part 5

Regina Imperatrix

Cast of Characters

PRINCE EDWARD, later **DUKE OF KENT** (1767–1820). The fourth son of George III, and father of Queen Victoria. He was strong and upright, a harsh disciplinarian as a military officer but a tender husband and father. After a controversial career as governor of Gibraltar and field marshal of the forces, Edward applied himself to producing an heir to the succession. He died, of pneumonia, only six days before his father, George III, and less than a year after the birth of a daughter, of whom he was enormously proud.

MARIE LOUISE VICTOIRE, DUCHESS OF KENT (1786–1861). The mother of Queen Victoria and of Feodora, princess of Hohenlohe-Langenburg. The Duke of Kent persuaded the widowed Victoire to marry him and move from Germany to England. The relationship of mother and daughter was tempestuous and septic; the estrangement that began in Victoria's teenage years was drawn into public view when she became queen. But they eventually reconciled, and when her mother died in 1861 Victoria was inconsolable.

GEORGE III (1738–1820). King of Great Britain (and then the United Kingdom) from 1760 to 1820, and grandfather of Victoria. Although he is the third-longest-serving monarch (behind Elizabeth II and Victoria) and led an upright, spartan life, George III is best known for his erratic, uncontrollable bouts of madness and for the loss of the colonies in the American Revolution. The specter of his insanity— and the possibility of its inheritance—would haunt Victoria (and arm her critics) for decades.

GEORGE IV (1762–1830). After serving as Prince Regent during George III's illness, Prince George Augustus Frederick became king on January 29, 1820. An extravagant, big-bellied man, George IV despised and persecuted his wife, Caroline of Brunswick, and lived instead with his mistress. His only child, Princess Charlotte, died giving birth. His relationship with his niece Victoria was at times strained, but he pleased her by giving her a donkey and staging Punch and Judy shows for her in his garden.

PRINCESS CHARLOTTE AUGUSTA OF WALES (1796–1817). The only child of George IV. She was much-loved and it was expected that she would be a great queen, but she died after a torturous labor, setting off a competition among her portly, middle-aged uncles to produce a legitimate heir to the throne. She also left behind a devastated widower, Victoria's dashing, ambitious, and kindly uncle Leopold.

WILLIAM IV (1765–1837). The third son of George III, and successor to his brother, George IV. He retired from the navy at age twenty-four and became king forty years later. By then, he had had ten illegitimate children with his mistress. He went on to marry the well-regarded Princess Adelaide of Saxe-Meiningen, but none of her babies survived infancy, which meant that when he died the crown passed directly to his niece Victoria.

ERNEST AUGUSTUS (1771–1851). The fifth son of George III became king of Hanover after Salic law barred his niece Victoria from succeeding to the Hanoverian crown. An extreme Tory, Ernest—also known as the Duke of Cumberland—was the subject of great fear and gossip due to his scarred face and reams of unproven rumors that he had bedded his sister, sexually harassed nuns, and murdered a valet.

PRINCE AUGUSTUS FREDERICK, later **DUKE OF SUSSEX** (1773–1843). The sixth son of George III. He disqualified himself from the succession by twice marrying women his father did not approve of, thereby contravening the Royal Marriages Act.

PRINCE ADOLPHUS, later **DUKE OF CAMBRIDGE** (1774–1850). The seventh son of King George III. He was also the grandfather of Mary of Teck (the wife and Queen Consort of George V) and the great-great-grandfather of Queen Elizabeth II.

VICTORIA'S HUSBAND AND CHILDREN

ALBERT OF SAXE-COBURG-GOTHA (1819–1861). Prince Consort to Queen Victoria. Born three months after Victoria at Castle Rosenau, near Coburg, Albert's childhood was marred by his parents' rather brutal marital breakdown. A polymathic, disciplined man, Albert aspired to greatness as well as moral goodness, and Victoria adored him. While clearly talented, he was a divisive figure: some called him "Albert the Good," but others dismissed him as "Albert der King"— a foreign interloper. He was universally feted for his brilliant staging of the Great Exhibition of 1851. His relentless hard work and poor health led to his early death in December 1861, at the age of forty-two.

PRINCESS VICTORIA ADELAIDE MARY LOUISE (1841–1901). The first child of Victoria and Albert. While she was a precociously clever child, once her brothers were born she would never be able to inherit the throne. At seventeen, she married the future emperor Frederick of Prussia. Her marriage was happy but her life in Germany was miserable; she felt alienated, misunderstood, and alone. Two of her sons died in childhood, and her eldest, Wilhelm, was deliberately cruel. Vicky and her mother confided in each other in vast reams of intimate letters for decades, and they died six months apart.

ALBERT EDWARD, PRINCE OF WALES, later **EDWARD VII** (1841–1910). The second child of Victoria, and first in line to the throne. The tempestuous, gregarious "Bertie" was never as clever as his older sister, and his parents judged him sorely for it. Victoria blamed him and his immoral escapades for the early death of his father and refused to allow him any serious responsibilities while she was alive. Despite his parent's reservations, Bertie would become an effective, well-liked king during his short reign. His son, George V, succeeded him.

PRINCESS ALICE MAUD MARY (1843–1878). Victoria's second daughter and third child. A rebellious child who was close to her older brother, Bertie, Alice's affectionate character was most obvious as she devotedly cared for her dying father, and then for her grieving mother. Her wedding to Prince Louis six months later was a grim occasion, and the marriage would be an unhappy one. While living in Darmstadt, she threw herself tirelessly into nursing, most notably during the Franco-Prussian War. She was only thirty-five when she died, from diphtheria, on December 14, 1878, exactly seventeen years after her father's death. She inherited the hemophilia gene from her mother and passed it on to several of her children, including Alexandra, the wife of Tsar Nicholas II, who would eventually employ Rasputin to heal her hemophilic son.

PRINCE ALFRED ERNEST ALBERT (1844–1900). The second son of Victoria and Albert, "Affie" would become the ruler of the tiny province of Saxe-Coburg-Gotha in Germany. A competent naval officer (though his long absences at sea would frustrate the queen), Affie had to abandon his naval career when he became the Duke of Coburg. He was a conscientious ruler, but his unhappy marriage and his son's suicide plunged him into a spiral of alcoholism. He died in July 1900, six months before his mother.

PRINCESS HELENA AUGUSTA VICTORIA (1846–1923). The third daughter and fifth child of Victoria, "Lenchen" married the unprepossessing Prince Frederick Christian of Schleswig-Holstein-Sonderburg-Augustenburg and had four children with him. An admirer of Florence Nightingale's, Helena became the president of the Royal British Nurses' Association in 1889. She lived near her mother but largely escaped the extremes of Victoria's maternal control as she carried out Victoria's secretarial work while also acting as a patron of several charities.

PRINCESS LOUISE CAROLINE ALBERTA (1848–1939). Born during a year of revolution, Louise would always be seen as untamed and capricious. She became a talented sculptor and indulged in indiscreet behavior, notably with her tutor, Joseph Edgar Boehm. The beautiful Louise married the Marquess of Lorne, who proved an unsatisfactory if companionate husband. Despite the disapproval of her mother, who was surprised by the bluestocking bent of some of her daughters, Louise encouraged the establishment of the National Union for the Higher Education of Women and served as its first president. She died at the outbreak of World War II, aged ninety-one.

PRINCE ARTHUR WILLIAM PATRICK ALBERT (1850–1942). Victoria's third son and seventh child. During four decades of military service, Arthur would become commander in chief of several armies. Perhaps sensibly, he acquiesced to his mother's choice of bride, a Prussian princess, and was rewarded with a happy marriage (at least by royal standards). On the death of his elder brother Affie, Arthur became the heir of the duchy of Saxe-Coburg-Gotha, but his intention of ruling as an absentee, from Britain, prompted the German emperor to select another candidate. Thus Arthur narrowly avoided fighting his own family in World War I.

PRINCE LEOPOLD GEORGE DUNCAN ALBERT (1853–1884). Victoria's fourth son and eighth child, and the first child she birthed with the aid of chloroform. An intellectual with strong conservative political views, Leopold's life was blighted by hemophilia. His protective mother and doctors prevented him from engaging in normal activities. Nevertheless, he attended Oxford, sat in the House of Lords as the Duke of Albany, married Princess Helena of Waldeck and Pyrmont, and became father to a daughter. Leopold died a few days before his thirty-first birthday in 1884, before the birth of his only son.

PRINCESS BEATRICE MARY VICTORIA FEODORE (1857–1944). Victoria's ninth and youngest child was also her most adored. Beatrice would be her mother's most constant companion after the death of Albert, though she had a brief respite from this frequently suffocating role when she married Prince Henry of Battenberg. Despite Victoria's reservations, "Liko" would prove to be a model son-in-law until his death in 1895. As an executor of Victoria's will, Beatrice spent years rewriting and destroying the queen's original journals and burning many of her letters, a grievous act of censorship.

VICTORIA'S GRANDCHILDREN

WILHELM II (1859–1941). Emperor of Germany, son of Princess Vicky, and first grandchild of Queen Victoria. Wilhelm's birth was breech, and traumatic; his arm was born twisted and useless, and he would spend the rest of his life concealing it and compensating for it. He loathed his mother and was a brute to her. He ostensibly adored his grandmother, but his aggressive ambition for his country made relations competitive and then hostile. As emperor, he would declare war on his British cousin George V.

GEORGE V (1865–1936). The second son of Bertie and grandson of Victoria, George V reigned from 1910 to 1936, his older brother, Eddy, having died unexpectedly in 1892. (George also married his brother's bride-to-be, Mary of Teck.)

MEMBERS OF THE ROYAL HOUSEHOLD

BARONESS LOUISE LEHZEN (1784–1870). Victoria's German governess and later lady of the bedchamber. Throughout Victoria's childhood, Lehzen was staunchly supportive, training her charge to be strong and defending her against critics and bullies. The queen relied heavily on Lehzen for guidance, a situation Albert would find intolerable. After a series of fights, Albert told the baroness to retire quietly to Germany; she packed her bags and left one morning as Victoria was still sleeping.

SIR JOHN CONROY (1786–1854). First as an equerry to the Duke of Kent, then as an adviser to his widow, Conroy manipulated his way into the heart of Victoria's family. Conroy was bent on acquiring personal power and tried to force Victoria to agree to make him her private secretary when she became queen. Victoria despised him and would never forgive his severe treatment; she banished him once she became queen.

LADY FLORA HASTINGS (1806–1839). A lady of the bedchamber and later lady-in-waiting to the Duchess of Kent. When Lady Flora developed an abdominal swelling, her court rivals gossiped that Sir John Conroy had impregnated her. Wanting to believe the worst, and buoyed by Sir James Clark's medical incompetence, Victoria did nothing to stop the rumors. When Lady Flora died after a long and painful illness, the young queen was booed in public and openly attacked in the press.

SIR JAMES CLARK (1788–1870). The queen's personal physician from 1837 to 1860. His long career in the royal household owed more to his diplomacy than to sophisticated medical ability. His demonstrated capacity for misdiagnosis and a desire to please the queen drew the court into a spectacular scandal in the case of Lady Flora Hastings.

BARON VON STOCKMAR (1787–1863). Trained as a doctor, he became a statesman and the unofficial diplomat of the royal household as secretary to Uncle Leopold, close adviser to Prince Albert, and nemesis of Baroness Lehzen.

LADY LYTTLETON (1787–1870). One of Victoria's ladies of the bedchamber and later lady superintendent—or manager—of the royal nursery. She was an astute observer of royal life who marveled at Victoria's innate "vein of iron."

LADY JANE CHURCHILL (1826–1900). A lady of the bedchamber from 1854 until her death in 1900, Lady Churchill often acted as the queen's intermediary. She would inform people of the queen's displeasure if they breached etiquette—being late for functions, for example, or laughing too loudly over dinner. She also read to the queen from novels written by the likes of Jane Austen and George Eliot. Lady Churchill loyally served Victoria for almost half a century, dying just a month before her queen. As she left behind no journals or memoirs, her discretion has remained impeccable.

GEORGE EDWARD ANSON (1812–1849). Prince Albert's private secretary and one of his most trusted advisers. Anson proved to be indispensable and frequently acted as a mediator between the often fractious royal couple. Albert was crushed by his sudden, early death.

SIR HOWARD ELPHINSTONE (1829–1890). A Crimean War veteran and recipient of the Victoria Cross, in 1859 Elphinstone was appointed as governor to Prince Arthur, and later to Prince Leopold.

SIR CHARLES PHIPPS (1801–1866). Keeper of the queen's Privy Purse and treasurer to the Prince of Wales. He was knighted in 1858 and was a member of the trusted inner circle present at Albert's deathbed.

GENERAL CHARLES GREY (1804–1870). A military officer and politician, and the queen's private secretary in the years immediately following the death of Albert. Much of his time was spent making excuses for Victoria's failure to appear in public.

SIR HENRY PONSONBY (1825–1895). The queen's loyal, insightful, and wryly funny private secretary. He served for thirty-eight years and was rewarded with a knighthood in 1879.

SIR ARTHUR BIGGE (1849–1931). He became the queen's private secretary in 1895 and was knighted in the same year. After the death of Victoria, Bigge served both Edward VII and George V, and was made a member of the House of Lords in 1911.

JOHN BROWN (1826–1883). A Highlander who was hired to work as a ghillie, or outdoor attendant, for Albert at Balmoral. He was summoned to England to help Victoria when she was mourning her husband. She quickly came to rely on him, and an intense relationship ensued, one that would become the subject of enduring scandal. Victoria's children loathed him, calling him "the Queen's Stallion."

When Victoria was buried, Brown's mother's wedding ring was on her hand. After Victoria's death, Edward VII burned any potentially compromising letters.

ABDUL KARIM (1862 or 1863–1909). The queen's Indian secretary and "munshi," or clerk. Karim's rapid rise in the royal household from servant to trusted adviser caused much resentment in the royal household, particularly among the queen's children, but Victoria was blind to his pretension and deceit. Following the queen's death, King Edward ordered a bonfire of the munshi's papers, so we can only speculate as to the true extent of his influence.

SIR JAMES REID (1849–1923). The queen's favorite personal physician. He attended to John Brown during his fatal illness in 1883 and delivered all four of Princess Beatrice's children. Reid's discretion, skill, and reliability made him indispensable to the queen. Reid was the one the queen entrusted with her final requests for burial. She died in his arms.

OTHER ROYALS

FEODORA, PRINCESS OF HOHENLOHE-LANGENBURG (1807–1872). Queen Victoria's much-loved half-sister, Feodora, was the Duchess of Kent's daughter by her first husband. When Victoria was just eight, the fetching Feodora married and moved to Germany. The half-sisters wrote to each other religiously for decades; Victoria was wretched when Feodora died in 1872.

LEOPOLD I, KING OF THE BELGIANS (1790–1865). Victoria's beloved uncle and widower of Princess Charlotte. Intent on betrothing Albert and Victoria from the time they were small children, Leopold was like a father to Victoria; he provided a stream of advice and took interest in her education, health, spiritual development, and marriage.

LEOPOLD II, KING OF THE BELGIANS (1835–1909). The son of Leopold I. His rule in the Congo was characterized by ruthless, barbaric exploitation and mass murder.

LOUIS PHILIPPE, KING OF FRANCE (1773–1850). Forced to abdicate after the revolution of 1848, Louis Philippe was exiled to Great Britain and lived at Claremont in Surrey. His daughter, Prince Louise-Marie, was the second wife of Victoria's uncle Leopold.

VICTORIA'S CONTEMPORARIES

THOMAS CARLYLE (1795–1881). A cantankerous but celebrated Scottish author and historian, Carlyle provided many eyewitness accounts of events during Victoria's lifetime.

CHARLES DICKENS (1812–1870). Dickens had no great reverence for the monarchy; he thought himself a greater celebrity than his sovereign and tried to avoid her. It was Victoria who greatly admired him and devoured his tales of the London underworld. The two did not meet until 1870, just three months before his death. She described him as "very agreeable, with a pleasant voice & manner."

FLORENCE NIGHTINGALE (1820–1910). A brilliant nurse who revolutionized medical care in the military, most notably in the Crimean War. She inspired generations of women, including the queen and her daughters Alice, Vicky, and Helena. Despite her own ill heath, Nightingale continued to lobby for structural and cultural change in hospital and health management. She was the first woman to be awarded an Order of the British Empire, in 1907.

ALFRED, LORD TENNYSON (1809–1892). The brilliant poet laureate, who lived near the queen on the Isle of Wight, became a confidant during her period of mourning, when his poems provided great comfort. He was awarded a peerage in 1883.

Prime Ministers

LORD MELBOURNE (1779–1848). The young queen's first and most completely trusted prime minister. Having endured a chaotic and painful personal life, Melbourne grew as attached to the eighteen-year-old monarch as she was to him. When his government eventually fell, Victoria was distraught. Later in life, she would be embarrassed by the intensity of her feelings for her first PM.

SIR ROBERT PEEL (1788–1850). Prime minister after the fall of Lord Melbourne's government. At first, Victoria resented him for ousting Melbourne and was irritated by his social reserve. But her respect grew as she witnessed his competence and willingness to fight for his beliefs despite personal cost. Although a conservative Tory, Peel was intent on reform and successfully repealed the unpopular, protectionist Corn Laws, making him a hated figure in his own party. Albert came to think of him as a father.

LORD RUSSELL (1792–1878). A liberal reformer and two-time prime minister. He was the architect of the 1832 Reform Act, a point to which some peg the beginning of the decline of the direct power of the monarchy. His great failure was his inability to come to the aid of the Irish during the famine of the late 1840s, poisoning relations with the impoverished country for decades to come.

LORD PALMERSTON (1784–1865). Foreign secretary and prime minister. Palmerston was initially popular with both Victoria and Albert, but later they clashed with him repeatedly over his liberal interventionist foreign policy and what they saw as an insulting lack of consultation. Victoria repeatedly called for his firing.

LORD DERBY (1799–1869). Derby served as prime minister three times, albeit in short-lived minority governments, and was leader of the Conservative Party for a record twenty-two years. Possibly his greatest achievement was ensuring the passage of the Second Reform Bill through Parliament in 1867, thereby doubling the size of the electorate and enfranchising large swathes of the middle class.

BENJAMIN DISRAELI (1804–1881). First Earl of Beaconsfield, flamboyant novelist, Conservative politician, and two-time prime minister. While he was a practicing Anglican, he was the first—and only—British PM to have been born Jewish. Disraeli's respectful flattery, facility with language, and entertaining anecdotes charmed Victoria. A skilled diplomat, Disraeli also pursued an aggressive foreign policy and pushed progressive legislation through Parliament.

SIR WILLIAM GLADSTONE (1809–1898). A Liberal leader and four-time prime minister, Gladstone was known as the Grand Old Man of British politics. He was a deeply religious man who retreated to his country estate to chop down trees for months at a stretch and had a curious obsession with rescuing "ladies of the night" from prostitution. Despite his obvious seriousness about governing, Gladstone never earned the respect of Queen Victoria. She would devote considerable energy to trying to prevent him from becoming PM.

EARL OF ROSEBERY (1847–1929). A reluctant Liberal prime minister who was coerced by Victoria into assuming the premiership instead of Gladstone. He held it for little more than a year.

LORD SALISBURY (1830–1903). Victoria's last prime minister, Salisbury served for three terms and joined her in vehement opposition to Irish Home Rule and its chief proponent, Gladstone. She would grow very fond of his genteel, respectful ways. A keen imperialist, Salisbury advocated a policy of "splendid isolation," eschewing the idea of forging alliances with other powers.

OTHER FIGURES

MADAME ALPHONSINE-THÉRÈSE-BERNARDINE-JULIE DE MONT-GENÊT DE SAINT-LAURENT (1760–1830). Often referred to as "Julie," she was the lover of the Duke of Kent for three decades before he married Victoria's mother.

ALEXANDRA OF DENMARK, PRINCESS OF WALES, later QUEEN ALEXANDRA OF GREAT BRITAIN (1844–1925). The wife of Bertie, "Alix" was elegant, kind, and forbearing. Although Alix's Danish heritage was something of an inconvenience, mostly due to the knotty, complicated Schleswig-Holstein question, Victoria often said she preferred her daughter-in-law to her own daughters. The British people adored Alix, too—while raising eyebrows at her husband's bacchanalian ways.

SIR JOSEPH PAXTON (1803–1864). A landscape gardener and architect who was responsible for the soaring design of the Crystal Palace for the Great Exhibition of 1851.

SIR JOSEPH EDGAR BOEHM (1834–1890). A distinguished Viennese sculptor to whom the queen gave more than forty royal commissions. Boehm was particularly close to Princess Louise, whom he tutored in the art of sculpture. Princess Louise was present when Boehm died suddenly in his studio; it was surmised that he had expired in the throes of vigorous sexual activity, speculation later further fueled by the destruction of Boehm's papers.

GENERAL CHARLES GORDON (1833–1885). An eccentric military hero much admired by Queen Victoria. In 1883, Gordon was sent on a mission to withdraw British and Egyptian troops from the Sudan after a local coup. Instead, Gordon dug in and a siege began. The reluctance of Gladstone to send reinforcements enraged Victoria and prompted public disgust. Gordon's subsequent murder was blamed on Gladstone's indecision. The queen never forgave Gladstone for this.

ARTHUR BENSON (1862–1925) and **LORD ESHER** (1852–1930). Two old Etonians who took upon themselves the monumental task of editing Queen Victoria's letters, a collection comprising more than 460 volumes of documents. Although they happily brought much of her writing out of the secretive, closeted archives and into public view, by expunging compromising episodes and anything they thought boring or trivial, such as motherhood, the two men warped our view of Queen Victoria for decades.

Compiled with assistance from Catherine Pope

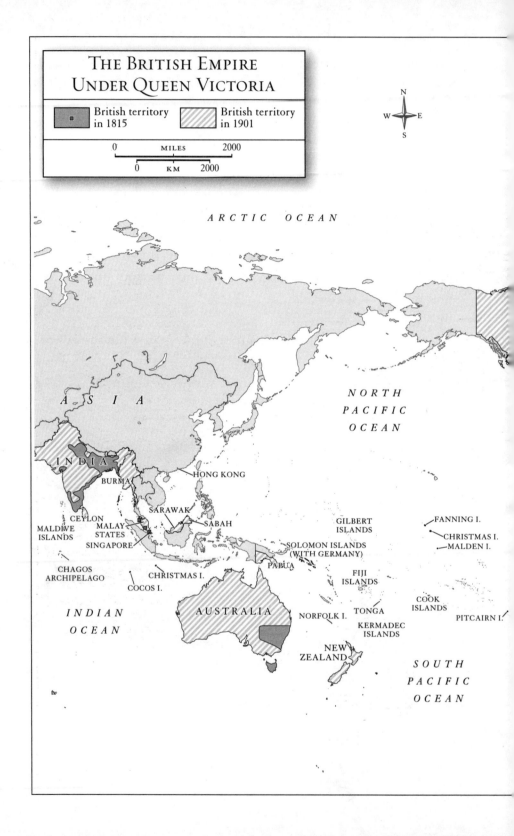

THE BRITISH EMPIRE UNDER QUEEN VICTORIA

British territory in 1815
British territory in 1901

MILES
0   2000

KM
0   2000

N
W   E
S

ARCTIC   OCEAN

ASIA

NORTH
PACIFIC
OCEAN

INDIA
BURMA
HONG KONG
CEYLON
MALDIVE
ISLANDS
MALAY
STATES
SARAWAK
SABAH
SINGAPORE
GILBERT
ISLANDS
FANNING I.
CHRISTMAS I.
MALDEN I.
CHAGOS
ARCHIPELAGO
CHRISTMAS I.
COCOS I.
SOLOMON ISLANDS
(WITH GERMANY)
PABUA
FIJI
ISLANDS
INDIAN
OCEAN
AUSTRALIA
NORFOLK I.
TONGA
COOK
ISLANDS
PITCAIRN I.
KERMADEC
ISLANDS
NEW
ZEALAND
SOUTH
PACIFIC
OCEAN

ARCTIC OCEAN

CANADA

UNITED KINGDOM
IRELAND
BRITAIN

EUROPE

NORTH
ATLANTIC
OCEAN

BERMUDA

IONIAN
ISLANDS
MALTA
CYPRUS

EGYPT

ANTIGUA
DOMINICA
ST. LUCIA
BARBADOS
TRINIDAD
BRITISH
GUIANA

BAHAMAS

JAMAICA

BRITISH
HONDURAS

AFRICA

GAMBIA

GOLD
COAST

NIGERIA

SUDAN

BRITISH
SOMALILAND

SIERRA
LEONE

UGANDA
PROT.

EAST-AFRICA
PROT.

SEYCHELLES

ASCENSION I.

ST. HELENA I.

RHODESIA

RODRIGUES
I.

EASTER I.

SOUTH
ATLANTIC
OCEAN

BECHUANA-
LAND

MAURITIUS

TRANSVAAL

NATAL
SWAZILAND

ORANGE-
FREE STATE

CAPE
COLONY

TRISTAN DA
CUNHA

FALKLAND
ISLANDS

SOUTH GEORGIA

SOUTH ORKNEY
ISLANDS

VICTORIA'S
ROYAL RESIDENCES

0   MILES   100

0   KM   100

SCOTLAND

BALMORAL
CASTLE

•Aberdeen

Braemar•

Perth•

Glasgow•   •Edinburgh

N
W   E
S

NORTH SEA

IRELAND

ENGLAND

IRISH SEA

Liverpool•

WALES

KENSINGTON
PALACE

•London

WINDSOR
CASTLE

BUCKINGHAM
PALACE

Southampton•

Isle of Wight

FRANCE

OSBORNE
HOUSE

English Channel

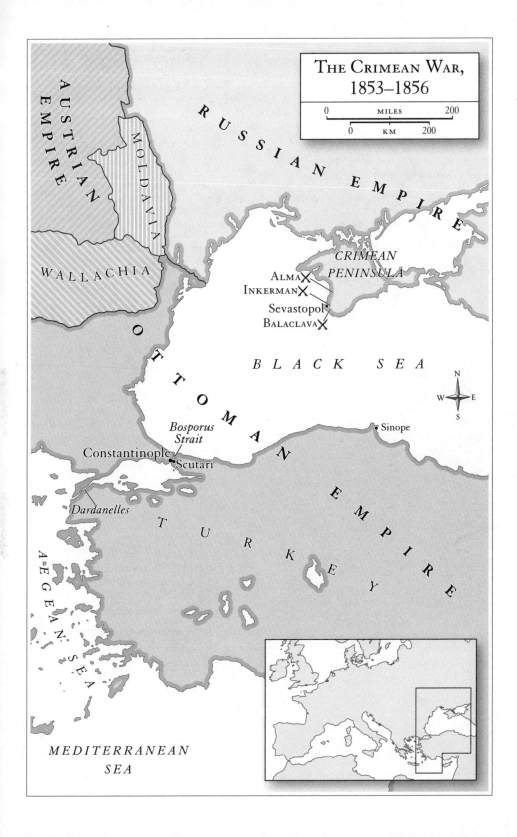

THE CRIMEAN WAR,
1853–1856

0 MILES 200

0 KM 200

AUSTRIAN
EMPIRE

MOLDAVIA

WALLACHIA

RUSSIAN EMPIRE

CRIMEAN
PENINSULA

ALMA ✕
INKERMAN ✕
Sevastopol •
BALACLAVA ✕

BLACK   SEA

N
W ✦ E
S

O T T O M A N   E M P I R E

Bosporus
Strait

• Sinope

Constantinople
Scutari

Dardanelles

T U R K E Y

A E G E A N   S E A

MEDITERRANEAN
SEA

NORTH SEA

DENMARK

SWEDEN

BALTIC SEA

SCHLESWIG

OLDENBURG

HOLSTEIN

Hamburg

MECKLENBURG-
SCHWERIN

POMERANIA

Danzig

WEST
PRUSSIA

EAST
PRUSSIA

Bremen

HANOVER

BRANDENBURG

Berlin

Warsaw

RUSSIAN
EMPIRE

NETHERLANDS

WEST-
PHALIA

Cologne

BELGIUM

RHINE PROV.

Dresden

SAXONY

SILESIA

Coburg

Frankfurt

Prague

BOHEMIA

Krakow

FRANCE

Nuremberg

MORAVIA

Stuttgart

BAVARIA

BADEN

WÜRTTEM-
BERG

Munich

Vienna

AUSTRIAN EMPIRE

HUNGARY

NEUCHATEL
(Prussia)

Budapest

SWITZERLAND

GERMAN UNIFICATION:

GERMANY, 1815

KINGDOM
OF
SARDINIA

Milan

Venice

Prussian territory

Boundary of German
Confederation in 1815

N
W   E
S

0   MILES   200

0   KM   200

TUSCANY
(Austria)

NORTH SEA

DENMARK

SWEDEN

BALTIC SEA

OLDENBURG

SCHLESWIG-
HOLSTEIN

Hamburg

Bremen

MECKLENBURG-
SCHWERIN

POMERANIA

Danzig
WEST
PRUSSIA

EAST
PRUSSIA

NETHERLANDS

HANOVER

BRANDENBURG

Berlin

Warsaw

RUSSIAN
EMPIRE

BELGIUM

WEST-
PHALIA

RHINE PROV.

Cologne

Dresden

SAXONY

SILESIA

Krakow

Coburg

Frankfurt

LORRAINE

Nuremberg

Prague

BOHEMIA

MORAVIA

FRANCE

ALSACE

BADEN

Stuttgart
WÜRTTEM-
BERG

BAVARIA

Munich

Vienna

AUSTRIAN EMPIRE

HUNGARY

SWITZERLAND

Budapest

ITALY

N
W E
S

GERMAN UNIFICATION:
Germany, 1871

	Prussian territory
	Boundary of German Empire in 1871

0   MILES   200

0   KM   200

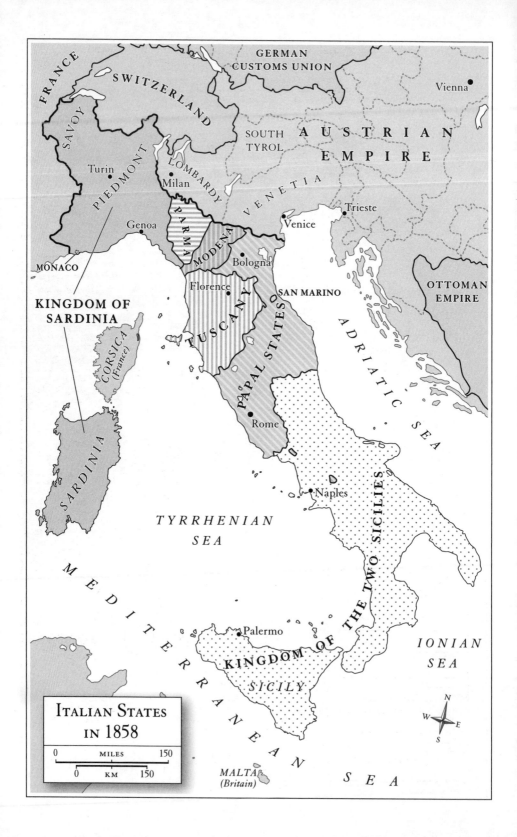

FRANCE

SWITZERLAND

GERMAN
CUSTOMS UNION

Vienna

SAVOY

PIEDMONT

Turin

LOMBARDY

Milan

SOUTH
TYROL

AUSTRIAN
EMPIRE

VENETIA

Venice

Trieste

OTTOMAN
EMPIRE

Genoa

PARMA

MODENA

Bologna

MONACO

**KINGDOM OF
SARDINIA**

CORSICA
(France)

Florence

TUSCANY

SAN MARINO

PAPAL STATES

ADRIATIC SEA

Rome

SARDINIA

TYRRHENIAN
SEA

Naples

KINGDOM OF THE TWO SICILIES

M
E
D
I
T
E
R
R
A
N
E
A
N

S
E
A

Palermo

IONIAN
SEA

KINGDOM OF THE TWO SICILIES

SICILY

N
W   E
S

ITALIAN STATES
IN 1858

0   MILES   150

0   KM   150

MALTA
(Britain)

FRANCE

SWITZERLAND

GERMAN
CUSTOMS UNION

Vienna

AUSTRIAN
EMPIRE

SAVOY

PIEDMONT

Turin

CEDED
TO FRANCE
IN 1859

1858

SOUTH
TYROL

LOMBARDY
1859
Milan

PARMA
1860

MODENA

VENETIA
1866

Venice

Trieste

Genoa

MONACO

KINGDOM
OF SARDINIA

CORSICA
(France)

SARDINIA
1858

1860
Bologna

Florence

TUSCANY
1860

PAPAL STATES

SAN MARINO

1860

Rome
1870

ADRIATIC
SEA

OTTOMAN
EMPIRE

1860

Naples

N

W   E

S

TYRRHENIAN
SEA

KINGDOM OF THE TWO SICILIES

IONIAN
SEA

ITALIAN
UNIFICATION
1859–1870

Kingdom of
Sardinia in 1858

Gained in 1859–60

Conquered by
Garibaldi in 1860

Gained in 1866

Gained in 1870

Palermo

SICILY
1860

0   MILES   150

0   KM   150

MALTA
(Britain)

MEDITERRANEAN   SEA

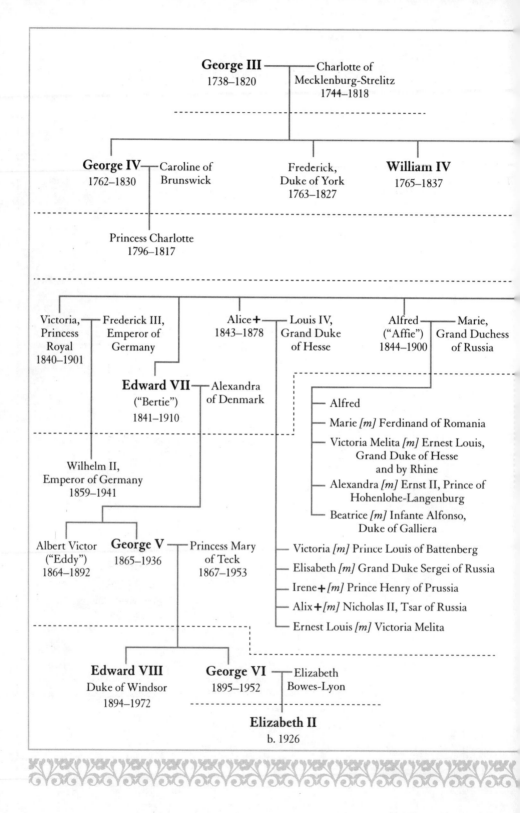

George III ———— Charlotte of
1738–1820   Mecklenburg-Strelitz
                1744–1818

George IV—Caroline of   Frederick,   **William IV**
1762–1830   Brunswick   Duke of York   1765–1837
                       1763–1827

Princess Charlotte
1796–1817

Victoria,—Frederick III,   Alice✚—Louis IV,   Alfred———Marie,
Princess   Emperor of   1843–1878   Grand Duke   ("Affie")   Grand Duchess
Royal   Germany   of Hesse   1844–1900   of Russia
1840–1901

Edward VII—Alexandra
    ("Bertie")   of Denmark   — Alfred
    1841–1910   — Marie *[m]* Ferdinand of Romania

                            — Victoria Melita *[m]* Ernest Louis,
                                 Grand Duke of Hesse
Wilhelm II,   and by Rhine
Emperor of Germany   — Alexandra *[m]* Ernst II, Prince of
1859–1941   Hohenlohe-Langenburg

                            — Beatrice *[m]* Infante Alfonso,
                                 Duke of Galliera

Albert Victor   **George V**—Princess Mary — Victoria *[m]* Prince Louis of Battenberg
("Eddy")   1865–1936   of Teck   — Elisabeth *[m]* Grand Duke Sergei of Russia
1864–1892   1867–1953   — Irene✚ *[m]* Prince Henry of Prussia
                          — Alix✚ *[m]* Nicholas II, Tsar of Russia
                          — Ernest Louis *[m]* Victoria Melita

Edward VIII   **George VI**—Elizabeth
Duke of Windsor   1895–1952   Bowes-Lyon
1894–1972

Elizabeth II
b. 1926

FAMILY TREE OF QUEEN VICTORIA

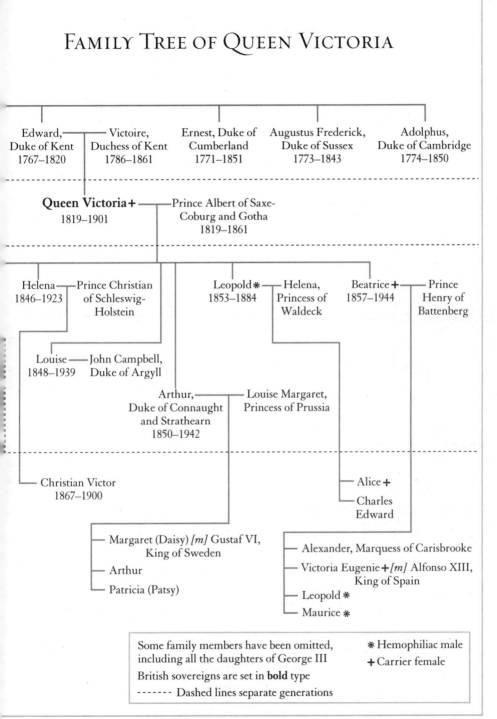

Edward, Duke of Kent 1767–1820 — Victoire, Duchess of Kent 1786–1861

Ernest, Duke of Cumberland 1771–1851

Augustus Frederick, Duke of Sussex 1773–1843

Adolphus, Duke of Cambridge 1774–1850

Queen Victoria+ 1819–1901 — Prince Albert of Saxe-Coburg and Gotha 1819–1861

Helena 1846–1923 — Prince Christian of Schleswig-Holstein

Leopold✶ 1853–1884 — Helena, Princess of Waldeck

Beatrice+ 1857–1944 — Prince Henry of Battenberg

Louise 1848–1939 — John Campbell, Duke of Argyll

Arthur, Duke of Connaught and Strathearn 1850–1942 — Louise Margaret, Princess of Prussia

— Christian Victor 1867–1900

— Alice+
— Charles Edward

— Margaret (Daisy) [m] Gustaf VI, King of Sweden
— Arthur
— Patricia (Patsy)

— Alexander, Marquess of Carisbrooke
— Victoria Eugenie+[m] Alfonso XIII, King of Spain
— Leopold ✶
— Maurice ✶

Some family members have been omitted, including all the daughters of George III

British sovereigns are set in **bold** type

------ Dashed lines separate generations

✶ Hemophiliac male
+ Carrier female

Introduction

One feels that the Queen is a woman to live and die for.

—EMILY TENNYSON

Such a little vixen.

—REV. ARCHER CLIVE

She was ready.

But when Victoria first sat on the throne, her feet did not touch the floor. Below the soaring arches of Westminster Abbey she was a mere dot, burning under the curious gaze of the gathered crowd, trying not to dangle her legs. Thousands thronged the streets of London before sunrise, hoping to claim a vantage point from which to glimpse Britain's new queen, who was just eighteen years of age and less than five feet tall. The previous kings had been profligates, philanderers, opium-addled, or mad; now the country was infatuated with "the fair white rose of perfect womanhood," their new ruler, the tiny teenager who was sitting uncomfortably in a large abbey festooned with gold drapes and exotic carpets as diamond-laden aristocrats stared at her.

Victoria's head ached under a heavy crown, and her hand throbbed—the ruby coronation ring had been jammed onto the wrong finger; it was later, painfully, removed with ice. Around her stood her older male advisers, in a state of disrepair. Her prime minister was half-stoned with opium and brandy, ostensibly taken to calm his stomach, and he viewed the entire ceremony in a fog. Her archbishop, having failed to rehearse, jumbled his lines. One of her lords tumbled down the steps when he approached to kiss her hand. But Victoria's composure was impeccable. Her voice was cool, silvery, and steady. Once, the thought of becoming queen had terrified her, but as she grew, she had longed to work, to be independent, and to have some control over her life. And what she dreamed of most of all was sleeping alone, in her own room, and escaping her mother's suffocating hands. Most teenagers are given an allowance; she was given a kingdom.

Few would have bet Victoria would become queen of the British Isles. Her father, after all, was not the first son of a king, but the fourth. It was, as so often with inherited power, due only to a series of tragedies—the deaths of family, including infants, a woman giving birth, and two corpulent uncles—as well as luck—her soldier father avoiding being murdered by mutinous troops and somehow persuading her mother to marry a middle-aged, almost bankrupt prince—that on June 20, 1837, the destiny of a nation wheeled, spun, and came to rest on the small frame of an eighteen-year-old girl. A girl who read Charles Dickens, worried about the welfare of Gypsies, adored animals, loved to sing opera, was fascinated with lion tamers, and hated insects and turtle soup; a girl who was bullied by those closest to her until her determination set like concrete; a girl whose heart was wound tight with cords of sentiment and stoicism.

It had not been simple. Before she reached the age of one, Victoria lost her father. Before she turned eighteen, she had become estranged from her mother. Many times the Crown almost slipped from her grasp; others had tried to wrest it from her for years. She had needed to draw on the innate iron vein in her character and cultivate a stubborn strength. But the toddler who stamped her feet, the child who slammed piano lids, and the teenager who stared down tormentors was now queen. The first thing she did when she got home from her coronation was to give her dog a warm, sudsy bath, laughing as he flicked soap onto her face and clothes.

We forget, now, how long Victoria ruled alone. She may have married Albert only a couple of years after she was crowned, but following his death, she ruled for thirty-nine years on her own. Yet we know little about this period. This is largely because of the enormous, enduring spectacle of her grief. To walk the streets of London today is to be reminded that Victoria mourned loudly and for a long time. It is clear to anyone, then and now, that she loved her German husband with a particular intensity: a sudden love that took her by surprise and lasted until her death. Two decades after Albert died, she was still erecting memorials—in Hyde Park his muscular statue juts into the sky, with strong golden thighs, surrounded by angels and the Virtues, looking godlike. Victoria never fully recovered, and when she later found happiness in the company of another man, she guiltily consulted a priest.

Yet the great volume of Victoria's grief meant that a myth sprang up almost immediately, which many still believe today: that she stopped ruling when Albert died, and that she had abdicated almost all of her authority and power to her clever husband when he was alive. When she was crowned, people were amazed that Victoria could think clearly and speak without stumbling; when she married, they were convinced she had deferred all major decisions to Albert; and when he died, she was castigated as a remote, grieving widow. All this is wrong. Queen Victoria was a decisive ruler who complained of the weight of her work while simultaneously bossing prime ministers about daily, if not hourly. "The Queen alone," said Prime Minister Gladstone, "is enough to kill any man." Yet our generation, almost as much as the Victorian, seems to fail to understand how such a woman could wield power ably and with relish. Part of the reason for this failure is the sheer difficulty of digging through the mass of legend and hyperbole to reach the real Victoria.

To properly understand this task, we must fly back to May 10, 1943, when the Second World War was raging. On this day, Adolf Hitler extended his dictatorship indefinitely, American troops were preparing to oust Japan from islands in Alaska, and Winston Churchill was arriving in Washington for a critical meeting with Franklin D. Roosevelt, a day before the Axis powers surrendered to the Allies in North Africa. Eighty-six-year-old Beatrice, Victoria's daughter, sat down in her home in Sussex, England, trembling. Decades earlier, she had been charged with the unfortunate task of editing the queen's voluminous diaries. She did this over ten years, writing them out in her own hand into blue copybooks and burning the originals, in one of the greatest acts of historical censorship of the century. Now she was an elderly woman who was occupying herself with translating her family archives as a distraction from the "anxieties" of war. That day, she pulled out a sheet of stationery to write a beseeching letter—never before published—to her great-nephew, King George VI, the father of Queen Elizabeth II. The most recent batch of archives had appalled her. Addressing him as "Bertie," she wrote:

> I have now received from the Librarian a book with short letters from my Father to my Mother, both in English & German, but of such an intimate nature, dealing with little personal momentary squabbles, which I cannot possibly undertake or deal with. There were also jottings about my mother's various confinements. These papers are of no historical or biographical value whatever, & if pried into could only be misconstrued to damage her memory. You may not know that I was left my Mother's library executor, & as such, I feel I must appeal to [you to] grant me the permission to destroy any painful letters. I am

her last surviving child & feel I have a sacred duty to protect her memory. How these letters can ever have been ... kept in the Archives, I fail to understand.

The Windsor Castle librarian, Owen Morshead, apologized to Sir Alan Lascelles, the Keeper of the Royal Archives, for having inadvertently sent "inflammable material" ("I know that the Prince and the Queen did not always agree during their early married years," he wrote matter-of-factly, "but I suspected no revelations within these particular covers"). The book was returned to Beatrice, and she quickly burned it.

In the following year, 1944, Beatrice died. What she had not been told was that before returning them to her, someone had taken photographs of these documents and slid them carefully into a section of the Royal Archives. They remain buried there today, piled neatly in a little white box tied up with ribbon. Why this happened is unclear. Was it the librarian who rebelled against orders and did not get caught? Or was it the order of the king to humor the old lady but preserve the evidence of his great-grandmother's marital conflicts? We know that George V and Queen Mary had been frustrated when watching Beatrice destroying her mother's private papers and disinfecting the remaining records. As some glimpses of Victoria's original diary still exist in the work of Theodore Martin, whom Victoria had commissioned to write a biography of Albert, it is clear that Beatrice made her mother tamer, less emotional, and more sensible in her rewriting.

The editors of Victoria's letters similarly warped the historical record. As Yvonne Ward has so adeptly demonstrated, Arthur Benson and Lord Esher, the two men entrusted with the task of culling and editing Victoria's correspondence, presented a skewed version of the queen. There were obvious trims—removal of too sharp a criticism of the French, or of her children, or deletion of words such as "vulgar" to sanitize her language—but further, "knowledge and particularly sharp or terse opinions which the Queen held were downplayed so that she might seem feminine and innocent. Her correspondence with women was omitted in order to avoid triviality. Her European correspondence was minimized to moderate any perception of foreign influences upon her." They cut any words that might have made Victoria seem "excessively assertive, unfeminine or insulting" as well as politically biased. Even worse, men wrote most of the letters in her official volumes; only four of every ten letters were in the queen's hand. Benson and Esher also cut out most letters to other women and references to her children, so Victoria's female friendships were scrubbed out, and her maternal confidences gone.

The photographs taken of the documents Beatrice destroyed during World War II—which are cited later in this book—are rare gems that provide insight into the intimate relationship between Victoria and Albert, in which he called her "child" and told her how to behave. But this correspondence also illuminates the extraordinary difficulty of trying to capture the mind and heart of a queen when her words were crafted, then rewritten, cut, concealed, and destroyed. It has been conservatively estimated that Victoria wrote an average of two and a half thousand words per day during her reign, a total of approximately sixty million words. Yet much of this material has been polished or glossed over or has vanished. Countless reams have been burned by her family, especially any correspondence relating to her Scottish intimate, John Brown, her Indian servant, Adbul Karim, and her most shameful episode as a young queen—the bullying of Lady Flora Hastings.

Queen Victoria remains buried under a mountain of myths, created by observers, sycophants, monarchists, republicans, and herself, and bolstered by the royal family ever since. Myths such as that when Albert died, she died too. That she loathed her children. That she was an impeccably constitutional, well-behaved queen. That she disliked power, lacked ambition, and loved only the domestic. That she was a simple product of the men who advised and shaped her, like a walking, talking Galatea. And, of course, that her servant John Brown was just a good friend. Then there are the myths of her own creation: that Albert was flawless and their marriage spotless. That he was king, and she only his supplicant shadow. All of this is nonsense.

Oscar Wilde believed that the three great personalities of the nineteenth century were Napoleon Bonaparte, Victor Hugo, and Queen Victoria. He described her as "a ruby mounted in jet"—a majestic more than a flattering image. She was indeed a great personality—but Victoria was also caustic and selfish, often dismissive, prone to self-pity, and obstinate. Millions died of starvation and disease during her reign, but she seemed blind to their plight. She was demanding, and rude to people she did not like. She despised elites, censured members of the House of Lords for hunting, drinking, and carousing all day, looked down on members of society who were idle and oversexed, often failed to support important reforms if she personally disliked their advocates, and frequently fled public duties for the peace and solitude of Scotland.

Victoria was acutely conscious of her flaws. Her dress was considered gauche, she was always fatter than she would have liked, and she surrounded herself with beauty out of a desire to compensate for her own lack of it. But she loved fiercely, was kind and truthful, had a keen sense of justice, despised racial and religious prejudice, and formed attachments to her servants that were so strong they were considered peculiar and even suspect. She also survived eight assassination attempts. By the end of her reign, Queen Victoria's prestige was phenomenal. Americans declared her the wisest woman in the world. Old women believed her touch would heal them, old men reported they could see more clearly after she visited them, and a seventy-six-year-old African American woman saved money for fifty years before traveling from the United States to talk to her for a few minutes.

The queen was born at a time of immense upheaval—the sleepy village that surrounded Kensington Palace would become a bustling metropolis by the end of her lifetime, with chimneys billowing smoke that clouded the sun, row houses crammed with five families per room, rivers clogged with sewage, and ships proudly sailing across the world to plant British flags on foreign continents. Uprisings would rattle the Church, the aristocracy, and Parliament. Under her reign, Britain would achieve a greatness it had not known before. This queen would rule a quarter of the people on earth, an epoch would be named after her, and her stern profile would forever be associated with a paradoxical time of growth, might, exploitation, poverty, and democracy.

Victoria was the most powerful queen, and the most famous working mother, on the planet. When we allow her to remain—as she has done in public memory for so long—submerged in her black piles of mourning, we forget that Victoria had been fighting for her independence, her prestige, and the honor of the Crown since she was a teenager, and did so successfully and in large part alone. We also forget that she fought for an empire and values she believed in and worked until her eyes wore out, that she advised, and argued with, ten prime ministers, populated the royal courts of Europe, and kept the British monarchy stable during the political upheavals that shook Europe in the nineteenth century. We forget that she loved again, that she giggled when grandchildren played at her feet, that she helped avoid a war with the United States, that she leapt upon opportunities to fire or anoint prime ministers. We forget that suffrage expansion and antipoverty and antislavery movements in the British Empire can all be traced to her monumental reign, along with a profound rethinking of family life and the rise of religious doubt. When she died, in 1901, she was the longest-reigning monarch in English history, and she remained so until 2015, when her great-great-granddaughter Elizabeth broke Victoria's record.

Victoria's legacy was enormous: a century, an empire, nine children, forty-two grandchildren. Today, outside Windsor Castle, amid ice cream stores and cluttered souvenir stalls, a statue of a portly woman stands in the middle of the road, unsmiling, looking over their heads to the distant horizon. The castle was built by William the Conqueror in the eleventh century and remodeled by a series of kings, including Charles II and George IV; Victoria found it large, gloomy, and "prison-like," but she is the monarch who shields it today. It is a mother who is the custodian of this castle, and who safeguarded the British people as they took firm steps toward democracy in a century roiling with ferment. It is a mother, who followed her husband from room to room while they fought, storming and crying, and who struggled to reconcile her innate resolve with her lack of self-esteem. It is an ordinary woman who was thrust into an extraordinary role.

Victoria grappled with many of the matters women do today— managing uneven relationships, placating resentful spouses, trying to raise decent children, battling bouts of insecurity and depression, spending years recovering from childbirth, yearning for a lost love, sinking into the strength of another when we want to hide from the world, longing to make independent decisions about our own lives and to shape the world we live in. She lusted after and fought for power at a time when women had none. Victoria's story is one of unmatched prestige and immense privilege, of defiance and crumbling, of meddling and mettle, of devotion and overwhelming grief and then, finally, a powerful resilience that defined the tiny woman at the heart of an empire. It is, above all, a surprising story of strength. What we have truly forgotten today is that Victoria is the woman under whose auspices the modern world was made.

Julia Baird
Shelley Beach
October 2015

Part 1

PRINCESS VICTORIA:
"POOR LITTLE VICTORY"

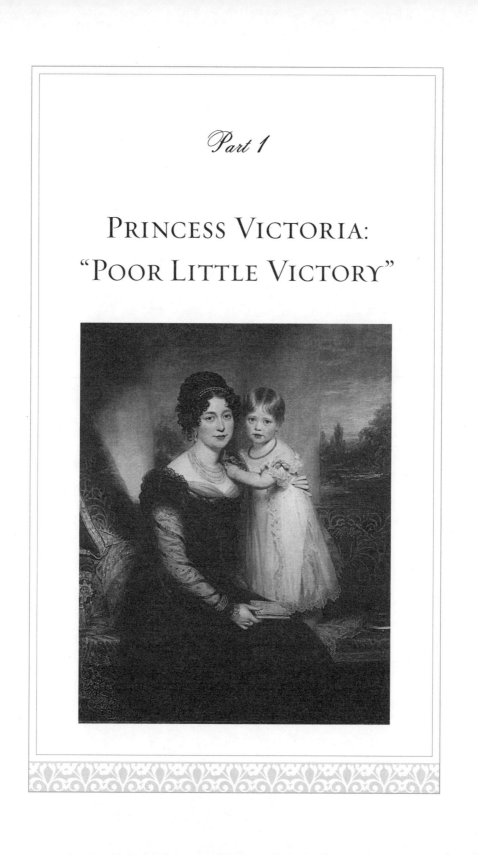

CHAPTER 1

The Birth of "Pocket Hercules"

My brothers are not so strong as I am.... I shall outlive them all; the crown will come to me and my children.

—EDWARD, DUKE OF KENT,
FATHER OF QUEEN VICTORIA

Queen Victoria was born, roaring, at 4:15 A.M., in the hour before dawn on May 24, 1819. In those first few seconds, she was like any newborn: naked, vulnerable, and wondering, wriggling in her mother's arms. Her spell of innocence would be brief. In moments, the most important men in the land—clergymen, chancellors, warriors, and politicians—would crowd into the room, pressing ruddy faces close to the baby girl who did not yet have a name. Within two decades, all of the men present at her birth who were still alive would be bowing to her as queen—something few could have guessed when she was born, as she was merely fifth in line to the throne. But this was an important child—one who would go on to command armies, select archbishops, and appoint prime ministers. From this moment, she would never be alone; an adult shadowed every step she took, tasted every mouthful of food, and overheard every conversation.

As the sky lightened, her mother, the Duchess of Kent, lay back on the pillows of her four-poster bed and closed her eyes, exhausted, breathing in the lilacs and mayflowers in the gardens below. On this cloudy spring morning, a light rain was falling, bringing relief after three weeks of intense heat. The room in Kensington Palace in which the baby was born was entirely white and smelled of lush new carpet. Outside the windows, sheep grazed and jays sang among the beech trees.

As was the custom in royal households, the men of the Privy Council had been summoned from dinner parties, the theater, and bed the night before. As the duchess lay writhing and breathing through contractions, His Majesty's ministers waited in an adjoining room. The duke had forewarned them that he would not entertain them, as he planned to stay next to his wife, urging her on. As tradition dictated, these high-ranking men listened to the cries of the duchess during the six-hour labor, then crowded the room once the baby arrived, to attest that it was in fact the mother's child. (In 1688, when Mary of Modena, the Catholic wife of James II, gave birth to a thriving boy, a majority of the public—fueled by Protestants unhappy at the thought of a healthy male heir—believed that she had in fact miscarried and that she had had another, live baby smuggled into her room in a warming pan. This was untrue, but it was one of the factors leading to the revolution that knocked James II off the throne.)

The duchess endured the presence of the men, who signed the birth certificate and a report of the baby's "perfectly healthful appearance." They murmured congratulations, then shuffled wearily back out into a city that was slowly waking; grooms in stables were fetching water, the scent of beeswax wafted from the nearby candle manufactory. Breakfast sellers were setting up stalls along the Great West Road, an old Roman highway that ran alongside Hyde Park and was the main route into London from the southwest. Workers hurried to factories through the mist among rattling mail coaches and market carts, and past thousands of weary cattle being herded to their slaughter.

Back in Kensington Palace, the Duke of Kent was restless with pride and excitement. In letters to friends, he raved about his wife's "patience and sweetness" during labor, and he praised the midwife, Frau Siebold, for her "activity, zeal and knowledge." In a curious coincidence that shows how tight-knit the worlds of the British and German royals were at the time, just three months later, Frau Siebold was to preside at the birth of Victoria's future husband, Albert of Saxe-Coburg and Gotha. The baby Albert, his mother cooed, was *"superbe—d'une beauté extraordinaire."* From infancy, Albert was praised for his beauty, just as Victoria was praised for her strength.

At birth Victoria was only fifth in line to the throne. But in the years before, her father, Edward, Duke of Kent—the fourth son of King George III—had dramatically revised his life when he realized his siblings were not producing heirs and that the throne could someday pass to him and his offspring. He already had a partner, a gentle Frenchwoman named Julie de Saint-Laurent. Edward had ostensibly hired her to sing at a party with his band in 1790, during his first stint as governor in Gibraltar, but she was really brought into his house to share his bed. Despite these unromantic beginnings, and the fact that even if they had married, the king would never have recognized their union, they formed a remarkably successful partnership, which lasted through postings in Canada and Gibraltar as well as a scandalous mutiny by Edward's troops.

But despite the three decades he had spent with the devoted Julie de Saint-Laurent, Edward had come to decide he needed a legitimate wife, one who would enable him to pay off his substantial debts, as princes were given additional allowances when they wed. When his niece Charlotte, the presumptive heir to the throne, died in childbirth, it also became clear that if he found a younger wife, she might be able to bear a child who could reign over England.

———

When the Duke of Kent urged his carriage westward from Germany weeks before Victoria's birth, he was trying to outrun the most unpredictable of rivals: biology. He wanted to get his heavily pregnant German wife to Britain in time to give birth to a baby he hoped might one day sit on the throne. The duke was certain any future monarch would be more loved if the baby bawled his or her first cry on England's soil. He looked down at his wife's pale face, lit by the gentle spring sun, and beamed. He was fifty-one and penniless: it was something of a miracle that he had found such a young, pretty, amiable wife. The thirty-two-year-old Princess Victoire of Saxe-Coburg-Saalfeld, a tiny principality much diminished by Napoleon's land grab in south Germany, was cheerful, short, and plump, with brown ringlets and apple-red cheeks. Recently widowed, Victoire had two children of her own, and had taken some persuading before agreeing to marry the Duke of Kent. But they had quickly settled into a fond companionship, and Victoire soon became pregnant.

When he began the long journey from Amorbach to England, the duke was not just racing to Great Britain; he hoped he was racing to the throne. Just a year before, the thought that the Duke of Kent might have been able to produce an heir to the throne would have been laughable. He was then only a distant fifth in line, after his older brother George, the Prince Regent. Next in line after George was George's only and much-loved child, Charlotte. Then, also ahead of the Duke of Kent were his other older brothers, Frederick and William. King George III, who was going mad, had fifteen children with his wife, Queen Charlotte, though only twelve were still alive. The seven remaining sons had precedence over their five sisters—and if any of the sons had children, the crown would pass down to their heirs, not to their siblings. (The British throne was until 2011 governed by male preference primogeniture, whereby the crown passed to the sons, in order of birth, before then being passed to the daughters, in order of birth.)

Charlotte, the only daughter of King George III's eldest son, the

Prince Regent who would become George IV, would ascend the throne after her father. Charlotte was a high-spirited, fetching young woman, who fell deeply in love with and married in 1816 the dashing Prince Leopold of Saxe-Coburg-Saalfeld. England cheered when she quickly became pregnant. But Charlotte hated feeling enormous— and constantly being told how big she was—and grew depressed. Her doctors put her on a strict diet in her final months, and drained blood from her. Many patients died from this dubious practice, the favored remedy for patients believed to have "bad humors," especially those who were already malnourished and ailing.

After a fifty-hour labor, Charlotte's son emerged stillborn. She was exhausted and bled heavily. Doctors plied her with wine and brandy, and piled hot water bottles around her, but they were unable to save her; she died on November 6, 1817. (Her accoucheur, or male midwife, Richard Croft, was so distraught that three months later, while attending another prolonged labor, he picked up a gun and shot himself in the head). Grief for Charlotte, the hopeful future queen of England, hung like a pall over the streets of London for weeks. Soon there was a national shortage of black fabric.

Suddenly, and unexpectedly, the succession had been opened up; the crown would now pass down through the aging brothers or their children, not to Charlotte, a young and beloved woman barely out of her teens. Who, they asked, would be the next heir to the throne?

King George III and Queen Charlotte led quiet and respectable lives, much like the British middle class. Their debauched sons, though, were unpopular, fat, and lazy. Oddly, the one son who was disciplined, upright, and truthful was the one his parents seemed to like the least: Victoria's father, Edward, the Duke of Kent.

By 1818, King George was deaf, blind, and deranged, suffering from what is thought by some to be a rare metabolic disorder called porphyria, although it was also quite possibly dementia or bipolar disorder. Residents of his castle could hear "unpleasant laughing" from the wings he wandered in, and he was often found strumming a harpsichord, wearing purple robes. He was haunted by apocalyptic visions of drowning in a large flood, spoke constantly to invisible friends, and embraced trees he mistook for foreign dignitaries. In 1811, at the age of seventy-three, he was declared officially mad.

The Prince Regent, later George IV, was friendly and mildly intelligent. By the time he reached his mid-fifties, he was a miserable man. He suffered from gout and took large doses of opium to numb the pain in his legs. His relationship with his wife, Princess Caroline, was toxic and brutal. The Prince Regent banned her from his coronation in 1821 (a door was slammed in her face when she arrived at Westminster Abbey clad in her finery). Three weeks afterward, Queen Caroline died. The cause is unknown; it was rumored that the king had poisoned her.

By the time the Prince Regent's daughter died, in 1817, the seven sons of George III were all middle-aged; the youngest was forty-three. So who would produce an heir? Ernest, the Duke of Cumberland, was the only one both officially married and not estranged from his wife.

When they were very young, King George III had decreed that none of the royal offspring could enter into marriages without the king's consent and the approval of Parliament. The resulting Royal Marriages Act of 1772 gave the princes a convenient excuse to wriggle out of any commitments to their lovers. They acted, Lord Melbourne later told Queen Victoria, like "wild beasts." The result was a large pile of illegitimate grandchildren—fifty-six in total, none of whom could ever occupy the throne. Charlotte had been the only grandchild produced from an officially recognized marriage. What was at stake, then, was not just this generation but control of the next. (Too far down the succession to count were King George III's five surviving daughters, who were all over forty and childless.)

Could such an enormous family have become extinct? It may seem ludicrous now to think that the Hanoverian dynasty, which began with King George I in 1714, could have ended with King George III's sons. It was entirely possible, though, given the behavior of his progeny. When Charlotte died, a hubbub surrounded the future of the throne, and Parliament insisted the four unwed brothers marry.

The brothers immediately powdered their hair and cast their eyes upon the royal courts of Europe. France was out of favor because of the decades-long battle with Napoleon. Germany was preferred, partly because it was thought that a Lutheran upbringing made for chaste and obedient wives. Three of the four quickly complied, marrying by mid-1818. The youngest of the royal princes, Adolphus, the Duke of Cambridge, sent a marriage proposal to Augusta, the German princess of Hesse-Cassel, to which she agreed.

Victoria's father, Edward, the Duke of Kent, was now fourth in line, and the only son who had adopted his parents' Spartan, disciplined lifestyle. He was more than six feet tall, proud and muscular, and called himself the "strongest of the strong." Though he privately conceded it was presumptuous, he boasted that he would live longer than his brothers: "I have led a regular life," he often said; "I shall outlive them all; the crown will come to me and my children." He was a composite of opposites that his daughter would later reflect: gentle and tough, empathetic and needy, severe when crossed and tender when loved.

Unlike his brothers, Edward was clever, eloquent, and a conscientious letter writer. He was a progressive who was in favor of popular education, Catholic emancipation, and the abolition of slavery. Despite his tyrannical military reputation, he had a kind heart. He was also extravagant: whims he indulged included a library of five thousand books dragged across the seas, fountains installed inside closets, bed ladders covered in velvet, and bright lights of every hue placed along driveways. He kept a hairdresser on staff for himself and his servants.

When the duke first asked for Victoire's hand, it was not guaranteed she would say yes. Her two children, Charles and Feodora, were just thirteen and ten, and the independent life of a widow was in many ways preferable to that of a wife. But days after Charlotte died,

Leopold, her widower, who was Victoire's brother, sent a letter urging Victoire to reconsider the Duke of Kent's proposal. Suddenly Edward had greater prospects: he was now much closer to the throne. Finally Victoire agreed. In response, Edward was tender and romantic, vowing to make his young bride happy.

Edward and Victoire were lucky: they were quietly thrilled with each other and settled into a domestic routine. On December 31, 1818, Edward wrote his new wife a loving note: "God bless you. Love me as I love you." As the new year rang in, three new brides were pregnant. They lay curled up next to their husbands, with rounded bellies and sweet hopes, thinking of the year ahead.

In 1819, the race began in earnest. On March 26, Augusta, the wife of the Duke of Kent's younger brother Adolphus, gave birth to a healthy son. On March 27, Adelaide, the wife of Edward's older brother William, produced a premature baby girl who lived only a few hours. And on March 28, Edward, the Duke of Kent, began his journey from Amorbach, Germany, to London. Victoire, at eight months pregnant, endured a 427-mile journey over rough roads and wild seas. The duke had worried that the trip might bring on an early labor. But Victoire was full of "joyful anticipation" at the life in store for her in England. As she rattled along next to her husband, her hands kept creeping to her stomach, her fingers tracing the skin where tiny feet kicked and limbs tickled inside her.

On April 18, the long caravan of children, nurses, midwives, clerks, doctors, and a string of servants, lapdogs, and parrots reached Calais, the French seaside town that overlooks the narrowest point of the English Channel. The Prince Regent had reluctantly agreed to let his brother use the royal yacht for the crossing. They crossed a week later. A gale was blowing, and Victoire's face was a pale shade of green; she threw up several times in the three-hour journey. After they finally landed in Dover, they went straight to Kensington. It was then much like a country village, and their large palace was dilapidated. The walls were damp, and the place stank with dry rot. The duke, who was an eager and lavish interior decorator, immediately bought curtains, fabrics, and furnishings: white for the bedrooms and red for the dining room. (He also privately sent anxious letters to friends, asking how his former partner, Julie, was.) As he and Victoire prepared for the birth of their daughter, who would reign over the British Empire for the better part of a century, few blinked. It was just another overspending, big-bellied prince with another pregnant German wife. The only people paying attention were those who had the most to lose from Victoria's birth: the royal family. Not long after she pulled the first fistfuls of air into her lungs, there were rumors that her wicked uncles were plotting to kill her.

CHAPTER 2

The Death of a Father

"Do not forget me."

—THE DUKE OF KENT, 1820

The Duchess of Kent was instantly smitten with her baby girl. She insisted on breastfeeding for six months, although most aristocratic women employed wet nurses then, often because their tightly laced corsets affected their ability to produce milk. While her peers raised their eyebrows, the public was pleased with the duchess's commitment to nurse, especially the bourgeoisie, who favored the practice themselves. Her decision was more significant than she would have known: as breastfeeding is a useful, if not ironclad, contraceptive, this meant that the duchess was unlikely to get pregnant again quickly. If she had, and had borne Victoria a brother, he could have taken the throne.

The duke was only briefly disappointed at not having a son. After all, under the Settlement Act of 1701, his daughter would be able to inherit the crown, if she had no brothers. Privately, while recognizing that her chances were slight—his older brothers might produce an heir yet—he still boasted: "Look at her well, for she will be Queen of England." Victoria's father would always regard his stout, pretty baby as miraculous. It was, after all, a dangerous thing to be born in the nineteenth century. Of every thousand infants, about 150 died at birth. Even then, the prevalence of measles, whooping cough, scarlet fever, and cholera meant that the likelihood that a child would survive to the age of five was little more than 70 percent. Children from poor, urban families who were not breastfed or were weaned too early had even slimmer chances.

It was also a common practice to give infants opium to stop their crying, and many babies lost their appetite and starved as a result. Predictably, the mothers were blamed for working long days in factories and leaving their children with strangers. A piece published in 1850 in *Household Words,* the journal edited by Charles Dickens, attributed this practice to "ignorant hireling nurse(s)" who managed eight or nine babies at a time by keeping them drugged. Concoctions called "Soothing Syrup," "Mother's Quietness," and a laudanum-based potion called "Godfrey's Cordial" meant "the quiet homes of the poor reek[ed] with narcotics." Karl Marx, writing in *Das Kapital* in 1867, described the "disguised infanticide and stupefaction of children with opiates," adding that their parents were developing addictions of their own.* Infant deaths were so common that parents

---

* At the time, as now, the drug use of the working class was of more concern than that of the upper and middle classes, and it drew attention away from the real issues: the long hours and onerous conditions the working class endured, let alone the lack of protections for women such as child care or maternity leave. Women were the mules of the Victorian world; they produced babies, cared for children, maintained the home, and, increasingly, labored in factories, but they had few rights and little recognition. Until late in the century, they remained the legal property of the men they married.

insured their newborns, and were typically paid £5 if they died, a practice that was thought to encourage infanticide. By 1900, 80 percent of babies were insured.

But Victoria bloomed with such vigor that the duke boasted that she was "rather a pocket Hercules, than a pocket Venus." She was a solid child, "a model of strength and beauty combined," according to her father, who personally oversaw the nursery schedule and operations. She was also quite chubby, with enormously fat legs: the duke's lawyer, Baron Stockmar, called her a "pretty little Princess, plump as a partridge." Victoria's uncles were not happy. The Regent, soon to be King George IV, hated his brother the Duke of Kent with a long-standing visceral passion.

Victoria was born at a glorious time in the British Empire. Four years earlier, in 1815, Napoleon had been defeated at the Battle of Waterloo, which ended a seventeen-year war with France. Britain had rejoiced at the humbling of the most powerful man and country in Europe. Now Napoleon was safely locked up on St. Helena, a tropical island in the South Atlantic, and, to the delight of the English, had embraced gardening. The Battle of Waterloo marked the beginning of Pax Britannica—a ninety-nine-year peace that would last until World War I. The empire expanded steadily, staining countries in Asia, Africa, Australia, and North and South America an imperial red (as maps then showed the British Empire to be). This growth was accompanied by enormous strength in manufacturing and a wealth of coal and iron production. The swift, seemingly unstoppable expansion of the empire in the nineteenth century made the British throne a glittering prize. At the end of the Napoleonic Wars, Britain was the world's only industrialized economy and the greatest naval power. But London was brimming with discontent.

In 1821, half of the British workforce was under the age of twenty. In the year Victoria was born, 1819, an act was passed to limit the hours children worked in factories and cotton mills to twelve; but it was rarely enforced. Children as young as five worked from dawn to dark in match and nail factories, gasworks, shipyards, and construction. In 1833, the Factory Act made it illegal for children under nine to work, though it applied only to textile factories. In 1834, it was made illegal to apprentice any boys under age ten as chimney sweeps or to "evil treat" any who were older—but, again, this act was ineffective and not enforced. Chimney sweeping became a great symbol of child abuse, with tales of children having fires lit under them to make them work faster, or getting stuck and dying in the winding dark crevices. By 1840, still only 20 percent of children in London had been to school.

The Industrial Revolution was rapidly accelerating, and the population shifted from country to city. At the beginning of the century, 20 percent of the British population lived in towns or cities; by the end of the century, 75 percent did. Slums spread across London, and in once-grand houses, sometimes thirty or more people lived in a single room. For most of those inhabiting slums and shantytowns, sanitation meant using a bucket and tipping it into an open drain. When Victoria was born, food was cooked in open fireplaces, horses carried messages, half of the population was illiterate, and a narrow band of property owners were the only ones with political power. By the end of her life in 1901, people traveled by subway, telegraphs shot messages across oceans, education was compulsory, and women had some basic rights.

At the time of Victoria's birth, the indulgent Prince Regent was far removed from the struggles of many of his impoverished subjects. The government passed the Corn Laws in 1815 to protect English wheat with tariffs; as a result the price of food had risen, which infuriated an overstretched working class. Common land, where country workers had collectively grazed animals, was enclosed into plots for which higher rent could be charged, creating much hardship. The rest of the world's demand for British exports had dropped along with wages and employment. Riots had erupted over the price of bread days before Victoria's birth; even in well-to-do areas around Kensington Palace, signs of poverty were visible.

Although Victoria was born in Britain, she was surrounded by Germans; even her bouts of crying were soothed with German lullabies (though she would not formally start learning the language until she was seven). Her blood was almost entirely Germanic. Her mother, her mother's daughter, Feodora, her uncle Leopold, and her governess were all German. All four of her grandparents were German, and her most recent British ancestor came from the seventeenth century. Between 1714 and 1901, all the Hanoverians who reigned over England married Germans—Victoria followed suit, as did six of her own nine children.

Germany was then a collection of states that had been bundled together in a union called the German Confederation in 1815 after Napoleon was defeated. (The country would not exist as one nation until 1871.) Some of these states had sided with France in the Napoleonic Wars, but the largest and most powerful—Prussia—was allied with England. One small state, Hanover, was, oddly, ruled from London by the English kings, who were Hanoverian by heritage. This century-long arrangement, begun in 1714 by King George, who was both British and German, would stop when Victoria became queen. Only men could rule Hanover.

On June 24, 1819, in a grand, high-ceilinged room on the top floor of Kensington Palace, a small crowd stood staring at the baby Victoria and her flustered parents. They were gathered around a gold baptismal font brought in from the Tower of London for the day. The rooms were draped with crimson velvet, which concealed a row of busts high up on the wall depicting the proud profiles of a clutch of emperors and pharaohs: Nero, Caligula, Cleopatra. (Protocol required that their faces be concealed to protect the sensibilities of the Archbishop of Canterbury.)

The Regent, who was irritated that the brother he despised had produced an heir, had insisted that the christening be small, private, and held in the middle of the afternoon. He did not want the ceremony to be elaborate, or in any way to signal that it was being held for a potential future monarch. No one was permitted to dress up or wear uniforms or gold lace. Even worse, the Regent did not permit the Duke and Duchess of Kent to name their own daughter. They had wanted to call her Victoire Georgiana Alexandrina Charlotte Augusta, but the Regent wrote to them beforehand to say he would not let the child be called Georgiana because he did not want a derivative of his own name, George, to be placed before that of the czar of Russia, Alexander (who had given the Duke of Kent money for his marriage and was the baby's godfather). The Regent said he would tell them at the ceremony which other names they could use.

At the christening, the Archbishop of Canterbury held the plump baby expectantly and asked the Regent, "By what name does it please Your Highness to call this child?" The Regent announced, firmly, "Alexandrina," and paused. The Duke of Kent offered up Charlotte as a second name, then Augusta, but the Regent shook his head. He also rejected the name Elizabeth. He did not wish this baby, a rival for the throne, to inherit any of the traditional, historic names of the British royal family. After the duchess burst into tears, the Regent finally said, "Give her the mother's name also, then, but it cannot precede that of the emperor." Alexandrina Victoria was an unpopular choice, as both names were foreign; the child was known as Drina until she was about four. After then, it was always Victoria. When attempts were made to change it to Charlotte or Elizabeth in Parliament in 1831 due to the belief that the names Alexandrina and Victoria were not then well-known in England, Victoria insisted her name remain the same.

The Regent left the christening without talking to his brother. His animosity did not abate: when the Duke of Kent brought little Drina to a military review on Hounslow Heath when she was just three months old, the Regent shouted, "What business has that infant here?" The royal uncles were not particularly fond of the child's mother, either. The Duchess of Kent had a heavy German accent and made little effort to learn English—though Lord Melbourne was later to infer that she knew the language well and it just suited her to pretend that she did not. Her speeches were written out phonetically: "Ei hoeve to regret, biing aes yiett so little cônversent in thie Inglisch." The royals had been pinning all their hope on the Duke of Kent's older brother, the Duke of Clarence, and his wife to produce an heir instead of the disliked Edward; little Victoria was "a real thorn in their side."

The unpopular Regent was a miserable creature. He had lost his daughter, Charlotte, and his only grandchild on the same day, and he hated his wife. He was rather fat and was dependent upon laudanum to ease the pain in his swollen legs. Aspirin was not patented as a medicine until 1899, and there were few painkiller alternatives. Laudanum—also known as tincture of opium—was legal in Victorian times. Laudanum was a concoction of herbs, opium, distilled water, and alcohol that was widely used as a general remedy to aid sleep, ease pain, stop diarrhea (commonly brought on by cholera or dysentery), curb menstrual cramps and flatulence, dull labor pains, and soothe earache, toothache, and sore throats. It was also used to treat hysteria and insanity and help with the "fatigue and depression" then common in the working class. It was a key ingredient in most patent medicines, and it was extremely potent and addictive. Those addicted to laudanum's soporific, transporting qualities included Mary Todd Lincoln, Samuel Taylor Coleridge, Charles Dickens, and Elizabeth Barrett Browning. Florence Nightingale took opium after she returned from the Crimean War, claiming that it helped her aching back. She wrote in 1866, "Nothing did me any good, but a curious little new fangled operation of putting opium under the skin which relieves one for twenty-four hours—but does not improve the vivacity or serenity of one's intellect." Dante Gabriel Rossetti's wife died from an overdose of laudanum. Many members of the royal family grew reliant on it, especially those with chronic conditions like gout.

The Duke of Kent thought a far better tonic than opium was the ocean. While most went to the seaside in summer, he decided to go in a bitterly cold winter in 1819 to provide some rest for Victoire, who had rheumatism. Doctors had recently discovered what they thought were the healing powers of the sea—it was claimed to cure weak chests, apoplexy, and even postnatal depression, or exhaustion as it was then called. Saltwater baths were highly recommended for nursing mothers. So the duke went to scout the Devonshire coast first to find a place for them all to stay. When he was there, he went to visit a fortune-teller. She told him that in the following year two members of the royal family would die. "Curious," he mused, "I wonder which ones?" One of them was to be his mad father, King George III; the second, he would not have guessed.

A few weeks later, he brought his family to a cottage nestled in a little glen not far from the shore. (On the way, they stayed with Bishop Fisher, an old tutor of the duke's. Little Victoria pulled his wig off—an early sign of the irreverence for episcopal authority that would continue throughout her life.) They moved in during a snowstorm on Christmas Day. It had been a harsh winter, and the house was exposed to vicious winds, but the duke was most content. He wrote a letter to a friend about how strong his baby girl was: "too healthy, I fear, in the opinion of some members of my family, by whom she is regarded as an intruder." Victoria was just eight months old but was the size of a one-year-old—and her father was convinced she had inherited the steel in his soul. Her first two teeth had cut through her gums "without the slightest inconvenience"; she barely flinched. When she was sleeping in her nursery at the cottage, a local boy hunting birds accidentally shot a pellet through her window. The duke said she stood fire just like a soldier's daughter.

On January 7, the Duke of Kent went for a long walk along the cliffs in a gale with his equerry, John Conroy. He walked back in the front door complaining the cold was making his bones ache. After he developed a fever, he was moved to a warmer room and bled twice, but he did not improve. The only doctor they could summon at such short notice, William Maton, spoke no German. Dr. Maton again bled, then cupped and leeched the duke. Cupping was at the time a common practice, wherein a cut was made in the skin and a heated cup placed over it. As the cup cooled, blood flowed into the vacuum. By the end of the duke's treatment, he had lost about three liters of blood. The duchess was mortified and angry, yet was unable to question the doctor's wisdom. She wrote that there was "hardly a spot on his dear body which [had] not been touched by cupping, blisters or bleeding. . . . He was terribly exhausted . . . by those cruel doctors." When the duke was told that night that the doctor wanted to bleed him again, he wept.

The duchess paced as her husband lay in pain, coughing and hiccuping. She refused to rest. Soon friends began to arrive at the cottage, including the duchess's brother, Prince Leopold, who came with his companion, the doctor and lawyer Christian Stockmar, who would have such a pivotal role in the court in years to come. As the duchess waited, Stockmar took the duke's pulse. He turned and said quietly, "Human help can no longer avail." The duchess stared at him, then walked back to her husband's side and took his hand. She had not changed her clothes or slept for several days. As the baby Victoria—whom she called by the diminutive "Vickelchen"—lay sleeping in her crib, the Duchess of Kent's older daughter, Feodora, was on her knees, praying. Dawn broke, and the duke was feverish and restless. He pressed his wife's hand, pulled her toward him, and whispered, "Do not forget me."

The Duke of Kent died at ten o'clock in the morning on Sunday, January 23, 1820. His death came as a great shock, given his usual rude health. "That Hercules of a man is no more," wrote Princess Lieven, the wife of the Russian diplomat to London. Poor Victoire was now a widow for the second time. She was widely disliked, almost penniless, and had few allies. She did not understand the language, the customs, or the people of the country whose tiny child, perhaps the future sovereign, she bore in her arms. There was some affection for her in the royal family, especially among the women, but this was soon quashed by her lack of tact as well as her competitiveness with those who might produce rivals for Victoria.

———

Even in death, the Duke of Kent was imposing. His coffin weighed more than a ton and was seven feet long—the pallbearers struggled to get it through doorways. He was buried at night in the family vault at Windsor on February 12 as his wife wept in her rooms (women were not allowed at funerals, ostensibly due to the belief they would lose control of their emotions). Theirs had been a happy union. Now she was alone and she would make the protection, instruction, and control of Victoria her life's greatest mission. But first she needed to learn how to survive.

It would not be easy. The duke had signed a will entrusting his child to his wife. He bequeathed everything to Victoire, though customarily men of this era left property to their male relatives (women were usually allowed only the interest on money in their estates). But his substantial debts forced his wife to rely on her brother Leopold's financial assistance and the hospitality of the Regent, her brother-in-law. The Regent agreed to let them stay at Kensington Palace. The sad crew traveled back to the palace in the cold London winter, with the eight-month-old Victoria distressed by the jerking of the carriage. She stood, crying on her sturdy legs, on her mother's knees and banged her fists on the closed windows of the coach, which was draped in black. With the death of her father, the twin recurring strains in the life of the girl who would become queen emerged: loss and endurance.

Six days after Edward passed away, his father, George III, died at Windsor Castle, and the Regent became King George IV. This meant that by January 29, 1820, Victoria had moved from fifth to third in line to the throne. As the stakes grew higher, her once-tender mother grew increasingly ambitious and obsessed with power. Victoria would need to learn to resist the woman who had only just weaned her when her father died. Victoria's mother said she was already showing "symptoms of wanting to get her own way" even as an infant. She would need to draw on this stubbornness as she grew. For it was in learning to defy the woman who gave birth to her that Victoria learned how to be a queen.

CHAPTER 3

The Lonely, Naughty Princess

[Victoria] is watched so closely that no busy maid has a moment to whisper "You are heir of England." I suspect, if we could dissect the little heart, we should find some pigeon or other bird of the air had carried the matter.

—SIR WALTER SCOTT, 1828

Victoria was a short-tempered and defiant girl. She hated sitting still, hated taking medicine, and hated being told what to do. When her piano teacher, Mr. Sale, told her she must practice just like everyone else, she banged the lid shut and yelled, "There! You see there is no *must* about it." The fact that there were many *must*s in her life just made her more rebellious. In 1830, her governess, Baroness Louise Lehzen, forced Victoria to document her outbursts in "Conduct Books." She sometimes recorded three tantrums a day, writing, "very ill behaved and impertinent to Lehzen." On August 21, 1832, she was *"very very very* terribly *NAUGHTY"* (the "verys" are underlined three times and the "naughty" four). On the afternoon of September 24, 1832, Victoria writes that she was *"VERY VERY VERY VERY HOR- RIBLY NAUGHTY!!!!!"*—all underlined four times—but in her journal she simply reported, "The heat was intollerable [*sic*]." When she made up stories for creative writing compositions, they were about children who were spoiled and disobedient and who needed to repent or be punished.

The young princess's stories also revealed how she wrestled with the need to be well behaved, and how she fantasized about being in- dulged and not corrected. In one story, written when she was seven, she described a "naughty girl" named An. She wrote (with spelling mistakes included):

Little An was pretty naughty greedy and disobedient. Nobody like to be near her for she was so unpleasant.

One day her Father gave a party and many fine people came; and little [A]n was allowed to come into the room. As soon as somebody adresd her she turned her back and gave no answer. As her dear Father wished to please her, so she was allowed to dine with her Papa; her Mother (who was her favorite) gave her whatever she asked for and gave her seetmeats in provu- sion. Ane sat between Lady D— and her Mamma; poor Old Lay D— was so plagued by An that she said to her Mother 'Mam your daughter is very ill behaving and troublesome.' Mrs G— who was the Mother of An flushed for anger. Indeed Mam I must beg your leave to go with my darling little Ane dear. She goes and leaves the room with An with a plate full of sweet- meats in her hand.

These are the words of a girl who was aware of both the appeal and the perils of being spoiled. Victoria was continually testing not just Lehzen but her tutor, the Reverend George Davys. When her mother offered four-year-old Victoria a reward if she behaved herself during Davys's first visit, she tried to negotiate, asking to have the reward first. When Davys suggested they study the letter *o,* she would say she preferred *h.*

Yet despite her temper, Victoria had a good heart, and was truthful. One day the duchess told Victoria's tutor, "She has been good this morning but yesterday there was a storm." Victoria piped up: "Two storms, one at dressing and one at washing." Some of her willfulness was fed by the fawning palace staff, as well as the great men who visited regularly. She became very conscious of her station. She once told a young visitor, Lady Ellice, who was trying to play with some of her toys, including a white satin doll's sofa and three dancing figures, "You must not touch those, they are mine. And I may call you Jane but you may not call me Victoria." It was as though she was actively encouraged to be superior, and so much sycophancy led to arrogance. Her half sister, Feodora, who was twelve years older, wrote to Victoria later about their mother's lady-in-waiting, Baroness Späth: "It was a sort of idolatry, when she used to go on her knees before you when you were a child." Bishops crawled on the carpets to play with her, and aristocrats sat in on her school lessons. She later confessed she knew she was the "idol of the house," and she sometimes dared people to defy her. Once, after being told that if she cried, her uncle the Duke of Sussex, who also lived in Kensington Palace, would punish her, she proceeded to scream herself hoarse whenever he walked past.

Perhaps surprisingly for a girl who lacked for nothing, had horses to ride, regular trips to the seaside, and attendants who doted on her, Victoria described her childhood as rather melancholy. She later complained that Kensington Palace was uncomfortable, dirty, and infested with beetles. Once, when asked what she would like for her birthday, she said she wanted the windows cleaned. But for all her toys, exquisite clothes, pets, and donkey rides, what she was truly lacking was friends. She later told her eldest daughter: "I had a very unhappy life as a child; had no scope for my very violent feelings of affection—had no brothers and sisters to live with—never had a father—from my unfortunate circumstances was not on a comfortable or at all intimate or confidential footing with my mother . . . and did not know what a happy domestic life was!" This was not just the grimness of hindsight—her sister, Feodora, later painted a similarly drab tale:

> To have been deprived of all intercourse, and not one cheerful thought in that dismal existence of ours, was very hard. My only happy time was going or driving out with you and Lehzen; then I could speak and look, as I like. I escaped some years of imprisonment, which you, my poor darling sister, had to endure after I was married.

Victoria was only nine when Feodora married and moved to Germany in 1828; she was devastated. From that time, she had only the crushing, constant surveillance of adults. She slept in her mother's room every night, with someone watching her until her mother came to bed, and even when she was watering flowers, a footman in scarlet livery hovered over her.

Victoria was ten years old when she discovered she was third in line to the throne. It was March 11, 1830, and she was at her little desk, trying to concentrate on her books. A sprig of holly was pinned to the front of her lace-trimmed velvet dress, to keep her chin up and her back straight. Outside, the sun was thawing the ground after a deep cold that had frozen parts of the Thames, and she was itching to be out on her horse, galloping sidesaddle across Kensington Gardens. Riding was the closest she got to solitude. She started leafing through Howlett's *Tables of the Kings and Queens of England,* then frowned as she came upon a page she had never seen before: a map of the British royal family tree that showed a line leading to the throne. Her uncle, the ill, reclusive King George IV, was the current king. Next was his brother, her uncle William. After that was her name. Victoria burst into tears: "I am nearer to the throne than I thought."

Thirty years later, Baroness Lehzen, who had initially been hired to teach Feodora but was appointed governess to Victoria when she was five, composed a glorified account of this moment. According to her, Victoria solemnly said, "Now, many a child would boast, but they don't know the difficulty. There is much splendor, but there is more responsibility." She then, Lehzen reported, put her forefinger in the air and declared, "I will be good!" These widely recounted remarks—far too formal and self-conscious for a child of ten—made a myth out of a daunting, distressing moment. And although many mothers may have preferred to tell their daughters such important news themselves, the Duchess of Kent was happy to have made Victoria aware of her situation as though by accident. (She had been recently prodded to by two bishops who came to assess Victoria's education; they told her she must tell her daughter.) Of course Victoria had a strong suspicion of her significance before this day—why else would so many bow and scrape to such a young girl? Especially while ignoring her half sister? But the confirmation was distressing. Decades later, Prince Albert revealed that the discovery of her nearness to the throne made Victoria "very unhappy." She had "cried much on learning it—& even deplored this contingency." Three months later her uncle, King George IV, died.

On the day that Victoria discovered her likely destiny, March 11, 1830, several children who would grow to be great figures of the Victorian age were also hunched over their books. Florence Nightingale, who was a year younger than Victoria, was constructing a pretend home in a playhouse in Winchester with her cousin, covering a sofa with heather and trying to get the damp out of the mossy beds. (Demonstrating a natural flair for organization, young Florence drew up a table headed "Vegetables" and "Fruits," which showed the cones, acorns, and various objects she and her cousin used to represent peaches, cucumbers, peas, and potatoes in her pretend pantry.) George Eliot—then Mary Ann Evans—was ten, and crafting immaculate compositions at her boarding school in Nuneaton. (Evans had an unusual upbringing: most mothers educated their daughters at home or

in schools that focused on obedience, sewing, drawing, and music.)
The future influential art critic John Ruskin was eleven and being
educated at home by his parents in Surrey. Charles Dickens had just
turned eighteen and was spending most days working in the British
Museum Reading Room, where he was learning shorthand so he
could start his career as a journalist. Alfred, Lord Tennyson, who was
a little older than Dickens, was unhappily studying at Cambridge.
All would be titans of their age, but forever dwarfed by the woman
who was once the teary ten-year-old in Kensington Palace.

Victoria trusted only one person: her governess. Baroness Lehzen,
the daughter of a Lutheran pastor from Coburg, was an eccentric,
single-minded, clever woman who dedicated her life to ensuring that
Victoria would be a forceful, intelligent queen. Victoria, who became
a prolific artist, drew affectionate portraits of her, with dark hair,
thoughtful eyes, and pointed nose and chin, looking serious, patient,
and kind. The one food she liked to eat was potatoes, and she had a
habit of chewing caraway seeds constantly to improve her digestion.
Lehzen was often criticized by those who resented her influence over
the young princess, but she was the only person who had solely Victoria's interests at heart. Because of this, she earned the young royal's
trust and affection, and she never betrayed it. When Victoria was ill,
Lehzen stayed by her side, quietly stitching doll clothes, as Victoria's
mother continued to visit friends and travel. If Lehzen fell ill, Victoria missed her. She wrote later, "The Princess was her only object and
her only thought. . . . She never for the thirteen years she was governess to Princess Victoria *once left* her." As princess and later as queen,
Victoria craved singular devotion.

Lehzen's greatest concern was that Victoria be protected, well
educated, and shaped into a strong-minded queen. She was often
blamed for Victoria's defiance and independence, but she was strict;
she had simply recognized Victoria's innate pluck and nurtured it.
She told Victoire, "I have to be sure not created, but nourished in the
Princess, *one* quality *which* is to test, consider and to stand firmly by

that which the Princess finds right and good." It was provocative then even to suggest that girls' minds were worth cultivating and that strength was an important quality in a young woman. While Victoria thought Elizabeth I a good ruler but a harsh and immodest woman, Lehzen told a member of Conroy's family that Elizabeth was the "model of perfection," adding that she would "pardon wickedness in a Queen, but not weakness." While not without her faults, Victoria was never weak. She was a quick, intelligent pupil who liked alchemy and hated Latin and anatomy. But her greatest passions were more dramatic than academic: dancing, singing, drawing, theater, opera, and ballet. Victoria was a girl who spoke and dreamed in emphatic italics.

It was often said that Victoria resembled the men in her family more than the women. This was in some ways unfortunate, given the male Hanoverian tendency toward thick builds and rounded faces, with weak chins, strong noses, and protruding eyes. It is true she would never be a great beauty, and always wrestled with her weight, though at times—especially as a child, when in love, or when laughing—she was certainly charming. Portraits show her lovely neck, delicate cheekbones, neatly arched eyebrows, and rosebud mouth. She seemed a sweet toddler: fair-haired, with a friendly face and wide blue trusting eyes. Lord Albemarle described her at age seven as a "bright pretty girl" who tended to flowers under his window in a large straw hat; he was amused to watch her water her little feet as liberally as the blooms. As she grew older, she grew slender, her hair darkened, and her expression grew more serious, imperious, and shy. The solemn paintings do not capture the lightness of her voice, or the grace and ease of her movement. Harriet Arbuthnot, a close friend of the Duke of Wellington, said Victoria at age nine was "the most charming child" she had seen: "a fine, beautifully made, handsome creature, quite playful & childish."

What was most unusual about Victoria's education was that her fiery spirit was not quenched—or that all early attempts to curb it failed spectacularly. Other girls then were taught to be meek and demure. The influential author Hannah More wrote earlier in the nineteenth century that, while boys were praised for having a "bold, independent, enterprising spirit," girls were not, and any such spirit should be suppressed when discovered. "Girls should be taught to give up their opinions betimes," More wrote, "and not pertinaciously carry on a dispute, even if they should know themselves to be in the right. . . . It is of the greatest importance to their future happiness, that they should acquire a submissive temper and a forbearing spirit." Victoria could not have been more different.

The young princess longed for what she called "mirth." She had a good sense of humor with great gifts of mimicry and repartee. Her grandmother described her as a comical, precocious clown. Victoria also loved dressing in costume. Her disguises included an old Turkish lawyer, with a large green shawl turban, a white beard, and a green cloak, a nun, a lady with a turban, and a bandit's wife with colored shawl and gold chains. Leopold frequently reminded her there was more to life than fun—exercise, for example, or learning—which was scant solace for a restless teenager. She retorted, "*pleasure* does more good than a hundred walks and rides." She told him that she "longed sadly for some gaiety."

Victoria was happiest when hosting visitors, and unhappiest when they left. When her cousins Princes Alexander and Ernest of Württemberg arrived in 1833, she was delighted, writing: "They are both extremely tall, Alexander is very handsome and Ernst has a very kind expression. They are both extremely amiable." They told her fascinating stories about Europe, and military campaigns, and she was bereft when they left: "We shall miss them at breakfast, at luncheon, at dinner, riding, sailing, driving, walking, in fact everywhere." In the summer of 1833, the charming Feodora and her two children, Eliza and Charles, came to stay at Kensington Palace. When they left, Victoria drew a picture of Eliza in her traveling dress to give to her young niece, and in a rambling fourteen-page diary entry, wrote:

It is such a VERY VERY GREAT HAPPINESS for me to have my DEAREST most DEARLY BELOVED sister with me in my room. . . . How I love her I cannot say. . . . It is TOO DREADFUL for me to think that in an hour I shall not see *Dearest* Feodora's *dear kind* sweet face, and the *little beauty* Eliza jumping about, and *good honest* Charles running about the room, any more. I was so dreadfully affected with grief at thinking of parting, that I fell round her [Feodora's] neck and we both cried *bitterly* and pressed each other in our arms *most tenderly*. . . . When I came home I was in such a state of grief that I knew not what to do with myself. I sobbed and cried most violently the whole morning. . . .

Just an hour and a half after Leopold left her place at Claremont, on September 21, 1836, after a six-day visit, Victoria wrote to tell him "how *very, very sad* I am that you have left us, and to repeat, what I think you know pretty well, *how much* I love you." The thought that he was leaving, and she might not see him for a year, she wrote, "makes me cry. . . . It is dreadful in this life, that one is destined, and *particularly unhappy me,* to be almost always separated from those one loves most dearly." She signed off as his "ever devoted and most affectionately attached Niece and *Child.*"

In the absence of friends, the little princess grew deeply attached to her pets. With the exception of some unfortunate canaries in the Kensington Palace menageries, whom she tortured, Victoria loved animals. Her favorite dog was a Cavalier King Charles spaniel called Dash, whom she played with for hours, dressing him up in red jackets and blue trousers and spoiling him with gingerbread and rubber balls at Christmas. Dash slept by her side when she was ill, and swam after her yacht when she was sailing. The young princess also spent many hours playing with her dolls. When she was nine, Victoria sent reports of her baby dolls to Feodora; sometimes they even wrote letters themselves. After one favorite baby had an unfortunate accident and lost its head, Feodora wrote, "I hope [baby] is almost recovered and that this serious bruise has no influence on its general health, and that it is not the less in favor for having been beheaded for a short while." But Victoria had found a better doll, writing, "Lehzen mended the baby, and I put her by, as a relick; but not withstanding this, I have got a lovely baby, which is called Clara."

By the time she was ten, Victoria was bored with her crowd of toy infants. By then she was engrossed in making a series of 132 sophisticated wooden dolls. She and Lehzen spent hundreds of hours carefully sewing clothes and copying figures from characters in the court, ballet, or opera. They painted them painstakingly, sewed their clothes, and listed them all in a book. Victoria took them traveling with her sometimes, and would carefully "arrange them" on beautifully upholstered chairs in each new environment, their somber little faces peering at her, all in a row.

In the absence of a father or any meaningful contact with her paternal uncles, Uncle Leopold became a crucial and adored figure. Some of the happiest moments of her childhood were spent at Claremont, his house in Surrey, to London's south. On seaside holidays, Leopold, Victoria, and Victoria's mother would be seen walking along the shore as children splashed and women wearing ankle-length bathing suits laughed in the shallows. Victoria sobbed when she had to return to Kensington.

Leopold's letters to Victoria show the warm side of the future king of the Belgians, who had been deeply wounded by the loss of his young bride, Charlotte. He was urbane, handsome, and elegant, but some, like his father-in-law, King George IV, thought him slick and ponderous. He became increasingly eccentric as he grew older. He often sported three-inch heels and a feather boa, wore a wig to prevent catching a cold, and propped his mouth open with wedges of gold as he slept, for reasons nobody could fathom. He also had a reportedly enormous sexual appetite, but he treated some of his lovers with contempt. In 1829–30, when Victoria was ten, he lured the beautiful Prussian actress Caroline Bauer to England on the pretense of marrying her, put her in a country estate, and visited her daily. Unfortunately for Caroline, he was very taken with the then popular pursuit of "drizzling": gold and silver tassels were taken from epaulettes and inserted into a machine, out of which came powder that could be melted into metal. Leopold occupied himself with drizzling for hours as Caroline sat so bored that she claimed she had "nearly unlearned laughing." In the months before Caroline's brother came over from Germany and demanded her return, Leopold drizzled enough thread to make a silver soup tureen. He gave it to Victoria.

Leopold took great interest in the welfare of the niece he called "dear little chicken." He regularly imparted moral lessons. First, he told her constantly to examine her own flaws and work hard. "A good heart and truly honorable character" were, he said when she turned thirteen, the "most indispensable qualifications for her future position." When she had her fourteenth birthday, he warned her not to be "intoxicated by greatness and success nor cast down by misfortune." Second, he taught her to be impartial, a lesson she would defy throughout her life. Third, he instructed her to be firm and decisive—but to wait before deciding. Fourth, study history and learn from it, and fifth, be watchful for hypocrisy. He also strongly advised the teenager whose ancestors had a tendency to plumpness to exercise and to refrain from her habit of eating too much or too quickly. When Victoria was fifteen, she urged Leopold to visit, if only just to be "an eye-witness of my extreme prudence in eating, which would astonish you."

King George IV was not a popular ruler. The Duke of Wellington considered him the worst man he had ever met, without a single redeeming quality. A reactionary Tory, the king fought the ongoing reform movement and had to be forced to assent to a bill allowing Catholics to stand for Parliament in 1829. William Makepeace Thackeray dismissed him as "nothing but a coat, and a wig, and a mask smiling below it." The extravagant king had also become a symbol of the gross excess of Britain's rich, as he drained public funds when the country was crippled by the cost of a war with France that had ended in 1815. When he became king at age fifty-eight, he weighed 245 pounds, had a fifty-inch waist, and was addicted to opium. His belly hung to his knees. (When Victoria was a small child, so chubby she could barely walk, Lady Granville had called her "le roi Georges in petticoats.")

Yet Victoria was delighted when, in 1826, she received an invitation to visit her uncle the king at the Royal Lodge in Windsor, where he was living with his mistress. The corpulent king, whose face was covered in greasepaint and topped with a wig, and whose large body glittered with imitation jewelry, presented Victoria with a miniature of himself. The sharp-eyed Russian ambassador's wife, Princess Lieven, said in spite of the "caresses the King lavished on her" she could see that "he did not like dandling on his sixty-four-year-old knee this little bit of the future, aged 7." But Victoria later described her "large and gouty" uncle as having "a wonderful dignity and charm of manner." By 1828, he had become a recluse who spent most days sleeping in his bed at Windsor Castle. The biographer Roger Fulford described George IV as a man who spent his final years "fondling an unpopular mistress, hoarding every garment he had ever worn, [and] clearing the streets before he went out for a drive that no one might see how the years had ravaged his appearance."

As the king grew weaker, the intrigue in Victoria's inner circle grew more intense, largely due to a man Victoria would come to hate. The manipulative, charming Captain John Conroy was a former soldier of Irish descent who had been her father's equerry and was now her mother's closest adviser. He had promised Victoire protection when her husband died, and he inveigled his way into her affections. He was occasionally kind to Victoria, but he also cruelly teased her, telling her once that she resembled the ugly Duke of Gloucester—an awful taunt for a young girl, and one that haunted her for decades. Victoria's chief playmate was Victoire, one of Conroy's six children, with whom she spent many hours riding, playing dress-up, and building cottages made of cards. But Victoria never really liked or trusted her. Mostly, though, she loathed Conroy, whom she believed had somehow hypnotized her mother. She took offense at his "impudent and insulting conduct," as well as the presumption that he could tell her what to do. He monitored her every move, and hungered for an official position—such as private secretary to the queen—that would enable him to control her.

Conroy was paranoid about members of the royal family wanting to kidnap or corrupt Victoria, so he and the duchess almost completely cut her off from them. He also fired Baroness Späth, the duchess's lady-in-waiting—whom Victoria loved and had known since her birth—because he believed that not only was she spoiling Victoria, she was spying for the king. The royal household was stunned by this sudden act—the baroness had been loyally serving the duchess for more than two decades. Victoria grew extremely worried that next, she would lose Lehzen—"the most *affectionate, devoted, attached* and *disinterested* friend I have."

The royal family grew angry at, and puzzled by, Conroy's disproportionate influence. In 1830, Victoria's aunt the Duchess of Clarence (later Queen Adelaide) wrote expressing concern that Victoire was becoming more isolated. The duchess conveyed the "general wish" of the royal family that she not allow Conroy "too much influence" over her. Conroy's family was, after all, not of high enough rank to be the only entourage of the future queen of England. The letter only fueled the shared paranoia of Conroy and the duchess. They spoke of little but the health of the king, and the air in the palace was thick with scheming.

At 3:30 a.m. on June 26, 1830, after a violent coughing fit, George IV suddenly cried out: "Good God, what is this?" He gripped the hand of his page boy, and reportedly answered himself: "My boy, this is death." Mourning was muted. It was decided that he had died of "obesity of the heart," though a great consumption of laudanum added to his decline. His brother William was thrilled. Now in his sixties, he had been preparing to be king for years, going on long, vigorous walks and drinking a medicinal tonic of lemon-flavored barley water. He had not accomplished much, apart from siring ten illegitimate children, and he was itching to wear the crown.

But the eleven-year-old Victoria heard the news with dismay. The next day, she woke hours before dawn in the cozy bed she took with her on all her travels, her chest tight with anxiety. At breakfast, complaining of a headache, she asked if she could go for a ride. She brandished her whip and held tight; she could have galloped for hours—pressing into the wind, her eyes stinging, the sun on her back. The throne could too soon be hers, but she didn't want it. She knew ambition was curdling her mother's heart, just as apprehension was gripping hers. It was now, when still a child who played with dolls, that Victoria's seven-year battle with her mother began, one that would deeply scar her. But her prayers would change once she realized her mother was seeking to snatch away her crown before it could be placed on her head.

CHAPTER 4

An Impossible, Strange Madness

The most formidably extreme of all [the eighteen-year-old Victoria's] extreme qualities was her strength of character. . . . No one was ever less the creature of whim or vacillating impulse. Once she had made up her mind what she ought to do, she adhered inflexibly to it. It was not in her to compromise.

—DAVID CECIL

Victoria was lying on her bed, furious. She had never felt sicker. Her head was pounding, she felt faint and nauseous, her fever had been high for days, and her cheeks had grown so hollow she barely recognized her own reflection. Standing next to her was Baroness Lehzen, chewing steadily on caraway seeds. Opposite was an over-wrought Duchess of Kent, who was dressed in bright silk and clenching her fists with frustration. Victoria's mother stood still, staring out of one of the hotel windows that overlooked the harbor shore at Ramsgate, which was bright with parasols and faces pink with the afternoon sun.

Conroy and the duchess wanted two things. First, for Conroy to be appointed Victoria's private secretary when she was queen (a peerage—and a place in the House of Lords—would have followed this, which was his greatest ambition). Second, for the duchess to become the regent and rule in Victoria's stead if the king died before Victoria turned eighteen—or twenty-one. Victoria was of such tender age, the duchess said, and they all lived together so closely. Would she not desire, and need, Conroy's wise counsel? But Conroy had needled and bullied Victoria for years; rather than have him run her future queendom, she wanted to banish him from her future queendom altogether. Victoria stared at her mother coldly: "No."

The group fell silent. Outside, they could hear the sounds of laughter and children at play. Suddenly Conroy swept into the room, lips thin with anger. He shouted at Victoria, accusing her of being a stupid, selfish, unreasonable fool. Her head was so full of rubbish, he said, with all her silly dolls and love of opera, that it was obvious that she could not rule on her own. And she *owed* him. After all, think of what he—and her mother—had done for her.

Conroy then forced a pen and paper into Victoria's hand, gripping it painfully, urging her to sign the document that would have appointed him private secretary. Victoria shook her head, grimaced, and pulled her beloved dog Dash closer. She saw the way her mother looked at Conroy, beseechingly, almost coy, and it made her sick.

Victoria did not write about this incident. Her diary was, unusually, blank for three weeks as she wrestled with illness and Conroy's bullying. It was only later that she revealed her trauma to Lord Melbourne: "All I underwent there; their (Ma's and JC) attempt (when I was still very ill) to make me promise *before* hand, which I resisted in spite of my illness, and their harshness—my beloved Lehzen supporting me alone." Part of Victoria's trauma came from distress that her mother was not taking her illness seriously; only Lehzen did. The duchess and Conroy shrugged off Victoria's cries for a doctor for days. Conroy did not want people to know Victoria was ill for fear she might be considered unfit to rule. (The local press was told one of the servants had been ill, and that Victoria only had a "slight cold.")

When finally summoned, Dr. Clark said she had "bilious fever," but it is more likely to have been tonsillitis, or even typhoid. It was clearly grave; she had been confined to bed for five weeks, at the end of which she could walk only a few steps at a time and her hair had fallen out in clumps. By the time she emerged from her room, limping and thin, she was incensed by her mother's lack of care. In contrast, her governess was dramatically praised: "My *dearest best* Lehzen has been & still is (for I require a great deal of care still) MOST UN-CEASING & INDEFATIGABLE in her *great* care of me. I am still VERY weak and am grown VERY *thin*." She studiously followed her doctor's advice, leaving her windows open, chewing food slowly, and lifting small clubs to build up her muscles. Slowly she recovered.

Had Conroy been a more astute observer, Victoria's refusal to hand over her power would not have come as a surprise. Warmth and persuasion would have been far more effective. As Leopold wrote to her, "He imagined he might get you into a sort of *captivity* which myself being near you, at your commands, was impossible, strange madness." Victoria had a quiet steeliness that stymied those who underestimated her. She would never forgive Conroy for the decade he spent bullying her. In 1833, the year she turned fourteen, she drew a picture titled "Amazons at War." In it, women with long streaming hair are riding into battle, their horses trampling men underfoot; one fires an arrow directly into the face of a male soldier, killing him.

The elaborate, strict regime concocted to spin a queen from a volatile teenager was called the "Kensington System." From the age of five, Victoria was not allowed to be alone, to walk downstairs without holding the hand of an adult, or to play with other children without a guardian. Much of the system was well intentioned, as a way of raising a proper queen. The duchess and Conroy also wanted to produce a progressive queen, a Whig like Conroy, instead of a Tory like the rest of the royal family. (In the early part of the nineteenth century, Whigs stood for abolition of slavery, equality for Catholics, expansion of the vote, and free trade, as well as a constitutional monarchy, where the king or queen acts as a head of state and the ability to make laws rests with Parliament.)

But the Kensington System was not solely, or even primarily, for the benefit of Victoria. Her half brother Charles of Leiningen defined the goals as (1) winning Victoria popularity by cutting her off from the royal court's bad morals and politics, (2) gaining regency (due to the need "to assure a pleasant and honorable future for the Duchess of Kent as well"), and (3) making Conroy private secretary. The monitoring carried out to achieve this, he wrote, was exhaustive, of even "the smallest and most insignificant detail."

Another, more sinister specter drove the scheme: the prospect of murder. The duchess and Conroy claimed to believe that Ernest, the Duke of Cumberland, was planning to kill his niece so he could become king; he was next in line for the throne after her. Conroy told the duchess that Uncle Ernest would poison Victoria's milk, kidnap her when she was weak, and let her die. Victoria scoffed at this idea, calling it "all Sir John's invention," but her mother was genuinely frightened. She made sure someone tasted Victoria's breakfast each morning.

At sixty-four, William IV was the oldest person ever to be crowned England's sovereign. After the French revolution of 1830, in which Charles X was overthrown, William IV tried to stem local republicanism by being more frugal than his opulent older brother and involving himself in politics. But his conservatism and coolness toward reform quickly alienated his increasingly restless subjects. In 1830, only 13 percent of men in England and Wales—those with property— could vote. Some small "rotten boroughs" still existed, where the local aristocratic landowner could effectively choose the local MP, and many manufacturing cities were entirely unrepresented. The half a million people living in Birmingham, Leeds, Manchester, and Sheffield, for example, had no representative in Parliament.

In 1830, impetus for change came when the progressive Whig Party swept into power. In 1831, when the Reform Bill failed to pass for the second time, the country erupted. Castles were burned down, homes were torched, and several hundred were killed or wounded in uprisings in Derby, mostly by the military. Four rioters were hanged. Politicians grew extremely nervous about the possibility of revolution if eligibility for the vote was not expanded. The next year, one million men gained the vote after the Reform Act was passed on the third attempt. Now 18 percent of the adult male population could vote. New cities that had boomed during the Industrial Revolution were given seats, and the most corrupt of the rotten boroughs were eradicated. The elected House of Commons grew in stature, while the House of Lords shrank. This decade marked the zenith of Whig efficiency: in 1833, slavery was finally abolished in almost all of the British Empire, three decades earlier than it was in America.

In November 1830, the Duchess of Kent wept with joy after the House of Commons passed a bill that provided an additional £10,000 for Victoria's household and education and made the duchess regent if William IV passed away without leaving an heir. (The next alternative—the Duke of Cumberland—was unimaginable.) "This is the first really happy day," she said, "I have spent since I lost the Duke of Kent."

From this point, the bitter hostility between the households of the king and the duchess seeped into public view. On one occasion, when the duchess was visiting Queen Adelaide and one of the king's (illegitimate) children came into the room, she froze and left immediately. She also took every opportunity to remind the king that her daughter was the next in line, deliberately provoking him by running up the royal standard to indicate when Victoria was at Ramsgate, and encouraging military salutes to "Her Royal Highness" when at sea. She and Conroy paraded Victoria across the country in what became the first of the royal tours, aimed at drumming up favorable publicity and exposing the princess to her future subjects. Victoria's diary entry of July 31, 1832, described such a trip, to Wales. She was astonished at the impact of coal mining in the country near Birmingham:

The men, women, children, country and houses are all black. The country is very desolate everywhere; there is coal about, and the grass is quite blasted and black. I just now see an extraordinary building flaming with fire. The country continues black, engines flaming, coals in abundance, everywhere smoking and burning coal-heaps, intermingled with wretched huts and carts and little ragged children.

It was a world Victoria passed through for only a brief moment, slack-jawed. Her characteristic candor was later edited out of official selections from her journals—complaints about ugly scenery, dense, demanding crowds, drunken townsfolk and an unfortunate episode when her carriage drove over a man on foot. She fought fiercely with her mother about the need to go on these exhausting trips at all. But her great popularity became evident as she traveled the country; Conroy's chutzpah aggravated the king.

The rift between the two families soon became a public soap opera. The duchess refused to attend William IV's coronation, believing he had snubbed Victoria by not allowing her to walk behind him in the procession. She sent the king a note saying Victoria had grazed her knee in a fall and they would not be able to attend. They went instead to the chalky, gray beaches of the Isle of Wight, ignoring the widespread condemnation of her impertinence that ensued. *The Times* wrote scathingly about the duchess's snub, attributing it to a "systematic, determined opposition" to anything the king wanted. In November 1833, the diarist Thomas Creevey described the duchess as "the most restless, persevering, troublesome devil possible."

In turn, William IV publicly humiliated Conroy at every opportunity. In the middle of a drawing room session, he told the Duchess of Kent's gentlemen—including Conroy—to leave on the grounds that only gentlemen of the king and queen were allowed to be there. When Conroy was ordered out of Victoria's confirmation ceremony in 1835, Victoria was furious. Her confirmation had been "one of the most solemn and important events and acts in her life" and she had gone with "the firm determination to become a true Christian." She walked out fuming, humiliated to be suffering on such a day, and on behalf of a man she despised, and to have such an important day ruined.

By her sixteenth birthday, Victoria had bloomed. Much to her annoyance, she was still just four feet eleven and also "unhappily very fat." Leopold wrote that he heard "a certain little princess . . . eats a little too much, and almost always a little too *fast*." She had terrible table manners, gobbling her food, picking bones, and doing "unmentionable things with her asparagus" (which probably meant eating it with her fingers). Still, as she grew older, she grew slender and people admired her skin and dramatically large blue eyes, her long, thick hair and robust health. At this age, the reins were slackened a little; she was allowed to read some novels, style her own hair, take Italian and singing lessons, and attend more of her mother's parties, where she would gaze with delight at the good-looking young men and dance with them as long as she was allowed. She adored music and opera; her teen idols were ballet dancers and singers—one of whom, the great Luigi Lablache, was hired to teach Victoria how to sing.

It was "generally known," writes Dulcie Ashdown, "that Victoria crossed the threshold into womanhood" at this age, although, thankfully, Victoria's "first menstrual period was never announced officially." Doubtless she was baffled by what was then called "the monthlies," "the turn," or "poorliness." Menstruation was not generally discussed, and most people believed women were incapacitated by it. Doctors advised girls to avoid dancing in heated rooms, stay out of the cold and rain, and try not to think too much. The writer James McGrigor Allan told the Anthropological Society of London in 1869:

> At such times, women are unfit for any great mental or physical labour. They suffer under a languor and depression which disqualify them for thought or action, and render it extremely doubtful how far they can be considered responsible beings while the crisis lasts. . . . In intellectual labour, man has sur-

passed, does now, and always will surpass woman, for the obvious reason that nature does not periodically interrupt his
thought and application.

What is most striking about Victoria is that apart from wanting to
be taller and thinner, she cared little about her appearance. She knew
she was no beauty and did not dwell on it. She joked about her looks
with her half sister, writing that she was "very happy to hear that the
portrait of my ugly face pleased you." Yet she genuinely took pleasure
from the aesthetic appearance of others—both male and female. Her
second cousin Charles, the Duke of Brunswick, particularly fascinated her, with his dark mustache and the fur-trimmed coat he wore
riding. She greatly admired the way he did his hair, which hung
"wildly about his face."

Victoria was considered a great catch. Many men became obsessed
with her, and a long list of potential matches was discussed in several
newspapers. Robert Browning wrote that when Victoria was ill, she
was "bent on marrying nobody but Lord Elphinstone," a dashing
man two years her senior. In February 1836, after she had recovered
and her doctor finally allowed her to go to St. James's Palace, Lord
Elphinstone sketched her portrait, watching her across the pews. She
sat self-consciously, dressed in a fancy gray coat from Paris, with the
weight of his gaze upon her. The Duchess of Kent made sure Elphinstone, an army captain and lord-in-waiting to William IV, was sent to
India. It was rumored that he and Victoria had fallen in love, and the
gossip alone was enough to see him banished. Other rumored suitors
included the Orange brothers, George Cumberland, the Duke of Orleans, the Duke of Nemours, one of the Württembergs, King Otto of
Greece, and even, rather oddly, Uncle Leopold.

But Leopold had already selected a mate for his niece—her first
cousin Albert—and openly tried to orchestrate their union. In May
1836, Albert and his brother Ernest made their first visit to Victoria
for her seventeenth birthday. Victoria adored her cousins, "so *very
very* merry and gay and happy, like young people ought to be." The

athletic Albert she found "extremely handsome." "His eyes are large and blue," she wrote, "and he has a beautiful nose and a very sweet mouth with fine teeth." But Albert was also frail, had a tendency to faint, and could not keep pace with his cousin. At her birthday ball at St. James's, Albert retired early; he had "turned as pale as ashes, & we all feared he might faint; he therefore went home." The next day, he stayed in his room all day without eating, due to a "bilious attack," before emerging looking "pale and delicate." Victoria wrote to Leopold, with a tinge of frustration, "I am sorry to say that we have an invalid in the house in the person of Albert."

At the end, Victoria politely thanked Leopold: "[Albert] is so sensible, so kind, and so good, and so amiable too," she wrote, adding that he had, "besides, the most pleasing and delightful exterior and appearance you can possibly see." But Victoria was not at all interested in marriage. She invited Albert's father to her coronation, but not his sons. They would not see each other again for three years.

Throughout this period, Conroy's behavior was genuinely puzzling. Where did his sense of entitlement come from? How could he presume to have a place at the royal table? Why would he tell Victoria, she wondered, that "his daughters were as high as me"? Years later, she was still mystified: "*Why* he outraged & insulted *me, I really never* cd understand." The answer lies in a tiny old church at Oxford, where the Conroy archives are kept in Balliol College. In a faded maroon journal, with a broken clasp and marbled pages, John Conroy's grandson recorded a secret message dated December 1868. It was written in code that seems to have drawn on Sir Thomas More's Utopian alphabet. It spells out: "Lady Conroy is said to be the daughter of the Duke of Kent." In other words, John Conroy believed that his wife, Elizabeth Fisher, was the illegitimate daughter of the Duke of Kent, Victoria's father, conceived while he was living in Canada, which would have made her Victoria's half sister. And this, of course, would have made Conroy Victoria's brother-in-law—an equal, not a subordinate. On his deathbed, John Conroy's eldest son, Edward, also confessed to this belief. It was technically impossible, self-serving, and untrue, but it explains Conroy's sense of familiarity and control. It was clear that Conroy did not want to advise the queen, he wanted to rule in her stead, with the duchess.

There can be little doubt there were erotic undertones to Conroy's relationship with the duchess, a woman who was alone for so many years. Victoria worried that they were lovers. The loathsome Duke of Cumberland had said so in front of her when she was just a little girl. The Duke of Wellington told Greville that Victoria had witnessed some "familiarities" between her mother and John Conroy, and that after she told Späth of this, Späth chastised the duchess. Victoria denied in her later years that her mother had ever taken Conroy as a lover, although that very suspicion weighed on her as a child. It is probable that the widowed duchess had developed an intense affection for a man known for an uncanny ability to bewitch women. It would certainly have explained his hold on her. King Leopold called Conroy "a real Mephisto" and told a nineteen-year-old Victoria that he ruled over the duchess with "a degree of power which in times of old one would have thought to proceed from witchcraft." Even in old age, the formidable queen shuddered at the thought of the man she called a "monster."

Conroy devised new strategies hourly: while combing his thinning hair, while flattering members of Parliament over bottles of wine, while enduring endless games of whist with the duchess. The more despairing he became, the more firmly Victoria stood her ground. She had learned control and patience in the face of persecution. It was her uncle King William IV who would finally, spectacularly, erupt over the overt, poisonous scheming. His rage would cause a scandal.

CHAPTER 5

"Awful Scenes in the House"

They plague her, every hour and every day.

—BARON STOCKMAR

King William IV was riding through the streets of London staring out his carriage window. It was a cool, windy day in August 1836, and he had just given a speech to mark the end of the session of Parliament.

He had waited years to be king, but now he could barely enjoy it. The endless calls for parliamentary reform were irritating. At first he supported reform, and was pleased to be liked for it. But then they became so greedy. He had not wanted to pass that reform bill, even though the lower classes had threatened rebellion. He told the prime minister that he would defend London, raise the royal standard at the military depot at Weedon, and fight to the death. Victoria could have joined him. But eventually he gave in and the bill passed. Even that didn't seem to satisfy the malcontents for long.

As the golden royal carriage made its way slowly past the Thames, the king remembered a time when you could catch salmon swimming upstream, when the river was a dull green, not dark with sewage. Soon it would be as black as the River Irwell in Manchester, where corpses were regularly found. He wiped his nose with the back of his forefinger, as was his habit, and stared out at the street chaos: an organ grinder making a racket, a man wearing a sandwich board advertising soap, little boys selling matches, street vendors hawking pies, an Indian beggar with a syphilis-ravaged nose playing the drums. The horses clacked noisily along the cobblestones, past piles of manure that splattered hemlines and turned streets to muck.

They pulled up in the driveway of Kensington Palace, which the king owned, even though the Duchess of Kent, Victoria, his younger brother the Duke of Sussex, and his sister, Princess Sophia, all lived there. A few months ago, the duchess had asked to move upstairs, farther away from the damp of the underground sewers, where mushrooms grew on the ceilings and workers found corks, cats, dead seals, false teeth, and even corpses. The doctor had recommended airier rooms after Victoria's sickness at Ramsgate—but the king refused the request.

He walked up the stairs, into the King's Gallery with its large windows overlooking the park, and stopped short. In direct defiance of his orders, it had been renovated. He counted: the duchess was now occupying seventeen rooms. During the three-hour drive to Windsor, the usually good-humored William IV thought about every slight the duchess had inflicted on him and his family. He had never liked his brother Edward anyway—and he was somehow now beholden to his ungrateful widow.

At ten o'clock that night, the king strode into his birthday party at Windsor. He walked over to Victoria, took her hands, and told her he wished he saw more of her. Then he said loudly to the Duchess of Kent that he knew she had taken apartments at Kensington "not only without his consent, but contrary to his commands" and that he "neither understood nor would endure conduct so disrespectful to him." He walked away from her, vowing to stymie her vulgar grasping for power.

The next night, August 21, one hundred palace guests sat in a row at the table for a birthday dinner, their faces shadowed with candlelight. The Duchess of Kent sat on the king's right, and one of his sisters sat on the left. William IV drained his goblet of wine and stood to speak, his rouged cheeks flaming, his large stomach straining against his corset:

> I trust in God that my life may be spared for nine months longer, after which period, in the event of my death, no regency would take place. I should then have the satisfaction of leaving the Royal authority to the personal exercise of that young lady, heiress presumptive of the Crown, and not in the hands of a person near me, who is surrounded by evil advisers, and is herself incompetent to act with propriety in the situation in which she would be placed. I have no hesitation in saying that I have been insulted—grossly and continuously insulted—by that person, but I am determined to endure no longer a course of behavior so disrespectful to me. . . . Amongst many other things I have particularly to complain of the manner in which that young lady has been kept away from my Court; she has been repeatedly kept from my drawing-rooms, at which she ought always to have been present. . . . I am King, and I am determined to make my authority respected, and for the future I shall insist and command that the Princess do upon all occasions appear at my Court, as it is her duty to do.

Victoria burst into tears. The servants cast furtive glances at the flushed face of the Duchess of Kent, who was composing retorts she would never utter. Piles of strawberry jelly, sponge cakes, and trifle were left untouched as the company quickly retired. The duchess fled to Claremont the next day.

By 1837, the atmosphere in Kensington Palace was suffocating as the rows grew fiercer, uglier, and more frequent. A miserable Victoria complained of headaches, strange pains, and weariness, and the duchess summoned her son—and Victoria's half brother—Charles of Leiningen to act as a mediator. Charles was shocked at Conroy's "terrible hatred" for, and harsh treatment of, Lehzen, but he had always liked Conroy and quickly took his side. He decided Victoria was being irrational and dismissed her loathing for Conroy as a "childish whim" spurred by Lehzen. His attempts at brokering peace failed: he was not able to persuade Conroy to apologize, Victoria to trust Conroy, or Leopold to tell Victoria to extend the regency until she was twenty-one. Victoria was crushed; even her brother had betrayed her.

In late May, Leopold, who was in Belgium, decided to send his trusted adviser Stockmar to England to assess the situation. The astute Stockmar decided the causes of the conflict were the "innate personality of the Princess," and "the behavior of Sir John towards the Princess herself." Sir John's problem, he said, was his abruptness, sense of entitlement, and the way that he acted as if he were "the regulator of the whole machine."

Yet Victoria held the trump card. Every day, she grew more aware of herself "and more conscious of her own strength," but the relentless harassment depressed her: "They plague her, every hour and every day," Stockmar told Leopold. Her mother openly chastised Victoria, reminding her of her youth and telling her that she owed all her success to her mother's good reputation. The woman who had insisted on breastfeeding her child and delighted in her fat cheeks had grown hard with anxious hunger for power, seduced by her own victim narrative of the long-suffering mother. She pointed out repeatedly that she had given up her life in another country to devote herself to raising a girl into a queen. Victoria soon stopped speaking to her.

In May 1837, King William IV decided to intervene. He wrote to Victoria a few days before she turned eighteen, telling her he would secure her independence on her birthday: he would apply to Parliament for £10,000 a year for her own use and allow her to appoint her own Privy Purse, or financial manager, who would answer only to her, and he would give her the power to create her own establishment. The king instructed his courier, the Lord Chamberlain, to ensure the letter was placed in Victoria's hands. Both Conroy and the duchess tried to grab the letter, but Victoria took it and read it carefully before passing it to her mother. The duchess was enraged, most of all because she thought the king showed no respect for her work as a mother. She knew her chance of securing a regency would expire in less than a week. She decided to reject the offer in Victoria's name without telling her.

After listening to her mother's tirade, Victoria went to her room. She wrote in her diary: "Felt very miserable & agitated. Did not go down to dinner." She would have loved to accept the king's offer but knew her mother would not allow it, and she still lived under her authority. Ignorant of any other option, Victoria had obediently copied out a letter her mother had written on Sir John Conroy's advice and sent it as her formal answer. She referred to her youth and inexperience and said she wished to remain in the care of her mother, who should have all her money. The king was not fooled: "Victoria has not written that letter."

On the morning of May 24, 1837, a bright flag bearing one word flapped against the gray, cloudy sky above Kensington Palace: VICTORIA. She had turned eighteen at last. The shop windows were shuttered as musicians played and minstrels danced along the flower-strewn streets of Kensington. At 7 A.M., a band of wind instruments and harps performed on the terrace under Victoria's window: "Here's a nation's grateful tears / For the fairest flower of May." Victoria, looking down from her window, asked if they could play it again.

She was relieved, writing in her journal:

Today is my 18th birthday! How old! And yet how far am I
from being what I should be. I shall from this day take the firm
resolution to study with renewed assiduity, to keep my attention always well fixed on whatever I am about, and to strive to
become every day less trifling and more fit for what, if Heaven
wills it, I'm some day to be!

The young princess had grown more excited about her destiny as
she had wrangled with her mother and ached for another life, one
that she could control and in which her mother would be forced to
answer to her.

When Victoria rode through the parks that afternoon with her
mother and brother, she was greeted with a roar of affection. The
mass of upturned faces on the sidewalks moved her: "The anxiety of
the people to see poor stupid me was very great, and I must say I am
quite touched by it, and feel proud which I always have done of my
country and of the English Nation." But the public cheer only high-
lighted how grim her home life was by comparison, and Victoria
grew despondent as the celebrations continued. Even a spectacular
birthday ball, and her pale yellow dress covered in flower blossoms,
could not lift her mood.

Lord Liverpool climbed out of his carriage at Kensington Palace on
June 15, 1837, under blue summer skies. He was wearing a gray suit
and a top hat—the top hat was now considered the mark of a gentleman, even though the first man to sport one in public, forty years
earlier, was arrested on the grounds that it had "a shiny luster calculated to alarm timid people." (Four women had fainted upon seeing
it, and pedestrians had booed.) Lord Liverpool, a Tory like nearly
everyone in the royal family and the younger half brother of the former prime minister, was one of very few people trusted by both the
duchess and her daughter. His task was to break the impasse.

Liverpool began by meeting with Conroy, who explained, as one man to another, that Victoria and Lehzen had taken an irrational dislike to him. First, he said, Lehzen had to go. Second, Victoria's "insurmountable objection to his being appointed to the situation of secretary or private political adviser" was ridiculous, as she would be unable to function without his guidance. She was totally unfit to consider matters of state, and while she was now eighteen, she was "younger in intellect than in years." Conroy explained that the princess was frivolous and "easily caught by fashion and appearances." Would Lord Liverpool make her see sense? Of course, all Conroy had in mind was her own welfare.

Lord Liverpool flatly rejected Conroy's request for an official position with the queen, telling him that he was very unpopular. As a concession, Liverpool said he might be appointed Keeper of the Privy Purse, who looked after the monarch's financial affairs, and receive a pension, if he did not interfere in politics and make his views "obvious to all." After "some reflection," Conroy agreed. The men shook hands.

Next was the recalcitrant princess. Victoria was waiting for Lord Liverpool, alone and prepared with a neat list of agenda items. She agreed that she would not have a private secretary and would entrust herself instead to the prime minister, Lord Melbourne. Working with Conroy, though, was out of the question. Surely Lord Liverpool was aware, she said, "of many slights & incivilities Sir John had been guilty of towards her," but beyond that "she knew things of him which rendered it totally impossible for her to place him in any confidential situation near her." She would not tolerate Conroy's occupying the position of Privy Purse. Lord Liverpool pushed for more information. What things did she know? Victoria would only say that she knew things about Sir John that "entirely took away her confidence in him, & that she knew of this herself without any other person informing her." Victoria had with her a letter that Lehzen had dictated, in which she refused to be bound by any promise. Finally, the teenager asked the former PM to open her tormentor's eyes "as to the difficulty of the situation in which they place me." She was firmly in command.

Lord Liverpool told the duchess that he could not change her daughter's mind. Conroy swore foully when he heard this. For the next few days, Victoria stayed in her room and spoke only to Lehzen. Conroy decided it was time for his final, desperate plan: locking Victoria up and forcing her to agree. His ally James Abercromby—a barrister who was then Speaker of the House of Commons—had told him that since Victoria would not listen to common sense, he should now use force. Conroy went to the duchess and declared that *"she must be coerced."*

As Victoria stared down relatives and bullies, in Parliament men were debating whether women should be allowed to observe parliamentary debates from the public gallery. On the day of Lord Liverpool's visit, June 15, a Mr. Grantley Berkeley had asked the House of Commons: "As to the presence of ladies . . . when they had a bouquet of flowers in their chamber, did they not find the air sweeter?" The honorable gentlemen did not, and voted against it.

When Victoria saw a band of Gypsies camped on the road near Leopold's English residence, Claremont House, she was captivated by their warmth. She visited them several times in January 1837, sketched pictures of them, sent them soup, and tried to arrange to have their children educated. When one of the young Gypsy women gave birth, Victoria had food and blankets delivered. She decided that if she was asked to sponsor the fatherless child, she would call him Leopold. The warm-hearted young Victoria did not show a shred of prejudice toward this illegitimate child. She envied and was fascinated by the cozy happiness in the Gypsies' homes:

> As we were walking along the road near to the tents, the woman who said she was called Cooper, who is generally the spokeswoman of the party, stepped across the road from the tents, & as we turned & stopped, came up to us with a whole swarm of

children, six I think. It was a singular, & yet a pretty & picturesc [*sic*] sight. She herself with nothing on her head, her raven hair hanging untidily about her shoulders, while the set of little *brats* swarming round her, with dark disheveled hair & dark dresses, all little things and all beautiful children. . . . The gipsies are a curious, peculiar & very hardy race, unlike any other!

At the time, Gypsies were maligned as lazy, uncouth, unwashed heathens, outcasts who drifted across Europe and filled the wards of workhouses. But Victoria thought them "falsely accused, cruelly wronged, and greatly ill-treated." Together she and Lehzen read a book called *Gipsies Advocate* by a Mr. Crabbe, which convinced them that poor people would respond to kindness. Conroy did not agree.

By 1837, King William IV was deaf and doubled over. Victoria rarely mentioned him in her journal, though when he fell seriously ill in May 1837, she felt sorry for him: "He was always personally kind to me." By mid-June, it was clear he was dying. The pressure on Victoria was enormous, and according to Stockmar, who visited on June 16, her mother had become extremely severe with her. If anyone outside the palace were aware that Victoria was an "oppressed Person," he wrote, everybody *"would fly to her assistance."* But no one did. Instead, Victoria learned, in the words of Stockmar, to "live on outwardly submissive and affectionate terms with people she distrusted and disliked."

Lehzen became a lightning rod for the discontent of the Conroy camp. By steeling Victoria's nerve, she was thwarting their plans. Conroy and his allies glared at her, mocked her, and spoke to her rudely. After Victoria's illness at Ramsgate, her half sister Feodora had been so worried Lehzen would be sacked that she wrote to the Duchess of Northumberland—then Victoria's governess—asking her to use her influence to help. When Conroy noticed that the Duchess of Northumberland had befriended Lehzen, she was "treated accordingly": the governess never saw Victoria alone, or came to know her, and she resigned in disgust. Victoria later wrote of what her singular ally Lehzen had *"endured"*: at times she had feared her life was at stake during the "awful scenes in the house."

At night, lying under her eiderdown quilt in her cot, listening to the tick of her father's old tortoiseshell clock, Victoria fantasized about revenge: she would make her mother sorry for having mistreated her; she would banish Conroy; she would host balls, invite the handsomest men she knew, dance and flirt all night, and feast on delicacies. The girl who had wept upon discovering her destiny had by that point become a determined teenager on the cusp of power. She wrote firmly to her uncle Leopold: "I look forward to the event which it seems is likely to occur soon, with calmness and quietness. I am not alarmed at it, and yet I do not suppose myself quite equal to it all; I trust, however, that with *good will, honesty,* and *courage* I shall not, at all events, *fail*." Those words would become her mantra: "I shall not fail."

Part 2

THE TEENAGE QUEEN

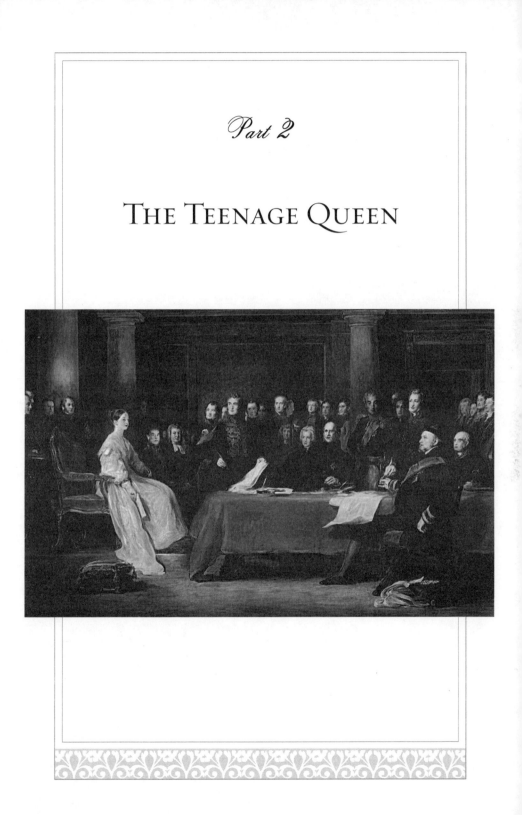

CHAPTER 6

Becoming Queen:
"I Am Very Young"

I was never happy until I was eighteen.

—QUEEN VICTORIA

It will touch every sailor's heart to have a girl Queen to fight for. They'll be tattooing her face on their arms.

—WILLIAM IV

At 2 A.M. on June 20, 1837, King William IV died with a sudden cry. Shortly afterward, his chamberlain, Lord Conyngham, and the Archbishop of Canterbury scrambled into a waiting coach and sped the twenty-one miles to Kensington Palace. They rocketed past milkmaids swinging pails and stableboys sweeping stable yards, washing carriages, and combing horses as the sky lightened. The men spoke curiously of Victoria, and of how little they, or anyone, really knew about her, so closely had her mother protected her. They arrived at the palace at five only to find the gates locked and the snoring porter deaf to their calls. Victoria lay dreaming as the men rang the bell repeatedly until the porter woke and ushered them into one of the lower rooms. They soon wondered if they had been forgotten. Twice they rang, and twice they were asked to wait. The Duchess of Kent finally woke Victoria at six.

When Victoria looked up into her mother's face, her stomach turned. She stood up, smoothed her long, loose hair, slid her feet into slippers, and threw a cotton dressing robe over her simple white nightgown. Her mother clasped her hand and escorted her down the dark, narrow stairs for the last time. Behind them walked Lehzen bearing smelling salts. When she walked into the room where the two men were waiting, Victoria closed the door behind her—shutting her mother and her governess out. The archbishop and lord dropped to their knees. Lord Conyngham told her that her uncle had died, kissed her hand, and gave her the certificate of the king's death. The archbishop told her God would be with her. She excused them, walked out, and closed the door. She then placed her head on her mother's shoulder and cried—for the king who had died, the uncle she had barely known, and the thrill of an emotion she barely recognized: release.

The first thing Victoria did was to ask for time alone. She ordered her bed to be moved out of her mother's room, put on an unadorned black dress, and pinned her hair on top of her head in a braided coronet. She then breakfasted with Stockmar, Leopold's trusted private secretary and adviser, whom Leopold gave to Victoria as a gift upon her becoming queen. She settled at her desk and wrote three letters: to Leopold, to her half sister, Feodora, and to the grieving Queen Adelaide, whom she insisted be addressed as Her Majesty. She wrote in her journal: "Since it has pleased Providence to place me in this station, I shall do my utmost to fulfill my duty toward my country; I am very young and perhaps in many, though not in all things, inexperienced, but I am sure, that very few have more real good will and more real desire to do what is fit and right than I have."

At 9 A.M. Victoria received the prime minister, "of COURSE *quite*

ALONE as I shall *always* do all my Ministers." The urbane Lord Melbourne immediately captivated her. During the meeting, he wrote a draft of her statement to the Privy Council, which was summoned to meet almost immediately, at 11 A.M. Across London, one hundred men frantically scrambled into official garb and rushed to Kensington Palace. There were other young queens then in Europe: the queen of Portugal (whom Victoria called the "fat queen") was just a month older than Victoria, and the queen of Spain was just six years of age (her mother was regent). But Victoria was the youngest queen Britain had known, and it had been 123 years since the last female monarch, Queen Anne. While the Privy Council—a group of former or current members of Parliament who advised the monarch— usually met monthly, few members attended with anything resembling regularity. Today, there was a record turnout.

When Melbourne asked her if she would like to be accompanied into the room, she replied, "No, thank you. I shall walk in alone." Her uncles the Dukes of Cumberland and Sussex led her to her throne. With the death of William IV, Cumberland had just become the king of Hanover, neatly ridding England of a widely loathed duke. Victoria swore her uncles in, then the Cabinet ministers and most of the Privy Counsellors. (With a gesture of kindness, she stopped the Duke of Sussex, who was "infirm," from kneeling—and kissed his cheek so he would not need to stoop to kiss her hand.) Victoria then read out the declaration Lord Melbourne had drafted for her:

> The severe and afflicting loss which the nation has sustained by the death of His Majesty, my beloved uncle, has devolved upon me the duty of administering the government of this empire. This awful responsibility is imposed upon me so suddenly, and at so early a period of my life, that I should feel myself utterly oppressed by the burden were I not sustained by the hope that Divine Providence, which has called me to this work, will give me strength for the performance of it, and that I shall find in

the purity of my intentions, and in my zeal for the public welfare, that support and those resources which usually belong to
a more mature age and to longer experience. . . . Educated in
England, under the tender and enlightened care of a most affectionate mother, I have learnt from my infancy to respect and
love the constitution of my native country. It will be my unceasing study to maintain the reformed religion as by law established, securing at the same time to all the full enjoyment of
religious liberty; and I shall steadily protect the rights, and promote to the utmost of my power the happiness and welfare, of
all classes of my subjects.

It was a triumph of public performance. The gathered men
gawked at the new queen, many of them touched to hear her speak
in her calm, silvery voice. Several wept. They seemed astonished that
a mere slip of a girl could read so well. The diarist Charles Greville,
who was there as the clerk of the Privy Council, wrote:

There never was anything like the first impression she produced, or the chorus of praise and admiration which is raised
about her manner and behavior, and certainly not without justice. It was very extraordinary, and something far beyond what
was looked for. Her extreme youth and inexperience, and the
ignorance of the world concerning her, naturally excited intense curiosity.

The accolades seemed to be unanimous. John Wilson Croker, a
Tory, said she was "as interesting and handsome as any young lady I
ever saw." The Duke of Wellington, who was visibly moved, declared, "She not merely filled her chair, she filled the room." "Our
dear little Queen in every respect is *perfection,*" gushed the Whig
politician and diarist Thomas Creevey. To the men assembled, she
was a child, or even an "infant queen," according to Lord John Russell. The simplest performance invited lavish praise.

———

The country was in love. The *Spectator* dubbed the infectious fever "Reginamania." A cartoon titled "Figaro in London" showed John Bull willing to cut off his ears if the little queen wanted him to. Writers rhapsodized about her attributes. Thomas Creevey described the time Victoria found the new lady-in-waiting Lady Charlemont, whom she had not yet met, in the corridor with a large armful of books from the library, and roared with laughter; and he added the fact that she was paying pensions out of her personal accounts for some unlikely people, such as the FitzClarences, the illegitimate cousins her mother had kept her away from but for whom Victoria nonetheless cared. Sallie Stevenson, wife of the American ambassador, wrote to her sisters in Virginia that everyone was "mad with loyalty to the young Queen. . . . In all societies nothing is talked about but her beauty, her wisdom, her gentleness, and self-possession. A thousand anecdotes are related to her goodness, and the wonderful address with which she manages everybody and everything." It had been little over half a century since Americans had successfully rebelled against King George III, and just a quarter of a century since they had fought England again in the War of 1812, but now even they were intrigued by the new queen.

The young queen charmed older men, often to their surprise. Lord Holland reported he came back from a visit "quite a courtier & a bit of a lover." "Though not a beauty & not a very good figure," he conceded, "she is really in person, in face, & especially in eyes and complexion, a very nice girl & quite such as might tempt." She may have gobbled her food while dining, and shown unattractive gums when she laughed, Creevey wrote, but he was prepared to overlook those handicaps because she "blushes and laughs every instant in so natural a way as to disarm anybody. Her voice is perfect, and so is the expression of her face, when she means to say or do a pretty thing." The artist George Hayter, who painted her portrait and would become a court favorite, was "quite in love with her" and "spoke most scientifically of the extraordinary character of her eye." Not all eyewitness accounts are reliable, though—Creevey, after all, reported that he had never seen a "more pretty or natural devotion" than Victoria had for her mother.

Some women—less concerned with how physically tempting the new queen was—feared for her, wondering what all the pomp, noise, and weight of obligation would do to a girl of eighteen. Even the tough-minded social reformer Harriet Martineau wrote, "We are all somewhat romantic about our young Queen, poor thing! What chance has she of growing up simple & good?" She saw little chance that Victoria could "turn out much."

As Melbourne walked out of Victoria's first Privy Council meeting, wiping tears from his eyes, Baron Stockmar approached and thrust at him a letter from John Conroy containing an audacious list of commands. "My reward for the *Past,*" wrote Conroy, "I conceive should be, a peerage—the red ribbon—and a pension from the Privy Purse of £3,000 a year." He was asking for more money than a government minister would have received. Melbourne dropped the paper and cried, "Have you ever heard such impudence?" In a day of mourning the king and celebrating the new queen, Conroy was thinking only of himself. Albert later wrote next to a list Victoria had made of the "monster's" demands: "The King had died that very morning."

In a flash, Victoria dismissed Conroy from her household, a moment that was as delicious in execution as it was in anticipation. To defuse tension, Lord Melbourne decided to give Conroy a pension and a baronetcy, and he promised that when he was able to create a new Irish peer, he would make Conroy one. He added that the queen assented to such a plan. This would prove to be an error of judgment. By granting Conroy a peerage that would take many years to eventuate—he needed to wait until an existing Irish peer died—he gave Conroy room to continue to scheme for revenge on Victoria. Conroy intended to stay in the Duchess of Kent's household until the queen fulfilled all her promises. (Lord Liverpool told Stockmar that Melbourne had been "duped.") Conroy never was made an Irish peer, and the hateful resentment of his family is still palpable in the scrap-books they kept, stuffed with clippings of newspaper articles critical of Victoria. They gloried in the moments when she stumbled, and relished attacks on her.

Victoria's sole mention of her mother in her journal on the day she became queen came at the end, when she wrote, "Went down and said good-night to Mamma, etc." The duchess was wounded. Earlier in the day, she had written to Victoria asking if she could take Conroy to her proclamation—underestimating, as ever, her daughter's vis-ceral hatred of him. The duchess argued that others would notice and "remarks would be made which you should certainly avoid the first day." The queen responded that it was Lord Melbourne's "decided opinion" that he should not go. The duchess wrote a condescending reply: "You do not know the world. S.J. [Sir John] has his faults, he may have made mistakes, but his intentions were always the best. . . . This affair is much tattled and very unhappily. Take care Victoria, you know your Prerogative! take care that Melbourne is not King."

From this day on, the duchess was forced to observe the etiquette that meant she would have to wait for Victoria to summon her before she could be seen. Victoria luxuriated in her controlled solitude. She met with the "very kind" Melbourne twice more that day. She then dined in her room, by herself. On this first day, she wrote the word "alone" five times in her journal—*"alone* . . . & of COURSE *quite* ALONE . . . *quite* alone . . . & alone . . . alone." At last.

A month later, Victoria appeared in Parliament to close the session. It was her first time there, and she was garbed magnificently in a white satin dress embroidered with gold, a crimson velvet robe and train trimmed with ermine and gold lace, and a tiara. As she walked into the House of Lords, she fixed her eyes on Lord Melbourne, who was walking in front with the Sword of State. An evening paper gushed: "Her emotion was plainly discernible in the rapid heaving of her bosom, and the brilliancy of her diamond stomacher, which spar-kled out occasionally from the dark recess in which the throne was placed." As would become customary at the young queen's early appearances, the great men of state wept openly. Lord Grey cried "from pleasure at the Queen's voice and speech," Charles Sumner declared, "I never heard anything read better in my life," and the Duke of Sussex was seen wiping his eyes when she finished. The American Sallie Stevenson, who was sitting in the diplomats' gallery, described her voice as "sweet as a Virginia nightingale's." Victoria's mother was overwhelmed when she watched her daughter, laboring under the heavy robes usually worn by men, finally sit on the throne. Outside, the police were unable to prevent people from clambering into the trees to try to get a glimpse of the queen; they hung on the branches like coconuts for hours in the rain.

In her new role, Victoria immediately established a routine. She rose at eight, read the Bible, and wrote dispatches until breakfast at ten, when her mother joined her. She saw her government ministers between 11:00 A.M. and 1:30 P.M. The two kings who had reigned before her had not been fond of hard work, so her industry was widely admired. She wrote proudly to her cousin Albert, with the hint of a boast, "I delight in the business which I have to do and which is not trifling either in matter or quantity." Uncle Leopold, who was now king of the Belgians, continued to advise her closely. He told her to be discreet, form her own opinion, and immediately change the conversation if people dared to bring up private matters without her consent. He also recommended she deliberate, just as Lehzen had: "Whenever a question is of some importance it should not be decided on the day when it is submitted to you." England's next ten prime ministers would be stymied by this approach.

Nonetheless, Victoria thrived on her new workload. She described it as "the *greatest pleasure* to do my duty for my country and my people, and no fatigue, however great, will be burdensome to me if it is for the welfare of the nation." She was finally useful and necessary to her country, and she was invigorated by it. When Leopold said she should spend more time at Claremont, his estate, she retorted, "I must see my ministers every day." Victoria had very little time off. As her maids tugged combs through her long, fine hair each day, she worked her way through large piles of papers and official boxes. She often worked late into the night.

Victoria had been queen for only a few weeks before remarks were made about her "slight signs of a peremptory disposition" and her "strong will." She was confident in her opinions. When she knighted Moses Montefiore, the first Jewish knight in English history, she dismissed any objections with "I was very glad I was the first to do what I think quite right, and as it should be." She also challenged conventions she considered redundant. She did not like the traditional gender segregation that occurred after dinner, for example, when the men went to another room to drink. She would not allow her male guests to do this for more than fifteen minutes, and she refused to take her seat in her drawing room until they walked in. Her female attendants were forced to stand too.*

The politician Arthur Ponsonby, the son of Henry Ponsonby, who would be Queen Victoria's private secretary later in life, wrote in 1933 that "from the first she showed a disposition to conform strictly to her own standard of conduct rather than adapt herself to some expected standard." Her self-reliance became "an abiding and dominant feature" throughout her life. But what he failed to note was that this trait would almost completely evaporate when she married. Victoria was most certain of herself when she was single.

---

* Even the public noticed that the girl who had been tightly controlled for years now delighted in exercising her will. When her mother and Melbourne told her it would be proper to go to a Hyde Park review in a carriage, she decided to ride in on a horse. Her decision inspired a ballad:

> I will have a Horse, I'm determined on that,
> If there is to be a review.
> No horse, no review, my Lord Melbourne, that's flat,
> In spite of Mama and you.

———

The relationship between Queen Victoria and her prime minister Lord Melbourne is one of the great platonic romances of modern history. Both the young, fatherless queen and the curiously apolitical politician had much to gain from the relationship—guidance for her and added status for him. Both fell a little bit in love. Victoria's infatuation had developed quickly. "I am so fond of him and his conversations do me much good," she wrote in her diary. She had been queen for only three days when she told Leopold, "My poor mother views Lord Melbourne with great jealousy." (The editors of her letters were later embarrassed by the intimate, affectionate way Victoria wrote about Melbourne, and they deleted some for fear people might conclude they were lovers.)

Melbourne, who had lost his wife and son, was able to devote himself to his new charge. He tutored Victoria in the ways of politics, but his greatest gifts to her were genuine affection and affirmation. Greville described it as a "passionate fondness" that he might have for a daughter, from "a man with a capacity for loving without anything to love." On August 30, 1837, Greville noted:

> [Victoria] has great animal spirits, and enters into the magnificent novelties of her position with the zest and curiosity of a child. No man is more formed to ingratiate himself with her than Melbourne. He treats her with unbounded consideration and respect, he consults her tastes and her wishes, and he puts her at ease by his frank and natural manners while he amuses her by the quaint, queer, epigrammatic turn of his mind and his varied knowledge upon all subjects.

The subjects they discussed were varied: diet, Dickens, chimney sweeps, her wicked uncles, her father and mother, teeth, Dr. Johnson, history, philosophy, and etiquette. There was always much to talk about. The political tumult had quieted somewhat after the 1832 Reform Act, but the working-class Chartist movement, which rumbled for decades in its fight for democracy and against corruption, was just beginning. The world took on a new fascination for Victoria now that she was part of it. In the year she became queen, Charles Dickens began the serialization of *Oliver Twist;* Caroline Norton published her radical pamphlet arguing that mothers should have some custody of their young children after divorce; and a national antislavery convention was held in America, in which British women were thanked for their support. Inventors patented the electric telegraph, the first daguerreotype was successfully exposed, and the Grand Junction Railway, which ran between Manchester and Birmingham, was completed. The momentum for massive change had begun to gather pace.

Victoria wanted to live in Buckingham Palace immediately. George III had bought it in 1761 and George IV had rebuilt it, but it was not yet an official royal residence, and the renovations and repairs were not finished. Victoria sent written instructions insisting it be done by July 13. A host of extra men were hired so her wishes could be met. "So much," wrote the wife of the American ambassador, Sallie Stevenson, "for a young Queen!" On July 14, the palace was in a state of chaos with maids scrubbing floors and workmen laying carpets, but Victoria was serene in the midst of it all. She summoned Sigismund Thalberg, reputed to be the greatest pianist on earth, to perform in late July, and asked Strauss to compose for her balls.

After the gloominess of Kensington Palace, Victoria was thrilled with the light and space of her new home; huge mirrors reflected the gardens outside and chandeliers sparkled in ballrooms. Her rooms were far away from her mother's. (Victoria never took a great interest in interior design, like George III and George IV; when she did, in later years, covering everything in tartan, it was generally considered an affront to the senses.) In time, Victoria would grow to hate Buckingham Palace, with its smoking chimneys, poor ventilation, and smells of rotting food, and she would feel oppressed by the dank air and crowds of London—as well as the soot that fell in black flakes on her gardens. But now it was centrally located, freshly painted, and sufficiently grand. She wrote to Feodora: "Everybody says that I am quite another person since I came to the throne. I look and am so very well, I have such a pleasant life; just the sort of life I like."

It was a wonderfully happy summer. Victoria spent it outside London, at Windsor, where she dined, danced, and did mostly as she pleased. On July 19, she held a reception at which her hand was kissed three thousand times. She loved the company, the attention, the praise. After a military review at Windsor Great Park, where she saluted the men as the officers did, she was thrilled: "The whole thing went off beautifully; and I felt for the first time like a man, as if I could fight myself as the head of my troops." On August 15, Victoria mounted a horse for the first time in two years; she had refused to ride for a long time because her mother had always insisted Conroy accompany her. She loved to assemble large groups of riders and gallop for hours, and she always thought she looked most alluring—and taller—when sitting on a horse.

When Victoria journeyed out in a carriage on the way to a banquet held by the Lord Mayor of London at the Guildhall in November, she was overwhelmed with applause. After years of being called selfish, stupid, and vain, it was enormously gratifying to be loved by so many. Finally Victoria was starting to believe that Feodora might be right to say, "You have it in your power to make thousands happy." It might soon be millions.

Two people, however, were distinctly unhappy. The duchess and the Machiavellian Conroy felt the icy winds of the queen's contempt. There were repeated scenes. Victoria had immediately announced that she would not change her mother's rank, and she did not even consider Conroy for private secretary or Privy Purse. They both knew that they would have little influence on the queen, if any. It was obvious to those in court circles too. Melbourne was now fully aware of the rift, even though the duchess had begged Victoria not to tell him, but did nothing to bridge it. Victoria started to pity her depressed mother.

It was a fool's mission, but the loyal duchess continued to try to rehabilitate Conroy. In November, she asked Victoria to allow him to come to the Guildhall banquet. If Victoria did not like him, then she asked her to "at least forgive, and do not exclude and mark him and his family." She continued: "The Queen should forget what displeased the Princess. Recollect I have the greatest regard for Sir John, I cannot forget what he has done for me and for you, although he had the misfortune to displease *you*." The duchess was miffed at what she believed to be her daughter's ingratitude. Pointedly, she gave Victoria a copy of *King Lear* for her nineteenth birthday.

With the additional income she earned as queen, Victoria began to pay off her father's debts, receiving formal thanks for having done so in October 1839. The duchess, however, continued to overspend, and she wrote cranky letters to Victoria asking for more money, despite her own allowance increase. In January 1838, Victoria wrote, "Got *such* a letter from Mama, oh! Oh! Such a letter." Her mother, she told Melbourne when she received another, was "plaguing" her. (All the letters between Victoria and her mother in 1837 were "eliminated" from official selections of her letters published shortly after her death.)

The bitter mother-daughter feud was now the talk of London, though observers were largely ignorant of the cause. Perhaps, guessed Greville, she had not only been "ill-used" by both of them in the past, but Victoria "secretly suspects the nature of her mother's connection" with Conroy. The duchess confided in Princess Lieven, who as the wife of the Russian ambassador was the eyes and ears of Europe, that she was hurt by "her own insignificance."

Conroy was now a lost and bitter man who by early 1841 was "pining to death for want of occupation." In a surprising career twist, he went to the countryside and studied the science of agriculture with his usual zeal, becoming a prominent advocate for a new style of farming. In 1852, he won a medal for the "Breeder and Exhibitor of the best pen of Fat pigs" from the Royal Agricultural Society of England. Victoria continued to honor her obligations to his family. She was still paying the pension for Conroy's daughter-in-law almost thirty years after he died.

Victoria's success as a new queen was almost too effortless at times, the praise too unqualified. As the men of state bawled into their handkerchiefs when she simply read aloud a statement someone else had written, it is clear that their expectations were extremely low because she was young and female. The members of the Privy Council were not just surprised but overwhelmed by the sight of the sheltered teenage girl maintaining her composure in public. As Lady Cowper (who was Lord Melbourne's sister) wrote, "I have never heard anyone speak a single word in dispraise of her, or find fault with her—this is indeed a rare happiness." Unfortunately, it was also to be a short-lived happiness. The sharp-eyed London footman William Tayler was cynical about Victoria's popularity in 1837: "The Queen is a new thing and please[s] the people very well at present, but I fear it won't last long as the people are to [*sic*] fickleminded to be satisfied with any one individual, King, Queen or subject." He was right.

CHAPTER 7

The Coronation: "A Dream out of *The Arabian Nights*"

> I shall ever remember this day as the *proudest* of my life.
>
> —QUEEN VICTORIA, 1838

> Poor little Queen, she is at an age at which a girl can hardly be trusted to choose a bonnet for herself; yet a task is laid upon her from which an archangel might shrink.
>
> —THOMAS CARLYLE, 1838

At midnight on the twenty-seventh of June, 1838—a little over a year since the death of William IV—London was humming with the sounds of saws, hammers, and planes. It was, happily for those still working, a cool night, with light winds. In Hyde Park, dwarves, giants, albinos, and obese boys in flimsy canvas tents were trying to get some rest before their day of performing; booth owners were pinning flags and banners to their tents; bakers were piling sweet goods into large baskets; and donkeys were braying as monkeys strained at leashes tied to carts, carriages, and poles. The bells of St. Margaret's Church, near Westminster Abbey, pealed until one o'clock in the morning, much to the annoyance of local residents. Shortly afterward, under a deep black sky, crowds of people began to wind through the streets toward the old, gray Abbey, trying to get the best seats for the coronation of Queen Victoria, which was to begin in just a few hours.

At five in the morning the Abbey doors opened to a great throng. Many revelers, leaving coronation parties and balls, had decided not to go to bed, wandering the streets half drunk before the sharp-elbowed scramble for viewing positions began. "The coronation day will in verity pass off like a dream to those folks," wrote one reporter. In the poorer parts of London, urchins in rags danced barefoot in the open streets and squares, laughing, screaming, and singing "God Save the Queen" until the pale dawn light blurred the sky.

Wide awake in bed at Buckingham Palace, Victoria was fighting a feeling that something "very awful" was going to happen to her that day. She tried to bury her head under her pillows during the twenty-one-gun salute as the sun rose just before four. It was impossible to get back to sleep because of the noise outside. She had already been queen for a year—coronations are usually held months after the death of a monarch so that they can be times of celebration, not mourning, and to allow sufficient time to prepare—but she was still nervous. Victoria had not been to a coronation before, had little idea of what to do, and was terrified of making a mistake. As Lord Melbourne was to tell her later, her own performance was "a thing that you can't give a person advice upon, it must be left to a person." Victoria's mother was no use either; her main concern was for Conroy, who would have been invited to the Abbey that day only if he were able to step over Victoria's corpse on the way.

Victoria could not bring herself to look outside until 7 A.M., when she peered out her window at the "curious spectacle" in the Green Park: throngs climbed the hill, the carriages of nobility and gentry rolled down toward the Abbey, ladies climbed into the specially erected seats in front of their clubs, soldiers marched, and the crowd jostled to get the best vantage point from which to see the queen. It had been raining heavily, and the crowd cheered when the sun finally came out that morning. Along the procession route, houses were decorated gaily with flags and flowers, and seats were lined with carpets and colored hangings, all the more brilliant as the beautifully dressed women sitting on top of them wore white or pale, summery colors.

Charles Dickens, who wrote a piece on the event for the *Examiner,* said that the world was "alive with men" waiting to see the queen. About four hundred thousand people had slept in the streets of London the night before. Greville wrote:

> It is as if the population had been on a sudden quintupled. Not a mob here or there, but the town all mob, thronging, bustling, gaping, and gazing at everything, at anything, or at nothing; the Park one vast encampment, with banners floating on the tops of the tents, and still the roads are covered, the railroads loaded with arriving multitudes.

Victoria was standing in front of the mirror, watching her dresser adjust the circlet of diamonds on her head, as Feodora walked into her room. The queen embraced her sister, then turned to her reflection and stared again, anxiety mixed with pride. Her petite, curvaceous frame had been tightly corseted into a white satin petticoat and red velvet dress. She was ready. When she finally stepped into her carriage at ten o'clock, her stomach clenching with nerves, the sun pierced the clouds and sailors hoisted the royal banner on top of the triumphal arch at the entrance to Buckingham Palace. When the first gun thundered, announcing her departure, those waiting miles away in Westminster Abbey, her destination, stood up. Theater owner Nelson Lee struck a gong in Hyde Park, and all the showmen of the fair unfurled their cloths, in rolls of flashing color, while the owners of booths and stalls pulled up canvas fronts and started hawking their wares. The show was beginning.

The three-mile drive to Westminster Abbey, up Constitution Hill to Hyde Park Corner, past the crowds at Piccadilly, St. James's, and Pall Mall to Trafalgar Square and Whitehall, took an hour and a half.

The composer Felix Mendelssohn, who was holidaying in England, described Victoria's coach as "golden and fairy-like, supported by Tritons with their tridents, and surmounted by the great crown of England." Victoria was overcome by the sight of her subjects, jammed on specially erected benches, on roofs clutching chimney pots, on parapets, in trees, and perched on one another's shoulders. As the eight gray horses pulled her magnificent carriage forward, Victoria looked in all directions, hoping to catch as many eyes as possible, beaming and waving. She wrote later:

> Many as there were the day I went to the City, it was nothing— nothing, to the multitudes, the millions, of my loyal subjects who were assembled in every spot to witness the Procession. Their good humor and excessive loyalty was beyond everything, and I really cannot say *how* proud I feel to be the Queen of *such* a Nation.

When the queen's carriage stalled in Whitehall, she saw some policemen "making more use of their truncheons than the circumstances seemed to require," and she made her displeasure known. She was forced to intervene several times, and repeatedly insisted that no harsh measures be used to clear the way for her. Felix Mendelssohn similarly could not understand why the police had resorted to violence that day. He spied some trying to restrain a drunken woman with bare shoulders and loose hair from dancing; each time they tried to stop her, she would shout the word "Coronation!" A member of the crowd calmed her by telling jokes and boxing her on the ear. Mendelssohn decided, "There are more drunken women here than drunken men: it is incredible how much whisky they can swallow." The yells of the crowd were deafening. "Their hearts," wrote Dickens, were "in their voices."

The new queen arrived at the Abbey just before noon, in the middle of a vast sea of waving handkerchiefs, gun salutes, and trumpet blasts.

"One had to pinch oneself to make sure it was not all a dream out of *The Arabian Nights,*" said the awestruck Mendelssohn. Reporters exhausted superlatives when writing about the vision that greeted Victoria when she walked into the Abbey, a diminutive figure under the Gothic arches. The Abbey was festooned in crimson and gold tapestries, with pews lined with peers and peeresses dressed in velvet, long rows of bishops' copes, a chancel and altar surrounded by purple drapes embroidered with gold, and brilliant oriental rugs on the floors. The women's elaborate diamond jewelry sparkled against pale skin. Even the author Harriet Martineau, who was no fan of religion, abbeys, or queens, was impressed, writing, "I have never before seen the full effect of diamonds. As the light travelled, each peeress shone like a rainbow. The brightness, vastness, and dreamy magnificence of the scene produced a strange effect of exhaustion and sleepiness." High up in the Abbey, Martineau ate a sandwich, read a book, and rested against a pillar while she waited.

As Victoria got dressed in the robing room in a red, ermine-lined mantle, with a very long train of crimson velvet, the ambassadors had entered the Abbey, to much excitement and admiration. There was a special cheer for England's old foe, the French general Marshal Soult. He was followed by the Duchess of Kent and the Duke of Sussex, then the Duke, Duchess, and Princess Augusta of Cambridge. The ambassadors' procession was particularly fancy and well received, for the sumptuousness of their carriages and, in some cases, for their flamboyant attire. The Russian ambassador was clothed in white fur. Austria's Prince Esterhazy was dressed in a suit made entirely of pearls and diamonds—even his boots were crusted with diamonds, which blazed as he walked across a bar of sunshine entering the Abbey. His spangly hat "cast a dancing radiance all round." When the sun was on him, Dickens wrote, he "glistened like a galaxy."

Then Victoria entered. The crowd stood as the anthem "I Was Glad" played. Behind her, eight trainbearers, all unmarried girls, wore silver and white, with pink roses in their hair. The Lord Chamberlain carried the end of her train. Ahead of her, Prime Minister

Lord Melbourne carried the Sword of State. He had taken a very heavy dose of laudanum and brandy to counter the effects of an upset stomach, was emotional and, in Victoria's words, *"completely over-come."* In his intoxicated state, he told Victoria that she appeared as though she were floating in a silver cloud. The recently elected Tory member of Parliament, and future prime minister, Benjamin Disraeli said Melbourne looked "very awkward and uncouth, with his great coronet cocked over his nose, his robes under his feet, and holding the great sword of state like a butcher."

Five hours of pageantry began. The Archbishop of Canterbury declared Victoria the "undoubted queen of this realm" as she turned to face the north, south, and west. She promised to uphold Protestantism before going to St. Edward's Chapel behind the altar, where she took off her robes and tiara and put on a linen shift and gold tunic, as was the custom. She then returned to the altar, sat in St. Edward's Chair, and was anointed under a gold canopy held aloft by knights of the garter. Not everything ran smoothly, due to lack of rehearsal and the fact that the Dean of Westminster was too sick to attend. Victoria whispered to Lord John Thynne: "Pray tell me what I am to do, for they [the ministers] don't know." She had to ask the Bishop of Durham what to do with the heavy orb. He told her to carry it, along with the scepter, as the robe made of gold and lined with ermine was placed around her shoulders. Unfortunately, the ruby coronation ring, which had been specially made for her little finger, was painfully forced onto her fourth finger.

London erupted with sound when the splendid new crown was placed on Victoria's head: forty-one Tower cannons thundered, drums beat, trumpets blared again. The peers and peeresses put on their coronets, the bishops their caps, the kings of arms their crowns. Those inside the Abbey shouted with abandon, shaking the vaulted roof. The crowd outside bellowed approval. Lord Melbourne gave Victoria "such a kind," "fatherly" look when she glanced at him. She also caught the eye of her "dearly beloved Lehzen" sitting directly above the royal box, and they smiled at each other. At the same time, two hot-air balloons rose over the city. Down below in Hyde Park, actors impersonating the queen and her entourage tried to enact the scene exactly the same way at the same time, as the beer-swilling audience shouted encouragement. The joy felt universal.

Seven-year-old Lord Salisbury—then known as Lord Robert Cecil—who was there as his father's page had been bored watching the woman who would appoint him prime minister several decades later perform her rounds of rituals. But once a neighbor swung him up on his shoulders to see the new queen wearing the crown, he was transfixed by what he later described as "an abiding vision of gorgeous color and light centered upon one slight lonely figure."

Sitting upright on a throne draped in gold, Victoria was still overwhelmed. Her mother burst into tears. Martineau said Victoria looked "so small as to appear puny." Her specially made Imperial State Crown was valued at £112,760, around $12.5 million in today's dollars, and had a Maltese cross on the top. A long trail of peers climbed the steps to the throne, one by one touching the crown and kissing her hand—not her cheek, though it was the usual custom, as it was decided that for a young girl, having six hundred older men kiss her cheek was an "appalling prospect." When her frail uncle Sussex struggled to climb the steps, the young Victoria threw her arms around his neck. There was a collective gasp when Lord Rolle, a large elderly man who was being supported by two men, fell and rolled down to the bottom of the steps, lying tangled in his robes. He was helped up and tried once more to ascend to the waiting queen, bolstered by shouts of encouragement, but Victoria instead stood up, walked toward him, kindly whispered that she hoped he was not hurt, and stretched out her hand so he could kiss it, endearing herself to all who saw and heard of the incident.

Victoria then took off her crown and received the sacrament. Eerily on cue, a ray of sunlight illuminated her head. The Bishop of Bath and Wells skipped a page of the order of ceremony and prematurely ended the coronation. The queen then had a brief interlude in the Confessor's Chapel, where the altar was covered with sandwiches and Melbourne drained a full glass of the priest's red wine. After that, the choir sang "Hallelujah" as she made a final, formal exit. She then returned to the robing room, where she tried to pull the ring off her throbbing fourth finger. Already self-conscious about her short fingers, Victoria had to soak her hand in ice water for half an hour before it would budge.

Outside the Abbey, Constable John Robinson was grappling with a man who was trying to force his way inside so he could ask Victoria to marry him. When a magistrate later asked the man, Captain Thomas Flower of the Thirteenth Light Dragoons, his profession, he replied, "Profession or business has nothing to do with the question. I am merely a candidate for the hand of Her Majesty." He had already been charged twice for disturbing the peace and had previously "created a great disturbance" at the Italian Opera House trying to gain admission to Victoria's box. He was declared insane and sent to Tothill Fields, a house of correction in central London. (Tom Flower was not the first man to attempt to propose to Queen Victoria. One had already been committed for stalking the princess, and another was arrested for trying to break into the Chapel Royal.)

Victoria had performed perfectly, her poise almost concealing the gaffes made by those around her. On the way back to Buckingham Palace, she was tired but relieved. The hordes kept cheering, and the ladies waved scented handkerchiefs from their positions on windowsills, balconies, and scaffolding. Victoria was starving, but as soon as she got back, she grabbed her little dog Dash and placed him in a tub to wash him, gently pouring water over his fur.

Once the procession had passed, at around 11 A.M., thousands of people started pouring into Hyde Park for the fair. It was a dazzling sight: almost one thousand booths spread across fifty acres. There were stalls, marquees, and tents displaying colorful banners and flags from all nations. There was plentiful beef, ham, chicken, salad, beer, and wine. Fairgoers wandered by stalls selling nuts, toys, gingerbread, ices, and oranges as bands played, men beat gongs, and acrobats tumbled past. They stopped to gaze at the fashionable panoramas and dioramas displaying landmarks and historical moments, including Niagara Falls (somehow contained in a box), the Death of Nelson, and the Capture of Napoleon. Most were there, though, for the drinking and dancing booths manned by clowns, "crowded to suffocation" and bedecked with curtains and British flags, where they smoked, caroused, and flirted. Within a few hours of the fair opening, the wife of a gingerbread worker gave birth. The baby was named Hyde Park and became a star attraction in its own right—the stall was kept open for days after the fair closed, and women brought presents for mother and child. The night of the coronation, a twenty-three-year-old man died in a dancing booth of suspected epilepsy, or, officially, "the visitation of God."

Some of the most popular booths and tents housed the "freak shows," a curious and usually cruel staple of Victorian entertainment. There were fat men and women, spotted boys, children with two heads, and animals with no heads. There were also dozens of monkeys, a skinny elephant, and fortune-telling ponies; a serpent handler; dwarves; "living skeletons"; twin giantesses from America; the two-headed lady; and the much-admired Madam Stevens, the "Pig-Faced Lady," who was actually a brown bear with shaved paws and a shaved face, dressed in white gloves, bonnet, shawl, cap, and dress, strapped into a chair and poked by a hidden boy with a stick when her master asked her a question.

Charles Dickens walked past one of the shows and laughed, shaking his head: Why was it that the canvas tents of the giants were always the smallest? He was the most celebrated author in England. He had left Twickenham, where he was on holiday, to watch the coronation celebrations in Hyde Park. So many people were snobs when it came to working-class pleasure, he thought: they accused them of all kinds of sinful and indulgent revelry—but look at how wonderful this was! It was a "very pleasant and agreeable scene." It was estimated that two-thirds of the population of London attended the fair. As Greville wrote, "To amuse and interest [the people] seems to have been the principal object" of the coronation. This was unusual, and it marked the beginning of a new era in the relationship between monarchy and citizenry.

Across England, Scotland, Ireland, and Wales, citizens of every kind participated in coronation festivities, both rowdy and orderly: picnics, official lunches, church services, street parties, dinners, and fetes. Those in workhouses and jails were given roast and boiled beef with vegetables, plum pudding, beer, tobacco, tea, and sugar. Paupers were given a coronation allowance. In Newgate, sheriffs gave prisoners beef, potatoes, bread, and a pint of strong beer. Those locked in solitary confinement were briefly allowed to mingle with the others. At country fairs, men over fifty ran races for a good waistcoat, and women over fifty competed for half a pound of snuff.

The queen rode past Hyde Park on the day after the coronation, after the rain cleared. Victoria, thrilled that Lord Melbourne had told her she had performed "beautifully—every part of it, with so much taste," stood on her balcony at midnight to watch the fireworks show that night. The crowd was dazzled by thousands of popping stars and lights, serpents, squibs, and rockets. But most exciting of all was the final spectacle—an illumination of Victoria in her full coronation robes, stretching across the sky in lights, twinkling.

The day after the coronation, Melbourne took to his bed with a strong dose of calomel. He did not return to the Cabinet for a week, but he found no sympathy at Buckingham Palace. On July 4, the queen wrote: "This is *most provoking and vexatious,* and makes me *quite cross,* for I'm *so* spoilt and accustomed to see this *kind* and I *may* venture to say *even dear* friend . . . *every day* that I'm *quite annoyed* and put out when my agreeable daily visit does not take place. . . . And I've a Council today . . . and there I must be, as it were, without the person who makes me feel safe and comfortable." (She hastened to add, knowing that a jealous Lehzen would be reading her entries, that he could be of comfort only when Lehzen was not with her.)

A few months later, the coronation was the centerpiece of Madame Tussaud's new premises at Baker Street. Victoria had allowed exact replicas of her robes to be made for the ambitious display that included a papier-mâché copy of the interior of Westminster Abbey and captured a moment that would not be repeated for more than a century: a young woman being anointed the ruler of millions. The British were "fundamentally royalist," Lady Cowper wrote to Princess Lieven: the queen "has only to show herself to be adored." At this instant, all was glorious, golden, and cloaked in sunlight; the pretty queen was ascribed every virtue. It was "impossible," wrote *The Champion and Weekly Herald,* given how young and lovely Victoria was, that "such a sovereign can have an enemy." This state of affairs would change swiftly. It was not poise or boldness that she lacked as a young queen, as she was shortly to find out. It was wisdom. This would cause her star to plummet as quickly as it had risen.

CHAPTER 8

Learning to Rule

You lead rather an unnatural life for a young person.
It's the life of a man.

—LORD MELBOURNE

Victoria immediately developed a crush on Lord Melbourne. Her prime minister was unattached and intensely appealing: good-looking and charming, with unruly dark hair and an air of studied nonchalance. She clung to each word he spoke, commented often on how well he looked, especially when he wore the red and blue Windsor uniform or when the wind ruffled his hair, and recorded his quips in detail in her journal. She loved him "like a Father," she wrote. "He has *such* stores of knowledge; such a wonderful memory; he knows about everybody and everything; *who* they were and *what* they did. . . . It does me a *world* of good; and his conversations always *improve* one greatly." She was a fatherless young woman who had been bullied by her mother's adviser; he was a widower who had been severely burned by the spectacular infidelity of his wife, and whose only child had died the year before. He loved being needed, admired, and important; she adored his affection and attention. As Greville astutely noted, Victoria's feelings were probably *"sexual,* although she did not know it." Gossips whispered about the inordinate amount of time they spent together. "I hope you are amused at the report of Lord Melbourne being likely to marry the Queen," wrote the Countess Grey to Thomas Creevey.

Victoria's faith in him was absolute—but not always deserved. Lord Melbourne was an unlikely leader, made prime minister for the second time two years before Victoria became queen largely because he was the least offensive candidate. He was not passionate about politics and couldn't muster sufficient energy to care about social ills, let alone combat them. At times, when reformers visited him to put the case for improvements such as narrowing the death penalty or introducing compulsory education, he would pull feathers out of a pillow, toss them up in the air, and blow them across the top of his desk as they spoke. William Lamb, as he was christened, was a privileged, clever, Eton-educated Whig who had spent much of his life avoiding conflict or exertion. From his insouciant demeanor, you would not have been able to tell that his private life had been one of excruciating betrayal and loss. His relationship with the young queen was rare, consuming, and strangely affecting. To understand why—and how his need matched hers—we must first understand how the humiliation and pain of Melbourne's private life had scandalized the aristocrats of London and caused him to cauterize his heart.

On the day that Lord Melbourne, then William Lamb, gave his maiden speech in the House of Commons in December 1806, a tiny boyish figure sat in the public gallery listening with rapt attention. It was his wife, Caroline Lamb, an impish, eccentric creature who that day had dressed in her brother's clothes. She was smuggled into the gallery—which at the time allowed only men—by the secretary of another Whig politician, Lord Morpeth. Her mother-in-law was furious.

Caroline Ponsonby was not considered particularly beautiful, but she was passionate, animated, and clever. Lord Melbourne was smitten, proposing to her almost as soon as he had the chance (once his older brother died, and he had become heir to an Irish peerage and considerable wealth). His family worried about her notorious rages and volatility, but Melbourne loved her, and they married in 1805. Their relationship was tempestuous, marked by his almost inexplicable tolerance of her destructive behavior. They had one child, a son who was epileptic and probably also autistic. The fact that Caroline was unable to have any more children was a source of great grief, and it amplified an already unstable emotional fault line. Just a few years into their marriage, William Lamb began receiving anonymous letters telling him of his wife's adultery.

Caroline's best-known lover was the glamorous poet Lord Byron, who was being feted by London after the publication of his adventures began in 1812, in *Childe Harold's Pilgrimage*. Caroline read it immediately and, after insisting they meet, declared him to be, in a phrase that has been immortalized since, "mad, bad and dangerous to know." They both were, in fact; their eyes locked in recognition as well as lust. "That beautiful pale face," she wrote on their second meeting, "is my fate." It was to be one of the most outrageous, legendary affairs of the century; a host of writers carved Caroline and Byron's escapades into fictional characters. The pair scandalized London that summer, so publicly and shamelessly did they conduct themselves. Byron was flattered by the attentions of the clever wife of a politician. She had thrilled to his beauty, his fame, and, most of all, his literary ability with an intensity that, in time, would cause them to suffer. They wrote reams of love letters—to one, lying in a folder in the archives of the British Library, Caroline attached a bloodied clipping of her own pubic hair—and attempted to elope (some still believe they were married in secret).

After four intense months, Byron spurned his lover. Caroline was shattered, and after a particularly dramatic incident in which she slashed her arms with broken glass at a ball, she was banished to the country estate of Brocket, where she was put on a regimen of a bottle of sherry per day. She broke furniture, smashed crockery, poked servants with broomsticks, and appeared semi-nude in public. She was often drunk and stoned from opium. It exhausted Melbourne, who turned gray at the age of thirty-six. His political career floundered, but he neither left his wife nor sought divorce.

There are three likely reasons Lord Melbourne stayed: his enduring love for her, his passivity (as a schoolboy he had walked away from fights he knew he would not win), and the fact that the mores of the Whigs were hardly puritanical. In the late eighteenth century, when Melbourne grew up, marital faithfulness was not a prized virtue. Marriages were seen as companionable contracts within which one should produce a male heir. Melbourne's own mother was, as he said himself, "a remarkable woman, a devoted mother, an excellent wife,—but not chaste, not chaste." She had many lovers, with whom she had several children. It was widely known that Melbourne's father was not his mother's husband, from whom he took his name, but one of his mother's lovers, Lord Egremont. What was surprising was that Melbourne stayed faithful to his own cuckolding wife. According to his biographer David Cecil, a married man was then thought peculiar if he did not have a "sprightly, full-bosomed" mistress. As for married women, "the practice was too common to stir comment."

But most people outside of the world of the Whigs condemned their sexual indulgence. They risked ridicule and, for the women, ruin if their amours were exposed in the press or in court. Caroline's openness shocked many people, especially when she wrote a thinly disguised book about her affair. *Glenarvon,* published in May 1816, was a bestseller, but it prolonged her husband's shame. The book, wrote biographer L. G. Mitchell, "threw buckets of ordure into the faces of the whole Whig world." Melbourne was devastated, but it would be years before his family persuaded him to separate. When Caroline was dying from dropsy, in January 1828, Melbourne traveled from Ireland to be by her side.

After his wife's death, Melbourne had two spectacular liaisons that ended in court. Both were with astute, amusing married women who had husbands to whom Melbourne tossed political favors until they decided to sue him. Both trials also detailed his personal predilection for whipping, and both ended with his shunning the women involved, even though he was acquitted each time. The first was his Irish friend Lady Branden, to whom he paid an annuity for the rest of his life. The second was the beautiful author Caroline Norton, a highly intelligent woman whose brutish husband abused her. When her openly affectionate relationship with Melbourne became the subject of gossip, Mr. Norton took it to court. Melbourne swore for the rest of his life that he and Mrs. Norton were never lovers, though many, including his brother, were dubious. The case, held in June 1836, was lost in nine days. Although he was exonerated, Lord Melbourne was depressed for months and unable to sleep or eat. He became cruel, telling Caroline Norton not to fight for custody of her three sons and advising her to return to her violent spouse. Mrs. Norton went on to fight for more rights for mothers, and in 1839 a law was passed allowing women to seek custody of children under the age of seven. Victoria was sympathetic to her cause, and she reprimanded Melbourne when he did not even show up to vote for the bill. He said, "I don't think you should give a woman too much right . . . there should not be two conflicting powers . . . a man ought to have the right in a family." Even though, or perhaps especially because, he had lacked any power in his own.

As his female friends could attest, Lord Melbourne was obsessed with discipline. He even discussed it with Queen Victoria, particularly when it came to spanking children. It seems to have sprung from his experiences at Eton, where corporal punishment was widely practiced, though he was flogged only three times in three years, to his disappointment. These beatings, he told the queen, "had always an amazing effect." For the rest of his life, he advocated whipping as punishment for children or maids. There is some evidence that he indulged in the practice with his wife, at least one of his lovers, and a young orphan girl called Susan Churchill who lived with their family for some time.* His victims seemed willing enough, though it would be questionable to assume consent from an orphan girl. L. G. Mitchell believes Melbourne was trying to punish all women for the sins of the one who had betrayed him. The one woman who would adore him unquestioningly was the queen.

"He is certainly a queer fellow to be prime minister," wrote Greville. He had no agenda for reform, no vision for a new, improved country, and no policies he wished to see made law. His canniness was often underestimated, but stasis was Lord Melbourne's preferred position. His favorite political dictum was "Why not leave it alone?" In this sense, he was not a man for his time; he embodied governments of the past that saw their central concerns as solely security, the avoidance of wars, and the managing of crises. At a time of tumultuous energy and massive change in England, the PM was most fond of the words "delay" and "postpone." The irony was that Melbourne was a Whig. Previous Whig PMs, most notably Lord Grey between 1830 and 1834, had enacted welfare laws, ended slavery, and ex-

---

* In a letter to her mother-in-law, his wife, Caroline, said Melbourne had called her prudish, and she implied that his bizarre practices had corrupted her morals: "[He] said I was straight laced amused himself with instructing me in things I need never have heard or known & the disgust I at first felt to the worlds wickedness I till then had never even heard of in a very short time gave way to a general laxity of principles which little by little unperceived by you all has been undermining the few virtues I ever possessed" (Lady Caroline to Lady Melbourne, April 1810, in Douglass, *The Whole Disgraceful Truth,* 53). In forty letters to Lady Branden, only four contain no mention of whipping (Ziegler, *Melbourne,* 106–7). Melbourne told her she should whip her children more often, and proffered it as a solution for a lazy maid: "A few twigs of a birch applied to the naked skin of a young lady produces with very little effort a very considerable sensation."

panded the vote. But Melbourne even once told Archbishop Whately
that he would have done "nothing at all" about slavery. Little wonder
that the Whigs had lost momentum by the mid-1830s. Melbourne's
government accomplished little in the seven years he was PM, from
July to November 1834 and then April 1835 to August 1841. He utterly failed to understand the root causes of any social uprisings. The
most significant parliamentary debates of his time were not about
which policies might transform a nation restless with inequality, but
"the degree of repression that was necessary to keep the discontented
workers—or more often the unemployed—securely in their place."

The rush of tenderness Melbourne felt for Victoria surprised and
pleased him. The year before she became queen, his only child, Augustus, had died at the age of nineteen. Doctors said he had the mind
of an eight-year-old. Nothing worked: the leeches regularly attached
to his skull, the starvation, the magnetizing of his head, or the scorching of his skull with caustic acid. He had lived with Lord Melbourne
after Caroline died, often spending hours staring into space. Melbourne had struggled to love him, but when he lost his only child, he
was reminded of the woman he once loved, of the loss of his small,
fractured family, and that he was again alone.

In Victoria, Melbourne suddenly had the child, the companion,
and the affection he had long craved. She told him everything. By July,
they were talking about, as she wrote in her journal, "*very* important
& even to *me* painful things." He responded kindly to her naked bids
for reassurance. When she complained, "Everyone grows but me," he
replied, "I think you are grown." She was not bashful or shy, he said,
she just had a "sensitive and susceptible temperament." Knowing how
much Victoria disliked her mother, he also harshly criticized the
Duchess of Kent. One diary entry of Victoria's detailed how Victoria
and Melbourne spoke about her mother "for a long time." He said: "I
never saw so foolish a woman." Victoria added, "Which is very true;
and we laughed at Stockmar's calling her 'such a stupid woman,'
which I'm sorry to say is also true." Their familiarity was striking.

Victoria and Lord Melbourne saw each other every day for about five hours. It was a cozy, domesticated relationship spent talking, eating large meals, playing chess, and riding across the parks. When Melbourne was near her, the shrewd Princess Lieven wrote, "he looks loving, contented, a little pleased with himself; respectful, at his ease ... and dreamy and gay—all mixed up together." They teased each other affectionately: Victoria poked fun at his accent—he pronounced gold as "goold" and Rome as "Room"—and his tendency to nod off in the middle of functions.

The little queen, who was the happiest she had ever been, listed Melbourne's witty epigrams and aphorisms carefully in her journal. She thought him and his irreverence hilarious: On reform: "You had better try to do no good, and then you'll get into no scrapes." On doctors: "English physicians kill you, the French let you die." On women: "It is very rare that women are kind to one another." On horticulture: "All gardens are dull, a garden is a dull thing." When the Duke of Richmond said it was shocking that people came out of prisons worse than when they went in, Melbourne responded, "I'm afraid there are many places one comes out of worse than one went in; one often comes out worse of a ballroom than one went in." He made Victoria "die with laughing."

Best of all, Melbourne made her feel safe. And yet he was far from the ideal partner for her. There were three things he failed to do: first, to smooth tensions with her mother (despite telling her how important it was to be seen as a dutiful daughter); second, to convince her she was the queen of an entire country, not just of the Whigs. The third was a failure to stimulate her nascent social conscience: he strongly impressed upon her that any uprisings, protests, or demands for change were driven by a small group of disgruntled individuals. He kept her from the reality of explosive growth during the Industrial Revolution, which saw an entire group of people thrust into urban poverty as ugly, crowded shanties mushroomed around large towns, given no opportunity for escape and no voice in Parliament.

The most troubling failure, in the long term, was the third point. Melbourne thought that children should be able to work instead of starve and that education would make people unhappy. He said he "did not like any of the Poor, but those who are poor through their own fault, I quite detest." He scoffed at Victoria's interest in the world Charles Dickens wrote about. When she told him on New Year's Day, 1839, about Oliver Twist's story of "squalid vice" and "starvation in the Workhouses and Schools," Melbourne replied, "I do not *like* those things: I wish to avoid them. I do not like them in reality and therefore I do not like to see them represented." Victoria argued with him in vain. For the rest of her life, she would fail to concertedly champion attempts to alleviate poverty or improve basic living and working conditions. Victoria's problem was not lack of concern about social ills but lack of exposure to them.

But in the short term, the greatest failing was the second: the failure to educate the queen on her constitutional duty of impartiality, as Leopold had done in the past and Albert would do in the future. Victoria was an unabashed Whig like her father and friends, and she used "we" in referring to herself and the Melbourne government. What she failed to realize was that Melbourne was naturally conservative and a Whig more by background than belief. He occasionally tried to convince her that Tories were not bad people and that she would need to work with them in the future, but she shrugged him off, calling opposition leader Robert Peel a "nasty wretch." When the Whigs won the first general election of her reign by a large margin, Benjamin Disraeli, a Tory, wrote: "It is a fact that the little Queen clapped her hands." The Tories watched the relationship between the queen and her chief minister bloom, annoyed. The prominent conservative Charles Arbuthnot said, "With the young foolish Queen against us we can have but little hope." Victoria still refused to talk about politics with anyone but the prime minister.

By the end of 1838, after little more than a year as queen, Victoria had grown bored with her shiny new life. The work was relentless, she was tired of the banquets and balls, and most of her companions were several decades her senior. She started to wonder if she was as able as she had once thought. By December, she was irritable, depressed, and fretting: "I felt how unfit I was for my station." People also wondered how Melbourne could stand it, the nights of "shilling whist with the Duchess of Kent [and] six hours a day of tête-à-tête with the Queen" and the need to put a "perpetual check on swearing and loose talk." It was curious behavior from the man who was supposed to be running the country. Melbourne became defensive about whether his life as mentor, tutor, and paternal court jester was distracting him from matters of state. Yet, at a vulnerable moment, when Greville congratulated him for his care of Victoria, he cried, "By God, I am at it morning, noon and night!"

Victoria also felt physically run down. Melbourne thought she looked "yellow." She overate out of boredom and opportunity. Melbourne told her that the simple solution was to walk, and to eat only when she was hungry; she responded that she should then be eating all day. Walking, she said, made her feel sick. Melbourne also told her to stop drinking beer, which she loved. By December, a "cross and low" Victoria found to her distress that she weighed 125 pounds—an "incredible weight for my size." People were starting to whisper that her dresses were being made larger, and that she was already losing her looks, at eighteen. Melbourne assured Victoria that wine was good for her, and that anyway, the best figure for a woman was "full with a fine bust." Lord Holland politely observed that she had "perhaps rather more appearance of a full habit of body than nice & nervous observers of health would quite approve."

Victoria was growing cross at her reflection. Not only was she getting fat, she thought, but her hair was dark, and her eyebrows were too thin (she asked Melbourne if shaving them would make them thicker; he advised against it). Her face was still youthful, of course, with creamy skin, large, expressive, and intense eyes, a straight nose, and a small pink mouth. It was not her appearance, really, that was the problem. She was sluggish; the unusually energetic queen described some days simply as "Dawdled." At the end of April she wrote, "This year I did not enjoy pleasure so much . . . quite changed from what I was last year." Victoria sank deeper and deeper into a funk. She put off bathing and brushing her teeth and came up with a myriad of poor excuses to avoid exercise. Her maids bore the brunt of her temper, especially her dressers, who had a task she now hated—helping her squeeze into increasingly tight clothes.

Victoria's temper flared over any breaches of etiquette, and she often upbraided her mother, whose very presence irritated her. She wrote on one such occasion, "I told Lord Melbourne that I had carried my point with Mama about coming up to my room without asking. She was angry at first. I had to remind her who I was." Melbourne did not escape her occasional outbursts either. One night in summer, she said his company bored her because he had been too ill to talk. She began to chastise him for snoring during sermons and overeating. She was jealous when other women commanded his attention at dinner, and when he spent nights at the popular salon at Holland House. She even once asked him if he thought Lady Holland prettier than her. No one, she scribbled in her journal, frowning, cared for him more than she did.

The stubborn will that had assisted Victoria so magnificently in her struggles against Conroy had now, with the heady indulgence of power, hardened into an imperious air. Stockmar compared her to her Hanoverian uncles, describing her as "passionate as a spoiled child." If she was offended, she threw "everything overboard without exception." She began to feel that a person in her position should not be told what to do or think—and Stockmar despaired that Lehzen was encouraging her in this, "just like the nurse who hits the stone that tripped the child up."

Sycophants and indulgent confidants surrounded the young queen. Her uncle Leopold had always advised her to be unbending, to show that once she had made a decision, "no unearthly power will make her change." An already stubborn young woman needed little encouragement to be more so, especially when so many were loath to contradict her. This would be painfully obvious in the twin calamities of the next few months, when her two great passions—her love for Lord Melbourne and her hatred of Conroy—would cause her to stumble spectacularly. She had learned how to love, and she had learned how to hate, but she had not yet learned how to rule. Victoria was woefully unprepared for what lay ahead.

CHAPTER 9

A Scandal in the Palace

[Melbourne] has a young and inexperienced infant in his hands, whose whole conduct and opinions must necessarily be in complete subservience to his views. I do him the justice to believe that he has some feeling for his situation.

—LORD ABERDEEN TO PRINCESS LIEVEN

They wished to treat me like a girl, but I will show them that I am Queen of England.

—QUEEN VICTORIA

The skies yawned blue above Lord Melbourne and Queen Victoria as they rode up the fashionable racecourse of Ascot in an open carriage on May 30, 1839. When they appeared, the sound of hissing penetrated the low murmur of voices. Then, when the queen walked out onto the royal balcony, a shout came through: "Mrs. Melbourne!" The crowd sniggered and turned to stare as Victoria blushed darkly. Uncharacteristically, Lord Melbourne looked bothered. The hissing came from two Tory women, the Duchess of Montrose and Lady Sarah Ingestre. Victoria raged. "Those two abominable women ought to be flogged!" she said, unaware that Melbourne might have been perfectly happy to carry out her commands. She knew why they were hissing. It was on behalf of Lady Flora Hastings, a friend of her mother and John Conroy, who had grown terribly thin in recent months. When Lady Flora walked into Ascot, she was cheered loudly and repeatedly. Victoria was incensed.

The thirty-two-year-old Lady Flora, who was from a powerful aristocratic Tory family, had been one of the Duchess of Kent's ladies-in-waiting for five years. Victoria decided that she was an "odious" spy, largely because she was close to Conroy, and told Lord Melbourne to be wary. But one night at dinner, Victoria and Lehzen noticed that Lady Flora's stomach was swollen. Lady Flora had spent Christmas with her mother in Scotland and had traveled back in January 1839 with John Conroy in a post chaise—or closed carriage—without a chaperone. Immediately upon her return, she went to see Dr. James Clark, complaining of strange pains and a sore stomach. He gave her rhubarb pills and lotion to rub on her belly. This appeared to be mildly effective, but while Lady Flora's abdomen did not grow larger, it did not diminish either. It was clearly rounded.

The imaginations of the royal court, particularly the ladies-in-waiting, began to stir. Was Conroy to blame? On February 2, Victoria spoke to Melbourne of the "awkward business." He told her to keep quiet, adding that doctors often made mistakes and that his own view of English doctors was not particularly high. But after she left, Melbourne immediately called Dr. Clark, who said that while he could not be sure without a proper examination, there was reason to be suspicious.

This, Victoria decided, was confirmation that Lady Flora and Conroy were lovers. Melbourne had told her he believed Lady Flora's closeness to Conroy made Victoria's mother jealous. Were the two women rivals? Victoria finally wrote in her diary, on February 2: "We have no doubt that she is—to use plain words—*with child*!! Clark cannot deny the suspicion; the horrid cause of all this is the Monster & demon Incarnate, whose name I forbear to mention, but which is the 1st word of the 2nd line of this page."

That word was "J.C."—John Conroy, who was twenty years Lady Flora's senior. Victoria was disgusted and quickly jumped from judging one woman to judging all women. It was enough, she wrote, to make one "loathe one's own sex; when they *are* bad, how disgracefully and disgustingly servile and *low* women are!! I don't wonder at men considering the sex despicable!"

The intrigue escalated with every foolish step Dr. Clark took. First, he spied on Lady Flora for a fortnight, sneaking glances at her stomach, puzzling over its shape from several angles. Dr. Clark, who had served as a naval surgeon in the Napoleonic Wars and was later called "perhaps the most incompetent royal doctor of all time," appeared to be ignorant of any other conditions that could lead to a distended stomach. He was confused by her ability to continue working and walking and functioning normally, which he told himself she would not be able to do if she were ill. He tried to examine Lady Flora under her stays; she refused (a delicacy that other doctors later said only added to her trouble). He then asked if she was secretly married. She denied it indignantly—by that point, her swelling had already subsided to a "remarkable degree," she wrote to her uncle later. But that did not stop a "coarse" Dr. Clark from telling her he had been persuaded by "the conviction of the ladies of the palace that I was privately married." Lady Flora tried to show him how her stomach had grown smaller. He then insisted she confess to save her character, but she refused.

> Upon which he told me, that nothing but my submitting to a medical examination would ever satisfy them, and remove the stigma from my name. I found the subject had been brought before the Queen's notice, and all this had been discussed, and arranged, and denounced to me, without one word having been said to my own mistress [the Duchess of Kent], one suspicion hinted, or her sanction obtained for their proposing such a thing to me. . . . My beloved mistress, who never for one moment doubted me, told them she knew me, and my principles,

and my family, too well to listen to such a charge. However, the edict was given.

Lady Flora consented the next day to a humiliating and "most rigid examination" by another doctor, Sir Charles Clark, as well as the man she called "my accuser," Dr. James Clark. Lady Portman was also present. It included a "full medical examination" that was, according to Lady Flora, rough, prolonged, and painful. They gave her what was, in essence, a certificate of virginity that stated that there were "no grounds for believing that pregnancy does exist, or ever has existed."

The fact that it had been considered necessary to establish, crudely, that Lady Flora was still a virgin, in a virgin queen's court, was a gross violation of her dignity and honor. When Lady Flora's brother, the Marquess of Hastings, heard, he rushed to London to determine who was to blame, to insist on reparation, and to defend his family's honor. He saw Lord Melbourne and baldly told Victoria she had received bad advice and needed to find out who the originator of the slander was so that they might be brought to punishment.

This forced examination had been a shocking error. Victoria sent a contrite note and visited an "extremely agitated" and ill Lady Flora. It was their first meeting since the intrigue had begun. The queen promised all could be put behind them for the sake of her mother. Flora accepted the apology, but told the queen, "I must respectfully observe, madam, I am the first, and I trust I shall be the last, Hastings ever so treated by their Sovereign. I was treated as if guilty without a trial." Victoria prayed it would all end.

Several factors ensured that this insult ballooned into a full-blown scandal that occupied London for months: Melbourne's refusal to quash the rumor or punish Dr. Clark (doubtless fueled by his lingering suspicion, fostered by Dr. Clark, that Lady Flora might still be pregnant); the fascination of the press with the tale; the ongoing acrimony between Victoria and her mother that warped all communication; the desire of Tories to discredit the Melbourne government; and the wounded rage of the Hastings family, who were bent on restoring the honor of Lady Flora and discovering who had started the rumor. The duchess, who was intensely loyal to Lady Flora, sacked Dr. Clark. Victoria refused to do the same.

This was an extremely embarrassing affair, and Melbourne was culpable. He continued to irresponsibly fan the gossip, pandering to the queen's dislike of anything to do with her mother's household. Greville was disgusted: "It is inconceivable how Melbourne can have permitted this disgraceful and mischievous scandal, which cannot fail to lower the Court in the eyes of the world, and from a participation in which discredit the Queen's youth and inexperience can alone exempt her."

He was right. The entire episode underlined Victoria's immaturity. At one stage, Melbourne suggested Lady Flora should be married off to stop the gossip: the queen wrote cattily, "This made me laugh excessively, for I said Lady F. had neither riches nor beauty nor anything!" Melbourne laughed too, she wrote, for he thought Lady Flora the ugliest woman he had ever seen. In portraits, Flora is not even remotely ugly. She was a slight, clever-looking woman, with thoughtful eyes, a small round mouth, and dark brown hair. Their shared bias made this pair spiteful and unpleasant.

Lady Flora's mother decided to appeal to the queen. On March 7, the Dowager Marchioness of Hastings wrote a strong letter to Victoria—through the Duchess of Kent—seeking her help. She asked her to refute "the slanders" with an act designed to show her indignation, and ended: "To a female sovereign especially, women of all ranks in Britain look with confidence for protection and (notwithstanding the difference of their rank) for sympathy." But Victoria had no sympathy; she decided the letter was foolish and, provocatively, sent it back to her mother without a word. This error of judgment would incite the beginning of a relentless, vitriolic, and public campaign by the Hastings family to expose the royal court and demand accountability. The dowager, who was unwell and mortified by what had happened to her daughter, then wrote to Lord Melbourne, asking for the removal of Dr. Clark. Melbourne responded that her demand was "so unprecedented and objectionable" that he would not reply to it, only deigning to confirm receipt of her letter.

Next the Hastings family went to the press. On March 24, Lady Flora's uncle sent the *Examiner* an account of the affair based on a letter his niece had sent him; it was published in full. Lady Flora blamed the Whig ladies-in-waiting, as well as "a certain foreign lady, whose hatred to the Duchess is no secret." The letter to her uncle is dated March 8, 1839, and in it Lady Flora pointedly praised the Duchess of Kent:

> I am quite sure the Queen does not understand what they betrayed her into. She has endeavored to show her regret by her civility to me, and expressed it handsomely with tears in her eyes. The Duchess was perfect. A mother would not have been kinder, and she took the insult as a personal one, directed as it was at a person attached to her service and devoted to her. She immediately dismissed Sir James Clark, and refused to see Lady Portman, and would neither reappear nor suffer me to reappear at the Queen's table for many days.

She ended by saying, "I blush to send you so revolting a letter, but I wish you to know the truth, the whole truth, and nothing but the truth—and you are welcome to tell it right and left." The press erupted. The problem was also political: the queen and her prime minister were Whigs and Lady Flora was a Tory. The paranoia of the Tories was fueled, and many Whigs believed this scandal was used as political leverage to cast aspersions on an unmarried queen and her ladies, as well as on the prime minister. Meanwhile, Lady Flora was now emaciated.

Victoria was too instinctively tribal to extend grace to the Hastings family. When the old dowager marchioness handed all her correspondence with Lord Melbourne to the *Morning Post,* Victoria called her a "wicked foolish old woman." She had stopped reading newspapers and said the editors should be hanged, along with the Hastings family. She did not understand the gravity of her mistake nor how compromised she had become by her closeness to Melbourne. The Tories, in the wake of the Hastings affair, mustered strength, and Melbourne was losing his grip on power.

Victoria shook her head. In front of her sat the Tory MP Robert Peel, a man she had always found cold and unpleasant. Three days earlier, on May 6, Lord Melbourne's political career had been dealt a fatal blow; his government won by only five votes a vote on a bill that would have enforced antislavery legislation in the Jamaican sugar trade. (The slenderness of the majority was enough to undermine his leadership.) Since then, it had been clear that Peel was the obvious choice for PM—and that he did not have the full support of his queen. No, she said to him, she would not remove any of the Whig ladies in her bedchamber simply because he was now prime minister.

Victoria, devastated by the loss of Melbourne, spent days crying uncontrollably. "The state of agony, grief and despair into which this placed me may be easier imagined than described! *All all* my happiness gone! That happy peaceful life destroyed, that dearest kind Lord Melbourne no more my minister. . . . I sobbed and cried much; could only put on my dressing gown." On May 7, she stood outside the Blue Room, where Melbourne was waiting to tell her he had to resign, trying to compose herself:

> It was some minutes before I could muster up courage to go in,—and when I did, I really thought my heart would break; he was standing near the window; I took that kind, dear hand of his, and sobbed, and grasped his hand in both of mine and looked at him and sobbed out, "You will not forsake me" . . . he gave me such a look of kindness, pity and affection, and could hardly utter for tears, "Oh! no," in such a touching voice.

That afternoon, Melbourne suggested she call on Wellington and Peel, adding that she should trust them but be cautious. He ended his memo, crucially, with "Your Majesty had better express your hope, that none of your Majesty's Household, except those who are engaged in Politics, may be removed. I think you might ask him for that." Victoria took the document from him and began crying again, in huge wrenching gasps. She held his hand for a long time, "as I felt in doing so he could not leave me." Melbourne was aware of the difficulty of Victoria's position. He had declined three dinner invitations from her that day, saying it would be inappropriate to meet during such delicate negotiations with his political opponent.

Victoria was heartbroken. Her desperate words revealed the raw wound of a teenager separated from the man she loved. When he left, Victoria sat down to write to him, tears blurring her vision:

> The Queen ventures to maintain one thing, wh. she thinks *is possible;* wh: is, that if she rode out tomorrow afternoon, she might just get a glimpse of Lord Melbourne in the Park; if he knew where she rode, she wld meet him, as she did Lord Anglesey, & various others,—& it wld be such a comfort; there surely cld be no earthly harm in this; for I may *meet anyone;* Ld Melbourne may think this childish but the Queen *really* is so *anxious* it might be; & she wld bear thro' all her trials so much better if she cld just see a friend's face sometimes.

That night she was unable to eat, and cried convulsively until nine. Victoria had lost a father at eight months, and now, at nineteen, had lost the central father figure in her life, the man who had backed her against Conroy and her mother and made her feel loved and charming for the first time. Her brother and sister were in Europe, and she had no peers. It was a searing loss.

When Victoria woke, she wept again. Melbourne warned her not to show disdain for Tories, particularly Peel, who was aloof and shy but a fine politician, but their meetings did not go well. She moaned:

"The Queen didn't like his manner after—oh! how different, how dreadfully different, to that frank, open, natural and most kind, warm manner of Lord Melbourne." When Peel first asked that she remove some of her ladies in-waiting who were aligned with the Whigs, she said she would only change male members of Parliament who were part of her household. She then shut the door and cried. Lehzen came to comfort her.

In her second interview with Peel, on May 9, Victoria was stronger, and unyielding. She had convinced herself that Peel's claim was outrageous, and decided that she should be loyal to her ladies, as they had been to her during the Lady Flora Hastings affair. Victoria spoke calmly:

> I said I could *not* give up *any* of my Ladies, and never had imagined such a thing. He asked if I meant to retain *all*.
>
> "*All*," I said.
>
> "The Mistress of the Robes and the Ladies of the Bedchamber?"
>
> I replied, "All."

Victoria never spoke about politics with her ladies, she said, and, besides, they had plenty of Tory relatives. She refused Peel's suggestion of changing only the senior ladies—the Mistress of the Robes had precedence over the other ladies—arguing that this had never been done before. Could it be right that her household attendants be plucked from her grasp simply because the government had changed? Her ladies were hardly politicians. (She repeatedly said that this had not happened to a queen before; Peel insisted it was different because she was queen regnant. He was right—there had been no woman as sovereign since 1714—but no queen has been asked to do the same since.)

After Peel left, pale and downcast, the Queen wrote triumphantly to Lord Melbourne:

[Peel had] behaved very ill, and has insisted on my giving up my Ladies, to which I replied that I never would consent, and I never saw a man so frightened. . . . I was calm but very decided and I think you would have been pleased to see my composure and great firmness. *The Queen of England will not submit to such trickery.* Keep yourself in readiness for you may soon be wanted.

Peel then bluntly told Victoria that if she did not agree to remove some of her ladies, who were married to some of his most vehement enemies, he could not form a government. Victoria, pleased by the prospect of Lord Melbourne returning, told Peel her mind was made up and she would write to him in a few hours or in the morning to give him her final decision. She scrawled excitedly that Peel had admitted weakness, and begged Melbourne to come immediately.

Melbourne's Cabinet argued for several hours about what to do. It was Victoria's letters that swayed them to return to government to protect the honor of the queen: "Do not fear that I was calm and composed," she wrote. "They wanted to deprive me of my ladies, and I suppose they would deprive me next of my dressers and my housemaids; they wished to treat me like a girl, but I will show them that I am Queen of England." Chivalry aside, her behavior was inappropriate; an opposition should not have been advising a queen on how best to defy the new prime minister.

On May 10, Peel resigned. In a chilly letter, he assured Her Majesty that he was thrilled that she had even considered him for the position of prime minister. The public was outraged. Victoria, however, was ecstatic. That night, she danced until 3:15 A.M. at a state ball she hosted for Czarevitch Alexander, son of Czar Nicholas I, whom she described as "a dear delightful young man." After he spun her around the dance floor, she pronounced, "I really am quite in love with the Grand Duke. I never enjoyed myself more." He squeezed her hand when he left, and kissed her cheek "in a very warm and affectionate manner." She told Melbourne, "A young person like me must *sometimes* have young people to laugh with." The Tory Duke of Wellington and Peel, however, were "very much put out."

With Melbourne back at the helm, all was in order once again in Victoria's world. But a pall had been cast over the court, and she was unable to shake feelings of despondency. Melbourne should have helped her understand that Peel only wanted those of her ladies who were married to Tory MPs gone. She soon asked Melbourne to help her find a Tory lady who could be quietly introduced into her household.* During the rest of her reign, Victoria was only ever asked to change the Mistress of the Robes, her highest-ranking lady. Her bias remained blatant, though. She was a Whig, like her parents, and she wanted a Whig to always remain prime minister. When crowds outside the palace hissed at Melbourne, the queen was furious: "Tories are capable of every villainy."

In the final years of her life, Victoria confessed she had blundered during what was called the Bedchamber Crisis: "Yes, I was very hot about it and so were my ladies, as I had been so brought up under Lord Melbourne; but I was *very* young, only 20, and never should have acted so again—Yes! it was a mistake." It was astonishing to think a queen had effectively dismissed a prime minister.

By April, Lady Flora Hastings had grown very weak. The campaign by the Hastings family had been successful; public sympathy was clearly with Lady Flora, who kept appearing in public so that people would not think she was pregnant. The distressed Duchess of Kent was convinced that Lady Flora was going to die, but even in

---

* When Peel became prime minister two years later, Albert's private secretary, Anson, told him not only that there were three prominent Whig women who would leave the household, but that they would have done so in 1840. Peel was astonished: "Had the Queen told me that these three ladies immediately connected with the government had tendered their resignation, I should have been perfectly satisfied and should have consulted the Queen's feelings in replacing them" (Ziegler, *Melbourne,* 298). Pride, haste, and heartbreak had prevented this matter from being resolved at the time.

June, Victoria was still dismissing Lady Flora's condition as a "bilious attack." The ongoing attacks had hardened her attitude to Lady Flora, and she resented, she said, having "to bear so much for *such* a woman." Lord Melbourne's advice continued to be immature and graceless. In early April, when Victoria decided Flora had been "exceedingly rude," Melbourne just advised her to be more distant. The next day, they shared gossip they had both heard: that Lady Flora had already given birth to a child. Her mother, Lady Hastings, was blamed for not detecting the bump and insisting she stay in Scotland. She told Lord Melbourne that if Lady Flora were to go away, it would be best if she stayed away. Lord Melbourne advised her that this would not put the queen in a good light. Victoria showed no signs of self-doubt in her journal, where she wrote of Lady Flora's impertinence, insolence, and still-rounded torso. Her entries reveal an alarming lack of remorse toward Lady Flora, and not the slightest sense of the continuing ordeal the sick woman was enduring. The Duchess of Kent repeatedly tried to make her daughter speak or at least write to Lady Flora, but Victoria would not shift an inch. She cited the impudence of the Hastings family and the affront of their decision to air the dispute in public. Lord Melbourne, as usual, told the queen that the Hastings family was in the wrong and encouraged her to remind them not to be rude. Victoria did not understand what she had done, nor what she had failed to stop. Lady Flora thought she lacked empathy: "It does not occur to her to feel for another."

But when Victoria finally went to see Lady Flora again at the end of June, alone, she was mortified:

> I found poor Ly. Flora stretched on a couch looking as thin as anybody can be who is still alive; literally a skeleton, but the body *very* much swollen like a person who is with child; a searching look in her eyes, a look rather like a person who is dying; her voice like usual, and a good deal of strength in her hands; she was friendly, said she was very comfortable, & was very grateful for all I had done for her; & that she was glad to

see me look well. I said to her, I hoped to see her again when she was better—upon which she grasped my hand as if to say "I shall not see you again."

Victoria left quickly. She started to pray that Lady Flora might suddenly revive, and soon it was all she could think and talk about. She began to have nightmares about the fine-featured aristocrat with the wandering eyes.

Flora Hastings died before sunrise on July 5, 1839. Lehzen told Victoria shortly after she woke up. She had died quietly, "& only just raised her hands & gave one gasp." Lady Flora made her last wish as her weeping family surrounded her: that a postmortem be conducted on her body that would finally, thoroughly prove her innocence. There were still rumblings in the court about a stillborn child. Even on the morning of her death, a protester wrote on a placard that Lady Flora died of a botched abortion. But the autopsy report, which Victoria waited anxiously for all day, showed Lady Flora had a grossly enlarged liver, which was pressing on her stomach. It also reported that "the uterus and its appendages presented the usual appearances of the healthy virgin state." Even in death, her chastity was probed.

Public fury was revived by the news; Victoria and Melbourne were hissed at in public, hats stayed on when the queen's carriage wheeled past in a gesture of disrespect, and voices stayed quiet when the royal toast was given amid whispers of murder. Victoria's mother told her she did not know "her own country," and on this occasion she was right. The queen had not been thinking of her subjects. For the first time in her life, she had been part of a clique, and it was a powerful one; and the pull of scandal, revenge, and bitchy gossip had been too great. Especially when it came to the sexuality of another woman, one she saw as an enemy due to her friendship with Conroy. (It was an example of what today we might call slut-shaming.) And not only did she have a crush on her enabler, he was the prime minister. It was intoxicating, and Victoria was too young to understand the consequences. This episode would long be considered an embarrassment: there is now no reference to Lady Flora's being ill or dying in Victoria's diary (a volume edited by her daughter Princess Beatrice), and most of Victoria's many letters about Lady Flora Hastings were later destroyed under the orders of her eldest son, King Edward VII. He and the editor had been shocked to discover Victoria's "precocious knowledge."

Flora Hastings's coffin was drawn out of the palace by carriage in the thick of night, in the hope of avoiding protests. The somber cavalcade rolled slowly to the East End of London, before finally landing at Brunswick wharf, Blackwall, at dawn. The body would be placed on the *Royal William* steamship, which would take her back to Scotland, the land of her ancestors. Crowds gathered to pay respects to the casket of the woman wronged by the royal court. One man shouted, "Ah, there's the victim, but where's the murderer?" and another shook his stick at the queen's carriage, crying, "What is the good of [Victoria's] gilded trumpery after she had killed her?" A few rocks were thrown at the royal carriage, despite the strong police presence lining the way from the palace to the docks.

Walking through the palace gardens on the day after Lady Flora died, Victoria had an overwhelming urge to roll in the green grass, over and over, until she was so dizzy she could somehow forget her shame. She was rarely named in press reports, but she was often directly blamed for Lady Flora's death. Some reporters bluntly accused the court of murder. Victoria often insisted she felt no remorse, but her own role troubled her deeply: "I can't think what possessed me." She swore she would never again leap to conclusions because of the way people looked. Victoria knew that her crown was tarnished.

The conviction Victoria formed that Lady Flora was catty and sly was wrong. Lady Flora was a woman of great pride, faith, and sensitivity. Throughout her extended period of torment, she wrestled with how to forgive those who hurt her. She would not sink to hating, she said: "For myself I feel this trial has been sent in love, it has drawn me closer to God, & shaken off some worldly feelings, & promoted deep heart-searching." When she took her last communion, lying in bed on June 20, the Bishop of London asked her if she had forgiven her enemies. She said she had, and that she held no bitterness toward them. The Duchess of Kent, who was kneeling beside her, cried. As she walked out of the room, she took the hand of Lady Flora's sister Sophia and asked, "Forgive my poor Child?"

Some claimed Lady Flora died of a broken heart. On July 20, 1839, her body was buried in the vault of an ancient church in Ayrshire, surrounded by the craggy mountains of southern Scotland. "The whole ceremony," wrote a reporter from *The Times,* "was most imposing." Several thousand people came to her funeral; she had become a martyr, especially for the Tories. "Her memory is embalmed by the sympathy and affection of a noble people," wrote *The Corsair,* adding that if the English court did not change, "there can be no safety for the life, for the happiness, or for the reputation of the Queen of England."

It was a gloomy summer for Victoria. She was lonely, moody, and on edge, and she felt fat. Having had her decisions challenged so publicly, she had become particularly sensitive to challenges to her authority. If she suspected that any of her ministers had not consulted her on a matter, she wrote heavily underlined, angry screeds, demanding an explanation. Harriet Martineau wrote that Victoria's unhappiness could be seen by anyone. The author blamed Melbourne:

At her accession, I was agreeably surprised at her appearance. The upper part of her face was really pretty, and there was an ingenuous and serene air which seemed full of promise. At the end of the year, the change was melancholy. The expression of her face was wholly altered. It had now become bold and discontented. That was, it is now supposed, the least happy part of her life. Released from the salutary restraints of youth, flattered and pampered by the elated Whigs who kept her to themselves, misled by Lord Melbourne, and not yet having found her home, she was not like the same girl that she was before.

The saga dragged on for months, with Lady Flora's brother publishing damning correspondence and Dr. Clark releasing a summary of his invasive exam. The darkness did lift for the queen, though, abruptly and spectacularly, just the day after Dr. Clark published his defense. Victoria woke depressed, with a terrible headache and sore eyes, to discover that someone had pelted her dressing room with rocks, smashing panes of glass into splinters. It was a mysterious but apt sign of what lay before her. That morning, as she tiptoed around the wreckage, a bilious Prince Albert stepped off a boat onto British soil and began his journey by land to see her. From the second he climbed out of his carriage at Windsor Castle, everything was different. Victoria would always remember October 10, 1839. On that day, her heart was blown to smithereens.

Part 3

ALBERT: THE MAN SOME CALLED KING

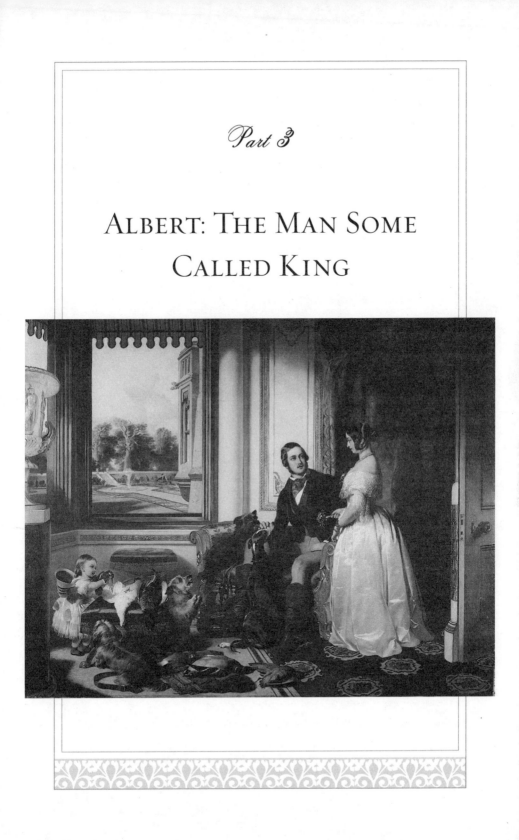

CHAPTER 10

Virago in Love

I told Albert that he had come like an angel of light to save me . . . for I *alone* could not have helped myself. I was young & wilful.

—QUEEN VICTORIA

Queen Victoria, even when she was most infatuatedly in love with Prince Albert, always addressed him exactly as if he were a little boy of three and she his governess.

—GEORGE BERNARD SHAW

Victoria stood at the top of the red-carpeted stairs at Windsor Castle staring down at her cousin Albert. He was climbing up the stone staircase with his brother Ernest, past a statue of George IV and suits of armor, to take the young queen's hand. It was early evening on October 10, 1839, and the two men had just arrived after traveling on an overnight boat trip through the rain from the Continent to Dover. Victoria stared at Albert in the flickering light, struck: though wan and still seasick, he was magnificent. He had filled out in the three years since she had seen him last; his chest was broad, his thighs muscular, and his face perfectly proportioned. The queen, suddenly self-conscious, stretched out her hand.

She was smitten. Victoria wrote in her journal that night: "It was with some emotion that I beheld Albert—who is *beautiful*." The next day, she went into further detail about the lure of his physical attributes: he was "so excessively handsome," with "such beautiful eyes, an exquisite nose, and such a pretty mouth with delicate mustachios and slight but very slight whiskers; a beautiful figure broad in the shoulders and a fine waist." It was a kind of lust she was powerless to contain. Looking at him made her stomach cartwheel: "I have to keep a tight hold on my heart." Just four days later, she would loosen her grip entirely.

Albert had spent the journey steeling himself for a difficult conversation. The proud German prince had resolved to tell "Cousin Victoria" that he would not drum his heels for years while she toyed with the idea of marrying him. He was tired of being left dangling and did not want to be dictated to. Victoria had wanted the two brothers to come several days earlier, but Albert told his brother Ernest to let her wait. He was well aware of her reservations. Albert's father had told him she was a "virago queen"—strong-minded and domineering—whose house was in turmoil. Albert considered her something of a hedonist, a woman who relished parties and sleeping late. They were a curious pair—the boy who happily wandered the woods around his summer residence, the Rosenau, looking for rocks, shells, and leaves to add to his natural science collection; and a girl who complained she hated walking because she got stones in her delicate boots, but would gladly dance until the soles of her shoes were as thin as sheets. As rolling gray waves slapped the prow of his ship, sailing across the English Channel, Albert rehearsed lines for the conversation he was dreading. How would you tell a young queen that you were not prepared to wait for her favor?

Victoria was extremely wary of marriage. After a stifling childhood, she was now finally free—finally able to do as she wanted. She had no memories of her parents together and had never witnessed a strong, happy marriage—save that of her uncle Leopold and his second wife,

Louise, who had been like a sister to her. She knew that most of her uncles had been unfaithful and unkind to their wives; why would she rush toward such a risk? Most girls of twenty may have been married or betrothed, but, as she wrote the year after she became queen, she wanted to "enjoy two or three years more" of her "present young girlish life" before "the duties and cares of a wife." She also worried about her workload, which "marrying now would render still more fatiguing." Besides, the country liked her the way she was, a young queen on her own. The whole subject, she declared, was "odious."

As for Albert, well, he was young and sickly, his English was poor, and he was lacking in sophistication. Their last visit, in 1836, had been uninspiring; Ernest had left thinking he was the one Victoria favored. Still, they kept in touch. Albert wrote her a letter congratulating her on becoming "Queen of the mightiest land of Europe." In it, he asked, "May I pray you to think likewise sometimes of your cousins in Bonn, and to continue to them that kindness you favored them with till now. Be assured that our minds are always with you." Victoria also directed Stockmar to accompany Albert on a tour of Italy, to broaden his education. It was a great success—the cerebral Albert was in raptures about the "inexhaustible source of knowledge," although he did not fancy the scenery or climate (in this sense, his tastes were the opposite of Victoria's; she far preferred sketching landscapes to trotting through museums).

Victoria was also a romantic and did not want love to be planned, or calculated; she wanted it to burst upon her with great, irresistible force. How could that possibly happen with her pale, serious cousin? In July 1839, a few months before their October meeting, Victoria tried to stop Albert from coming to visit. She begged Leopold not to let her cousin get his hopes up: "for, apart from my youth and my *great* repugnance to change my present position, there is *no anxiety* evinced in *this country* for such an event." If her marriage were rushed, it "might produce discontent." Her cousin sounded wonderful on paper, but as she sensibly pointed out, she "may not have the *feeling* for him which is requisite to ensure happiness." She asked

Leopold to cancel the visit and be perfectly clear to Albert that there was *"no engagement."* All signs pointed to disappointment. She even hinted, in a letter to the increasingly frustrated Albert, that she had a crush on another gentleman from the Continent: "We have had the Grand Duke of Russia here for some time. I liked him extremely."

Victoria had not been wanting for suitors. She was powerful, vivacious, and young. Newspapers in the United States reported rumors that President Martin Van Buren, then a fifty-four-year-old widower, "thinks seriously of making an offer" to her. The *Daily Advertiser* saw "no reason why he should not *offer,* or why he may not stand as good a chance as the namby-pamby princes and kings of Europe." A succession of men from the New World and Old had been suggested as possible husbands for the "rose of England," but she was not interested in any of them.

And, as was becoming a pattern, Victoria was under the strong influence of a particular opinion: that of Lord Melbourne. He had warned Victoria against marrying Albert on three counts: he was a German, a cousin, and a Coburg. Given that his mother-in-law was also his aunt, was there not a chance that Albert would side with her? (Victoria, certain of Albert's loyalty, "assured him he need have no fear whatever on that score.") Melbourne's most forceful argument was simply that this marriage was *"not* NECESSARY." On this point they agreed. There was some self-interest behind Melbourne's argument, as he did not want their cozy intimacy disturbed. Victoria, too, told Lord Melbourne she hoped he would not remarry, when his sister was urging him to.

Most of all, the willful Victoria was concerned that marriage would mean she might no longer be in charge; that in becoming a wife, she would not be able to be the kind of decisive and controlling queen she liked. In April 1839, in the midst of the Lady Flora Hastings debacle, she and Lord Melbourne had discussed how they might be able to boot Victoria's mother out of the palaces Victoria inhabited. One possibility was marriage, though Victoria said it was a "schocking [*sic*] alternative" to her current life. She said she was "so accustomed to have my own way, that I thought it was ten to one that I shouldn't agree with any body." Melbourne said, perhaps unwisely, "Oh! But you would have it [your own way] still." This was the model of marriage planted in Victoria's mind. Her power would remain intact; her future husband, then, would be more of a traditional wife. She would rule, and he would trail behind.

Albert was sick of it. His uncle Leopold warned him of Victoria's hesitation and inflated the wait from a two- to a four-year delay. Albert interpreted this as rejection and prepared to tell her he would not stand idly by. She had initially underwhelmed him, anyway. "Cousin Victoria is always friendly toward us," he wrote when they first met as teenagers. "She is not beautiful by any means, though extremely kind and bright." His famous relative had been presented as his destiny throughout his life, but now that they were both twenty years old, he was worried he would soon look like a fool: "If after waiting, perhaps for three years I should find that the Queen no longer desired the marriage, it would place me in a ridiculous position, and would to a certain extent ruin all my prospects for the future." His future hinged on the whims of a young queen. He walked into Windsor Castle, nauseated and exhausted, and looked up at the small figure looming above him on the stairs, the most powerful woman in the world.

On October 13, Victoria told Lord Melbourne that her opinion about marriage had changed. She had spent the last three days in a state of agitation, scribbling in her journal while listening to Haydn symphonies, sneaking looks at Albert as his greyhound stole food from her fork. Albert was so "amiable and good tempered," she said to Lord Melbourne, owning up to her own bad temper, and confessing that she now recognized "the advantage of beauty." When she told him of her intentions, the prime minister advised her to think about it for a week. But the next day, she told him her mind was made up. A kindly Melbourne changed tack and assured her she would be much more comfortable, "for a woman cannot stand alone for any time, in whatever position she may be." Throughout her life, this message would be repeated to Victoria: women cannot, and should not, rule alone. "Thank you," said a flushed Victoria, "for being *so fatherly*."

Now came the excruciating part. As a ruling queen, it was convention that Victoria must do the proposing. It really was tantamount to informing him of her decision, but to a protected young woman, who did not have a father and did not confide in her mother, the prospect was nerve-racking. She and Albert had never discussed anything like love or marriage; her stomach clenched every time she thought of it. That night, to her delight, Albert squeezed her hand while saying good night. This was encouraging.

Finally, on Tuesday, October 15, at twelve-thirty, Victoria sent a summons when Albert was out hunting. He walked into his room to see the note lying on his dressing table. Half an hour later, he went to see her. Victoria asked him to sit down, then tried to make some idle talk. She was trembling a little, and speaking too quickly:

> I said to him that I thought he must be aware *why* I wished him to come and that it would make me too *happy* if he would consent to what I wished (namely to marry me); we embraced each other over and over again, and he was so kind, so affectionate; Oh! To *feel* I was, and am, loved by *such* an Angel as Albert was too *great a delight to describe*! He is *perfection;* perfection in every way—in beauty—in everything!

Albert accepted instantly. Victoria told him she was not worthy of him, lifted his "dear hand," and kissed it repeatedly before she called for his brother Ernest. Then, tellingly, Albert went to pay his respects to Lehzen—the woman Victoria truly thought of as her mother. Victoria's diary entries on that day and the several following are striking for their unrepressed joy. It was as though she had chanced upon the prospect of happiness with unaffected surprise: a blind woman stumbling on a marble statue, unable to stop caressing it. Victoria wrote to her uncle Leopold later that day:

> He seems *perfection,* and I think that I have the prospect of very great happiness before me. I love him MORE than I can say, and shall do everything in my power to render this sacrifice (for such in my opinion it is) as small as I can. He seems to have great tact, a very necessary thing in his position. These last few days have passed like a dream to me, and I am so much bewildered by it all that I know hardly how to write; but I do feel very happy.

For almost a month, Victoria kept her secret from her mother. In her contentious biography of the queen published in 1840, Agnes Strickland wrote that the betrothal was "sanctioned" by the Duchess of Kent. Victoria firmly scribbled in the margins: "Never. The Duchess of Kent never knew anything of it until the Queen told it to her a few days before the Prince left." Victoria distrusted her mother and had persuaded Albert that her mother would tell people and cause mischief. The duchess clearly suspected something was afoot; twice she burst into Victoria's room without knocking, when she knew she was with Albert, which Victoria thought most indiscreet. Finally, the queen summoned her mother to her room on November 9. The Duchess of Kent threw her arms around Victoria and wept; she knew her daughter had not asked for her blessing, but she told her she would give it to her anyway. Albert then came into the room, hugged Victoria, and stood holding her hand. An emotional duchess said they were so young—Victoria replied that Albert was so steady—and vowed that she would never meddle in their marriage. She also gushed, inappropriately, about other men who had wanted to marry Victoria.

The duchess's joy shriveled somewhat as she returned to her room. She was unable to sleep, knowing Victoria had waited so long to tell her. She fretted about who had known before she had, wondering if the couple had decided to marry too quickly. She worried about where she was going to live and wrote Victoria several letters on the subject of her housing, which her daughter shrugged off as a nuisance. Her mother, she said, was a "great plague."

Inside the lovers' cocoon, though, all was sunlit. Albert was charmed by the queen's euphoric proposal and her lack of guile. He wrote to his grandmother:

> The Queen sent for me alone to her room a few days ago, and declared to me in a genuine outburst of love and affection, that I had gained her whole heart, and [that it] would make her intensely happy if I would make her the sacrifice of sharing her life with her, for she said she looked on it as a sacrifice; the only thing which troubled her was that she did not think she was worthy of me. The joyous openness of manner in which she told me this quite enchanted me, and I was quite carried away by it. She is really most good and amiable, and I am quite sure heaven has not given me into evil hands, and that we shall be happy together.

It was Victoria's passion that had hurtled the pair forward, but Albert's slower yet certain devotion would follow soon after. They behaved like besotted lovers. He took her hands in his, warming them, marveling at how small they were. He sat near her as she worked, blotting her ink when she asked. Victoria crept up behind him and planted her lips on his forehead, and chased him as he left, for one last kiss. Albert had a clinical, pragmatic mind, and he struggled to match Victoria's passionate pronouncements, responding by demurring: *"Liebe Kleine, Ich habe dich so lieb, ich kann nicht sagen wie"* (Dear Little One, I love you so much, I cannot say how). He was genuinely delighted and surprised by the magnitude of her love, which had sprouted so swiftly. In mere weeks, Victoria had pivoted from being a woman who relished being and ruling alone, to one who was entirely consumed with passion for her beloved. At times Victoria overwhelmed him with barely concealed lust: "I said to Albert we should be very very intimate together, and that he might come in and out when he pleased. . . . Oh! how happy I shall be, to be very very intimate with him!"

Albert was floored, telling Stockmar he was "often at a loss to believe that such affection should be shown to me." But his happiness was checkered; he was distraught at the thought of leaving Germany. Even when the queen, his *Vortrefflichste* (incomparable one), spent hours describing the glorious future they would share, he was preoccupied by what he would be losing. He wrote to his grandmother: "Oh, the future! does it not bring with it the moment when I shall have to take leave of my dear, dear home, and of you! I cannot think of that without deep melancholy taking possession of me." Albert was conscious that he was not just getting married but accepting a job, and that his work would be "decisive for the welfare of so many." Albert had spent years contemplating the possibility of marrying into great power. He wrote to his brother just months earlier, on his twentieth birthday, that they should strive for general education and "elasticity of the brain," which he believed was what gives "great men such power to rule over others." Albert was aiming for greatness.

Because Victoria modeled an orthodox marriage for her age, with a large clutch of children, and was photographed looking up adoringly at her husband, or placing her hands on his shoulders as he read, it is easy to forget how unconventional her relationship was. She was the most famous woman in Britain, with palaces, a large staff, and immense responsibility. He was relatively unknown, and from a small, poor German duchy. Victoria had been advised by her prime minister to seek a consort she could control, who would bend in obedience to her plans. Albert could see how stubborn and strong his fiancée was. In the three years since he had last seen her, he observed that she had barely grown an inch, "but she has acquired much greater firmness." In many ways Victoria's role was that of the man; she was the one to propose, to give Albert a ring first and ask for a lock of his hair. She was not obliged to take his name, just as women who married kings were allowed to keep theirs. The affectionate words she used to describe him were often womanly; he was her beautiful, "dearest Angel."

In the most conventional of senses, Victoria had procured herself a wife. Melbourne was her intellectual companion and Albert was her object of desire. In the days after the proposal, she continued to record her lengthy conversations with Melbourne, while "dearest" Albert flitted through scenes as a beauty, a fine dancer, and a dinner companion. His words and ideas were not given the same weight as Melbourne's, although she did briefly touch on his great dislike of Russians, the French, and, alarmingly, Jews. Lord Melbourne dismissed this anti-Semitism—which Victoria did not share—as typically German. Victoria did not linger on it. She confessed twice to Lord Melbourne that falling in love had made her quite stupid. Yet while the young queen may have admired Albert's athletic physique—especially when he wore tight white pants "with nothing under them"—it was his constantly whirring, polymathic mind that would endear several generations to the serious German prince who liked going to bed early.

Albert was a curious boy: after he uttered his first cry at birth, he "looked about him, like a squirrel." As a child, he was confident and certain in his views; when he was a teenager, he met Pope Gregory XVI and discussed art with him in Italian. He created a natural history museum with his brother, wrote poetry, collected donations for a poor family in his village whose house burned down, and composed music. When he was eleven he wrote in his journal: "I intend to train myself to be a good and useful man." He instinctively adhered to a code of honor from an early age: When he was a boy, playing a game of knights, his group was attacking an old ruined tower that others were hiding in. One friend suggested sneaking in through the back entrance, which would have meant easy victory; Albert objected, saying it would not be the right thing to do and "most unbecoming in a Saxon knight."

While he was droll and had a gift for mimicry, Albert was also delicate, asking to be carried upstairs even at the age of four. The fair-haired, cherubic child tired easily, and would sometimes slip off his chair after falling asleep at the table. His mother, Princess Louise, adored him, describing her son as "superb, an extraordinary beauty, with large blue eyes . . . and always jolly." Albert inherited his mother's gaiety, sense, and wisdom, but he never really knew her. His father, the Duke Ernst of Saxe-Coburg and Gotha, was a notorious philanderer and was blatantly unfaithful to his vivacious wife—who called him her "master." Eventually, when she began to have flirtations of her own—and began spending a lot of time with an equerry four years her junior—he accused her of similarly immoral behavior. Duke Ernst threw her out in a rage, and he retained full custody of their children.

Louise, who was then only twenty-three years old, was bereft. Her sons, only five and six years old, were sick with whooping cough on the night she left; they thought she was crying because they were sick. She pined for her sons, once disguising herself as a peasant woman so she might go unnoticed at a local harvest festival and gaze at them from afar. Duke Ernst never sent her any news of them, despite her repeated requests, and cruelly intercepted the letters she sent.

The fact that Albert so strongly resembled his mother, not his father or brother, has prompted some to suggest Duke Ernst was not his father—rumors that are unfounded. The press occasionally aired incorrect claims, fueled by anti-Semites, that Albert's real father was a Jewish baron, the court chamberlain. Duke Ernst's own suspicions were that Albert's father was his childhood friend Alexander Graf zu Solms. He sent Louise back to live with her family for some time as punishment, exiled zu Solms, and conducted a bogus official inquiry that went on for years. In a clear example of the glaring double standards of the time, Louise was accused of many scandalous, fictitious liaisons, called a harlot and a "shameless little sinner." The biographer Hector Bolitho examined the divorce papers in the archives of the Duke of Saxe-Coburg and found "there was not even a hint in the documents that the Duchess had been unfaithful, with either Jew or Christian, until at least four years after Prince Albert was born; he was already in the schoolroom when his mother was divorced, in 1826. Seven months later she married Alexander von Hanstein, named in the proceedings as a co-respondent." Louise was treated exceedingly unfairly, given her husband's own conduct. It was the woman who was cast out, not the man, and it was the children who suffered.

In 1831, Albert's mother died of uterine cancer in Paris, just months before the riots against the monarchy that Victor Hugo described in *Les Misérables*. She was only thirty years old. Her wish was to be buried with her second husband, the man who had loved her despite her scarlet reputation. Albert and Ernest refused to accept this; once their father had died, in 1846, they dug up her coffin from St. Wendel in western Germany and reburied it in the ducal tomb in Coburg next to their father. They shifted the coffins again in 1860 into a grand mausoleum they built especially for their parents in Coburg. Though it may have been wrong to overrule the wishes of their mother, the brothers were trying to achieve what had escaped them when their mother and father were alive—united parents. For the rest of his life, Albert would be viscerally horrified by infidelity, the behavior that tore his own family apart and took his mother from him. Albert always spoke of Louise "with tenderness and sorrow" and was tortured by accounts of her painful illness. In a tellingly gentle gesture, one of the first gifts he gave Victoria was a little turquoise star pin that had belonged to her. His determination to be faithful was so deeply held that it never appeared to be a struggle for him; it created a cocoon in which Victoria always felt safe. Both had lost parents at an early age, and while Albert did not have a rift with his father as Victoria did with her mother, both ached for an idyllic domesticity they had dreamed of as children.

Victoria sat in front of the Privy Council on November 23, 1839, wearing a simple morning dress. Dangling from her wrist was a bracelet with Albert's tiny face peering up from it. Eighty-three peers sat in a room on the ground floor of Buckingham Palace, staring at her expectantly. Victoria felt slightly ill. She lowered her head, tried to still her trembling hands, and read out a declaration Melbourne had written the night before:

> I have caused you to be summoned at the present time, in order that I may acquaint you with my resolution in a matter which deeply concerns the welfare of my people, and the happiness of my future life. It is my intention to ally myself in marriage with the Prince Albert of Saxe-Coburg and Gotha. Deeply impressed with the solemnity of the engagement which I am about to contract, I have not come to this decision without mature consideration, nor without feeling a strong assurance that, with the blessing of Almighty God, it will at once secure my domestic felicity and serve the interests of my country. I have thought fit to make this resolution known to you at the earliest period, in order that you may be fully apprised of a matter so highly important to me and to my kingdom, and which I persuade myself will be most acceptable to all my loving subjects.

Victoria then walked out as soon as it was polite to do so, leaving a tearful Lord Melbourne behind. She was still shaking the following day. In a letter to Albert, who had returned to Germany two weeks before, she described it as "an awful moment," to have to declare such intimate news to strangers.

After the meeting had ended, the Duchess of Gloucester— formerly Princess Mary—asked Victoria if she had been nervous.

"Yes," Victoria responded, "but I did a much more nervous thing a little while ago."

"What was that?" asked the duchess.

"I proposed to Prince Albert."

The news was greeted with muted enthusiasm. Albert was considered a decent choice as a bridegroom. Critics pointed out that he was young, inexperienced, and poor, while others spoke favorably of his musical and poetic skills. The public had many questions about their queen's fiancé. Beyond a superficial curiosity, most people wanted to know how much power he might wield, the amount he would be paid, and what could be done to ensure that a foreign prince would not exert too much influence over the queen.

The *Spectator* was dismissive. The husband of a great British queen, they wrote, must surely be emasculated:

> A gilded puppet, who can perform no action becoming in elevated birth and exalted station; who can follow no pursuit worthy of a warrior or a statesman; whose entire importance is reflected; and who can avow no opinion (except perhaps on an article of dress, a piece of furniture, or a horse), even though the fate and character of his wife be at stake, without violating the Constitution of the country that has adopted him!

Historically, husbands of queens had not been widely loved in England. And they had been spectacularly unsuccessful at siring their wives. Philip II of Spain was not particularly attached to Queen Mary I, the titian-haired Roman Catholic daughter of Henry VIII who executed more than 280 Protestants and was known as Bloody Mary. It was a political marriage of convenience, and they ruled jointly, although Philip could not make decisions without his wife's consent and his reign ended with her death. Mary, who was thirty-eight when they married, had no offspring, and died at forty-two. When the Protestant Mary II was told she had to marry her Dutch cousin William, she cried for two days. She grew fond of him, but she, too, was unable to bear children. After invading England, they demanded co-regency for pragmatic reasons: Mary had a stronger claim to the throne, but William provided strength through his Protestantism, following the Glorious Revolution and the overthrow of her Roman Catholic father, James II. They reigned together from 1689 to 1694; William ruled alone after she died when she was only thirty-two. Mary II's younger sister, Anne, who was queen of Great Britain from 1702 to 1714, was devoted to her husband, Prince George of Denmark, but she had a torturous time trying to bear children. Obese and lame with gout, she had seventeen pregnancies, twelve of which ended in miscarriages. Four of her remaining children died before their second birthdays, and her last son died when he was eleven. In Victoria's case, there was no obvious reason for a dual monarchy—she was popular, and was old enough to rule on her own—especially given that Albert was a foreign prince.

Underpinning much of the grumbling about Albert were certain subterranean prejudices: against Germans, and against marrying cousins. The latter practice was common at the time in bourgeois circles, and aristocratic families often encouraged it, to keep their family close. In 1874, George Darwin wrote to his father, Charles, citing statistics from the registrar general that showed cousin marriages to be "at least three times as frequent in our rank as in the lower!" It was especially common among the great family clans, such as the Darwin-Wedgwoods, where about 10 percent of marriages were with first or second cousins. Those who married cousins were in esteemed company, including the writer Margaret Oliphant, the daughters of Thackeray, Elizabeth Gaskell, the poet laureate Robert Southey, Anthony Trollope's aunt, the parents of Lewis Carroll, and John Ruskin. Cousins married in the novels of Dickens, Emily Brontë, Thomas Hardy, Thackeray, and Trollope. Even characters in children's books fell in love with their cousins: "When Benjamin Bunny grew up," Beatrix Potter wrote, "he married his Cousin Flopsy. They had a large family, and they were very improvident and cheerful."

In his book *Fertilisation of Orchids,* published in 1862, Charles Darwin criticized "perpetual self-fertilisation" and suggested that marriage between near relations was "likewise in some way injurious." For four decades, he had struggled with a host of mysterious illnesses that made him dizzy, nauseous, bloated, exhausted, anxious, faint, and depressed. He passed many of these symptoms on to his children, and fretted about heredity; how much of all of this was a consequence of the fact that his own parents were cousins, and that he had married his own cousin? Following an increasingly heated debate on the subject in the mid-1800s, his son George decided to determine whether inbreeding was bad and began collecting data with the help of his father. (Florence Nightingale had raised similar concerns; she wrote in 1852 that "intermarriage between relations is in direct contravention of the laws of nature for the well-being of the race; witness the Quakers, the Spanish grandees, the royal races, the secluded valleys of mountainous countries, where madness, degeneration of race, defective organization and cretinism flourish and multiply.")

The Darwins found no evidence to substantiate the belief that consanguinity caused blindness or deafness; only a small percentage of inhabitants of mental asylums were the offspring of cousins (3 to 4 percent). The only troubling discovery was that a low percentage of men who had rowed for Oxford or Cambridge were the offspring of cousins. Yet, reflecting the prejudice of the age, George Darwin concluded there were few risks in cousin marriage for aristocrats and the bourgeoisie, but greater risks for the poor. But by the end of the Victorian age, despite the successful marriage between Victoria and Albert, most people condemned the practice. By then, the medical establishment was unanimous in their opposition. Modern studies have established that children whose parents are cousins are at greater risk of cognitive defects, intellectual and developmental disabilities, and being stillborn.

But perhaps the more serious issue was Albert's German heritage. Lord Melbourne had harsher things to say about marrying Germans—who he said never washed their faces, and smoked too much—than he did about cousins. In the mid-nineteenth century,

Germany was disparaged as an untamed, backward place, even though it was a popular tourist destination. Author Henry Mayhew said in 1864 that Germans were uncivilized, "starving, cringing, swaggering" people who lived "in an offensive state of dirt and slovenliness." Germany then consisted of a group of states in a loosely configured federation formed after the Napoleonic Wars, which were under pressure from reformers who wanted a united country with popular elections and a single emperor. Far from filthy peasants, the most refined and sophisticated German intellectuals, composers, and poets of Victoria's age were beginning to infiltrate British intellectual circles. In the 1800s, while there was lingering hostility toward France, the great foe of the Napoleonic Wars, there was a great revival of interest in German philosophy, writing, and thought, led by Madame de Staël, as well as, later, writers such as Thomas and Matthew Arnold, Dickens, Goethe, Carlyle, Coleridge, and George Eliot. The anti-German sentiment was partly due to the fact that German consorts and spouses were thought to have an insidious influence on the monarchy: between the years 1714 and 1901 every single British monarch had married a German. Victoria, who was half German, contentedly followed this tradition.

But the greatest problem for Victoria was not Albert's country but the God he prayed to. The queen of England could marry anyone she liked—but not a Catholic. After the pro-Catholic King James II was hurled off the throne in the Glorious Revolution of 1688 and replaced by the Protestant William III, an act was passed that prohibited any English monarch from being a Catholic, or marrying one. This is still the case today. Albert was a strict Lutheran with a strong personal faith, but Catholics dominated his family. Suspicions were raised when Victoria's address to the Privy Council did not have the word "Protestant" in it. (Foolishly, given the intense anti-Catholicism in the country and Victoria's crucial position as Defender of the Faith, Melbourne had advised taking it out.) After the Duke of Wellington raised the matter in Parliament, and the Tory papers made snide remarks, it was reinserted in the official version. When Albert went back to Germany to prepare for the wedding, he drew up a detailed family history proving his impeccable religious credentials. Martin Luther, after all, had composed psalms in Coburg.

Further hurdles followed as Victoria tried to procure status and money for her beau. The vote on Albert's annual income was humiliating. Melbourne had proposed that he receive £50,000, the same amount as previous consorts. The Tories emphatically voted against this and his income was set at £30,000. Albert, embarrassed and annoyed, chastised Victoria for failing to utter even one word of sympathy: "for those nice Tories have cut off half my income (that was to be expected), and it makes my position no very pleasant one. It was hardly conceivable that anyone could behave as meanly and disgracefully as they have to you and me. It cannot do them much good, for it is hardly possible to maintain any respect for them any longer." Victoria vowed, "As long as I live, I will never forgive those infernal scoundrels with Peel—nasty wretch—at their head."

Next came the question of precedence. Victoria wanted Albert to be placed after her in the country's official hierarchy, which meant he would follow her in official processions, but her uncles and the Tory leaders objected. Victoria was enraged, again: "Poor dear Albert how cruelly are they ill-using that dearest Angel! Monsters! you Tories shall be punished. Revenge, revenge!" She blamed the Duke of Wellington, who had railed about Albert's religion in Parliament and failed to support the proposal for a higher income. It took considerable persuasion on Melbourne's part to procure an invitation for the duke to her wedding, and even then Victoria would allow him to come only to the ceremony and not to the wedding banquet.

Albert was an introvert unused to expressing emotion. As he confessed to Victoria later in the year, "I am usually (alas!) of a rather cold nature, and it needs a pretty strong appeal to move me." But he wrote his fiancée many letters with assurances of his love, trying valiantly to respond to her fervor. On November 30, he wrote a particularly long, rambling letter from Coburg:

Dearly beloved Victoria—I long to talk to you; otherwise the separation is too painful. Your dear picture stands on my table in front of me, and I can hardly take my eyes off it. . . . [W]hat a delight it must be to walk through the whole of my life, with its joys and sorrows, with you at my side! . . . Love of you fills my whole heart. . . . Think sometimes with love of your Albert, whose heart beats truly and honourably for you, and whose dearest wish is that your love may continue. . . . I kiss you a thousand times. May Heaven bless you!

Albert fretted when Victoria's letters were delayed for nine days by an erratic postal service. His love was genuine.

But terse words sometimes followed the sugary sentiments. When it came to the business of court, Albert attempted to assert his will, especially regarding the men who would form his household. Albert was desperate to ensure they would not simply be Whigs, the party his future wife was allied with, but men of honor, standing, and intellect. "If I am really to keep myself free from all parties," he wrote, "my people must not belong exclusively to one side . . . above all do I wish that they should be well-educated men and of high character." Albert was dismissive of the suggestion that Lord Melbourne's private secretary should be his treasurer: "I know personally nothing of Mr. George Anson, except that I have seen him dance a Quadrille." Albert campaigned for weeks, urging Victoria at least to allow him, a man who was leaving his home behind, to choose the men who would be closest to him. Surely it was more important to please Albert than Mr. Anson? Albert wrote forcefully:

I have exhausted all my arguments on that point, and written myself nearly blind to make you understand how distasteful it all is to me. It was the first and only request with which I appealed to your love, and I do not wish to make a second; but I declare calmly that I will not take Mr. Anson nor anybody now.

But Victoria and Melbourne had their way. Mr. Anson was appointed. The only concession was that Anson had to resign from Melbourne's staff. Soon he and Albert would laugh about this dispute, for they became close friends. It was one of the few—or possibly only—instances in which Albert was—eventually—glad not to win. But his original instincts were correct, and he was wise to insist the Crown be above politics. William IV had been a Tory, Victoria was an avowed Whig, but Albert firmly steered her toward the view that nonpartisanship was crucial for a sovereign. His success in doing so helped guard the Crown from revolution.

Albert's early letters reveal him to be confident and determined to be heard and respected. He calmly expressed his displeasure at being overruled or dictated to, and then moved on to blow Victoria kisses. When he was arguing with his fiancée about the suggestion that someone handle his finances, he was clear about the prospect of fiscal emasculation. "As the Queen's husband," he wrote early in January 1840, "I shall be in a dependent position, more dependent than any other husband, in my domestic circumstances. My private fortune is all that remains to me to dispose of. I am therefore not unfair in requesting that that which has belonged to me since I came of age nearly a year ago (and indeed belongs to any grown man) shall be left under my control." He ended this forceful letter: "With burning love for you, I remain, your faithful, Albert." He told Victoria that she should not confuse business with personal matters, and that disagreements do not mean "failure of my love towards yourself, which nothing can shake."

One of the things Victoria was most certain of was that Albert must not be seen to exercise any undue influence upon her, or possess any independent power. Although Leopold had pushed Albert to request a place in the House of Lords, Victoria refused. What she wanted for her husband was royal rank: she asked Melbourne if there was any possibility he could become king. The prime minister said no, that she was the monarch and he was the spouse, meant for "support and assistance" in difficult times. The problem for Victoria, then, would be how to reconcile the role of a wife with that of a powerful queen. Bucking the traditional role of an at least outwardly submissive wife would be painful and unprecedented.

Six weeks before the wedding, on December 29, 1839, Melbourne wrote a letter to Albert—at Victoria's prompting—laying out guidelines. First, it was crucial that Albert and Victoria be seen to agree on all matters. Second, he should not dabble in politics himself: "It will be absolutely necessary that your Highness should be considered as sanctioning and countenancing the policy pursued by the actual government of the Queen." Third, he should choose men generally sympathetic to the government for his household. Albert was irritated. He wrote to Victoria, "I hope Lord Melbourne does not think we want to lead a life of strife and dissension instead of love and unity; one's opinions are not to be dictated, for an opinion is the result of reflection and conviction, and you could not respect a husband who never formed an opinion till you had formed yours, and whose opinions were always the same as yours." Albert would not be a trophy husband. Victoria always adored him, and their marriage was a happy one. But what she did not discuss, except with her eldest daughter after Albert had died, was the conflict and struggle of their marriage, the toll it took, and how hard she labored to make it work. At the heart of the struggle was the fact that both of them loved power: Victoria for the freedom it brought to her as a woman living in a century when most of her sex lacked it, and Albert for the license it gave him to lead, influence, and effect change.

As she stood trying to stay still for a series of fittings for her white lace wedding dress, Victoria mentally scrolled through the lists of chores to be done for the wedding. She must not forget to tell Albert, she thought, as the seamstress pinned ivory folds to her now-slender torso, that he should not shave for the wedding. If there was one thing she would insist upon, it would be that he keep the thin mustache he had when she met him. She was so impressed by it that she told Lord Melbourne that all the cavalry should be made to grow one, which Melbourne "saw no objection to." She wanted it to be part of an official uniform. It is a curious image: rows of uniformed men on horseback, all wearing identical narrow mustaches because of an infatuated young queen. The thought of Albert was almost enough to overcome Victoria's nerves; the thought of all the fuss and pomp and scrutiny of her wedding day was making her feel queasy.

In the days leading up to her wedding, Victoria was preoccupied with a fight to make Parliament—especially the Tories—understand that Albert, as her husband, should be recognized as the preeminent man in her kingdom—both well respected and well remunerated. Her prayer on New Year's Day, 1840, was simple: "From the Tories, dear Lord, deliver us." Victoria's antagonizing of the Tories would also antagonize Albert. Her groom was determined to puncture Melbourne's influence: he would make the prime minister suffer for the foolish mistakes Victoria had made in her first year as queen. Albert did not just want to be good; he wanted to be great.

CHAPTER 11

The Bride: "I Never, Never Spent Such an Evening"

If I were Queen
What would I do?
I'd make you King
And I'd wait on you.

—CHRISTINA ROSSETTI

You forget, my dearest Love, that I am the Sovereign, and that business can stop and wait for nothing.

—QUEEN VICTORIA

As her wedding loomed in the early weeks of 1840, Victoria became increasingly agitated. The weather was dismal—windy, cold, and wet. She grew pale and thin, she could not eat or sleep, she was feverish, her entire body ached, and she had a terrible cold. Even writing letters exhausted her. Dr. Clark examined her and, in another case of misdiagnosis, told her she had the measles. As Victoria lay in her bed watching rain streak the dirt on her windows at Kensington Palace, trying not to panic, doubts crawled through her mind. Hadn't she enjoyed the last two years of her life as an independent woman more than any others? That pure freedom was about to slip from her grasp. She closed her eyes and thought of the preparations humming across the city: cakes being baked, shoes polished, coats fitted, gardens trimmed, carriages cleaned, and large casks of Scottish whisky and carts piled high with food for the wedding feast being rolled along the streets.

The questions drummed persistently in the twenty-year-old woman's mind: What would life be like after making her vows? She dreaded the thought of having children. The ways of a man and his wife, alone together, seemed mysterious. Was she good enough for Albert? Would his eye turn to other, more comely women in a few years' time, as Lord Melbourne had so unkindly suggested? Why did so many people think Albert would interfere politically, when it was clear she was the ruler, the one in charge? Would he try to control her or criticize her? Would the sacrifice be too much for him? She felt, at times, so unworthy: he was so handsome, and she so plain. Her pride was ingrained, and her strength had become habitual, but love had humbled her. In a poem printed five days after the wedding, Elizabeth Barrett (later Browning) wrote: "If ye say, Preserve the queen! oh, breathe it inward low / She is a woman, and beloved! And 'tis enough but so." Victoria had learned, in just a few years, how to be a queen, but how did one learn to be a wife?

Lord Melbourne's sole task was to boost Victoria's spirits in the days before the wedding. It was normal, he assured her, to feel anxious. When she reminded him of her former determination to remain single, he said getting married was natural; it was her job as monarch that was "very unnatural." The man whose own marriage had been torturous and humiliating offered realistic advice: "it's a great *change*—it has its inconveniences; everybody does their best, and depend upon it you've done well; difficulties may arise from it." Victoria recorded his words carefully, adding, "All this is so true." There was also a quiet need to shine and feel pretty. She pointed out to her prime minister, a little shyly, that she had lost weight and must look awfully stressed. He insisted that she looked "very well." He added that he had seen an article in a Scottish newspaper in which the reporter described Victoria as having "a large searching eye, an open anxious nostril, and a firm mouth." Lord Melbourne repeated this compliment several times, with tears rolling down his face. It was, he said approvingly, "a very true representation, can't be a finer physiognomy." While few women today would be flattered to hear they had open, anxious nostrils, the queen smiled and responded, "I am sure none of your friends are as fond of you as I am." He replied, "I believe not." His gentle encouragement could have come from a father.

Victoria's measles turned out to be nerves, which were calmed the moment she saw Albert. When he arrived at Buckingham Palace, she was impatiently standing at the front door: "seeing his *dear dear* face again put me at rest about everything." Albert, though so ill from his crossing that he likened himself to a wax candle, was unruffled and resolute. The only jarring note was a rather formal letter Albert had received from Victoria as he left his Coburg home. She would not agree to a two-week honeymoon, she wrote, despite his desire for at least two weeks alone together. She said, somewhat condescendingly, that she was just too busy:

> Dear Albert, you have not at all understood the matter. You forget, my dearest Love, that I am the Sovereign, and that business can stop and wait for nothing. Parliament is sitting, and something occurs almost every day, for which I may be required, and it is quite impossible for me to be absent from London; therefore two or three days is already a long time to be absent. I am never easy a moment if I am not on the spot, and see and hear what is going on. . . . This is also my own wish in every way.

Her love for her husband was deep, but so was her love for her work, and her sense of duty. This is what is often forgotten in accounts of Victoria's consuming relationship: when she fell in love with Albert, she had no intention of stepping back from her tasks of correspondence, reading Cabinet documents, and consulting with the prime minister. Victoria thought she would be able to do *more* work with Albert by her side, not less. She knew, though, that she would need to be careful not to evirate her husband, the majority of whose income derived from the simple fact that he was married to the most famous woman in the world.

When the archbishop asked the queen if she would like to remove the word "obey" from the marriage service, she insisted it remain. It was not, for her, a call to subservience, but a reminder that she could not, or perhaps would not, dominate the man she married, as she did the rest of her household, her Cabinet, and her millions of subjects. At the time of her wedding, she was as contradictory and complicated as she would be throughout her life: publicly vowing to obey her husband at precisely the same time she privately overruled his wishes.

Victoria wanted a simple wedding: a plain dress, a small group of guests, and a restrained ceremony. This was, of course, a difficult desire to accommodate for a queen. Melbourne managed to persuade her to have a more elaborate celebration, which he thought suitable for a monarch. He counseled her to try to overcome her public shyness and discomfort with being looked at. He had convinced her to invite not only the Duke of Wellington but also Lord Liverpool, despite her determination to have a wedding entirely devoid of Tories. Melbourne also persuaded her that the ceremony should take place in the Chapel Royal of St. James's Palace, even though she thought it was hideous. Victoria sighed, "Everything [is] always made so uncomfortable for Kings and Queens."

Certain things Victoria insisted on. While Albert wanted her to have only daughters of mothers he considered virtuous in her bridal party, Melbourne advised her, with the glorious hypocrisy of the privileged, that this kind of morality was a problem only for the lower classes. She decided to ignore Albert's wishes and chose her twelve bridesmaids according to rank. She even, daringly, included the daughter of the notorious Lady Jersey, who had been the mistress of George IV. She also wanted Albert to sleep under her roof on the night before their wedding, and shrugged off the objections of her mother and prime minister as "foolish nonsense." She knew she would sleep better if he was nearby, and she joked with Lord Melbourne: "I declared laughing I would show that I could *sometimes* have my own Will, though I was so seldom allowed to have it—which made Lord M. laugh." The prime minister and the queen chortled together as Albert awaited instructions, biding his time.

The skies were black and brooding on the morning of February 10, 1840. Victoria slept deeply and late, waking at 8:45 A.M. It was the last time she would be in her bed on her own, she thought happily. She peered out the window at the darkness and sat to write a letter to her groom:

> Dearest,—how are you today, and have you slept well? I have rested very well, and feel very comfortable today. What weather! I believe, however, the rain will cease. Send one word when you, my most dearly beloved bridegroom, will be ready. Thy ever-faithful, VICTORIA R.

Victoria stood still as she was carefully buttoned into her white satin dress, with a flounce of lace and a six-yard train edged with orange blossoms. Her hands shook slightly as she pinned Turkish diamonds to her ears and looped them around her neck before fastening a sapphire brooch from Albert on her breast. She held her feet out as her maids tied the ribbons of her delicate white satin slippers around her ankles. Her dress sat low on her shoulders, displaying her smooth ivory chest, and her hair, parted severely in the middle, was looped into low buns on either side of her head.

Victoria's clothes had been carefully chosen to display her patriotism. The fabric of her dress was from the Spitalfields, the historic center of the silk industry in London, and two hundred lace makers from Devon had labored on it for months. The pattern was destroyed afterward so that no one could copy it. Her gloves were stitched in

London and made of English kid. Victoria had commissioned a huge swath of handmade Honiton lace for her dress, in an attempt to revive the flagging lace industry (machine-made copies had been harming the trade). She stood in front of her mirror and stared at her reflection disbelievingly. On her head she wore a simple wreath of orange blossoms and myrtle. In portraits she looks young and pale, hovering between anxious and dreamy.

The queen had asked that no one else wear white to the wedding. Some have wrongly interpreted her choice of color as a signal of sexual purity—as Agnes Strickland later gushed, she had chosen to dress "not as a queen in her glittering trappings, but in spotless white, like a pure virgin, to meet her bridegroom." Victoria had chosen to wear white mostly because it was the perfect color to highlight the delicate lace—it was not then a conventional color for brides. Before bleaching techniques were mastered, white was a rare and expensive color, more a symbol of wealth than purity. Victoria was not the first to wear it, but she made it popular by example. Lace makers across England were thrilled by the sudden surge in the popularity of their handiwork.

As Victoria made her way to her golden carriage, the crowd clamored. She kept her eyes down, and "a hurried glance around, and a slight inclination of the head, was all the acknowledgment returned."

The torrents of rain and violent winds deterred "vast numbers" of well-wishers, but the public anticipation could not be dampened. There are few things as certain to knit British hearts as a royal wedding, and London had been thrumming with excitement for weeks. *The Satirist* complained: "We are all going stark staring mad. Nothing is heard or thought of but doves and Cupids, triumphal arches and white favors, and last, but not least, variegated lamps and general illuminations." The cantankerous historian Thomas Carlyle was, as usual when it came to royal events, wearily wondering why such a great fuss was being made: "Poor little thing." (Even from a distance, he said, he could correctly tell that the woman hated by the Tories had "an abundance of obstinate temper.")

Still, after a year of hissing, name-calling, and savaging by the press, it seemed as if London was once more in love with their queen. A small number were obsessed. Victoria had a clutch of farcical, fixated stalkers, some of whom grew quite distressed by the upcoming nuptials. Several were committed. One devoted man stationed himself outside the gates of Kensington Palace and followed her carriage when it appeared each day. Another, Ned Hayward, sent a torrent of letters to the Home Office desperately seeking to propose to Victoria. He finally tried to stop her horse to hand a letter to her himself, but was arrested. Another gentleman, believing that he was the rightful king and that Victoria would be an excellent housekeeper, climbed over the Windsor Castle gate and declared, "I demand entrance into the castle as the king of England."

The wedding excitement was so ubiquitous that Charles Dickens joked with his friends that he, too, was a victim of it. In a letter to the eccentric poet Walter Savage Landor, he wrote: "Society is unhinged here by her majesty's marriage, and I am sorry to add that I have fallen hopelessly in love with the Queen." Three days after the wedding, Dickens wrote a letter to a friend pretending to have been one of Victoria's pursuers:

> On Tuesday we sallied down to Windsor, prowled about the Castle, saw the corridor and their private rooms—nay the very bedchamber . . . lighted up with such a ruddy, homely brilliant glow—bespeaking so much bliss and happiness—that I, your humble servant, lay down in the mud at the top of the long walk, and refused all comfort.

Dickens returned, he joked, with "pockets full of portraits" that he "wept [over] in secret."

———

Souvenir marriage medals were proudly displayed by the damp crowd waiting to see the bride. The police stood in stiff rows along the muddy route from the palace to the chapel, pushing back rowdy onlookers. Burglars began creeping through the alleys and backyards of London, taking advantage of the fact that the bobbies would be distracted for a day. Meanwhile, along the route from the palace to the chapel, tree branches were collapsing under the weight of the people clinging to them.

When Victoria arrived at St. James's crimson and gold Chapel Royal, she went to her waiting trainbearers, all in white dresses of her design. She gave each of them a small turquoise brooch in the shape of an eagle, as a symbol of courage and strength. Albert waited at the altar, looking dashing in a bright red, tightly fitted uniform decorated with the collar and star of the Order of the Garter, the highest order of chivalry in Britain, with his blue eyes fixed on his solemn little bride as she approached. Florence Nightingale, who, like most, thought Albert a "remarkably agreeable looking youth," reported that a Mrs. Lefevre, who stood close to Victoria during the ceremony, said she was

> perfectly composed and spoke distinctly and well but that every orange flower in her head was quivering and she was very pale and her eyes red as if she had not slept. But she signed her name like a lion and was so anxious that PA should appear to advantage that she touched his elbow whenever he was going to do wrong, showed him where to sign his name and put him right when he set the ring on the wrong finger. After the marriage she cleared up and looked quite happy.

The next day, the only report Victoria wanted to correct was that she had cried: "I did not shed one tear the whole time." She had been trained in the art of composure and did not intend to be seen as an unsteady queen.

———

After the ceremony, the newlyweds snatched half an hour together in Victoria's room before facing the crowds at the wedding banquet. Victoria placed a ring on Albert's finger as he said there should never be any secrets between them. (She wrote in her journal twenty-three years later, "There never was.") Victoria then changed into another white dress, edged with swansdown, and a bonnet with an enormous brim—a hat she could hide inside.

The feast was a frenzy of nodding, curtsying, beaming, and hand-shaking. The couple finally left at four in the afternoon, trotting off in simple fashion as the sun started to poke fingers through the clouds, with three coaches accompanying them and people cheering and running alongside. Greville complained that they "went off in a very poor and shabby style" in an old traveling coach, but the queen did not notice; as the sun singed the clouds red before sinking into black, it was just "I and Albert alone, which was SO *delightful*." This would be a refrain throughout her marriage: what she wanted most of all, always, was to be with Albert alone.

After a three-hour journey, the exhausted couple arrived at Windsor Castle. Victoria had a headache; she changed and lay on the couch, mentally scrolling through images of her chaotic day. Albert played the piano as she rested. It was so much quieter than London; what a relief. She thought back on the past few hours: the look on dear Melbourne's face as he tried to stem his tears. The happy moment when Albert placed a ring on her finger and it was done. The rippling, jostling ocean of faces lining the route to the chapel; and at the palace, the thick heat of goodwill, the deafening applause, the sight of elegant Albert in his uniform. The mad cheering of the boys at Eton as they rolled into Windsor. The profundity of the service. "The Ceremony was very imposing, and fine and simple," she wrote in her journal, "and I think *ought* to make an everlasting impression on every one who promises at the Altar to *keep* what he or she promises."

What she liked about it most of all, though, was that as they stood before the archbishop, they were called simply Victoria and Albert. For the rest of her life, she thought with a swelling joy, she would just be Victoria to her Albert. She wasn't a queen or ruler, but simply a wife and lover. She rolled onto her side and looked at her husband as his fingers glided along the piano keys, playing one of his own compositions. Albert looked up and came over to her, kissing her. By 10:20, they went to their room, as Victoria spelled out, "*of course* in *one* bed." She lay by his side, in his arms, and on his chest, smiling in the darkness as he whispered to her.

Victoria woke the next morning after a night of little sleep. She lay still, staring at Albert's face in the early light, marveling at him and his pale throat, which she had seen only glimpses of before. He was "beautiful, angelic." She was sated and thrilled with an intimacy her mind had strained to imagine. Luckily for her, the mortifying tradition of the court coming to peer at the royal couple when they first climbed into the same bed had gone out of fashion with George III. She was also lucky in that Albert seems to have been a competent, tender lover. Victoria's wedding night was the closest thing she had known to bliss. Her elation was palpable in her journal entry:

> I NEVER, NEVER spent such an evening! MY DEAREST, DEAR Albert sat on a footstool by my side, and his excessive love and affection gave me feelings of heavenly love and happiness I never could have hoped to have felt before. He clasped me in his arms, and we kissed each other again and again! His beauty, his sweetness and gentleness,—really how can I ever be thankful enough to have such a *Husband*! Oh! This was the happiest day of my life!

It was a kind of lustful enchantment. Over breakfast, Victoria gazed at him, again noticing how he had no neckcloth on under his black velvet jacket and was "more beautiful than it is possible for me to say." The next day, she was cooing in otherworldly tones: "Already the 2nd day since our marriage; *his* love and gentleness is beyond everything, and to kiss that dear soft cheek, to press my lips to his, is heavenly bliss. I *feel* a purer more unearthly feel than I ever did. Oh! was ever woman so blessed as I am!" It was the small, intimate gestures she loved the most: when Albert put on her stockings for her, when she watched him shave. He slid into bed next to her, kissing her over and over; they fell asleep with arms entwined. After Lord Melbourne remarked that she looked "very well," she replied that Albert's "kindness and affection" were "beyond everything." In these days, it was Albert's touch that she wrote about, as well as his handsome appearance, while continuing to faithfully record the subject and nature of every conversation with her Lord M.

Historians have long acknowledged that Victoria had a high libido—some have implied she was some kind of sexual predator who devoured a tolerant but exhausted husband. She was undoubtedly extremely passionate, the fact of which clashes with the strong associations Victoria often carries of dour old age and puritanical condemnation. Given how fraught sex was at the time for women—with limited access to contraception and abortion, and no pain relief for childbirth—Victoria's unbridled and unabashed physical enjoyment of her husband is remarkable.

In the nineteenth century, it was assumed that women with strong libidos were pathological: female desire was considered dangerous and potentially explosive, and it was thought that women's animal nature would overwhelm their weak will and they would lose control. Women were dubbed "nymphomaniacs" for dreaming, thinking about, or having what was considered to be an excessive amount of sex. Some were given clitoridectomies or had leeches placed on their perineums. Others were told to abstain from meat and brandy, use hair pillows, douche with borax, have cold enemas, or adhere to strict vegetable diets. In 1886, a doctor reported that the most likely candidates for nymphomania were virgins, widows, or women with blond hair aged sixteen to twenty-five. Projection was prevalent in the Victorian medical profession.

Most female illnesses were thought to derive from troublesome pelvic organs. The greatest sources of knowledge about the female organs were assumed to be male gynecologists, which made the bodies of women a secret even, or perhaps especially, to themselves. (The 1858 Medical Registration Act specifically excluded women from becoming qualified doctors.) Sex education for girls was unthinkable. British doctor and author of books on masturbation William Acton even argued that some married couples were so ill informed that their marriages were never consummated. (You cannot help but feel some sympathy for Dr. Acton's wife, given his 1857 declaration: "The majority of women (happily for them) are not troubled with sexual feeling of any kind.") Many women tried to avoid orgasms because they were told they led to pregnancy. In 1877, Robert Tait wrote:

> The majority of women enter the married state with but a very hazy notion of what its functions are . . . there is a false modesty on these subjects ingrained in our English life which has to be paid for in much suffering amongst women.

For many married women, sex was a chore, not something to be enjoyed. Given the ignorance surrounding women's bodies, Victoria's delight in sexual pleasure was genuinely countercultural. Albert did not record his views on sex, but it is clear that he satisfied his wife. And he certainly admired her, writing to his brother approvingly about her oft-praised bosom. Just a few months after his wedding he told Ernest, somewhat defensively, that Victoria had "changed much to her advantage" and had looked lovely at the previous night's dinner: "She had a very low-necked dress, with a bunch of roses at her breast which was swelling up from her dress."

Despite the intensity and obvious physicality of his relationship with Victoria, who was certain she was the only woman to whom Albert had ever made love, there has been some speculation that Albert was gay. What made Albert's contemporaries skeptical was the fact that Albert appeared immune to the charms of London's great beauties, whose names he too often forgot; he did not flirt and was not impressed with appearance. When Albert turned eighteen, he had jokingly promised Stockmar he would "pay more attention to the ladies." Stockmar said Albert was just "too indifferent and too reserved" around the opposite sex, adding, "He will always have more success with men." This was partly true. Albert loved his wife, but socially and intellectually he preferred male company. This preference was obvious to the likes of Lady Clarendon, a politician's wife, who struggled to make conversation with him at dinner and noted that the only women he spoke to were royalty. While he did not enjoy the after-dinner port drinking and male banter that were then the custom—usually leaving to play chess alone or sing duets with Victoria—his closest friendships were with men.

There is no evidence that Albert had a physical relationship with a man, but many have suspected he did. Lytton Strachey stated that Albert did not take after his cheating father for two possible reasons: either because of his "peculiar upbringing" or because of "a more fundamental idiosyncrasy," which was "a marked distaste to the opposite sex." Others point to the male friendships he developed at Bonn University and Albert's close relationship with Christoph Florschütz, a gifted scholar who shared a small attic room with Albert and Ernest for fifteen years. Albert credits Florschütz, not his father, for the happiest years of his life. His intense attachment to his tutor is unsurprising, given the absence of his mother. Some have also pointed to the strong culture of homoeroticism at many male colleges such as those that comprised Oxford and Cambridge and public schools such as Eton in the nineteenth century, and there is no reason to think Bonn would be exempt. Intimate behaviors—passionate declarations of love, sharing of beds, and kissing—that today would be called homosexual did not attract a label.

It is extremely unlikely that the discussion about Albert's sexuality will ever move beyond speculation. He and Victoria had an intimate and satisfying marriage, and Victoria was the chief protector and creator of the memory of Albert. No one seriously gossiped about it while he was alive, at a time when homosexuality was not considered an identity but something people occasionally dabbled in, often as teenagers and young men and women. According to Michel Foucault, the beginning of the categorization of homosexuality as an identity did not come until 1870.

And ultimately, the fact that Albert did not ogle or admire other women was one of the things Victoria loved most about her husband. It made her feel secure, protected. It was also excellent revenge on the popular, pretentious society women who circled the royal court. She told Melbourne happily "of Albert's not caring greatly for beauty, and hating those beauties who are so feted, and wishing to spite them always." Victoria flew into a fury when Melbourne suggested that that sort of interest in women was apt to come later. It was a stupid thing to say, and Victoria fumed: "I shan't forgive you that." She did, though, of course, the very next day. Melbourne apologized and said he had only been referring to Albert's shyness.

The marriage between Victoria and Albert is one of the greatest romances of modern history. It was genuine, devoted, and fruitful. Together, they ushered in an era when the monarchy would shift from direct power to indirect influence, and from being the fruit of the aristocracy to becoming the symbol of the middle class. They restored and raised the stature of the monarchy, preserving it from the revolutions that toppled the aristocracies and royal families in Europe during the same years that Victoria and Albert were widely feted in Britain. Albert would grow to surpass his wife, for a short time, in influence, but not in longevity, stamina, or sheer will. Albert would soar; Victoria would endure.

In giving Albert free rein to work alongside her as she carried nine children, Victoria was soon to discover that the clever, intellectually restless Albert was a great asset. She spent roughly eighty months pregnant in the 1840s and 1850s—more than six years in total—and even longer recovering from childbirth. During this time, she was able to hand off work to a brilliant, trusted deputy. But her husband had no intention of being a subordinate partner, and this sparked the fiercest fights of their marriage. Even as a boy, Albert had displayed "a great dislike to being in [the] charge of women." He had then married a woman who was in charge of an empire. As he and Victoria embarked on married life, each tried to assert his or her will in what had traditionally been the most unequal of relationships: husband and wife, and monarch and spouse. In this case, the spouse held the trump card: he would never have to bear children.

CHAPTER 12

Only the Husband, and Not the Master

[Acknowledging] one important truth [will make a successful marriage]—it is the superiority of your husband, simply as a man. It is quite possible you may have more talent, with higher attainments . . . but this has nothing whatever to do with your position as a woman, which is, and must be, inferior to his as a man.

—SARAH ELLIS, *THE WIVES OF ENGLAND*, 1843

In my home life I am very happy and contented; but the difficulty of filling my place with proper dignity is that I am only the husband, and not the master in the house.

—PRINCE ALBERT, LETTER TO
PRINCE WILLIAM OF LÖWENSTEIN, MAY 1840

The pistol cracked loudly. Heads swiveled, and the horses drawing the carriage startled and stopped. On the footpath stood a short, slender teenage boy holding a gun in each hand, gazing fixedly at the queen. It was June 10, 1840, a cloudy, warm Sunday afternoon. People milled about the park on foot or horseback, and had been curiously scrutinizing the royal carriage, which often drove past at this time on weekends, on the road leading from Buckingham Palace to Hyde Park Corner. Albert, who had noticed "a little mean-looking man" folding his arms over his chest just before he fired, grabbed his wife's hand, crying, "My God! Don't be alarmed!"

Victoria just laughed. She had thought someone was shooting at birds in the park. "I assured him I was not the least frightened, which was the case. It never entered my head, nor did it his, after the first shot, that it was meant for me." It was. The man's name was Edward Oxford, and he was an unemployed public house potboy from Birmingham with vague dreams of revolution. He was dressed respectably in a brown frock coat, light trousers, and a silk waistcoat. He stood still, staring with intense, dark eyes at the royal couple.

A second shot punched the air. Victoria ducked and this time the bullet whistled above her head, lodging in a wall opposite. Albert ordered the driver to keep going as onlookers seized Oxford and hauled him to the police. A defiant Victoria continued riding up Constitution Hill, stopping off at her mother's house at Belgrave Square to tell her what had happened. The young couple, married for four months now, took a leisurely route back to the palace, going through the park, to give Victoria "a little air" and "to show the public that we had not, on account of what happened, lost all confidence in them," as Albert told his grandmother. Victoria's calm was reported admiringly in the papers the next day.

By the time the queen and Albert returned to Buckingham Palace in their open carriage, there was a swelling crowd of Londoners who had taken off their hats and were roaring in support. A cavalcade of gentlemen and ladies who had been riding in the park clustered around the queen's carriage, escorting her home. It was, she wrote in her journal, like a "triumphal procession." But when she finally returned to her room, Victoria sat on her bed, pale and shaken, showing vulnerability for the first time. Albert slid his arms around her and kissed her, praising her bravery. Victoria knew she had narrowly avoided death, writing: "Our escape is *indeed* providential." Later, Albert showed her the pistols "which might have finished me off."

She ended her day's journal with a prayer of thanks, and then she curled up tightly next to Albert, trying not to think of what might have been. But God had saved the queen, and a rising tide of popular sympathy drowned out any lingering thoughts of the past year's scandals of Lady Flora Hastings and the Bedchamber Crisis.

Victoria continued to appear in public that summer after the attempted shooting, riding in an open carriage, unbowed. She had quickly grasped that demonstrating bravery in public with what modern leaders would call great "optics" would evoke a powerful response from her subjects. She was beginning to understand how to behave—not just as a woman and queen, but as an emblem of her country—as Britannia, who knew how to rule and how to lead. King Leopold, writing with great haste from Laeken after he heard of the incident, told Victoria: "That you have shown *great fortitude* is not to be doubted, and will make a very great and good impression." She knew, now, the importance of symbolic strength.

In the grungy borough of Southwark, the police were rifling through Edward Oxford's bedroom in search of a motive. They seized upon a sword, a cap with red bows, bullets, gunpowder, and documents pertaining to a club called "New England." The vital clue seemed to be a memo implying he had been prompted to act by "some communications of an important nature from Hanover." This ignited some public panic: Was Victoria's greatly feared uncle—the much-maligned, scar-faced former Duke of Cumberland, now the king of Hanover—trying to kill the queen before she could produce an heir to take his place as first in line to the throne? The silver pistols Oxford had wielded bore the monogram *ER,* which some speculated stood for Ernestus Rex, king of Hanover. All of the documents, however, appear to have been written by Oxford himself; they were merely a ruse.

At the police station, the man Lord Melbourne called "a little vermin" was "thoroughly enjoying the attention." When questioned, Oxford was disdainful, self-possessed, and cocky. He laughed sporadically. He was eager to know how the queen and Prince Albert had responded to his attack. Told that neither of them had been scared or alarmed, he shrugged and fibbed: "Oh, I know to the contrary; for when I fired the first pistol, Albert was about to jump from the carriage and put his foot out, but when he saw me present the second pistol, he immediately drew back."

Leopold was surprised by the attack; not only had Victoria been a liberal monarch, "one should think that your being a lady would alone prevent such unmanly conduct." In truth, Oxford suggested it was precisely because Victoria was female that he wanted to kill her. He told the constables his real motive was that he did not think a great country like England should be ruled by a woman. Oxford was charged with high treason and sent to Newgate Gaol, then to an asylum, where he spent twenty-seven years before emigrating to Australia.

Seven men tried to kill Victoria between 1840 and 1882: unemployed youths, a cabinetmaker, a potboy, a chemist's assistant, an agricultural laborer, and a former army officer. All of them became brief media celebrities before vanishing. All were odd, some were insane and some perfectly lucid, and most were sent to Australia, which was at the time serving as a remote prison for England's criminals. Some attributed the sudden spate of attacks on a young, powerful woman to a strange, contagious "erotomania," in which men who had fancied themselves lovers of the queen were "turned to jealousy by continued disappointment." After a second assassination attempt in 1842, the poet Elizabeth Barrett (later Browning) wrote to a friend puzzling over "this strange popular mania of queen-shooting."

> I am very angry. . . . Who shot George the fourth? Not even I—says the sparrow. Poor Victoria! Let the coolness be what it may, there is an undercurrent—she is a human being and a woman!—And is moreover conscious that of those who reproach her most, nobody has said that she has not wished to benefit her people according to her light. And the end of it all

is,—she is set up for a mark to such little boys in her dominions as are pleased to play with pistols! It is worse than bad. I hear that people go now to see the poor queen leave the palace for her drive with a disposition to be excited, with an idea of seeing her *shot at:* there is a crowd at the gates every day!

Victoria's reaction to each attack was the same: she was defiant and brave, but inwardly shaken. Why did so many men, in their derangement, want to marry her, subdue her, or shoot her? Even the powerful, privileged queen was not safe from violence.

That June afternoon, Albert's first thought had been for their unborn child. When Edward Oxford shot at Victoria she was almost four months pregnant, which makes her boldness even more surprising. At the time, there was a superstitious belief in maternal impression—the belief that events disturbing the minds or spirits of pregnant women could harm, deform, or derange their unborn children. (The biography of Joseph Merrick, known as the Elephant Man—one of the most heart-wrenching of the Victorian "freaks"—provides this theory as an explanation for his deformity: his mother was startled and trampled on by an elephant when he was in her womb. The still-mysterious genetic disease he suffered from—thought to be neurofibromatosis or Proteus syndrome—had nothing to do with his mother's uterus, but this idea defined the sad life of the Elephant Man. Victoria sent him a handwritten note each year.)

Victoria's true and more practical concern, though, was not maternal impression but maternal mortality. Conservative estimates of the number of women who died giving birth in 1840s England are about four to five women per thousand. She had written a few months earlier that falling pregnant and having a great many children was "the ONLY thing I *dread*." Laboring women died mostly from puerperal fever, for which there was no cure, despite the liberal doses of opium and brandy administered by doctors. When the Female Medical Society told doctors not to deliver children with hands dirtied by dissection rooms, *The Lancet* scoffed. Doctors claimed that the problem was not contamination but excessive "mental emotion" of the women who died. Victoria was also haunted by the death of her beloved cousin Charlotte, the onetime heir to the throne who had died in childbirth. Upper-class women weren't exempt from the dangers of labor. In 1839, Princess Marie of Württemberg, the wife of her cousin, had died after giving birth to a boy.

Victoria was furious when she discovered her worst fear had been realized within a few weeks of her wedding. She confided in her grandmother the Dowager Duchess of Saxe-Coburg and Gotha: "It is spoiling my happiness; I have always hated the idea and I prayed God night and day for me to be left free for at least six months, but my prayers have not been answered and I am really most unhappy. I cannot understand how one can wish for such a thing, especially at the beginning of a marriage." If she had a "nasty girl," she declared, she would drown her.

Victoria loved being married and wanted to spend every second with her new husband. Carrying a child would interrupt her new-found peace. Without pregnancy, she later wrote to her eldest daughter, married life was "unbounded happiness—if one has a husband one worships! It is a foretaste of heaven." Once, when speaking to Victoria about someone else, Lady Lyttelton used the phrase "as happy as a queen," before realizing what she had said. "Don't correct yourself," said Victoria; "a Queen *is* a very happy woman." This was a queen who ran into Lady Lyttelton's room in her dressing gown to drag her to come and see "the most lovely of all rainbows!" This was a queen who earnestly bent over tulips, geraniums, and queen bees as Albert explained their curious characteristics. Victoria soon declared in her journal that she now preferred the countryside to London.

Victoria refused to let her round belly change her life dramatically or mark her as weak. She shocked onlookers at a ball when obviously pregnant by dancing more than Lord Holland thought "a nurse or man midwife" would have approved. She refused to sit down at parties or stay indoors during wild weather. She boasted to her sister

Feodora that she was in rude health: "I am wonderfully well. I take long walks, some in the highest wind every day and so am active, though of a *great* size, I must unhappily admit." Just a few weeks before the birth, Lady Lyttelton described her as "very active; out walking before ten this morning, and seeming determined to bear up and complain of nothing." Albert tried to keep her still by reading or singing to her as she lay on the sofa.

Charles Locock, her chief accoucheur, was taken aback by Victoria's frank approach to pregnancy: "She had not the slightest reserve, & was always ready to express Herself, in respect to Her present situation, in the very plainest terms possible." Locock took a great dislike to the queen, suggesting she lacked delicacy because she openly discussed her body with him. He inappropriately and maliciously confided in female friends that her body was shaped like a barrel: "She will be very ugly and enormously fat. . . . She goes without stays or anything that keeps Her shape within bounds; . . . she is more like a barrel than anything else." It was only recently that the idea that all pregnant women must wear corsets had begun to fade, and they still labored in petticoats, gowns, and chemises.

Albert tried to reassure his wife about the looming labor. Solicitous, thoughtful, and intelligent: Albert's strengths were increasingly obvious. The women of the royal household gushed about his blue eyes, "simple tastes and pleasures, and happy, active temper." He was credited with raising the quality of the conversation in the court to include science, art, and botany, above the usual gossip of the palaces. Albert was a serious man, who encouraged Victoria to read constitutional histories with him at night, but he also made her laugh. When he told his wife that she should just smile in public, like a dancer, he leapt into the air and pirouetted as he said it, to make his point.

Yet Albert was not as happy as the queen he loved. Part of this was due to the stifling nature of the royal household. He missed his family. He was bored by the conversation and usually preferred to play double chess on his own. He often nodded off during concerts and dinners. The time seemed wasted to him. Albert wanted to use the luster of the court to invite and attract great literary and scientific minds. The queen was reluctant, though; those people made her feel insecure. She worried that her education had been lacking, as Albert had told her, and as Melbourne told Anson, "She is far too open and candid in her nature to pretend to one atom more knowledge than she really possesses on such subjects." She was thrilled that her husband did not care to dawdle with the men after dinner, but she seemed oblivious to the fact that he was just bored.

The prince had long bouts of melancholy from which his wife was unable to shake him. Two weeks after the wedding, when Albert's father returned to Germany, Victoria found him sobbing in the hallway; he brushed past her without talking to her. She crept into his room, concerned. He turned to her, his eyes red, and told her quietly that she would not understand what it was like to leave behind a golden life and affectionate family. He was right—Victoria had been glad to pull up the drawbridge behind her when she married, leaving her mother, Conroy, and other vexatious people behind. Troubled, Victoria wrote afterward: "God knows how great my wish is to make this beloved Being happy and contented."

But the true hurdle to Albert's happiness was sizable. He was impatient to become, effectively, king. He was ambitious, intellectually restless, and appalled by the thought of being seen as a decorative spouse while his wife trod the carpeted halls of power. He also wanted to help Victoria avoid the kind of serious missteps she had made when she first became queen. He wanted to occupy the same elite, exclusive podium of sovereignty as Victoria. The people close to Albert saw the imbalance right away. His brother Ernest remarked on how Victoria had ensured "a quiet, happy but an inglorious and dull life for him" while "as queen she moves on another level."

Victoria was perfectly happy with the arrangement. She knew Albert wanted to be the household head and agreed this was his rightful place. She had even, unsuccessfully, sought the title of King Consort for him in February 1845, five years into their marriage. But the ques-

tion was, what did being the head of the household mean? Surely it
did not mean relinquishing her job. She was protective of the crown
she had fought for and intended to keep her marriage separate from
her work, continuing to meet with Melbourne and her ministers on
her own. But Albert refused to be shut out or relegated to a second
place. In his view, the husband should control all of his wife's affairs.
How does a man establish his natural authority in such a context? he
wondered. He wrote to his friend Prince William of Löwenstein in
May: "In my home life I am very happy and contented; but the difficulty of filling my place with proper dignity is that I am only the
husband, and not the master in the house."

Albert's fundamental belief was that women were not meant to
rule, and certainly not by themselves. His hometown, Coburg, was
under Salic law and insisted on male sovereigns; that is why the
crown of Hanover went to the next in line, the Duke of Cumberland,
when Victoria became queen (making her the first Hanoverian to be
monarch only of England). Baron Stockmar, King Leopold, and Ernest all shared Albert's views. In 1850, Albert told the Duke of Wellington that he believed it was his duty to

> fill up every gap, which, as a woman, the Queen would natu-
> rally leave in the exercise of her regal functions—continually
> and anxiously to watch every part of the public business, in
> order to be able to advise and assist her in any moment in any
> of the multifarious and difficult questions brought before her,
> political, or social, or personal . . . to place all his time and pow-
> ers at her command as the natural head of her family, superin-
> tendent of her household, manager of her private affairs, her
> sole confidential adviser in politics, and the only assistant in her
> communications with the officers of the Government, her pri-
> vate secretary, and her permanent minister.

This was an extremely broad and comprehensive set of duties. But
the times suited Albert's aspirations. In the nineteenth century, only

an infinitesimal number of aristocratic women had more money and power than their husbands. Most women were chattels without rights to their bodies, money, property, or children. Various philosophies sprang up to justify this position: women, by their nature, belonged in the home, and they could gain some prestige or status by having children and not sleeping with other men. By being, in other words, moral guardians of the hearth.

This meant there was substantial cultural support for Albert's jockeying, as major intellectuals of the era agreed that women were innately inferior. John Ruskin argued in 1864 that women's natural state was "true wifely subjection." Women's power was not for battle, he said, "and her intellect is not for invention or creation, but for sweet ordering, arrangement, and decision." Charles Darwin agreed, writing in 1871 that natural selection meant women were lesser than men. He conceded that women were more tender, intuitive, and perceptive, and less selfish, but added: "Some, at least, of these faculties are characteristic of the lower races, and therefore of a past and lower state of civilization." When wives promised to obey their husbands, it was for good reason. As the author Sarah Stickney Ellis wrote in 1843, one thing that women must be certain of before marriage was "the superiority of your husband simply as a man." She dedicated her popular book *The Wives of England* to the queen. "It is quite possible," Ellis continued, "you may have more talent, with higher attainments, and you may also have been generally more admired; but this has nothing whatever to do with your position as a woman, which is, and must be, inferior to his as a man." The illogic of this position fueled the restlessness of generations of women.

But Victoria was taught to believe all of this, and Albert encouraged her in thinking her education and abilities lesser than his. The paradox of their marriage is that as her love and contentment grew, her confidence in herself wilted. It was best, her male advisers said, that she satisfied herself with her domestic life.

In May, after three months of marriage, Albert decided to broach the subject of his role directly with his wife. After Victoria's twenty-first birthday, which she said was the happiest she had ever had, Albert complained that she did not speak to him about politics or even "trivial matters." Victoria confided in Lord Melbourne, telling him that while Albert was unhappy about a "lack of confidence," she honestly didn't want to do anything about it. Lord Melbourne described the exchange in a conversation recorded by Albert's private secretary, Mr. Anson:

> She said it proceeded entirely from indolence; she knew it was wrong, but when she was with the Prince, she preferred talking upon other subjects. My impression is that the chief obstacle in her Majesty's mind is the fear of difference of opinion, and she thinks that domestic harmony is more likely to follow from avoiding subjects likely to create difference. My own experience leads me to think that subjects between man and wife, even where difference is sure to ensue, are much better discussed than avoided, for the latter course is sure to beget distrust.

All the men in Victoria's life backed Albert's quest for more power. They told the queen to trust him, to lean on him, to confide in him. Even her beloved uncle Leopold agreed "there should be no concealment from him on any subject." The sharp-eyed Baron Stockmar was the only one to advise Albert not to be too hasty in his quest for the keys of power. He told Anson that while it was true that the queen should "by degrees impart everything" to her husband, there was "a danger in his wishing it all at once." The danger was that Albert might make a mistake or overreach, and not be asked for his help again. Stockmar also suggested that the young Victoria's problem was more ignorance than indolence, and that she just did not understand much of what she was being told of her ministers' plans and bills.

Victoria ignored these urgings and continued seeing her ministers alone, although even they were starting to feel sorry for her husband.

Albert was still not allowed to see the state papers or sit in the room while the queen spoke to Lord Melbourne. She resented his attempts to give her advice or direction. When a box of official state papers arrived with a blunt note directing her to "sign immediately," Albert took offense on her behalf and told her not to reply for a day or two, lest they think her a mere bureaucrat. Victoria picked up her pen and signed instantly. Having spent her childhood fortifying her spine, Victoria was not easily bent to another's will. Even so, now her childhood allies were saying the same kinds of things her enemies had: that she was not capable of fully comprehending politics, and she should relinquish control. She could shrug this off when it came from Conroy, but it would be far more fraught when it came from her husband.

The one person who did not believe Victoria should submit to Albert was Baroness Lehzen, a woman also well practiced at resistance. Lehzen had told her protégée that she believed Albert should have the same role she did: influential but invisible, a remarkable status for a woman whose official role had been governess. But soon after marrying, Albert had decided Lehzen had to go. The baroness's sphere of influence had widened: she now managed Victoria's finances and acted as her secretary, controlling her diary and processing invoices for payment. Albert believed the woman who had stood stoutly by Victoria's side in her troubled teenage years now controlled her to an unhealthy extent. When out walking on the terrace one day with the queen, Lady Lyttelton noticed "Mme. De Lehzen's pale face (the only face I ever see that seems to feel what is going on *at all*) with her usual half-anxious, smiling, fixed look following the Queen from one of the castle windows." Lehzen saw everything. To Victoria, this was reassuring. To Albert, it was ominous.

Albert's skill came in intuiting that he would not win his power through force or demands, but watchful tenderness. As his wife's waist expanded and contracted during a round of pregnancies, he would encourage her to lean on him. Albert tried a strategic kind of patience—he would have his way through will, intelligence, and, most of all, his complete wooing of and caring for his wife. She decided to give him what he wanted and needed. It was a sweet kind of capitulation.

Nine days before Edward Oxford cocked his gun at the pregnant Victoria, Albert gave a speech to the Anti-Slavery Society, which he had labored over, despite its being only 165 words long. The five or six thousand people in the crowd cheered loudly, which, he said, "rewards me sufficiently for the fear and nervousness I had to conquer before I began my speech." Albert craved respect. He took his duties seriously—and was rapidly charming the court. It was, Lord Holland wrote to Lord Granville, "now all the fashion to praise Prince Albert." One woman, sitting next to him at a dinner, wrote eagerly of their "deeply interesting conversation on the most important subjects": "upon religious principle, its influence on Sovereigns and its importance in the education of children; and upon modes of worship, our views respecting them . . . also on the management of children generally; on war and peace; on prisons and punishment." The Prince Consort was a natural polymath.

Albert's deliberate execution of a long-standing plan to rule England did not mean that he loved Victoria any less. The position of husband to the queen of England was part of a path chosen for him when he was an infant, which meant that his marriage was also his career, and he had always been philosophical about it. He knew it would be difficult and "plentifully strewn with thorns," but he decided it would be better to be so "for some great and worthy object than for trivial and paltry ends." In the weeks after the wedding, Albert's brother Ernest reported on his brother's progress to their uncle Leopold. In unpublished letters in German archives, Ernest "reported that Albert had done the correct thing by not hesitating to speak his opinion on everything. This had led to all orders within the household and stables being directed through him and thus he had become 'the great channel through whom the Queen's will' was expressed." The more vulnerable and earthbound his pregnant wife grew, the more Albert's official status rose.

In the months following the assassination attempt, the men around Victoria began quietly to prepare for the possibility of her death—whether from gunfire, childbirth, or some unanticipated cause. On July 2, three weeks after the shooting, Melbourne told Victoria he wanted to discuss a subject of "great importance and one of great emergency"—perhaps Victoria knew what he was referring to? She did not. "It is about having a Bill for a Regency," he said. When in July 1840 Albert was given the legal right to rule in the place of his wife in the event of her death, he wrote triumphantly to his brother Ernest: "I am to be Regent—*alone*—Regent, without a Council. You will understand the importance of this matter and that it gives my position here in the country a fresh significance." Melbourne told Victoria the reason for Parliament's decision was entirely Albert's good character, even though it meant that if the English queen were to die, a German prince would be in charge.

In August, the Prince proudly perched on a throne next to Victoria's at the prorogation of Parliament after Melbourne discovered that precedent allowed this. In September, he was made a Privy Counsellor, and he boasted to Stockmar that he was being handed a stream of "interesting papers." He had been "extremely pleased" with Victoria in the past few months, writing somewhat condescendingly: "She has only twice had the sulks . . . altogether she puts more confidence in me daily." In November, just before she gave birth to their first child, Victoria successfully asked that Albert's name be included in the liturgy, as her child's would be.

But the queen wouldn't slow down—she worked hard throughout her pregnancies. She was preoccupied by what was then known as the Eastern Question: the impact of the decline of the immense Ottoman Empire. Founded in 1299 and centered in Turkey, at its time of greatest reach, in the sixteenth and seventeenth centuries, it spanned vast tracts of southern Europe, the Middle East, North

Africa, the Horn of Africa, and Western Asia. But after decades of sluggish economic growth and inept administration, the empire that linked the Mediterranean, Aegean, and Black Seas had grown weak: Czar Nicholas called it the "sick man of Europe." England and France wanted to prop up Turkey and keep Russia out of the Mediterranean. But when the Ottoman sultan died and his teenage son became leader in 1839, the Turkish viceroy in Egypt tried to break Egypt away from Turkey. England, Russia, Prussia, and Austria were supporting Turkey, but France supported Egypt. War was narrowly avoided, and a peace agreement was signed in London in 1840. Victoria told King Leopold she gave "these affairs my most serious attention" and joked: "I think our child ought to have besides its other names those of Turco Egypto, as we think of nothing else. . . . I hope I have done good."

Before long, Albert arranged to have his and Victoria's heavy wooden writing tables pushed together so they could work side by side. Just before the birth of their child, he wrote to his brother: "I wish you could see us here and see in us a couple united in love and unanimity. Now Victoria is also ready to give up something for my sake, I everything for her sake. . . . Do not think I lead a submissive life. On the contrary, here, where the lawful position of the man is so, I have formed a prize life for myself."

Victoria gave birth three weeks early, on the afternoon of November 21, 1840. Her contractions had begun the night before, as she had woken to the sound of rain tapping her windows. She roused Albert and spent the next few hours racked with pain. (Characteristically, she later claimed that once labor had begun, she was not the slightest bit nervous.) Unusually for the era, Albert was with her during her labor, along with the doctor and nurse. In the next room sat men of state, an archbishop and bishop, as well as Lord Melbourne, cocking their ears as the queen panted and tried not to yell. (Lord Erroll, Lord Steward of the Household, boasted later that the door had been left open, so he had full, clear view of the queen.) Once the ordeal was over, a red, wriggling baby girl was brought out for inspection. She was in perfect health, but her parents were disappointed by the gender (as were many of their subjects). When the doctor told the queen, "Oh, Madam, it is a Princess," she responded, "Never mind, the next will be a Prince."

Victoria lay back against her pillows in her canopied mahogany bed, declared herself to feel much better, and looked at her husband proudly as he smiled and stroked her hand: "Dearest Albert hardly left me at all & was the greatest comfort and support." Soon, though, he was gulping down a quick lunch before dashing downstairs to represent the queen in the Privy Council for the first time. She was relieved; she had survived, she was alive. Outside, cannons boomed. Albert was ecstatic. He had become a father and a proxy for the queen in the same day.

Victoria spent two weeks in bed after giving birth, as was then customary. Her baby was brought to her twice a day when she was in her dressing room, and she watched her being bathed once every few weeks. She called her "the Child" until she was christened Victoria Adelaide Mary Louisa almost three months later. In later years, Victoria would reveal that she did not find babies endearing, especially newborns, with their scrawny mottled limbs and startled reflexes. (She has been criticized for calling infants "froglike"—but this is not simply derogatory; anyone who has nursed, bathed, or blown air on the stomach of a days-old baby will know that their limbs splay in an alarmed fashion called the Moro reflex. They do resemble frogs lying on their backs.) Because of this, an enduring myth that the queen lacked all maternal instinct has taken root in almost all major biographies.

As Yvonne Ward from La Trobe University has demonstrated, the selection of Victoria's published letters was made by two men, who rejected her correspondence with other women on matters such as babies, teething, and pregnancy as softer and less relevant. This has meant that Victoria's starkly rebellious and countercultural remarks to her daughter Vicky—about the trials and difficulties of birth, written after most of her nine children were grown—are relied on as evidence that she despised her offspring. These letters sound a note of repugnance about the physical toll of bearing children—and, in Victoria's case, of bearing such a great number of children. She did not say in these letters what effect childbearing had on her body, but she spoke often of suffering; it would not have been gentle on the small frame of a woman who did not reach five feet. It is likely that her uterus prolapsed in these years, and there is evidence she suffered enduring, painful gynecological problems. But the words she wrote in her journal at the time of having her children reveal a tenderness and optimism that have been forgotten.

Victoria was, in many ways, a doting mother. Her diaries reveal her affection and love for her children, and how much she delighted in playing with them. Three weeks after Vicky was born, she called her "our dear little child" who got "daily prettier": "She has large, bright, dark blue eyes and a nice little nose and mouth, a very good complexion with a little color in her cheeks, very unusual for so young a Baby." Four weeks after the birth, she wrote: "It seems like a dream, having a child." Her journal in early 1841 is a record of contentment: showing off her bright, pretty little girl, playing with Vicky as Albert played the piano nearby, or watching as Albert pushed Vicky around on a sledge outside. She laughed at her daughter's attempts to sit up, and danced her on her knee. She was such a "dear" baby, she wrote repeatedly: "She is such a darling." She clasped her with one arm on her lap, letting her play with trinkets as she wrote in her journal.

On Christmas Day 1840, Victoria marveled at her great luck: "This day last year I was an unmarried girl, and this year I have an angelic husband, and a dear little girl five weeks old." When Vicky was eighteen months old, Victoria wrote she had become "quite a little toy for us & a great pet, always smiling so sweetly when we play with her." The queen spent more time with Pussy, as she nicknamed her daughter, than was expected of her. Lady Lyttelton, who became the children's governess in 1842, wrote that Victoria had the child with her "constantly" and fretted about her development: "The Queen is, like all very young mothers, *exigeante,* and never thinks the baby makes progress enough or is good enough. She has her constantly with her, and thinks incessantly about her, and seems also more and more devotedly fond of the Prince."

Motherhood was a surprise to Victoria. The young girl who had envied Gypsies their cozy domestic life was now astonished to find herself at the center of a loving family. Albert was consistently gentle, attentive, and kind. Looking back on this time in later years, the queen was rhapsodic, writing in the third person:

> The Prince's care and devotion were quite beyond expression. . . . He was content to sit by her [the queen] in a darkened room, to read to her, or write for her. No one but himself ever lifted her from her bed to her sofa, and he always helped to wheel her on her bed or sofa into the next room. For this purpose he would come when sent for instantly from any part of the house. As years went on and he became overwhelmed with work this was often done at much inconvenience to himself; but he ever came with a sweet smile on his face. In short, his care of her was like that of a mother, nor could there be a kinder, wiser or more judicious nurse.

It was Albert who took on the traditionally feminine role in some ways, as Victoria regained her strength. He was the tender nurturer and the vigilant parent. He was the one Pussy ran to, and the one who lifted her in the air and waltzed around the room, trying to make her giggle. Victoria was not the slightest bit jealous; she adored Albert too, and the maternal instinct was not at the time glorified and elevated above the paternal. He was simply the more natural parent. Victoria told Leopold: "Our young lady flourishes exceedingly. . . .

I think you would be amused to see Albert dancing her in his arms; he makes a capital nurse (which I do not, and she is much too heavy for me to carry), and she already seems to [be] happy to go to him." All Victoria wanted was for her children to resemble their father.

The children fascinated the inquisitive, intellectual Albert. When Pussy was two and a half, he wrote to his stepmother about his love of being a parent:

> There is certainly a great charm, as well as deep interest in watching the development of feelings and faculties in a little child, and nothing is more instructive for the knowledge of our own nature, than to observe in a little creature the stages of development, which, when we were ourselves passing through them, seemed scarcely to have an existence for us. I feel this daily in watching our young offspring, whose characters are quite different, and who both show many lovable qualities.

Albert commissioned the favored royal artist Edwin Henry Land-seer to paint a pastel portrait of himself on his twenty-third birthday, to give to Victoria. In it, he carefully cradles the tiny princess and gazes down at her adoringly. Albert's care was a way of healing the brokenness of his childhood home. He wrote to his brother: "Wedded life is the only thing that can make up for the lost relationships of our youth."

Relieved of much of the physical burden of child-rearing by her servants, Victoria was up walking within a month, and planning a trip to Windsor. Her letters to her uncle Leopold in early 1841 started to veer from talk of babies to foreign policy: "Your little grand-niece is most flourishing; she gains daily in health, strength and, I may add, beauty; I think she will be very like her dearest father; she grows amazingly; I shall be proud to present her to you. The denouement of the Oriental affair is most unfortunate, is it not?" When Leopold wrote back delightedly wishing she would have a large and happy family, she snapped, telling him not to harbor any illusions. She still saw herself as the leader of the country, first and foremost, and that's where her responsibility fell:

> I think, dearest Uncle, you cannot *really* wish me to be the "Mamma *d'une nombreuse famille,*" for I think you will see with me the great inconvenience a *large* family would be to us all, and particularly to the country, independent of the hardship and inconvenience to myself; men never think, at least seldom think, what a hard task it is for us women to go through this *very often*.

And so, when she found herself pregnant again just three months after giving birth, Victoria wept and raged. She did not have the aid of the natural—if imperfect—contraceptive of breastfeeding, as she refused to nurse her children as her own mother had done, and birth control was widely considered sinful. Some women tried to coat their vaginas with cedar oil, lead, frankincense, or olive oil, in the belief that this might prevent the "seed" from implanting. In 1838, many aristocrats used sponges "as large as can be pleasantly introduced, having previously attached a bobbin or bit of narrow riband to withdraw it." But there is no evidence Victoria was even aware of such a thing. Women were also advised to have sex around the time of ovulation if they wanted to avoid pregnancy, which we now know to be precisely the time that most conceive. The queen was miserable, later telling a grown-up Vicky that the first two years of her married life were "utterly spoilt" by pregnancy. She had to unglue herself from her husband's side, and later complained that she enjoyed nothing at that time. Albert, though, was relishing his new life.

By the end of 1840, the brass keys to the rectangular red confidential dispatch boxes were in Albert's hands. Inside were the documents revealing the thinking of the prime minister, the Cabinet, and the other men wrangling with the great social, economic, and geopoliti-

cal issues of the decade. Albert, slipping the key into the lock for the
first time without his wife watching, was thrilled. A large part of his
success, he knew, was due to the fact that his wife was lying supine,
needing to be lifted from sofa to bed, but he had also earned it. His
secretary and champion, Anson, remarked:

> This has been brought about by the fact of the Prince having
> received and made notes of all the Cabinet business during the
> Queen's confinement, this circumstance having evinced to the
> Queen his capacity for business and power to assist in searching
> and explanation. . . . [He was now] in fact, tho' not in name,
> Her Majesty's Private Secretary.

It had taken the prince only two days after the birth to persuade
his wife to have the boxes sent to him instead of her. On November
24, he boasted to his brother, who was in charge of a tiny German
duchy: "I have my hands very full, as I also look after Victoria's political affairs."

Albert had muscled, charmed, and earned his way into his new
place as head of the house and functional monarch. In July 1841,
when Vicky was eight months old, Anson recorded how satisfied he
was:

> The Prince went yesterday through a review of the many
> steps he had made to his present position—all within eighteen
> months from the marriage. Those who intended to keep him
> from being useful to the Queen, from the fear that he might
> ambitiously touch upon her prerogatives, have been completely
> foiled. . . . The Court from highest to lowest is brought to a
> proper sense of the position of the Queen's husband. The coun-
> try has marked its confidence in his character by passing the
> Regency Bill *nem. con.* The Queen finds the value of an active
> right hand and able head to support her and to resort to for

advice in time of need. Cabinet Ministers treat him with deference and respect.

On their first wedding anniversary in 1841, Albert gave his wife a brooch crafted in the shape of a cradle with a baby in it: "the quaintest thing I ever saw & so pretty," wrote Victoria. This year, she declared, had been "perfect happiness." Albert was responsible for this, but his own visions stretched far beyond nursery walls. He loved music, art, science, sanitation, and symmetry, and he wanted to broaden their reach in Britain. Once he had been allowed entry to the most powerful political discussions, Albert would slave for a country that still viewed him as a foreigner. There remained only two substantial blocks to his power: Lord Melbourne and Baroness Lehzen, the two people Victoria was closest to. To get what he truly wanted, he needed them gone.

CHAPTER 13

The Palace Intruders

When a woman is in love, her desire for public power becomes less and less.

—HECTOR BOLITHO

In the early hours of December 3, 1840, a short, ugly teenager was lying under a floral chintz sofa in the queen's sitting room in Buckingham Palace. Edward Jones, an unemployed errand runner, had been hiding for hours hoping to glimpse the queen. He lay awake listening to the sounds of the palace—the baby princess wailing intermittently; the night nurse pacing the nursery, softly singing lullabies; the odd footsteps and snoring of night watchmen. Just three hours earlier, the queen had been sitting on the very sofa he was now underneath; he hugged himself at the thought of it. The baby Princess Royal was actually asleep in the room next door! As the wind rustled the trees outside the window, he wondered if he should venture to the kitchen for more provisions before morning broke. Would there be more delicious potatoes in the larder? Cheese? Jones had been hiding in the palace for a couple of days, and he knew nighttime was best spent scavenging, exploring, and hunting for new hiding spots.

In the anteroom next door, Mrs. Lilly, the monthly nurse charged with taking care of the baby princess, was awake, listening to the soft grunting sounds coming from the ornate cradle next to her bed. Suddenly, the door to the queen's sitting room creaked loudly. Mrs. Lilly called out, but no one responded. She sat up, and yelled loudly when the door opened farther: "Who is there?" The door slammed shut.

Mrs. Lilly ran from her room, woke Lehzen, and sent for Kinnaird, the page then on watch. Kinnaird scanned the sitting room and peered under a corner of the tightly stuffed sofa, upon which Victoria had been wheeled into her bedroom earlier in the night. He suddenly jerked upright, then slowly backed away. Lehzen glared at him and marched to the sofa, pushing it away from the wall. She placed a hand over her nose as her eyes flew wide; the teenager hiding underneath was covered in filth, and stank. He was seized and taken downstairs, where he said he had not meant any harm, he had only come to see the queen. Albert and Victoria slept soundly as the women scrambled to pin down the intruder just fifty yards away.

The news ignited London. Much like Edward Oxford, the would-be assassin, this palace intruder enjoyed being grilled by the authorities. He boasted that he "sat upon the throne" and "saw the Queen and heard the Royal Princess squall." He had scaled the garden wall and climbed in through a window, and spent three days in the palace, hiding under beds and in cupboards. Jones was the type of young man who might have succeeded on Fleet Street; he had dreams of writing a scandalous book about the royal couple and insisted this was the only reason he had trespassed—he wanted to "know how they lived at the Palace," and especially to hear the conversations between the queen and her husband. His father claimed Jones was disturbed, and doctors appeared to confirm this by declaring the shape of his head to be "of a most peculiar formation." But because he was unarmed and had not stolen anything, the Privy Council sentenced him to only three months' hard labor.

The security at the palace was notoriously lax in those times. Vagrants and drunken soldiers were often found passed out on the palace lawns, having climbed over the low walls, which were concealed by heavy, low-hanging tree branches. Many of the watchmen were elderly, having been promoted as recognition of long service, and often slept on the job. The Boy Jones, as the London newspapers called him, had broken in once before, in December 1838. He was captured by police in St. James's Street, following a chase, and was found wearing two pairs of trousers and two overcoats. When the bulging top pair of pants was pulled down, several female undergarments fell out. He had been to the queen's bedroom and dressing room, stealing a letter he found there, along with a portrait and the underwear. His actions were described as "youthful folly," and he was acquitted.

Three months after Lehzen found the Boy Jones, he broke into the palace a third time. He was discovered at 1:30 A.M. with meat and potatoes from the pantry hidden in his handkerchief. This three-time achievement earned him celebrity status. Charles Dickens wrote to the boy's father soon after to request a meeting with the "Palace Victim," more out of curiosity than admiration (he doubted the popular belief that the Boy Jones was smart, but unfortunately did not write about their meeting). The American novelist James Fenimore Cooper, author of *The Last of the Mohicans,* called on Jones's father when he was visiting London and offered to take his son to America, where he thought a clever boy would thrive. A meeting was organized, but Cooper was surprised to meet "a dull, undersized runt, remarkable only for his taciturnity and obstinacy."

Prince Albert used the story of the Boy Jones's repeated trespassing as a pretext to scrutinize the complicated, inefficient, and wasteful palace administration. He was determined to rid the palace of all intruders, including Baroness Lehzen, who had taken on greater re-

Edward, the Duke of Kent, was a proud, militaristic man. He doted on his baby daughter and boasted that, despite the odds, one day she would be queen.

Victoire, Victoria's German mother, would always remain an outsider in England, but she longed for greater power herself.

The robust little Victoria was likened to a king in petticoats; the young princess had a fondness for dolls and a tendency to throw tantrums.

When the eighteen-year-old Victoria was told the king had died, she was ready to become queen. But her governess hovered behind the door, holding smelling salts.

By 1851, their wedding clothes had grown more snug—but Victoria liked to reenact the moment, even eleven years later, to remind her public she was still bride to her handsome groom.

American painter Thomas Sully was eager to capture Victoria's "sweet tone of voice" and "gentle manner" in her coronation year. She was praised for her poise, maintaining composure while the men around her fumbled lines and stumbled down stairs.

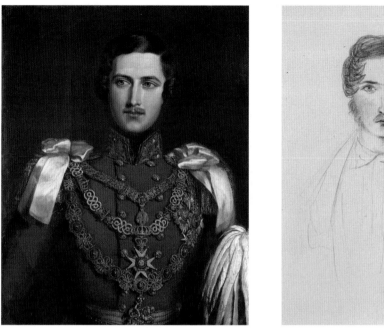

Albert was "excessively handsome," wrote a smitten Victoria in her journal. She was so taken by Albert's "delicate mustachios" that she asked that all soldiers in the British army be ordered to grow them.

In 1859, as she turned forty, Victoria was a woman in her prime—with nine children, a country that had avoided revolution, and a husband she adored. She thought this portrait, by court favorite Franz Xaver Winterhalter, magnificent.

VICTORIA'S CHILDREN

Vicky, the eldest child of Victoria and Albert, was precociously clever. She married when she was a teenager and went to live in Prussia, where she struggled with a hostile public and a cruel son, the future Kaiser Wilhelm II.

Victoria (here with Bertie, Vicky, Alice, and Alfred) was a strong disciplinarian who was deeply involved in the lives of her children.

Osborne House, on the lush, tranquil Isle of Wight, was the first private home owned by the royal family. Victoria, who longed for quiet and pure air, was thrilled: "all our very *own*."

Bertie was a sociable boy whose charm outweighed his intellect; his parents had his skull inspected for faults. Keenly conscious of their disappointment, the future King Edward VII rebelled and flirted with debauchery.

Victoria and Albert doted on Beatrice, their youngest child (sketched by Victoria here). Victoria fell asleep holding her on the night Albert died, and maintained a strong grip on her forever afterward.

The Great Exhibition of 1851 was the most shining achievement of Victoria's reign, its success largely due to Albert. "We are capable," she wrote, "of doing almost anything."

Baroness Lehzen, Victoria's governess, was intent on teaching her young charge to be a strong, stubborn queen. Albert would decide she had too much influence over his wife, and later forced her to leave.

King Leopold I, Victoria's uncle, provided steady advice and tender concern for the fatherless princess. He also encouraged her to marry her cousin Albert, thereby placing a fellow Coburg on the pinnacle of British power.

Victoria became infatuated with her droll prime minister, Lord Melbourne, and he in turn adored her. Later, both Victoria and the editors of her letters would be embarrassed by her effusive affection for an older man.

Former army officer John Conroy was desperate to control the throne and tried to bully the teenage Victoria into handing over power to him and her mother. Victoria despised him.

Lord Tennyson's poems provided solace for the grieving, widowed Victoria. He was one of the few to recognize how lonely she was on "that terrible height."

Victoria found Robert Peel stiff and reserved; not long after being made queen, she prevented him from becoming prime minister for a time so she could keep Lord Melbourne in power. But Albert admired him, and eventually she did too.

Royal Residences

Immediately upon becoming queen, Victoria wanted to live in the light, spacious Buckingham Palace. Eventually its poor sanitation and ventilation would make it oppressive.

Victoria was never entirely at home in the large spaces of Windsor Castle, but after Albert died there in 1861, she took great care to preserve his rooms exactly as they had been when he was alive.

Albert worked closely with renowned architect Thomas Cubitt to build Osborne House in Italianate style, a perfect summer retreat for his family.

sponsibility for the nursery as well as the queen's finances during Victoria's confinements before and after she gave birth. The prince, who craved structure, despised the ineptitude obvious in the running of the royal residence. He decided to implement new order for Victoria, instilling discipline in everything from her daily schedule to her finances and shambolic palaces.

First, Albert gave Victoria a routine to follow every day. They breakfasted at nine, took a walk, then wrote and drew together and had lunch at two. Victoria saw Lord Melbourne in the afternoon for a few hours, before going out for a drive in a pony phaeton, with Albert or with her mother and ladies. Dinner was at eight. Albert ensured this schedule was followed as closely as possible, thereby curbing Victoria's appetite for late nights.

Second, the prince tried to curtail expenditure. He was staggered to discover that in 1839 the queen spent £34,000 annually on charities and pensions alone, roughly £2.6 million in today's terms. He devoted particular time to the financial records of the Duchy of Cornwall, which provided substantial income for Victoria in 1840, mostly from its tin mines—£36,000, about a third of which vaporized in costly administration. He successfully pruned, restructured, and budgeted—and within a couple of years, had enough money to buy a private house for his family on the Isle of Wight. (He continually denied requests for money from his family in Coburg.)

Third, the prince turned to the parlous state of Victoria's homes, especially Buckingham Palace, where they spent several months a year. It was large, grand, and situated on the finest real estate in London, but ventilation was poor, the heating was patchy, and frequent gas leaks led to the odd explosion in the kitchen. The servants' quarters were crowded and the nursery inadequate for their growing brood. The palace reeked of fecal fumes: the brick floor of the kitchen was the roof of the sewer that gurgled beneath the larder and ovens. The toilet on the floor above the queen's dressing room often overflowed in front of the window. After dozens of cesspools overflowing with sewage were discovered underneath the floors at Windsor Castle in 1844, Albert replaced all the old Hanoverian commodes with modern flushing water closets.

In the first year of Victoria's reign, a commissioner of the Department of Woods and Works inspected Buckingham Palace after complaints of bad smells and declared the lower floors to be squalid and uninhabitable. In the kitchen, he found "the remains of garden stuff and everything else the most filthy and offensive." The roofs leaked and the drains had holes in them, yet little was done. Three years later, Albert asked Stockmar to help him conduct another, more comprehensive review. They found an archaic and extraordinarily inefficient structure, with responsibility split between the Lord Chamberlain and Lord Steward, with some input from the Master of the Horse and the Office of Woods and Works. Lamps in Buckingham Palace were provided by the Lord Chamberlain's office, cleaned by the Lord Steward's office, and, mostly, lit by the Master of the Horse. The windows were always dirty, as the inside and outside were never cleaned at the same time: while the Lord Chamberlain's office was responsible for the interior of the palace, the Office of Woods and Works was in charge of the exterior. The Lord Steward's staff prepared and laid the fires, while the Lord Chamberlain's lit them. Broken windows and cupboards were unattended to for months because before fixing them, the chief cook had to prepare and sign a requisition, which then needed to be signed by the Master of the Household, authorized by the Lord Chamberlain's Office, and given to the Clerk of the Works, under the Office of Woods and Forests. Albert appointed one officer to live in the palace and represent all three departments.

Next were the servants. Up to two-thirds of palace servants were unsupervised at any given time, so they did much as they pleased, disappearing at will. The staff was known for rudeness. Rarely was anyone available to show guests to their rooms; many got lost in the labyrinthine corridors. Albert identified a series of scams and perks that servants had abused for decades: people outside the palace often forged the signatures of the queen's ladies when ordering carriages, charging the cost of their ride to the royal household; fresh candles were put out each day while the footmen pocketed the previous day's, many unlit; and expensive staff dinners were offered to those with only tenuous connections to the royal court. Albert slashed salaries, sometimes by as much as two-thirds, to account for the fact that many servants worked in the palace for only half the year.

Last on Albert's agenda was what he called the "moral dignity of the Court." The gambling tables disappeared from Windsor. No one was allowed to sit down in the queen's presence—or in Albert's. (The wife of Lord John Russell—who was later prime minister—was allowed to rest in a chair after she had just given birth, "but the Queen took care when the Prince joined the company to have a very fat lady standing in front of [her].") Ministers had to back out of the room when visiting the queen, as it was considered poor etiquette to show a monarch your backside. Court dress was obligatory. (If a woman did not want to wear the appropriate styles she needed to get a doctor's certificate explaining how it would be injurious to her health, and then seek permission from the Lord Chamberlain's department.) Punishment was given for "dishonest and sexually loose behavior." A strict new code of conduct was carefully framed and hung in the bedrooms of maids of honor. Victoria's name has long been associated with the puritanism Albert championed in her court, but he, not she, was the true advocate of these standards. Melbourne quickly realized that while Victoria "did not much care about such niceties of moral choice," Albert was "extremely strait-laced." The prince insisted on "spotless character," while the queen did not care "a straw about it." No one was exempt from Albert's standards. Even his own brother had been a cause of fury due to his sexual licentiousness that had resulted in severe "visitations" of venereal disease. Yet Victoria would do little to stem her husband's fervor; the Albert era, at least inside the palace, had begun.

Meanwhile, the political sphere was fizzing with speculation about when Lord Melbourne's increasingly unpopular Whig government would be ousted by Sir Robert Peel's Tories. Ever prepared, Albert had begun secret negotiations with Peel, sending his secretary, Anson, to try to forge a deal that would avoid the embarrassment of the Bedchamber Crisis, in which Victoria had stymied Robert Peel because of her fondness for Melbourne. Albert also maneuvered himself into discussions with Melbourne, communicating to the PM that he did not believe a pregnant Victoria (she was expecting their second child) was able to cope or "go through difficulties" herself, and that he wanted the prime minister to include him in any conversations with the queen on the matter.

On May 9, 1841, Anson met with Peel to discuss the ladies in Victoria's household. On Albert's behalf, Anson offered the resignations of three senior ladies-in-waiting whose husbands were prominent Whigs, and thus allies of the outgoing Melbourne: the Duchess of Sutherland, the Duchess of Bedford, and Lady Normanby. Peel, after many protestations that his greatest aim was to protect the dignity and feelings of the queen, accepted. He also asked that Victoria formally notify him that those three positions were vacant. The change should come from her and not be seen as a condition of Peel's forming a government.

After the previous debacle, Peel was extremely grateful for Albert's diplomatic intervention. In a twenty-seven-page memorandum, stored in the archives of the British Library, Peel's excitement, ill-concealed triumph, and gratitude are evident, as is his anxiety that nothing be interpreted as a slight to the queen. The men openly acknowledged Albert's intellectual superiority to the queen, Anson quoting the prince, who said that the queen had a "natural modesty upon her constitutional views" and was likely to accept the arguments of men more experienced than she was. There was some truth to this—Melbourne advised his successor to write fully to the young queen, and "*elementarily,* as Her Majesty always liked to have full knowledge upon everything which was going on."

Most historians have assumed that Victoria, then in the second trimester of her second pregnancy, went happily along with the arrangement her husband made without asking her. But the change

in prime ministers—facilitated by her husband behind her back—
was a trying time for her. In the first week of May, she and Melbourne talked about the need to resolve the question of her ladies
before she sent for Peel. While they were still discussing it, Albert
acted without consulting her, offering Peel the resigations of the
three Whig ladies. Victoria was surprised, writing on May 9: "My
kind excellent Ld Melbourne told me that Anson had seen Peel
(which I had no idea of, but which of course Albert must have
known)." The aside is significant—why had her husband not told
her? At the end of the day, she wrote, she "felt very low." That
night, she had nightmares about losing Melbourne and woke up
exhausted and depressed, writing: "Oh! if only it were a dream!"
Every time she thought of the prospect of losing her dear Lord Melbourne again, Victoria felt like crying. She told Leopold it was
"very, very painful" but she was determined to be philosophical, especially now that she had Albert. After reading through the Anson-
Peel memoranda from May 1841 closely, she added one caveat: Peel
must understand that the queen was the one who appointed her
ladies, not him. She insisted on this as a *"principle,"* underlining it
emphatically. Peel agreed.

Victoria was torn between political expediency and loyalty. A few
weeks later, she worried that she had capitulated to Peel too easily.
Albert said her ladies were influencing her; Victoria cried for some
time and admitted that the family of the Duchess of Bedford—who
had not wanted to go—had left a letter for her. Anson wrote: "The
Queen was the whole day much depressed and said it weighed heavily on her mind and felt she had been hurried and compromised by
the Prince and Lord Melbourne." She knew that she now effectively
had no choice but to do as her husband suggested.

Victoria was often uneasy about what she felt was an abdication of
her role to Albert. When Lord Melbourne told her that her husband
had met with a triumphant reception at an event, she responded, "I
don't like it—first of all because I don't like his being absent from me,
and then because I dislike his taking my part in politics or in the gen-

eral affairs of the country." But Albert was politically dexterous. He and Anson were wooing current and future prime ministers and arranging meetings behind Victoria's back. On May 15, Albert was in the room when Melbourne arrived to meet with Victoria; this time, he stayed.

In June, when Melbourne's government lost a debate on foreign sugar duties, Peel forced a vote of no confidence and Parliament was dissolved. Victoria was glum, but an aging Melbourne was philosophical: "Why, nobody *likes* going out but I'm not well—I am a good deal tired, and it will be a great rest for me." Victoria overtly displayed her bias by visiting influential Whig houses during the elections, but to little effect. The Conservatives returned with a large majority on August 19. For the first time, the queen did not go to the opening session.

Nine days later, Melbourne was finally forced to resign. He and his queen said goodbye a few hours after their last official audience, "in the starlight" on the Windsor terrace. The queen wept. Melbourne told her tenderly, "For four years I have seen you daily and liked it better every day." When they said a final farewell at Claremont four days later, she sobbed. Victoria was much more amenable to Peel than she had been two years ago, but she still told Melbourne she was "dreadfully affected" at parting with him. Her journal is full of descriptions of how "wretched" she felt, of her "heavy heart" and "melancholy presentiments." She was accustomed to seeing him every day; before this, the longest she had gone without seeing him was eleven days. A month later, she was still struggling with the change, spending far less time with the new PM than she had with Lord Melbourne. The queen's correspondence with Peel was cooler and more businesslike; the affection had instantly drained from the relationship.

Albert was ready to work. He and Peel had much in common: shyness, an inclination for intellectual conversation, a love of art and literature—especially German writers and Dutch painters—and a commitment to social reform (though not to increasing the number of those eligible to vote, as Peel had opposed the 1832 Reform Bill). Albert even managed to persuade Peel to accept his veto of official appointments on the grounds of dubious moral behavior, including that of the surprised Duke of Beaufort. (When the duke's wife died, he had married her half sister, which was prohibited by Church of England canon law.) Curiously, Peel agreed.

England's new leader was a brilliant man, who had excelled at classics and mathematics at Christ Church, Oxford, entered Parliament when he was only twenty-one, and been appointed home secretary thirteen years later. When in the Home Office, Peel had established the Metropolitan Police Force, called "bobbies" after him ever since. He was earnestly committed to ensuring workers were protected and campaigned for many years to repeal the Corn Laws, the tax on imported wheat that protected local landlords and pushed up the price of bread, causing much misery among the working classes and unemployed. He was the first prime minister to grapple seriously with the urgent challenges of the burgeoning population, Industrial Revolution, and recession. But he was never particularly well liked, partly because he was reserved and awkward. Lord Ashley described him as "an iceberg with a slight thaw on the surface." Greville called him "vulgar," "more like a dapper shopkeeper than a Prime Minister," who cut jellies with a knife. Victoria liked to be charmed, and Peel was incapable of it. His smile had been likened to the gleam on the silver plate of a coffin lid. They had little to say to each other, and she was irritated by his manner of "a dancing master giving a lesson." She would like him better, Greville observed, "if he could keep his legs still."

It was a hot summer, and the pregnant Victoria suffered constant headaches. She had lost her beloved prime minister, fought with her husband, and fretted over the health of her fussy baby daughter. She was often depressed, telling Leopold that her "present heavy trial, the heaviest I have ever had to endure," of losing daily contact with Melbourne, was "a sad heartbreaking." At the end of August, Melbourne wrote urging her "to pick up [her] spirits."

Albert, usually more prone to melancholy than his wife, was buoyant and upbeat. Everything was unfolding as he had hoped. He was extremely pleased by the timing of Melbourne's exit, which allowed him to become the queen's sole confidant. He told Anson to remind Melbourne that "his view had always been that from this moment [he] would take up a new position, and that the Queen, no longer having Lord Melbourne to resort to in case of need, must from this moment consult and advise with [him]." Albert was also canny in persuading Victoria's most trusted allies to speak in his favor. He asked Anson to tell Melbourne to "urge the Queen to have no scruple in employing the Prince."

Melbourne agreed that Albert should naturally step into his place, but he warned him not to alarm Victoria by making her think "the Prince was carrying on business with Peel without her cognizance." Melbourne then dutifully wrote the queen a letter praising Albert and nominating him—not Peel—as his true replacement, praising his "judgment, temper and discretion."

As Melbourne's dominance faded and Albert came to the fore, Victoria began to recognize a new source of comfort in her life. She now knew love: a love that was safe, deepening, and enduring. Looking back as a wife and mother, she was embarrassed by the way she had behaved when infatuated with Lord Melbourne. She wrote in her diary on October 1, 1842: "Looked over & corrected one of my old journals, which do not now awake very pleasant feelings. The life I led then was so artificial & superficial, & yet I thought I was happy. Thank God! I *know what* REAL happiness means!"

This realization followed her for months; "real happiness" was a major milestone as she matured and bloomed in her marriage. In December 1842, Victoria talked to Albert about what had been her "unbounded affection and admiration of Ld. Melbourne." She said she did not really know where it came from, "excepting the fact that

I clung to someone, and having very warm feelings." Albert told her she had "worked [her]self up to what really became at last, quite foolish." Albert was perhaps too sensible to have ever worked himself up into anything foolish, but he was too dismissive of his wife's feelings. Melbourne had made Victoria feel safe in her vulnerable first years as queen, and her affection for him was genuine, and reciprocated. It was painful to say goodbye.

Lord Melbourne became a somewhat sad and lonely figure in his decline. He gazed wistfully at the palace as he rode by, and waited for letters from Victoria in the years after his resignation. He hoped he might be called back to Parliament in 1846, but the queen told him she had refrained for the sake of his health. He wrote to Victoria when he heard she had postnatal depression, saying he, too, had been depressed: "I know how difficult it is to fight against it." His biographer David Cecil says Melbourne longed for the queen. His days with Victoria had been the happiest and most fulfilling of his life—she had adored and needed him. When her name was mentioned, his eyes welled with tears.

The queen still sent Melbourne letters and presents and lent him money, but her attention was divided; at a ball in April 1842, there was such a long queue of people waiting to say goodbye to her that Melbourne slipped out into his carriage, downcast. He wrote to her the next day, telling her that as he drove past the palace he could see into her room, "so as to be able to distinguish the pictures, tables, etc., the candles being lighted and the curtains not drawn. Your Majesty was just setting off for the Opera." He suffered a stroke soon after, and died in 1848.

Baroness Lehzen and Albert clashed repeatedly as she tried to protect her territory and he tried to expand his. Stockmar told Lord Granville that Lehzen was "foolish" to contest Albert's influence, and not to recognize that her position was different now that Victoria was married. Even Leopold, once a friend, described her as a "great future danger" for Albert.

The men of the court began to scrutinize and circle her. In December 1840, when Anson returned from a ten-day trip, he fumed that Lehzen had "meddled and made mischief wherever she has had the opportunity since I left." While Melbourne assured him that Victoria's love for Albert could not be diminished by Lehzen's interference, Anson was not sure: "She was always in the Queen's path, pointing and exaggerating every little fault of the Prince, constantly misrepresenting him, constantly trying to undermine him in the Queen's affections." There is little evidence Lehzen actually did this—she had previously praised Albert as "such a good and humble-minded person"—but it is clear she stiffened Victoria's resolve to retain her prerogatives. John Conroy had schooled Lehzen, and her instincts were to protect the queen. It was important that Albert recognize, she said, that "the Queen would brook no interference with the exercise of her powers of which she was *most jealous*." Here was the heart of the dispute: the fight over the powers of the queen.

The hostility soon spilled into public view. When Albert told Lehzen to leave the palace in 1842—something, she retorted, that he had no right to do—she stopped talking to him. Lehzen resented Albert's trying to change things she and Victoria had agreed upon. Albert thought she was rude, disrespectful, and hungry for power—and had been promoted above her rank. He was livid when he found Lehzen, a commoner and staffer, holding Pussy on her lap—sitting down—in the nursery. (Even wet nurses were advised to breastfeed standing up out of respect for their infant royal charges.) When she neglected to tell Albert that Captain Childers, one of the queen's courtiers, had fallen in love with the queen, he accused her of incompetence. Lehzen insisted she had told the Lord Chamberlain instead of Albert only because Albert had been so rude to her that it was impossible to talk to him.

When a woman like Lehzen threatened Albert's authority, he became unusually nasty. She was generally viewed, as Albert's biographer Roger Fulford put it, as a "spinster gremlin." Albert referred to her as *die Blaste*—the hag—in letters to his brother. When she got jaundice that Christmas, he called her "the Yellow lady." Albert blamed her for Victoria's shortcomings: what he believed to be a substandard education—even though she was a better linguist, fluent in English, German, and French, with some Italian—and her anxiety about conversations with scholars and politicians much older than she. He was particularly critical of Victoria in the months before Lehzen left, but once she was gone, Albert described her to his brother as "the most perfect companion a man could wish for."

Lehzen was jealous of Albert, but she was not the gremlin of his imagination. Lord Holland praised her as having "sense and information, great judgment and yet greater strength of mind." The acerbic Greville described her as a "clever agreeable woman" who was "much beloved by the women and much esteemed and liked by all who frequent the Court." Georgiana Bloomfield, a lady-in-waiting, said she was a "kind and motherly" figure to the women in the court, especially the younger ones. Likewise, Lady Lyttelton thought she was kind, helpful, and devoted. But Albert would not stand any rivals in Victoria's affections, and instead of accommodating his ambitions, Lehzen fought them, just as she had fought Victoria's mother and Conroy years ago. She was punished for standing up for her queen.

During Victoria's second pregnancy, the queen's ladies marveled at her robust health. But in truth the young mother was feeling unwell, "wretched," "low and depressed." She had not wanted to have another child so quickly and deeply resented the limitations on her life—as though her "wings were clipped." She grew less interested in her work, and frequently erupted in tantrums.

On November 9, 1841, a fat, healthy baby was born. Victoria was thrilled it was a boy, but felt low after a torturous birth. She wrote in her journal:

> I will not say much, but my sufferings were really very severe and I doubt that I should have died but for the great comfort and support of my beloved Albert. . . . At last at 12 m[inutes] to

11 I gave birth to a fine, large boy! Oh, how happy, how grateful did I feel that Almighty Providence has so greatly blessed me and preserved me so mercifully through so many days and trials. Though tired I felt very well once the child was there.

Albert gave her a jeweled brooch featuring the crest of their son; she then fell into a deep sleep for the rest of the day, relieved, again, that she had not died. But Victoria felt nothing for him when she held him in her arms; no love, or even affection. She would suffer from postnatal depression for a year. Throughout November, Albert continued to lift her from bed to chair. She felt weak and depressed and had trouble sleeping. Members of her household watched her nervously, suspicious that her grandfather's madness would eventually emerge and overwhelm her.

It took many months for Victoria to shake her sadness, one she found inexplicable, as Albert made her so happy. Her nerves "were so battered," she told Leopold in April 1843, that "I suffered a *whole year* from it." She later told her eldest daughter that the problem was having two children in such quick succession: "Bertie and I both suffered and the former will ever suffer from coming so soon after you." As the first boy, Albert Edward—later Edward VII—was born to be king, but his older sister would always be smarter, prettier, and more loved.

On January 16, 1842, Albert and Victoria drove as fast as they could back to Windsor from Claremont. They had spent a short break at Leopold's English estate in an attempt to cure Victoria's melancholia, but had been summoned back early because Pussy, whose health had been poor for months, was getting worse. Albert had long blamed Lehzen for problems in the nursery, but when his infant daughter grew ill, he was anxious and angry. Pussy became weak and unsettled when she was just a few months old, and neither Lehzen nor the wet nurse was able to soothe or fatten her. The queen wrote: "'Til the end of August she was such a magnificent, strong fat child, that it is a great grief to see her so thin, pale and changed." Dr. Clark gave her ass's milk and chicken broth with cream, which she was unable to keep down, as well as mercury-laced calomel, and the appetite-suppressing laudanum. The birth of a little brother, the boy her parents had longed for, only made little Pussy worse. The day after he was born, Victoria wrote: "Saw both children, Pussy terrified and not at all pleased with her little brother."

They were silent for much of the trip: so many children died before even learning to walk. When the coach pulled in to the rectangular courtyard at Windsor, they ran up the stairs to the nursery. There, they were shocked at the sight of a thin, hollow-eyed Pussy, who nonetheless beamed and gurgled at them. Albert said something in anger, which prompted the nurse to respond aggressively. He turned to Victoria and muttered, "That really is malicious." Victoria erupted, upset: did he want her, the mother, out of the nursery?

Both lost their tempers: Albert told Victoria she had an irrational infatuation with Lehzen, and said the pair of them had neglected their child—did they want to kill her? Victoria in turn accused him of wanting to control everything, including the nursery; of being jealous of her position, of her treasured friendship with Lehzen; of thinking the worst of her; of not allowing her to make her own decisions. After taking over much of her ceremonial role, she was incensed that Albert now wanted to control the care of their babies too. The months of subterranean tension had finally erupted. She was sorry, Victoria shouted, that she had ever married him.

Albert was infuriated and appalled by such a public scene. Muttering "I must have patience," he returned to his rooms and refused to talk to Victoria for days. Stockmar acted as an intermediary. Victoria wrote to him that same day, immediately contrite, saying the argument was like a bad dream. She wanted him to tell Lehzen there had been a "little misunderstanding," to calm Albert and say the queen was too upset to see anyone. Still recovering from Bertie's difficult labor just a few weeks earlier, she could not stop crying. "I feel so forlorn and I have got *such* a sick headache! I feel as if I had had a dreadful dream. I do hope you may be able to pacify Albert. He seems so very angry still. I am *not*."

He was. Albert was not going to temper his words anymore. He would force the queen to choose between her husband and her governess. He wrote to Stockmar:

> Lehzen is a crazy, common, stupid intriguer, obsessed with lust of power, now regards herself as a demi-god, and anyone who refuses to acknowledge her as such, as a criminal. . . . I on the other hand regard Victoria as naturally a fine character but warped in many respects by wrong upbringing. . . . There can be no improvement till Victoria sees Lehzen as she is, and I pray that this come.

Victoria's passionate fits came and went, but Albert's anger was white, cold, and enduring. He was willing to inflict pain on his wife. He wrote to her, in icy tones, a couple of days later: "Doctor Clark has mismanaged the child and poisoned her with calomel and you have starved her. I shall have nothing more to do with it; take the child away and do as you like and if she dies you will have it on your conscience." Victoria told Albert that she forgave him his "thoughtless words" and asked him to tell her if he was worried about something. But Albert stormed in a letter to Stockmar: "Victoria is too hasty and passionate for me to be able often to speak of my difficulties. She will not hear me out but flies into a rage and overwhelms me with reproaches of suspiciousness, want of trust, ambition, envy, &c, &c."

The men were in agreement: the queen must surrender. Stockmar wrote a confidential note to Victoria threatening to resign if such scenes recurred. The queen wrote back quickly: "Albert must tell me what he dislikes, & I will set about to remedy it, but he must also *promise* to listen to & believe me; when (on the contrary) I am in a passion which I trust I am not very often in now, he must not believe the stupid things I say like being miserable I ever married & so forth which come when I am unwell."

Victoria accepted that she had faults. She had been having these outbursts—which Albert called "combustibles"—ever since she was a child. But Albert seemed unable to accept that occasionally she needed to vent or storm. Instead he rebuked her and urged her to train her emotions: a Sisyphean task.

Victoria continued to defend Lehzen. She reasonably pointed out that she wanted to look after her former governess out of kindness and loyalty, and to keep her in the house as a reward for a lifetime of service. She acknowledged, though, that their position was "very different to any other married couples" because "A. is in my house and not I in his," but, ultimately, that she would submit to him because she loved him. She promised to try to tame her temper, writing on January 20, 1842:

> There is often an irritability in me which (like Sunday last which began the whole misery) makes me say cross & odious things which I don't believe myself & which I fear hurt A. but which he should not believe, but I will strive to conquer it though I knew *before* I married that this would be a trouble; I therefore wished *not* to marry, as the two years and a half, when I was so completely my own mistress made it difficult for me to control myself & to bend to another's will, but I trust I shall be able to conquer it.

Three months later, Lady Lyttelton was appointed governess. She was the perfect choice: sweet, competent, old-fashioned, and mild-mannered. The children adored her and she pleased both the prince, whom she deeply admired, and the queen, whose "vein of iron" she recognized instantly. It was agreed that Pussy had simply been fussed over too much, and that the doctors did little good.

———

On July 25, without consulting his wife, Albert fired Lehzen. He then lied to Victoria, telling her that Lehzen wanted to go back to Germany for the sake of her health. She would be out of the palace in two months. He added that he approved of this. That night, Victoria wrote in her journal: "Naturally I was rather upset, though I feel sure it is for our and her best."

Ever conscious of protecting Victoria, Lehzen was cheerful and comforting when an agitated queen walked into her room. She repeated Albert's line, "saying she felt it was necessary for her health to go away, for of course, I did not require her so much now, & would find others to help me." Victoria left the room, momentarily relieved. As she later sat next to her husband, playing a duet on the piano, she fought a desire to cry. It was done. Albert had willed it. She wrote in her journal: "Felt rather bewildered & low, at what had taken place, & naturally the thought of the coming separation from my dear Lehzen, whom I love so much, made me feel very sad."

On the night of September 29, 1842, Victoria dreamed of Lehzen. This was the woman who had smiled at her in Westminster Abbey when the heavy crown of England was placed on her head, who had given her strength when John Conroy had tried to usurp her power, who had held cold cloths to her brow to calm the fever that almost took her life at fifteen. The woman who had been closer to her than her mother. She dreamed that Lehzen had come into her room to say goodbye, embracing her with her usual tenderness. Victoria woke choked with grief: "It was very painful to me. . . . I had heard it mentioned before—that odd feeling on waking—but I had no experience of it. It is very unpleasant."

Downstairs, the baroness was buttoning her jacket. She stooped to take the last of her bags down to a coach waiting in the courtyard of Windsor Castle. The sky was whitening; she hurried down the stairs. She did not want to disturb Victoria, as she knew they would both struggle to maintain composure. Over breakfast that morning, Victoria received a letter from her "in which she took leave of me in writing, thinking it would be less painful than seeing me. This naturally upset me, & I so regret not being able to embrace her once more. . . . I can never forget that she was for many years *everything* to me."

With great dignity, the baroness returned to Germany to live with her sister, who died only a few months later. Lehzen lived alone for the rest of her life, supported by the generous annual pension Victoria provided. Her devotion to the queen never faltered. In 1858, she stood for hours on the platform of Bückeburg station waiting for a train bearing Victoria and Albert, who were on their way to visit the newly married Vicky. As the carriages rolled through the station without stopping, Lehzen stood there waving a handkerchief, trying to catch a glimpse of Victoria.

Lehzen had been the brace that steeled Victoria's spine as it grew; she was enormously proud of her. Victoria visited her one last time, in 1866, after Albert died, at Reinhardtsbrunn. They hugged each other and cried; Victoria knew that Lehzen, though now frail, would understand the magnitude of her grief. Lehzen spoke constantly about her queen in her last months, when her mind was wandering and she was confined to her bed with a hip fracture. She died in 1870, at the age of eighty-five. Victoria ruled for another three decades.

By the end of 1842, Albert's rivals were gone. Melbourne had resigned and Lehzen was exiled to Germany. Albert had the keys to Victoria's boxes, control of her finances (from both the civil list and private estates), and access to her ministers. By now he was not simply representing but overshadowing the queen. In his role as private secretary—the position John Conroy had coveted—he drafted letters, read state papers, advised the queen on every matter, and dominated meetings. With Peel, he prepared to do the work of a king: an unusually active, disciplined, and competent king. He was ready to start the real work on the "higher and graver things."

There was much to do. The issues that concerned Albert most were army reform, education (especially science and geology), slavery, working conditions, and foreign relations, most particularly the relationships with Germany and France. He cared deeply about music, art, housing, and architecture. He took up an official role in groups including the Royal Agricultural Society, the Philharmonic Society, the British Association, the Society for Improving the Condition of the Laboring Classes, the Statistical Congress of All Nations Conference, the National Education Conference, the Dublin Exhibition, the Great Exhibition, the Society of the Arts, the Society for the Extinction of Slavery, and the Royal Commission for Fine Arts (the latter in connection with the building of the new Houses of Parliament). He worked late into the night and rose early so he might have time to labor on his special projects. Albert was an inordinately driven man, and happily for Britain, his work would soon be put to transformative uses.

Albert also ensured that the Christmas of 1841 was delightful. He imported pine trees from Coburg—popularizing the Christmas tree tradition, though they were hung from the ceiling as well as being placed on the floor as they are today—and they skated, built snowmen, and rode sledges across crunchy snow. Victoria could hardly believe she had two children, a one-year-old daughter and a two-month-old son, and such a *gemütlich,* or cozy, domestic life. On Boxing Day, from Windsor Castle, Anson reported with satisfaction that the queen "interests herself less and less about politics" and was a "good deal preoccupied with the little Princess Royal."

Albert, in turn, became more and more preoccupied with politics. Across the Channel, Europe was simmering with revolutionary zeal. The British royals seemed remarkably immune to the threat of the guillotine for now, but there was no telling how quickly the wind could shift. The prince had fought for his place as man of the house, ensured the hedges were properly trimmed and the palace cleaned, the queen's closest friends sidelined or sacked. He now turned his attention to the state of England and the survival of the British monarchy. Albert was determined to usher in a new era: one of a noble, nonpartisan, unbiased monarchy. He was also determined not to make the same mistakes as his wife. He would rule without favor. And he would no longer be mocked as a compliant, docile spouse; his mastery over his wife would be recognized and respected. The Albert epoch had begun.

CHAPTER 14

King to All Intents:
"Like a Vulture into His Prey"

He is become so identified with her that they are one person, and as he likes and she dislikes business, it is obvious that while she has the title he is really discharging the functions of the Sovereign. He is King to all intents and purposes.

—CHARLES GREVILLE, DECEMBER 16, 1845

In the mid-1800s, the month of January was often the worst for those scraping a living from the streets of London. The summer stench of manure, tobacco, rotting fish, unwashed bodies, tanneries, chemical works, coal fires, and the cesspools beneath houses was replaced by a gnawing cold. The air grew bitter after the sun sank into a pale sky. Emaciated cats scavenged for food, and "pure-hunters" trawled the sewers for nails, coins, or bits of rope in the dark, often fending off large rats. The cold stiffened the limbs of corpses often left in gutters and narrow alleys for want of graveyards: young women who died in childbirth, men who froze in their sleep, skeletal babies with mysterious diseases. The cold also whistled through window cracks of tiny rooms where families huddled together for warmth. And in the enormous and poorly heated Buckingham Palace, the same cold forced Prince Albert to wear long johns to bed and a wig to breakfast. In London, the soot fell in flakes like snow, leaving a grimy black patina on hats, roofs, and upturned faces. The German prince longed for the crisp clean air of the country.

On the afternoon of January 27, 1846, as the royal carriage pulled up outside the Palace of Westminster, the sun was a pale pink smudge behind a forest of chimneys. A large, excitable crowd had gathered to watch members of Parliament walk past in their top hats and tailored frock coats. They shouted out the names of those they recognized. One man sold veal and eel pies; another was roasting chestnuts on the street corner. A woman hawking pork sausage clambered over the litter piled up in the gutter. A boy of about twelve, dressed in red, darted behind carriages to scoop up horse manure, placing it in a bucket by the side of the road; it would later be sold to farms and nursery gardens outside London. A crowd of children barely dressed in dirty rags chased a mangy dog down the street.

Prince Albert was coming to Parliament that day to support his friend the prime minister, Sir Robert Peel, during what was to be the defining political debate of Peel's career. Peel, the son of an industrialist, had come to believe that the tariffs placed on a range of foreign goods were hindering free trade and economic growth and unfairly pushing up costs for ordinary British citizens. Landowners, who were strongly supported by most Tories, argued that removing the tariffs—or "Corn Laws"—would ruin them. Peel spurned the wishes of his party as he advocated for their total repeal over the next three years. It was both political courage and career suicide. Victoria and Albert admired Peel's stand, and had decided to support him after he sent series of memos on the Corn Laws to Albert. The hardworking Victoria shared Peel's disdain for idle and privileged lords, writing in her journal in 1846:

[Peel] added that it made one impatient to see "gentlemen, who did nothing but hunt all day, drink Claret & Port Wine in the evening, & never studied or read about any of these questions, then proceed to lecture & interfere with the Ministers." It does make one more than impatient & when one thinks how Peel sacrifices his health, his comfort, his time, & even his Party connections, solely for the good of the country to be only rewarded by abuse & shameful ingratitude, it quite makes one's blood boil.

It was approaching 4:30 P.M. Police had lined the street since one o'clock, holding back the dense crowd, who noisily cheered any member of Parliament who opposed the Corn Laws. Inside Westminster, Peel walked into the House of Commons, bowed gracefully to the Speaker, and walked to the center of the Treasury Bench. He was self-assured and patrician: a tall, handsome man with fair hair and fine features, a long, thin nose, a high forehead, and dark, grave eyes. Observers described his manner as that of a banker or a "dapper shopkeeper." The crowd stared at him coldly, four hundred aristocrats in all, boots muddy from the day's hunt.

A hush descended when Prince Albert entered the Strangers' Gallery. Lord George Bentinck, a Tory with a passion for horse racing, rolled his eyes: Did this German prince really think he could bring royal favor into the debate? First it was the queen with Melbourne; now, Albert with Peel? It seemed highly irregular, and wrong, to have this interference from the monarchy. Even "moderate men," Disraeli later claimed, were bothered by his presence.

At 4:48 P.M., Peel rose, shook out his cuffs (a mannerism that particularly annoyed Victoria), cast a glance around the chamber, and began to speak. He did not stop for three hours. Albert rushed back to the palace afterward, as Victoria was heading to dinner, and reported that the speech had been "very comprehensive & excellent." The debate ground on over a series of late nights. In late February, Lord George Bentinck—who was the cousin of Privy Council clerk and diarist Charles Greville—rose to his feet and poured scorn on the prince in an electrifying speech. (His wrath would earn him the leadership of the protectionist Conservative Party in the House of Commons. This party formed when the Tory Party split in two over the Corn Laws—the free-trade Peelists went with the prime minister, while the others regrouped as the Conservatives.) Lord George Bentinck was a striking figure with a red-tinged beard, dressed in a long frock coat, a velvet waistcoat, and a sizable turquoise stone that bulged from a gold chain around his neck. Peel, he said, had abandoned the honor of the aristocrats. And Albert was guilty of "listening to ill advice" and allowing himself to be "seduced" by Peel to "come down in this House to usher in, to give éclat, and, as it were, by reflection from the Queen, to give the semblance of the personal sanction of Her Majesty to a measure which, be it for good or for evil, a great majority at least of the landed aristocracy of England, of Scotland, and of Ireland, imagine will be fraught with deep injury, if not ruin, to them."

Attending the debate was the prince's only overtly partisan action, and it was a mistake. The Tories had been suspicious of the throne since Victoria was crowned, and Albert, who wanted to be influential but neutral, had vowed to have no appearance of bias. In Theodore Martin's biography of Albert, commissioned by Victoria, the queen defended her husband: "The Prince merely went, as the Prince of Wales and the Queen's other sons do, for once to hear a fine debate, which is so useful to all princes. But this he naturally felt unable to do again."

By the time Parliament voted in March, the royal family was holidaying on the unspoiled Isle of Wight. Victoria was leaving the beach when a servant came running down, red-faced, with a box from Peel: the House of Commons had repealed the Corn Laws with a strong majority. Victoria stared at the letter, relieved. Albert viewed Peel as a kindred spirit and, eventually, like a second father. He wrote to Stockmar that the Tory leader "shows boundless courage, and is in the best spirits; his whole faculties are roused [*er fühlt sich*] by the consciousness, that he is at this moment playing one of the most important parts in the history of his country." (Repeal was not, it should be noted, an individual achievement. The Anti–Corn Law League, which came largely from the middle class, was a polished, well-funded, and unified political group. The group's leaders were clever orators and effective in placing aristocrats on the defensive by castigating them as wealthy landowners, inert politicians, and morally bankrupt leaders. Middle-class opinion was marshaled and aristocrats were criticized in a way they never had been before; it was a significant political shift.)

Robert Peel, who had inherited something of a mess, was a great contrast to Lord Melbourne, the last of the Georgian prime ministers, with his laissez-faire philosophy and marked immunity to the heaving, toiling energy of the age. Melbourne had been unmoved by the problems plaguing the country during the early years of Victoria's reign: economic depression, high unemployment, rampant crime, and poverty. After the inertia of Lord Melbourne, Peel led what was called a "real working government." In two years, he turned a deficit into a surplus despite cutting more than half the tariffs in his first budget in 1842. After 1845, wheat was the only primary product that was still heavily protected. He introduced an income tax of seven pennies on the pound for those who earned more than £150 per year—equivalent to a rate of 3 percent. (When Peel announced that the queen had agreed to have her income taxed, it caused a "very great sensation" in the House.) He reformed the banking system, regulated companies, and grappled with burgeoning complex issues spurred by industrialization and rapid urbanization. He knew the urgency of simmering public anger. The economic and political analyst Walter Bagehot said Peel was as "afraid of catching revolution as old women are of catching cold."

The mid-1840s in England were dominated by debates about two vegetables: potatoes and wheat. The devastating failure of the Irish potato crop in 1845, following a very wet summer and a blight that spread from America to Europe, finally gave the Corn Law debate some urgency. The artificially high prices that resulted from the tariff made grain too expensive for the Irish poor, and most of it was exported to England, removing a crucial alternative food source from the ravaged country. Peel argued that "the removal of impediments to import is the only effectual remedy." Victoria became increasingly worried about reports of the "extreme distress" of the Irish, who lacked dignity even in death, when their bodies were tossed into the ground without rites or coffins. She decided to limit palace bread rations to a pound per person per day.

The response of the British government to the tragedy in Ireland was appallingly inadequate. In the first phase of the famine, in 1845 and 1846, the British acted to set up a relief organization, invest in public works, and fund soup kitchens. They gave the Irish £7 million, which was merely one-tenth of the money raised for the Crimean War a few years later. But in 1847, as the famine worsened, their actions only aggravated the hardship: the Irish Poor Law Extension Act steered the impoverished away from handouts and into overcrowded workhouses where they labored under horrific conditions. Those who occupied more than a quarter acre of land were refused relief; many were forced to give up their holdings. No substantial attempts were made to remove the dependence on the potato, improve agriculture, or change the tenancy system. Staggeringly, food continued to be exported from Ireland to England during the famine years. Unfortunately, the repeal of the grain tariffs would do little to help the Irish.

The English had a deep, enduring belief in the importance of laissez-faire. The government was loath to intervene, ostensibly on the grounds that those suffering should be able to hoist themselves out of their misery and poverty without requiring aid. Kindness, it was feared, would corrupt them. There was also a profound and long-standing prejudice against the Irish in England. As the wry Anglican cleric Sidney Smith wrote: "The moment the very name of

Ireland is mentioned, the English seem to bid adieu to common feeling, common prudence and common sense, and to act with the barbarity of tyrants and the fatuity of idiots." The young queen was not immune to these feelings. She swung from anger at the landlords for taking wheat rations for themselves to disgust at the Irish who murdered those landlords. When hearing of the murder of one man as he was driving home in his carriage, she wrote: "Really they are a terrible people, & there is no civilized country anywhere, which is in such a dreadful state, & where such crimes are perpetrated! It is a constant source of anxiety & annoyance." She did not visit Ireland until 1849, twelve years into her reign.

In the 1840s, political attention was turning, in general, to the way the working class lived and worked. In May 1842, the first parliamentary report on the employment of children was accompanied by shocking illustrations of six-year-olds chained to coal carts. According to the report, the youngest children employed were responsible for ventilating the mines, keeping the trapdoors shut until a coal car needed to pass through, then opening and shutting them correctly. These children, called trappers, were aged between four and ten. The *Examiner* reported that what they hated most was the dark in the dungeons: they used to beg colliers for candle stubs. Women and older children were put to use drawing the coal carts along passageways too narrow for grown men. They crawled along the ground like animals through puddles and piles of rocks. The girls sometimes worked stripped to the waist like the boys, men often went naked in the intense heat, and rape and sexual assault were common in the mines and pits. There were concerns that women who worked there would no longer be suitable for marriage.

These stories stoked the public imagination and provided impetus for change, which only occurred incrementally, against great resistance. The Coal Mines Act of 1842 made employment of all females and boys under ten under the ground illegal, and ensured that inspectors would enforce the law. The Factory Act of 1844 limited the working day for those in textile factories to six and a half hours for children between eight and thirteen, and twelve hours for women. In 1847, a bill was passed legislating a ten-hour working day. By the end of the decade, there had been a dramatic shift. By 1851, only 2 percent of children aged five to nine worked, and only a quarter of ten- to fourteen-year-olds. Over the course of Victoria's reign, the living conditions of most of her subjects improved considerably; more people voted, and more had basic protections at work. The modernizing of the country had truly begun.

Meanwhile, in that spring of 1842, Buckingham Palace was frantically preparing for a ball. On May 12, the fanciest, richest, and most decorated personages of England would gather dressed in costumes made from English silk as an expression of support for the impoverished silk weavers of the Spitalfields. It had been Albert's idea, and Victoria thrilled to it. For weeks, seamstresses labored over their costumes in Spitalfields; Victoria painted hers in her journal with watercolors.

The ball was a resounding success. Jewelers across London were emptied of diamonds. The queen wore a stunning gown lined with miniver, a silver surcoat embroidered with gold flowers, open hanging velvet sleeves, a velvet demi-train edged with fur, and armlets studded with precious gems. A gold crown crusted with jewels sat on her head. Albert wore a scarlet velvet cloak lined with ermine and edged with twelve hundred pearls and gold lace. A brooch fastening his cloak sparkled with diamonds, emeralds, rubies, topazes, and other precious gems. Under this was a robe of gold and blue brocade slashed with diamond-studded royal blue velvet. His sword hilt was also covered in diamonds. Victoria's crown kept slipping, and her heels made dancing difficult, but she declared that the night could not have gone better: Never did England display its "supremacy in female beauty" more decidedly than on this night, wrote *The Illustrated London News*. The queen danced until 2:45 A.M.

The contrast could not be starker: the bejeweled aristocrats sparkling under candelabra and the children working all day in darkness, begging for candle stubs. This was a time when the opulence of the royal court was considered a subject of pride, a symbol of English might and wealth. The reaction to this ball, however, revealed the rising temperature of resentment toward the wealthy. The *Odd Fellow,* a satirical working-class paper, wrote: "A number of benevolent peers and peeresses have resolved to disguise themselves as starving weavers, in order to give her Majesty some faint idea of the extensive misery now existed. When this group enter[s], her Majesty will be deeply affected, and the newspapers will have observed next morning that she shed tears."

The scorn was palpable. The *Northern Star* compared Victoria to Nero, playing a violin as the flames devoured the city. Using money wrung from the poor by their monopoly of the market, the aristocrats were renting diamonds and feasting to excess in a "childish display of the waste of thousands." Victoria meant well with the Spitalfields ball, and briefly the weavers were overwhelmed with work, but this was short-lived. The decline of the industry was inevitable.

At a time when most working-class people lived in misery, Victoria was more readily stirred by compassion for individuals she met than by reform movements. She worried about whether widowed women had enough money to live on and whether dwarves who performed for her were well treated. She worried about the well-being of orphans, wounded military veterans, and victims of sexual assault. When she saw how "lonely" child offenders jailed on the Isle of Wight spent months in solitary confinement, she was troubled by their sad existence. (Always aesthetically tuned, she also puzzled over how unattractive they were, "really frightful" looking.) She asked that "the most deserving boy" in each ward be pardoned. But when Lord Shaftesbury—an aristocratic politician who campaigned for two decades for the rights of the working poor—introduced an amendment to a bill to cut working hours to ten a day, she opposed it, agreeing with Peel that it would cripple economic productivity. While Albert labored over plans to lift people out of poverty and to

improve the housing of the working class, Victoria needed more vi-
sual, immediate, individual prompting.

Despite his obvious good grace, Albert still struggled to be fully accepted in England. Victoria was infuriated by the continuing hostility
from her family toward her husband. Her uncles were often jostling
for precedence, insisting they be placed before the German prince,
which led to farcical situations in which Victoria and Albert were
physically shoving them out of the way at formal events. At a wedding in July 1843, Albert, who had just recovered from a bout of the
flu, strongly pushed the king of Hanover (the Duke of Cumberland)
down the altar steps, and Victoria sprinted from one side of the altar
to the other so she could pass the pen to Albert after signing the register.

Victoria fretted that Albert's pride would be hurt. She was furious
when in Germany the king of Prussia snubbed Albert by placing an
Austrian archduke in the seat next to Victoria, thereby demonstrating his precedence. (It took years before she would agree to accept
any more hospitality from the Prussians.) In June 1842, she spoke to
Peel about "dear Albert's *awkward* & painful position, & its being so
strange that *no* provision had been made for the position of the
Queen's Consort, which I wished could be defined for futurity." She
had worried, she wrote, "that the position of a Prince Consort must
be painful and humiliating to any man," so much so "that at times I
almost felt it would have been fairer to him for me not to have married him. But he was so good & kind & had loved me for myself." She
tried but failed to have him formally recognized as King Consort.
Finally, in 1857, Victoria used her royal prerogative to make him
Prince Consort by Royal Letters Patent.

Albert's isolation became starker when his father died in January
1844. He had not seen him for four years. While Albert wept in private, he complained to Stockmar that they had "a great cold public
around us, insensible as stone." Duke Ernst had not been a perfect

father: he had betrayed Albert's mother, had plagued him for money, had tried to seduce the ladies of the royal court, and had been angry when Albert's first boy did not bear his name. But Albert had loved him, and he was devastated. Victoria shared her husband's distress, writing in her diary: "We shall not see his like again." Albert was "wretched & desolate, though comforted & happy in the intimate love we bear one another." Every time she stared at her husband, her eyes filled with tears.

Albert saw his father's death as a sign that he must now dedicate himself to the second part of his life, to his wife and growing family. His home was now England, more than ever. He no longer had a paternal home to return to, writing to his brother Ernest: "Our little children do not know why we cry and they ask us why we are in black; Victoria weeps with me, for me and for all of you. Let us take care of [our wives], let us love and protect them, as in them we shall find happiness again." The grief drew Albert and Victoria closer: "[Victoria] is the treasure on which my whole existence rests," Albert wrote. "The relation in which we stand to one another leaves nothing to desire. It is a union of heart and soul, and is therefore noble, and in it the poor children shall find their cradle, so as to be able one day to ensure a like happiness for themselves."

Albert, always practical, declared himself just a week later to have recovered from his father's passing. He was ready to "fortify [him]self by constant activity" and devote himself to his family. The prince returned to Germany to comfort his brother and arrange his father's affairs. This was the first time he had left Victoria since marrying, and letters he wrote to his "dear little wife" were full of sweet reassurance and love.

When Albert returned after the two-week separation, Victoria ran downstairs at the sound of his carriage. She was so excited she lay awake next to him for most of that night, watching him sleep, "agitated with joy and thankfulness."

The queen had much to be thankful for. Throughout the 1840s, she continued to lead a charmed life with her husband: her children were flourishing, they had found respite in Scotland and the Isle of Wight, and she was delighted by the coziness and warmth of their domesticity. She wrote glowingly in her journal about their children playing on the floor as she and Albert sat reading by lamplight. They went for long walks, played skittles, and drank cowslip tea. Late in 1843, she expressed regret at having to leave Buckingham Palace for another residence, but she knew she had nothing to complain about: "I have been so happy there—but *where* am I not happy *now*?"

Victoria gave birth to their third child in April 1843. The baby was named Princess Alice Maud Mary, but she was nicknamed Fatima, because she was such a chubby baby. Victoria was relieved to have survived another labor. Just two days later, she was bored: "It is rather dull lying quite still and doing nothing particularly in moments when one is alone." She was rolled in her bed to the sitting room, then in an armchair to dinner. She examined jewels that Indian princes sent as presents and waited for Albert to return to her side. Albert was busy adding to his list of responsibilities and hosting official receptions on the queen's behalf. While she was heavily pregnant with Alice, Victoria had agreed to see the Duke of Wellington, but Albert saw several other ministers for her, as she felt tired. Albert met with Peel and they decided that titles held by Victoria's "rather peculiar" uncle Sussex, who had died just days before Victoria gave birth to their third child, should now go to Albert: the office of Knight Great Master Order of the Bath and Governor of the Round Tower.

Soon Victoria became pregnant again with her fourth child. On August 6, 1844, she gave birth to a boy whom they named Alfred Ernest Albert. He was beautiful, with a thatch of long dark hair, blue eyes, and a big nose. The labor was grueling, and Victoria's suffering was "severe," but the joy of her "immense, healthy boy" erased the memory of the pain. Albert was once again with his wife throughout. As the family grew, Albert started planning for their future. At the christening of the boy they would call "Affie," Albert was already plotting the marriage of his four-year-old Vicky to the king of Prussia's twelve-year-old son. Albert's plan was for Bertie to be the future king, Affie to be the Duke of Coburg—if his brother did not produce any heirs—and Vicky to be a linchpin in Europe as the wife of the Prussian king. While Victoria and Albert could not possibly have foreseen the tectonic shifts in Europe over the next century, some of the alliances they made for their offspring would prove extremely difficult for England in later years, and heartbreaking for their children.

As Victoria produced four babies in the first five years of marriage, Albert took on ever broader responsibilities. Peel appointed him the chairman of the Arts Commission for rebuilding of Parliament, which oversaw the artworks to be installed in the new Parliament house after the Palace of Westminster burned down in 1834. He was also offered the chancellorship of Cambridge University, where he made an impressive, lasting contribution by modernizing and broadening the curriculum. Much of his time was also taken up with the remodeling of Osborne House, their family residence on the Isle of Wight, and Buckingham Palace throughout the 1840s. He added a farm, kennels, and a dairy to Windsor Castle and drew up designs for workers' dwellings. Stockmar attributed Albert's relentless, rapid development to "a practical talent, by means of which he in a moment seizes what is really important in any matter, and drives his talons into it, like a vulture into his prey; and flies off with it to his nest."

Albert's curiosity was rapacious. He studied his new country like a man cramming for an exam, poring over architectural plans, visiting art galleries, craning his neck inside the machines of factories he visited. He archived everything he could, including precious manuscripts held at Windsor such as the Leonardo da Vinci collection. Albert was in the fortunate position of being able to have many of his bold ideas implemented; he lobbied successfully to outlaw dueling, and he designed helmets for the army, cribs for the nursery, and model farms for his children. His pigs won first prize at agricultural fairs. Perhaps his greatest triumph was overcoming "all impertinent sneering" about his horsemanship, showing the British he could ride "boldly and hard." Victoria was disgusted that he had been criticized in the first place.

Albert's industry, thrift, prudery, religious devotion, and desire to harness the steaming activity of the century in many ways encapsulated the Victorian age better than Victoria did. It also made him a candidate for what we might today call burnout. Albert was driven but delicate. When the couple traveled on a train for the first time, a short trip from Slough to London in 1843, Albert suffered motion sickness and was unsettled by the speed of forty-four miles per hour. Victoria loved it: "I find the motion so very easy, far more so than a carriage and cannot understand how any one can suffer from it." Albert was a man surrounded by luxury and comfort, but he denied himself rest and allowed workaholism to undermine his health. Had he not, the century might have been better known as the Albertine age.

By 1845, Albert was effectively king. In December, Lord Lansdowne and Lord John Russell visited Windsor and were struck by his firm grasp of the crown:

> Formerly the Queen received her Ministers alone; with her alone they communicated, though of course Prince Albert knew everything; but now the Queen and Prince were together, received Lord L. and J.R. together, and both of them always said *We.* . . . It is obvious that while she has the title he is really discharging the functions of the Sovereign. He is King to all intents and purposes.

Victoria was then pregnant with her fifth child. She described her husband as a deputy who was smarter than she was; she was at times in awe of his abilities. The editors of Victoria's letters, Arthur Benson and Lord Esher, testified to how hard Albert worked and how palpable his assistance to the queen was. He arranged and annotated the queen's papers and wrote "innumerable" memoranda. But Victoria continued to be queen. While drafts of the queen's replies were often in Albert's handwriting, she corrected and rewrote parts of them, and she drafted much of her correspondence herself. Benson and Esher write:

> A considerable number of the drafts are in her own hand, with interlinear corrections and additions by the Prince; and these so strongly resemble in style the drafts in the handwriting of the Prince, that it is clear that the Queen did not merely accept suggestions, but that she had a strong opinion of her own on important matters, and that this opinion was duly expressed.

It would be wrong to assume, as some have, that Albert's efforts and opinions obliterated Victoria's. When it came to matters such as religious tolerance, for example, Victoria had firm opinions from an early age. When Robert Peel wanted to improve tertiary education for Catholics and provide more funding for the Catholic Maynooth training college for priests, Victoria supported him despite the surge of protest in England. She was remarkably progressive about religion: "I blush for the form of religion we profess, that it should be so void of all right feeling, & so wanting in Charity. Are we to drive these 700,000 Roman Catholics, who are badly educated, to desperation & violence?" Victoria praised Peel for standing up against a "tide of bigotry, and blind fanaticism."

Peel's Corn Law triumph cost him his career. On June 25, the prime minister lost an important vote in the House of Commons, partly because the protectionists had combined to vote against him. He resigned and retired, and the Whigs came to power once more. The queen, who had grown fond of Peel, told him she and the prince considered him "a kind and true friend." Peel asked for a portrait of Victoria and Albert with the Prince of Wales—who had been born just after Peel became PM—in the "simple attire" he had often seen them in. Peel's greatest asset was his single-minded determination to do the best for his country, and his greatest flaw was his inability to convince his party that it *was* the best. He is still remembered as a party traitor.

Victoria learned of Peel's political demise while she was recovering from the difficult birth of her fifth child, a plump, strong girl, Princess Helena Augusta Victoria, in May 1846. While she was saddened, her domestic contentment had made her more philosophical. It was an utter contrast to her response to the loss of Melbourne five years earlier. "Really when one is so happy & blessed in one's home life, as I am, Politics (provided my Country is safe) must take only a second place." These words have been oft quoted to underscore the queen's supposed dislike of politics. But a mere two weeks after giving birth to her fifth child, and watching poisonous political opponents savage an effective leader she had grown to admire, she was simply speaking a truth many politicians think at times of crisis: family matters more than anything else. The caveat she added is important here, too: *provided her country was safe*.

Lord Melbourne had gone, and now Robert Peel had too. But the royal couple no longer had need of mentors. By the time they both turned thirty in 1849, the queen and her prince were operating as a formidable joint force. The prime minister, the prominent Whig Lord John Russell, was tasked not only with placating and aiding the Irish, who were starving by the thousands, but also with managing his arrogant foreign secretary, Lord Palmerston, whom Victoria and Albert grew to detest. Their battle with him would shape the next era of British foreign policy and demonstrate the force of the queen and her prince when they agreed, and fought together.

CHAPTER 15

Perfect, Awful, Spotless Prosperity

The two young people were for several years even more foolish about their babies than are most affectionate young parents, and in spite of public demands on their time they spent a large portion of each day playing with their human toys.

—CLARE JERROLD

There was a quiet, a retirement, a wildness, a liberty and a solitude.

—QUEEN VICTORIA ON SCOTLAND

He was only twenty-five inches tall and weighed a mere fifteen pounds, but General Tom Thumb was not at all nervous on the day he was to meet Queen Victoria. The American boy was six years old, though his age was usually advertised as twelve or fourteen. Charles Sherwood Stratton, who had stopped growing when he was only seven months old, looked like a miniature man. He had blond hair, black eyes, rosy cheeks, and perfectly tailored clothes. The confident American entertainer burst through the doors leading to the Queen's Picture Gallery, where Victoria and Albert were waiting for him, and walked firmly along the long stretch of carpet.

Gasps were heard from the crowd. His manager, P. T. Barnum,

who was then "renting" him from his parents, later wrote that he looked like "a wax doll gifted with the powers of locomotion." Tom Thumb marched past some of the world's greatest artwork— Rubenses, Van Dycks, Rembrandts, and Vermeers, mostly collected by King Charles I—and stopped in front of the petite queen. For once she found herself looking down on someone. Then he bowed deeply: "Good evening, *ladies and gentlemen*!" The court roared at the breach of etiquette: he had failed to address the queen as Your Majesty. The queen then took Thumb's hand and walked him around the gallery, asking questions. He told her he thought her picture gallery was "first-rate" and the royal household laughed. For the next hour, Thumb sang, did an imitation of Napoleon, and gave a seamless performance.

Barnum had been instructed, as all guests were, to bow his way out of the room. The picture gallery was a considerable distance— about fifty meters long—and, as Barnum tells it, Thumb's little legs could not keep up with Mr. Barnum's; when he fell behind, he turned and ran a few steps, before backing out again, then running again. He kept up this routine until the gallery was rocking with laughter. The excitement agitated Victoria's poodle; he began barking, and Thumb was forced to fend him off with his cane, which made people laugh even harder.

Victoria, who became worried that Barnum was not treating Thumb gently enough, described him as "the greatest curiosity, I, or indeed anybody ever saw":

No description can give an idea of this little creature, whose real name was Charles Stratton. . . . He is American, & gave us his card, with Gen: Tom Thumb, written on it. He made the funniest little bow, putting out his hand & saying: "much obliged Mam." One cannot help feeling very sorry for the poor little thing & wishing he could be properly cared for, for the people who show him off tease him a good deal, I should think.

It was 1844, and this was the first of Thumb's three successful trips to Buckingham Palace during a three-year tour of Britain and Europe. Victoria gave Thumb money and presents, but her greatest gift was her attention, which endowed him with prestige and publicity. General Tom Thumb became the height of fashion; carriages lined up outside his exhibition rooms in Piccadilly. Thumb rode through the London streets in a tiny but elaborate red, white, and blue carriage pulled by pretty ponies. He soon adopted court dress: an intricately embroidered chocolate-colored velvet coat and short pants; a white satin vest with colorful patterns; white silk stockings and shoes; and a wig, cocked hat, and fake sword. He and his famous showman master, Barnum, knew how to delight a crowd. Barnum claimed his young protégé became a "great pet" to Prime Minister Robert Peel, as well as to the Duke of Wellington. The queen invited him to perform for her again in 1856.

Victoria was highly entertained by the "curiosities," as they were then called: exotic animals or unusual men and women, from horse whisperers to dwarves and court jesters. Not long after she married Albert, Victoria met the "Lady of the Lions," the first woman known to enter large cages of lions and tigers and exit unscathed. She performed in the courtyard of Windsor Castle as the queen watched from a window. Afterward, Victoria sent for the woman and praised her courage. "Poor girl," said Victoria. "I hope and pray you will never get hurt. God bless you!"

Victoria's kindness to the vulnerable and her curiosity about the unique endured throughout her life. When a couple billed to be the tallest couple in the world got engaged, she asked them to visit her at Buckingham Palace and gave the bride a wedding dress and a diamond ring. In her late seventies, the queen requested regular shows from the handsome muscleman Eugen Sandow. When an elephant called Charlie, who performed for her once, killed a man who had been teasing him, Victoria wrote a letter to his handler expressing her regret.

These were happy years. Victoria struggled with her pregnancies and rapidly multiplying brood, and she fretted about instability in Europe, but during the same period, she asserted her rights, gave her husband ample leeway to execute his plans, and delighted in her family. She and Albert sang along as Felix Mendelssohn played private concerts; constructed a theater to stage plays at home, and feasted on fine food and wine. Victoria indulged sometimes perhaps too much: "A Queen does not drink a bottle of wine at a meal," wrote Stockmar to her sternly. What she really yearned for was privacy, solitude, and smaller homes by the sea and in the Highlands. Two of her best-loved words were "cozy" and "snug"—both encapsulated in the German word *gemütlich*.

It was on the Isle of Wight, with its lush fields and chalky cliffs sloping into a gray sea, that Victoria and Albert first made their own home. The island had an enchanted air; walking paths were crowded with flowering thickets and overhanging branches; rabbits leapt about on the headlands; nightingales sang in the trees. The sea could be seen from almost every room in the light, breezy house, which was called Osborne. Victoria had stayed on the island as a girl, and when Peel notified them that an estate was available, Albert was able to negotiate a reasonable price, paid for by his own prudent budgeting. He relished the chance to design and remodel a house unhampered by intervention from a government department. He hired the renowned builder and draftsman Thomas Cubitt and was involved in everything: the Italianate floor plan and façade, the arrangement of art and china, the gardens, the beach, the soil, the sewage, the planting of the trees. Albert constructed an icehouse, a small lake to be used for fighting fires, a beach hut lined with mosaic tiles for Victoria, and a floating pool moored in the sea for the children. (Victoria used a wooden bathing machine, from which she slid discreetly into the sea.) He also designed the nursery cribs; the lamps over the slate billiard table, which swung out to be cleaned; the sliding doors in the

drawing room that were mirrored to reflect the lights of the chandeliers at night; and the Swiss Cottage, where the children grew plants,
collected rocks, and played in their model fort with their model guns.
At Christmas he composed hymns for the family to sing to the ac-
companiment of wind instruments.

This home was, for Victoria, a "perfect little Paradise." She delighted in the spring, the lambs and nightingales and foliage ("the
trees seem covered as with feathers"). Albert thrived there. In May
1845, Victoria wrote: "It does my heart good to see how my beloved
Albert enjoys it all, and is so full of admiration of the place, and of all
the plans and improvements he means to carry out. He is hardly to be
kept at home a moment." It was, she noted three years later, a form of
therapy for him. Albert loved gardening; he experimented with turning raw sewage into fertilizer, and was keenly disappointed when he
could not find a way to make others follow suit, especially given the
state of the sewers in London. He also gained a reputation as a man
who treated his employees well.

The Victoria of Osborne House is a warm, lighthearted woman in
the flush of her young marriage. The writing desks were dotted with
framed portraits of the family and casts of baby feet and hands: fat,
creased palms, dimpled elbows, smooth young faces—she and Albert
were parents capturing the moments of youth that sprint past unmarked if you don't throw butterfly nets over them. A painting displayed in the expansive yellow drawing room shows the subtle wit
and playfulness of the couple at that time. It depicts three women
sitting under trees heavy with green leaves, dappled by the afternoon
sun. One of them, smiling mysteriously, is leaning on another. At
first, it looks like an innocuous, dreamlike summer's picnic. On closer
examination, the shape of a man's back can be traced under the skirt
of the woman lying back with the smile on her face, and an extra pair
of feet can be seen coming out from her petticoats. This painting, *La
Siesta* by Franz Xaver Winterhalter, is thought to be the first that the
queen bought. It is charming to think of a saucy Victoria laughing

over the scenario with Albert, slyly showing the painting to visitors without pointing out the hidden man.*

In the late summer or fall, the family traveled north to the sparsely populated low-lying mountains of Scotland. Victoria first went in 1842, when she was struggling with depression after Bertie's birth. She and Albert were captivated by the remote stillness and beauty of the untamed Highlands. The family would wander up into the wild, solitary hills; Albert hunted or deer-stalked while Victoria drew or chatted with the ghillies—the locals who worked as attendants, especially on hunting, fishing, or walking expeditions—and the children played. Albert admired the "severe and grand character" and "remarkably pure and light" air, and the fact that the people were "more natural, and marked by that honesty and sympathy which always distinguishes the inhabitants of mountainous countries, who live far away from towns." It reminded him of his childhood home in Germany.

Victoria and Albert took their first trip to the "pretty little Castle" of Balmoral in September 1848. They walked up the hills for miles, toward ever more glorious views, in utter silence: "It was wonderful not seeing a human being, nor hearing a sound, excepting that of the wind, or the call of blackcock or grouse. It filled me with peculiar feelings of admiration & solemnity," wrote Victoria. The introverted Albert loved the "complete mountain solitude, where one rarely sees a human face," and he wanted mostly to hunt: "I, naughty man, have also been creeping stealthily after the harmless stags, and today I shot two red deer." He took his hunting very seriously, and Victoria anxiously waited to hear how many hides he had collected: when he got

---

* It should be noted that while Michael Hunter, the curator of Osborne House, says that "the arrangement of the composition is rather suggestive," he also points out that the painting has been restored in the past; "it would be interesting to ascertain—by X-ray examination—to what degree it has been overpainted by a restorer." Correspondence with the author, February 12, 2015.

none, she almost cried. They spent afternoons working, replying to a flurry of reports from the outside world, about Ireland, an unstable Europe, unrest in India; but the mornings were still and undisturbed.

The queen shed her inhibitions at Balmoral and befriended the locals. She gave the tenants of her local cottages new petticoats, chatted with the women for hours, and sometimes joined them for tea. She found them simple, straightforward, and refreshingly unpretentious: "They are never vulgar, never take liberties, are so intelligent, modest and well bred." The royal couple were smitten with the Highland life: they sported tartan, Albert studied Gaelic, and the queen and children took Scottish dancing lessons. Charles Greville was struck by the simplicity of their existence there: "They live there without any state whatever; they live not merely like private gentlefolks, but like very small gentlefolks; small house, small rooms, small establishments."

Scotland would remain the place where Victoria felt happiest, and the most herself, for the rest of her life. She could sit in mud cottages and chat endlessly about anything. She could dance with Highlanders without snooty aristocrats raising eyebrows, and giggle with her ladies while clambering down slippery hills in the most beautiful, remote terrain. (In her diary on September 11, 1849, she wrote of one man who had taken care of her on one sojourn and would be so important to her in future years: the handsome "J. Brown.") Not all were charmed by her enthusiasm: after enduring a dinner party full of long, awkward silences at Osborne House, Lady Lyttelton watched the men play billiards with some envy as the queen began to talk about "her wild Highland life, and very pleasantly—that Scotch air, Scotch people, Scotch hills, Scotch rivers, Scotch woods, are all far preferable to those of any other nation in or out of this world." "The chief support to my spirits," Lady Lyttelton added, "is that I shall never see, hear or witness these various charms." But this was the great magic of their new Scottish home: Victoria and Albert loved it more than anyone else did.

———

During these years, Victoria occasionally fretted that her contentment might not last. She longed to freeze time. Sitting alone in her room on New Year's Eve as 1847 gave way to 1848, she wrote:

> When one is as happy as we are, one feels sad at the quick passing of the years, & I always wish Time could stand still for a while. This year has brought us much to be thankful for; the Children are so well, & the 2 eldest decidedly so improved. I have thought over my faults,—what I have to avoid, & what to correct, & with God's help & perseverance on my part I hope to conquer my shortcomings.

Victoria bore one child after another without ever ceasing her work. She vowed to try to make herself a better person for her husband. But her attitudes toward her job, her children, and the havoc motherhood wreaked on her body oscillated. She was robust yet constantly exhausted, adoring yet often resentful of Albert, proud of her family yet increasingly aggrieved by the sacrifices required of her. Victoria's power and triumph as a monarch rested on her ordinariness as a mother and her obvious contentment as a wife. She was the Domestic Queen, and she was worshipped for it. But all the while, a sense of the injustice of the lot of women—which she would not express in words until she was a grandmother—took root and bloomed in her heart.

The worst part was the physical toll. The wear on Victoria's body is apparent in her private, growing distaste for the physical part of child-rearing; she did not write of pain, discomfort, or damage to her body in her journal, but being pregnant, she said, made her feel like an animal.

Victoria had a "totally unsurmountable disgust" for breastfeeding. She was incensed when her daughter Alice decided to nurse her children herself, later in life, and a heifer in the Balmoral dairy was soon named Princess Alice. Victoria viewed it as vulgar, and inappropriate for upper-class women. She also believed it was incompatible with performing public duties, perhaps a persuasive argument in the days before breast pumps existed. Until commercial baby foods became widespread in the 1860s, most women in the Victorian middle class, and even aristocrats, combined breastfeeding with animal milk or mashed foods until the baby was a few months old. Wet nurses were expensive and frequently suspected of somehow corrupting their charges with dubious morals. But Victoria did not hesitate to employ them, believing it better for the child if a woman who was less refined and "more like an animal" suckled them. She summoned her eldest son's first wet nurse, Mary Ann Brough, from the Isle of Wight to suckle the Prince of Wales when she was still in labor.*

For all her privilege, the queen shared with other women a complete lack of control over the messy, often debilitating process of bearing children. Eight in ten women gave birth less than a year after their weddings, just like Victoria. Most Englishwomen at the time were carrying or nursing babies for an average of twelve years: in total, Victoria spent sixteen. Yet Victoria produced almost double the era average of 5.5 children. Many historians have glossed over this achievement, ignoring the physical and emotional toll it took, the helplessness it engendered. She told her daughter that childbearing was "a complete violence to all one's feelings of propriety (which God knows receive a shock enough in marriage alone)."

Victoria's greatest comfort in the early child-rearing years was Albert. Her husband was far more involved in the lives of his children, and sufferings of his wife, than the average Victorian male. He was

---

* Thirteen years later, Mrs. Brough slaughtered her own six children in their beds, cutting their throats before unsuccessfully trying to slit her own. She was found to be insane. Reports trumpeted the fact that she had once nursed the Prince of Wales; Victoria and Albert, who were then already worried about Bertie's mental capacity and glum disposition, read these reports nervously. ("The Murders at Esher Coroner's Inquest, Esher, Monday Night," *The Times,* June 13, 1854, 12, column C.)

entirely comfortable in the nursery. He also "superintended the principles" of his children's upbringing, which were, he wrote in 1846, "difficult to uphold in the face of so many women." The Prince Consort was with Victoria during her births, carried her through her confinements, and humanely ended the practice of having a dozen men of state present in the next room as the queen gave birth. He was similarly tender with his children. Lady Lyttelton wrote of a nurse struggling in vain to get a glove on the tiny hand of the Prince of Wales—the boy was then two and a half years old—and finally throwing it away in frustration. She wrote:

> It was pretty to see [Albert] just coax the child on to his own knee, and put it on, without a moment's delay, by his great dexterity and gentle manner; the Princey, quite evidently glad to be so helped, looking up very softly at his father's beautiful face. It was a picture of a nursery scene. I could not help saying: "It is not every Papa who would have the patience and kindness," and got such a flashing look of gratitude from the Queen!

As the children grew, Albert was a figure of fun, instruction, and care in their lives: ordering the nursery, proudly showing the babies to visitors, organizing the christenings, planning their lessons, building cottages and forts, taking them to the theater, to the zoo, and to see Madame Tussaud's waxworks. Victoria describes him noisily and eagerly flying a kite with his two elder sons, playing hide-and-seek with Vicky and Bertie, showing Bertie how to turn somersaults in piles of hay. The sight of him giving the children rides on his back and pulling them along the floor in a large basket delighted her. She wrote: "He is so kind to them and romps with them so delightfully, and manages them so beautifully and firmly." He jiggled a child on each knee while playing silly songs on the organ.

In 1859, Victoria told her firstborn, the eighteen-year-old Vicky, that Albert took the care of his family very seriously: "Papa says that the men who leave all home affairs—and the education of their children to their wives—forget their first duties." Victoria blamed bad parenting for the wasted lives of her uncles: "It seems that George III cared very little for his children." For many years, Albert taught the children for an hour a day himself. He also carefully monitored their security, after receiving threatening letters of "the most horrid kind" aimed at the children, in the years when Victoria was shot at regularly. He always kept a key to the children's apartments in his pocket and ensured that they were formidably fortified with "intricate turns and locks and guardrooms, and various intense precautions."

For Victoria, dailiness was an important part of parenting. She visited her infants every day in the nursery and showed them off proudly. Even her ladies-in-waiting commented on how many hours she spent with her babies. In an 1844 memorandum on education, Victoria stated that children should be "as much as possible with their parents, and learn to place their greatest confidence in them in all things." She read and prayed with her sons and daughters, and taught them about the Bible: the faith she wanted them to learn was one of kindness, tolerance, and love, not "fear and trembling." Reports on her children appeared almost daily in Victoria's journal: picking primroses, violets, and anemones in the woods near Osborne, hunting for Easter eggs, watching sheep being washed at the farm, laughing at the clowns at the circus, romping in her dressing room when she was disrobing, visiting the wild bears at the zoo, and digging potatoes in the gardens. On her wedding anniversary in 1852, Victoria wrote gratefully that while children were "often a source of anxiety and difficulty," they were "a great blessing and cheer & brighten up life."

When their eldest son, the Prince of Wales, was still an infant, Victoria and Albert began concentrating on his education, an important task for a future king. He was a willful child who had hurricane-like tantrums as a toddler just like his mother—they exhausted him so much that afterward he lay on the floor as though asleep with his eyes open. They were inevitably disappointed with Bertie, who hated learning, was never destined to be a scholar, and whose progress was always compared unfavorably with that of his precocious older sister, Vicky. When he was five, the queen described him as "a very good child & not at all wanting in intellect." Just a year later, she said he was "more backward" than his sister. (Greville said bluntly that the queen thought he was stupid.) When he was eight, his parents asked a phrenologist to examine his skull. The findings confirmed their fears: an "inaptitude for mental labour, and an aversion to it at particular times; and that . . . the organs of Combativeness, Destructiveness and Firmness [were] all large. The intellectual organs are only moderately developed." Bertie's affectionate, sociable nature was unfortunately overlooked in the drive for academic accomplishment. It was never going to be easy being the son of a man like Albert.

By the end of the 1840s, foreigners landing in London were struck by the fervor of the people's love for Victoria. As the Reverend D. Newell stood waiting for the queen to arrive at a public dedication for Lincoln's Inn, which housed a barrister's guild, he saw a "tide of human beings flow from all directions" to see the queen. It was impossible to get a glimpse, he said, but "the occasion was not lost to us, since, in the midst of this mighty confluence of Britons, we could, in a sense see and feel the strong pulsations of a nation's heart." Victoria credited her family for this. In October 1844, she wrote to Leopold: "They say no sovereign was ever more loved than I am (I am bold enough to say), & *this* because of our domestic home, the good example it presents." The queen was acutely aware of her symbolic power and understood her people with a canny intuition. Victoria represented a sweet, simple home life rather than idle excess, and this would help to inoculate the English monarchy from the revolutions that gripped Europe in the coming years, as other countries rose up against the idle excess of their monarchies.

For as Victoria and Albert gamboled at Osborne and trekked the green hills of Scotland, clouds of dissent were gathering over the Continent. In a room in Brussels in 1848, two men named Karl Marx and Friedrich Engels were producing *The Communist Manifesto,* urging the working class to "arise ye starvelings from your slumbers." As

Buckingham Palace was being enlarged and beautified, European royalty were pushed off their thrones. While Albert was surveying with pleasure his own tranquil abodes, angry hordes swarmed through palaces in Paris, Berlin, Vienna, Prague, and Budapest. In May 1848, he wrote to Stockmar smugly from Buckingham Palace: "All is well with us, and the throne has never stood higher in England than at this moment."

CHAPTER 16

Annus Mirabilis:
The Revolutionary Year

The uncertainty everywhere, as well as for the future
of our children, unarmed me & I quite gave way to
my grief.... I feel grown 20 years older, & as if I
could not any more think of any amusement. I tremble at the thought of what may possibly await us here
though I know *how* loyal the people at large are.

—QUEEN VICTORIA, APRIL 3, 1848

The man known as the Citizen King of France stared in the mirror as he slowly slid a razor down his cheeks. His wife, sitting behind
him, smiled for the first time in days as her husband's bare face
emerged from the auburn whiskers that had framed it for many
years; he looked suddenly shy, and exposed, like a child. Louis
Philippe had been shorn of his crown just a few days earlier, at the
age of seventy-four. After eighteen years on the throne, he was forced
to abdicate in favor of his nine-year-old grandson during a bloody
revolution that saw the streets of Paris burn. He and his wife, Marie-
Amelie, had fled for safety. They had not slept for many days. Louis
Philippe patted his pocket, making sure for the hundredth time that

the falsified "Mr. and Mrs. William Smith" identification papers were safe. They left the house in Paris, traveled by boat to Le Havre on the coast, and, in the black of night, boarded a waiting steamship. All they had with them on the journey to England was a tiny suitcase and the clothes they were wearing. Their escape was close: just two hours after they left, police came to the house they had been hiding in to try to arrest the king.

In the preceding years, the gulf between rich and poor in France had widened; the working classes toiled in intolerable conditions, and the cost of living spiraled. The once-loved King Louis Philippe had become increasingly unpopular. When the government outlawed a series of banquets organized to raise funds to support opposition, thousands gathered on the streets to protest. On February 22, 1848, fifty-two people were killed during violent riots. As an angry rabble streamed to his palace, the king, surrounded by panicked advisers, decided to abdicate. Dozens of family members made their way in clusters of two and three, in carriages, trains, boats, and on foot, with their nurses, maids, and courtiers, to England; in France, the revolutionaries drank and danced in the palace, raiding the royal closets. Among the king's offspring traveling to England were Albert's cousin Augustus and his wife, Clementine (the third surviving daughter of Louis Philippe), and Victoire of Saxe-Coburg-Kohary, a close cousin of Victoria, who was married to the eldest surviving child of the deposed king and queen of France. When Louis Philippe stepped from the steamship onto the safety of British shores, wearing the captain's overcoat and concealing his eyes with enormous goggles, he almost wept with relief.

Victoria took in her royal friends, but she disapproved of their capitulation. She thought the king should have stayed to fight. Giving up was not just cowardly, she believed, but unnecessary. The twenty-eight-year-old Victoria, belly swollen with her sixth child, had nerves of iron. She wrote repeatedly in her diary over the next few months that she thought the king of France had made a mistake.

Another tender point was that Louis Philippe had double-crossed Victoria only two years earlier. The French king and British queen had initially enjoyed a period of warm relations, partly because his eldest daughter, Louise, had married Victoria's uncle Leopold and had always been kind to the younger British queen. In 1843, Victoria became the first British monarch to visit a French counterpart in more than three hundred years. She was taken with the beauty of their castle at Eu and the ease of their manners. Queen Marie-Amelie told Victoria that she thought of her as a daughter. But one thing the royals did not discuss during the visit was the sensitive subject of Spain. Louis Philippe had long dreamed of aligning his country with Spain and had quietly arranged for one of his sons to marry the Infanta Luisa, the younger sister of the thirteen-year-old Queen Isabella, who ruled Spain with her mother as regent. Louis Philippe had concocted a complicated plot. He hoped that Queen Isabella would marry her cousin the Duke of Cadiz, who was thought to be either gay or infertile, and leave no heirs, so that the Infanta Luisa could marry the Duke of Montpensier, his son, and produce an heir with him.

Victoria, though, wanted Queen Isabella to marry a Coburg cousin. After protracted intrigue, during Victoria and Albert's second visit to Eu in 1845, the English and French foreign ministers agreed that neither of them would present a suitor for the Infanta Luisa until her elder sister had children. This agreement evaporated in 1846 when Lord Palmerston foolishly showed the French ambassador a dispatch that said a cousin of Victoria's was a candidate for Queen Isabella's hand. In a snap, the two girls were engaged to the Duke of Cadiz and the Duke of Montpensier. An "extremely indignant" Victoria told Queen Marie-Amelie that her husband had breached a promise. The tensions endured for almost two years, until the protests in Paris began.

Victoria quickly forgot her grudge. She was genuinely appalled at the uprisings, and despite past intrigues she still loved her French family. "Humbled poor people they looked," she wrote on March 7, the day after she greeted Louis Philippe and Marie-Amelie at Buckingham Palace. Victoria, who was then heavily pregnant, sent clothes for the refugees and lent them her uncle Leopold's grand estate, Claremont, to stay in for as long as they needed. Augustus and Clementine and their children lived with her in Buckingham Palace. Clem, who was pregnant with her fourth child, was the same age as Victoria, and the two women grew close as they tried to fathom the events of the past month. Victoria was distressed to hear that Louis Philippe's daughter-in-law Helene, the mother of the next king, had had her children torn from her in the melee: "What could be more dreadful!"

Anxiety and sadness radiated through the palace. "Poor Clem," Victoria wrote in her journal, "says she can get no sleep, constantly seeing before her those horrible faces and hearing those dreadful cries and shrieks." She spent months worrying about her guests. She fretted when they grew too thin, and described her cousin Victoire as looking "like a crushed rose."

The European revolutions of 1848, called the "Springtime of the Peoples," started in Sicily in January, spread to France in February, and quickly spread across Europe. The most violent uprisings occurred in Poland, the Austrian Empire, Germany, and Italy as well as France. The reasons were disparate and mostly unconnected, but in many countries it was the eruption of the working and middle classes—grouped in unusual and temporary coalitions—after decades of exponential change. They had endured a rise in basic living costs, crop failures, crowded cities, parliaments run by the idle and apathetic rich, and repressive monarchs. The voices of dissent grew louder and louder as they debated ideal forms of democracy, socialism, incremental liberalism, and republicanism.

As the rebellion spread, Victoria's attitude swung from fear to horror. This kind of chaos was anathema to a monarch. In her diary, she referred to the revolutionaries as a "mob of bloodthirsty ruffians," "the dreadful rabble," and "people [who] are going on in a disgusting way." The queen did not like hordes, nor did she like the French.

This was clear in her correspondence. When Arthur Benson and Lord Esher edited her letters for posthumous publication, they censored her harshest anti-French views to avoid embarrassing her son, King Edward VII, about an ally. The original letters, in the Royal Archives, reveal her secret desire for the French citizenry to be punished for rebelling. A letter she wrote to Leopold in April 1848 reads: "In France, really great things go on *dreadfully,* & for the sake of morality there *ought* to be some *great* catastrophe at *Paris* for *that* is the hothouse of Iniquity from wherein all the mischief comes." While she privately believed that Louise Philippe should not have abdicated, she wrote: "The recollection of Louis XVI *and the wickedness and savageness of the French mob* is enough to justify all and everybody will admit that." (The words in italics were later deleted by Benson and Esher.)

England was mostly spared the revolutionary fervor that was sweeping the Continent. In March, just two weeks after the uprising in Paris, a much-hyped meeting in Trafalgar Square ended only in the destruction of Prince Albert's skittle alley and the arrest of the young leader, who burst into tears. Victoria wrote impatiently that the "foolish" protests were scaring her French relations. The next day, Albert told her some of "the mob" had broken her mother's windows at her London home and had contemplated attacking Buckingham Palace, but were deterred by the sight of numerous guards. There was really no danger, she wrote in her journal, but "after the horrors of Paris, one cannot help being more anxious."

The queen spent her days poring over dispatches from Europe and soothing her French guests. Albert, who thought princes were better placed than any politician to advise on foreign policy, had been devastated to hear of turmoil in his beloved Germany. He sensibly cautioned his brother, the Duke of Coburg and Gotha, against using or extending military power to quell the local riots. Albert was also concerned about the growing confidence of the Chartists in England, who had garnered strength in recent years with the release of many of its leaders from jail. The Irish had also grown desperate after several bitter winters of starvation, and financial speculation had created instability and panic. Chartists had danced until dawn in the streets of London when they heard France had become a republic, shoving their king from his throne.

On March 18, in the thick of the turmoil, Victoria gave birth to her fourth daughter, Louise Caroline Alberta. She had almost forgotten she was pregnant until the excruciating labor began.* When baby Louise was just a couple of days old, Victoria and Albert were forced to leave London in fear of their lives. The Chartists had declared a massive meeting of half a million people for April 10 in London, which most expected to turn ugly, if not incendiary.

Victoria, who was still recovering from the difficult labor, lay on her bed and sobbed:

> The sorrow at the state of Germany—at the distress and ruin all around, added to very bad news from Ireland & the alarm in people's minds at the great meeting which is to take place in London on the 10th are trying my poor Albert very much. . . . Yes, I feel grown 20 years older, & as if I could not any more think of any amusement. I tremble at the thought of what may possibly await us here though I know *how* loyal the people at large are. I feel very calm & quite prepared to meet what God may send us, if only we are spared to one another to share everything.

The royal family retreated to the woods of Osborne, where they awaited news from London with some trepidation. Victoria quickly

---

* The pretty, plump girl grew up to be a strong-minded sculptor with far more sympathy for social movements, such as suffrage, than her mother. On the first birthday of her "good little child," Victoria wrote: "She was born in the most eventful times, & ought to be something peculiar in consequence." Queen Victoria's Journal, Sunday, March 18, 1848.

regained her composure, boasting in a letter to Leopold: "Great events make me quiet & calm; it is only trifles that irritate my nerves." Albert's equerry, Colonel Phipps, stayed behind and walked through the streets of London, eavesdropping on random conversations, trying to gauge the reaction to the queen's exit. He wrote: "Her reputation for personal courage stands so high, I never heard one person express a belief that her departure was due to personal alarm."

Back in London, military-style preparations were being made for the April 10 meeting. Volunteers swarmed police stations, with an astonishing eighty-five thousand men signing up to be special constables on the day of the meeting. Volunteers included Prince Louis-Napoleon Bonaparte, who would later become emperor of the French. The hero-worshipped, elderly Duke of Wellington was placed in charge of the army once again, for the last time. The government seized control of the telegraphic system to ensure that revolutionaries could not broadcast false information, and a Removal of Aliens Act was rushed through Parliament to give the home secretary powers to remove any foreign citizen against whom allegations had been made. The Chartists boasted of a petition bearing five million names, so enormous it was rolled up like a large bundle of hay and pulled by four horses. They hoped for revolution, but at the very least they planned to wring some compromises out of Parliament.

On April 10, under a bright blue sky, the Chartists trekked to four meeting points around London, holding banners that read LIVE AND LET LIVE. A phalanx of four thousand Metropolitan Police surrounded Kennington Common—formerly used for public executions and cricket matches—and a further eight thousand regular troops were hidden at various points around London. Four batteries of artillery were installed along bridges, and armed ships were anchored at key points along the Thames. Armed men lined the Mall to prevent access to Buckingham Palace. Prime Minister Lord John Russell lined his windows with parliamentary papers, and his pregnant wife accompanied him to the safety of Downing Street for fear the sound of cannons firing would trigger early labor. In the empty government buildings, which were barricaded with boxes of papers, men with guns hid behind pillars and curtains, peering out every few minutes to see if the rioting had begun. The troops were told to fire if necessary.

The reports of tight security had rattled Feargus O'Connor, the leader of the Chartists and the MP for Nottingham. He had been unable to sleep for several days. He had decided, turning in his bed the night before, that he would approach the demonstration with a spirit of conciliation. He could have ordered the Chartists to attack, in the hope that troops and police would crumble and defect as they had in many European countries, but his instincts told him this was futile. On the day of the protest, his fears were confirmed: only twenty-three thousand turned up, just one-tenth the number hoped for.

O'Connor stood on the stage erected at Kennington surrounded by flags reading NO SURRENDER! and told supporters not to fight with the police. Most obeyed, and only the odd skirmish erupted. The leaders agreed to deliver their petition—later found to contain a host of fake names, including "Queen Victoria"—to the Houses of Parliament in three hansom cabs. Lord Palmerston called it "the Waterloo of peace and order." Victoria was thrilled at the triumph of British lawfulness:

> What a blessing! . . . The loyalty of all classes, the excellent arrangement of the Troops & Police, the efficiency of Special Constables, high & low, Lords, Shopkeepers.—& the determination to put a stop to the proceedings,—by force if necessary,— have no doubt been the cause of the failure of the Meeting. It is a proud thing for this country, & I trust fervently, will have a beneficial effect in other countries.

Albert, too, was relieved, although he continued to monitor the ongoing rumbles and Chartist meetings—some reaching fifty thousand in number. He remarked to Stockmar on their sophisticated organization, with secret signals and carrier pigeons. He also wrote to

Prime Minister Russell, telling him his personal research found a dismayingly large number of unemployed persons in London, mostly because the government had cut its budget for capital works. He suggested the government look at ways to create jobs and resume schemes to assist those without work. He also reminded the prime minister that the government was obliged to help the working class at a time of distress.

The Prince Consort was unable to shake a sense of gloom about Europe in 1848. The recent death of his grandmother had saddened him, and he had grown quite depressed. The work was relentless: "I never remember to have been kept in the stocks as I am just now. The mere reading of the English, French, and German papers absorbs nearly all the spare hours of the day; and yet one can let nothing pass without losing the connection and coming in consequence to wrong conclusions." In March 1848, he had begged Stockmar to travel to be with him and bear some of his burden: "My heart is heavy. I lose flesh and strength daily. European war is at our door. . . . I have need of friends. Come, as you love me."

Victoria tried to convince him not to be too black about the future, but Albert was so "overwhelmed with business" that insomnia struck. Every morning, he woke early, unable to sink back into sleep. Victoria would often wake to see Albert staring at the bedposts, turning over problems in his mind. He rose at seven, walking to his desk and turning on the green lamp as his wife slept. "I am not half grateful enough for the many ways in which he helps me," Victoria wrote, a little guiltily.

The ugliness of the violence in Europe had a lasting effect on the queen. She remained spooked by the constant, albeit low, threat of an attack. The Chartists' curse seemed almost biblical: in June 1848, heavy rain at Osborne saw thousands of toads swarming across the terrace and slopes, "like a plague." Three days later, there were false reports of Chartists coming to invade the family's private home; laborers stood on the lawns armed with sticks. Just four days later, Victoria was genuinely frightened riding home at night from the opera;

she had been warned that Chartists would strike in stealth, in the dark. As their carriage rumbled along toward the palace, a man ran up to the open window on Albert's side, mumbling the words "a real murderer" over and over. He was quickly arrested—and found to be mad—but Victoria was stiff with fear for hours.

Every day, Victoria and Albert woke to another batch of urgent dispatches from Europe, and they passed them back and forth to each other across their adjacent wooden desks. The workload was extraordinary. In 1848, twenty-eight thousand dispatches came to them from the Foreign Office alone, on everything from the Chartists and the European revolutions to the devastating impact of increased tariffs on sugar in the West Indies (which were also struggling with the economic impact of the abolition of slavery) and the ambitious king of Sardinia. Victoria and Albert jointly wrote letters, corrected drafts sent from the foreign minister and PM, fired off letters to a host of political figures, both domestic and foreign, and prepared memoranda on events. They were intensely involved in all correspondence with other countries. They helped their government craft a nuanced British response that was supportive of legitimate governments and assisted allies and relatives where they could. Uncle Leopold and his relatively tranquil Belgium remained a beacon of peace in Europe for them.

The foreign secretary at this time was Lord Palmerston, a man who had an unshakable belief in his own diplomatic skills. Known as Lord Cupid because he had charmed women as a bachelor, in 1848 he was still a good-looking fifty-four-year-old, now married to Lord Melbourne's clever sister Emily. The queen had found him pleasant when she was a teenager, but now she and Albert were suspicious of him. One winter's night in 1839, he was found in the bedrooms of one of the ladies-in-waiting, allegedly forcing himself upon her before screams rang through the corridors and he fled the room. Palmerston insisted he was merely lost; in truth, he was simply letting himself into a room he thought was occupied by Lady Emily Lamb, to whom he was then engaged. Albert remained uncertain, though, and used the story to argue against Palmerston a decade later.

Lord Palmerston was a unilateral liberal interventionist who tended to support European rebels and independence movements. A Whig minister who had started out as a Tory, he had a starkly different approach to foreign policy from that of Victoria and Albert. The couple had their own biases, wanting to maintain a close alliance between France and England and backing Austria in its territorial hold of Italy (Palmerston wanted Italy to be independent and united and secretly funneled arms to Italian rebels). Albert wanted to see a strong Prussia leading a united Germany. But the royal couple clashed with the foreign secretary over style as well as policy. They resented Palmerston's failure to consult them or heed their advice, and his tendency to send off dispatches without their review. As early as 1841, Victoria had reprimanded him for disregarding procedure. Palmerston wrote a typically smooth response, assuring the queen he would make sure it would never happen again, while blithely continuing in practice to ignore her. Victoria and Albert considered him a danger.

Victoria believed foreign policy was a core part of the monarch's role because it involved questions of peace and war. She felt upholding "the dignity, the power and the prestige" of Britain was one of the most important aspects of her job. While Palmerston was willful and impulsive, she saw herself as above political intrigues and better able to "maintain at all times a frank and dignified courtesy towards other Sovereigns and their governments." In her view, Palmerston had a ministerial duty to keep her fully informed, to seek her consent, to take her advice, and not to change documents or policies after she had sanctioned them.

On August 20, 1848, Victoria wrote a reprimanding letter to Palmerston after discovering that a "private letter" addressed to her had been "cut open at the Foreign Office." She reproached him again a few days later for failing to update her on the feud between Austria and Sardinia. A series of high-minded, dictatorial dispatches by Palmerston to Spain and then Portugal—which ignored the advice of the prime minister, the man who was his superior—also infuriated the queen. Palmerston was eager to help pry Italy away from Austria and make Venice a republic, which Victoria thought abominable: Why help these foreign rebels when they were wrestling with their own rebels in Ireland?

Victoria and Albert privately called Palmerston "Pilgerstein," or the devil's son. (This was later edited out of their official correspondence.) Victoria told Prime Minister Lord John Russell that she could no longer see Palmerston socially, as she would not be able to treat him with respect. She mused with Russell about how to get rid of him—perhaps a foreign posting might suit, for example in Ireland. Victoria thought Russell showed a "lamentable weakness" in failing to confront Palmerston, but the PM was loath to jeopardize the support of the Radicals and Liberals that Palmerston commanded. A steady stream of angry correspondence passed between the queen and her foreign secretary, especially in the years 1848 to 1851. Victoria often wrote daily in her journal about how much she despised Palmerston.

But outside the palace, Palmerston was hugely popular, the only government minister to have a public following. He was widely viewed as a democratic hero, and was prone to grand, dramatic gestures. In 1850, he got embroiled in a dispute when a Portuguese man, Don Pacifico, had his house pillaged while living in Athens. Pacifico's attempts to seek an immense amount of compensation from the Greek government were unsuccessful. Because Pacifico was born in Gibraltar, he appealed to the British government as a British subject. Palmerston, incredibly, ordered a fleet to be sent to Piraeus to demonstrate official support for him. Victoria and Albert were furious and the House of Lords condemned his actions, but after a long, inspired piece of oratory, Palmerston's misstep was hailed by the House of Commons as an act of heroism. They cheered his idea that every British citizen must be forcefully defended, wherever they happened to be. Buoyed by this broad support, Palmerston ignored Victoria and Albert's suggestions on a draft dispatch to be sent to the British minister in Greece. The queen said she could not consent to "allow a servant of the Crown and her Minister, to act contrary to her orders, and this without her knowledge." This pattern continued for years— Palmerston's unilateralism, Victoria's objections, and Lord John Russell's reluctant intervention, followed by insincere apologies from Palmerston. When Don Pacifico's vastly exaggerated claims were finally settled years later, he was awarded only a small sliver of his original demand. For this paltry sum, Victoria thought, England had almost gone to war, angered Greece, and alienated France.

In August 1850, on the heels of the Greek debacle, Victoria wrote to Prime Minister Russell firmly laying out her complaints against Palmerston and outlining her expectations that she be fully, promptly, and respectfully informed by her ministers. Otherwise, she said, she would use her constitutional powers to dismiss him. Palmerston came to see Albert with tears in his eyes, insisting that he had thought his only difference with the queen was one of policy. His contrition was short-lived, and soon after, the skirmishes began again.

In 1850, the Austrian general Julius Jacob von Haynau, a despotic, sadistic man who had treated rebels in Austria brutally, visited England. He was recognized by some workers, who threw missiles at his head and dragged him along the street by his long, gray mustache. Victoria was horrified that a foreign statesman should be assaulted in her country; but the liberal Palmerston thought "the Austrian Butcher" deserved it. In contrast, when the rebel Hungarian leader Lajos Kossuth made a tour to England during which he delivered speeches railing against the Austrian and Russian emperors, Palmerston was eager to host him. He was forced to cancel the invitation after the Cabinet objected and Victoria threatened to sack him. But just ten days later, Palmerston received a deputation of Radicals who called the Austrian and Russian emperors despots and tyrants. Greville declared this provocative act "an unparalleled outrage."

Lord Palmerston's final, most costly mistake was his unilateral declaration of support for Louis-Napoleon when the French king arrested the leaders of the National Assembly in Paris in December

1851 and declared himself the emperor for life in a coup d'état. The British government had decided to remain neutral, instructing the ambassador to refrain from backing either side. Palmerston, however, congratulated the French ambassador and gave his support to the coup, which was extremely embarrassing for the British government. Lord John Russell finally dismissed him, and Victoria was elated.

The queen could not be persuaded that a revolution could be a good thing. In August 1848, she stated, "I maintain that Revolutions are always bad for the country & the cause of untold misery to the people. Obedience to the laws & to the Sovereign, is obedience to a higher Power, divinely instituted for the good of the *people,* not of the Sovereign, who has equally duties & obligations." For Victoria, hierarchy was divine: men were the heads of their households, and the sovereign was the head of state. She believed that peace in both her marriage and her country required obedience—even though her own was rarely forthcoming. A strong strain of liberal sympathy had emerged in Europe, but for now, her country was safe, and little had changed.

In Ireland, the 1848 potato crop had again failed and people on the streets of Dublin were crying for food. The British Parliament was so nervous about the possibility of rebellion that they suspended habeas corpus so that people in Ireland could be arrested without a warrant. The subterranean anger in the impoverished country threatened only to get worse. In 1848, made nervous by events in Europe, Victoria was of the firm belief that any restive Irish should be "crushed" and taught a lesson. Even then, her views were considered strident.

The Great Potato Famine, one of the greatest calamities of the century, had sown hatred in Ireland toward the British, and prompted mass emigration. The Irish population had ballooned in the early nineteenth century, but between 1846 and 1851 it plummeted from eight million to about six and a half. About one million died of starvation, and others died from dysentery and cholera. Of those left, three million depended on government assistance for survival. The failure of the English to stem the vast number of deaths permanently estranged the two countries. Between 1801 and 1841, there had been 175 commissions and committees on the state of Ireland—all foretold doom, and none enabled the Irish to climb out of the deepening ravine of poverty the country was slipping into. Many subsisted on water and potatoes.

Some historians have called the deaths of more than a million starving people a genocide—but it was caused mostly by bigotry and ignorant neglect, not deliberate mass murder. Many British politicians were more intent on reforming the Irish economy and implementing their free-market ideals than on preventing deaths. Much of the reluctance to do anything was driven by anti-Irish prejudice and a belief that the Irish were weak, prone to criminality, and reliant on others; many viewed the famine as a sign of God's disapproval as well as evidence of defects in the Irish character. The blame for this has, somewhat unfairly, fallen on Victoria's shoulders. She was called "the Famine Queen" and accused of neglect and a lack of sympathy. She donated £2,000 (worth roughly £200,000 today), the largest single donation to Irish relief, but it was criticized for not being enough; she published two letters urging the public to donate to Ireland; rationed bread in her household; ordered swaths of Irish poplin; and agreed to order that days of fasting be observed in support of the poor. She donated another £500 in 1849.

It would be a long stretch to blame Victoria for the famine, though she could have done much more for what had become an unpopular cause, and several of her public gestures were made at the insistence of her prime minister, Lord John Russell. She was initially critical of tyrannical landlords, but when some of those she knew personally were murdered, her sympathy for their tenants waned.

Albert was as troubled by the root causes of the revolts as he was by the results. He had far more sympathy for the working class than for aristocrats, describing them as having "most of the toil and least of the enjoyments of this world." In a meeting he chaired in May 1848 of the Society for Improving the Condition of the Working Classes, he said that while the model lodging houses, loan funds, and ground allotments the government had established were important, any improvement in conditions "must be the result of the exertion of the working people themselves," not dictated by capitalists. He devised four core principles for the improvement of the condition of the working classes: education for children with practical training in industry, improvement of housing, a grant of land allotments with cottages, and the establishment of banks especially for savings. The press reports praised him.

Politicians on the hard right resented Albert's political activism. He told his brother in May 1849 that the "ultra Tories" hated his working "energetically . . . against their plans." He was known for his dislike of the aristocracy, and he was clear about the purpose of his work: "The unequal division of property, and the dangers of poverty and envy arising therefrom, is the principal evil. Means must necessarily be found, not for *diminishing riches* (as the communists wish), but to make facilities for the poor. But there is the rub." Such remarks show that Albert was grappling with the questions raised by the European revolutions—and hoping to stem local unrest by addressing them. Unlike his wife, who was intent on quashing dissent, he was eager to prevent it. His views were rare in his echelon.

Albert was careful to treat his own staff well, and he earned plaudits for his attempts to improve the lives of those caught within unequal structures. For example, when he was master of Trinity House, ballast heavers gave him the title of Albert the Good after he helped redress their situation when he discovered they were only given work through publicans who insisted they drink before they work, putting them in a sorry state. He also organized a superannuation scheme for servants after reading a report on workhouses and noting the disproportionate number of former servants who were inmates. A bad reference from a single boss could thrust them into poverty. Seventy percent of servants in England or Wales—almost seven hundred thousand—ended up in workhouses or on charity. It is these kinds of initiatives that reveal Albert's flashes of brilliance, as well as his scope and potential as an acting monarch.

In the end, Ireland did not revolt, largely because the people were too hungry. Britain escaped the turbulence of 1848 unscathed. Whig aristocrats still ruled Parliament, Victoria still wore the crown, and Britain continued to inch across the globe, annexing land and dominating the seas. At the end of the year, Louis-Napoleon Bonaparte was elected president of France. There were repeated scuffles in Prussia and Austria, but Europe was mostly stable again. The major democratic changes demanded by the rioters in 1848 were not made in most countries until the late 1860s. As the historian Miles Taylor writes: "Both to contemporaries and to posterity, 1848 was the year in which British peculiarity seemed to be underlined once again." Britain avoided revolution for several reasons: a loyal middle class who loved their queen, a government that applied force ruthlessly when needed, and canny politicians like Peel who introduced laws lowering the cost of food. Plus, by transporting the most radical dissenters to far-off colonies such as Australia, the government was able to siphon off some of the greatest political leaders of the Irish independence and Chartist movements. And ultimately, Britain was just not then the land of the revolutionary. Victoria was immensely proud of that.

On June 29, 1850, former prime minister Robert Peel's horse tossed him off and trampled on him, breaking his collarbone, shoulder blade, and a rib that pierced his lungs. Crowds stood for hours outside his house in London, waiting for policemen to read a series of grim medical bulletins and scanning the faces of his friends as they came and went. Three days later, he died. Victoria described Albert as suffering dreadfully, observing that he had "lost a second father"— the man who had been his ally in his rise to power. Albert wrote to the Duchess of Kent: "Blow after blow has fallen on us. . . . And now death has snatched from us Peel, the best of men, our truest friend, the strongest bulwark of the Throne, the greatest statesman of his time." Peel was hugely popular in death. Almost half a million men gave one penny each to a fund established in his name to buy books for workingmen's clubs and libraries.

It had been a hard few years for Victoria and Albert. "Every day," the prince wrote in July 1850, "brings fresh sorrow." In the late 1840s, several close friends died in astonishingly quick succession; each loss was a blow, and the prince grew even lonelier. In November 1849, Prince Albert's private secretary and close friend George Anson died at thirty-seven. Albert mourned him like a brother, wrote Victoria. The dignified Queen Adelaide, the widow of King William IV and Victoria's aunt, passed away in December 1849. In July 1850, Victoria's uncle the Duke of Cambridge died. Then, in August 1850, Louis Philippe, the former king of the French, died in exile at Claremont. In October, Uncle Leopold lost his much-loved second wife, Louise. Victoria was inconsolable.

Only Stockmar, the faithful family adviser who now lived in Germany, remained to counsel the prince; Albert wrote to him often, begging him to come to England. Albert rose an hour before Victoria to respond to letters and worked until midnight. He began to look "pale and fagged," as Victoria put it, putting on weight and waking early, still plagued by insomnia.

Despite his melancholy, Albert's determination did not flag. On the cusp of turning thirty in 1849, he was finally ready to rule on his own. England was at peace, Victoria was content, and Albert was now acting as monarch, with his wife's permission. If there were to be an Albertine age, with its strains of prudence, religious earnestness, industry, energy, and determination, it would be the coming decade. In the 1850s, the prematurely aged, troubled, but gifted Prince Consort would reach his full powers.

CHAPTER 17

What Albert Did:
The Great Exhibition of 1851

We are capable of doing almost anything.

—QUEEN VICTORIA, APRIL 29, 1851

As black clouds slowly parted in the London sky, a vast crowd of people lined the streets. They perched on rooftops, ladders, and boxes and stood jammed together on the banks of the Serpentine River. In Buckingham Palace, Prince Albert was buttoning up a stiff field marshal's uniform. Nine-year-old Bertie was stepping into a tartan kilt. Ten-year-old Vicky was waiting patiently as a wreath of pink wild roses was pinned to her hair. But the crowd mostly wanted a glimpse of the queen. Victoria glittered with diamonds: hundreds of them were sewn into the pink silk of her dress, clasped around her throat, placed carefully on her head. Across her chest she wore the Order of the Garter, a star on a broad blue ribbon. She glanced at her reflection, then smiled: the first of May 1851 was going to be one of the greatest days she and her country had known.

Outside, as the crowds waited for the royal carriages to appear, they watched a determined man with a wooden leg awkwardly work his way up a large elm tree. What had taken a boy five minutes took him fifty; when he finally reached an unoccupied branch, face ringed with sweat, he grinned triumphantly as loud applause broke out from the crowd. Moments later, distant cheers signaled the first sighting of the queen.

On cue, the sun emerged as Victoria's closed, steel-lined carriage trotted quickly along the streets. Police estimated there were seven hundred thousand people crammed in the streets craning to spy her tiny figure. She flushed with a genuine pride in what Albert had created. All appeared as though in a dream; heat on the damp ground created a fog that made the spectacle seem unreal. At last, she thought as she scanned the crowds packing the streets and bobbing in little boats, her husband would be properly recognized by England for his brilliance.

Through the clearing mist, the Crystal Palace gleamed in the sunlight, flags fluttering on every corner of the massive building, constructed of one million square feet of glass. The *Morning Post* described it as a "stupendous cliff of crystal, beautiful beyond the power of language to describe." When Victoria entered the enormous structure with Albert, her two eldest children, and the royal court, cannons boomed, trumpets sounded, and the organ played "God Save the Queen." Victoria ascended her temporary throne—an Indian chair draped with a rich scarlet elephant cloth surrounded by statues, a gushing fountain, and wildly colored carpets. She sat upright, clasped her hands together, and gazed at her husband with undisguised adoration.

The Great Exhibition of 1851 was the most brilliant moment of her reign thus far. Around her, tens of thousands of people crowded the corridors of the marvelous structure that had been built in just seven months by two thousand laborers. And it was all due to her

Albert, who stood stiffly in his red and black uniform. He was exhausted but still spectacular to look at. She had woken that morning to see him lying awake, alert, and anxious. The day passed without a glitch (save for the enthusiastic Chinese mandarin who, after prostrating himself before the queen, was thereafter mistaken for a diplomat, and joined the official procession). Victoria would always remember it as a fairy tale:

> The tremendous cheering, the joy expressed in every face, the vastness of the building, with all its decorations & exhibits, the sound of the organ (with 200 instruments & 600 voices, which seemed nothing), & my beloved Husband the creator of this great "Peace Festival," inviting the industry & art of *all* nations of the earth, *all* this, was indeed moving, & a day to live forever.

To Victoria, Albert was now more than a husband; he was a "creator," godlike and a subject of awe. That afternoon, the couple appeared on the royal balcony at Buckingham Palace for the first time. Intoxicated by the attention, Victoria struggled to give adequate expression to the joy, marvel, and thrill of the moment. "Albert's dearest name is immortalized with this great conception," she wrote. "It was the happiest, proudest day of my life, and I can think of nothing else." In contrast, Albert soberly described the opening as "quite satisfactory." It was the culmination of months of work. The entire structure was a symbol of progress: a place of great beauty where science and creativity met industry. Perhaps most of all, it was a showcase of global unity, the glory of empire, and the moral superiority of Britain. Half of the exhibition space was given to foreign countries, to give it an international flavor. It was the first time many citizens were made aware of the riches of these far-flung countries, of the reach and bounty of the British Empire. Dozens of globes were on display, featuring the shapes of the continents and the celestial heavens above. One contraption depicted the globe as an animal curled inside its shell, pushing and pulling the ocean's tides with its heartbeat.

———

It would have taken at least twenty full working days to view the whole of the Exhibition. There were four sections: Raw Materials, Machinery, Manufacture, and Sculpture and the Fine Arts. The sights on display were wondrous: sperm whale teeth, elephant tusks, nude sculptures, gas fittings, buttonless shirts for bachelors, three-story beehives, enormous jewels, furniture, fertilizer, three-hundred-blade knives, fountains flowing with perfume, diamond-encrusted tartan socks, a collapsible piano, a double piano (Queen Victoria thought the sight of two people playing at each end "had a ludicrous effect"), flowers made from human hair, rhubarb champagne, cake that crumbled into beer, garden benches made of coal, floating deck chairs, a carriage drawn by kites (the "charvolant"), a pulpit with tubes extending to special pews for the hard of hearing, and a hollowed-out walking stick made for doctors that contained enemas. The most popular American exhibits were a reaping machine, the Colt revolver, reclining chairs, a bed that could be converted into a suitcase, and a vacuum-sealed coffin designed to preserve corpses until distant relatives arrived.

Volunteer patrolling policemen were required to demonstrate one of the most popular exhibits: a device, set like an alarm clock, that tilted a bed and rolled out its sleepy inhabitants, possibly into cold water, at the inventor's suggestion. A metal mannequin changed shapes for fitting clothes. There were also likenesses of the queen made of hair, zinc, and even soap, which prompted the economist Walter Bagehot to quip, "It must be amusing to wash yourself with yourself."

Six million people visited the Exhibition over its five-and-a-half-month span. Many London luminaries made the pilgrimage. Charlotte Brontë described it as "vast, strange, new and impossible to describe." It seemed quite magical to her, and the hordes filing through seemed "subdued by some invisible influence." While she stood in a crowd of thirty thousand people, "not one loud noise was to be heard, not one irregular movement seen; the living tide rolls on quietly, with a deep hum like the sea heard from the distance." The wife of the novelist Anthony Trollope, Rose, had a folding tapestry screen in the exhibit; she was delighted to win a bronze medal in her category. Visitors came from every class, and picnicked between pillars or around fountains. Happily for the crowds, for the first time, something resembling a flushing toilet—"monkey closets" or "retiring rooms"—were provided, at a penny per visit.

The idea for the Exhibition had been floating in Albert's mind since he saw the Frankfurt fairs, begun in the sixteenth century, as a child. The same idea had occurred to Henry Cole, an energetic civil servant famed for making the first Christmas card and helping to launch the penny post. Cole returned from an exhibition in Paris in 1849 to discuss the idea with Albert, a fellow member of the Royal Society of Arts (Albert was then the president). Albert suggested the fair be international, and it was begun.

For Albert, the Exhibition was an occasion with serious moral and patriotic underpinnings. "England's mission, duty and interest," he wrote to the prime minister, Lord John Russell, in September 1847, "is to put herself at the head of diffusion of civilization and the attainment of liberty." He recognized the dawning of a new age and saw England as the moral beacon for the world. In a speech aimed at drumming up public support, given at a banquet at Mansion House in March 1850, he outlined his vision:

> We are living at a period of most wonderful transition, which tends rapidly to accomplish that great end, to which all history points—*the realization of the unity of mankind*. . . . Gentlemen— the Exhibition of 1851 is to give us a true test and a living picture of the point of development at which the whole of mankind has arrived in this great task, and a new starting-point from which all nations will be able to direct their further exertions.

Albert was appointed the chair of the royal commission oversee-ing the Exhibition. The design of the structure came from an unex-pected candidate: a gardener named Joseph Paxton. He had doodled a large, arching glass palace—based on a conservatory he had built at Chatsworth House in 1837, partly inspired by water lilies—while sit-ting in a railway board meeting. When he published the sketch in *The Illustrated London News* on July 6, the reaction was glowing (al-though art critic John Ruskin called it "a cucumber frame between two chimneys"). It was quickly accepted: only ten months remained before the Exhibition was due to open. Some objected to his ambi-tious, unusual design: Would trees need to be cut down? Would it smash in storms? Cave in under the weight of the visitors? Be smeared in bird droppings? Hundreds of men were employed to stamp up and down the top level of the structure; it was declared solid and se-cure. Hawks were brought in to rid the park of sparrows that might soil the glass, at the suggestion of the Duke of Wellington; astonish-ingly, it worked. The final creation, Albert declared, was "truly a marvelous piece of art."

The public opposition was intense. Critics railed about crowds, crime, noise, plague, assassinations, riots, and revolution. Politicians said it would attract socialists, who would meet in the park, as well as thieves, pickpockets, vagrants, prostitutes, and foreigners of dubious hygiene who might spark epidemics. An extreme Tory MP called it "the greatest trash, the greatest fraud, and the greatest imposition ever attempted to be palmed upon the people of this country." Others said food supplies would be endangered, the surrounding park would be defiled, and the silver cutlery of those dwelling nearby stolen. There were fears of Roman Catholics using it as a chance for propa-gandizing and of women neglecting their housework.* One member

---

* A cartoon in *Punch* showed a man standing horrified as a servant explained that his wife would be at the Crystal Palace until tea time. It was headed "Awful Re-sult of Giving a Season Ticket to Your Wife." (Another showed "Mama" going missing—sneaking off to a remote refreshment room with a handsome man.)

of Parliament said he wished "that hail or lightning might descend from Heaven" to prevent the Exhibition from taking place.

Albert worked like a man possessed to secure funding, government support, and public approval of his project, fighting back against what he saw as lack of imagination and fearmongering. He began to lose sleep and to experience rheumatic attacks again. He wrote to his stepmother, two weeks before opening day: "Just at present I am more dead than alive from overwork. The opponents of the Exhibition work with might and main to throw all the women into panic and to drive myself crazy." But he persisted, obtaining support from guarantors. In less than two years, the structure was built. The vice president of the Royal Commission wrote that without Albert, "the whole thing would fall to pieces."

The corridors of the Exhibition rang with the sounds of pistons pumping up and down, steam whistling from pipes, an almighty din of machines. There were machines for wiping shoes, spinning cotton, folding paper, purifying sugar, making envelopes, stirring chocolate, sending electric telegraphs, cutting stone, manufacturing medals and spikes and candles, grinding wheat, extracting oil from linseed, rolling and wrapping cigarettes, weighing gold, carbonating soda water, and even drawing blood (by a mechanical leech). It was a grand and miraculous sight, and a prescient sign of the coming Machine Age. Of the millions of people who filed past these creations, staring at them with wonder, very few comprehended how much these mechanisms would transform their lives in the decades to come.

The queen was one of the most enthusiastic observers, visiting the machine section several times and spending hours with guides who taught her how the devices worked. It was, she wrote, "excessively interesting & instructive, & fills one with admiration for the greatness of man's mind." She was particularly captivated by the sight of cotton-cleaning machines.

On July 9, a guide showed her the electric telegraph, which she declared "truly marvelous." The practical application of the science, which had seemed abstract and uninspiring before she met Albert, was now fascinating. He had stirred a new, real excitement in her about the potential usefulness of knowledge. Albert's ability confidently to apply theory to the everyday, and to conceive an incredible future, continued to impress her. Behind the hiss of the machines could be heard the gentle staccato beats and intermittent chiming of hundreds of watches—wooden, waterproof, stop—marking the speeding of time that began in the Industrial Revolution a century before. England had entered the second half of the nineteenth century, and the Exhibition defined as nothing else did the booming, steaming industry, creativity, and inventive spirit of the Victorian age. Queen Victoria visited the Exhibition forty times in five and a half months.

Not all were so rhapsodic. Local tradesmen and thespians complained bitterly about the loss of trade. Charles Dickens thought it a jumbled mess. He had briefly served as a member of the Central Committee of the Working Classes for the Great Exhibition, intended to include and accommodate the needs of the working class, but it was disbanded—at Dickens's urging—after four months. He believed their task was hopeless. He had grown irritated with the notion of the year being marked as one of untrammeled success and sunshine, when so many people were living in squalor. Early in 1851, Dickens suggested in *Household Words* that a second exhibition be held, of "England's sins and negligences." When he finally went to the Crystal Palace, he described it as "terrible duffery." He wrote in July 1851:

> I find I am "used up" by the Exhibition. I don't say "there's nothing in it"—there's too much. I have only been twice. So many things bewildered me. I have a natural horror of sights, and the fusion of so many sights in one has not decreased it. I am not sure that I have seen anything but the fountain and per-

haps the Amazon. It is a dreadful thing to be obliged to be false, but when anyone says, "Have you seen?" I say "Yes," because if I don't he'll explain it—and I can't bear that.

Thomas Carlyle was similarly glum. The only thing the writer admired was the structure itself, which he alternately called a "Gigantic Birdcage," a "big Glass Soapbubble," and "the beautifullest *House,* I fancy, that ever was built in the world." The rest he disdained, calling it the "Exhibition of *Wind*dustry."

Despite his good intentions, Albert's aloofness, relentless work, and lofty ideas annoyed many in the aristocracy. Lady Lyttelton crisply observed that the Exhibition would only "increase the contempt for the Prince among all fine folk." Llewellyn Woodward called him "something of a prig." Albert's warmth and humor did not translate in public, and he could come across as awkward and tactless. Because of this, he surprised many who personally met him. When Carlyle encountered Albert at Windsor Castle in 1854, he was immediately impressed, describing him as a "handsome young gentleman, very jolly. . . . He was civility itself, and in a fine simple fashion: a sensible man withal." They had an extensive conversation about art, Martin Luther, and Saxon genealogy. Albert was most comfortable in the company of people like Carlyle: intellectuals, scientists, and artists, whom he regularly visited in their studios—almost too comfortable, muttered some of the aristocrats.

Still in their early thirties, the powerful couple were confident in the advancement of their public image by 1851. In the Exhibition's opening week, newspapers crowed about the superiority of Britain, evident in the well-behaved crowds, the devotion to the monarch, and the nation's inventions. Superlatives flowed: the Exhibition was greater than the pyramids, declared the *Bristol Mercury*. Albert had proved himself to be "no alien" but a true Brit, "native and [to] the manner born." Victoria was certain the Exhibition had cast a kind of spell over London, and she crowed when Lord Aberdeen told her that even Parliament was going smoothly because of it. She would spend the rest of her life preserving and polishing this moment.

While the glass behemoth in Hyde Park showcased the wondrous expanse of the globe, a woman named Florence Nightingale was stewing about the narrowness of her world. Unlike Victoria, she was bound by middle-class expectations for women, and despite her crisp intelligence, she was unable to do what she wanted. Nightingale, who dreamed of becoming a nurse, was locked in fierce disputes with her family, who wanted her to stay at home. Her older sister threw hysterical fits whenever Nightingale traveled to another country to visit convents and hospitals. Her mother dismissed her dreams as folly and mad ambition. Nightingale felt trapped by convention and the dullness of society, and she begged her family to allow her to "follow the dictates of that spirit within." She became depressed, spending long days in bed, refusing food, and contemplating suicide. Her days were spent yearning for a life in which she could use her brain, and her nights were spent wishing for death: going to bed after a day at home, she wrote, was like going to her grave.

In 1852, Nightingale wrote a remarkably prescient essay, initially intended as a novel, titled *Cassandra*. It was named after the beautiful red-haired Greek goddess who had the gift of prophecy but who was cursed by Apollo after she spurned his advances. This meant that although she would tell the truth, no one would believe her warnings. As a young woman, Cassandra yearned to be allowed to devote herself to helping others, and to use her brain, as men did. Cassandra was, of course, Florence Nightingale. She wrote:

> Why have women passion, intellect, moral activity, and a place in society where no one of the three can be exercised? . . . Now, why is it more ridiculous for a man than for a woman to do worsted work and drive out every day in the carriage? Why should we laugh if we were to see a panel of men sitting around

a drawing room table in the morning, and think it all right if they were women? Is man's time more valuable than women's?... Women themselves have accepted this, have written books to support it, and have trained themselves so as to consider whatever they do as *not* of such value to the world or to others.

This essay, written during the Exhibition, is a stark reminder that Victoria's ambitions had vanished behind the far brighter, higher visions of her husband. Nightingale wrote: "Behind *his* destiny woman must annihilate herself, must be only his complement. A woman dedicates herself to the vocation of her husband. . . . But if she has any destiny, any vocation of her own, she must renounce it, in nine cases out of ten." "Awake," she cried, "ye women, all ye that sleep, awake!" She could very well have been addressing Victoria directly. But the nature of the queen's job meant that she was largely freed from domestic concerns; it was not a public life she yearned for, as Florence Nightingale did, but the private. Her diary shows how tightly politics was entwined with her daily life, how conscientiously she worked, and how carefully she tried to inform herself. She cared desperately about her country. Her own ambitions of rule were slowly being buried under the weight of wifely devotion and maternal exhaustion, but her grand passion was intact. Florence Nightingale's passion was to stretch her mind and heal the sick. Queen Victoria's was Albert.

Being married to Albert, though, had made her think that the act of governing was for men; that power was, perhaps, inherently masculine. For Victoria to hold this view, she had to bury her own instincts. But the more she devoted herself to Albert, the more she feared a fundamental incompatibility between being a good wife and being a good ruler. "Good women" of the era did not even work, let alone possess immense power. When she grew bored with her job, or when Albert demonstrated a greater natural ability, she put it down to her gender—what other explanation could there be? Albert, she told Uncle Leopold on February 3, 1852, "grows daily fonder and

fonder of politics and business, and is so wonderfully *fit* for both—
such perspicacity and such *courage*—and I grow daily to dislike them
more and more." It was not just her: "We women are not *made* for
governing—and if we are good women, we must *dislike* these masculine occupations; but there are times which force one to take an interest in them *mal gre bon gre* [*sic*; "whether one likes it or not"], and I
do, of course, *intensely*." It would take decades for Victoria to stop
pretending that being a good woman required eschewing power. She
did not readily defer to anyone, but she would be fully comfortable
reigning over an empire only when she was without a husband.

On June 27, 1850, Victoria was physically assaulted by one of her
subjects. She was out visiting the Duke of Cambridge when a small,
pasty-faced man named Robert Pate emerged from the crowd surrounding her carriage and Victoria felt herself "violently thrown by a
blow to the left of the carriage." He had smashed a brass-plated cane
into her face. Her bonnet was crushed, and the metal tip bruised her
forehead and left a red welt (the mark remained for many years).
Victoria was livid:

> Certainly it is very hard & very horrid, that I, a woman—a de-
> fenceless young woman & surrounded by my Children, should
> be exposed to insults of this kind, & be unable to go out quietly
> for a drive. This is by far the most disgraceful & cowardly thing
> that has ever been done; for a man to strike *any woman* is most
> brutal & I, as well as everyone else, think this *far* worse than an
> attempt to shoot, which, wicked as it is, is at least more compre-
> hensible & more courageous. The Children were much shocked,
> & poor Bertie turned very red at the time. It is the 2nd time that
> Alice & Affie have witnessed such an event.

It seemed to her "like a horrid dream." Pate, a former British
army officer, whose lawyers argued that he had had a lapse of reason,
was transported to Tasmania, but Victoria never forgot this incident.

Half a century later, in 1899, when an auction house tried to sell the famous metal cane, a stern letter was sent from Osborne and the cane was withdrawn from sale.

When Victoria next gave birth, in April 1853, to a frail child she named Leopold, she took chloroform during labor for the first time. (She had not been so fortunate when Arthur was born, three years earlier.) Dr. Simpson, an anesthetist, was brought from Edinburgh to administer it. He soaked a handkerchief with a small amount of chloroform and inserted that into a funnel the queen could inhale through. She wrote in her diary: "The effect was soothing, quieting and delightful beyond measure." Victoria's example encouraged a generation of women to try the first kind of pain relief available in childbirth. In doing so, they were ignoring the objections of doctors who suggested it might sexually arouse women, who would then try to seduce them while in labor, and priests who insisted that it was wicked to try to opt out from the consequences of original sin. It was a small step in the long march women took over the next century to try to gain control over their bodies. Thousands of relieved mothers across England followed the queen's example. Dr. Simpson's first patient in 1847 was thrilled: the baby was nicknamed Anesthesia.

Before the Exhibition closed in October 1851 and was moved from Hyde Park to Sydenham, where it remained until 1936 when it was destroyed by fire, it had returned a surplus of almost £200,000. Albert planned to invest the money in four institutions to house raw materials, machinery, manufactures, and art on a site near the Crystal Palace. From this vision sprang the complex of museums in South Kensington including the Victoria and Albert Museum, Albert Hall, the Museum of Natural History, the Imperial College, and the Royal College of Music. Albert ended 1851 with a rare feeling of completion and unmitigated success, writing to his brother, "I cannot complain of the past year. The Great Exhibition, which caused me so much work and trouble, ended in an astonishingly satisfactory measure."

The Prince Consort was contented but dangerously exhausted by the strain of running the Exhibition, as well as the jousts with Palmerston. Photos show a man with heavy jowls, a widening girth, and a ponderous look, far from the eager, lean youth he was ten years before, when he married Victoria. He had never stopped working, and his family demanded his time and caused concern. Victoria and Albert constantly worried about their eldest son, Bertie. As they tried to enforce a rigorous education, in line with the expectations for a future king, Bertie would fly into inarticulate rages—"gusts of elemental fury," as Albert's librarian put it. Victoria also fretted about their baby, Leopold, who was thin and did not thrive. It was some time before they understood that he had hemophilia (in this case hemophilia B, a condition passed on by affected males or asymptomatic females). Three of Victoria's daughters went on to transmit the gene, with disastrous consequences for the royal houses of Europe, especially in early-twentieth-century Russia.

Ten years on, strains were beginning to show in Victoria and Albert's marriage. The differences in temperament are obvious in the cool letters Albert penned after their disagreements, urging Victoria to be rational. The volatile Victoria was starting to resent the toll childbirth was taking—she had borne eight children by 1853—and the fact that Albert was exempt from this burden. She would storm and rage, demanding to be heard, following him from the room if he left. Albert cautioned her to control herself and talk to God. He began one long memo, written in May 1853—not long after Leopold was born—with "Dear Child" and urged his wife to "consider calmly the facts of the case." She had erupted over a minor disagreement and he reminded her that he had not caused her misery, but had merely triggered it because she had been "imprudently heaping up a pile of combustibles." He was unable to help her, because if he analyzed her complaints, she got angry; if he ignored her, she felt insulted; if he left, she would follow him.

Albert, an analytical workaholic, struggled to comprehend the gales of hormones released by childbirth, and was bewildered by what he saw as his wife's lack of reason. (As he once told her, "a long closely connected train of reasoning is like a beautiful strain of music.") He couldn't understand when her upset stemmed from something deeper. Victoria, who wrote in her diary about how grateful she was for Albert's "untiring love, tenderness & care," sometimes wept with frustration when she read the stern memoranda from her husband. Her needs were much simpler than he recognized and she resented being lectured to.

A hint of the essential problem in their communication is contained in a letter he wrote in February 1855: "What can I do to you, save, at the most, not listen to you long enough when I have business elsewhere?" Victoria wanted only to be heard and be held. But it was still mostly a happy, supportive marriage. They ate together, walked together, talked for hours, and shared everything. During their sojourns in Scotland, while Albert hunted stags, Victoria would draw with chalks or paint—her diaries are jammed with exuberant descriptions of joyful days, beautiful skies, indescribably lovely Highland landscapes: mountain peaks, woods, sunsets. It was here that they were happiest. The sentimental Victoria mimicked Lot's wife each time she left, mournfully looking back over her shoulder.

CHAPTER 18

The Crimea:
"This Unsatisfactory War"

We are and indeed the whole country is *entirely* en-grossed with one idea, one anxious thought—the Crimea.... I feel so *proud* of my dear noble Troops, who, they say, bear their privations, and the sad disease which still haunts them, with such courage and good humor.

—QUEEN VICTORIA TO
KING LEOPOLD OF THE BELGIANS

Numbers have, I feel confident, died from sheer want of attention. I visited the field, and the groans of the wounded went through me.

—YOUNG NAVAL OFFICER, 1854

Early in the morning of February 28, 1854, Victoria stood at her drawing room window in Buckingham Palace as crowds cheered below, waving handkerchiefs tied on sticks. When the clock chimed seven, Victoria, who had hurriedly dressed at dawn in a dark green woolen dress with a matching shawl and bonnet, took a deep breath. She pushed the door open and stepped onto the balcony to a gust of noise from the crowds. With her opera glass, she stared proudly at the troops below—the last battalion of the Guards due to embark to the

Crimea. She was surprised: unusually, not one soldier seemed to be drunk!

A Scottish infantry regiment—the Scots Fusilier Guards—stood erect in crimson tunics, black trousers, and tall bearskin caps, rifles glinting in the sunshine. The British soldier was confident and unquestioned after the brilliant success ending the Napoleonic Wars. Victoria longed to be one herself. "On such an occasion" as war, wrote the thirty-four-year-old queen, "one feels wretched at being a woman."

The Guards, known for their height and courage, took off their headdresses and gave three massive cheers—which, Victoria wrote, "went straight to my heart." She watched the hats twirl in the air as they threw them toward the balcony, yelling, "God Save the Queen!" The men then turned and marched, disappearing from sight down Pall Mall, along the Strand, and across Waterloo Bridge to the terminus of the South Western Railway. Dozens of wives were accompanying their men to war, walking alongside the troops. They preferred the uncertain fate of joining their husbands to the worry of staying behind.

Back in Buckingham Palace, the young princes Bertie and Arthur played with a wind-up stuffed lion that stretched its jaws and swallowed toy Russian soldiers whole. Victoria went for a walk, received visitors, and saw a play. As she sat watching the actors struggle with their lines, her mind strayed to the soldiers. Later, she wrote: "I shall *never* forget the touching, beautiful sight I witnessed this morning."

The Crimean War was, in many respects, an unnecessary one. "God forbid!" Victoria had cried, when she first mentioned the possibility of conflict. Few could fathom why Britain should rush to defend Turkey against Russia—they had little in common with either country and there had been peace in Europe for forty years, since the end of the Napoleonic Wars in 1815. But the Russian czar Nicholas I— a despot who ruled over a backward country populated by more than twenty-two million serfs—was now eyeing the weakening Ottoman

Empire to his south. Over the past few decades, the Ottoman—or Turkish—Empire had stagnated economically, had been slow to modernize, and had endured a series of ineffective governments that too readily capitulated to the demands of European countries. Czar Nicholas called it the "sick man of Europe" and wanted to carve it up and distribute the spoils. It was a geographically crucial region: Constantinople linked Europe with Asia by land and sea; it was there that the Black Sea met the Mediterranean. If Russia were to edge south into Turkey, it could potentially block crucial chains of supply—especially Britain's route to India—and expand its sea power through its naval base at Sevastopol. In 1853, as Russia moved troops south into the lower Danube (into the modern Romania), the rest of Europe—especially France, Britain, Austria, and Prussia—looked nervously to the east.

The war began, ostensibly, with an argument over access to shrines in Palestine. But the real heart of the dispute was who would act as the protectors of the Christians in Muslim Turkey: Catholic France or Orthodox Russia. The Ottoman Empire, which at its height occupied large swaths of Africa, Europe, Asia, and the Middle East, was predominantly Islamic, but contained thirteen million Orthodox Christians out of a population of about thirty-five million. Russia had been the head of the Eastern Orthodox Church since the fall of the Byzantine Empire in 1453. Czar Nicholas wanted to be the guardian of these Christians caught under Muslim rule in the Ottoman Empire and to shield them from persecution. This claim was his means to wedge further into an unstable region. When the Ottoman leaders decided to grant protectorship to France, Russia invaded Ottoman territories, now modern Romania and Moldova.

Louis-Napoleon Bonaparte, who had been popularly elected as president in 1848 and declared himself Emperor Napoleon III in 1852, was keen to regain France's status in Europe (and boost his domestic popularity by acting as the champion of Catholics). Britain, in turn—the greatest naval power in the world—needed to protect the trade routes into India through Egypt and the eastern Mediterranean, which would be threatened if Russia controlled the Black Sea. Lord Palmerston campaigned for the need to fight, and he rallied the British public behind him. After weeks of clumsy, protracted diplomatic crossfire, a series of misunderstandings were taken as snubs from the Russians, and with the aid of belligerent press and politicians, the country found itself gradually maneuvered into war.

Victoria fretted about leaving London for Scotland at the end of the summer of 1853 while talk of war simmered, but she was assured by Lord Aberdeen—who had been made prime minister in 1852— that she would not be excluded from crucial decisions. She was outraged, then, to discover in October that Lord Palmerston had persuaded the prime minister to send troops to the Black Sea in a defensive position of war, without seeking her consent. Albert was also urgently concerned about a drift toward conflict. He wanted the four neutral powers—Britain, France, Prussia, and Austria—to act in concert to avoid it. He also worried about the precariousness of an exclusive alliance with France. The couple left Balmoral immediately and returned to Windsor to demand an explanation from Lord Aberdeen.

Victoria was increasingly concerned that England was assuming the risks of a European war, offering support to Turkey without having bound it to any conditions. She furiously lobbied her ministers, but she was unable to slow the momentum to fight. On October 23, Turkey declared war on Russia. On November 30, the slaughter of four hundred Turks at Sinope galvanized British support. Russia would not turn the Black Sea into a "Russian lake," declared *The Times*.

The winter of 1853 was raw, dark, and cold. The sun disappeared for days at a stretch, and with it Victoria's hopes for peace. Five days before Christmas, she wrote: "It is an anxious state of things." On the first day of the new year Victoria tried not to think of the looming conflict as she was pushed about in a chair on the frozen lake at Windsor, lined up with other ladies of the court. Vicky and Alice, now thirteen and ten, were learning to skate; Victoria watched them curiously and decided to try it herself, wobbling while holding on to someone's arm. The children made snowmen as deer wandered past.

On February 25, 1854, the Cabinet determined that England would send a summons to Russia to evacuate the Danube. If Russia refused or failed to reply, they would act. Lord Aberdeen, the prime minister, came to see Victoria afterward and complained that he had "terrible repugnance" to all forms of war. Victoria, finally convinced by the now inevitable, sat upright: "I told him this would never do, that it was to save more bloodshed & a more dreadful war, that it was necessary, it should take place *now,* for that a *patch up* would be very dangerous." She was resigned. It was time to be calm and pray for a short, relatively bloodless war. And England had a crucial ally: over the winter, France and England had inched closer together, overturning a deep-rooted enmity to fight together for the first time in two centuries.

Russia refused to move, and Britain prepared to go to war. It had been a peculiar, inexorable drift, comprised of ultimatums, brinkmanship, and a populace perceiving insults from distant barbarians, all of it inflamed by interventionist politicians and newspapers. With defter diplomacy, the involvement of Britain and France could easily have been avoided. But public opinion had been whipped into a frenzy. The poet Arthur Hugh Clough wrote to the American author Charles Eliot Norton in Boston, "Well, here we are going to war, and really people after their long and dreary commercial period seem quite glad; the feeling of the war being just, of course, is a great thing." Thomas Carlyle thought it was a "mad business," but he wrote in his journal in the spring of 1854, "Never such enthusiasm seen among the population." There was some resistance, from Lord Aberdeen and others, but Victoria's mood mirrored her subjects'. On March 28 the war began.

Six months later, dead cats and dogs bobbed gently on the surface of the Scutari harbor in Turkey, grotesque in the sunlight. It would be some hours before the ship *Colombo* would arrive, carrying piles of corpses and soldiers wounded at the Battle of Alma on September 20, maggots squirming in untreated wounds. This was the first battle of the war, and while it was hailed as a victory for Britain and France, losses were heavy. The stench was so bad that the captain was sick for five days afterward. All the blankets were thrown overboard before the ship's anchor was lowered through the flotsam drifting on the harbor.

The inefficiency of the military was deadly. It had taken four days to remove the injured from the battlefield onto the ship, and several men died from cholera before it set sail on September 24. No stretcher bearers were provided for the wounded: an officer spoke of a man carrying his comrades as "a great brawny son of Neptune handling a poor wounded soldier the same as a careful nurse would a small baby." Russian women stared down at their injured enemies from the cliffs above. A young naval officer described the battle's aftermath:

> You can have no idea of their sufferings; men who had under-gone amputation being carried down on men's shoulders a distance of six miles. . . . I never saw such want of arrangement. The military have made scarcely any. I met some officers who told me that until they got a little brandy-and-water from some naval doctors, they had not put a single thing between their lips for two days, and they had been 36 hours on the field without ever seeing a medical officer. Numbers have, I feel confident, died from sheer want of attention. I visited the field, and the groans of the wounded went through me.

Of the 27 wounded officers, 422 wounded soldiers, and 104 Russian captives the *Colombo* was carrying, only half had been medically examined before boarding. There were only four doctors on the ship, and most men weren't treated until almost a week after the battle. *The Times*'s correspondent described the upper decks as "a mass of putridity." There were so many bodies lying motionless on the decks that the officers were unable to get below to their sextants for navigation and had to guess the way to Scutari. This delayed the trip a further twelve hours; thirty men died en route. The lucky ones were dragged slowly up the hill by the elderly pensioners who had been brought to work as an ambulance corps and who were, wrote the correspondent, "totally useless."

The lack of basic preparation was astonishing. The British military had sent troops into battle with virtually no forward planning for medical treatment. In the hospital at Scutari, there were no orderlies or nurses. There was not even material to make bandages to dress wounds. While twenty-three thousand British died in the two-and-a-half-year-long Crimean War, only four thousand of these were killed in action; the rest succumbed to disease, illness, and neglect (this was made worse by the fact that the Turkish barracks that had been lent to the British for use as a hospital were built over sewage pipes and overflowing cesspools, with poor ventilation). It was soon obvious—especially to the woman who would become an emblem of the Crimean War, Florence Nightingale—that many of the fatalities could easily have been avoided.

Back in England, *The Times* began a campaign for better care for the wounded and published accounts that differed dramatically from the official reports. The soldiers, they said, were being treated like savages. *The Times*'s Constantinople correspondent and future editor, Thomas Chenery, thundered:

> What will be said when it is known that there is not even lint to make bandages for the wounded? The greatest commiseration prevails for the sufferings of the unhappy inmates of Scutari, and every family is giving sheets, and old garments to supply their wants. But, why could not this clearly foreseen want have been supplied? Has not the expedition to the Crimea been the talk of the last four months?

In October 1854, a scorching editorial in *The Times* called for citizens to donate money to provide basic supplies for the Crimean campaign. That winter, more than £20,000 poured into *The Times*'s fund.

Every person employed by the Great Exhibition donated a day's salary, and the Victoria Theatre donated one night's ticket sales. And while in her family's summer home at Derbyshire, Florence Nightingale devoured accounts of the war. Like Victoria, Florence had a longing to participate in the matter at hand—in this case, to impose order and efficiency on a morass made by underprepared men. She hated war but regarded it as a part of life. What she truly loathed was inefficiency, incompetence, and stupidity. On Tuesday, October 10, 1854, Florence traveled to London. On Thursday, she told Lord Palmerston, then the home secretary and a friend of the Nightingale family, that she would like to go to Turkey, with one other nurse, at her own expense. On Friday, she was given letters of authorization and introduction from Dr. Andrew Smith of the Army Medical Department. Her trip was quickly arranged. On October 21, Florence Nightingale set sail for Scutari, with a motley crowd of eager nurses, now forty in total. In one short week, the history of medical care in Britain—and the world—had been permanently altered.

Victoria was determined to be an involved monarch, and she told her uncle Leopold: "My whole soul and heart are in the Crimea." She was constantly anxious as she waited for news of battles. The war had been immediately plagued by massive problems of disease and illness, which were easily spread in the humid Mediterranean summer. Thousands died from dysentery, diarrhea, and cholera before they had even cocked a gun at the enemy. William Howard Russell, the *Times* correspondent, saw dead bodies bobbing in the Scutari harbor.

Victoria was infuriated by *The Times*'s reports—the treatment of the men was appalling, but it was also embarrassing to have their incompetence revealed to enemies and allies alike. Why let the Russians know where they had fallen short? In May 1855, a year after the war began, a Lieutenant Colonel Jeffreys told her that "the misery, the suffering, the total lack of everything, the sickness, &c." had not been exaggerated. Victoria told him that the newspaper reports just encouraged the Russians. She wrote in her diary:

He admitted that this was a great misfortune, but that on the other hand they felt certain things *ought* to be made known, else they would not be remedied, & the country *must* understand what has been going on. . . . The trenches, badly drained, were full of water so that one had to lie up to one's waist in it. This was even the case with the Officers, who hardly had had time to change their boots, being constantly obliged to turn out in the night. What must it then have been with the poor men? They had to lie down in their wet clothes, frequently being unable to change them for 1 or 2 nights. They froze & when they did pull off their boots, portions of their feet would come off with them! This Col: Jeffreys himself had seen, & could therefore declare to be no exaggeration of the newspapers.

Victoria did everything she could: harangued her minister about the evident disorganization and negligence, argued for more troops, lobbied for medals to be made quickly to give to the returning men, tried to find employment for disabled veterans, visited returned wounded soldiers in the hospital, and agitated for better military hospitals. She told Lord Panmure, the war minister, that her "beloved" troops were constantly in her thoughts.

Victoria's natural empathy is most obvious in her detailed, careful accounts of meetings with wounded soldiers. Her journal for the year 1854 is crammed with stories of bullet wounds and ravaged faces, feet disfigured by frostbite, mouths emptied of teeth by scurvy, the sadness of empty sleeves and trouser legs. She visited soldiers in hospitals frequently, and she was always distressed at the sight of these "brave, noble" men. She tried to find reasons to be optimistic: their scalps had been torn apart by gunshot, but their faces looked good; they would survive, some even return to war. She wished she could visit them every day.

A few things buoyed her: reports that her messages to the troops were encouraging them; the British military successes against the Russians; the avowals that her men were uncomplaining and noble in the most gruesome of circumstances. Much of this was propaganda fed to the queen by generals who did not wish to upset her. Victoria's wartime diary reveals how frequently those around her spun even the worst news into something positive, how eager the generals were to assure her that their men did not mind suffering for their country. Sir John McNeill, who had been sent to investigate the Crimean hospitals as a sanitary commissioner, gave Victoria "most interesting, gratifying, & comforting accounts of the state of the brave Army" and downplayed the newspaper reports. He described the army camp as a kind of Eden: "The Camp was one of the happiest imaginable; singing, dancing, playing games went on, & there was an incredible disregard of danger: 'the soldiers no more minded shot & bullets, than apples & pears.' . . . There is not 'one man in that Army, who would not gladly give up his life to prove his devotion to Yr Majesty.'"

Victoria clutched at these assurances as well as any accounts of heroism. On October 9, 1854, for example, she was given the "satisfactory" dispatch from Lord Raglan—the Commander of the British troops in the Crimea—about the Battle of Alma: "We also read the sadly large list of casualties with deep interest. The Battle was most brilliant & most decisive, but very bloody. Never, in so short a time, has so strong a battery, so well defended, been so bravely & gallantly taken."

That night, Victoria joined her children dancing reels at Balmoral.

The battle of Alma, just north of Sevastopol, on September 20, 1854, had been the first decisive victory for the allies. This was followed by the chaotic Battle of Balaclava on October 25, in which the British and French light cavalry, armed only with lances and sabers, confronted rows of Russian men armed with guns. The bullets wounded or killed about 240 out of 660 of the British Light Brigade alone (a total of 737 allied soliders were killed or wounded or went missing in the battle). Tennyson's sad refrain was published just a few weeks after the charge was made: "Theirs not to make reply, / Theirs not to reason why, / Theirs but to do and die. / Into the valley of Death /

Rode the six hundred." The charge of the Light Brigade was forever memorialized as a moment of glorious sacrifice, as needless slaughters ordered by shortsighted generals so often are.

Victoria trembled when listening to Lord Raglan's dispatch about the terrible outcome at Balaclava; that night she lay awake for hours. She came down to breakfast the next day only to receive another, even worse dispatch. She trembled throughout her morning walk, lunch, and dinner. The military tried to assure her that the battle had been a great victory despite the fact that no advance had been made. Victoria, who had not known war in her lifetime, was stunned: "What an awful time! I never thought I should have lived to see & feel all this!" She swung from grief to pride and back again: her empathy and imagination made her wretched. Thoughts of the men and their widows consumed her. She slept fitfully, and she repeated the word "anxious" dozens of times in her diary.

The war finally came to hinge on the small Russian-controlled port of Sevastopol, on the Black Sea. It was the fort there that the allied armies of Britain, France, Sardinia, and the Ottoman Empire had intended to capture as soon as they landed in the Crimea. But it was not until the Battle of Inkerman on November 5, 1854, which had broken the Russian resolve, that the port was encircled and the siege began. It dragged through the winter of 1854; the fort had been engineered by brilliant Russians in the early 1800s and proved nearly impossible to penetrate. The queen and her ministers waited every day for news. By Christmas 1854, the public mood was glum; people devoured Russell's daily accounts of the misery, lack of provisions, and failure to capture the Russian citadel. Lady Lyttelton wrote to a friend: "The gloom and weight on one's spirits are dreadful; it appears to me that war never before was so horrible."

Victoria was an involved commander in chief, and she was a part of all discussions to do with the war, even though she believed herself not especially competent in military matters. She wrote to the Duke of Newcastle: "The Queen feels it to be one of her highest prerogatives and dearest duties to care for the welfare and *success* of her army." Albert worked alongside her, writing memoranda that summarized various disputes and political wrangles. When, in January 1855, a motion to hold an inquiry into the conduct of the war was carried by a large majority, the prime minister, Lord Aberdeen, resigned. Lord Palmerston was made prime minister, to the satisfaction of Victoria and Albert, who thought he would make a far better PM than foreign secretary.

Yet along with the war came something strange: an outbreak of hostility toward Albert. As Stockmar pointed out, distrust of the prince stemmed from the fact that he was an outsider; he did not dress, ride horses, or even shake hands in the "true orthodox English manner." His reserve and "severe morality" were evident in the fact that he refused to swear, gamble, or keep a mistress. Protectionists had resented his showcasing of foreign industry at the Great Exhibition. Then there was the inescapable fact that he was German.

Suspicion of foreign influence ran deep in Britain. Many resented the prince's advising the queen in any capacity; some argued that it was unconstitutional for him to advise the sovereign on state affairs, to discuss them with ministers, or to be informed of them at all. For thirteen years, the fact that he shadowed the throne had gone largely unremarked. Now, at a time when he was campaigning openly against the mismanagement of the war and arguing for extra troops to be sent, he became a victim of wartime xenophobia. He was accused of excessive intervention, an almost sinister influence over the queen, and a desire for personal power in the lead-up to the war. He was blamed for blocking Palmerston's push to war against the Russians, as well as for the fact that Palmerston had briefly retired from the Cabinet over a dispute about a reform bill. False rumors spread that Albert had been charged with treason.

Victoria called the attacks "abominable," "unwarrantable," "horrid," "infamous and *now* almost ridiculous." A wounded Albert responded by cutting back some of his commitments until the matter was resolved in Parliament. Victoria disagreed with his retreat, thought it seemed guilty, and criticized Albert for being "afraid to do what I should think to be right." She pressed her ministers who dined at her table to support a public, parliamentary repudiation of the gossip. Gladstone assured her the critics were just excited about "the Eastern Question & their desire for war." Lord Aberdeen dismissed it as antigovernment propaganda of no consequence. When Parliament opened on January 31, 1854, Russell led the debate in the lower house that defended Albert's role as a key adviser. This subdued the critics, and Victoria reported three weeks later that the jeering had stopped in the crowds.

Many of the rumors were right, though: Albert was intensely involved in the queen's work and had, in many ways, usurped her role. He was now regularly meeting with prime ministers alone, and he had gained the respect of the Cabinet and foreign leaders; the French emperor Napoleon III, who met him in September 1854, declared that "he had never met with a person possessing such various and profound knowledge." Victoria would mention these meetings casually in her diary, though she remained keenly engaged in political affairs throughout her pregnancies and confinements. Albert saw their relationship as one befitting two people in the traditional biblical model of marriage, in which the man is the master of the woman.

Reading through their correspondence around this time, Lord Esher remarked that they "were the real Ministers of the Crown, and even Palmerston, now and then, had to take a back seat."

But at the same time that Albert was suspected of wielding too much power, he was mocked for having too little. The prospect of a woman's having a more powerful job than her husband was constant fodder for cartoonists in those decades and inspired a host of apocryphal stories. In one, credited to the painter E. M. Ward, Albert is dining with the Council of the Royal Academy when a royal messenger arrives and tells him the queen needs him urgently. Albert nods, then returns to his dinner. After sending away two more messengers, he finally climbs into his carriage, only to tell his driver to bypass the palace and go directly to Claremont, the country house owned by Uncle Leopold.

A story related by the Edwardian biographer Lytton Strachey is perhaps the most widely told. Albert locks the door behind him in his room; Victoria comes up and bangs her fist on it:

> Victoria: "Open the door!"
> Albert: "Who is there?"
> Victoria: "The Queen of England!"
> *Silence. A torrent of knocking.*
> Victoria: "Open the door!"
> Albert: "Who is there?"
> Victoria: "The Queen of England!"
> *Silence. More knocking.*
> Victoria: "Your wife, Albert."
> The door immediately swings open.

But it was obvious to all who met them that Albert was the dominant figure; an understanding had developed between the two that Albert's talents were superior. An unpublished letter he wrote to his brother in March 1841, not long after their wedding, provides a glimpse of his views of women's intellectual inferiority. He wrote:

> That you are frequently in society including excellent artists is pleasing to hear. However, I cannot agree that you can only gain in conversation with brilliant/clever ladies/women. You will lack in manliness and clarity of your perceptions of the world; for the more brilliant those ladies are, the more confused they are about general ideas and principles. I would prefer to see you in close and intimate traffic with older men who are experienced in life and have achieved something and reached a balance within themselves and with humanity in general.

Albert was not particularly interested in women, clever or not. Unlike many other politicians and aristocrats, he had not grown up surrounded by cerebral women—such as the reformer writer Elizabeth Montagu or Lord Melbourne's mother, Elizabeth Lamb, who ran salons and were at the center of sophisticated cultural life in nineteenth-century England. Albert had been motherless since he was young; he had had a male tutor, a male lawyer, and a household full of men. Rather than encouraging his wife to have faith in her own abilities, he instructed her on her need for "improvement."

Victoria was now calling Albert her "Lord & Master." On their fourteenth wedding anniversary, in 1854, she sighed: "Few women are so blessed with *such* a Husband." She rifled through her desk to find their marriage service: "I feel so impressed by the promise I made 'to love, cherish, honour *serve* & *obey*' my Husband. May it ever be duly impressed on my mind, & on that of every woman." She scoffed at women who dominated their husbands, particularly Lady John Russell, the wife of the prime minister. When the queen of Portugal died, Victoria bemoaned the loss of "a most devoted, loving wife, an exemplary mother & an affectionate true friend." She did not mention the fact that her friend was also a monarch.

The higher Victoria pushed Albert, the lower she sank in her own estimation. The queen was increasingly showing signs of lacking confidence in her own abilities, a change from her teenage pluck. Little wonder, as her husband told her that her eldest daughter was more intellectually capable than she was. Eighteen years after her accession, she wrote: "I trust I have tried to do my duty, though I feel how incompetent, I, as a woman, am, to what I ought to be. I often think what a blessing it would be, were dearest Albert King, instead of me!" Victoria was well educated and intellectually curious; she discussed astronomy with Lord Rosse, including topics such as the weight of the stars, and distant planets like Jupiter. But she was frequently intimidated and increasingly uncertain. In October 1854, after several months of dispatches from the front in the Crimean

War, she hesitated before writing about the war in her journal: "I am so little versed in military matters, that I shall be unable adequately to describe what the difficulties consist in, but will try to put down in a few words, what I mean."

The qualities that had enabled the queen to fight for her crown were the same qualities Albert now said were ruining her character and ability to rule: stubbornness, obstinacy, strength, self-belief. She longed to please him. On his thirty-fifth birthday, in 1854, she dressed carefully in pink and white muslin, watched his face closely as he opened his presents, and pondered how unworthy she felt. (She would pass this fear on to Vicky, too, who was a prodigiously clever, precocious child and later the intellectual equal of her husband, Fritz; in that era, it was the lot of a woman tied to a clever and dominant man.) Surely "*no* wife ever loved & worshipped her husband as I do," she wrote. Victoria was overjoyed when every man in uniform was told to stop shaving above his top lip, just like Albert. By August 4, 1854, she was told the mustaches were "very popular" among the Guards. She wanted her children to resemble Albert, her soldiers to mirror Albert, her ministers to consult Albert, and her subjects to respect Albert.

The prince's ambition was impatient and large, and he genuinely wished to assist his wife. When the Duke of Wellington offered him the position of commander in chief in 1850, he declined because Victoria needed his help:

> The Queen, as a lady, was not able at all times to perform the many duties imposed upon her; moreover, she had no private secretary who worked for her, as former sovereigns had. The only person who helped her, and who could assist her, in the multiplicity of work which ought to be done by the sovereign, was myself. I should be very sorry to undertake any duty which would absorb my time and attention so much for *one* department, as to interfere with my general usefulness to the Queen.

Sitting in his room in Windsor Castle on April 6, 1850, bent over the green lamp he had brought from Germany, Albert wrote a memo on his understanding of his unusual role:

> This position is a most peculiar and delicate one. [It] requires that the husband should entirely sink his *own individual existence* in that of his wife—that he should aim at no power by himself or for himself—should shun all contention—assume no separate responsibility before the public, but make his position entirely a part of hers—fill up every gap which, as a woman she would naturally leave in the exercise of her regal functions—continually and anxiously watch every part of the public business, in order to be able to advise and assist her at any moment in any of the multifarious and difficult questions or duties brought before her.

In 1857, Albert was at last made Prince Consort, to Victoria's great satisfaction. By this time, Greville wrote, the queen was dwarfed by her husband's staggering command of policy detail, and "acts in everything by his inspiration." Albert assumed his command without affirming hers. Instead of relying on a wide range of advisers, Victoria relied only on him; her dependence was total, and her confidence was damaged. But Albert underestimated her intelligence, as well as her stamina and strength.

As the war marched on through 1855 and 1856, Victoria grew jealous of the woman she called "the celebrated Florence Nightingale."* She pored over newspapers for mention of the "Lady of the Lamp," and she wrote at length in her diary about how the soldiers loved the

---

* Victoria did not mention the Jamaican-born nurse Mary Seacole, who worked in the Crimea running an army provision store—the much loved "British Hotel," built from driftwood, at Balaclava—and tending to the ill, dressed in her brightly colored clothes, on the battlefields.

formidable nurse. She wished that she, too, could be mopping the brows of her wounded troops. Victoria spoke about her soldiers in a maternal way; when she personally gave the men their Crimean War medals in March 1855, she was emotional, writing how rare it would be for "the rough hand of the brave and honest soldier" to come into contact with the queen's small, smooth one. She was pleased to hear that many had cried that day.

The queen gave Nightingale a brooch on January 20, 1856, inscribed "Blessed are the Merciful." Later that year, she invited the now widely renowned nurse to Balmoral. Victoria wrote to her in January 1856: "It will be a very great satisfaction to me, when you return at last to these shores, to make the acquaintance of one who has set so bright an example to our sex." Nightingale quickly agreed, hoping to seize an opportunity to lobby for a royal commission.

When they met at Balmoral, Victoria found Nightingale thin, slight, and careworn—she had contracted what was called "Crimean fever" during the war (thought to be typhus). Traveling incognito as "Mrs. Smith" with her aunt, she had returned home suffering from chronic brucellosis, a savage bacterial infection that dogged her for the rest of her life. Victoria was surprised: she had been expecting a cold, severe woman and found someone "gentle, pleasing and engaging, most ladylike and so clever, clear and comprehensive in her views of everything." But the queen most admired Nightingale's single-mindedness:

> Her mind is solely and entirely taken up with the *one* object to which she has sacrificed her health and devoted herself like a saint. But she is entirely free of absurd enthusiasm ... truly simple, quiet, pious in her actions and views, yet without the slightest display of religion or a particle of humbug. And, together with this, an earnest wish never to appear herself— travelling under a feigned name so as not to be known, and refusing all public demonstrations.

Nightingale spoke mostly about the lack of "system and organization" in the military medical care, which had led to so much suffering in the Crimea, and how important it was that it be improved. Victoria was thrilled when Nightingale thanked her for her "support and sympathy saying that, to a man, the soldiers had *all* deeply felt and appreciated my sympathy and interest." Albert discussed the subject with Nightingale at length, agreeing that matters had become even worse since the war ended. Nightingale was taking care with her words, eager to excite sympathy and support for her cause. (Her success was becoming widely known; just a few years later, she would be asked by the United States government for advice on how to care for the wounded in the American Civil War.) She spent the next month at the home of Sir James Clark, near Balmoral, startling Victoria by cutting all her hair off in an attempt to get rid of a lice infestation contracted in hospital. A royal commission into health in the army was agreed upon by the end of her stay, to her great satisfaction.

Nightingale's initial conclusion was that Victoria may have been curious, but was "stupid—the least self-reliant person she had ever known"; she would send for Albert if she found herself stuck for conversation. But Nightingale changed her views dramatically once she had spent more time with the queen. As for Albert, she decided he "seemed oppressed with his situation, full of intelligence, well up in every subject," but was capable of being greatly wrong. "He thought that the world could be managed by prizes and exhibitions and good intentions." He was, she concluded ominously, "like a person who wanted to die." What precisely she meant is unclear, and it was an observation made in hindsight in 1879. It may have been his exhaustion or ill health, but it was a chilling insight from a woman whose expertise lay in trying to help people to live.

An inevitable part of being a queen at a time of national crisis is incongruity. As the violence and bloodshed continued in the Crimea, Victoria wrote about the moonlight on the sea, the snow, blooms, blue skies, and the "peculiar and soothing effect" of a sunny week at Osborne. As soldiers sailed for the East and shivered on hillsides without tents or warm clothes, Victoria was hunting for Easter eggs with the children, playing with stuffed mice, and hiding quietly in the heather as Albert hunted deer.

The children were all shooting upward, and the eldest, Vicky, had suddenly matured. In 1855, during the war, while the royal family was up at Balmoral, Frederick William, the only son of Prussia's Emperor William I, asked Victoria and Albert if he could marry their accomplished, smart daughter, who was almost fifteen. They accepted gladly, making him—and the men of state they confided in—promise not to tell Vicky until she was confirmed a year later, aged sixteen. Victoria was thrilled, telling Leopold, "He is a dear, excellent, charming young man, whom we shall give our dear child to with perfect confidence. What pleases us greatly is to see that he is really delighted with Vicky." She had been worried that her daughter was not pretty enough for her suitor. But her heart ached too; soon she would lose her beloved daughter to Prussia.

Victoria's mother, the Duchess of Kent, was now a doting grandmother and a crucial part of the family, their estrangement long forgotten. Both mother and daughter looked back on the conflict caused by Conroy with regret. The duchess wrote to Victoria that the death of Conroy in 1854 grieved her: "[He] has been of great use to me, but unfortunately has also done great harm." She went on to ask her daughter not to dwell on the past, when "passions of those who stood between us" had sparked mistrust. A wiser Victoria reassured her mother that those days were long gone.

Victoria constantly fretted that she might lose all her hard-won happiness. On her thirty-fourth birthday, in 1853, she wrote: "*What* blessings do I not enjoy! often I feel surprised at being *so* loved, & tremble at my great happiness, dreading that I may be *too* happy!" Osborne was "paradise," with its nightingales, roses, and orange flowers. She was a woman staunchly, though nervously, content.

———

The Crimean War was the only war involving more than two European powers between 1815 and 1914. It marked an interruption of the long peace that stretched from the end of the Napoleonic Wars to the First World War. It had not taken long for Britain to realize they had little in common with their allies the Turks, who were running a largely corrupt, despotic empire; they soon abandoned their uneasy alliance with the French too. The two-and-a-half-year-long Crimean War would always be associated with official cluelessness, and it exposed the incompetence of the British parliamentary elite as well as the military. Florence Nightingale's task was mammoth: it would take a nurse who pioneered the use of pie charts to demonstrate the folly of generals.

In the fall of 1855, the long-awaited news finally came: after a 349-day siege, Sevastopol had fallen to allied troops. Victoria and Albert walked up the hill of Craig Gowan after dinner and lit a bonfire (it had been built the year before, following false news that the fort had fallen). The gentlemen of the Scottish village, clad in nightgowns, boots, and jackets, came, along with servants, foresters, and workmen. As the queen watched the figures dance around the flames from below, firing guns into the blackness, drinking, and playing the pipes, her thoughts drifted, as always, to the soldiers. Many had died, many had returned maimed, and the pact agreed to at the war's end did not score any major concessions for Britain, but the fighting was now over. After months of negotiating a treaty that only served to restrain Russia for a few years, the hefty weight of the war rolled from Victoria's back. Albert returned from the bonfire and reported that it had been "wild & exciting beyond everything."

CHAPTER 19

Royal Parents and the Dragon of Dissatisfaction

A *family* on the throne is an interesting idea. It brings down the pride of sovereignty to the level of petty life.

—WALTER BAGEHOT, 1867

I go on working at my treadmill, as life seems to me.

—PRINCE ALBERT, AUGUST 6, 1861

For centuries, the jade-green river Thames had coursed through the heart of London, crowned by large flocks of swans and crowded with fish; it bustled with barges and sustained millions of livelihoods. The fetid sewage that accumulated on its riverbanks in the early nineteenth century also provided a decent living for those who could put up with the smell. So-called mud larks, usually children of seven or eight, collected rubbish from the river, roaming the banks and pipe ends with kettles and baskets dangling from their arms, hunting for pieces of coal or wood, copper nails, or any salable rubbish. Men crawled through sewers scavenging for anything useful: nails, rope, coins, bolts, cutlery, metals, or buttons. Henry Mayhew's definitive midcentury account of London's poor recounts "many wondrous tales" of men losing their way in the labyrinths flowing with sewage or of "sewer-hunters beset by myriads of enormous rats." The work was filthy, but surprisingly lucrative.

A century earlier, the river named Tamesis by Caesar was clean. But when the water closet replaced the cesspool in the mid-1800s, channeling the city's sewage to the river in large murky pipes, the water turned to black in less than half a century. At the same time, the capital's population ballooned. In 1801, there were 136,000 houses in London. By 1851, there were 306,000. Those living near the river noticed an increasing acidity and murkiness in the water.

By the mid-1850s, eighty million gallons of human waste from more than three million Londoners was draining down the Thames each year. The problem seemed insurmountable. In 1852, the chief engineer of the Metropolitan Sewers Commission, Frank Forster, died, and his death was attributed to "harassing fatigues and anxieties of official duties." The next year, a cholera epidemic raged through the city, killing almost twelve thousand. This finally convinced scientists that disease was not borne by foul air, but by water. Yet the government, crippled by inertia and lack of will and urgency, failed to act.

The royal family was insulated, but not exempt. Buckingham Palace often reeked of leaking excrement and crawled with rodents. Victoria watched her dogs chasing rats around her bedroom at Windsor, praising one for "valiantly" triumphing; "the rat made an awful noise, though he was killed right out pretty quickly." Victoria employed a personal ratcatcher, Jack Black, who strode around corridors in blazing red topcoat, waistcoat, and breeches, wearing a belt set with cast-iron rats. When Victoria and Albert rode along the Thames in a barge, they grew sick from "the fearful smell!"

By June 1858, the smell was so bad that lime was scattered in the river beneath the Houses of Parliament, and sheets soaked in bleach hung from ceilings inside so the gentlemen could speak without having to hold handkerchiefs over their noses. In the early summer, a long dry spell had dwindled the supply of fresh water coming from upland areas, and the water temperature was at a record high. A thick mass of black sewage stretched for eighteen miles. The resulting crisis became known as the Great Stink. Much of the city business ground to a halt; the courts rushed through cases to avoid prolonged exposure to the fumes. Charles Dickens wrote that the "most horrible" Thames had a "most head-and-stomach distracting nature." Some Londoners spontaneously vomited when suddenly exposed to fumes. The stench was no respecter of class; all were affected. The country Victoria ruled was struggling to keep pace with the rapid modernization of the century; industry was flourishing, trade was expanding, and the Thames had become one of the busiest waterways in the empire. But the government was scrambling to ensure that the most basic of rights were provided to her subjects: clean water, clean air, and sanitation.

Victoria was more preoccupied with the world inside her palaces. Her ninth child, her beloved Beatrice, was born on April 14, 1857. Albert and the doctor again gave Victoria chloroform to numb the pain, which she found a "great relief." Dr. Clark advised her that, given the wear on her physically, and the fact that she was almost thirty-eight, this should be her last baby. Worried that this might affect her intimacy with Albert, Victoria asked her doctor, "Can I have no more fun in bed?" During her ninth and final pregnancy, she had struggled with a bad cough and exhaustion, all while grieving the death of her half brother, Charles, a Bavarian soldier and politician. By the end, Albert told his brother that Victoria was "hardly able to do what is expected of her." But the robust queen bounced back cheerfully from the grueling labor. Two months after the birth, Victoria was strong enough to dance all night. "I have felt better & stronger this time, than I have ever done before," she wrote happily. "How I also thank God for granting us such a dear, pretty girl, which I so much wished for!" She named her Beatrice, she said, because it meant "blessed." This baby girl would be an enormous comfort to her mother. After watching Beatrice gurgle and play in her bath, Victoria wrote: "A greater duck, you could not see & she is such a pet of her Papa's, stroking his face with her 2 dear little hands." Both parents were infatuated. Albert declared her "the most amusing baby we have had."

Beatrice quickly flourished; she was a godsend, a child of grace. Victoria doted on babies over the age of four months, especially the fat ones. She wrote on Beatrice's first birthday: "She is so engaging, & such a delight to kiss & fondle. If only she could remain, just as she is."

Less than a month after Beatrice was born, India erupted into a spontaneous, brutal mutiny. It was a war of independence fought on political grounds—the Indians rebelling against the rule of the British—and religious, the Hindus and Muslims against the Christians. The revolt followed a broadening of British influence in India. From 1848 to 1856, Lord Dalhousie, the governor-general of India, had introduced reforms, most controversially through the "doctrine of lapse" whereby he annexed land when the Indian ruler was "manifestly incompetent" or died without an obvious male Indian heir, in an attempt to bring the entire country under British control. He had also built infrastructure—railways, irrigation canals, telegraph lines, post offices, roads, and bridges—and increased the land owned by British India by more than a third, including the vast Punjab in the north. He centralized and westernized the public service and administrative branches of government, and he tried to clamp down on abhorrent local practices such as female infanticide and human sacrifice. Some changes—such as legalizing the remarriage of Hindu widows in 1856—were made too rapidly; that was seen as an assault on the Indians' faith and way of life. The Indians knew their soldiers far outnumbered the British; five Indian soldiers to one British soldier was the common ratio.

The immediate cause of the rebellion was the introduction of the Enfield rifled musket in 1853. The cartridges used with this musket were smeared in pig and cow fat and were designed to be torn open with the teeth, which was offensive to both Muslim and Hindu soldiers (whose religions ban or discourage the eating of pork and beef). They feared they were going to be forcibly converted to Christianity by their British rulers. The cartridges were eventually replaced, assurances made about respect for religion, and an allowance made for soldiers to open cartridges with their fingers—although rumors persisted that the offending grease remained. The catalyst came on May 9, 1857, when eighty-five Indian men at Meerut station were sentenced to ten years in prison for refusing to load their guns. The next day, in reaction, three Indian regiments killed British officers and their wives. They then marched south to Delhi and butchered as many Europeans as they could (around fifty, at closest count).

As the mutiny spread, Victoria tried to goad the Cabinet into action. British troops were currently en route to Asia, to fight for greater recognition of British trade and diplomacy in the Second Opium War in China. They were instead diverted to India, delaying the Chinese war by a year. It was a brutal conflict; both sides committed atrocities. At Cawnpore, 350 Britons were under siege from 3,000 Indian mutineers for three weeks. A local prince who sided with the rebels offered the British safe passage down the River Ganges if they would abandon their entrenchment in Cawnpore. The British agreed, and they piled into rowboats moored at the river's edge. Suddenly bugles sounded, the Indian oarsmen dived into the river, and the Indians fired cannons at the British group, killing nearly everyone. Saber-bearing Indian troops rode into the water to slice up any who had escaped the grapeshot. The 125 women and children who survived were imprisoned in a nearby villa and slaughtered a month later. The British arrived the day after the massacre and walked past wells piled with mutilated corpses. There were tiny red hand- and footprints on the walls of the huts and children's shoes with the feet still in them. Reprisals were swift and savage. Before being led to the gallows by the British, mutineers were made to lick blood from the floor.

Victoria was sickened and unable to sleep, haunted by the thought of toddlers trapped in the villa. It made her "blood run cold." She asked her former lady-in-waiting Lady Canning, now the wife of the governor of India, to let those "who have *lost* dear ones in so dreadful a manner *know* of my sympathy. A woman and above all a wife and mother can only *too* well enter into the agonies gone thro' of the massacres."

The British public bayed for revenge. The rebels were maimed, killed, stripped naked, and tortured for sport. One British unit drank and listened to a band while they watched hundreds of rebels hanged. When the enlightened Lord Canning, the governor of India, chastised his troops for this behavior, the press blew raspberries and clamored for bloody reprisals. Victoria offered support to Lord Canning, calling the vengeful cries "shameful." While those responsible for the carnage should be punished, she said to him, "to the nation at large—to the peaceable inhabitants, to the many kind and friendly natives who have assisted us . . . these should be shown the greatest kindness. They should know there is no hatred to a brown skin— none, but the greatest wish on their Queen's part to see them happy, contented and flourishing."

In July1858 a peace treaty was signed. Parliament abolished the East India Company, which had governed most of India since 1601, and instead took direct responsibility for the governance of the country. Victoria promised legal protection for the religious belief and worship of her Indian subjects and insisted that all should be given jobs according to education and ability, not class or creed. Her views were enlightened when compared to the reports she had from British officials returning from India, who complained of Indians behaving "like animals."

In January 1858, in the last months of the mutiny, Vicky married her Prussian prince, Fritz. Albert had approved of the match; not only was Fritz from a country he hoped would lead a united Germany, but he was a man with liberal beliefs despite his strict militaristic upbringing. As Vicky's views dovetailed with her husband's, they would both find themselves uncomfortably at odds with the conservative Prussian royal family. The alliance would not prove to be as effective as Albert had hoped.

Victoria was more nervous at her eldest daughter's wedding than she had been at her own; at least then, she said, she knew she would be going home with Albert. She trembled so violently on the frosty morning before the ceremony that her image was blurred on the daguerreotype for which she posed with Vicky and Albert; the other two were perfectly still. The seventeen-year-old Vicky was elegantly dressed in white rippled silk trimmed with lace and wreaths of orange flowers and myrtle. The wedding was held in the Chapel Royal at St. James's Palace on January 25, 1858—the same place where Victoria and Albert had wed eighteen years earlier. (Victoria had written to the Earl of Clarendon stamping out any suggestion that the wedding might take place in Berlin: "It is not *every* day that one marries the eldest daughter of the Queen of England.") On the way to the chapel, Victoria, wearing a mauve velvet dress, struggled not to cry: "I could hardly command myself." She was proud of her daughter's poise, but sobbed when she bade her farewell a few days later: "My breaking heart gave way. . . . What a dreadful moment, what a real heartache to think of our dearest Child being gone & not knowing how long it may be before we see her again!"

On February 2, snow fell as Albert walked through the thousand-strong crowd at Gravesend to escort his teenage daughter to the yacht that would ferry her to a new life in Germany. Nearby, small girls sprinkled the paths with flower petals. Albert had dreaded this moment: he was very fond of the astute, gifted daughter who so resembled him—his favorite child and a kindred spirit. The thought of separation was "especially painful." As the two of them stood in her cabin, Vicky buried her face in Albert's chest, soaking it with tears. She felt she owed her father more than anyone else. Albert stared ahead, his arms around her. He wrote to her the next day, assuring her of his love, despite his stiffness: "I am not of a demonstrative nature, and therefore you can hardly know how dear you have always been to me, and what a void you have left in my heart."

In the days after the wedding, Victoria was restless with worry. As she had told Leopold: "She is so much improved in self-control, and is so clever (I may say wonderfully so), and so sensible that we can talk to her of anything—and therefore shall miss her sadly." What consoled her was that the twenty-six-year-old Fritz, Prince Frederick William of Prussia, was decent, kind, and obviously in love. Then it became quickly obvious that the distance would draw mother and daughter closer. That year, Victoria and Vicky began a torrent of letters that they sometimes wrote daily, totaling almost four thousand over four decades.

It was the threat of war in Europe, though, that most preoccupied Victoria and Albert in 1858 as their daughter settled into her new Prussian palace. Italy was then divided into many states, with Austria ruling the north, incorporating Lombardy, Venetia, and Tuscany (and their capitals, Milan, Venice, and Florence), and the push to unify it had gained strength. There were three Italian wars of independence between 1848 and 1866, which ultimately concluded with a united Italian peninsula. Austrian rule had remained intact after the first war in 1848; a decade later, another began when France was drawn in to help the Italian nationalists (Napoleon III wanted Italy to unite under a Sardinian king). The British were suspicious about the French intentions. Victoria believed Italy would merely be France's stepping-stone toward the Rhine, and Victoria and Albert were concerned that the ambition of Napoleon III—a close friend they were losing faith in—would ignite a full-blown European war.

In March 1859, after Napoleon III lent his support, the leader of the powerful, democratic northern Italian state of Piedmont-Sardinia mobilized. In April, Austria sent an ultimatum demanding they disarm. When they refused, Austria declared war. England remained staunchly neutral, despite public support for Sardinia. Albert and

Victoria were influential in pushing the Cabinet to maintain this neutral stance, sending a torrent of letters to the bellicose Lord Palmerston and Lord John Russell. The interventionist ministers wanted to help France, but Victoria and Albert reined them in repeatedly. They were often at odds with Palmerston over his sympathy for the Italian nationalists during the years that he was prime minister, from 1855 to his death in 1865 (apart from an interlude in 1858–59 when Lord Derby was PM). But on July 11, 1859—the same day that London's Big Ben tower clock struck for the first time—a preliminary peace between France and Austria was unexpectedly agreed upon (it was confirmed by a treaty signed by all three parties in November, and Lombardy ended up being ceded to Sardinia). A full-scale war had been averted, and the royal couple had played a crucial part in staying Britain's hand.

Victoria and Albert were now at the height of their powers. As one of the editors of the queen's letters, Lord Esher, later observed, the work of the queen, with Prime Ministers Peel, Aberdeen, Palmerston, and Derby, "was of immense value. . . . [Victoria] had on several very vital occasions stayed the action of a Minister, when such action involved risks and perils which reflection convinced him and his colleagues they were not justified in incurring." Without "the tenacity of the Crown," he wrote, England would have been drawn into the Austro-Italian war of 1859.

But the question of whether Albert was starting to intervene in government affairs more than was appropriate remained. By 1859, almost two decades after he had married Britain's queen, he was showing signs of increasing stridency. He frequently fought with government ministers to get them to change course. In 1905, reading through the correspondence, Lord Esher noted that this tendency may have only increased with time:

> The Prince Consort was taking a stronger hold than ever of the helm of State and there were constant battles between him and the Ministers, he acting in the Queen's name. . . . That there

was friction is beyond doubt. Had he lived, his tenacity might have hardened into obstinacy, and the relations between him and a Government founded—like ours—on democratic institutions, would have become very strained.

The role of the monarchy under Albert's leadership, then, was of forceful influence, which urged the government to exercise restraint in foreign policy and democratization, to erode the authority of the aristocracy and exert influence through a web of royal connections that spanned Europe in a network of carefully planned and delicate backdoor diplomacy. Victoria and Albert were among the most skillful diplomats of their time, meeting with kings and queens, writing to emperors and empresses, and trying to sway them through friendship or argument. Albert planned to seed the British royal bloodline in the courts of Europe with his offspring. The first step was placing Vicky in the royal court of Prussia, which was a strategic triumph, though her life there would be miserable.

On January 27, 1859, Victoria became a grandmother. She ran along the castle corridors to tell Albert about the birth of Vicky's first child, Frederick William Victor Albert, the future Kaiser Wilhelm II. Victoria then sent out a flurry of telegrams as bells rang in the town below Windsor Castle and illuminations flared. She had at first been horrified to discover her daughter had become pregnant so quickly; she called it "horrid news." Vicky, sounding like her father's daughter, responded that she was proud to create an immortal soul. Victoria rolled her eyes at the suggestion that birth was some kind of spiritual endeavor: "I think much more of our being like a cow or a dog at such moments; when our poor nature becomes so very animal and unecstatic." Once the child was safely born, Victoria felt "relieved from a great weight," given how perilous childbirth still was. But two days later, she learned the birth had been "very severe"; the baby had been in breech position and had almost died. Albert advised rest, cold baths, and sea air. Vicky sent her mother a locket with a clipping of her grandson's hair.

Victoria had berated her daughter for "choosing" a delivery date when she could not be there with her, and sent in her stead a bottle of chloroform, Dr. James Clark, and the curiously named midwife Mrs. Innocent. Victoria carefully recorded every detail of Vicky's recovery: when she first lay on a couch, when she was able to sit up in her armchair and get to her feet, when she was able to walk. It was only when Vicky came to visit in May 1859 that Victoria learned that her grandson's left arm had been injured at birth and hung weakly from its socket, paralyzed. When Victoria finally met little Willy in 1860 on a trip to Germany, she described him as a "fine fat child, with a beautiful white soft skin." Victoria was an adoring grandmother, who believed her children's offspring to be "the best children I ever saw."

In the late 1850s, as she approached the age of forty, the queen grew slender and content. She was at last relieved from the cycle of childbearing and delighted in the privacy of the Isle of Wight and the freedom of Scotland. She and Albert often stayed in a small granite and wood hut above Loch Muick, spending hours floating on the lake fishing for trout before going to bed early, "so peaceable & happy in this little cottage, far away from all human habitations." The working poor who inhabited the cottages near Balmoral Castle continued to be startled by unannounced visits from the queen. Victoria and Albert undertook long expeditions through remote parts of the Highlands, where they traveled incognito and stayed in inns. They loved the game of anonymity, evading questions from curious passersby and trying to guess how their cover had been blown if they were recognized. Once, the giveaway was the crown on the dog cart and the marking on the bedsheets they brought along that made the locals suspect they were wealthy visitors from Balmoral, compounded by the fact that Victoria wore so many rings. One morning, the royal group realized they had been found out when they woke to the sounds of drums and fifes and saw that their elderly landlady had donned a fancy black satin dress adorned with white ribbons and orange flowers.

On one of their 1859 expeditions, when they had reached the top of the second-highest mountain in Britain, Ben Muich Dhui, Albert described the queen as "particularly well, cheerful and active." Her expeditions were lighthearted; they giggled as they slipped down escarpments and slid on rocks, and they laughed at the wry ghillies. Victoria grew particularly fond of her "invaluable Highland servant" John Brown, a man she would later call her best friend, who guided her horse, carried her shawls, and lifted her over rocky, steep terrain. She often mentioned how much she had laughed. A common refrain then was "Oh! if only the time did not fly so fast!" The last note in Albert's diary in that year is "We danced in the New Year." Victoria, in these halcyon days, was always dancing: waltzes, trots, and especially reels. Albert could rarely match her stamina on the ballroom floor, but it didn't matter. As she got back on her feet in the weeks after giving birth, she knew that if she could dance, she was ready to turn her face to the world again.

Walking through the gardens at Buckingham Palace on June 1, 1859, along the muddy lake edge where pale pink flamingos poked their beaks into the water, Victoria relished the new intimacy that had blossomed between herself and her eldest daughter. They talked about everything: "We so completely understand one another. She is a dear, clever, good affectionate child & we are like 2 sisters!" Once Vicky grew up, her relationship with her mother shifted to more equal footing: they had both married and borne children.

Yet Albert remained the adored instructor, nurturing his daughter morally and intellectually. He told her to win hearts by thinking of others, and encouraged her to be punctual, and serene about the fickle moods of the public. He set her complex translation tasks and offered to look through the Prussian budget to help her understand it better. Albert also made her promise that she would tell him "faithfully the progress of her inner life," a strikingly thoughtful gesture from an intense father to an intense daughter. In return, he promised to nurture that inner life as fulfillment of his "sacred duty."

The abstract, philosophical nature of Prince Albert's brain is illustrated in his letters to Vicky. When she said she was homesick, for example, her mother warmly assured her she was missed. But her father wrote an analysis of the condition of homesickness. Assuring her it was a natural state, he explained it was "a painful yearning, which might exist quite independently of, and simultaneously with, complete contentment and complete happiness." It was a dualism, he said, in which "the new I" cannot disconnect from "the I which has been": "Hence, the painful struggle, I might almost say, spasm of the soul."

Victoria wanted to know everything, and demanded a level of excruciating detail about Vicky's new life—her reception, her housing, her health, her clothes, her rooms, her daily routine. She told Leopold that, never having been apart from her daughter for any real length of time, she was "in a constant fidget and impatience to know everything about everything. It is a great, great trial for a Mother who has watched over her child with such anxiety day after day, to see her far away—dependent on herself!" Shortly after the wedding, Victoria wrote and told Vicky to leave "descriptions of great things" to others, "but give me your feelings—and your impressions about people and things, and little interior details. 1st: What dress and bonnet did you wear on landing? And what bonnet the next 2 days? 2nd: What sort of rooms had you at Cologne and Magdeburg? 3d: Did you dine with your people at Cologne and did you sup at Magdeburg at 12? 4: What cloak did you wear on the road, and have you been drawing? 5: How do you like the German diet—and how do your poor maids bear this hurry scurry?"

Victoria was often guilty of micromanaging her children's lives, showing concern but also an oppressive zealousness and control. When giving Vicky various instructions, Victoria wrote: "So you see, dear, that though alas far away (which I shall never console myself for)—I watch over you as if I were there." She was also frequently critical. She reprimanded Vicky for not eating enough during the day, for capitalizing too many words, for not numbering pages correctly, and for mixing up the date of her accession. She told her to not laugh too loudly or stoop when she wrote, to maintain dental hygiene—"few people have good teeth abroad"—to be tidy for the sake of her husband, and to have no familiarity with anyone in her court except her parents-in-law. "I really hope," she wrote, "you are not getting fat again? Do avoid eating soft, pappy things or drinking much—you know how that fattens." She also warned her daughter against neglecting her husband or duties because of too much love for her babies. "No lady, and less still a Princess," she said, would be fit for her husband or her position if she "overdid the passion for the nursery." Victoria insisted that she saw her youngest children being bathed and put to bed only about four times a year.

Vicky was somewhat surprised at her mother's sudden overwhelming fondness for her, given how harsh a disciplinarian she had been in earlier years. But the two women concurred in their belief that Albert was a demigod. It was to Vicky that Victoria confided tales of her unhappy childhood, how she had no outlet for what she knew as her "very violent feelings of affection." This was why, she said, she owed everything to Albert: "He was my father, my protector, my guide and adviser in all and everything, my mother (I might almost say) as well as my husband. I suppose no one ever was so completely altered and changed in every way as I was by dearest Papa's blessed influence. Papa's position towards me is therefore of a very peculiar character and when he is away I feel quite paralysed." The queen was unaware how vulnerable this utter dependence would one day leave her.

Bertie was one subject the women disagreed on. Victoria regularly railed against her secondborn, while Vicky rarely said a word in return. In March 1858, Victoria told her daughter she was "wretched" about Bertie, who was then sixteen and preparing for his confirmation the next month by reading sermons to his mother. Over the next few months he would travel to Rome and begin his studies at Oxford, but Victoria despaired of his constant laziness. She called him ignorant, dull, and far from handsome, "with that painfully small and narrow head, those immense features and total want of chin." She decried his hanging "Coburg nose"—just like his mother's—his putting on weight, his large mouth, and his new hairstyle. The fashion was to cut the hair short and part it severely in the middle, which Victoria said "makes him appear to have no head and all face."

Victoria described her children the same way she described most people: bluntly and often harshly. Of her son Leopold, for example, she wrote: "He is tall, but holds himself worse than ever, and is a very common looking child, very plain in face, clever but an oddity—and not an engaging child though amusing." Helena suffered from features "so very large and long that it spoils her looks." The attractive Arthur, Alice, and Louise were praised and held up as foils. When Vicky told Victoria that Bertie, while visiting her in Germany, was charming, his mother scoffed in reply: "I think him very dull; his three other brothers are all so amusing and communicative." Vicky's heart sank; defending him was a vain exercise.

Victoria was now the most famous working mother in the world. Her image, that of a mother-queen, made a once remote-seeming monarch instead a figure of ordinary flesh. Walter Bagehot wrote in 1867 that having a family on the throne "brings down the pride of sovereignty to the level of petty life." Victoria simultaneously reigned over England and appeared as though she were solely concerned with her domestic life. In England at the time, women who had jobs were pitied, but the 1851 census found one in four wives and two in three widows worked. In the second half of the nineteenth century, the ranks of working women swelled rapidly and became respectable. It was still believed, though, that men were enhanced by work, while women were weakened by it. But the queen worked without guilt.

Yet it is only at this stage, when Victoria was steeped in the contentment of motherhood, that we begin to see the creeping anger she felt at what childbearing required of women. She called it the *Schat-tenseite,* or shadow side, of marriage: little discussed, or even properly understood, except by the women who bore children. When Vicky suggested that a married woman had more liberty in society than an unmarried woman, the queen responded that in one sense that was true, but in another, physical sense, it wasn't:

> Aches—and sufferings and miseries and plagues—which you must struggle against—and enjoyments etc. to give up—constant precautions to take, you will feel the yoke of a married woman. . . . I had 9 times for eight months to bear with those above named enemies and I own it tired me sorely; one feels so pinned down—one's wings clipped—in fact, at the best . . . only half oneself—particularly the first and second time. This I call the "shadow side" as much as being torn away from one's loved home, parents and brothers and sisters. And therefore I think our sex a most unenviable one.

The hidden world of nineteenth-century motherhood—of medical ignorance, and lack of pain relief—made Victoria shudder when she thought of what her daughters might go through. When looking at suitors for Princess Alice in 1860, Victoria was gloomy: "All marriage is such a lottery—the happiness is always an exchange—though it may be a very happy one—still the poor woman is bodily and morally the husband's slave. That always sticks in my throat."

Even the angelic Albert failed to understand the lot of women. Victoria wrote angrily to Vicky in 1859 that Albert sometimes "sneered" at her and other women for their bodily trials. Vicky had been complaining that one of her husband's cousins despised women and thought they were only good for decoration. Victoria responded:

> That despising our poor, degraded sex is a little in all clever men's natures; dear Papa even is not quite exempt though he would not admit it—but he laughs and sneers constantly at

many of them and at our unavoidable inconveniences, etc., though he hates the want of affection, of due attention to and protection of them, says that the men who leave all home affairs—and the education of their children to their wives—forget their first duties.

The Prince Consort grew tired of Victoria's complaints about the debilitation of pregnancy. When she was entering into the middle trimester of her last pregnancy in the fall of 1856, Albert accused her in a letter of being demanding and selfish. By writing, he had intended to calm her, but he also showed impatience with her complaints about the physical constraints she railed against:

I, like everyone else in the house make the most ample allowance for your state. . . . We cannot, unhappily, bear your bodily sufferings for you—you must struggle with them alone—the moral ones are probably caused by them, but if you were rather less occupied with yourself and your feelings and took more interest in the outside world, you would find that the greatest help of all.

Albert urged his wife to let God's goodness lift her out of the pain, "degradation [and] indignation" she described to him. What no historians have mentioned as a factor in her ambivalent attitude toward childbearing is the cost to her physical—and mental—health, which she kept hidden for the rest of her life.

In many ways Victoria was not a natural mother. Albert told her that the reason she did not enjoy the children was because she mistakenly thought the job of a mother was to discipline: "The root of the trouble lies in the mistaken notion that the function of a mother is to be always correcting, scolding, ordering them about and organizing their activities. It is not possible to be on happy friendly terms with people you have just been scolding." When Bertie was still a boy, his governor—then Lord Clarendon—described "the Queen's severe way of treating her children" as "very injudicious," especially with the strong-willed, self-certain Bertie.

In June 1856, Vicky burned her arm when a candle she was using to melt wax to seal a letter set her sleeve on fire. Victoria was at her daughter's side every day when the wound was carefully dressed.

Sometimes Victoria's children bored her, and sometimes they delighted her. She wrote fondly of the sweet, pretty "Lenchen" (Helena), her amiable, selfless Alice, and the hemophiliac Leopold, who struggled with ailments but was "a clever, honest & well intentioned boy." She clearly favored Beatrice, Vicky, and Affie, the last of whom she described as a "sunbeam in the house" and "so like his precious father." When speaking of Arthur, she said, "Children are a great comfort to me at such times, for their happy innocent unconsciousness is refreshing and cheering to one's heart." When Albert refused to allow her to take her younger children with her to visit Vicky in Prussia in 1858, she called him a "hard-hearted and a great tyrant." Not long after, when Affie was sent away for several months to join HMS *Euryalus,* a steam frigate heading for the Mediterranean via Gibraltar, she told Vicky that "Papa is most cruel upon the subject. I assure you, it is much better to have no children than to have them only to give them up! It is too wretched." She and her children watched eclipses and comets through telescopes, gazed at the ugly whale-headed storks at the zoo, and marveled at a remarkable performance from the American "horse whisperer," who was able to tame wild horses almost instantly into submission. Mostly theirs was a life of stability; the closeness between Victoria and Albert was the pole that the family, and the nation, circled. Their children grew up observed and controlled, but they formed their own alliances and rebellions, like Alice and Bertie, who sneaked out for cigarettes.

Victoria consulted calendars obsessively. She marked important dates and anniversaries in her diary—not just birthdays and wedding days, but the day Albert arrived in England before their engagement, the day they got engaged, the day Albert arrived in England for their marriage, the day Fritz declared his intention to marry Vicky, the day Vicky and Fritz were officially engaged, and the day they married. She noted anniversaries of battles, the fall of the French Orleans family, the opening of the Great Exhibition, the day Vicky burned her arm badly, and the time Albert jumped out of his carriage in Coburg, scratching his face. Victoria clutched at time with the manner of a woman unused to contentment and terrified at the possibility of it ending. She disliked change.

The year 1860 ended on an anxious note. Victoria was worried about war. She told Vicky she was sick of "horrid" politics and the Continent in general and one day wanted to escape to Australia with the children. Albert kissed her head and told her to trust in God; he would protect them as he had done before. Victoria was also concerned about the health of her mother. When the Duchess of Kent rallied after a bout of illness in 1859, Victoria wrote to Leopold that she had never suffered as she had in the four hours she spent waiting to hear whether her mother was going to survive: "I hardly myself knew how I loved her, or how my whole existence seems bound up with her, till I saw looming in the distance the fearful possibility of what I will not mention." She felt guilty about her bullheadedness as a teenager. Loss was her greatest fear.

On March 16, 1861, after several months of ill health, back pain, and infection, the Duchess of Kent died. Victoria was sitting on a footstool holding her mother's hand when she realized she had stopped breathing. As a tearful Albert bent to pick her up and take her to the next room, she was overwhelmed: "My childhood, all seems to crowd in upon me." She wrote to her uncle Leopold, her mother's brother: "On this, the most dreadful day of my life, does your poor brokenhearted child write one line of love and devotion. *She* is gone!"

Victoria cried for weeks, lying in her room with curtains drawn. She slept and ate poorly, thinking of how silly her estrangement from her mother had been two decades earlier and of how much she missed her. She adopted her mother's Scottish terrier, commissioned a bust, combed through her letters, and began disposing of her possessions. Vicky returned from Germany to be with her, and her youngest child, Beatrice, occasionally cheered her with her "sweet innocent little voice & prattle."

But Victoria, then forty-one, had plunged into a depression, which she described as an oppressive, fatiguing cloud. She could not bear loud conversation or crowds. A fortnight after her mother's death, she was only conscious of a great emptiness, a "blank, or desolation," "*Sehnsucht* and *Wehmut*" (yearning and nostalgia). A daily bout of uncontrollable weeping was her only relief. Her headaches were severe and frequent; she was grateful for the fact that the rubber wheels on her pony carriage made no noise. Just the sound of Bertie's voice sent her wild with irritation.

Soon, whispers of madness began to circulate; they were never far away, given the fate of the queen's grandfather King George III. Albert told his brother, "Victoria is very well and I cannot understand how these horrid, vile rumors about her mental state could arise. They have annoyed me tremendously as I know what the consequences may be."

Yet Albert too, aware of Victoria's capacity for longing and nostalgia, cautioned her not to founder in her grief. Her great task in life was, he said, "controlling her feelings." He wrote a memorandum to her several months after her mother had died, in October 1861:

My advice to be less occupied with yourself and your own feelings is really the kindest I can give for pain is felt chiefly by dwelling on it and can thereby be heightened to an *unbearable extent.* . . . If you will take increased interest in things unconnected with personal feelings, you will find the task much lightened of governing those feelings in general which you state to be your great difficulty in life.

Victoria was a naturally sentimental, sometimes clingy person who grew greatly attached to people and places; she hated leaving Osborne, then Balmoral, and she held her breath waiting for Albert to return whenever he left on business. She carefully recorded the comings and goings of all her family in her journal and lamented anyone's absence. She was peculiarly vulnerable to strong grief, and there was a part of the mourning process that gratified the queen, as though she were pressing on a sore. She told Vicky in April that she didn't want to be "roused out of" her grief. It was this that thwarted Albert's campaign against her self-absorption.

On Victoria's forty-second birthday, in 1861, she asked that no music be played outside her window. She wanted only to relish Albert's "tender love and affection," in what had become an intimate birthday ritual. Her dear husband, she wrote poignantly, was her "all in all, whom God will I am sure ever bless for years to come, & never let me survive!" As she grew older she also grew nervous about the prospect of losing anyone close to her. On Feodora's fiftieth birthday, Victoria, having only just lost her half brother, Charles, wrote: "May God long preserve this dear, & *only* sister! I tremble so now for all those dear to me!"

Albert's health was fragile; he had chronic stomach problems involving violent cramping; he suffered from the cold and had frequent headaches, fevers, toothaches, and, especially, catarrh. Too much work and excitement, he told Stockmar in May 1859, kept his "mucous membranes in a state of constant irritation." Sometimes stress led to bouts of vomiting. Victoria blamed it on overwork, and was always impatient for him to recover. She privately believed he made too much of a fuss, as though he were suffering from a Victorian form of "man flu." While Albert chastised his wife for emotional frailty, she chastised him in return for physical weakness. (This was the woman who, after all, was unfazed by multiple assassination attempts.) She complained to Vicky in a letter in 1861:

Dear Papa never allows he is any better or will try to get over it, but makes such a miserable face that people always think he's very ill. It is quite the contrary with me always; I can do anything before others and never show it, so people never believe I am ill or ever suffer. His nervous system is easily excited and irritated and he's so completely overpowered by everything.

Women, she said, were "born to suffer."

The Prince Consort was deeply exhausted. In September 1860, on a trip to Coburg to visit his brother, Ernest (now Duke of Saxe-Coburg and Gotha), Albert dived out of a moving carriage when his horses bolted. He was bruised and scratched. Stockmar, looking at Albert's minor cuts, said quietly to Ernest: "God have mercy on us! If anything serious should ever happen to him, he will die." Ernest also reported signs of morbidity in the maudlin Albert. When they went out together for their last walk in Coburg in October, Ernest said, "Albert stood still, and suddenly felt for his pocket handkerchief. . . . I went up to him and saw that tears were trickling down his cheeks . . . he persisted in declaring that he was well aware that he had been here for the last time in his life." Albert was depressed, and "the dragon of his dissatisfaction" gnawed at him.

The father of nine was unable to stop working. Life, in his mind, was an interminable treadmill. He saw himself as a kind of indentured pack animal, writing to his brother: "Man is a beast of burden and he is only happy if he has to drag his burden and if he has little free will. My experience teaches me every day to understand the truth of this more and more." His endless, solitary deer-stalking escapades seemed unable to ease his fatigue. Victoria had become intensely dependent upon him, and she resented his absence in a fashion that became oppressive. When he went to Aberdeen for one night to give a speech, she told Leopold, "I feel so lost without him." She had forgotten her own colossal strength. It lay dormant for years as she worshipped and relied on her ailing, driven husband.

On a Saturday in June 1861, a great fire erupted in London. Victoria and Albert, down in the gardens of Buckingham Palace, saw the sky light up in a peculiar way and went up to the palace roof to watch the flames.

> The sight was fearful, the sky quite lurid, & the flames shooting up furiously . . . lighting up the whole town & giving a terrifying aspect of destruction. . . . The whole scene was weird & striking, Westminster's white towers rising to the right of the conflagration, the moon shining beautifully, the night warm & still interrupted by the striking of "Big Ben" in the Westminster Tower, & the Tattoo from the Barracks.

It was thought that the Tooley Street fire began by spontaneous combustion in the middle of warehouses jammed with jute, hemp, cotton, and spices. The fire soon burned a quarter of a mile along the south bank of the Thames, creating a hundred-foot wall of flames. Spectators rowed up and down the river, which glowed gold in the firelight. The fire would burn for two more days, and would not be completely extinguished for two more weeks; six people died, including the chief of the fire brigade when a warehouse collapsed on him.

Victoria stood on the roof of her palace and watched for hours, staring at the smoke and bursts of red flame. What she did not realize, as she eventually turned her back on the fire to go to bed, was that before the end of that year, her own happy life would be destroyed.

Part 4

THE WIDOW OF WINDSOR

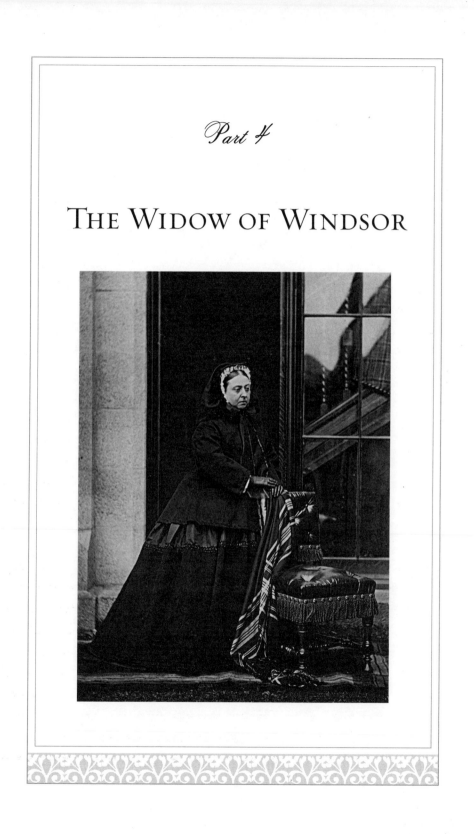

CHAPTER 20

"There Is No One to Call Me Victoria Now"

I tremble for the Queen.

—CHARLES GREVILLE,
DECEMBER 14, 1861

Bertie thrust his head out of the window and scanned the grounds of the military camp of Curragh. The last post had sounded hours ago at the curfew time of 9:30 P.M. He quickly walked out of his headquarter hut past two small tents and his guards, who didn't notice him. Making his way through the blackness, he found the hut he was looking for and poked his head through the door. Inside, the voluptuous Irish actress Nellie Clifden was waiting. His friends had smuggled her into the camp as a treat for the nineteen-year-old Prince of Wales.

"Fast women" were increasingly common in the 1860s, a decade of a forgotten but determined progress toward emancipation. Single women began to rebel in greater numbers: smoking, flirting openly, mixing freely with unmarried men. Books of that era are peppered with complaints about the looseness of the younger generations. Some young women even embraced the term "fast," which was astonishing to polite society. One novelist wrote: "Oh, that any British maiden should unblushingly, nay, and without the slightest feeling of shame, even glory in such a title! But so it is, in the year 1861." Even in 1868, while traveling in Switzerland, Victoria noticed among a crowd who gathered to see her "independent young English ladies, specimens of the present most objectionable 'fast young lady.'" She added: "Some were no doubt American."

Pretty Nellie Clifden is commonly described as a woman of "easy virtue." Bertie became intoxicated with her world of the theater, so different from the tightly laced royal court. He reveled in the thrill of the illicit when he was with her and in the fun to be had at the clubs where his cachet as heir was unparalleled. He drank, smoked, tipped whisky over the heads of sycophants, and flirted with women. His jokes were laughed at, his desires indulged, and—best of all—his parents were absent. Puffing on his black pipe, he wrote about Nellie in his engagement diary in code.

6 Sept.	Curragh—*N.C.* 1st time
9 Sept.	Curragh—*N.C.* 2nd time
10 Sept.	Curragh—*N.C.* 3rd time

The eldest son of the pious, brilliant Albert grew up with daily reminders that he had somehow failed his parents and would never meet their expectations. Albert's Teutonic discipline, regimented schedule, and labored moral instructions failed to change his son. Although he was an entertaining and kind young man, the story of "poor Bertie," as Victoria called him, was always one of disappointment. He followed an exacting seven-day school schedule that failed to inculcate a love of learning. His father decided he lacked the ability to concentrate, with a mind "of no more use than a pistol packed at the bottom of a trunk"—useless.

Even Bertie's secret fling at Curragh in the summer of 1861 was conducted in the crucible of failure. Albert had decreed that Bertie "should be subjected to ten weeks course of infantry training, under the strictest discipline which could be devised, at the Curragh Camp near Dublin" so he might develop some discipline and fiber. Bertie performed poorly, and his superior officer told his parents that he would not be able to command a battalion by the end of his stay. Victoria and Albert visited the Irish camp and watched him go through his drills and perform a junior role without distinction (although Victoria thought he looked fetching in his uniform). During that visit, Albert was left with a sinking feeling: Would his son ever be good at anything? What kind of king would he become? There was an unmistakeable irony: Bertie would have the title Albert had always craved, and yet he would not deserve it. Both parents regretted that their eldest was more like his mother than his father. Bertie was Victoria's "caricature," and in a man, the queen sighed, that was so much worse. Victoria had perhaps been more interested in books and learning as a child, but she and her son shared a volatility, a hot temper, and a love of fun.

What Albert and Victoria failed to recognize was how their son could represent the throne not through intellect but through cheer. Bertie's 1860 trip to Canada and America, the first made by an heir to the British crown, was a smashing success. In Canada, when he was eighteen, he opened bridges, danced vigorously, and even agreed to wheel a French acrobat across the Niagara Falls in a wheelbarrow, although his minders stopped it. He was immensely popular in the United States, where he traveled incognito between engagements. In New York, he was given a standing ovation, and a ballroom floor collapsed under the weight of the crowd gathering to see him. American newspapers also reported he had overt flirtations with the ladies, "whispering sweet nothings." The queen, briefly, approved, and found Bertie very talkative on his return. She attributed his enthusiastic reception in America as coming "principally from the (to me incredible) liking they have for my unworthy self." The next king of England was destined to rebel for decades.

Prince Albert first heard the rumors of his son's thespian liaison with Nellie Clifden from Baron Stockmar, then in Germany, who had stumbled upon the story in European papers. The gossip had been swirling about the London clubs for weeks. The subterranean Hanoverian streak Albert feared in his son had now spilled into public view; the embarrassment caused to the monarchy by Victoria's uncles seemed likely to resume. Albert felt physically ill, and his gut flared with pain. Sexual looseness was Albert's psychological Achilles' heel: his own family had been destroyed by infidelity, and his only brother had contracted syphilis. Albert was incapable of viewing trysts as casual, inevitable, or meaningless; for him, they could only contain the seeds of ruin. In the nineteenth century, this kind of affair could mean not just scandal, but disease, pregnancy, court cases, and financial ruin.

On November 16, four days after he heard the rumors about the affair from Stockmar, Albert sat down to write to his son. It was a strikingly harsh letter, especially as it was not unusual for aristocratic men to dabble with women before marriage. It began: "I write to you with a heavy heart upon a subject which has caused me the greatest pain I have yet felt in this life," the discovery that his son, a prince, had "sunk into vice and debauchery." Bertie had always seemed ignorant and weak, he wrote, but "depraved" was a new low. His father warned him of nightmarish scenarios: this "woman of the town" could have a child—and take him to court if he denied it. She could offer "disgusting details of your profligacy" and Bertie himself could be cross-examined, mobbed, and humiliated. Bertie, shamed and guilty, begged his forgiveness. Albert told him nothing could restore his innocence. Victoria shared her husband's disgust: "Oh! that boy— much as I pity him I never can or shall look at him without a shudder."

It was decided: Bertie must get married. Vicky had been thumb-

ing the almanac of eligible European princesses for months, searching for an appropriate bride for her younger brother. She had fixed
on Princess Alexandra of Denmark, who turned seventeen in December 1861, for her beauty, her aristocratic but unaffected manner,
and her kind disposition. It was arranged that they would meet, casually, at a German cathedral while sightseeing, in 1861. Vicky had half
fallen in love with Alexandra—or Alix—herself, and thought if Bertie was not taken with this woman, he would not be taken with anyone. Bertie liked her, but he was in no rush to marry. A frustrated
Victoria wondered if he was "capable of enthusiasm about anything
in the world." The only serious drawback was Alix's homeland. One
of the major political disputes of the 1860s was between Germany—or
Prussia—and Denmark over the Schleswig-Holstein duchies. The
Germans wished to gain control of the mostly Danish duchies in
order to gain access to the North Sea; Holstein was part of Germany,
and Schleswig was majority Danish but aligned with Holstein. It was
difficult, then, for the heir to the throne of England to align himself
with the foe of Prussia; however, Prince Albert declared that Bertie
would marry the princess—but not the country. The union would not
be a "triumph of Denmark." Time was short, for the beautiful Alexandra had other suitors.

Albert was ill and unable to sleep, haunted by visions of a dissolute
future for his son. He decided to visit Bertie at Cambridge in November, where he was studying, and went for a long walk with him in the
rain. Bertie's remorse was genuine, and by the end Albert, his clothes
soaked through to his skin, forgave him for the Nellie Clifden debacle. As Victoria walked in the forest, she prayed her fatigued husband
would sleep that night.

It would be unfair to blame Bertie for Albert's insomnia. The
Prince Consort was forty-two, but he had the poor health of a man
much older. He worked fiendishly, and as he sank deeper into his Sisyphean tasks—committees, engagements, matters of state—he grew
more irritable, and he lost his temper with Victoria more frequently.
She complained to Vicky that he was "very often very trying—in his

hastiness & over-love of business." It was her role, as always, to cheer him up. Victoria was always far more buoyant than Albert, but she was increasingly frustrated with him, too. She was unable to penetrate the dark cloud he now inhabited.

More than anything, the Prince Consort was lonely. He felt isolated in the court, and he did not have a close friend to confide in. He had lost Anson and Robert Peel, and the elderly Stockmar had moved to Germany. He was acutely distressed when he heard their cousin, young King Pedro of Portugal, had died of typhoid at twenty-four. He regarded the industrious, good Pedro as being like a son—the son he had wished Bertie would be. He was also lonely in his marriage. As he told Stockmar, "many a storm" had "swept over" his relationship with Victoria. Much as she tried, she could not talk to him at length on the matters that consumed him most. Spiritually, they were well matched; intellectually, they were not. Victoria knew this, writing later that she had prayed often "to be more fit society for him." Stockmar was the only one he could talk to unreservedly.

Albert's constitution had always been fragile. As a boy, according to his old tutor Florschütz, he was "never very robust." His brother Ernest reported that his "physical development did not keep pace with the quick unfolding of his remarkable mental powers; he needed protection." He never grew into a healthy adult, as was hoped, and his stomach was a constant source of complaint. Nor were their palaces particularly comfortable. He was often shivering, partly due to Victoria's insistence on a chilly environment; she thought warm air caused colds and ruined one's complexion. Both believed that bracing baths and cold showers were good for the immune system. (Albert joked with Vicky that her mother would be annoyed to wake and find he had lit a fire in that morning hour he had to himself, to work, write, and get warm.)

Soon Albert's depression turned into passivity, and eventually into fatalism. He toyed with the thought of dying. A man of strong Christian faith, toward the end of 1861 he told Victoria he would not fight death if it came. If struck by a grave illness, he would submit to it: "I do not cling to life. You do; but I set no store by it. If I knew that those I love were well cared for, I should be quite ready to die tomorrow."

When he returned home to Windsor from Cambridge, Albert was sick and suffering neuralgic pain in his back and legs. Victoria blamed Bertie and hinted at "a great sorrow and worry" to Vicky, "which upset us both greatly—but him especially—and it broke him quite down." She had never seen him "so low." Albert also confided in Vicky that he was at a "very low ebb." It was a warm day when he went to see the Eton volunteers go through their maneuvers, but Albert was shivering in a fur-lined coat; he felt as though cold water were being poured down his spine.

That weekend of November 30, 1861, Albert drafted the most important document of his career. The Civil War had broken out in America, shortly after Abraham Lincoln was sworn in as president. On April 19, 1861, the Union established a naval blockade to prevent any goods or supplies—especially arms—from going in or out of the Confederate South. On May 13, Queen Victoria issued a proclamation of neutrality, forbidding British subjects to join either side. Then, on November 8—as Albert prepared to go out into the rain at Sandhurst—a British mail-carrying ship called the *Trent* was intercepted by the USS *San Jacinto* in the Bahama Channel near Cuba. Two men on board, Confederate diplomats heading to Europe, were captured and taken from the *Trent*.

Northerners were furious that the British-owned *Trent* had ferried Confederates, though Lincoln did not want to risk war over the matter. The British public was angry, too, at the insult to their neutrality and free movement. "Bear this, bear all!" was the cry; surely war must be the consequence of such a provocative act. Victoria scribbled to Vicky: "The great and all absorbing event of the day is the American outrage! They are such ruffians!" The Cabinet decided it was a gross violation of international law. A memo was drafted by the foreign secretary to the British ambassador in Washington, with a series of strongly worded demands. It was sent to Windsor Castle on November 29.

A feeble Albert rose at 7 A.M. on November 30, after a sleepless night, to draft a response. He was worried that the curtness of the foreign secretary's reply might provoke the Union, effectively forcing Britain to go to war with the United States. Victoria agreed. Jamming a wig onto his head for warmth and wrapping his velvet dressing gown around him, Albert toned down the demands, employed far more diplomatic language, and gave the Lincoln administration a way out by indicating that the British assumed the *San Jacinto* must have acted without the Union's knowledge or approval:

> The United States Government must be fully aware that the British Government could not allow its flag to be insulted, and the security of her mail communications to be placed in jeopardy, and Her Majesty's Government are unwilling to believe that the United States Government intended wantonly to put an insult upon this country, and to add to their many distressing complications by forcing a question of dispute upon us, and that we are therefore glad to believe that upon a full consideration of the circumstances, and of the undoubted breach of international law committed they would spontaneously offer such redress as alone could satisfy this country, viz. the restoration of the unfortunate passengers and a suitable apology.

Albert brought it to Victoria wearily, saying, "I could hardly hold my pen." It was the last memorandum he ever wrote.

After making some corrections, Victoria sent it to her ministers. The amendments were universally approved, and the final version hewed closely to Albert's suggestions. (Lord Palmerston—who had been wandering the corridors of Windsor Castle for days, leaning on his cane and arguing that Albert should receive better medical treatment—had been particularly pleased with the response.) The

Confederate men were released. While no formal apology came forth, Lincoln's administration eventually condemned the *San Jacinto*'s actions. War with America was avoided.

By Monday, December 2, only opiates could bring relief to the lethargic Albert. Victoria had never seen him so ill, and she was "terribly nervous and distressed." By December 4, as Albert wandered between his bedroom and dressing room, seeking rest, the public received the first notice of his illness, which was described as a "feverish cold." The queen was thrilled if Albert fell asleep for just an hour. Some have surmised that Dr. James Clark decided to conceal the gravity of the situation from the royal family, out of concern for them, but he was also plainly inept. He failed to call for further medical help, and he had an unhelpful tendency to claim imminent recovery before a serious decline. Lord Clarendon later remarked that the doctors there were "not fit to attend a sick cat."

On December 6, Victoria woke at 3 A.M. to check on Albert, though he did not smile or acknowledge her when she came near. As she later watched him drink tea and eat two rusks, she was unable to shake the feeling that he was elsewhere: "Sometimes he has such a strange wild look." Later, he seemed to rally, and was sitting up and talking, still weak but with a stronger pulse. He even asked to see the plans of the house Alice would live in with her fiancé, Louis, the future Grand Duke of Hesse. Victoria was growing so anxious that she frequently asked Dr. Jenner to check on her after examining Albert. Eighteen-year-old Alice, who exhibited a patient strength and a remarkable maturity during this time, sat and read to her father for hours.

By December 7, Albert was often incoherent, repeating such phrases as "I'm so silly." Victoria sat motionless on her bed in her room, feeling as "if my heart must break." She remained in an "agony of suspense" until the doctors came to her and said they had finally diagnosed the problem: it was gastric and bowel fever, which usually took a month to clear. Victoria was consumed by her own needs and kept thinking how awful it was to be deprived of her husband. Alice tried to cheer her up, and took her driving. Half of the month had already passed, she reminded her. As Victoria sat next to a silent Albert, tears dropped in a steady stream onto the sheets. It was as though she were "living in a dreadful dream." He would have to stop working so hard, she thought. She could barely contemplate two more weeks without him.

The next day, Albert asked to be placed in the King's Room—now called the Blue Room—which was cheerful and sunlit. A piano was wheeled next door so he could listen to chorales. His eyes brimmed with tears as Alice played for him. He drank tea at three-hour intervals, with a little wine. Victoria glumly made her way to church, where she was unable to focus on a word of the sermon. When she returned to Albert, he smacked her hand when she was trying to explain something to the doctor. But he later smiled and stroked her face—*"liebes Frauchen"*—before falling asleep as she read to him. The doctors said they were very pleased with his progress, a patronizing fudging of the situation. The royal household had been trained to tiptoe around the volatile and sensitive queen, but they were only contributing to her eventual trauma and shock.

As he grew fainter, Albert veered from lucidity to confusion, from testiness to tenderness. On December 11, he rested against Victoria's shoulder as he ate breakfast. She cried when he said kindly, "It is very comfortable like that, dear Child." He then said, as though startled, "Let us pray to the Almighty!" Victoria glanced at his flushed face and reassured him that he always prayed, plenty. "But not together," Albert replied, grabbing her hands and cupping them in his before bending to pray. The last sermon Albert had heard at Balmoral before coming to Windsor was on Amos 4:12, "Prepare to meet Thy God, O Israel!" Once Victoria was out of the room, he told his daughter Alice he was dying.

Meanwhile the doctors told Victoria she had absolutely no cause for concern and predicted Albert would be better in a week. But his shallow, gasping breaths tormented her. She woke at 4 A.M. on December 13 and asked for a report, but she was told Albert was sleep-ing. He took no notice of her when she visited him at 8 A.M. that day. As he was wheeled into the next room, he didn't even glance at the sublime Raphael Madonna he had said helped him live. He lay pant-ing, staring out the window at the clouds, straining for sounds of the nightingales that reminded him of Rosenau. Victoria stayed by his side, leaving only for short intervals to walk or go for drives. She tried to remain calm when in the room with Albert, but lost control when outside, praying and crying "as if I should go mad!"

The doctors slid brandy down Albert's throat every half an hour in a futile attempt to strengthen his pulse. They continued to tell the queen that they had seen much worse cases recover. It was, Victoria wrote, "a time of awful anxiety, but still *all* full of hope. It was a crisis, a struggle of strength." The last sentence—her last journal entry for some days—reported the words of the doctors that "there was no rea-son to anticipate anything worse." She went to bed miserable on the night of December 13, asking to be woken every hour with updates. She curled up tight, a tiny figure alone in the large bed that she and Albert normally shared, thinking how just a short time ago Albert had been stalking deer at Balmoral. She wished they were still there, and not at the cavernous and overlarge Windsor. Until just recently, the public could wander the parks outside the castle, and the Eton boys often tore about the terraces or went poaching in the park. Vic-toria had never liked the sprawling Windsor Castle, and she would soon come to hate it.

At 6 A.M. on December 14, there was wonderful news. Mr. Brown, who had been a royal doctor since the year Victoria was crowned, came to tell her there was "ground to hope the crisis is over." Outside, she heard faint sounds of dogs howling in the kennels and birds squawking in the aviary. The sun was climbing in a brilliant blue sky. She went to see Albert an hour later, padding down the corridor in slippers, her long hair falling down her back, but she was taken aback when she arrived: "The room had the sad look of night-watching, the candles burnt down to their sockets, of doctors looking anxious. I went in, and never can I forget how beautiful my darling looked, lying there with his face lit up by the rising sun, his eyes unusually bright, gazing, as it were on unseen objects, and not taking notice of me." He looked like a saint.

Bertie had, until now, been kept ignorant of his father's condition. Victoria was still angry with him and had not wanted him to come, worried that he might upset Albert. In some of Albert's jumbled ramblings over the past few days, one word could be discerned: "Bertie." Alice, who had always adored Bertie and had been his sidekick in various rebellious capers, finally decided she must tell him Papa was "not so well" and to come at once. The telegram reached Bertie while he was hosting a dinner party at Cambridge on the night of December 13; he boarded a train to Windsor two hours later. He arrived at three in the morning, and was shocked by the state his father was in. Albert never recognized the face of his son by his bed.

At 10 A.M., the doctors told Victoria that they were still all "very, very anxious" but that Albert had rallied. When she asked if she could go out for air, they asked her to return in fifteen minutes. She wandered, dazed, out onto the terrace with Alice, began crying and could not stop. Alice placed her arms around her and stared across the park, mute, as a military band played in the distance.

Victoria was exploding with grief. The man who had left his homeland for her over twenty years ago now lay pale on his bed, soaked in sweat, taking no notice of anyone. His hands and face had a "dusky hue." Albert folded his arms and raised his hands to style his hair: "Strange! as though he were preparing for another and greater journey." Twice that afternoon, Albert called Victoria *Frauchen* and kissed her tenderly. Finally, later that night, she walked into the anteroom and collapsed onto the floor, sobbing. When her spiritual counselor the Dean of Windsor told her to steel herself for a great trial, it made her cry harder: "Why? Why must I suffer this? My mother? What was *that*? I thought that was grief. But that was *nothing* to this."

In a few minutes, Dr. Clark asked Alice to fetch her mother. Victoria wiped her eyes and walked quickly to the Blue Room. When Alice told her hope was gone, she "started up like a Lioness rushed by every one, and bounded on the bed imploring him to speak and to give one kiss to his little wife." Albert's eyes opened but he did not move; she leaned in to kiss him over and over. She then knelt next to her husband and took his hand. It was already cold, and his breathing was faint. "Oh no," Victoria said, staring into his face. "I have seen this before. This is death."

Alice stood on the other side of the bed with her hands folded, and Bertie and Helena stood at its foot.* Behind them stood Victoria's nephew Prince Ernest of Leiningen and his wife, Marie, the four royal doctors, and Albert's valet and top equerries. Clustered in the grand red-carpeted corridor outside the room stood a grave group of men of the royal household.

Albert took three long, gentle breaths, and then it was over. Victoria stood, kissed his forehead, and pressed his hand to her face. She cried out in a howl of anguish that chilled her children's hearts and echoed in the castle's thick stone corridors: "Oh! my dear Darling!" She dropped to her knees, numb and distraught, as the clock chimed 10:45 P.M.; the castle was surrounded by black night. Her family stood, stricken, looking at the woman who ruled millions but had loved only one. What would become of her now?

Before retiring to bed, Victoria went up to the nursery. She lifted a warm, sleepy Beatrice out of her cot and held her tight, rocking si-

---

* Arthur, eleven, and Louise, fifteen, had said goodbye to him earlier that evening and been sent to bed. Four children were absent: Vicky was pregnant and stuck in Berlin, Affie was in Mexico with the navy, and four-year-old Beatrice was not allowed to enter the sickroom. The fragile Leopold, now aged eight, had just been diagnosed with hemophilia and was on a recuperative trip—after a bad bout of bleeding—in southern France. Also crowded in the room that day were General Robert Bruce (Bertie's governor); the Dean of Windsor, Gerald Wellesley; Sir Charles Phipps (Albert's private secretary); and General Charles Grey.

lently in the darkness. She walked back to her room and placed four-year-old Beatrice in her empty bed, curling up next to her. Veering from wild grief to numbness, and sedated with opium, she cried all night. Albert's nightclothes were laid out next to her. Alice lay in a small bed at the foot of hers, and she woke to cry with her mother. The tenderness of the children was remarkable. Little Beatrice stroked Victoria's face when she finally woke, saying tenderly, "Don't cry. Papa is gone on a visit to Grandmama."

For a long time, Victorian doctors disagreed on what killed Prince Albert. Victoria had not allowed an autopsy. Most assumed he died of the deadly typhoid that the poor drains of Windsor could easily have exposed him to, or perhaps a perforation of the bowel. Others have since guessed it was bowel cancer, a peptic ulcer, or a gastrinoma. The most recent and plausible theory, put forth by Helen Rappaport, is that it was Crohn's disease, an inflammatory bowel condition exacerbated by stress, whose symptoms matched Albert's. (This syndrome was not identified by the medical community until 1913.) Albert's feverish signs, Rappaport argues, may have been the deterioration of a chronic gastrointestinal inflammation, which would explain his stomach problems and his toothaches.

The next morning, bells tolled across England. Preachers hastily rewrote sermons on death. Sheets of black material descended on coats, dresses, arms, swords, buckles, fans, flags, and houses across London. The country had not mourned in such a way since the death of Princess Charlotte almost half a century earlier. Doubts about the foreign prince evaporated as the British began to realize what they had lost. The papers trumpeted the virtues of the German now called "the most important man in the country." Politicians grew nervous about what his death might mean. Lord Clarendon, who had long admired Albert's "motives, sagacity and tact," said it was a "national calamity, of far greater importance than the public dream of." He worried, too, as everyone did, for Victoria:

No other woman has the same public responsibility or the same motive for being absolutely guided by the superior mind of her husband. This habit, or rather necessity, together with her intense love for him, which has increased rather than become weaker with years, has so engrafted her on him that to lose him will be like parting with her heart and soul.

It was true. The proud queen became a wretched woman who would forever be defined by her loss. After she was carried out of the King's Room, she said quietly, "There is no one to call me Victoria now." She asked her household not to desert her. She knew how much sympathy her subjects had for her, as reports across the country trickled back: "Even the poor people in small villages, who don't know me," she wrote, "are shedding tears for me, as if it were their own private sorrow." Her subjects ached for her. "The peasants in their cottages," wrote Richard Monckton Milnes, "talk as if the Queen was one of themselves."

The children were heartbroken to lose their father. Vicky, pregnant and marooned in Europe, was desperate with the pain of separation. A horror-struck Bertie threw himself into Victoria's arms and vowed to devote his life to comforting her. Alice was devastated but stoic, and she cared for her mother selflessly and gently, as she had done for her father in his final days. Alfred heard the news when he was still at sea near Mexico and couldn't return home until February. The eight-year-old Prince Leopold, far away in France, could only cry: "Oh! I want my mother!" The young Beatrice continued to somehow miraculously cheer her mother up. The nine fatherless children were now under the pall of the depressed court: clad in crackling, heavy dark crêpe, they were forbidden to laugh or show any kind of enthusiasm for life. It was a heavy burden for children who needed comforting themselves.

Victoria did not attend her husband's funeral. Arthur and Bertie were sad little figures who tried to conceal their sobs in front of the rows of solemn old men. Victoria had made one change to the funeral service, though. After reading the draft of proclamation asking that God "bless and preserve" the queen "with long life, health and happiness," she struck out "happiness" with her black pen. She wrote the word "honor" instead: she could not conceive of a life that might contain happiness now.

Christmas 1861 was a grim affair. Lady Augusta Bruce described it as agony, as though an "impenetrable cloud" had settled over all of them: "The whole house seems like Pompeii." The royal household all received mementos of Albert as gifts. Victoria sat silently in her drawing room while people talked quietly around her. She would slide her hand into her pocket and finger Albert's red handkerchief and gold watch, thinking forlornly that it hardly seemed fair that his watch was still ticking while he had gone. She had once bemoaned the passing of time; now every hour seemed interminable. She made sure all of her husband's timepieces were wound daily, and that visitors continued to sign his guest book, next to hers. People had to understand: Albert might have died, but he hadn't gone.

While nursing her grief, Victoria grew to hate being in the watchful eyes of the public: the peering opera glasses, rows of politicians or commoners craning their necks on footpaths or leaning into her carriage. Eyes followed her everywhere. She couldn't bear it. Victoria longed for yawning vistas empty of people, for the sight of the sea, for solitude. And what comforted her most of all was her own grief: an excessive, indulgent, loud, unembarrassed, demanding, and scandalous grief. For a woman who was unable and unwilling to suture her raw, bloody heart, the solace of poetry had, for now, entirely overshadowed politics. Would anyone understand when she cried that losing her husband was like "tearing flesh from my bones"? She did not describe herself as the queen anymore, but signed herself as the "brokenhearted Widow."

CHAPTER 21

"The Whole House Seems Like Pompeii"

I have, since he left me, the courage of a lioness.

—QUEEN VICTORIA

When Alfred Tennyson heard that the queen of England wanted a private audience, he was glum. "I am a shy beast and I like to keep in my burrow," he complained to his friend the Duke of Argyll. The poet asked two questions: how to greet her when he entered, and whether he needed to back out of the room. The duke, a Scottish peer whose son would marry Princess Louise, advised Tennyson on how to behave: to bow low respectfully or kneel, and offer her his hand if it felt natural to do so, and that the queen would walk out when finished. It was April 1862, only four months after Albert had died. The Duke told Tennyson: "Talk to Her as you would to a poor Woman in affliction—that is what she likes best." Tennyson was warned not to refer to the Prince Consort as "late," but to re-member the "strong reality" of the queen's "belief in the *Life presence of the Dead.*"

The fifty-three-year-old poet dressed in a suit and black stockings for his trip to Osborne House on a bitterly cold day. He lived nearby, only miles from the queen's residence on the Isle of Wight. He was shown into Victoria's drawing room and stood with his back to the fire as he waited for the queen. When Victoria entered, she was pale but self-possessed. She stared quietly at him: the poet who had cap-tured her grief so perfectly. Tennyson had written *In Memoriam* after the death of a close male friend, and Victoria had returned to it hun-dreds of times, adding her own notes and underlining the words in her thick black ink:

> *But I remain'd, whose hopes were dim,*
> *Whose life, whose thoughts were little worth,*
> *To wander on a darken'd earth*
> *Where all things round me breathed of him.*

He looked a bit peculiar, Victoria thought, but she found there was "no affectation about him." Tennyson knelt to kiss her hand. Victoria sat down and told him how much his poem had comforted her, as well as his recent dedication of *Idylls of the King* to Albert. Tennyson told her that Albert's death was a great loss to the country, his eyes welling. He thought Victoria very pretty, like a sweet, sad statue. When Victoria asked if he wanted her to do anything, he re-sponded only that she might shake the hands of his two boys. She invited his sons, Hallam and Lionel Tennyson, to Osborne in May the next year, along with their parents.

The Tennyson family—Alfred, his wife, and their children—were smitten with the queen, whom they found to be "beautiful, not the least like her portraits," and utterly without pretense. Even ten-year-old Hallam wrote: "The Queen is not stout. Her Majesty has a large mind and a small body to contain it therein." Tennyson's wife,

Emily, remarked on her easy familiarity, and how there was no shy-ness between them. "One feels," Emily wrote, "that the Queen is a woman to live and die for."

Tennyson provided great solace to the queen, with his fierce belief in the immortal soul and his ability to make her feel understood. She wrote in her diary:

> Had some interesting conversation with [Tennyson] and was struck with the greatness and largeness of his mind, under a certainly rough exterior. Speaking of the immortality of the soul and of all the scientific discoveries in no way interfering with that, he said: "If there is no immortality of the soul, one does not see why there should be any God," and that "You can-not love a Father who strangled you," etc.

Twelve years earlier, in 1850, Albert had insisted that Tennyson be appointed poet laureate. In 1862, Alice sent a message to the poet ask-ing if he could write something to mark her father's death. Tennyson wrote a dedication for the *Idylls*, in which he declared him "Albert the Good." In it, he urged Victoria, in words she recited to herself in her blackest hours, to endure:

> Break not, O woman's-heart, but still endure;
> Break not, for thou art Royal, but endure;
> Remembering all the beauty of that star
> Which shone so close beside Thee that ye made
> One light together, but has past and leaves
> The Crown a lonely splendor.

The first few months without Albert were horrendous. Victoria struggled to sleep, woke feeling wretched, and had violent pains in her face, with frequent headaches. It all felt like a "hideous dream." She missed Albert's help constantly: when arranging papers, select-ing art, placing paintings on walls, talking about politics or the army, meeting with people, placing sketches in travel albums, supervising the clipping of bushes, consulting with her children's doctors, arranging rooms for visitors, and hiding Easter eggs, which she had never done before.

Everything triggered the memory of Albert. The sight of trees and plants upset her, because he had known all their names. So did the sounds of singing birds, especially nightingales. She sought out his possessions and went through his papers, his favorite art—especially the Raphaels—and his guns and rifles. What upset her most of all were the calendar reminders of his absence: Christmas, Easter, anniversaries, and birthdays. Victoria spent the day before her forty-fourth birthday, in 1863, on the couch, crippled by a headache. The next day, the pretty presents from her children failed to cheer her: "What I felt so dreadfully was that there was *nothing* from my beloved one." The next year, the day for her was "empty" and she felt ill. She dined alone in her room.

Some began closely scrutinizing Victoria for signs of madness. The household was aware of Victoria's acute sensitivity and tendency toward depression. There was also the widespread Victorian belief that women lacked resilience, were frequently manic or hysterical, and were unable to cope with the vicissitudes of life. Lord Clarendon said they had all seen Victoria's mind "tremble in the balance" when she lost her mother. With Albert's death, the risk seemed even higher. The "loss of her reason," he said, could cause a "national calamity."

Others noted Victoria's calm and stoicism in the initial stages of her grief. Four days after Albert died, Florence Nightingale said she was astonished to see "this nervous, anxious, fidgety woman behaving with a firmness which would dignify a hero." Lord Clarendon assumed she was dutifully following Albert's instructions not to submit to her pain. In truth, she was in a state of shock that later gave way to grief. When she did openly mourn, she was judged quickly and unfairly. Eyebrows arched when she said to Queen Augusta of Prussia, "I could go mad from the desire and the longing." And when

Clarendon was summoned to Osborne a few weeks after Albert had died, he complained: "The Q. showed embarrassing emotion."

Victoria decreed that the entire court would mourn for an unprecedented official period of two years. (When this ended, her ladies and daughters could discard the black and wear half mourning, which was gray, white, or light purple shades.) Many of her subjects decided to join them in mourning. Her ladies were draped in jet jewelry and crêpe, a thick black rustling material made of silk, crimped to make it look dull. Victoria had worn black for much of the decade before her "angel" had died, honoring the deaths of various relatives and dignitaries. The serious, exacting ritual of mourning had always appealed to her. Now, Victoria would wear her black dresses (or "widow's weeds") for the rest of her life. Who cared about how she looked? She abandoned corsets, stepped into white underwear trimmed with black ribbon, and settled into unapologetic middle age. There would be no need for corsets in heaven.

Albert's belongings and rooms were preserved exactly as they were when he was alive. Victoria hung his photo above his side of the bed. Each day, servants carefully laid out his ironed shirts and pants in the Blue Room and provided clean towels and hot water for shaving, which grew cold as his clock ticked and blotting paper sat unmarked. His remains were interred in a burial site on the Windsor grounds, and Victoria arranged for a sculptor, Baron Carlo Marochetti, to model effigies of Albert and herself, at the same age, to be placed on their tombs. It was as though she, too, had died at age forty-two. At Windsor, she went to the mausoleum every day to pray and gaze at his statue, and she visited the Blue Room every night.

Servants grew accustomed to tiptoeing around the queen and speaking in whispers in corridors. Grim company though she might have been, Victoria still insisted on gathering her children around her and keeping them close. She wanted to compensate somehow for the loss of their father, telling Arthur and Leopold's tutor, Howard Elphinstone, that "she is anxious NOT to *separate* herself *more* from them than is *absolutely necessary,* as now that God has taken their adored Father away who united *everything* requisite to attach them to Home ... the Queen wishes her boys, especially the young ones, to become very intimate with her and to *imbibe* the views and habits entertained by both of us." She wanted them to breathe the air Albert would have breathed, though the atmosphere became suffocating.

The entire household revolved around Victoria's sensitive mental state. Those returning after an absence, like eight-year-old Leopold, were cautioned she could not bear "noise, excitement, etc." Bertie was warned not to be frivolous, gossipy, and shallow. Victoria refused to allow her children any alternative or a respite from grieving. Instead of protecting them from the pain, she insisted they flounder in it. She grew irritated with the children when they laughed or talked loudly, viewing it as a sign that they were unmoved by their father's death. She corralled her children into small, black-clad groups for various bleak photographs in which they posed gazing upward at cold white busts of Albert's head, and she distributed the images to the public. She wrote at the bottom of one such image: "Day is turned into night."

The queen wanted the public to see how extraordinary Albert was. She canonized him better than any pope could a saint, commissioning books of his speeches and a biography as well as a host of portraits and public memorials. Paintings showed him clad in golden armor, standing in the clouds. Albert the Good, the Handsome, the Knightly, the Celestial Being was clad in a "crown of righteousness." Victoria wanted to cement his reputation as a man who inspired people's better angels, a man from whom Louis-Napoleon had walked away feeling "more disposed to do good."

Victoria also pined for her husband physically. She had chosen a sultry portrait of herself as a young woman of twenty-four to place in his hands in his coffin. In it, her head leaned back against a red couch and her large blue eyes were cast over her left shoulder. Her pale décolletage was exposed, and her hair tumbled down one side of her bare neck. This was a woman only one man had known. Even in death, Victoria continued to desire him. She had a marble cast taken

of his face and hands, and she stored the hands near her bed. Sometimes she pulled them close and pretended the cold stone was warm
skin. It was dreadful, she said, going to bed by herself: "What a contrast to that tender lover's love! All alone!" She closed her eyes when
she slid between the sheets, wrapped an arm around his dressing
gown, and pulled his coat over her.

The queen openly wished her grief would kill her. She wrote to
Albert's childhood tutor, Herr Florschütz: "My only wish is to follow
him soon! To live without him is really no life." She consoled herself
with the thought that he was near her, and she would meet him in
their "eternal, real home." Without that thought, she said, she would
"succumb." She revised her will, appointed guardians for her offspring, and prayed to die.

Victoria managed to hold a council on January 6, just a few days
after Albert died. She asked the men of the Cabinet to organize their
affairs to account for her anguish, and said she did not have the stamina or fortitude to see them through a time of chaos. She told Lord
Clarendon pitifully that "her mind was strained to its utmost limit—
that she had never before had to think, because the Prince used to
read and arrange everything for her, saving her all trouble, explaining to her things which she had to sign, etc." She claimed a change of
ministry would kill her—"and most *thankful* she would be for that
result"—through sheer madness. Once, she tapped her forehead dramatically and cried, "My reason, my reason!" knowing well the impact this would have.

She also appealed to the leader of the opposition, Lord Derby, for
calm. On June 16, 1862, six months after Albert's death, the queen
asked Lord Clarendon to tell Lord Derby "that if the Opposition succeeded in turning ministers out of office, they would do so at the risk
of sacrificing her life or reason." She said this would apply only to the
current session of government, which went through to August. Some
interpreted this as support for the prime minister, her old foe, Lord
Palmerston, rather than what it actually was: a desire for peace and
stability. After her message was sent to Lord Derby, no more attacks

were made on the government in that session, sparing Victoria a potentially enormous workload.

Victoria was surrounded by those who believed, just as Albert had, that she could not rule alone. The elderly Palmerston, who had fainted several times on hearing of Albert's death, said, "The Queen would be less a national loss." Benjamin Disraeli, too, said, "We have buried our sovereign." She believed it herself. The robust queen who had waved troops off to war and given birth to nine children had been reduced to a lonely, weeping widow. By 1864, more than two years after Albert's death, people were openly asking whether she might abdicate. But Bertie was not respected or particularly liked, and many people knew he had been blamed for his father's death. The relations between Bertie and his mother were at a dangerously low ebb. Victoria refused to allow Bertie to take over any of her or Albert's duties or even be gainfully employed, despite pressure to do so. Victoria was annoyed by the sight of him, and even complained about his "ugly" legs. She prayed that she would outlive him. The prime minister grew increasingly concerned about her "unconquerable aversion" to her son. The Prince of Wales existed in a liminal state of "enforced idleness." In February 1862, just a few weeks after his father died, he was sent off to the Middle East for a trip Albert had planned. Victoria was relieved.

In death, Albert was not just dominant and clever, but omnipotent and omniscient. Victoria began to construct a myth that would have been implausible when Albert was alive: that of her utter helplessness, uselessness, and worthlessness. She grew furious if anyone suggested she had ever done anything at all when it came to the children or business: "They ought to have known it was all *him,* that he was the life and soul of the family and indeed of all her counsels." When explaining why she didn't want to open Parliament in 1864, she described herself as a small rabbit that had haplessly bounded into the world of politics, "trembling and *alone.*" Constructing this fiction gave her an excuse to dwell on, and magnify, her loss. Shrinking herself and inflating Albert became a way to explain both her grief and her reluctance to reenter the world: If he had been everything, what could she possibly do without him? If the man she mourned was like a god, then surely all should grieve, or at least respect her grief, as the loss was everyone's.

Victoria was now saddled with the chores of two people, one of whom had been a prodigious workaholic. Her loss of confidence was extreme. Even just reading out a declaration for Bertie's marriage to a small group was "very trying"; her pale face distressed her children. In conversation, her conviction faltered and old insecurities returned. When talking to an aristocratic guest about turmoil in Italy and Poland in April 1863, she wished that she had been "surer of my facts to have been able to talk more myself." She went back through the binders of Albert's opinions and studied them closely. This was surely the best way to advocate for the policies Albert would have wished her to promote.

When Florence Nightingale had visited the royal couple at Balmoral during the Crimean War, she had been struck by the difference between the bored, frivolous court members and Victoria and Albert, both consumed with thoughts of war, foreign policy, and "all things of importance." Even before Albert's death, she thought Victoria conscientious "but so mistrustful of herself, so afraid of not doing her best, that her spirits are lowered by it." With Albert gone, "now she is even doubting whether she is right or wrong from the habit of consulting him." Nightingale found this touching, a sign that "she has not been spoilt by power." She had developed a great fondness for Victoria, shy in "her shabby little black silk gown." She could see she had depth; that the queen could not "now go through the vain show of a drawing room."

Victoria never attended or held another public ball. Alice's wedding, held at Osborne House in July 1862, was more like a funeral. A solemn Victoria sat on a chair, hidden from view by her four protective sons. She fought her tears throughout and could not stop thinking that she had planned this wedding with Albert. She found the "hustle" unbearable and skipped the reception, dining with Alice and

Louis on her own in a separate room. Victoria grew fond of her new son-in-law, Prince Louis of Hesse-Darmstadt in Germany, but she admonished Alice for not spending enough time in England. Another child was lost to her. Victoria decided she must have one married daughter living with her, and she determined to find a "young, sensible Prince" for Helena to marry who could live in one of her homes.

Her children were hurdling puberty, growing taller, exploring other lands, falling in love, having babies of their own, and trying to shape their lives around the sinkhole caused by their father's death and their mother's grief. In April 1863, Alice gave birth to a girl at Windsor. The eighteen-year-old Alfred got up to mischief with women in Malta. At each event marking their growth—confirmations, weddings, christenings—Victoria felt increasingly desperate. It was not just that she missed Albert's company; she also resented being on her own. She hid in corners, behind her children, or up in church closets, trying to shrink to nothing.

Victoria seemed to take for granted that her houses swarmed with sympathetic companions. Her depression meant she was more troubled by departures than buoyed by arrivals. Even when she felt desperately alone, her life was always full of people: her numerous, kind children, her ladies-in-waiting, relatives, friends, politicians, priests, poets, servants, and ghillies. She even saw her childhood governess Lehzen on a trip to Germany in 1862, and they were both "much moved." The queen did not lack for affection; what she lacked was peers. As she stood alone on that "terrible height," peering longingly into the heavens, behind her stood a crowd of people, watching closely. She didn't want a crowd; she only wanted Albert.

When Bertie married the beautiful Alix of Denmark on March 10, 1863, Victoria sat in a closet high above the altar of St. George's Chapel, Windsor Castle. (She had walked a covered path through the Deanery to avoid being seen.) When Benjamin Disraeli raised his eyeglass to see her better, he received a wintry glare and dared not look again. Guests were allowed to wear colors, but the ladies and royal daughters were in the colors of half mourning, mostly lilac and white. Victoria was wearing a black silk gown with crêpe, and a long veil with her cap, feeling agitated. When she saw her children walk into the chapel, Victoria wanted to sob. Bertie bowed to her while waiting for Alix, and he kept looking up at his mother with an anxious expression. When the trumpets sounded, she thought of her own wedding and almost fainted.

Thirty-eight people thronged the dining room for a family luncheon, but Victoria ate quietly next door with Beatrice, who was now almost six. That night, she went to bed miserable. Her children kept leaving her. Vicky, Alice, and now Bertie had their loved ones next to them, but she had only Albert's gowns to clutch: "Here I sit lonely & desolate, who so need love & tenderness, while our 2 daughters have each their loving husbands & Bertie has taken his lovely pure sweet Bride to Osborne,—such a jewel whom he is indeed lucky to have obtained . . . Oh! what I suffered in the Chapel!"

She knew she should not be envious of her children, but could hardly bear it. Her consolation was that poor Bertie was at last settled, he seemed content, and Alix was a "jewel." She woke the next day with a heavy head cold, feeling rotten.

Lord Palmerston once quipped that there were only three people who understood the Schleswig-Holstein conflict: the Prince Consort, who was now dead; a German professor who had gone mad; and himself, who had now forgotten it. For Victoria, while the politics were complex, her allegiances were fairly simple. Denmark had ruled the two duchies for decades, but the Germans—led by the dominant, belligerent Prussians—continued to eye them hungrily. Victoria supported British neutrality and was keen to avoid a general war after the disaster in the Crimea, but her sympathies were with Prussia. When the king of Denmark died in November 1863 and was succeeded by Alexandra's father, Christian IX, the Prussians prepared to strike, with Austria's backing.

The battle split the family. Alix, who naturally supported her homeland, Denmark, went into premature labor in January 1864, and gave birth to a son, Albert Victor. The next month, Prussia and Austria invaded Schleswig. When Bertie, loyal to his wife, argued that the British should intervene to support Denmark, Victoria asked Clarendon to tell him to tone down his views. After all, his brother-in-law Fritz, Vicky's husband, was fighting in the Prussian army. It became a taboo subject at family dinners.

Victoria's heated correspondence on the subject contradicts her self-portrait in those years as a "poor hunted hare." She fired off letters and memoranda full of conviction, urging neutrality. She grew so absorbed that she seemed hardly aware that she was working. Queen Sophie of the Netherlands said to one of the ladies, "She has the *habit* of power and once taken it is hardly possible to live without it." Victoria continued to see herself at the center of the government's foreign policy, directing Palmerston to ensure that when she traveled to Coburg, "*no step* is taken in foreign affairs *without* her *previous sanction* being obtained." She lobbied the Cabinet in a manner that indicated she did not wish to be contradicted. When writing to Vicky in 1863 about the frictions in Europe, Victoria bemoaned the loss of Albert's help, but she added that in spite of her broken heart she still had the many "eyes of Argus": "I have, since he left me, the courage of a lioness if I see danger, and I shall never mind giving my people my decided opinion and more than that! Yes, while life lingers in this shattered frame, my duty shall be done fearlessly!"

Not all appreciated the roars of the lioness. On May 10, 1864, an "impertinent" Palmerston informed her that people had come to believe she had strong "personal opinions" on the Schleswig-Holstein question. Some thought she had influenced the government in not going to the assistance of Denmark, breaching her constitutional duty of impartiality. On May 26, Lord Ellenborough insinuated that Victoria had not been as neutral as previous monarchs such as George III. There was, he said, a "strong impression on the Continent, and especially in Germany" that in matters relating to Germany, Her Majesty's ministers had difficulty "carrying out a purely English policy," which had undermined their authority and influence. Victoria launched into a torrent of self-pity in her diary:

> What a cruel accusation, against a poor unprotected widow, who is no longer sheltered by the love & wisdom of her beloved Husband, when I only live on to work & toil for the good of my country & am half torn to pieces with anxiety, sorrow & responsibility, seeing this Country lower itself & get more & more into difficulties,—& above all, have always sought to be so impartial! Such monstrous calumnies have made me feel quite ill. Oh! to be alone, & not to have any one to shield me, it is too dreadful!

She told Lord Granville it was her "duty to God & my country" to stop them going to war in Europe, despite much public support for it. Granville diplomatically assured her that she had saved the country from "many a false step." By June, Denmark was defeated. By October, Holstein and the German-speaking parts of Schleswig were ceded to Prussia and Austria.

This became Victoria's new template: weep with the women and dictate to the men, all while cushioning herself with a dramatic, large grief. As she withdrew completely from public view into her far-off mansions and castles, though, the tremendous public sympathy for her began to sour. Someone tied a sign to the Buckingham Palace gates: "These commanding premises to be let or sold, in consequence of the late occupant's declining business." It was pulled down, and the police presence doubled, but it appeared again just a few days later.

The snow was falling lightly in the Scottish Highlands on October 7, 1863, and Victoria spent the day riding with Alice and Helena, stopping for tea before turning back home. It was dark, and the guide could not see the road well; Victoria's servant John Brown kept hopping off the box of the carriage to help him. Twenty minutes later, the

carriage began to tip—Alice said slowly, "We are turning over"—
and the women were thrown to the ground. This was a pivotal moment for Victoria. She wrote in her diary afterward that she had just
a moment to think "whether we should be killed or not" but decided
"there were still things I had not settled & wanted to."

> I came very hard with my face on the ground, but with a
> strength I should not have thought myself capable of, I man-
> aged to scramble up at once, saw Alice & Lenchen lying on the
> ground, near the carriage, both the horses on the ground &
> Brown calling out in despair, "the lord Almighty have mercy
> on us! Who did ever see the like of this before, I thought you
> were all *killed*!"

Victoria spent the next few days in bed with raw meat on her black
eye, nursing a sore neck and a sprained thumb that would remain
crooked forever. Her "helplessness" was very trying, Victoria sighed,
yet she had shown that her grief-fueled wish to die was overruled by
a stronger, subliminal will to live.

Gradually, with regular visits to Albert's body in the mausoleum
at Frogmore, trips to Osborne, long hours of prayer, treks around
Balmoral, and the kindness of her children, Victoria grew calmer. On
the third anniversary of Albert's death, while thousands walked
through the mausoleum to get a glimpse of Albert's grave, she seemed
more philosophical. She told her friend Countess Blucher, also a
widow:

> Lonely & weary as my life now was I yet realized & felt more &
> more, how necessary I was to my Children & Country & to the
> carrying out of dearest Albert's wishes & plans. For all this I
> must try & live on for a while yet! My suffering is as great as
> ever but there is resignation & submission, which was so hard
> for me at first.

Victoria, despite herself, gradually became more serene. Alice urged her mother to get back in her carriage, on the horse, into public view. At first, after Albert died, she had struggled even to walk. People commented on how thin she had grown; but she wanted to wrinkle and age to show the wear of grief and outward signs of the cracks in her heart. She checked eagerly to see if gray hairs had sprouted. But soon pink cheeks and occasional bouts of animation betrayed her still-robust constitution. Victoria would live another thirty-seven years.

CHAPTER 22

Resuscitating the Widow of Windsor

All those who are in waiting *on me* bear the sable garb, which I think suits best *our sad sisterhood.*

—QUEEN VICTORIA TO
LADY WATERPARK, SEPTEMBER 1864

An English lady in mourning is a majestic and awful spectacle.

—GEORGE BERNARD SHAW

On January 16, 1862, just a month after Albert died, more than two hundred men and boys were trapped in the lowest pit of the New Hartley mine. The cast-iron beam of the pumping engine had snapped and fallen into the single shaft, entombing the miners below. When their bodies were found six days later, they looked as if they had fallen asleep on the floor. The youngest boy was only ten. Victoria was distraught, declaring "her heart bled for them." Eleven months later, after she had returned from a ceremony consecrating Albert's remains, she was given a handsome Bible with the signatures of many "loyal English Widows" inside, including eighty women who had lost their husbands in the Hartley disaster. Victoria sat at her desk and wrote to her "kind sister widows," telling them that what comforted her in the loss of her husband was "the constant sense of his unseen presence" and the idea of being united with him someday.

In her fervent embrace of widowhood, the queen turned what was usually a sign of lost identity into something noble and significant. Bereavement crossed all divisions. "I would as soon clasp the poorest widow in the land to my heart," she wrote, "if she had truly loved her husband and felt for me, as I would a Queen or any other in high position." She invited Lady Eliza Jane Waterpark to attend her after her own husband had died, with the words "I think that we understand one another, and feel that *Life* is ended for us, except in the sense of duty." It was a gloomy life. The queen promised she would only ask Lady Waterpark to do things in harmony with her feelings, and added, "All those who are in waiting *on me* bear the sable garb, which I think suits best *our sad sisterhood*." This sisterhood provided Victoria with a steady flow of emotional counselors, women she talked and wept with. (Lady Geraldine Somerset, lady-in-waiting to the Duchess of Cambridge, sighed, "The dreary painful effect of all this mass of black all round one [was] altogether too inexpressibly sad and dreadful.") When Abraham Lincoln was assassinated in 1865, Victoria wrote to his wife, Mary, with her condolences. No one could better appreciate, she wrote, what she was going through than this "utterly broken-hearted" queen. Mary Lincoln responded that she knew Victoria could understand.

In the Victorian era, women mourned more loudly and longer than men. Widowers were far more likely to remarry and go back to work, usually reentering the world after a few weeks of seclusion. In the second half of the nineteenth century, one in three women aged fifty-five to sixty-four was widowed, but only one in seven men. For most women, writes Patricia Jalland in her fascinating study *Death in the Victorian Family,* "widowhood was a final destiny, an involuntary commitment to a form of social exile." Yet the queen had a choice; her exile was voluntary and had privileges others' didn't, and some people were privately critical of her lack of stoicism. The Scottish author Margaret Oliphant, for example, had endured the death of her own husband in 1859 and that of three of her children in infancy. She provided for her remaining offspring with her wits, writing dozens of books. When Victoria met Oliphant in 1868, four years after the author lost her last surviving daughter, she noted approvingly that Oliphant was a simple widow. But Oliphant did not approve of the queen. She wrote to her publisher:

> If any of us ordinary people were to treat our friends and visitors and society in general in the same way [Victoria does] we should . . . lose both visitors and friends. I doubt whether *nous autres* poor women who have had to fight with the world all alone without much sympathy can quite enter into the "unprecedented" character of the queen's sufferings. A woman is surely a poor creature if with a large happy affectionate family of children around her, she can't take heart to do her duty whether she likes it or not.

But no one could force the queen to do anything she did not want to do. The innate steel that helped drive a teenager to seize a crown now drove a woman to insist upon a clamoring and unrepentant grief.

Behind palace doors, Victoria continued to work. Her year was now split between Windsor, Osborne, and Balmoral. She avoided Buckingham Palace as much as possible, as it was too keen a reminder of the past. She continued to correspond forcefully with her ministers, to involve herself in awarding honors and approving appointments, and to insist on her right to scrutinize all ministerial recommendations for posts, often raising objections or making suggestions, especially when it came to bishops and archbishops. She retained her power, but this work was hidden from the public.

The voices calling for Victoria to show herself continued to clamor. This made her furious. She chastised anyone who dared press her for not understanding how fragile she was. In 1863, Victoria's secretary, Charles Phipps, told Palmerston that her three doctors were "very decidedly" of the opinion that appearing alone in public in full dress would be "most undesirable" for her health. Her doctors were loath to put this in writing for fear it might be misconstrued.

On April 1, 1864, *The Times* officially protested Victoria's absence. That December, on the third anniversary of Albert's death, *The Times* complained again. Just days before, Victoria had told Lord Russell that she could not open Parliament because it would give her "moral shocks." She had felt safe with Albert next to her, but now that he was gone, "no child can feel more shrinking and nervous" than she did at the thought of appearing in public. She wrote to Lord Russell:

> Her nerves are *so* shattered that *any* emotion, *any* discussion, *any* exertion causes much disturbance and suffering to her whole frame. The constant anxieties inseparable from her difficult and unenviable position as Queen, and as mother of a large family, (and that, a *Royal family*), without a husband to guide, assist, soothe, comfort, and cheer her, are so great that her nervous system has no power of recovery, but on the contrary becomes weaker and weaker.

Physically, Victoria was more robust than she would admit. Mentally, she was fragile. Her great anxiety caused headaches, faintness, and rheumatic pains in her face and legs. In May 1866, Victoria told Lord Russell that she continually feared "some complete breakdown." She often declared she was likely to die soon. The thought that thousands of eyes would rest on her sent her into a severe form of agitation. When out in public, she trembled from head to toe and often struggled to compose herself. She had been shot at, clubbed in the head, abused, and widowed; what she wanted now was to feel safe, to have someone who would protect her. Her refuge soon materialized in a most unlikely person.

The trusted Scottish ghillie John Brown was sent for in the winter of 1864 to lead Victoria's pony at Osborne. Her doctor had ordered Victoria to continue to ride, and in the Highlands she grew accustomed to Brown's leading her: "A stranger would make me nervous. . . . Alas! I am now weak & nervous, & very dependent on those I am accustomed to & in whom I have confidence." A tall, handsome, protective man, Brown cheered Victoria with his brawny authority and calm strength. He arrived in December; in February she made his position permanent under the title of the Queen's Highland Servant. By November, he was designated John Brown, Esquire. Brown began to occupy an unusually elevated place in the household, traveling with her from London to Scotland and even to Europe. Victoria was charmed by his loyalty: "He is *so* devoted to me—so simple, so intelligent, *so unlike* an ordinary servant, and so cheerful and attentive." He was precisely the tonic a forlorn, lonely queen needed.

Victoria finally opened Parliament in February 1866 for the first time since Albert's death. She made sure that the prime minister, Lord Russell, knew it was a "very severe trial" for her. When the day arrived she was agitated and unable to eat. She wore plain evening dress, with a small diamond and sapphire coronet on top of her widow's cap. The wind whipped her veil as she rode silently in an open carriage past curious crowds, many of whom had not glimpsed her for years. At the crowded House of Parliament, where she used a different entrance to avoid the gallery with "staring people," Victoria felt she was going to faint. The next day, she told the prime minister she was "terribly shaken, exhausted and unwell from the violent nervous shock" of the effort. It was only for the sake of her children and country, she said dramatically, that she had any desire to live.

But gradually she began to do more in public, holding court at Buckingham Palace, reviewing troops at Aldershot, attending the wedding of her cousin opening waterworks, and unveiling a statue. When her daughter Helena married on June 12, 1866, Victoria even gave her away (though the archbishop told her it was "not usual" practice for a woman to do so). In 1867, she opened Parliament again, though she insisted that she not be asked to do it the following year. For the last thirty-nine years of her reign, Victoria opened Parliament only seven times, and not once did she read out her own speech. This was done for her by the Lord Chancellor.

As Victoria grieved through the 1860s, a concerted push for democracy sparked a spate of riots, public marches, and demonstrations. John Bright, the radical leader of the Reform League that sought an expansion of the suffrage, spoke at mass meetings across England. In 1867, the Second Reform Bill—which doubled the number of men who could vote in England and Wales from one to two million—was passed in Parliament. Victoria was wary of democratization, but she strongly supported the bill once it was evident that it had majority support in the House of Commons. She viewed herself as the queen of the poor, often lamenting "the frivolity of the higher classes & the little feeling they had for those beneath them." But her impact on this crucial piece of legislation was minimal.

But politically, Victoria had lost none of her fire. Prime ministers had grown used to being pummeled by an assertive queen who insisted she was ailing and weak. Lord Stanley was reprimanded for sending dispatches that had not received Victoria's approval, just as Palmerston had been, years before. She batted most official requests away, even those she eventually complied with. She frequently resisted hosting foreign dignitaries and asked the British government to pay if she did. In 1867, for example, the Earl of Derby, a Whig who had replaced Lord Palmerston as prime minister, begged the queen to postpone a trip to Osborne for three days so she could meet the sultan of Turkey for ten minutes at Buckingham Palace. Her response was scorching: "The word *distasteful* is hardly applicable to the subject; it would be rather nearer the mark to say extremely inconvenient and disadvantageous for the Queen's health." Still, she agreed to postpone her trip for two days, asked the sultan to come a day earlier, and dispatched her doctor to Lord Derby so he might relay the fragile state of her nerves, thus emphasizing again how great the burden was. She threatened again a "complete breakdown," saying she refused to be bullied or dictated to. This was Victoria's unique and effective negotiating tactic: to plead helplessness in a manner of hostile combat, and to insist on her weakness in repeated shows of strength. Her ministers were ill equipped to handle a cantankerous, obstinate queen. Only one realized that the lonely queen wanted to be feted, flattered, and adored.

Benjamin Disraeli understood the power of charm. In 1868, he swept into office, declaring of himself to the queen, "He can only offer devotion." Though he was a Tory, when he was made prime minister, Victoria heralded it as a victory for the working class. He had no position or fortune and was the son of a Jewish man, which was almost unheard of in political circles. Disraeli had been refused a job under the leadership of Prime Minister Peel and had been instrumental in forming the protectionist Conservative Party when the Tories split over the repeal of the Corn Laws. He was regarded as a peculiar, if talented, outsider who had a flair for writing popular novels. When he became prime minister, Disraeli proudly declared he had "climbed to the top of the greasy pole."

Disraeli was a singular character. He had dressed as a dandy in ruffled shirts, dyed ringlets, and colored stockings for decades, aping Lord Bryon, the poet who had seduced Lord Melbourne's wife back in 1812. At the age of twelve, he had converted from Judaism to Anglicanism after his father had a disagreement with their local synagogue; this allowed him to contemplate a political career, as Jews were at the time precluded from holding office. He adored his wife, Mary Anne Lewis, a winsome, clever, wealthy widow who was some twelve years older than he.

Disraeli was also a successful popular novelist with a fondness for florid sentiments. His great talent with words was put to good use in his relationship with the queen. He hoped, he wrote,

that, in the great affairs of state, your Majesty will not deign to withhold from him the benefit of your Majesty's guidance.

Your Majesty's life has been passed in constant communication with great men, and the acknowledgement and management of important transactions. Even if your Majesty were not gifted with those great abilities, which all now acknowledge, this rare and choice experience must give your Majesty an advantage in judgment which few living persons, and probably no living prince, can rival.

When Victoria next saw Disraeli, she greeted him with "a very radiant face."

It was not just that Disraeli made an art form of flattery. In his confiding missives to the queen, he made politics entertaining for her for the first time since Lord Melbourne. He explained political events and debates clearly, in great detail and with style. Victoria told a friend she had never had such letters before. Disraeli wisely deferred to her wishes on appointments, especially when it came to men of the church, saying he was delighted to obey her commands. He also treated her with respect. After Victoria published *Leaves from the Journal of Our Life in the Highlands* in 1868, drawn from her journals, it quickly sold out its print run of twenty thousand. Disraeli would then, in conversation, smoothly refer to "we authors." He could not convince her of everything, but he was so successful in manipulating her that he eventually managed to convert the once unequivocally Whig queen to the cause of Tory conservatism.

But Disraeli's first term as PM lasted only ten months. He was trounced by his greatest political rival, the Liberal William Gladstone, in the December election. Gladstone was an imposing, cerebral man with hawklike eyes, and strong Christian faith, whom Albert had approved of; their eldest sons had traveled together. Gladstone, often called "the People's William," was a popular, frugal chancellor who was intent on reform. What he lacked was the delicate tact required to manage a prickly sovereign—the kind of tact that men like Melbourne and Disraeli possessed. His wife had told him to "pet the Queen," but he could not understand how. Nor was he able to explain policies in a simple way. He frequently baffled Victoria, who hated feeling stupid or patronized. Dean Wellesley tried to explain it another way: "You cannot show too much regard, gentleness, I might even say tenderness towards her."

Proving himself to be both farsighted and politically courageous, Gladstone said his great mission was "to pacify Ireland." In his first term, from December 1868 to early 1874, Gladstone was primarily preoccupied with disestablishing the Protestant Church of Ireland— as it was known, although it was a minority church in communion with the Church of England—of which Victoria was head. This meant legally separating the church from the state and freeing the Irish—most of whom were Catholic—from paying tithes to it. Victoria did not support this bill—she argued that land rights should take precedence, and that extreme nationalists would be provoked. Undoubtedly a greater personal concern was that Scotland might follow suit—and perhaps even England—and remove her as the head of their church as well. But the overwhelming majority in the House of Commons—which Gladstone called the "emphatic verdict of the nation"—forced her to recognize that the decision was not hers, and that a collision between the two houses of Parliament would be "dangerous if not disastrous." After initially scheming against it, she aided Gladstone by working as a mediator and helping to broker a compromise with the House of Lords. She even—reluctantly—postponed a trip to Osborne to ensure the passage of the bill (while strongly reminding Gladstone that such an accommodation was very uncommon and must not be regarded as a precedent). The Irish Church Act passed in 1869.

Albert's work had been performed in full public view; he made the monarchy obviously productive as well as respectable. Without him, Victoria shrank from view, and public resentment toward the expensive, mushrooming monarchy spread. The royal family was incurring greater and greater costs with each marriage and new birth, and Bertie's behavior was profligate. Between 1871 and 1874, eighty-five Republican Clubs were founded in Britain, protesting, among other things, the "expensiveness and uselessness of the monarchy" and Bertie's "immoral example." Gladstone wrote to Granville in 1870: "The Queen is invisible and the Prince of Wales is not respected." The economy was weak, the royals were overpaid, and France had become a republic in 1870; why shouldn't Britain follow suit?*

One of the greatest threats to public safety came from the Fenian Brotherhood, which was founded in America in 1858 with the aim of overthrowing British control of Ireland and establishing an Irish republic. In 1866, the Brotherhood unsuccessfully tried to invade Canada from America. In 1867, they began a campaign of terror in Britain, blowing up a prison wall and killing a policeman. Three members were executed in reprisal and became martyrs. The resulting overblown panic irritated Victoria, and she advised her ministers to respond to any threat of violence by simply suspending habeas corpus, which would mean people could be arrested or detained without cause, but they considered this inappropriate. On December 20, 1867, she was told that eighty members of the Fenian Brotherhood had set out in two ships from New York and were coming to attack the British government. One hundred Scots Fusiliers set up camp in the Osborne stables as ships patrolled the beaches below. Victoria felt trapped, but was even more annoyed when no threats materialized.

Three months later, on a trip to Australia, a Fenian shot Victoria's twenty-three-year-old son Prince Alfred in Sydney. He was on his way to Cabbage Tree Beach to "see the aboriginals, as they were then ready for some sports," when he was shot in the back and fell on his hands and knees. The bullet lodged in his abdomen. For three days, he later told his mother, he could not breathe. The Irish assailant, who was about thirty-five, fair, and well dressed, was later executed.

---

* Helena was given a dowry when she married in 1866, Louise was awarded a dowry in 1871, Arthur was given a grant when he turned twenty-one in July 1871, and Prince Alfred an annuity at turning twenty-one, then again when he married in 1873.

The Sydney Morning Herald described the shooting as a "gigantic calamity, affecting all classes of the people." Like other British revolutionary movements, the Fenian Brotherhood fizzled after this and disappeared for some years.

Albert wanted Germany to be unified and powerful. He had embedded his eldest daughter, Vicky, in the Prussian court in the hope of bringing his liberal ideals to the state he hoped would lead a future German nation. In the 1860s, the canny and opportunistic Prussian diplomat Otto von Bismarck was bent on unifying all German states under Prussian rule. By 1871, he had largely succeeded. The Crimean War in 1854 and the Italian War in 1859 had destabilized alliances between the great powers of Europe—Great Britain, France, Austria, and Russia—leaving a vacuum that Bismarck capitalized on with his well-organized and well-resourced army. "The great questions of the time," he said in 1862, "will not be resolved by speeches and majority decisions but by iron and blood." In 1866, he invaded Austria with Italian support, in what became known as the Seven Weeks' War. Prussia decisively defeated Austria, and the resulting treaty saw twenty-two states unified in a North German Confederation, with Bismarck as its chancellor and leader. But Austria, which had led the German Confederation since the end of the Napoleonic Wars in 1815, was excluded.

In the new federation, Schleswig, Holstein, and Hanover became Prussian states. Victoria agreed with Albert, telling Lord Stanley: "A strong, united, liberal Germany would be a most useful ally to England." But she distrusted Bismarck and thought his aggressive conduct "monstrous." Her son-in-law, Vicky's husband, Fritz—whose uncle was then king of Prussia—also disapproved of forcing unity through violence, as Bismarck was doing. Fritz had thought it would be "fratricide" to go to war against Austria, but he was proved wrong when Prussia triumphed. Victoria urged the king of Prussia to make acceptable compromises to secure peace and prevent a wider war from erupting.

Around the dining table, the wars made for awkward conversation. Vicky was married to a dovish Prussian prince who fought for the Prussians, Alice to a German prince who fought for the Austrians, Bertie to a Danish princess, and Helena to a German prince born in Denmark. When Victoria began to plan Louise's future at the end of 1869, she abandoned Albert's insistence on clever geopolitical matches. She wrote to Bertie: "Times have much changed; great foreign alliances are looked on as causes of trouble and anxiety, and are of no good. What could be more painful than the position in which our family was placed during the wars with Denmark, and between Prussia and Austria?" Instead, the beautiful Louise married a subject—a poetry-loving Liberal politician named John George Edward Henry Douglas Sutherland Campbell, Lord Lorne. (The couple lived separately and did not have children; rumors endure about Lorne's sexuality. Louise, a talented sculptor, harbored her own secrets; she had allegedly had an affair with the sculptor Joseph Edgar Boehm, who is thought to have died while making love to her. A recent biographer claims she bore a child who was quietly sent out for adoption.) But Helena married Prince Christian of Schleswig-Holstein, despite her mother's political objections.

The royal brood continued to multiply. Bertie's relationship with his mother improved after he married Alix, though Victoria still refused to allow him official responsibilities. Alice, a great admirer and friend of Florence Nightingale's, worked as a nurse in the Austro-Prussian war of 1866 and was happily married, though she later became somewhat estranged from her mother when she angered her by suggesting that she go out in public more. When Vicky lost one of her children, Sigismund, at just twenty-one months to meningitis, Victoria was desperate that she could not be with her to comfort her. She continued to fret about the hemophiliac Leopold, and after he suffered a hemorrhage in 1868, Victoria decided he would be her "chief object in life." She kissed him good night religiously. Even when he was well, Victoria felt "in constant anxiety about him." The constant thought that nagged her throughout her children's lives was how the loss of their father had affected them. She tried to compensate for his absence, but felt herself to be unequal to it. So instead she controlled, chastised, commanded, and adored her children, in a storm of moods. In her journal, she stopped drawing the cozy domestic scenes that had filled the pages when Albert was alive. From now, it was mostly the remote hills of Scotland that she etched in quiet moments.

On December 10, 1865, four years after Albert's death, Victoria's beloved uncle Leopold died. She was "stupefied and stunned" by the loss of her surrogate father. At forty-six, to be a sovereign, a single parent of nine children, and the matriarch of a family often fractured by warring European countries was a heavy load to bear without the sage counsel and company of a close relative. In the absence of this, Victoria had determined that her north star would be Albert's legacy, and she repeatedly vowed to carry out his wishes. But in truth, she found it easier to erect statues than to execute his ideas.

Victoria's grief was lengthy and noisy. The public wondered: Why could she not turn up at Parliament and fulfill her role as monarch? Why could she not briefly put aside her own suffering to do the work for which she was paid? But there are at least two things that must surely temper the scorn for a woman who failed to function properly for years. First, Victoria was not unwilling to work; she was unwilling to appear in public. The acute anxiety she experienced after Albert's death resembled a kind of social phobia, of which she was conscious but which she was unable to control. Second, it is only in recent years (since the mid-1980s) that psychologists have begun seriously to examine the nature of enduring grief—a complicated, traumatic, or prolonged grief—to understand why some suffer more acutely than others. It is a controversial subject, as many resist pathologizing understandable grief, but it is now in the appendix of DSM-5 (*Diagnostic and Statistical Manual of Mental Disorders,* fifth edition), as Persistent Complex Bereavement Disorder (PCBD). Studies of this disorder, which affects an estimated 10 percent of the bereaved, shed light on why Victoria might have been especially vulnerable to a deep, consuming mourning.

Women are more likely to experience protracted grief than men, and they are particularly susceptible if they have lost a parent in childhood, have been bullied or had controlling parents, have lost a supportive spouse they were highly dependent on, or if the death was sudden and unexpected. Other contributing factors include a history of mood disorder and an insecure attachment style. Victoria was ripe to grieve. While Victorians tolerated extensive mourning, Victoria's seclusion definitely exceeded what people thought appropriate for a widowed queen. The initial sympathy had faded by the mid-1860s, just a few years after Albert's death.

Today, psychotherapy and antidepressants would probably be prescribed, as well as regular exercise and a good diet. Instead, the queen who could control an empire but not her own heart gathered other sad women around her and wallowed in misery. She hated being told that she would be happy again. To suggest that things would improve seemed grossly disloyal to the memory of Albert. And the thought of a replacement was impossible, making the loss even starker. When a senior religious figure told Victoria she must think of herself as a bride of Christ from now on, she replied, "That is what I call twaddle."

Time lessened the anguish. But Victoria missed it when it faded, writing to Lady Waterpark: "The *violent* grief is *past*—I almost grieve for *that,* for there is sweetness even in *that,* but the constant black and the constant cloud are ever abiding." Still, she said, she was ready to "struggle on cheerfully." She had spent almost three years saying she wanted to die, but now said she wanted to live for her family and friends. As she grew stronger and happier, she was able to delight in nature again. Slowly she resumed recording beautiful scenes in her journal. In the thick of night in November 1866, Affie asked Victoria's maid to wake his mother to tell her the sky was full of falling stars. She rolled out of bed reluctantly and wrapped her dressing gown around her. When she stood at the window, she saw an extraordinary spectacle of large, bright stars, and meteors shooting like rockets across the sky. She remained there for half an hour and sent her servants to wake as many people as possible. She did not want anyone to miss it.

CHAPTER 23

The Queen's Stallion

Brown was a rude unmannerly fellow . . . but he had
unbounded influence with the Queen whom he
treated with little respect. . . . It was the talk of all the
household that he was "the Queen's Stallion." He was
a fine man physically, though coarsely made.

—WILFRED SCAWEN BLUNT

God knows, how much I want to be taken care of.

—QUEEN VICTORIA, 1865

John Brown was, most of all, a physical presence. When the ghillie
was with Victoria, he rowed her boats, steered her around dance
floors, and guided her up steep Highland paths. He lifted her onto
her horse, tackled assailants, carried her when she was unable to
walk, and perched on top of her carriages. There is little left of Brown
in the diaries Victoria's daughter Beatrice edited; he emerges suddenly as though from the shadows, summoned when needed, when
rivers were too deep, horses too stubborn, tracks too rocky, roads too
wet. A reader would not be able to tell, though, from these scattered
entries, that Brown was almost always nearby. He traveled with the

queen everywhere: in just a few years, she would be unashamed to declare him her best friend. Gossips suggested he was more than this; even Victoria's children called the strapping Scot "the Queen's Stallion." How else to view the remarkably unusual relationship between a sovereign and a servant? As a ruler, Victoria was a firm adherent of protocol. But as a woman, she obeyed her instincts. The muckrakers could rot. John Brown made her happy.

Always drawn to the direct, the unassuming and unaffected, Victoria had been instantly impressed by the young ghillie working at Balmoral. In 1850, when she was thirty-one, she described him as "a good looking, tall lad of 23, with fair curly hair, so very good humored & willing." He was wholly obliging when asked to come and care for the queen more than a decade later, after Albert had died. He was to be the most intimate friend of her life—more than Lehzen, Melbourne, or any of the others who had come and gone. Victoria spent eighteen years in the company of John Brown, almost as long as she spent with her beloved Albert.

In the late 1860s, Victoria was still something of a recluse. When she appeared at a garden party at Buckingham Palace in 1868, the crowds disoriented her. She had been in seclusion for almost seven years. Her journal entries in those years were flat, dull, and repetitive, devoid of her usual enthusiasm and curiosity (with occasional exceptions, such as her description of the visit of two conjoined girls from South Carolina, the children of slaves, who sang duets for her). The sediment of grief had compressed her world; even dramatic foreign events were, at least initially, described in the context of her feelings. Her days were still dogged by death. In 1870 alone, she lost Countess Blücher, General Grey, her doctor James Clark, and her old loyal governess, Lehzen. In 1872, the loss of her sister Feodora was "irreparable." The sad but resilient Victoria was surviving so many of the important figures in her life. As her old intimates slowly vanished, the queen ate too much, let out her skirts, and battled with rheumatism, toothaches, and headaches.

But as her subjects waited for the queen to appear, the rumors swirled about the man who had captured her affection and monopolized her attention. Had this tall Scot spirited her away? Victoria felt no sense of guilt when she was charged with neglecting her queenly duty up in Scotland: she saw herself as the sole arbiter of what that duty entailed. She refused to defer trips to Balmoral, even when needed to open Parliament or manage a ministerial crisis. Sir Thomas Biddulph, the Keeper of the Privy Purse, said, "The Queen will talk as if she were Mrs. Jones and might live just where she liked." The men of state scratched their heads as the queen's carriage rattled through the streets with a familiar six-foot-four figure on top of it: Brown, in his kilt, glaring protectively at anyone who might approach his queen.

What shocked people most was Brown's familiarity. It was unthinkable that a man could address a queen in such a fashion as he did. The Tory lord chancellor, Lord Cairns, was dumbstruck while watching him at a Ghillies' Ball—where royals and aristocrats danced with servants—in Balmoral: "I did not conceive it possible that anyone could behave so roughly as he does to the Queen." A barrister once observed Brown trying to pin a plaid shawl on the queen, when Victoria moved and the pin grazed her chin. Brown then cried, "Hoots, wumman, canna ye hold yer head still!" The empress of Russia reported that Brown treated Victoria "like a small child."

Yet what others saw as impertinence was to Victoria a refreshing lack of reserve. And this frankness was a hallmark of the intimacy she had craved from the moment she had lost Albert. When walking on steep slopes in the Highlands with Victoria and her other ladies, Jane Churchill fell, having tangled her feet in the hem of her dress. Picking her up, Brown said bluntly, "Your Ladyship is not so heavy as Her Majesty!" Victoria laughed at this: "I said 'Am I grown heavier do you think?' 'Well, I think you are,' was the plainspoken reply."

Many found the queen's blatant disregard for propriety and gossip galling. An indignant Lord Derby listed in his journal all that the queen was doing to "create suspicions":

Long solitary rides, in secluded parts of the park: constant attendance upon her in her room: private messages sent by him
to persons of rank: avoidance of observation while he is leading
her pony or driving her little carriage: everything shows that
she has selected this man for a kind of friendship which is absurd and unbecoming her position. The Princesses—perhaps
unwisely—make a joke of the matter, and talk of him as "Mamma's lover."

Victoria even tolerated and ignored Brown's alcoholism. When he
lay passed out, drunk, in his room one afternoon, unable to take her
riding, Henry Ponsonby* simply hopped onto the carriage instead.
Not a word was spoken. (Victoria overlooked her servants' drinking.
When she received a report that a footman who was an alcoholic had
dropped a lamp on the stairs, she just wrote "poor man" in the margin.) Brown increasingly acted as an intermediary, annoying those of
high rank. Instead of seeing the queen as hoped, they met with a
blunt, bearded Scotsman who had little time for niceties. When the
mayor of Portsmouth came to see her, to ask if she could come to a
military review, Brown simply stuck his head in the room and said,
"The Queen says sartenly not." The mayor retreated, stung. Derby
worried that no one was willing to tell the queen about how the rest
of the world perceived Brown, and her relationship with him.

What Victoria failed to recognize was the impact Brown had on
her children, who despised him and would devote considerable energy to destroying any record of their mother's intimacy with a ghillie.
His drinking, cussing, and bossing were not as appealing to the

---

* The diplomatic Ponsonby had served as an equerry to Albert, and was made the
queen's private secretary in 1870. As a Liberal, he would be a strong democratic
influence in the royal household, along with his feminist wife, Mary Bulteel,
whom the queen found intimidatingly clever. She grew reliant on Ponsonby,
though, and appreciated his tolerance for Brown—whom he called "Child of
Nature."

younger people in the house. Bertie, Alfred, Louise, and Leopold particularly grew to loathe Brown. They thought him coarse and presumptuous, and they were irritated by their mother's fondness for him. When Louise was engaged and planning her household, she told Ponsonby, "I won't have an absurd man in a kilt following me about everywhere."

Victoria, a woman who believed that her deceased husband still had a presence in the physical world, was drawn to Brown's seeming sixth sense, thought to be common to Highlanders. When the royal family left Balmoral in 1861, Brown told her he hoped she would keep well and that "above all, that you may have no deaths in the family." There were three that year, including Albert's. Brown's words circled repeatedly in Victoria's mind, "as if they had been a sort of strange presentiment." This convinced her of his mystical powers. Many still believe she used Brown as a medium during séances to try to reach Albert; this is possible, given her interest in spiritualism, but has never been proved. One writer called Brown "Rasputin in a kilt." (The empress Alexandra Feodorovna, who would later be captivated by the real Rasputin, met John Brown when she visited her grandmother Victoria with her mother, Alice.)

Victoria doubled Brown's salary, gave him a house for his retirement at Balmoral, promoted him to "the Queen's Highland Servant," and decorated him with awards. She ordered the Balmoral property manager to trace Brown's family tree and was thrilled when he linked him to Scotland's most prestigious clans. She knew Brown came from fine stock.

For five years after Albert's death, the queen remained hidden to the public. But in 1867, thousands flocked to the annual Spring Exhibition of the Royal Academy. On display was a large canvas, a painting, by Sir Edwin Landseer, titled *Her Majesty at Osborne, 1866.* In it, the queen sat sidesaddle on a sleek dark horse, dressed in her customary black. She was reading a letter from the dispatch box on the ground, next to her dogs. Opposite was a tall figure in a black kilt and jacket

solemnly holding the horse's bridle. Was *this* what the queen had
been doing with her time in the years since Albert's death?

It caused a scandal. The *Saturday Review* art critic wrote: "If anyone will stand by this picture for a quarter of an hour and listen to the
comments of visitors he will learn how great an imprudence has been
committed." It was not long before the gossip became crude: Were
the queen and Mr. Brown lovers? Was she pregnant with his child?
Had they secretly married? In 1868, an American visitor said he was
gobsmacked by constant, crass jokes about the queen commonly referred to as "Mrs. Brown." "I have been told," he wrote, "that the
Queen was insane, and John Brown was her keeper; the Queen was a
spiritualist, and John Brown was her medium."

Victoria adored the painting and ordered an engraving. She refused to change her behavior. When it was delicately suggested to her
in 1867 that she not take Brown with her to a military review in Hyde
Park, because they expected crowds to mock him, she was furious.
She crushed the idea with her customary mix of self-pity and obstinacy, claiming it would make her nervous and upset, that Brown was
a comfort to her. The Cabinet, after a lengthy discussion about her
mental health, decided not to press her. Her physician Dr. Jenner had
informed them that any "strong excitement (and very little excites
her) would cause her to vomit violently." And that if she had not been
provided this relief by "Nature," "the effect on her mind might be
dangerous." The men of state stared at one another across the Cabinet table: The queen would have a vomiting fit if they asked her to
leave Brown at home? And if she could not vomit, then she might go
mad? The review was postponed.

In quiet moments, staring out at the misty Highlands or the green
lawns of Windsor, Victoria felt a nagging sense of guilt. Did the fact
that her grief was easing mean that she was being disloyal to Albert?
Was it wrong to take consolation in another's company? She confided
in Dean Wellesley, who assured her that "a settled mournful resignation" was entirely appropriate, and was a more enduring evidence of

love than initial, blinding grief. He went further, telling her that she should consider this comfort a gift from God.

There are few subjects as wildly speculated about and poorly documented as Queen Victoria's relationship with John Brown. Most of the rumors are unfounded. The story of Victoria popping out of a carriage, disappearing into a cottage to give birth to John Brown's child, then emerging beaming and bearing champagne, for example, is risible for anyone who has ever given or witnessed birth. Most of the accounts rest on tantalizing tales of documents that have mysteriously disappeared over the years. The author E. P. Tisdall claims to have received a version of a letter allegedly in Victoria's writing telling John Brown she adored him, pieced together from the rubbish bin where Brown had allegedly left it after tearing it up. But this letter has been lost, and its veracity and claimed semblance to Victoria's writing were never tested.

One oft-repeated tidbit came from one of Bertie's notorious lovers, Catherine Walters. When Bertie commissioned the sculptor Joseph Edgar Boehm to capture her beautiful features, Boehm told Walters he had seen much suspect activity in the three months he spent at Balmoral carving a statue of Brown at the queen's request. Walters then confided in a friend:

> Brown was a rude unmannerly fellow. . . . He had unbounded influence with the Queen whom he treated with little respect, presuming in every way upon his position with her. It was the talk of all the household that he was "the Queen's Stallion." He was a fine man physically, though coarsely made, and had fine eyes (like the late Prince Consort's, it was said) and the Queen, who had passionately been in love with her husband got it into her head that somehow the Prince's spirit had passed into Brown and 4 years after her widowhood being very unhappy allowed him all privileges. . . . She used to go away with him to

a little house in the hills where, on the pretence that it was for protection and "to look after her dogs" he had a bedroom next to her, the ladies-in-waiting being put at the other end of the building. . . . Boehm saw enough of his familiarities with her to leave no doubt of his being allowed "every conjugal privilege."

Rumors of a marriage have been found not just in newspapers but in the diaries of the prominent and powerful. One minister who had served as Victoria's chaplain, the Reverend Norman Macleod, confessed on his deathbed in 1872 that he had married the queen and John Brown—a story that was recorded by someone several points removed. Given Victoria's belief that widows should not remarry, and the fact that Brown had almost married someone else in 1870, this is unlikely. But it is entirely possible there was some kind of promise or exchange or ritual, in which Brown gave his queen his mother's wedding ring; he had, in effect, renounced marriage to serve and love only her.

What we can also be certain of, though, is that the royal family has taken every measure possible to destroy any evidence of the relationship between Victoria and Brown, both when Victoria was alive and after her death. Bertie's hatred of his mother's Highland servant survived his accession as Edward VII, and the family was deeply embarrassed that their matriarch and monarch was besotted with a commoner who drank and swore. Much has been lost. Which is why even the faintest new shred of information can tell the loudest story.

In a small town near the southernmost tip of the Scottish Lowlands, not far from Berwick-upon-Tweed, the archives of Sir James Reid, Victoria's doctor for twenty years, are kept in a stone mansion. Dr. Reid was a solid, respected man whom Victoria trusted and relied on from 1881 to the end of her life; she died in his arms. She had given strict instructions that Sir James alone—known for his tact and discretion—would lift and move her body after her death. He kept immaculate diaries in a tiny, neat hand, where he recorded daily movements and medical appointments. On one day, in 1883, he recorded a most curious sight. Opening the door to Victoria's room at Windsor Castle, he saw her flirting with John Brown as she "walked a little."

Brown says to her, lifting his kilt, "Oh, I thought it was here?"

She responds, laughing, and lifting up her own skirt, "No, it is here."

It is unclear from the note exactly what "it" might be. What is clear is that Sir James was sufficiently interested in this exchange, and thought it significant enough, to record it in his little black journal. It revealed an extraordinary level of intimacy. We will never know the precise nature of that intimacy, but this snippet, which has not been published before, suggests there was a closeness that exceeded what was normal not just for a queen and her servant but for any male and female friend. Elizabeth Longford, the first to have full access to Victoria's diaries, and author of a remarkably insightful biography published in 1964, has long insisted Victoria would have had only a platonic relationship with Brown. She wrote recently that if Brown had been Victoria's lover, "one or other of her numerous courtiers, equerries, ladies-in-waiting, dressers, 'rubbers,' readers or other attendants would at some point have accidentally seen something." What Longford did not know is that Sir James did.

Perhaps the incident that gives the greatest pause, only discovered through the preservation of the doctor's notebooks outside the Royal Archives, is the report of Bertie being blackmailed with a cache of letters between Victoria and Alexander Profeit, the manager of Balmoral, who was thought to have intensely disliked Brown. There were about three hundred letters in total between Victoria and Profeit, and Profeit's son knew how significant and potentially lucrative his discovery was in the years after Victoria's death. Sir James Reid was dispatched to procure the letters from Profeit's son on Bertie's behalf, which he did successfully in 1905, after six months of negotiations. It is not known how much money was exchanged for these missives, nor their contents. They were burned immediately. Reid took some notes on the letters in a green notebook, which was destroyed upon his death. All we have is his remaining description of these notes in his journal. These letters, he wrote, were "very compromising."

Despite all this, researchers have shied from concluding Victoria was in love with John Brown. To do so, it is implicit, would be to suggest that Victoria and John Brown had a burning, consuming, and enduring sexual relationship. Victoria never hid her relationship with Brown—surely she would have been less defiant if they were full-blown lovers. But their relationship was undeniably flirtatious, intense, and proximate. They spent many hours alone on the moors, drinking whisky—or what John Brown called "sperruts"—and stayed in remote locations with rooms near each other. It is difficult to imagine that such a passionate, lonely woman could have been immune to the attraction of a rugged Scot. We will never know what actually occurred; whether he held her hand, or put his arms around her as they sat, isolated and miles away from human eyes in the mountains near Balmoral. There are a thousand possibilities for intimacy on the spectrum between lover and friend. Victoria might have curled up against him once or twice to remind herself what it was like to feel the heat of another body next to hers; she was more than a full foot shorter than Brown. To those who imagine that perhaps brief moments of tenderness would not conflict with the morals and manner of a monarch, it is of little significance what form their physical relationship took.

What is certain is that Queen Victoria was in love with John Brown. This, in fact, is the true scandal. It was not a love she had known with Albert, in which she was the devoted inferior who worked on "improving herself," under the guidance of a man she saw as a god, not an equal. She never knew the love of her father, for a long time she distrusted the love of her mother, and Lord Melbourne was more of a mentor than a jovial companion. Her love for John Brown was unique. He was seven years younger than Victoria, and an impossible chasm stood between them socially. Even so, he treated her like a woman, not a queen. Victoria thought of marriage as something between a "master" and an adoring, ostensibly subservient wife. The thought that a marriage could occur between a woman who ruled the world and a man who tended her horses was absurd to her and would violate her basic conception of the relationship. But she loved him, as a woman who loves the man who protects and adores her.

Because the relationship was so improbable, Victoria could allow herself to think of it as an ardent best friendship. It is clear, from Reid's glimpse into their private world, that there was a level of intimacy between them that would have scandalized society. The extent or nature of their physical relationship we will never know. Victoria's relationship with Brown was like a second marriage, with a remarkably different power dynamic—and one that, much as she would have refused to admit it, suited the queen very well. Gradually, the color crept back into her life. When Louise got married the next month, her mother wore rubies as well as diamonds.

Over in Europe, Otto von Bismarck was dreaming of a united Germany that would emerge as a continental superpower. Bismarck's appetite had been whetted by the 1866 Austro-Prussian war, after which twenty-two northern German states formed a confederation, led by Prussia. Now he wanted to exploit any opportunity to draw the states together more tightly under a centralized government, encompassing those in southern Germany that were still independent, including Bavaria and Hesse-Darmstadt. He believed one way to achieve this was to provoke neighboring France into a war, in order to force the southern German states to join with the militarily muscular northern states to fight their common enemy. France was threatened by Bismarck's overt ambition, and when a Prussian prince was considered as a possible king of Spain, France roared with disapproval. The Prussian prince's name was eventually withdrawn, but subsequent diplomatic slights (exaggerated by a manipulative Bismarck, who redrafted a crucial dispatch) convinced France to attack: it declared war on Germany in July 1870. After South Germany joined with the North, the Prusso-German army had roughly twice as many soldiers as the French.

After the ugliness of the Crimean War sixteen years earlier, Victoria was desperate to maintain Britain's neutrality. She pored over the accounts of the wounded in newspapers, and repeatedly urged Gladstone to increase the number of British troops as an "absolute necessity." She demanded to know the readiness for war, numbers in the army and navy, and the state of the dockyards.

Victoria could see little point to the conflict, and was miserable about her sons-in-law going to war. She insisted, "The only way is to leave matters as quiet as possible, and to let people quiet down. For me to attempt to do anything, beyond preaching neutrality and prudence would be useless." Her heart, though, was with Germany. (This did not stop her from agreeing to Britain's continuing sale of arms and horses to France, though, which outraged Prussia.) She prayed only for the war to end, and comforted Vicky and the heavily pregnant Alice; both daughters tended to the wounded in hospitals as they waited for news of their soldier husbands. Back in the Highlands, Victoria stopped at the Balmoral local store and bought calico for bandages.

The war lasted less than a year. After the Battle of Sedan in September 1870, the French leader Napoleon III surrendered and was captured along with 104,000 of his men. Prussia's win was decisive. Their numbers were superior, thanks partly to the use of conscription as well as to their railways, their use of Krupp steel artillery, and their well-coordinated mobilization. This marked the end of the balance of power in Europe, whereby Britain and France had been dominant for half a century. Now the German empire was rising. Germany scooped up Alsace and half of Lorraine, which France would try to win back in the First World War. Germany was now officially unified under King William I of Prussia; it became a single country in

January 1871. At the same time, Italy captured and annexed the Papal States, which had been under the direct rule of the Pope since the 700s and had lost their protector in Napoleon III. The landscape of European power was shifting every year.

In the midst of the war, France had become a republic when the revolutionary Paris Commune staged a coup on September 4, 1870. The French empress Eugénie came to hide in England. A sympathetic Victoria went to meet her, recording the story of her flight and horror in exacting detail—from the gamin who recognized her under her hat and cloak and called out *"À la guillotine!"* to the hellishly uncomfortable trip, riding sandwiched in a carriage on rocky roads. The British Isles were once again spared revolution; their stout queen was in no danger.

As Victoria grew older, she gradually leaned more toward conservatism. In her youth, she had taken a keen interest in the life of the poor as described by Charles Dickens, but she had not gone on to take an interest in the causes of poverty and frequently blamed those protesting against it. She supported the first of the Irish Land Acts in 1870, which meant tenants would be compensated for any changes they made to their property, but she hastened to point out to the prime minister the "apparent want of sympathy with the landlords." It was unfair, she wrote, to cast the "entire blame" of the problems with the landlords, and said the tenants should not be led to think that they could misbehave.

This did not mean the queen did not wish for the lot of the poor to improve. When she met Charles Dickens in March 1870, she described him as "very agreeable, with a pleasant voice and manner." When Dickens died, just three months later, at age fifty-eight, Victoria wrote: "He had a large, loving mind and strongest sympathy with the poorer peoples. He felt sure that a better feeling, and much greater union of classes would take place in time. And I pray earnestly it may." Yet the queen did not suggest or contemplate any steps that might alleviate this poverty, as her husband might have done when he was alive.

Victoria favored escape over exploration. She wrote enormously popular books about her time in Scotland—*Leaves from the Journal of Our Life in the Highlands* in 1868 and *More Leaves* in 1884—that were domestic and sweetly focused on her family, and the books fomented a belief that she was idling. But as Arthur Ponsonby pointed out, Victoria was as opinionated as ever:

> It would not require much research to pick out a date recording some colorless, unimportant incident and to find it in her correspondence on the same day some letter to the Prime Minister or the Private Secretary expressing in her most vehement language her desire to interfere in high matters of national importance. But this was all excluded from the volumes and the general public, including radicals and even republicans for a short time, were satisfied there could be no harm whatever in a monarch who spent all her days so innocently in a Scottish retreat.

As a single parent, she felt the weight of her children's welfare acutely. Her correspondence continued with her adored Vicky. Victoria had also warmed to Bertie since he married the sweet-natured, elegant Alexandra of Denmark, and she praised his popularity while still warning him off his fast, reckless behavior. Bertie, who lived in Sandringham House at Norfolk, continued to drink, gamble, and woo women as his wife battled through a series of illnesses and pregnancies. The queen's attempted control of Bertie's and Alexandra's social life was the subject of much chatter.

In 1869, the husband of one of Bertie's alleged lovers—Harriet Mordaunt—exposed his peccadilloes in what would be a scorching scandal. As he sat to write a letter to his mother, Bertie felt sick, remembering how disappointed his father had been about Nellie

Clifden just before his death. On February 10, 1870, he wrote to the queen: "It is my painful duty (I call it painful, because it must be so to you to know that yr eldest son is obliged to appear as a witness in a court of justice) to inform you that I have been subpoenaed by Sir C. Mourdaunt's Counsel to appear as a Witness on Saturday next at Lord Penzance's Court." The queen supported her son, and believed him to be innocent. The prime minister, W. E. Gladstone, followed suit. After confident testimony from Bertie in court, the judge declared Harriet insane. Bertie went on blithely carousing and womanizing. He was unconcerned by the slanders made against his name, but he was widely considered a roué.

It was now her middle children Victoria was struggling with. At twenty-six, Affie drank heavily and had indulged in an affair with a young woman at Malta when he was stationed there. His mother distrusted his reserved manner and found him "touchy, vague and willful." She and twenty-seven-year-old Alice, though, had reached a rapprochement of sorts. Victoria criticized Helena for producing "excessively plain" babies, for ill health and pudginess, and for looking older than her twenty-four years. Louise's marriage was fraught and unhappy. The intellectual Leopold was straining against his confinement at home as he fought off various hemorrhages and leg injuries. His siblings protested what they saw as their mother's overprotective attitude toward their sickly, stifled brother; Victoria staunchly insisted they would do better not to think of what Leopold was missing out on, but everything he could still do. Her children were ungrateful, and foolish to not take her advice, she thought. Being head of a family and sovereign at once was almost more than a person could bear. It was too bad Bertie was such a disappointment.

The youngest children were still sweet and adored. Arthur, who still strongly resembled his father at twenty, troubled his mother only when he parted his hair down the middle. Beatrice, thirteen, was the most overtly favored, and the child Victoria was most intent on keeping home with her. Victoria tried to delay her adulthood, preventing her from going out at night and postponing her societal "coming out" as long as she could. "She is the last I have," Victoria wrote plaintively, "and I could not live without her." As grandchildren ran giggling around her palaces, Victoria doted on them—especially the good-looking ones—while simultaneously complaining about how many there were. She experienced diminishing returns when it came to her grandchildren: she was interested in perhaps two to three of them, but "when they come at a rate of three a year," she told an apologetically maternal Vicky, "it becomes a cause of mere anxiety for my own children and of no great interest."

In the decade after Albert died, Victoria became increasingly selfish. Her grief and depression, unchecked, led her to view all interactions through a self-centered lens—even foreign affairs were, initially, assessed according to the impact on her state of mind. Those who were most attuned to her needs, like John Brown and Beatrice, were praised. Those who weren't, like Gladstone, were shut out. She accused her children of not understanding her burden. When her daughter Louise got engaged, Victoria wasn't happy for her; she was saddened by the thought of losing another daughter. When Affie got married in St. Petersburg, she refused to go. It was just depressing, she wrote to Vicky, when the children married. It was the first wedding of one of her children that she missed, but she confided in Vicky, "I dislike now witnessing marriages, very much, and think them sad and painful, especially a daughter's marriage." She also missed her grandchild Willy's confirmation in Prussia. When Willy's mother, Vicky, protested, Victoria responded, "I am very tired."

The queen's candor also applied to the dignitaries who swept through her palaces. When she met the author Thomas Carlyle, for example, she described him as "a strange-looking eccentric old Scotchman, who holds forth, in a drawling melancholy voice, with a broad Scotch accent upon Scotland and upon the utter degeneration of everything." (He, in turn, gushed about her "kindly little smile," and her "rather attractive" appearance. It was impossible, he told his sister, "to imagine a politer little woman.")

By 1870, people regarded Victoria with something approaching panic. How could they get her to appear in public again? Her children and ministers all shared the same dim view: her seclusion was damaging the monarchy. The longer she stayed out of sight, the more her subjects' fondness for her dwindled. Ponsonby was despondent: "If she is neither the head of the Executive nor the fountain of honor, nor the center of display, the royal dignity will sink to nothing at all." Even Disraeli was glum. He worried that the monarchy was in danger, not from any republican movement, or hostility, but from "gradual loss of prestige": the queen had made people believe they could do very well without her. There was a growing sense that affection for the monarch was not self-replenishing, but could be exhausted by her absence.

At the end of 1871, Victoria fell ill—the worst she had felt since she had typhoid as a teenager. When she was still recovering, Bertie suddenly collapsed into a fever with symptoms eerily similar to those Albert had suffered exactly ten years earlier. The family panicked. Three times, Victoria journeyed to Sandringham, where Bertie lived with Alix, expecting to kiss a cold brow. She stood apprehensively behind a screen in his room and listened to his breathing. She had never loved him more than in those moments, when she thought she might lose him. Thousands of letters and telegrams poured in; the public grief was extraordinary. Crowds swarmed around newspaper offices, waiting for bulletins. Priests cried out to God in their Sunday sermons, asking for Bertie to live. The nation warmed to the sight of a family miserably teetering on the precipice of great loss. Just as the British had failed to recognize Albert's gifts until he had died, one newspaper mused that perhaps the same was true of Bertie. He had gifts of another class, more popular than intellectual: a "geniality" in performing ceremonial duties, an "English love of sport," and lastly a characteristic of great use in a royal: an "apparent willingness to place his services at the disposal of anyone who wants a foundation stone laid or a bazaar opened."

The fact that Bertie survived was considered miraculous. A thankful Victoria wrote: "We all feel that if God has spared his life it is to enable him to lead a new life." Gladstone leapt at the chance to capitalize on the revived affection for the monarchy and suggested a rousing thanksgiving service be held on February 27, 1872, in St. Paul's Cathedral. Victoria was bored in the church, and found St. Paul's "cold, dreary and dingy," but the roars of millions who stood outside in the cold under a lead-colored sky made her triumphant, and she pressed Bertie's hand in a dramatic flourish. It was "a great holy day" for the people of London, *The Times* declared gravely. They wished to show the queen she was as beloved as ever. Their delight at seeing her in person was as much a cause for celebration as Bertie's recovery.

This moment revealed something that Bertie would quickly grasp though his mother had not: the British public requires ceremony and pageantry, and the chance to glimpse a sovereign in finery. It was not a republic her subjects were hankering for, but a visible queen. As Lord Halifax said, people wanted their queen to look like a queen, with a crown and scepter: "They want the gilding for their money." Victoria considered it intrusive, but her son instinctively understood the importance of this kind of performance. He rose to wave and bow to the country that his mother expected to love her regardless.

Just two days later, Victoria was shot at again as she drove into Buckingham Palace. She credited Brown's "great presence of mind and quickness" for grabbing the man by the throat and forcing him to drop the pistol—"Brown alone saw him spring round and suspected him." For this, she created a new category of award—the "Victoria Devoted Service Medal," for a "very special act of devotion to the Sovereign," which was gold and bore her head on one side. (Brown appears to have been the sole recipient of this medal.) She also pinned a silver medal for "long and faithful service" to his broad chest with satisfaction. Brown had not just restored her enthusiasm for living, he had saved her life, she thought over and over as they rode for miles over the Highlands.

———

Victoria still longed to crawl into smaller and smaller homes. She grew more introverted as she aged, and her hatred of noise grew to rival her hatred of heat. The sounds of children yelling and screaming annoyed her, and she was convinced that her nerves—strained by work, anxiety, and rebellious children—would never recover. She wrote to Vicky:

> I know that you have many great difficulties—and that your position is no easy one, but so is mine full of trials and difficulties and of overwhelming work—requiring that rest which I cannot get. The very large family with their increasing families and interests is an immense difficulty and I must add burden for me. Without a husband and father, the labour of satisfying all (which is impossible) and of being just and fair, and kind—and yet keeping often quiet which is what I require too much is quite fearful.

The only place she could get complete rest was in the tiny cottage called Glassalt Shiel, hidden in the firs on snow-covered hills around the ink-black Loch Muick in the Highlands.

Gradually her strength returned. She began to dance and travel again. She even allowed herself to look at her sheet music once more, her piano duet books bringing back memories of Albert. Finally, her recollections brought more joy than pain: "The past has seemed to rush in upon me in a strange & marvellous manner."

Victoria rarely dreamed of Albert. Instead, she dreamed of her mother: "Married life has totally ceased," she wrote, "and I suppose that is why I feel as though I were again living with her." On her fifty-second birthday, in 1871, Victoria wrote: "Alone, alone, as it will ever be." She had no husband, no official partner in her duties as ruler and mother. But she did have Brown, a man whose relationship defied categories: best friend, consigliere, confidant, companion, intimate. "No one loves you more than I do," Victoria told Brown, often. He would answer seriously, "Nor you—than me. No one loves you more." He was closer to her than her own children and was the only person, said Henry Ponsonby, who could "fight and make the Queen do what she did not wish." When she was ill, sons and daughters were not called for: Brown was. Had her family come, cried Victoria's financial manager (or Keeper of the Privy Purse), Thomas Biddulph, "that would have killed her at once." As she explained to Vicky,

> When one's beloved Husband is gone, & one's Children are married—one feels that a friend ... who can devote him or herself entirely to you is the one thing you do require to help you on—& to sympathize entirely with you. Not that you love your Children less—but you feel as they grow up & marry that you can be of so little use to them, & they to you (especially in the Higher Classes).

On January 1, 1877, Victoria sent a card to Brown with a picture of a chambermaid on the front. She wrote on it: "To my best friend JB / From his best friend V.R.I." Inside, it read:

> I send my serving maiden
> With New Year letter laden,
> Its words will prove
> My faith and love
> To you my heart's best treasure,
> Then smile on her and smile on me
> And let your answer loving be,
> And give me pleasure.

Brown answered with his life.

CHAPTER 24

The Faery Queen Awakes

"I don't know what you mean by your way," said the
Queen, "all the ways about here belong to me."

—LEWIS CARROLL,
THROUGH THE LOOKING-GLASS

What nerve! What muscle! What energy!

—BENJAMIN DISRAELI ON
QUEEN VICTORIA, NOVEMBER 26, 1879

One morning in June 1875, while breakfasting in the cottage at
the aptly named Frogmore, Victoria suddenly noticed an "immense
number of little frogs" swarming the grounds of Windsor Castle.
There were thousands of them, "hopping & crawling all over the
grass & paths, which seemed to increase . . . making the grass look, as
if it were alive!" Horrified, she ordered her servants to sweep the
paths for hours, until they were clear of the "disgusting" creatures.
The tiny frogs made her skin prickle. A naturalist told her the frogs
had come from far away to breed in the pond at Windsor but would
soon disperse, much like a plague of locusts. Victoria, who would
go to some lengths to save the life of an old turtle and wept at the

thought of dogs in pain, still found the sight of the frogs "quite dreadful."

A year later, they were gone. The paths at Windsor were swept, the lawns trimmed, and the hedges clipped. The queen's life was an ordered and comfortable one; she bent nature, and the world, to her liking. But the political landscape around her was rapidly evolving as the Turkish Empire declined, the Austrian hold on Europe was slipping, and a unified Italy and Germany were growing in influence. Europe was heaving after Turkish mercenaries committed bloody acts of barbarity against rebelling Bulgarians (then part of the Ottoman Empire). In July 1876, while on a train to St. Petersburg, the Russian poet Ivan Turgenev wrote a poem, "Croquet at Windsor," which likened the croquet balls Victoria was happily whacking to the severed heads of Bulgarian women and children rolling around the feet of Turkish militia. The hem of her dress was soaked in blood. The Russian press refused to publish the poem for fearing of offending Victoria; handwritten copies were passed around instead.

The Turkish atrocities were gruesome. The skulls of Bulgarians were carried on spikes or piled on carts, pregnant women were ripped open and rows of fetuses brandished on bayonets, children sold into slavery and harems, women savagely raped, people locked inside churches and burned alive. "Christian heads," wrote one correspondent, were "tossed about the market place, like balls from one Turk to another." Yet few in England could work up outrage over what would become one of the greatest atrocities of the Victorian age. Disraeli dismissed it as "coffee house babble." The queen was sure the stories were exaggerated. The Turks, after all, were their allies. The British had spent years helping to protect their borders from the barbaric Russians.

Parliament was inexcusably slow to investigate the actions of the Turks. By downplaying the nature of the atrocities even when their extent became apparent, Disraeli grossly underestimated the public mood. He planned to continue to shore up a weakening Turkey against Russia's advances, largely to protect the British trade route to

India. His instincts were wrong. It was left to the newspapers—in particular the *Daily News,* which published a report on June 23 estimating the number of dead Christians as between eighteen and thirty thousand—to press the politicians to properly investigate.

Since the Ottoman Turks had taken possession of nearby Bulgaria—which perched on the western side of its northern border—five hundred years before, the Bulgarians had chafed at their (mostly military) rule. When they rebelled in 1876, the reprisals were swift. Most acts of reprisal were carried out against Christians by *bashi-bazouks,* harsh mercenaries who themselves had to be restrained occasionally by the Turkish forces they worked for. Victoria described them as "horribly cruel mutilators . . . with narrow faces, and pointed beards, dressed in no uniform . . . with many knives stuck about in their belts." She was loyal to the stubborn Disraeli, but she began to realize there was truth to the rumors.

More than two decades after the Crimean War, Turkey—the sick man of Europe—threatened to collapse again. The Eastern Question wasn't resolved. There were now two competing matters of concern for Britain: the stability of their ally Turkey, and the fate of Christian subjects in Turkish lands. Agitators argued that the rest of Europe should intervene to protect the Christian subjects. The other side worried this would only give Russia permission to go to war with Turkey on behalf of the Orthodox Christians in Bulgaria who looked to Russia for protection. Russia still was determined to break Turkey up and gain an entrance to the Mediterranean Sea through Constantinople, just as Britain was determined to keep it together, to maintain their authority in the region and their access to India.

Upon reading of the atrocities in the papers, Gladstone, who was now sixty-six and in a state of semiretirement after resigning from the leadership of the Liberal Party, was enraged. It was not just a battle of civilization against tyranny, he thought, but darkness against faith. As a Christian, who had been occupied writing theological tomes since his resignation, he was particularly angry about the religious persecution of other Christians. From his bed, he wrote a thunderous pamphlet calling on the Turks to leave Bulgaria. His most famous work, *Bulgarian Horrors and the Question of the East,* came out on September 6, 1876, and was an instant bestseller. Two hundred thousand copies sold in the first month. But Victoria, who favored realpolitik over high-mindedness and interventionism, said he was just adding "fuel to the flame."

Gladstone had a better knack for reading the mood of the people than did Disraeli; this was clear now. He was a fit, intellectual man who was fond of bow ties and wore a habitually serious expression. He had been in the House of Commons for forty-four years, serving in a host of positions. As the Turkey debate raged, he quickly became the most authoritative figure in the opposition. He also loathed Disraeli: their mutual contempt and competition made for the greatest political rivalry of the century.

By late 1876, the country was galvanized, and pressure mounted on the government to act. Public opinion was building on Gladstone's side, seeing the need to act to protect the Bulgarians. Thomas Carlyle—with John Ruskin (who called Disraeli and Gladstone "two old bagpipes")—led some of the hundreds of meetings organized against the Turks and protesting their presence in Bulgaria. Charles Darwin contributed fifty pounds to a relief fund. Victor Hugo satirized the tendency of men like Disraeli to dismiss the horrors as overblown: "The child that was thrown from the point of one lance to another was in fact only pierced with a bayonet." Oscar Wilde, then twenty-two and studying the classics at Oxford, and earning a reputation as a long-haired, decadent aesthete with a fondness for carrying sunflowers, sent Gladstone a copy of his poem "Sonnet on the Massacre of the Christians in Bulgaria."

But Victoria—who had performed mysterious mental acrobatics in order to blame Russia somehow for the Turkish atrocities and to hold Gladstone responsible for whipping up anti-Turkish sentiment— was angry. Gladstone was a mere "mischief maker and firebrand." The increasingly conservative queen chastised her daughter Vicky for showing sympathy to the liberal cause. By Victoria's rationale, the British Empire's prestige would be upheld if Britain made it clear to Russia that they would protect Turkey's interests if the Russians invaded Constantinople. Her Cabinet was divided on the subject, but Disraeli agreed; together they acted secretly to communicate this to the Russians in August 1877, an extraordinary act especially given that not even the foreign minister was aware of it. There had been much dissection of the disastrous Crimean War in the two decades since it ended, and many both inside and outside Parliament were of the view that if Britain had been more emphatic about protecting Turkey, Russia would not have invaded in the first place. Victoria and Disraeli's core concern was protection of British power.

Disraeli erred by refusing to unequivocally condemn the atrocities in public. He worried that improving the lot of the Balkan Slavs might cause problems domestically; it would make Irish autonomy look more logical. But his aims were unclear, aside from breaking up the affronting League of the Three Emperors—an alliance between Germany, Russia, and Austria-Hungary that Bismarck formed in 1873. The aim of the League was to control Eastern Europe—"which Disraeli regarded as an affront to British prestige." For Gladstone, foreign policy was about morality. For Disraeli, it was about power.

Benjamin Disraeli was an unlikely prime minister. He dressed like a dandy in lurid velvet suits, with rings over his gloves and a curl in the middle of his forehead. He affected a goatee, rouged cheeks, and a faintly weary, quizzical expression. He had inveigled his way into the center of British society through charm, but Disraeli was an outsider (he remains Britain's only prime minister of Jewish descent). In between his two stints as prime minister, he wrote a bestselling novel, *Lothair*—his sixteenth. A talent for popular fiction at that time, in the mid- to late nineteenth century, was considered somewhat suspect: instead of occupying himself, as other gentlemen did, with "classical, historical or constitutional studies," he wrote a "gaudy romance" that to some "revived all the former doubts as to whether a Jewish literary man, so dowered with imagination, and so unconventional in his outlook, was the proper person to lead a Conservative party to victory."

But in 1874, Disraeli defied his critics. His Conservative Party won a majority of seats in Parliament for the first time since 1841. A delighted Victoria wrote conspiratorially to Vicky: "Did you ever see such a universal and overwhelming result of a Dissolution against a Minister as there is against Mr. Gladstone? It shows how little he is trusted and how unpopular he is!" Albert had liked Gladstone, with his intellectual rigor and devout faith. But Victoria was suspicious of him and had come to the conclusion that he was "a great misfortune." She considered him bright, but a terrible statesman, pushing legislation simply for the principle at great political cost. Vicky shared her father's liberalism and naturally identified with Gladstone, but she also felt he was contradictory and "incomprehensible"—a poor politician. Victoria was genuinely puzzled by his popularity and crowed when it dissipated: "Mr. Gladstone is a very dangerous Minister—and so wonderfully unsympathetic."

Gladstone was also remote and charmless. Worse, he was no fun; no ribald asides or juicy tidbits of gossip. The poet and novelist Emily Eden said Gladstone didn't talk, he just lectured: "If he were soaked in boiling water and rinsed till he was twisted into a rope, I do not suppose a drop of fun would ooze out." His briefings were complicated and boring. Victoria complained he spoke to her as though she were a public meeting. A smug Disraeli said, "Gladstone treats the Queen like a public department; I treat her like a woman." Gladstone's grand oratorical talent was lost on his queen, and she grew to resent what appeared to be condescension. He utterly lacked the warmth and intimacy that Melbourne, Brown, and Disraeli had all provided. In the words of Lady Rosebery, "Mr. Gladstone may be a marvel of erudition, but he will never understand a man, still less a woman."

Disraeli understood women. After sitting next to Gladstone, one woman declared, "I thought he was the cleverest man in England.

But when I sat next to Disraeli I thought I was the cleverest woman." It was the greatest essence of charm: a singular, flattering focus. Even when Victoria disagreed with Disraeli, she found him charming, telling Lord Rosebery, "He had a way when we differed . . . of saying 'Dear Madam' so persuasively, and putting his head on one side." Victoria's favor was still significant enough to matter to a prime minister; it would be a source of sustenance for Disraeli and sorrow for Gladstone.

Victoria budded in the presence of a man who charmed her, who confided in her and sought her approval. Albert had made people feel stupid—as did Gladstone. But Disraeli made Victoria feel like her best self again. When he came to visit Osborne, he thought she might even embrace him: "She was wreathed with smiles and, as she tattled, glided about the room like a bird." Sensitive to his gout, the queen even asked him to sit down—the first PM she had granted that honor to since Lord Melbourne. Like Melbourne, Disraeli was also mourning the death of his wife, Mary Anne, with whom he had spent thirty-three years. He developed a genuine, deep affection for Victoria. "I love the Queen," he told the Dowager Lady Ely after his wife's death, "perhaps the only person in this world left to me that I do love."

In many ways, Disraeli was the opposite of Albert. His biographer Robert Blake described him as "proud, flamboyant, quick-witted, generous, emotional, quarrelsome, extravagant, theatrical, addicted to conspiracy, fond of backstairs intrigue." He saw women as intellectual equals, unlike Albert. Writing about his male secretary, Montagu Corry, Disraeli said, "I like him much better than any other man, but, as a rule, except upon business, male society is not much to my taste." Even his fiction was written mostly for women. It was probably unfortunate for him that women couldn't vote; not surprisingly, he was sympathetic to the idea of female suffrage.

Disraeli's foppish dress, flamboyance, fondness for Turkish baths, close male friendships, and love of older women have led some historians to suggest he was gay or bisexual. There is no definitive evidence to support this and he did have a long-lasting, happy marriage. William Kuhn parsed Disraeli's books for signs of homoeroticism and effeminacy, arguing that the stories were autobiographical in a time when same-sex love needed to be kept secret: sodomy had been punishable by death as recently as 1861. Kuhn concludes that Disraeli "embraced a sort of doubleness, a conscious ambiguity, such that sexually and romantically he loved both men and women," and that he was "more than just friends" with Montagu Corry. In his view, Disraeli might have been "what today we might call gay." His great biographer, Robert Blake, simply suggested he was like the flamboyant Oscar Wilde, who had sexual relationships with men while married to a woman—and the parallels are obvious.

In the spring of 1877, Russia finally invaded Turkey, in a bid to support the Bulgarians and unite Orthodox Christians. Victoria took it as a personal slight. With each passing month of the war, her resolve grew and her hatred for the Russians hardened under the guise of patriotism. "I rejoice," she said, "at every Russian defeat." Ponsonby blamed Disraeli for simplifying the dispute as a chess game between queen and czar. Disraeli played his hand cleverly, restraining the queen with his Cabinet's division, and prodding his Cabinet with the queen's staunchness. Victoria dismissed those who disagreed with her as fools or traitors. In her mind, she and Disraeli stood for "the Imperial policy of England," while Gladstone was a mere "sentimental" crusader. She began mentioning "the British Lion" in her correspondence, threatening he will "bite, now that he is roused." Russia must know Britain was ready to fight if necessary.

In times of crises, Victoria's strengths and weaknesses flared in tandem: her loyalty, patriotism, and sense of duty alongside her inability to see an opponent's position, a stubbornness, and a propensity to frame things as epic black-and-white struggles between good and evil. She saw the vacillators as weak and lacking in resolve, telling Disraeli she'd like to go and whip the Russians herself. When Victoria was unable to bend the parliament to her will, she was miserable. She threatened to abdicate five times between April 1877 and February 1878, rather than witness her country "kiss the feet of the great barbarians." She decried the MPs as lacking patriotism and decency: "It is a miserable thing to be a constitutional Queen and to be unable to do what is right. I would gladly throw all up and retire into quiet."

Missives flew out of Victoria's castles and homes like clouds of bats. Disraeli told his friend Lady Bradford that "the Faery [as he had grown fond of calling her] writes every day and telegraphs every hour." Disraeli and the queen were now working as partners, and Victoria referred to the two of them as "we." When Disraeli gained the support of his party to recall Parliament, increase British forces, and engage in direct mediation, she rewarded him by a show of public support. For the first time since she visited Lord Melbourne at Brocket in 1841, she went to Hughenden Manor, the home of the prime minister, for lunch.

In the summer of 1878, Victoria received eleven thousand telegrams during the four weeks she was at Balmoral—most of them about the Eastern Question. In March of that year, the Russians had imposed the secret Treaty of San Stefano on Turkey, which had created an alarmingly large, independent Bulgaria. But the Congress of Berlin, which began on June 13, superseded this agreement; for a month Disraeli and Lord Salisbury, the foreign secretary, negotiated new terms between Russia and Turkey with the help of Prussia and Austria, and destroyed the Treaty of Stefano without war. Bulgaria was made independent, but smaller, and less threatening not just to neighboring states, but also to Britain. Disraeli also managed to snare Cyprus for the British—without apparent justification. He updated the queen by letter each day. The tenacious, vital seventy-three-year-old spent weeks lobbying, maneuvering, socializing, and smoking cigars with a champagne-drinking, corpulent Bismarck until the deal was completed and Disraeli was spent. This agreement remained in place until 1918; Russian expansion into the Mediterranean had been checked and Europe preserved, for now. Bismarck exalted his new British friend: *"Der alte Jude, das ist der Mann"* (The old Jew, that is the man).

Disraeli returned on July 16 to cheering crowds and rapturous acclaim: it would be his greatest moment as prime minister. War had been avoided, and Britain had gotten what it wanted. Victoria sent him a letter and a nosegay. Flowers had long formed a part of their friendship: she sent him primroses and snowdrops from Osborne that he called a "faery gift." Victoria was now as fiercely partisan a Tory as she had been a Whig under Lord Melbourne. After the victory in the negotiations at the Congress of Berlin, she swore revenge against the Liberals: "The harm they have done their country is irreparable & I can never forget it." She was older, but her strength grew, her energy returned, and she unwittingly followed Albert's advice to immerse herself in something external in order to bury misery. She opened Parliament three times while Disraeli was PM. And she never did forgive Gladstone.

Queen. Church. Empire. This is how Disraeli defined his party's philosophy, and how he shaped Tory rhetoric for a century to come. Victoria was his enchanted sovereign, to whom he brought titles and vast tracts of land, simply to please her. The spoils of empire were gratifying trophies. The first thing Disraeli managed to procure was a share of almost half of the Suez Canal, purchased from a bankrupt Turk, the khedive of Egypt, for £4 million in 1875. The rest of the shares were French, and as three-quarters of the ships going through the Canal were British (mostly bound for India), Disraeli leapt at the chance to prevent full French control. The next day, Victoria wrote approvingly to Albert's biographer Theodore Martin that Disraeli had "very large ideas and very lofty views of the position the country should hold. His mind is so much greater, larger and his apprehension of things great and small so much quicker than that of Mr. Gladstone."

Benjamin Disraeli almost single-handedly modernized the Tory

Party. Politics, in his view, had to center on social justice, reform, and the well-being of the British. His government was a socially progressive one, marking a radical shift from the Tory Party of the aristocracy and the upper middle class to a new party of democracy and the masses. He had outmaneuvered Gladstone in 1867 by defeating him on the Reform Bill, which expanded suffrage to all households—and would have given wealthy men more than one vote—then introducing his own, slightly more progressive bill. When this bill failed, he simplified it to household suffrage alone; when it passed, he took credit for the entirety of the reform. It was masterful politics, cementing his place as future party leader, outraging Gladstone and prompting a redefinition of conservatism. Disraeli had, one commentator said, perceived a new kind of Tory voter in the working classes as a sculptor sees "the angels in the marble." Working-class Toryism has been a defining feature of British politics ever since, for the likes of Stanley Baldwin, Winston Churchill, Harold Macmillan, and Edward Heath—as well as, most recently, for Margaret Thatcher and John Major. But Disraeli was as pragmatic as he was principled. As soon as he had passed the Second Reform Act, he labored to ensure his Conservative rural seats would be protected from newly enfranchised working-class voters who might oust the Tories.

Under Disraeli's leadership, slums were torn down and replaced with new housing, and measures were put in place to encourage savings. In 1875, he passed a series of enlightened acts protecting labor rights, arguing they were as important as property rights. Two of the laws ensured that workers would have the same recourse as employers when contracts were breached, and made peaceful picketing legal, protecting unions from charges of conspiracy. The Agricultural Holdings Act meant tenants could be compensated for improvements to property. The Public Health Act made pavements and street lighting mandatory, established local sanitary authorities, and mandated that new buildings would have running water and drainage. The 1878 Factory Act ensured that no child under ten would be allowed to work, that ten- to fourteen-year-olds could only work for half of the day, and women no more than fifty-six hours a week. Other new laws provided funds to be loaned to cities for the creation of working-class housing. Gradually, Victoria watched England become a fairer, more modern country.

Then there were the laws Disraeli pushed through simply to please the queen. The first was the Public Worship Regulation Act in 1874, intended to cleanse the church of Roman influences. (Gladstone opposed it.) The second was the Cruelty to Animals Act in 1876, which forced researchers to demonstrate that any experiments with animals involving pain were absolutely necessary, and ensured they would be anesthetized if so. Finally, Disraeli forced through legislation to give Victoria the title of Empress of India, despite strong opposition and accusations that this was merely about ensuring that the queen had precedence over her daughter-in-law the Grand Duchess Marie (daughter of Alexander II of Russia)—who insisted that she be addressed as "Her Imperial Highess" rather than "Her Royal Highness"—as well as her daughter Vicky, who would become an empress when Fritz inherited the Prussian throne. Others suggested it was a maneuver intended to give her children a higher position at the German courts, an accusation Victoria called "an absolute falsehood." She had considered the title to be informally hers ever since Britain took over India in 1858, and opposition to it perplexed her. After all, Bertie had just had a most triumphant trip to India, where he swashbuckled through tiger and elephant hunts and charmed his hosts. On May Day 1876, the queen was formally announced Empress of India. It was one of her proudest moments. She dipped her quill in the well and carefully signed "Victoria R & I" (*Regina et Imperatrix*).

But tragedy continued to lurk in the wings of Victoria's life. She was growing older, well into her fifties now, and with each year the losses and heartbreaks mounted. One morning in May 1873, Alice's two boys, Ernest and Frederick William (called Fritz or "Frittie"), were playing hide-and-seek. Alice walked away from them for a moment, stuck her head out the door, and called for the nurse to come and take the children. Suddenly the toddler Fritz walked to the window, scrambled onto the window ledge, and toppled over, landing on the balcony below. His mother's shriek pierced the walls; bystanders turned their heads on the streets below. The little boy, a hemophiliac, was unconscious. He had not broken any bones, but his brain hemorrhaged, and he died.

Almost exactly three years later, in 1876, Helena's baby boy had a series of convulsions and died. Wretched and distant in Scotland, Victoria kept having visions of the baby in front of her, a child she had thought would recover. The family buried another tiny coffin, this time in the vault of St. George's Chapel, Windsor. Victoria placed a locket containing the child's hair around her neck: Why was there such unending sorrow? she thought. Poor Helena. And poor Alice. When the Duke of Hesse-Darmstadt died in 1877, Alice's husband, Louis, succeeded him, and Alice's workload trebled. She must arrange for a holiday for the poor girl, Victoria thought. Even during the war, while pregnant, Alice had waddled about hospitals, bandaging soldiers and cleaning up. In the summer of 1878, Victoria paid for the whole family to have a holiday at Eastbourne, a popular seaside resort on England's south coast.

Sickness never seemed far from the sprawling royal brood. Late in 1878, diphtheria infected Alice's family in Hesse-Darmstadt. Alice watched over her five children, red-eyed with worry. On November 16, her three-year-old daughter May died. Soon Alice, too, fell ill. When the queen heard Alice had been stricken, she cried, sent her doctor to Hesse, and waited nervously for reports. She consulted with Bertie and Leopold and, superstitiously, went to pray in the Blue Room, where Alice had nursed her father during the blackest days of her life. On December 14, the day Albert had died, Alice passed away: exactly seventeen years later. She was only thirty-five.

John Brown brought Victoria the telegrams, and stood by her side as she sobbed:

That this dear, talented, distinguished, tender hearted, noble minded, sweet child, who behaved so admirably, during her dear Father's illness, & afterwards, in supporting me, & helping me in every possible way,—should be called back to her Father, on this very anniversary, seems almost incredible, & most mysterious!

The grief drew the family closer. Bertie was ill over the loss of his adored, naughty childhood ally, and he stuttered to Victoria, "The good are always taken, the bad remain." Then, just three months later, Vicky's youngest child, Waldemar, died from diphtheria. Vicky was devastated, again. She wept when her visits to England ended; she wanted to come more often, but Victoria would not always allow it. Vicky's precise, philosophical brain—which Albert had so carefully tended—was of little use in her new role as a wife and mother. "On the whole," she told Victoria wistfully, "one may say that unintelligent women are the happiest, if going through life as smoothly as possible really constitutes happiness." Her eldest child, William, the future kaiser, whose wasted arm had troubled her so much, was growing up to be rude, hateful, and disrespectful.

From now on, Victoria would take an especially keen interest in Alice's offspring, her five motherless grandchildren. What she didn't know was that one of them would be blamed for starting a revolution. Alice's daughter Alexandra, who married Czar Nicolas II, passed the hemophilia gene to her son Alexis. She would fall under the sway of the soi-disant holy man Rasputin because of his apparent unearthly ability to calm the boy and even stop his bleeding.

In 1879, the queen turned sixty. She was, at last, sprouting gray hairs. She felt older, and the loss of Alice had "shaken the elasticity out" of her. She was now considerably rounder, and she seemed to have shrunk in height. Lady Cavendish wrote in her diary on March 17, 1879, that while the queen at a wedding carried herself beautifully in long, sweeping black-and-white attire, "I do think H.M. has grown down and is a shorter woman than ever." Victoria insisted on being painted with a serious expression, worthy of a monarch, while privately dismissing her "ugly old face." In the eyes of her granddaughter Sophie, though, she was like a little doll: "My dear Grandmama is very tiny—a very, very pretty little girl." She had grown stronger in the heat of the affection of her two men—Brown and Disraeli. It was almost unthinkable that in just four years, the two great buttresses of her life would vanish from it.

Part 5

Regina Imperatrix

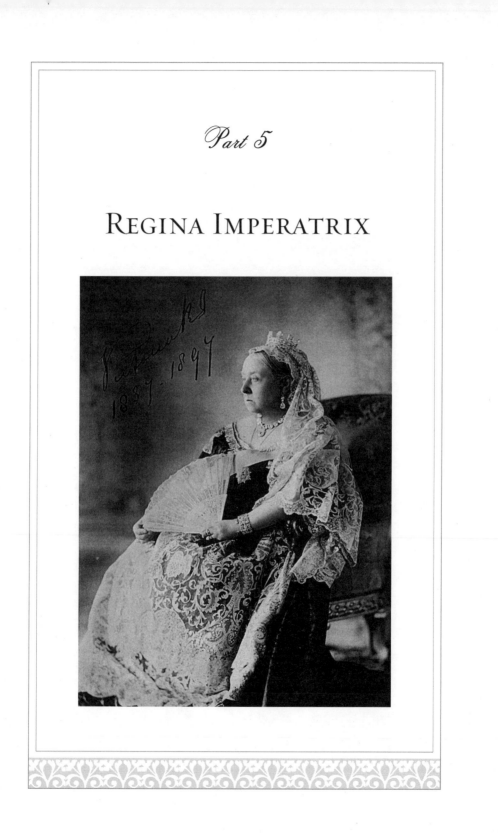

Enough to Kill Any Man

The Queen alone is enough to kill any man.

—WILLIAM GLADSTONE

It is difficult to pinpoint a precise moment when dislike calcifies into loathing. But for Victoria, 1880 was, at the very least, a year when her ill will toward Gladstone morphed into barely concealed hostility. In April 1880, a telegram with the news that Disraeli had lost the parliamentary election arrived in Baden-Baden, Germany, where she was holidaying. Disraeli was not prepared for such a result, nor had he prepared his Faery Queen. "This is a terrible telegram," she told her private secretary, Henry Ponsonby, who was shocked by the language she used. Disraeli wrote that he was devastated: "His relations with your Majesty were his chief, he might almost say his only, happiness and interest in this world. They came to him when he was alone, and they have inspired and sustained him in his isolation." Victoria responded conspiratorially that she hoped they would be able to write to each other "on many a *private* subject and without anyone being astonished or offended, and even better without anyone knowing about it." (She had done this before, with Melbourne. It was not strictly illegal, but it undermined the convention that monarchs do not correspond with members of the opposition as it might be perceived as undermining the government.)

Even worse than losing Disraeli was the thought that Gladstone might replace him. Victoria traveled back to England later that month preoccupied: how could she prevent "the People's William" from becoming the People's Prime Minister? She told Disraeli it would be impossible to send for Gladstone and ask him to form a government "as I could only say that I cd not trust him or give him my confidence." (Nor was she technically obliged to, as he had earlier resigned as the leader of the Liberals.) Henry Ponsonby told her repeatedly she must call Gladstone, but Victoria took several days to consult with other Liberals in an attempt to avoid it. On April 4, she wrote: "She will sooner *abdicate* than send for or have any *communication* with that *half mad firebrand* who wd soon ruin everything & be a *Dictator*. Others but herself *may submit* to his democratic rule but *not the Queen*." Another bout of self-pity erupted: must a "no longer young" widow really take on a man who had been the enemy of her government?

But Gladstone was far older, more prepossessing, and more authoritative than the two other possible candidates who shared the leadership of the Liberal Party, which was now in power. Both had the right of refusal: Lord "Harty-Tarty" Hartington—the Liberal leader in the House of Commons—and "Pussy" Granville, the Liberal leader in the House of Lords. Disraeli, who had spent two days closely advising Victoria on his successor after he resigned on April 21, told her to call for Hartington. After Hartington said he could not form a government without Gladstone as a minister, Victoria instructed him to ask Gladstone to see if he would serve under Hartington. Gladstone was "stunned" he should have even been asked: surely it was obvious, after his stellar oratorical performance in the election, that he had the confidence of the people and should be PM. Reluctantly (because he had opposed the law that made her Empress of India), Victoria then turned to Granville, Gladstone's close friend. He told her Gladstone was supported by the British public and assured her that the Grand Old Man was unlikely to lead for more than a year.

Devoid of other alternatives, on April 23, Victoria grumpily summoned Gladstone to Windsor. He said, pointedly, later that she greeted him with "[the] perfect courtesy from which she never deviates." Gladstone informed her he wanted to be both prime minister and the Chancellor of the Exchequer, which she considered excessive but did not challenge. Victoria then chastised him for some of the "very strong language" he used against Disraeli during his Scottish campaigns, and she unsuccessfully tried to have Hartington appointed Secretary of State for War. Five days later, her private secretary, Ponsonby, told her Gladstone wanted to appoint the Radical Joseph Chamberlain and the republican Sir Charles Dilke to his Cabinet. Victoria told Ponsonby firmly that she had to be "reassured about the views of both" before she would consent to their being made ministers. She had already given Ponsonby an extraordinary list of instructions for Gladstone—that he must not change the foreign policy, nor the British rule in India, cut projected spending, or bring in "democratic leaning." Still, wrote Gladstone after his awkward meeting with the monarch, "All things considered, I was much pleased."

On that cold night when they met at Windsor, the stars were particularly bright. As the wind stirred the trees below her windows, Victoria stared at Gladstone's craggy face, wondering how long he might be fit to occupy his post. He was seventy, ten years older than Victoria, but in full vigor and energy—unlike Disraeli, then seventy-five, who had suffered from bad health throughout his entire prime ministerial term. Still, she asssured Disraeli that Gladstone looked "very ill, very old and haggard, and his voice feeble," and that he had told her twice that he would not be in office long—a promise that was not kept.

Disraeli could have done little to prevent his defeat. The mood of the country had shifted, and his victory at the Treaty of Berlin was already forgotten. The British had won recent battles in Afghanistan and South Africa in a bid to maintain and expand their enormous empire, but at great cost, with many bloody losses in battles. But more importantly, the economy had slowed after three decades of uninterrupted growth. In 1877, unemployment was 4.7 percent; by 1879, it had risen to 11.4 percent. Farmers were struggling, but Disraeli refused to introduce the measures of protection that had been rolled back in the first few years of Victoria's reign, and that neighboring countries had reinstated. Disraeli wrote to Lord Lytton, "The distress of this country is the cause & the sole cause of the fall of the government over wh. I presided." He was publicly sanguine but privately deflated, and tired.

Gladstone had also waged a staggering, unprecedented campaign strategy. In what became known as the Midlothian campaign, he pioneered American-style electioneering in Scotland, directly addressing crowds of thousands in a series of mass public meetings. He spoke in rousing, thunderous oratory, attacking Disraeli, focusing particularly on his "pestilent" foreign policy, which he saw as stamping on the rights of small countries to determine their fate. Ten thousand Zulus in Africa had been killed, Gladstone thundered, "for no other offence than their attempt to defend against your artillery with their naked bodies, their hearths and homes, their wives and families." He also spoke of "the sanctity of life in the hill villages of Afghanistan." Gladstone argued for virtue in foreign policy—meaning less intervention—and thereby tapped into the mood of fatigue among the electorate.

Gladstone preached a gentler colonialism, supporting the principles of local autonomy and self-government—the same position he favored for Ireland. Gladstone even vowed to give independence to the South African Transvaal, which had been annexed by Britain in 1877. He was wary of further expansion in Africa and the Pacific, and called brutally obtained new swaths of land "false phantoms of glory." Victoria was furious: she saw wars as a necessary means of protecting her empire. She dismissed Gladstone as "an American stumping orator" and was personally insulted by his attacks on foreign policy for which she thought she shared ownership with Disraeli. But hordes came to hear Gladstone speak—one crowd in Edinburgh was twenty thousand strong—and reports of his speeches spread rapidly. His niece was tickled to observe him on his return, uncharacteristically "a little *personally* elated." Disraeli—whom Victoria had elevated to the House of Lords as the Earl of Beaconsfield in August 1876—refused to read his opponent's speeches.

So it was: the Grand Old Man of England became its leader again. "The downfall of Beaconsfieldism," he wrote, "is like the vanishing of some magnificent castle in an Italian romance." He had vanquished his great rival. What Gladstone lacked, however, was a detailed plan. He had been so intent on undoing Disraeli he had neglected to form a detailed legislative agenda of his own.

The election loss sapped an already fatigued Disraeli. In the spring of 1881, he was struck again by bronchitis. When he lay ill in his house in London, wrapped in a red dressing gown and attended by his homeopath, Victoria sent doctors and daily bouquets of his favorite primroses. When he was asked if the queen should visit, Disraeli retorted, "No, it is better not. She would only ask me to take a message to Albert."

Benjamin Disraeli died calmly in the hour before dawn. It was April 19, a year after he'd lost the election. John Brown was the one who told the queen, and was especially regretful as Disraeli had always treated him with respect. Victoria summoned Disraeli's loved secretary, Montagu Corry, and questioned him for hours about her "truest kindest friend's" final moments. Even Gladstone said the most "extraordinary man" in England, perhaps Europe, had passed.

The flamboyant statesman had not wanted a state funeral; he asked only to be buried quietly next to his wife, Mary Anne, at his home at Hughenden. Gladstone saw this as another annoying affectation, saying, "As he lived so he died. All display without reality or genuineness." But Victoria understood. The sweet little primrose had become a symbol of what she considered their shared distaste for excess. Both lived in homes drenched with fancy blooms, yet both praised the humble primrose. She sent bunches of them to his funeral, with a card labeled "his favorite flowers from Osborne." Gladstone rolled his eyes. (He insisted Disraeli preferred lilies and had only been humoring the queen.)

Their names will always be twinned as the greatest modern political rivalry in Britain: Gladstone and Disraeli, the Lion and the Unicorn. Disraeli had been bitter about Gladstone to the end, and missed few opportunities to attack him. When Gladstone sat to write a tribute to his rival in Parliament after his death, he had an attack of diarrhea. Giving that speech, he later told a friend, was one of the worst experiences of his life. Gladstone's problem was his strong streak of honesty: what he really wanted to say was that a fraudulent Disraeli had exploited "the weak side" of Victoria's subjects. Still, Victoria briefly softened toward him as a result of his kind words about her friend.

Forty years after she was made queen, at sixty Victoria was finally certain of herself. Now a firm Tory, she scoffed at what she saw as the softness and incompetence of Gladstone's Cabinet. It was not she who had changed, she told herself, but the parties: the Liberals had drifted to socialism, while the Conservatives were true liberals and true defenders of the empire. Disraeli had continued to correspond with her in his yearlong retirement, writing a total of twenty-two letters. Most of this correspondence was personal, but once he strayed into unconstitutional territory. In January 1881, Victoria objected to words contained in her Speech from the Throne—text that had been given to her to read aloud, by Gladstone's office—that declared British soldiers would leave Kandahar. She would not deliver the speech with those words contained in it; her ministers would not present it without them. After a heated Cabinet meeting at Osborne, several ministers threatened to resign. A furious Victoria said she had not been treated with "such want of respect" in all her years as queen. She glared stonily at her Cabinet, recording how they "nearly tumbled over each other going out."

The subject of the dispute was an important one—whom did the queen speak for when she opened Parliament? When Sir William Harcourt, the home secretary, told her the speech was really "the Speech of the Ministers," her rage grew. Disraeli contradicted Harcourt and assured her—incorrectly—that his claim was "a principle not known to the British Constitution" and "only a piece of Parliamentary gossip." Leopold, who liked to intervene in politics, and whom Victoria thought the smartest of her children, also backed his mother, arguing it was obviously the sovereign's speech. Victoria finally agreed to give the speech as it was, while condemning the paragraph on Afghanistan in a letter to Gladstone. It was another instance of her asserting her authority, but not getting her way.

It was no simple feat to coax a single-minded sovereign out of solemn seclusion. To Disraeli Victoria owed her resurgence as a politically active monarch, which may in the end have been his greatest revenge against Gladstone. She was reenergized and now convinced of her right to interfere in politics, and had stopped talking about her work as a great burden. She even threatened her ministers with greater intervention than the Constitution allowed. She told Granville in June 1881, "A Constitutional Sovereign *at best* has a *most difficult* task, and it *may* become *almost* an *impossible one,* IF things are allowed to go on as they have done of late years."

While the role of the monarch in British politics dwindled to one of constitutional consigliere as the franchise was expanded and the House of Commons grew in influence, Victoria continued to demand space. The fact that she had been encouraged to respect her own judgment just before she inherited a new prime minister with mostly opposing views created the perfect conditions for battle. Unsurprisingly, the Grand Old Man of British politics (GOM) thought Disraeli had "over-educated [his] pupil a little." When the queen insisted upon intimate details of Cabinet meetings, as Disraeli had given her in the past, Gladstone thought it "intolerable."

As the queen jostled for power and demanded to be heard, British women were also growing more restless and began arguing for the right to their own incomes, to divorce on the same terms as men, to protection from violence, and to shared custody of their children. (For most of the century, men were given full custody of children if they divorced or separated from their wives.) Victoria little understood the torment, because she had no need to—and little interest in or sympathy with it. Her own private struggles, and those of her children, consumed her.

Unknotting the idea that women were the property of their husbands took decades. Until 1870 all of the money women earned belonged to their husbands, and until 1882 their property did too, even after a divorce or separation. According to the centuries-old principle of coverture, English law saw a wife not as a separate entity but a "femme covert," who was under the "protection and influence of her husband, her baron or lord." The status of a wife, in other words, was that of a servant. The Second Married Women's Property Act of 1882 established wives as distinct entities—"femme sole"—who could own, inherit, and rent property and represent themselves in a court of law. Gradually women won more rights to care for their children after divorce; from 1886 the welfare of the children could be taken into account when determining if women could have some (limited) custody over their children.

The first bill for women's suffrage was debated in Parliament in 1870. It was soundly defeated, but there was a small victory—women who owned property were allowed to stand for election to school boards. (Elizabeth Garrett Anderson, the first woman to qualify as a doctor in Britain—in 1865—stood and was elected to her local board five years later.) Activist Emmeline Pankhurst formed the Women's Franchise League in 1889 with her barrister husband Richard, with the aim of procuring the vote for women in local elections. (The Pankhursts had a rare egalitarian marriage, and their three daughters, Christabel, Sylvia, and Adela, all became influential suffragettes.)

Victoria had no sympathy for suffragettes. She wrote to Albert's biographer, the Scottish poet Theodore Martin, "The Queen is most anxious to enlist every one who can speak or write to join in checking this mad, wicked folly of 'Women's Rights,' with all its attendant horrors, on which her poor feeble sex is bent, forgetting every sense of womanly feeling and propriety." She remarked of one woman, Lady Amberley, who had attended a women's suffrage event, that she "ought to get a *good whipping*." "Let woman be what God intended," she snorted, "a helpmate for a man—but with totally different duties and vocations."

The deceptive part of being queen was that, while the job was the same as that of king, it *sounded* like a female position and therefore seemed appropriate. Victoria supported women's being "sensibly educated" and "employed whenever they can be usefully," but not their entering the serious professions or voting. Throughout her life, Victoria was a paradox: a model of female authority in a culture preoccupied with female domesticity. And, tellingly, four out of five of the queen's daughters became advocates of women's rights.

Victoria described herself, conveniently, as "anomalous." She protested that women should not hold power, all while being increasingly vigilant about the protection of her own power. She did, after all, chortle when Lord Dufferin told her a group of women had argued they should be given the vote because "men were seldom fit for the work." Lord Dufferin may as well have been talking about her attitude toward Bertie—Victoria considered herself far more capable of leadership and political work than her eldest son, and the idea of abdicating for his sake was anathema to her.

The idea of young girls in the dissecting room, confronted by body parts "that could not be named in front of them," made the queen queasy. She and Gladstone agreed for once: the idea of training women as doctors was "repulsive." (She did, though, support women training to be obstetricians or to work with poor female patients in India, whose religion prevented them seeking medical advice from men.)

The queen reserved a peculiar scorn for women who were "fast," especially those who engaged in traditionally masculine activities like hunting game. When Lady Charles Kerr fractured her skull while riding a horse, Victoria considered it a teachable moment. She wrote to Vicky in 1872:

> May it be a warning to many of those fast, wild young women who are really unsexed. And to the husbands, fathers and brothers too who allow their wives, daughters and sisters to expose themselves in such an unfeminine way. In other respects this poor young thing was very quiet and not very strong—but imagine her going down alone to hunt while her husband was walking about in London!

"Fast" women were blamed for many things in Victorian England: a loosening of moral codes, the masculinization of ladies, and an epidemic of venereal disease that had crippled the British defense forces in the Crimea, in India, and in England. By 1864, almost a third of all British troops were admitted to the hospital for syphilis or gonorrhea. Because it was not the soldiers who were blamed but the women they slept with, the solution decided upon was simple: the army and navy needed clean prostitutes. In 1864, the first of the Contagious Diseases Acts introduced official brothels for the military.

The laws also included extraordinary provisions for the monitoring of women walking in public: police could arrest any woman suspected to be a prostitute, without evidence. Women could be exposed to humiliating internal examinations for VD, either in a hospital or on the spot, and registered at the local police station for regular checkups (or imprisonment). If they protested, they were jammed into straitjackets and their legs pried open with clamps. If a woman was found to have VD, she could be detained in a hospital for three months. In what Ronald Pearsall called a "certain climate of hunting the whore," sex workers—not their clients—were blasted from pulpits and Parliament alike. It was probably the most potent, public example of the Victorian double standard under which women were punished for sexual behavior while men escaped scrutiny and condemnation.

Still, many men regarded prostitutes as essential to the social fabric. Tolstoy, for example, could not imagine London without its "Magdalenes." "What would become of families?" he wrote in 1870. "How many wives or daughters would remain chaste? What would become of the laws of morality which people so love to observe? It seems to me that this class of woman is *essential* to the family under the present complex forms of life." Divorces were still rare, and men were supposed to delay marriage until they were financially solvent. Unemployment created a swath of single men.

Prostitution was the subject of much speculation but little rigorous research in England at the time. Estimates of the number of female sex workers in London at midcentury ranged between 80,000 and 120,000, out of a total population of 2.3 million men and women. A significant number were infected with venereal diseases, most commonly syphilis, which also ravaged children born to them. Before the discovery of penicillin, the treatments used were ineffective; the widespread use of mercury in tablets, baths, and creams only led to teeth falling out, kidney failure, poisoning, and mouth sores. (The preventive treatments—oil, vinegar, and alcohol—were similarly useless.) It was almost impossible to have safe sex then—condoms were available by midcentury, but still remained expensive—and for women to control their own reproduction.

In the last half of the century, a woman named Josephine Butler waged an impressive and effective campaign against the sexual exploitation and abuse of women—trying to expose what she saw as the hypocrisy that meant that the moral shame belonged only to the women, not the men who sought them out.* The 1871 Royal Commission on the Contagious Diseases Acts, for example, declared there was no comparison to be made between prostitutes and their clients: "With the one sex the offence is committed as a matter of gain, with the other it is an irregular indulgence of a natural impulse." Yet, as one sex worker said after being imprisoned, "It did seem hard, ma'am, that the Magistrate on the bench who gave the casting vote for my imprisonment had paid me several shillings a day or two before, in the street, to go with him."

Bracebridge Hemyng declared that sex workers were "poisoning the blood of the nation." The country's "Great Social Evil" became a magnet for the most energetic, fervent reformers of the age: evangelistic Christians who worked in earnest to reform and rehabilitate prostitutes. The most famous of them all was William Gladstone, who developed a nearly crippling obsession with "rescuing" the loveliest strumpets of Britain. He was the greatest friend to prostitutes the political world knew. And he was convinced that this was why the queen hated him.

Gladstone was an eccentric and upright man. Tall and lean, he spent up to four months at a stretch swinging an ax at trees at a country estate, thinking through the questions that consumed him. He was constantly self-reproving and intent on honing his character, fulfilling his godly mission, and doing the work of Christ on earth. His days were bookended by prayer. He went to church daily and delivered a weekly sermon to his servants. Lord Salisbury told Victoria that it was difficult to imagine Gladstone could listen to a sermon

---

* Once a woman had "fallen" into prostitution, it was frequently asserted that an early death was inevitable. One expert estimated that after women decided to "turn a trick" in Victorian England, they had, on average, only four years left to live. According to the admission registers of the Lock Hospital in Edinburgh, nine out of ten prostitutes "disappeared by the age of thirty." For many young women, it was just a temporary occupation before marriage.

without "rising to reply." Even mealtimes were a chance for virtue: he advocated chewing each mouthful of food thirty-two times—once for every tooth—before swallowing. He would live to the age of eighty-nine, no small achievement in the Victorian age.

It is not clear when Gladstone's fetish for "fallen women" began, though it is clear that the period of greatest activity was around 1850, when he had been in Parliament for eighteen years. He started work for a charity called the Church Penitentiary Association for the Reclamation of Fallen Women in 1848, before moving to a personal kind of vigilantism. He spent hours talking to sex workers he met in the streets, trying to persuade them to choose another life. He read them Tennyson and Thomas Malory, arranged for them to have their portraits painted, and grew deeply attached to them.

The tall, somber politician was particularly drawn to beautiful prostitutes, something that did not escape comment. In 1852, he described one of his great interests as "half a most lovely statue, beautiful beyond measure." His colleague Henry Labouchere said, "Gladstone manages to combine his missionary meddling with a keen appreciation of a pretty face." Concerned colleagues tried to warn Gladstone about possible ramifications of his behavior, but he refused to stop. Sex workers called him "Old Glad-eye." He tried to rescue somewhere between eighty and ninety prostitutes over the five years following 1849, but he had little success. He admitted, "There is but one of whom I know that the miserable life has been abandoned *and* that I can fairly join that fact with influence of mine."

Most biographers have assumed these encounters were chaste, driven by sexual titillation, not consummation. When a Scottish man tried to blackmail Gladstone in 1853 after spying him in conversation with a prostitute, Gladstone alerted the police and courts himself without compunction—not usually the conduct of a guilty man. But when his diaries were published in 1968, a more ambiguous light was cast. Racked with shame, he would sometimes flagellate himself after meeting with prostitutes, drawing a tiny symbol of a whip in his diary (which appeared for the last time in 1859). Roy Jenkins, his biographer, says his "religio-sexual emotional crises" were "exceptional more for the abjectness of the guilt which they produced than for the strength of the temptation." While it is extremely unlikely that he had full sexual relationships with these women, Gladstone himself guiltily acknowledged the "carnal" nature of his forays, that they were a kind of sexual temptation that lured him onto dangerous rocks. They were the "chief burden" of his soul. And if they were not carnal, he wrote, "they would not leave such a void." (In mysterious diary entries, Gladstone describes two hours he spent with the beautiful and statuesque Elizabeth Collins as "strange, questionable, or more," followed by a symbol of a whip. His thoughts of the courtesan Marion Summerhayes "required to be limited and purged.")

Toward the end of his life, Gladstone told his sons that he believed that stories about him, "whether true or false," must have made their way to Victoria, causing her coldness. (He later assured his son Stephen, a priest, that he had never "been guilty of the act which is known as that of infidelity to the marriage bed.")* It was improbable that Victoria's hostility was due to the stories she heard about Gladstone and sex workers; she frequently said he was a good man, but a weak statesman and a "madman." Her dislike was not moral, but visceral; she spent years trying to unseat William Gladstone. It had nothing to do with his own infatuations, and everything to do with the fact that he did not know how to treat the queen.

———

* This was just before Gladstone died in 1898. As the biographer H.C.G. Matthew concludes, it was a "precise and obviously qualified declaration," a statement that was not used by his son Herbert when he was later defending his father's reputation in court in 1927 against libelous suggestions made by Captain Peter E. Wright that Gladstone had spoken "language of the highest and strictest principle" in public, while in private it was his practice "to pursue and possess every sort of women." Herbert's lawyers thought the reservation implicit in the statement might suggest to the jury that Gladstone's relationships with the dozens of sex workers he befriended were in fact not entirely innocent. The court confirmed Gladstone's moral character.

In 1886 the Contagious Diseases Acts were finally repealed. They had been ludicrously ineffective: the rate of VD in the army was exactly the same it had been in 1865, unchanged by twenty years of the law. Women were now no longer blamed as sole carriers of disease, and public attention had slid to men. There was even some suggestion that women were being exploited. Some, like George Bernard Shaw, even dared to suggest it was time to critically examine it. In 1893, Shaw wrote in the preface to his play about sex workers, *Mrs. Warren's Profession,* that prostitution is caused not by "female depravity" or "male licentiousness," but the "underpaying, undervaluing and overworking" of women. Prostitutes continued to be the object of contempt as well as pity and desire, but the fight over double standards had energized a generation of women to whom Victoria was an unwitting, prickly muse. The slow march toward women's suffrage had begun. Victoria would inspire but not support it; she sat like a prickly muse, the most powerful woman in the world, who spent her days trying to control men.

And men continued to shoot at her. Brown was with the queen when another madman fired bullets at her as she alighted from the train at Windsor on March 2, 1882. It was the seventh attempt on her life; a train conductor stopped the man—Frederick McLean—and two local Eton boys attacked him with umbrellas. Britain was furious. But the queen lapped up the sympathy the attack invoked, as she had always done. "It is worth being shot at," Victoria said with satisfaction, "to see how much one is loved."

Florence Dixie was an unconventional woman. A writer, traveler, feminist, and war correspondent, Lady Florence Dixie hunted game in Patagonia, wrote travel books, corrected Charles Darwin on factual errors, and played a key role in establishing women's soccer in Britain. In 1880, she went to South Africa as the foreign correspondent for the *Morning Post* during the First Boer War, following the British annexation of the Transvaal in 1877, when Disraeli was prime minister. Lady Florence Dixie held some controversial views—that firstborn daughters of the king or queen should be able to inherit the throne, that boys and girls should be educated together, that women should be able to wear trousers, and that marriages should be equal. She also, fatefully, later moved to a house near Windsor Castle (she was forced to place her pet jaguar in a zoo because he kept killing all the deer in the park surrounding the castle).

In the afternoon of March 1883, Lady Florence Dixie, then twenty-six, was out walking when, she said, two men clad in long gowns and veils pushed her to the ground and tried to stab her. Eventually her Saint Bernard dog, Hubert, scared them away. Initially the attack was blamed on the Irish republican Fenians, who were provoked by Lady Florence Dixie's support for Home Rule for Ireland, though doubt was cast on the veracity of her claims.

Troubled by such an assault occurring only two and a half miles from the castle, the queen sent a kind note to Lady Florence Dixie and tried to establish what had happened. John Brown combed the area for hours in the wintry air, looking for answers on Victoria's behalf. He then spent a week carrying around the queen, whose knee was badly swollen from a sprain. All the while, Brown was battling a fierce cold. The next weekend, Brown came down with erysipelas, a painful syndrome wherein the entire face swells, including ears and eyelids. He had not taken a single day off in eighteen and a half years at Windsor Castle, and Victoria was "vexed" that he could not attend her.

Two days later, he was dead.

Victoria was distraught. "He was the best, the truest heart that ever beat," she wrote to Brown's sister-in-law Jessie McHardy Brown. Her grief, she said, was "unbounded, dreadful & I know not how to bear it, or how to believe it possible." She had fallen downstairs on March 17, 1883, ten days before Brown's death, and had been unable to walk unaided since then. From this time on, she would be, to her embarrassment, clutching the backs of chairs to make her way around rooms, and hobbling with two sticks. She needed to be carried upstairs, and moved from carriage to train in a special chair. Some of her subjects suggested various remedies—including a Mrs. Cash, who thought the queen's legs might be improved if she rode a tricycle. Ponsonby, who had a keen eye for the absurd, wrote to his wife: "Fancy the Queen on a tricycle."

The similarity to 1861 and the death of Albert was stark. Her heart was smashed open again, the old wound seeping a new grief. The queen told the Earl of Cranbrook on March 30 that she had not just lost her "truest and dearest" companion, but an unprecedented friendship, writing about herself in the third person: "The Queen feels that life for the second time is become most trying and sad to bear depriving of all she so needs." A few days after Brown died, she told Ponsonby:

> The Queen is trying hard to occupy herself but she is utterly crushed & her life has again sustained one of those shocks like in 61 when every link has been shaken & torn & at every turn & every moment the loss of the strong arm & wise advice, warm heart & cheery original way of saying things & the sympathy in any large & small circumstances—is most cruelly missed.

It is often assumed that Tennyson told Victoria she was "all alone on a terrible height" after Albert's death; it was actually after John Brown's that he said those words. It was then that she was finally alone. Victoria was so touched when Tennyson wrote to comfort her about Brown's death that she asked him to come and see her. Though he was shaky on his legs and half-blind, he told her that he could see how isolated she was and vowed to do whatever he could to comfort her, with the little time he had left to live. The old poet told his son afterward that he had cried leaving the queen, for she was "so womanly, and so lonely."

Victoria wrote to Tennyson to thank him for his kindness, saying of Brown:

> He had *no* thought but for me, my welfare, my comfort, my safety, my happiness. Courageous, unselfish, *totally* disinter-

ested, discreet to the highest degree, speaking the truth fearlessly and telling me what he thought and considered to be "just
and right," without flattery and without saying what would be
pleasing if he did not think it right. . . . The comfort of my daily
life is gone—the void is terrible—the loss is irreparable!

The Court Circular contained twenty-five lines about Brown, and
the queen's "grievous shock"—it had only five for Disraeli when he
died. Bells tolled, pipers were forbidden to play near the castle, and
Victoria ordered that the tartan plaid she and Brown had taken on
their Highland treks be used as a pall on his coffin. She devoted herself to ensuring Brown would be remembered as more than a common servant—or as a "domestic," as Gladstone clumsily wrote to her,
failing to recognize the obvious and outsized affection his queen had
for the man. Gladstone hoped she would "select a good and efficient
successor." Victoria did not want and could not imagine a successor;
people, to her, were irreplaceable. Albert was irreplaceable and so
was John Brown. Her heart may have been pocked with holes, but
she would not attempt to plug them.

Instead, Victoria commissioned tie pins, busts, monuments, and
statues of Brown, commissioned lines from Tennyson to place on his
tombstone, dedicated cairns and seats to him. Then, still buoyed by
the recent success of the publication of her Highland journals, she
announced she would write a memoir of John Brown, intended, she
said, only for private publication. Here her advisers took an uncharacteristically robust stand. Henry Ponsonby wrote nervously, asking
Her Majesty's forgiveness "if he expresses a doubt whether this record of Your Majesty's innermost and most sacred feelings should be
made public to the world." He worried that strangers would misun-
derstand her words, attracting the wrong kind of attention, which
would be "painful for the Queen." Victoria replied, "I certainly *cannot* agree," and told him she had to correct the impression that Brown
was just a servant, when he was "a great deal more than that." That
is what she wanted the world to understand.

A draft of the memoir was then passed to Randall Davidson, the young new Dean of Windsor, who was the spiritual head of the priests at Windsor Castle's St. George's Chapel and had quickly earned Victoria's respect. They spoke for hours after Brown died, in a conversation he described as "most touching, solemn and interesting, but terribly difficult." Davidson panicked when he discovered Victoria had written a memoir about Brown, and found that Victoria had quoted heavily from Brown's diary. Victoria had already dedicated *More Leaves from the Journal of a Life in the Highlands* to Brown, to her family's disgust. It was full of more sentimental tales of a tame life in the wild Highlands. (In 1884, a satirical version of *Leaves* and *More Leaves* lampooned Victoria's relationship with Brown: "We make it a point to have breakfast every morning of our lives.... Brown pushed me (in a hand-carriage) up quite a hill and then ran me down again. He did this several times and we enjoyed it very much.... He then put me in a boat on the lake and rocked me for about half an hour. It was very exhilarating.")

The Dean told Victoria she should not publish a memoir of Brown, making the unusual argument that some among the "humbler classes" would not be "worthy of such confidences." When Victoria insisted she would publish it, he offered to resign. She froze him out for two weeks, then resumed relations. The book was never published. It is little wonder that Ponsonby relished the chance to burn Brown's diaries, although the loss of these—and Victoria's *Life of Brown*—is a great one. Bertie further destroyed remnants of Brown when he became king, and even had Brown's rooms at Windsor Castle—which Victoria had sealed off after his death—made into a billiard room.

But Victoria ensured Brown would not be forgotten. She allowed her adoration to become public because to her, a relationship of a powerful woman with a servant could never be a marriage, or even a serious romance. She could never call him "Master"; she was his Mistress. Yet they spoke a language of a singular kind of love. Author Tom Cullen claims he found an extract from the queen's journal, copied out by Victoria and sent to Hugh Brown (John's brother) after John Brown died. She revealed that Brown had pledged to care for her until he died, saying, "You haven't a more devoted servant than Brown." Victoria continued: "Afterwards so often I told him no one loved him more than I did or had better friend than me: and he answered 'Nor you—than me. No one loves you more.'"

In 1884, a year after Brown died, Victoria was still glum, fretting about turmoil in India, Egypt, and Ireland, convinced that life "does become sadder and sadder and harder." Then she was told her hemophiliac son Leopold had fallen in Cannes and injured his knee. Shortly afterward, he convulsed and died of a brain hemorrhage. His wife was then expecting their second child. Victoria's grief was assuaged by the fact that she knew how unhappy Leopold had been, after a "succession of trials and sufferings" and tormented by "such a restless longing for what he cld not have," which had only increased as he grew older. An intense, troubled intellectual, Leopold yearned to lead a normal life but was stifled by his mother's protectiveness and frustrated that his illness gave her constant cause for anxiety. His existence was miserable—bruising easily, being held in contempt by some in the court, and even cruelly bullied by John Brown and his brother. He was considered to be "very ugly" and awkward by his vigilant mother. He died just ten days before his thirtieth birthday.

Hemophilia was poorly understood in the 1800s, though it had been the subject of extensive research, especially in Germany. Few hemophiliacs survived into adulthood; the median life expectancy was only eleven. Death could result from a fall from a horse or a chair, or the pulling of teeth. It could result from the slightest injury: a barber died after scratching his nose with scissors, as did a baby who sliced its lip on a cigar holder in 1860. Childhood games could be fatal; children died from bruises as well as cuts. In the face of medical impotence, the life of a parent of a hemophiliac was one of ceaseless vigilance, guilt, and worry. "No one knows the constant fear I am in about him," wrote Victoria, who ensured she was always near her son.

In 1868, when Leopold was fifteen and was recovering from another hemorrhage, the *British Medical Journal* published a leading article that argued Leopold should not engage in strenuous exertion. It was thought that he had "weak veins" or some kind of male menstruation; it was not until 1891 that researchers showed that the blood of hemophiliacs took longer to clot. Victoria followed the best experts, who advocated healthy food, attention to hygiene, avoidance of violent boyhood games, and rest. So Leopold devoured towers of books, earning the title "the Scholar Prince."* He had forceful, conservative views on politics; Victoria would miss them.

As he grew older, Leopold tried desperately to assert his independence. In 1878, when he was twenty-five, he refused to travel north to Balmoral with his mother and went to Europe instead. To Gladstone, it appeared as though he wanted to either "live or die hard." He wanted to find a wife and live like a normal man. Marriage for hemophiliacs was taboo and extremely rare then—there were concerns about offspring, as well as longevity and the ability to earn an income. Leopold's doctor was of the firm view that marriage should not be entertained because of the prospect of passing on "so dreadful an entail of disease."

Victoria knew that for her fragile son to marry was "such a risk

---

* Leopold's condition—which in the 1860s was already described as "weak veins"—provoked a broader, important discussion about the cause and treatment of hemophilia. From the 1870s, the British royal family was acutely aware that their bloodline was being questioned, and Victoria continued to insist she had not inherited any such affliction. Cases of spontaneous mutation—or de novo cases—were entirely mysterious. (Stephen Pemberton, *The Bleeding Disease: Hemophilia and the Unintended Consequences of Medical Progress* [Baltimore: Johns Hopkins University Press, 2011], 35.) The only hypothesis with any evidence was intermarriage, according to a treatise published by John Wickham Legg in 1872. There is no record of this being discussed with Victoria, and given that genetics was not properly understood until the end of the nineteenth century, it is unlikely that a conversation took place.

and experiment," but she allowed it. In April 1882, he married the redoubtable, plucky Princess Helena of the German state of Waldeck. The night before the wedding, he had slipped on an orange peel and bled dangerously. On his wedding day, his mother watched him closely, "still lame and shaking," "on the most important day of his life." For the first time in forty-two years, Victoria wore her white wedding veil over her black garments. Now, less than two years later, Leopold was dead and she wore only black, again.

CHAPTER 26

"Two Ironclads Colliding": The Queen and Mr. Gladstone

Mein Gott! That was a woman! One could do business with her!

—OTTO VON BISMARCK

Sometimes the oddest of men make the greatest of heroes. A thin, shabbily dressed man, General Charles George Gordon was widely viewed as arrogant and deluded. As a young boy, he amused himself by playing pranks on his schoolmates, and fantasized about being a eunuch. As a military cadet, he bullied his juniors by beating them with hairbrushes or brooms. By the time he was a lieutenant in the British army, he was a fanatically devout Christian who eschewed material comforts, insisted on low pay, and longed to die. He had fought in the Crimean War, he said, hoping to be killed. As with Napoleon III, Gordon's penetrating blue-gray eyes were thought to be the secret to the mysterious control he exerted over large swaths of men, especially, in his case, opposing tribal forces in China and Africa. When not at war, Gordon tended to the sick and poor in workhouses in Kent and rescued street urchins. He also had an unexplained and possibly dubious predilection for the company of boys.

This eccentricity was no obstacle to Gordon's celebrity. In the middle of the century, as Victoria fretted over the Eastern Question and the collapse of the Ottoman Empire, Gordon played a crucial role in quashing the Taiping Rebellion in China, a brutal civil war that ran from 1850 to 1864, in which at least twenty million people died. The man who led the "Ever Victorious Army," which was composed of Chinese soldiers, to a series of wins became known as "Chinese Gordon," and his name would become the stuff of imperial legend.

In 1882, despite Gladstone's reluctance, the British had occupied Egypt, which was then nominally a Turkish province. The British policy was somewhat muddled, but the initial intention was to help the Egyptian throne fend off a military mutiny and economic ruin, as well as to protect the Suez Canal and the British investments made in Egypt after it opened in 1869. Not long after, in neighboring Sudan, a charismatic mystic emerged and declared a holy war for independence from that nation's Turko-Egyptian rule. The mystic called himself Muhammad al-Mahdi—the Islamic Messiah. In 1883, the Sudanese government tried to quash him, but failed. The Egyptian forces there were not strong enough to repel the rebels, and it soon became clear the Egyptians in the Sudan would need to be evacuated, along with any British citizens. Gladstone's Cabinet equivocated about intervening. The queen did not. She wanted to crush the Mahdi underfoot, but others, especially Liberals like Gladstone, wanted all troops withdrawn.

General Gordon seemed an unlikely candidate to solve this quandary. Now fifty-one, his fame had faded, and he was due to go to the Congo, where he suspected—or hoped—he might die. Politicians who publicly admired him called him deranged in private. Gladstone's secretary, E. W. Hamilton, called him a "half cracked fatalist." Sir Robert Hart, a British consular official in China, decided he was "not all there." But after Gordon gave an interview to the notorious publisher W. T. Stead about how he would manage the Sudan crisis as he had done in China—and how Sudan's capital of Khartoum must not be abandoned, but fortified—the cry "Gordon for the Sudan" erupted in the hawkish London press.

At first, Gladstone resisted the pressure to send Gordon on an ill-defined mission. He wanted very little to do with Egypt, preferred to abandon the Sudan altogether, and did not want to waste time or resources securing more land. Why send an aggressive adventurer to manage a retreat? Still, assuming the mission would be short, he capitulated on the grounds that Gordon could advise on strategy without executing it himself. It was a vain hope: Gordon was a maverick with a scorching disdain for authority. He thought the British Cabinet was full of charlatans, and believed he answered to a far higher authority, in heaven. Events play on us, he told his sister: "We are pianos."

And so the concerto began. Gordon sent a characteristically blunt telegraph to the governor in Khartoum: "Don't be a funk. You are men, not women, I am coming. Tell the inhabitants." He successfully managed to evacuate 2,500 women, children, and wounded before the rebelling Mahdists surrounded the city and trapped him inside. He dug in to fight. The British government spent the summer of 1884 wondering whether to send forces to rescue him; he had been told to leave the Sudan, not occupy it. Gordon was aware of his rogue status, writing in his journal on September 19: "I own to having been very insubordinate to Her Majesty's Government and its officials, but it is my nature, and I cannot help it." His insolence endeared him even more to the public. The Radical Cabinet member Charles Dilke, who had backed both the sending and the rescuing of Gordon, had warned in March after receiving a dozen "extraordinary" telegrams: "We [are] obviously dealing with a wild man under the influence of that climate of Central Africa which acts even upon the sanest men like strong drink."

Months passed as the government debated whether to send any troops, and if so of what kind and size, and by what route to send them. An irate Victoria urged Gladstone to support Gordon, whom she thought was a "most extraordinary man." She grew extremely anxious about his safety and decided to contact her generals directly. When she was reprimanded by the war minister, Lord Hartington, she retorted: "The Queen always has telegraphed direct to her Generals, and always will do so. . . . The Queen won't stand dictation. She won't be a machine." She then directly contradicted her prime minister's advice, telling General Wolseley, when he was sent to Khartoum, to ensure that the soldiers stayed in the Sudan. Her position at the head of the empire, she complained to Vicky, provided no pleasure, as "in spite of warning and writing, cyphering and speaking . . . nothing [was] done till the pistol is pointed at their breast." She "trembled" for Gordon's safety, she told the prime minister on February 9, 1884, as Gordon was making his way from Cairo to Khartoum: "If anything befalls him the result will be awful."

The siege of Khartoum began on March 13, 1884. The British army did not march to relieve him until November of that year.

After a siege that had lasted more than three hundred days, Gordon was killed by the Mahdists; they barbarically wedged his severed head in a tree at their camp. He had been murdered on January 26, 1885. Just two days later, the British relief expedition arrived at Khartoum. Ten days later, the news of Gordon's death reached London. Victoria roared with rage. This was to her a deeply personal humiliation. She blamed the government: "On their heads," she wrote to Vicky, "rests the precious blood of Gordon and thousands!" Her own conscience was clean: "I warned, urged without ceasing all in vain. [But] Mr. Gladstone . . . will be forever branded with the blood of Gordon that heroic man."

It was time, the queen decided , to take a highly irregular step. She sent a telegram *en clair*—so everyone could read it, it was not secret—to Gladstone; the foreign secretary, Lord Granville; and the war secretary, Lord Hartington. The stationmaster of the Carnforth Junction train station handed the telegram to the prime minister as he was racing back to London from North Lancashire—where he had been staying with the Duke of Devonshire—following the news of Gordon's death. He unfolded it and read the queen's harsh words: "These news from Khartoum are frightful and to think that all of this might have been prevented and many precious lives saved by earlier action is too fearful." Incensed, Gladstone swore he would never again shadow the cobblestones of Windsor, and he considered resigning.

A carefully crafted, firm reply was sent to the queen that night. Gladstone wrote that while he did not "presume to estimate the means of judgment possessed by Your Majesty," according to his information and recollection, he was "not altogether able to follow the conclusion which Your Majesty has been pleased thus to announce." In other words, she was wrong. The British forces, under Lord Wolseley, might have reached Khartoum in time to save Gordon, he wrote, if they had not been delayed by advancing by a circuitous route along the river, "upon the express application of General Gordon." He was technically correct, but it was not exactly the point. Victoria had urged action ten months before it was taken; it was not a matter of days.

Suffering "overaction of the bowels" again, Gladstone fell ill, his hands mottled with a rash. He went to see a play on February 19, 1885, the same day the news of his general's death broke, and he barely mentioned Gordon in Parliament—hardly the elaborate lamentation Victoria knew Disraeli would have delivered. Gladstone was right that strategically, Khartoum meant little to the British Empire, but he was disastrously wrong about what it would mean to his party to lose a general of Gordon's standing. The Tories were delighted that they had been so effortlessly handed this ammunition, a symbol of apparent lack of Liberal imperial ambition. The GOM, or "Grand Old Man," nickname was flipped to MOG—Murderer of Gordon.

By now, Gladstone was struggling to conceal his contempt for his strong-willed queen. He began Cabinet meetings by reading out Victoria's dictums, then jammed her letters back in his pocket, saying dismissively, "And now, gentlemen, to business." In April 1885, he called Victoria's views "quite worthless." What he failed to comprehend was that Victoria had an uncanny knack for speaking the mind of many of her subjects, for better or ill. She had developed better political instincts than many of her ministers. And sometimes Victoria did intervene successfully. In 1884, for example, Parliament was in gridlock over the Third Reform Bill, which extended the vote to agricultural workers. Victoria generally favored electoral reform, but she disliked the disruption it caused. She was sanguine about this bill but horrified by the calls of some Liberals for the abolition of the House of Lords. She called on Gladstone to restrain "some of his wild colleagues and followers," and argued that the position of monarch would be "utterly untenable" if there was no balance of power left.

Victoria had insisted the Liberals meet with the Tories, who were adamant they would pass the Reform Bill only if a redistribution bill was introduced at the same time. The meeting resulted in the House of Lords agreeing to pass the Reform Bill as a freshly negotiated redistribution bill was introduced into the lower house. Lord Granville praised the queen's "powerful influence," and Henry Ponsonby credited her for "incessant hammering at both sides to be moderate and insisting on their meeting." When Gladstone thanked her, she responded theatrically: "To be able to be of use is all I care to live for now." She was in her mid-sixties now and focused on her work. Victoria's success at negotiating that compromise persuaded her of two things: the prescient possibility of creating a third, centrist party, and the effectiveness of her own influence.

But foreign policy was one area where Victoria's influence stalled during Gladstone's tenure. Gladstone was naturally averse to jingoism and further expansion for expansion's sake, but his country remained imperialist. He was reluctantly prodded into colonial wars in South and North Africa, as well as Central Asia. As his biographer Roy Jenkins wrote, Gladstone got "the worst of both worlds. . . . From the beginning a government elected on a largely anti-imperialist platform found itself uncomfortably squelching in too many imperial quagmires." The resulting foreign policy was incoherent—while British forces withdrew from the Transvaal in 1881, they occupied Egypt in 1882; while the Cabinet sent Gordon to rescue the British in the Sudan, they refused to rescue him when he was surrounded. In Windsor Castle, a marble bust of General Gordon sat in a corridor as a cold reminder of his death.

For seven excruciating months in 1884, there had been glacial silence at the royal table. From May to November, Beatrice and her mother refused to talk to each other, instead pushing notes across the table to communicate, while their knives and forks clinked against china. The large block of ice Victoria regularly had placed on the dining tables to cool the summertime air was barely needed. It was bitterly awkward, especially given their usual closeness. Victoria's youngest child had, to this point, shown only obedience. But now she had fallen in love with the handsome Prince Henry of Battenberg, right under Victoria's nose.* When the dutiful, shy twenty-seven-year-old Beatrice confessed that Prince Henry had snatched her heart, Victoria was predictably selfish and melodramatic: "Pleasure has for ever died out of my life."

Victoria had long dreaded this moment. She had tried to prevent the word "wedding" from being uttered in front of Beatrice. She had ensured her daughter was never left alone in a room with a man and never danced with anyone but her brothers. She had delayed her confirmation. She wanted to protect her beloved youngest daughter from an institution she viewed with skepticism; after all, Victoria now claimed to hate marriage. She had adored her own, of course, but

---

* It happened at the wedding of Alice's eldest daughter, Victoria, to Henry's older brother, Louis. Victoria had been distracted by the discovery that Alice's widower, Louis, the Duke of Hesse, had just married his mistress, a Russian divorcée. She instantly arranged to have the marriage annulled, dispatching Bertie to tell the hapless woman. (She went on to bear the duke's child, but gave it up for adoption.) "We are a close family when we all agree," Bertie said. And somewhat brutal.

thought that incessant pregnancies were traumatic and painful, the loss of a child was an unbearable wrench, and most marriages were miserable. Her own family bore this out. Vicky was miserable in Prussia, bullied by disapproving and controlling parents-in-law; Louise had married a man suspected to be gay and had taken on a series of lovers; Alice had died in a far-off land; only the introverted Helena lived contentedly with her husband nearby. Victoria said glumly, "The longer I live the more I think marriages only rarely are a real happiness. The most are convenience—not real happiness—though of course when it is, it is greatly valued but how rarely it lasts."

To modern eyes, Victoria's control of Beatrice seems stifling and selfish, and in many ways it was. But it was also common practice in the nineteenth century for youngest daughters to devote themselves to their surviving parents. Everything else had to be sacrificed for that. Many middle-class daughters chafed against the confines of the spinster existence; it is remarkable that the biddable Beatrice did not. She now had a chance at happiness, though, with "Liko." Beatrice could be stubborn too, matching her mother's obstinate silence with her own. Liko was a catch: dashing, kindly, and charming. The silence finally shattered when three male protectors—Bertie; Alice's widower, the Grand Duke Louis of Hesse; and his brother, Prince Louis of Battenberg—came to plead Beatrice's case. Victoria laid out her conditions of approval: the couple must live with her, always, and have no homes of their own. A worn-down Beatrice—and Liko, who had few assets anyway—quickly agreed.

The wedding took place on a hot, sunny day in a church near Osborne on July 23, 1885. Only a small crowd witnessed it; notably, Victoria refused to invite Gladstone. Beatrice wore white lace and orange blossoms, just as her mother had, and borrowed her mother's veil. She looked, said an emotional Victoria, "very sweet, pure & calm." The night before, the queen had slipped out of a crowded soiree with Beatrice, walked her to her room, and hugged her hard, crying. She was, in a sense, letting go of her last child, after more than four decades of motherhood. She left red-eyed and lay in her bed staring out her window at the illuminations strung up around the villa and gardens, praying Beatrice would be happy and never leave her. Victoria was "utterly miserable" after the wedding, though she was soon won over by her spirited, pliable son-in-law (even, somewhat shockingly, allowing him to smoke with his companions after dinner). Beatrice was relieved to have gained some independence from her moody, controlling mother.

Beatrice quickly became pregnant with the first of four children. It would soon become obvious that she was a carrier of the dreaded hemophilia. One of her sons—who was also named Leopold—inherited the disease. Beatrice's only daughter, Victoria Eugenie, would become immensely unpopular when she married King Alfonso XIII and passed the affliction on to the Spanish royal family.

On the day that Gladstone's government fell in 1885, four months after the death of Gordon, Victoria cheered "like a schoolgirl set free from school." The government was defeated on a minor matter—a proposal to increase beer duty—but it had struggled with legitimacy ever since the death of General Gordon. The government was also deeply divided on the boiling question of Irish independence. Parliament was dissolved, and the Tory Lord Salisbury became prime minister—a role he would fulfill three times. During his first tenure, he headed a minority government in June 1885 that lasted only several months.

A tall, balding man with a thick beard, Salisbury was a Conservative who had resigned in 1867 over the passage of Disraeli's reform bill. His suspicion of change dovetailed neatly with Victoria's. Their relationship was a comfortable one and Victoria grew extremely fond of the genteel Lord Salisbury. He was courteous, intellectual, funny, and shared his queen's opposition to Home Rule.

Salisbury was also the first of Victoria's prime ministers to be younger than she was, and the last of the aristocratic politicians to lead the British government from the House of Lords. The man his biographer Andrew Roberts called the Victorian Titan would win smashing majorities for the Tories in 1895 and 1900, cementing a long stretch of Conservative rule.

Victoria relished the time she spent with Salisbury, and told one of her bishops that he had "an equal place with the highest among her ministers, not excepting Disraeli." His daughter Violet once remarked, after watching them converse in France: "I never saw two people get on better, their polished manners and deference to and esteem for each other were a delightful sight."

The respect was mutual. Salisbury believed that the queen had an uncanny ability to reflect the view of the public; he felt that when he knew Victoria's opinion, he "knew pretty certainly what views her subjects would take, and especially the middle class of her subjects." Salisbury and the queen also shared a concern for the living conditions of the poor. He had written an article in 1883 arguing that poor housing led not just to poor health but poor morality. This nexus had also piqued the interest of Victoria. She had been appalled by the Reverend Andrew Mearns's account of nearby slums in a report called *The Bitter Cry of Outcast London,* published in October 1883. It described outrageous overcrowding and contained accounts of incest, and it was promoted by that great self-styled vigilante against dirt, vice, and exploitation in London, the publisher W. T. Stead.* Victoria, who was

---

* As the editor of the *Pall Mall Gazette,* Stead would go on to conduct a spectacular exposé of the child sex trade in London—*The Maiden Tribute of Modern Babylon*—in 1885, with the help of feminist reformer Josephine Butler. Victoria was horrified by the publication of the gruesome tales for public consumption, and when Stead was arrested for obscenity, she refused to intervene. Gladstone, who was surprisingly uninterested in the stories, hurried reform through Parliament, conscious that Stead might have the names of some compromised MPs. (Gladstone said he was "not well satisfied with the mode in which this mass of horrors has been collected, or as to the moral effect of its general dispersion by sale in the streets." July 15, 1885, Matthew, *Gladstone,* 541–42.) But the age of consent was raised from thirteen to sixteen, and penalties were strengthened. Stead, who was on the *Titanic* when it sank, dying in the icy North Atlantic waters, had gained a lasting fame.

then still mourning the death of Brown a few months earlier, wrote to Gladstone saying she was distressed by stories of "the deplorable condition of the houses of the poor in our great towns" and asked whether a public works program should be begun, and if an inquiry would be conducted into it. In the face of Gladstone's reluctance, she lobbied other, more sympathetic politicians and clergy. In February 1884, a royal commission was appointed to look into the housing of the working classes; Salisbury served on it, along with Bertie.

In 1885, when Salisbury was prime minister, he introduced an act into the House of Lords that made landlords responsible for unhygienic housing and gave local government boards the power to close down unsanitary residences. These laws were incremental but important; they helped prod the public into thinking about what might be done about conditions in the slums, and further investigations and housing trusts followed.

In January 1886, Salisbury resigned after being defeated on a land bill vote. The eighty-six Irish nationalists in Parliament had stacked the numbers against him, hopeful that Gladstone—who now supported Home Rule—would return to power. Victoria began a concerted and forceful campaign to ensure Gladstone would not become prime minister again. First, she refused to accept Lord Salisbury's resignation. Second, she tried to create a coalition between moderate Whigs and Conservatives to keep the Liberals out. She told George Goschen, a moderate Liberal Unionist, that to change the government would be "very disastrous," adding, "I am terrified for the country." She urged him to create a coalition with centrist Tories and back away from supporting Gladstone, because he would only "ruin the Country if he can." She told Salisbury she would refuse any "objectionable people" if Gladstone came in. She ended a memorandum self-pityingly: "What a dreadful thing to lose such a man as Lord Salisbury for the Country—the World—and *me*!"

There was no option Victoria would not explore in order to prevent Gladstone from returning as prime minister. She even asked Lord Tennyson—who had just accompanied his friend Gladstone on a sea cruise to Scandinavia—to try to discourage Gladstone from standing in the upcoming election. Tennyson protested he had little influence over him.

Victoria's intervention was extraordinary: she did not disguise her antipathy to Gladstone, she tried to push—and keep—him out of power, she actively sought to form other coalitions and governments, and she expected to have a pivotal say in who was selected for the Cabinet. There was no pretense of partiality. Victoria's ministers and secretary repeatedly warned her that public knowledge of these machinations would expose her to criticism and possibly scandal. The moderate Liberal Goschen bluntly refused to visit her for fear it might "compromise" the situation (a view for which she chastised him). He advised Victoria to send for Gladstone, arguing the Liberals were still in Gladstone's thrall.

Nervous that the press might discover Victoria's reluctance to call for Gladstone, Ponsonby leapt into action, asking if he might send for him immediately, to "put an end to the nervous excitement." Passive aggression was Victoria's final resort. Ponsonby raced to find Gladstone late at night, when he was just about to change into his nightshirt, to ask if he would form an administration; when he found him he said, "Your Majesty had understood from his repeated expression of a desire to retire from public life that he would not accept office and therefore in sending this message she left him free to accept or not." It was not a warm embrace.

The Grand Old Man, who was by now inured to the queen's disapproval, accepted and became PM once again. Ponsonby outlined the queen's choices for the Cabinet selection: she would not accept Charles Dilke, who had been named in a scandalous divorce case and was an outspoken republican. Gladstone grumbled but agreed. The queen also objected to the inclusion of his friend Lord Granville, to which Gladstone also acquiesced. Later, he also agreed not to appoint Hugh Childers to the War Office, which he considered a "great sacrifice." (He was made home secretary instead.) Victoria reminded him that her objection was not for her own sake, but "for the country's." What she was most eager to ascertain was Gladstone's precise intention with Home Rule: Was he only going to investigate the Irish call for autonomy, as he said? Or was this just a diplomatic paving of the way toward implementation? It was the defining issue of British politics in that era: Should the mutinous Irish be allowed to self-govern? Gladstone's fervent belief that this issue should at least be considered seriously cost him dearly. It would be his greatest, most farsighted, and yet most self-destructive quest.

By the 1880s, the Irish Question dominated the British Parliament. Ireland was suffering from a protracted agricultural depression, ruinous bouts of famine, and relentless bursts of violence. Support for the Irish republican Fenians was growing. Even as early as the 1840s, before the potato famine, Gladstone had viewed Ireland as a "coming storm." In the decades following, he watched the clouds blacken. When he was told he was going to be prime minister in 1868, while chopping down trees at his estate, he paused to declare, "My mission is to pacify Ireland."

And he tried. First, he freed Catholic farmers from having to pay tithes to the church when he disestablished the Church of Ireland in 1869. Next, he tried to tackle the culture of (mostly absentee) landlordism by providing protections for Irish tenants. In 1870, he passed laws that ensured evicted tenants could be compensated for improvements they had made to properties during their stay. In 1881, he introduced the Second Irish Land Act, which provided some genuine security by allowing tenants to apply for fair rent, fixed tenure, or freedom to sell their lease. (The bulk of Irish farmers did not own their land, and instead leased it from landlords, the majority of whom lived in England. In 1870, only 3 percent of agricultural holdings were occupied by owners.)

The most gargantuan task, though, was Home Rule. This was anathema to the bulk of the House of Lords, to many of his Liberal colleagues, and to the queen herself. The parlous Irish economy, the aftershocks of the famine and sustained depression, and the rumbling republican violence and agrarian unrest were a collective source of embarrassment to Britain. As the British Empire tried to extol liberty and, at times, the recognition of native people's rights on the world stage, the charge of hypocrisy closer to home was too obvious. Gladstone believed the cycle of anger was a cancer metastasizing on the British body politic.

The queen was not convinced Ireland deserved or needed autonomy. She thought Gladstone was "always excusing the Irish," and reminded him often of the opposition to his "dreadful" bill. In fact, the violence ended up somehow being his fault. His insistence on stirring up debate, she said, caused unrest and made Ireland a "complete state of terror." The queen advocated martial law and tried to tighten her grip in Parliament. She encouraged those who opposed it, no matter their party, to band together to protect the empire and defeat the Home Rule bill. She repeatedly rebuked a weary Gladstone and asked him to write a memorandum on his precise intentions. Gladstone's letter, setting out his wish simply to "examine" the matter of self-government, did not placate her, even though his determination was driven in part by recognition of the will of the Irish. Victoria told him he should never interpret silence from her as approval on this matter, that she could "only see danger to the Empire" in his course, and that she could not give him her support "when the union of the Empire is in danger of disintegration and serious disturbance." Gladstone pointedly reminded her of her legal responsibilities, writing that he was "most humbly sensible" of her desire "to give an unvarying constitutional support to those who may have the honor to be Your Majesty's advisers." He knew well that the queen's support varied wildly, but that legally she was obliged to give it. But, much like General Gordon, Victoria saw herself as answering to a higher power.

When Gladstone addressed the House of Commons on Home Rule in April 1886, his oratory was electrifying. The bill before them would allow for a separate parliament and government in Dublin, which would control all Irish affairs except foreign policy, defense, and trade. (It also removed Irish MPs from Westminster, which many Liberal MPs objected to, as it would erase votes they often relied on.) "This, if I understand it," Gladstone said in his strong, upward-lilting voice, "is one of those golden moments in our history, one of those occasions which may come and may go, but which does not often return."

But the moment went. On June 8, the bill was defeated, 341 to 311. The Liberals split, with 93 voting against. The Liberal Unionists separated from the Liberal Party and aligned with Conservatives in their opposition to Home Rule until 1914. Gladstone's foresight was greater than his political skill, and he struggled to corral a sufficient number of colleagues.

For Victoria, this was victory. When she received a telegram from Gladstone on July 20, 1886, saying his government would resign, she wrote in her diary: "I cannot help feeling very thankful." Gladstone's dedication to the measure made no sense to Victoria, who thought he had become "almost fanatically" earnest "in his belief that he is almost sacrificing himself for Ireland." She was, as ever, adept at sniffing political winds—and fanning them when she could. She busily encouraged prominent politicians who opposed the bill, and continued to urge moderate Liberals to find common ground with moderate Conservatives.

That summer and fall after the vote in 1886, dozens were killed in sectarian riots in Belfast and several hundred arrested. Gladstone did not give up, even after he had resigned. In 1887, he wrote in his diary: "One prayer absorbs all others: Ireland, Ireland, Ireland." He went on to fight for Home Rule again in the 1892 election, and managed to push through a watered-down bill in 1893: a version that was quickly, soundly rejected by the House of Lords. Gladstone's commitment to Irish self-government was fascinating: principled yet politically impossible. The House of Lords would never have supported him. Instead of bringing unity to the Isles, he had split his party, and he would be blamed for keeping Liberals out of office for the better part of two decades. But if Britain had passed Gladstone's bill in 1886, it would have been spared thirty-five years of turmoil and bloodshed.* Gladstone was right—it was a unique opportunity, blown.

In these years, through the 1870s and 1880s, Victoria was in her political prime. She proved more adept with the levers of power than most of the men around her. Many of her contemporaries struggled to understand how—or if—a woman could exercise such power. Arthur Ponsonby wrote that his father, Henry, who had become Queen Victoria's private secretary in 1870, would have found his job intolerable if he had merely been "dancing attendance on an obstinate middle-aged lady who knew little of what was going on and cared less." But Ponsonby soon gained "a high opinion of her powers and was constantly amazed at her industry." He considered her a "clear, sensible, honest thinker, who was in some things an excellent woman of business." But it can be difficult to glean from the accounts of these men exactly how effective she was. Their attitudes so often seemed to reflect Samuel Johnson's view of women preaching: it was just surprising to see it done at all.

What is more startling today is to discover what a robust and interventionist ruler Victoria was. She regularly stretched the boundaries of her role. She tried as hard as she could to ensure she and the foreign secretary would decide matters of foreign policy together, without their needing to be canvassed in the Cabinet. She bypassed the prime minister to give her own directives to generals. She tried to prevent Gladstone from gaining and keeping power. "The Queen was less ready to yield to ministerial dictation than is commonly sup-

---

* Both houses of Parliament did not pass Home Rule until 1914, and it was then postponed because of the outbreak of war. It was not until 1921, upon the signing of a treaty after a guerrilla war by nationalists, that Ireland was granted independence. Southern Ireland seceded the following year—and was called the Irish Free State—while Northern Ireland remained under British rule.

posed," wrote Sir Edmund Gosse in 1901. Yet Victoria so carefully cultivated the image of a compliant, reclusive, and domesticated queen that the books that emerged after her death were considered radical for implying she had her own mind. The extent of her interference in politics—and the audacity of her reach—did not become apparent until the 1920s and 1930s, when the letters of the final years of her reign were published. Even Lord Salisbury—PM three times while Victoria was queen—wrote: "I may say with confidence that no Minister in her long reign ever disregarded her advice, or pressed her to disregard it, without afterwards feeling he had incurred a dangerous responsibility. . . . She knows what she is talking about." As one of the editors of her letters, Lord Esher, pointed out, the queen always gave way to the views of a united Cabinet, but would "not always yield at once to the opinion of a single Minister."

So what exactly was the constitutional role of the queen then? Britain has no written constitution, but rather a host of pieced-together materials: statutes, judgments, authoritative works, treaties, and conventions. In 1867, during the queen's reclusive mourning period, Walter Bagehot, in his seminal work *The English Constitution,* noted there was no clear articulation of the monarch's constitutional role anywhere. Yet he argued that the lack of comprehension of the queen's role added to her prestige: "When there is a select committee on the Queen, the charm of royalty will be gone. Its mystery is its life. We must not let in daylight upon magic. We must not bring the Queen into the combat of politics, or she will cease to be reverenced by all the combatants; she will become one combatant among many."

Bagehot decided the monarch had three rights: "the right to be consulted; the right to encourage; and the right to warn." While the monarch was the "face" of democracy, he wrote, his or her role was primarily ceremonial and symbolic. But it was not until after Bertie ascended the throne that this ceremonial, symbolic kind of monarchy would become the norm. Victoria exercised many other rights beyond what Bagehot suggested: the right to berate, withdraw support, shape Cabinets, scheme against prime ministers, and instruct military officers.

The first function of a royal family, wrote Bagehot, was to sweeten politics "by the seasonable addition of nice and pretty events." Their second function was to provoke loyalty among the uneducated or simple-minded: "to be a visible symbol of unity to those still so imperfectly educated as to need a symbol." The third was to welcome foreign ministers and dignitaries. The fourth was to provide an example of morality (while noting that many of Victoria's ancestors failed at this). The last was to provide stability during times of transition, which would serve as some kind of "disguise" for changes of government.

The monarch's greatest powers came into play during the collapsing and creating of governments. When a party was divided and unable to choose a leader, the monarch might, wrote Bagehot, "pick out from the ranks of the divided party its very best leader," provided the monarch was unprejudiced. But who would be the judge of the monarch's discernment? Bagehot concluded that, due to the early acquired feebleness of hereditary dynasties, few monarchs would be actually equipped for such a task: "Probably in most cases the greatest wisdom of the constitutional king would show itself in *well-considered inaction.*" Yet the power, it is clear, was there, and Victoria took it when she could, even when the party was not divided. Technically, division could occur only when there was more than one person who could command a majority of politicians in the Commons. This happened only once in Victoria's time, in 1894. Yet she also chose Lord Aberdeen in 1852 and Lord Rosebery in 1894—these men were legitimate royal selections. During the split over Irish Home Rule in 1886, Victoria tried to push the Duke of Argyll to create a new party of moderates to "save the country and the Constitution." She also encouraged Liberals who opposed Home Rule to form a separate group of Liberal Unionists.

It is clear Victoria also believed she had the power to dismiss a prime minister, and ministry, though this was never exercised. When the king of Greece sacked his entire Cabinet in 1892 for "leading the country to bankruptcy," Victoria thought he was entitled to do so: "but whether it is wise to exercise this right must depend on circumstances." She objected to certain men being made ministers, but she did not think she could dismiss them once appointed. Her protests were often at least ostensibly on moral grounds—as in the case of Henry Labouchere, who had cohabited with his actress wife before marrying her—as well as personal grounds (Labouchere had also criticized the monarchy). As he did with Dilke, Gladstone protested but accepted the veto, and left both men out.

Despite being the head of the executive, kings and queens were supposed to agree with the advice given by their ministers. But the idea of just stamping policies handed to her was insulting to Victoria: she was not a "mere machine." Stockmar, after all, had told her the monarch was the "permanent Premier" and the prime minister merely the "temporary head of the Cabinet." Disraeli had also encouraged an inflated sense of her place, calling her the "Dictatress" and "Arbitress." Henry Ponsonby tacked in the other direction, spending many anxious years trying to ensure that Victoria relied on the advice of her ministers, and not simply on her own mind. But she never vetoed a Cabinet proposal, even as she fought to defeat them. When Gladstone pushed through a bill to disestablish the Irish church, for example, Victoria simultaneously indicated her opposition to it and offered her assistance in passing it.

By the end of Victoria's reign, England was drawing closer to becoming a democracy—two-thirds of men could now vote (although still no women), and the monarch's powers were substantially diminished. As queen, Victoria carried out a job undergoing continual redefinition. She worked furiously to maintain her powers, but did so in private. She was a clever and forceful political calculator, but she cannily presented herself to her subjects as an ordinary mother trotting about Scotland. This was evidence of her sharp political intuition; she knew the country loved her when she appeared to be one of them, but with her ministers, she clung tenaciously to her unconventional powers. She had watched Bismarck erode the influence of the German emperor, Vicky's father-in-law, and she had no intention of allowing the same to happen to her. She tried to ignore the fact that Gladstone was the leader of his party and had popular support, but she was forced to acknowledge it when her scheming proved to be futile. What she was insisting on—with threats of abdication if she did not get her way—was her own relevance.

By the 1880s, Gladstone had come to view his queen as "somewhat unmannerly." She pushed him harder than she had pushed any other prime minister—and he pushed back with almost equal force, calling her demands for information on Cabinet disputes "intolerable" and "inadmissible." He wished she'd step down for Bertie and admitted that his confidence in the monarchy had been shaken. Over time, he cared less about what she thought of him. Her dislike was so naked and obdurate that by 1886, the time of Gladstone's second premiership, he had grown resigned to her reprimands and barbs. He was keenly aware that she would delight in his government's falling after a few months, following the Irish split.

In 1881, he wrote of an audience with the queen: "Received with much civility, had a long audience, but I am always outside an iron ring: and without any desire, had I the power, to break through." He wrote to Charles Dilke: "I am convinced, from a hundred tokens, that she looks forward to the day of my retirement as a day if not of jubilee yet of relief." He was right, and yet the two of them lived on together, horns locked, into improbable old age. Victoria perpetually underestimated Gladstone's potential longevity. Every time she saw him, she described him as being in a state of illness and deterioration. She, too, was growing old, walking with the help of a stick and having daily massages to try to soothe pain in her sciatic nerve and alleviate her rheumatism.

It is quite possible Victoria was jealous of Gladstone, as his secretary, Edward Hamilton, concluded, especially of his extraordinary hold over her subjects. She frequently cautioned him from campaigning as he had done in the Midlothian campaign. She told him to mind his words, treating him much like a teenager requiring perpetual monitoring, even though he was a decade older than she. She sent him notes before he was due to give big speeches: in 1881 she told him to be "very cautious," in 1883 to be "very guarded in his language." In September 1883 Hamilton wrote:

> She feels, as he [Gladstone] puts it, aggrieved at the undue reverence shown to an old man of whom the public are being constantly reminded, and who goes on working for them beyond the allotted time, while H.M. is, owing to the life she leads, withdrawn from view. . . . She can't bear to see the large type which heads the columns of newspapers by "Mr. Gladstone's movements," while down below is in small type the Court Circular. . . . She finds Herself with a Prime Minister whose position in this country is unique and unlike that of anyone else of whom She has had experience, or of whom indeed any of Her predecessors had experience.

Of all the statesmen Victoria worked with, Gladstone was the most visionary. He was utterly unlike the bruised, wisecracking Lord Melbourne, who had preferred inaction to effort. Gladstone wrestled with the greatest questions of his time, vowing to press ahead even if he had to do so alone. He would not have had patience for polls or focus groups—he preferred to try persuasion and leadership. He introduced the first national schooling laws in the Education Act of 1870, cracked the political clout of Irish landlords with the Ballot Act of 1872, disestablished the Anglican Church in Ireland, tried to stamp out the purchase of votes with the Corrupt Practices Act, introduced the test of merit for employment of civil servants, and stopped the practice of men paying for official positions in the army.

Perhaps there has not been more controversy over Victoria's veering across constitutional lines because she rarely did so successfully;

had she managed to push Gladstone from power, or managed to persuade one of her centrists to form a government, people would have been shocked, and she would have been condemned. Her subjects pictured her ambling around Scotland, not shoving a popularly elected prime minister from his perch. Theirs was a great clash of wills and personalities.* Ponsonby grew so tired of passing politely angry missives from Victoria to Gladstone and back again that, during one protracted dispute in 1884, he instructed the prime minister to write directly to his queen. Ponsonby told his wife, Mary, that he had no desire to put his "finger in between two ironclads colliding."

* The irony was that one of the few things Victoria and Gladstone agreed on was that it was nonsense to give women the vote, or any political power. The old man protested that it might cause women to undermine the source of their power: "the delicacy, the purity, the refinement, the elevation of her own nature." Victoria agreed, even while firing rounds of letters and telegrams into her prime minister's camp, demanding his surrender.

CHAPTER 27

The Monarch in a Bonnet

The symbol that unites this vast Empire is a Crown not a bonnet.

—LORD ROSEBERY

They wanted her to wear a crown. That was, after all, what monarchs did. Surely, at her Golden Jubilee, the queen would wear a sparkling reminder of her fifty-year reign, a symbol of her height, command, wealth, and singularity. But Victoria shrugged off the pleas of her prime minister and family. In 1887, she wore a bonnet to her Golden Jubilee, with a plain black dress. She refused to wear the traditional violet velvet robes and the ceremonial crown, or to carry the heavy scepter and orb as she had done so carefully at her coronation half a century ago. There were kings and queens, princesses and princes, great men and women of Europe who dazzled in their plumage, jewels, and finery; but Victoria rolled behind them in her carriage, small and clad in black. This was her hallmark and her instinct, and it was entirely original: she was the queen who wore a bonnet, not a crown. She appeared at the top of the world's mightiest empire as the meekest of figureheads.

On June 21, 1887, the brilliantly sunny day of the thanksgiving service in Westminster Abbey, Victoria sat in her carriage, shielding her face with a parasol. Fifty years ago, she had been an excited, pretty teenager: the "rose of England." Today she was a white-haired widow who had given birth nine times, lost a husband, two children, five grandchildren, and her most loyal friend and companion. Instead of thundering through parks on horseback, as she had done as a young girl, she was now pushed around in pony chairs, lame and often exhausted. As she looked around on that bright June day, the deafening roars, the cheers, and the ocean of grinning, upturned, squinting faces overwhelmed her. The Duchess of Cambridge, a lady-in-waiting, described the "masses and millions of people thronging the streets" as looking "like an anthill."

A mob of workingmen ran alongside Victoria's carriage, cheering and shouting as loudly as they could: "You go it, old girl! You done it well! You done it well!" She nodded at them, laughing, as her eyes reddened with tears. Before her were rows of her royal men: her three sons, five sons-in-law, and nine of her grandsons. The swords of the Indian cavalry flashed in the sun. Cream-colored horses pulled state carriages filled with royals, mostly from Europe. Victoria had forty-three family members in the Westminster Abbey procession, including the spouses of her children and grandchildren. Once inside, she sat on top of the scarlet and ermine robes draped over her coronation chair in Westminster Abbey—but, pointedly, "in no way wore them around her person." She looked down at the members of the House of Commons sitting below her. She scanned their faces, unable to see Gladstone, though he was there.

The women who attended wore mostly pale colors, white and gray, in the plain morning dress Victoria had prescribed. It was the men who strutted: in scarlet uniforms, embroidered civil suits, and purple velvet episcopal copes that swept the ground. The most glamorous participants were those from the far-flung colonies, "chiefs of Eastern climes" who sported pebble-sized diamonds and emeralds, strung along chests and woven into turbans.

The queen did make one concession: for the first time in twenty-five years she trimmed her bonnet with white lace and rimmed it with diamonds. Within days, fashionable women of London were wearing similar diamond-bedecked bonnets. One reporter noted this trend disapprovingly at a royal garden party at Buckingham Palace in July, the month after the Jubilee: "Her Majesty and the Princesses at the Abbey wore their bonnets so trimmed in lieu of wearing coronets. It is quite a different matter for ladies to make bejeweled bonnets their wear at garden-parties."

Across England for several days, there were fairs, picnics, regattas, sporting tournaments, and dinners for the young, poor, and elderly. For children, the anticipation was magical. A twelve-year-old Winston Churchill wrote to his mother from school: "I can think of nothing but Jubilee." The two days of celebration concluded with a party for thirty thousand schoolchildren in Hyde Park. They stuffed themselves with meat pies, buns, and oranges, as well as milk, lemonade, and ginger beer. For entertainment, there were six military bands, twenty Punch and Judy shows, a hundred "lucky dip" barrels, eight marionette theaters, nine troupes of performing dogs, ponies, and monkeys, one thousand skipping ropes with "Jubilee handles," ten thousand little balloons, and forty-two thousand other toys. Giants strolled alongside pygmies.

From the northern part of Scotland to the southernmost tip of England, "beacons flamed from most of the hills, and bonfires were lighted and kept blazing until daybreak." More than a thousand fires were lit in the fifty-two counties of England and Wales alone, and as far north as the Orkney Islands, where locals struggled to see the flames because the skies were still light with the midnight summer sun. The blazing pride of empire lit up the heights of the British Isles.

The celebration was unprecedented: there had been some feeble attempts to celebrate George III's Silver Jubilee in 1785, marking twenty-five years, but few people came.

Now London was like an enchanted city, flickering with gaslight, oil light, limelight, electric light, candelabra, and fairy lights. So many lamps illuminated the city that in some parts it was brighter than day. A Mr. Breidenbach of Bond Street arranged for jets of violet-scented perfume to be sprayed fifty feet into the air, then lit up by electric lamps.

Through it all, Albert was a ghostly figure conjured by the persistence of Victoria's mourning. When the morning of June 20 broke, Victoria was, as ever, keenly aware of her solitude. She wrote in her diary: "The day has come and I am alone." It had been twenty-five years since her husband died. An entire generation had grown up without knowing him, but still she stood there doggedly dressed in black, trying to honor him, certain that the cheers reflected an understanding of how she had suffered without him. After the Jubilee, Victoria wrote a letter thanking her subjects for her kind reception on the way to and from Westminster Abbey: "It has shown that the labor and anxiety of fifty long years, twenty-two of which I spent in unclouded happiness, shared and cheered by my beloved husband, while an equal number were full of sorrows and trials, borne without his sheltering arm and wise help, have been appreciated by my people."

When three million of her subjects donated to a "Women's Jubilee Offering Fund," raising £75,000, Victoria decided to commission yet another statue of Albert (although she gave the bulk of the money to establish the Queen's Jubilee Nursing Institute). Thanks to Victoria, Albert abided (although she did alter some of his strict rules: she allowed women thought to be innocent parties in divorce cases to join the Jubilee; she even contemplated extending this privilege to such women from other countries, although Lord Salisbury counseled her against it "on account of the risk of admitting American women of light character"). It was a time for leniency—across the empire, prisoners were set free, except those who were cruel to animals, a sin Victoria considered unforgivable.

As usual, Victoria's reflections on her loneliness were made in the thick of a large crowd of relatives. She craved public expressions of love from her offspring. While reading over the speeches of her children prepared for the Jubilee, Victoria wrote to Ponsonby: "The Queen approves of these answers, but always wishes the words 'my dear Mother' to be inserted. Not only on this occasion, but always . . . the Queen wishes it should never be omitted when her children represent her."

The surviving seven royal children, now scattered across the globe, congregated in London to toast their mother's long reign. Affie, now forty-two, was stationed in Malta with his family, as the commander in chief of the British fleet in the Mediterranean. Arthur, then thirty-seven, was commander in chief of the Bombay army and living happily in India with his wife—and would soon be joined by his three children. Vicky, forty-six, was living in Prussia, miserable and deeply unpopular, persecuted by a suspicious press, the anti-British Chancellor Bismarck, and her own children, especially her eldest, Wilhelm.

The other children were still in England: Beatrice, who had just turned thirty, was pregnant with her second child and cheerfully ensconced with her new husband, Liko. When the baby girl, Ena, was born a few months later at Balmoral, Liko called her the "little Jubilee grandchild." Louise was not yet forty, and miserable in her marriage to the Marquess of Lorne. Helena was forty-one, and deeply engrosssed with her charity work; in the year of the Jubilee, she became president of the newly founded British Nurses' Association.

Bertie, of whom Victoria had grown fonder in recent years, was a portly forty-five and had five children, but seemed scarcely closer to ascending the throne than he had twenty years before. W. T. Stead sniped at him in the *Pall Mall Gazette:* "Will the Prince of Wales, 'the fat little bald man in red,' who looked so unimpressive beside his splendid German brother-in-law in white, ever reign over us?"

Sometimes it seemed as if Victoria was a permanent fixture on the landscape of Britain.

A week after the Jubilee ceremony, Vicky's husband, Fritz, was operated on for a growth on his larynx. It was declared to be nonmalignant, and Vicky's hopes that her husband might be cured were raised. The small lump had first been discovered in his throat in May, and several clumsy, painful attempts were made to remove it with red-hot wire, but every time it was sliced off it reappeared. Six German doctors diagnosed throat cancer, and they recommended a dangerous operation that would have resulted in Fritz's loss of voice and could have been fatal. A British specialist, Dr. Morell Mackenzie, had rushed to Prussia to see him, at Vicky's request. Dr. Mackenzie removed a lump from Fritz's throat and said it was benign. The German doctors insisted something was wrong; Dr. Mackenzie took another piece out and again said it was not cancerous. Vicky was desperate to believe Dr. Mackenzie, but her reliance on an English doctor angered the locals, as well as her eldest son, Wilhelm, who began to plot to oust his father from the succession.

Wilhelm was a proud, often cruel, and talentless man who harbored a particular kind of hatred for his mother. The painful breech birth Vicky had suffered meant he had to be wrenched from her womb, causing partial paralysis of his left arm due to nerve damage (this is now known as Erb's palsy). This made his left arm fifteen centimeters shorter than his right, something he tried to disguise for years by resting it on swords or other props. The medical establishment was ill equipped to deal with such a disability, which was considered shameful at the time. The treatments used to try to repair his arm were horrific. One such treatment, first applied when he was a few months old, was "animal baths." Twice a week, a hare was killed and sliced open; Wilhelm's limp arm was slid inside the still-warm body in the hope that some of its life force would magically transfer to the baby boy. Willy was also jolted with electric shocks and strapped into a metal contraption that forced his head upright. He blamed his mother for his shame, and for his years of unsuccessful, painful treatments: he would never forgive her.

As a militaristic conservative who favored state rule, Wilhelm believed he was the true patriot in his family. He "fancied himself of enormous importance," Vicky told her mother. He thought he was more Prussian than his progressive father, Fritz, and was a great admirer of Bismarck and all things associated with "despotism and Police State." Victoria was so irritated by her twenty-eight-year-old grandson's haughtiness that she did not want to invite him to her Golden Jubilee. Vicky had to plead his case, especially as any signs of division between England and Germany would only exacerbate her own problems as a liberal British woman in conservative Germany. Willy had hoped to leave his sick father behind in Prussia and go to London on his own. From England, Victoria regarded his scheming with irritation. Even Chancellor Bismarck recognized Willy was too immature to rule, that he was impetuous, "susceptible to flattery and could plunge Germany into war without foreseeing or wishing it." It turned out to be a matter of character, though, not maturity, for this was precisely what happened years later, when Wilhelm's eagerness for war would far outstrip his competence at waging it.

In November of 1887, it was determined that Fritz in fact had cancer; Dr. Mackenzie concurred at last. Willy quickly embarked on a naked grab for power, persuading the Prussian emperor—his grandfather, Fritz's father—to authorize him to sign any documents on Fritz's behalf. In February 1888, Fritz had a tracheotomy. By March 23, Wilhelm was deputy emperor, working at the German Foreign Office and leading a host of parliamentary committees. He prepared his proclamation speech and kept a detailed plan of his succession in his desk. Fritz knew he was already dismissed as dead; the hurt only deepened when Wilhelm's siblings, Charlotte and Henry, switched to support their brother. Vicky complained to Victoria: "People in general consider us a mere passing shadow soon to be replaced by *reality* in the shape of William!" It seemed painfully unfair to Vicky that her own husband was so ill when he stood ready to inherit the throne; the emperor was now ninety, and sure to die soon. She was certain her husband would be a great, humane leader of Prussia, and a forceful advocate for parliamentary democracy.

In March 1888, an increasingly feeble Fritz finally became Emperor Frederick when his father died. Victoria was elated that her daughter was now empress: "It does seem an impossible dream." Victoria, by now a ruler with a half century of experience under her belt, instructed them both to be firm and to demand respect, despite Fritz's illness.

Fritz was a voiceless emperor. He scribbled instructions on paper and breathed through a cannula while his eldest son waited impatiently for him to die. Vicky's nerves were raw, and her neuralgia sometimes confined her to bed. She spent her days knitting or crocheting next to her husband as he pressed a bag of ice cubes to his throat, hovering outside his door to listen to him breathing, or accompanying him on carriage rides as he struggled with coughing fits. Vicky was isolated and misunderstood; her British origins had made her deeply unpopular. Her private letters were leaked to the press and published in full. All three of her children also attacked her, accusing her of causing her father's illness or of ensuring that his medical treatment was poor. Even when Vicky smiled, it was pointed to as evidence of callousness.

The ruling elite drummed their heels and gossiped about Vicky. Bismarck's son Herbert considered Fritz's looming death "good fortune"; he would be glad to be rid of a man married to a woman with a "totally English outlook" that might mean a disastrous foreign policy. The nobility, and Chancellor Bismarck, worried Fritz might try to make Vicky regent. Even the idea of Vicky signing documents for Fritz was opposed by Bismarck and her own son Henry, who said, "Hohenzollern Prussia and the German Reich must not allow themselves to be led by a woman." The sad empress was surrounded.

It was time for her mother to intervene. Victoria decided she would go to Prussia on her way back from a holiday in Italy in April 1888 to see Fritz and show support. While she was there, she would confront the old statesman Bismarck, one to one. There was, simultaneously, another delicate diplomatic operation at stake. Vicky's daughter Princess Victoria wanted to marry Prince Alexander of Battenburg—"Sandro"—who had resigned as king of Bulgaria in 1886 after a seven-year reign. Fritz had given his daughter his approval. Bismarck, whose own son had his eye on the pretty princess, strenuously objected on the grounds that it would anger Russia, especially the new czar, Alexander II, who was Sandro's cousin. Sandro was tall, strikingly handsome, and adored by Queen Victoria, although she had cautioned Vicky to wait to get full approval. (She had also been told that Sandro had fallen in love with a particularly beautiful opera singer.)

When Victoria walked into Fritz's room, he handed her a nosegay; it would be the last time she would see him. She then saw Bismarck in her rooms at Charlottenburg Palace. (Lord Salisbury urged her to bring a minister with her, but she refused.) It is unclear exactly what happened during the forty-five minutes they spent alone together, but Bismarck wiped a handkerchief across his brow when he walked out. Shortly afterward, he declared, "*Mein Gott! That* was a woman! One could do business with her!" A man to whom the concept of female authority was anathema, Bismarck later amended his remarks to sound more patronizing: "Grandmama behaved quite sensibly at Charlottenburg." Poor Vicky sobbed as she said goodbye to her mother. But Victoria's visit had been a triumph, as she had reminded the Germans of the power that their empress's mother wielded. A jealous Willy sniffed: it was "high time the old lady died."

Fritz occupied the throne for only ninety-nine days: he died on June 15, 1888. He was, by then, a "perfect skeleton." The day before, he had written in a note to his wife: "What is happening to me?" Vicky had sat by his bed for hours, holding out a sponge soaked in white wine for him to suck on. After he drew his final breath, jamming his eyes shut, Vicky placed his sword on his arm and kissed his hands and feet. Wilhelm immediately jerked into action. His forces—scores of Hussars in scarlet coats—quickly surrounded the house. He cordoned off the telegraph office while they searched Fritz's study for evidence of liberal plots.

The new kaiser went to his mother's room and ransacked it, accusing her of hiding secret documents that he believed would be sent to England. Vicky stood watching him, weeping. (She had also anticipated this: Vicky had already brought a cache of Fritz's private papers over to England during the Golden Jubilee and hidden them in an iron safe in Buckingham Palace. Later, when Fritz realized he was dying, he had arranged for a doctor to smuggle his war diaries to the British ambassador in Berlin, eager to preserve an accurate record of the part he had played in the Franco-Prussian and Austro-Prussian wars and the unification of his homeland.) Later, when Vicky tried to walk onto the terrace to clip some roses to place on Fritz's body, a guard grabbed her arm roughly and escorted her back in.

Sitting alone in her room, stunned, Vicky wrote to her mother, who would understand better than anyone: "I am a widow, no more his wife. How am I to bear it? You did, and I will do." Victoria sympathized: "I had not the agony of seeing another fill the place of my Angel Husband, wh I always felt I *never* cd have borne!" And the place had been filled by a son who not only ruled over her but despised her. Even his friend Herbert von Bismarck described Wilhelm as being "as cold as a block of ice. Convinced from the start that people only exist to be used . . . after which they may be cast aside." Wilhelm buried his father as quickly as possible, conveniently forgetting to open his instructions for his funeral.

The nationalistic new kaiser was deeply ambivalent about Britain, which marked a significant shift in British-German relations. He dressed in British uniform when visiting his grandmother, whom he loved, and he enthusiastically raced yachts around the Isle of Wight. But he also felt a deep rivalry, focusing on building up Prussia's navy to try to compete with Britain's. He would end up warring with his mother's family, leading them to change the royal family's name from Saxe-Coburg-Gotha to Windsor in the First World War, when Britain was fighting Germany. Wilhelm dramatically snubbed Bertie, refusing to meet him in Vienna not long after becoming kaiser, because of something Bertie had said at Fritz's funeral. Victoria was shocked, thought him obnoxious and pretentious and his wife "odious." She only grudgingly allowed him to visit her at Osborne in 1889, where his affection and excitement about being allowed to wear a British admiral's uniform disarmed her. Wilhelm gushed: "The same uniform as St. Vincent and Nelson; it is enough to make one quite giddy."

What would have happened if Fritz's cancerous throat had not prematurely ended his life? Germany would have been under the rule of a liberal, compassionate emperor, a leader who wanted to improve the lives of the working class and who especially despised the anti-Semitic movement. "As a modern civilized man, as a Christian and a gentleman, he found it abhorrent," wrote Vicky; he tried to counter it where he could. His son Wilhelm was the opposite, stirring up and championing anti-Semitism, writing in 1927 while in exile in the Netherlands that "press, Jews & mosquitos . . . are a nuisance that humanity must get rid of in some way or another. I believe the best would be gas?" The father would certainly have fought what the son fostered.

Democracy made no sense, Victoria declared, when it only resulted in the reelection of a man like William Gladstone. He became prime minister again in 1892, the third time in a dozen years. It was, she wrote, "a defect in our much-famed Constitution to have to part with an admirable Govt like Ld Salisbury's for no question of any importance, or any particular reason, merely on account of the number of votes." In the Court Circular, Victoria provocatively proclaimed the resignation of Salisbury "with regret." It really was too much to have to call for "an old, wild incomprehensible man of eighty-two and a half." The aging of Gladstone, her senior by a decade, galled the queen. She described him as "much aged . . . his face shrunk, deadly pale, with a weird look in his eye, a feeble expression about the mouth, & the voice altered." He was bent, she pointed out, and walking on a stick. But so was she.

The older they grew, the closer Gladstone had to sit to Victoria's side because of his increasing deafness. They both loathed their meetings and struggled to make conversation; it had become "a farce," said the queen. To her disdain, Gladstone tried once again to introduce "gradual self-government" for the Irish in 1893, which resulted in fistfights in the Commons. The House of Lords threw it out with a resounding vote of 419 to 41. Gladstone would not live to see the Irish govern themselves.

On February 28, 1894, after eighteen more months as prime minister, the elderly Gladstone walked slowly up the stairs at Windsor. He steeled himself for the queen's reaction to his resignation. He had been politically destabilized lately by his lack of support for shoring up the navy, at a time when Germany was increasing in maritime strength. But Gladstone said his decision to go was driven by his physical deterioration; he could no longer properly see or hear. The Grand Old Man and his unsympathetic queen spent an awkward half hour together, trying to drum up small talk, eventually resorting to discussing the fog and rain, as well as Victoria's impending trip to Italy. Victoria's relief was obvious. "I never saw her looking better," wrote Gladstone. "She was at the high point of her cheerfulness. Her manner was personally kind throughout." By contrast, several of his ministers wept at the news. Gladstone called them "that blubbering Cabinet." His career had spanned six decades; he had been prime minister for a total of twelve years, and a Privy Counsellor (part of a group of politicians who advised the sovereign) for fifty-three.

The queen's response to Gladstone's letter of resignation was brief and graceless. She acknowledged after "many years of arduous labor and responsibility," he was "right in wishing to be relieved at his age of these arduous duties, and she trusts [he will] be able to enjoy peace and quiet, with his excellent and devoted wife, in health and happiness, and that his eyesight may improve." She continued, abruptly, "The Queen would gladly have offered a peerage to Mr. Gladstone, but she knows he would not accept it." Gladstone felt this like a slap. After so many decades, no sign of warmth? Surely she could at least offer a fragment of praise, or even just recognition? Wouldn't his departure thaw her a jot? He likened their farewell to the end of a holiday in 1831 that he'd taken in Sicily. He had ridden around on a mule the whole time. While he had been "on the back of the beast for many scores of hours" and it had done him no wrong and rendered him "much valuable service," Gladstone reflected, "I could not get up the smallest shred of feeling for the brute. I could neither love nor like it."

The day after Gladstone gave his last, rousing speech in the House of Commons, he went to Windsor with his wife, Catherine, for dinner with the queen and stayed the night. The next morning, Catherine went to see Victoria, sobbing throughout their meeting. She wanted to try to repair the relationship, she wanted to assure her strangely fragile husband that the rancor between him and the queen would not fester or be widely known. She asked Victoria twice to understand that her husband was devoted to her, "whatever his errors." Then, wrote Victoria, Catherine "begged me to allow her to tell him that I believed it which I did; for I am convinced it is the case, though at times his actions might have made it difficult to believe." Catherine was clever; she shared memories of Albert, and of how long they had all known one another. Victoria wrote: "I kissed her when she left."

After all the decades of conflict, Gladstone was haunted by the queen's rudeness to him when he resigned. He could not fathom why she dismissed him with the "same brevity" used in "settling a trades-

man's bill." He wrote on March 10, 1894, in his diary that in his relationship with the queen there was "something of a mystery, which I
have not been able to fathom, and probably never shall." He wanted
his family to "keep in the background" his poor relationship with the
queen in their later years. At least now he was free from any obligation to talk to her.

Victoria had not bothered to ask Gladstone who should replace
him. She chose Lord Rosebery, a moderate Liberal who was bashful,
anxious, and imperialistic. Most gratifyingly, he had assured Victoria
he would not argue for Home Rule. After an initial tussle over his
desire to introduce bills to disestablish the Welsh and Scottish
churches, they had an amicable relationship. The queen's clarity and
decisiveness took the new prime minister aback. Aged forty-six, he
was substantially younger than the queen, a reversal of the dynamic
of previous years. His government was largely ineffective, with a divided Cabinet and a series of social reforms quickly dismissed by the
House of Lords. The government lasted only until June of the next
year. Victoria was sad to see him go. Unusually, she even preferred
Rosebery personally to the Tory leader, Lord Salisbury, with whom
she was more usually politically aligned. But at the 1895 election, the
Tories had a thumping win. Victoria's party of preference was back
in power.

At the core of the queen's world were her children and grandchildren, and she remained preoccupied with their lives. She delighted in
the little grandchildren who crawled under her legs and flashed dimpled smiles; her love for small children, wrote Arthur Ponsonby, was
now "all embracing." She was now known as "the Grandmother of
Europe": her descendants thronged the courts of the Continent, and
would go on to populate the royal houses of Germany, Russia, Spain,
Greece, Romania, Portugal, and Norway. The beautiful Princess
Alix of Hesse, Alice's daughter, agreed to marry the Czarevitch
Nicholas of Russia. Three weeks before the wedding in 1894, she was

hurled into public view when her husband's father, the Russian czar, died. She and her husband, now the czar, and their children would later die in the Russian Revolution.

It always seemed bitterly unfair to Victoria to bury a grandchild, and especially an heir. But on January 14, 1892, Bertie lost his eldest child, Prince Albert Victor, known as Eddy, to pneumonia. Eddy was only twenty-seven and was due to marry his cousin, Princess Mary of Teck, in just a few weeks (he had wanted to marry another cousin, Alix of Hesse, but she had rejected him). Eddy's younger brother George grew close to Mary in their grief, and he married her himself in June. (In 1910, he became King George V.) Alix and Bertie were devastated by the loss of their good-looking, genial son; Alix kept a shrine to him for the rest of her life. It was the second child she had buried, as their youngest had died only twenty-four hours after his birth. Eddy's death has been the subject of unfounded or unproven gossip for a century. In his lifetime, he was rumored to have been a client of a homosexual brothel, the father of an illegitimate child, as well as, scandalously, Jack the Ripper. (More than a hundred men have been linked to the gruesome murders of prostitutes in London in 1888, around the impoverished Whitechapel district, but the killer has never been identified. The accusation that it was Eddy has been disproved.)

As Victoria's carriage rolled out of the palace gates during her Golden Jubilee celebration in 1887, a tall, thin Indian man with intense eyes stood watching at a window. Abdul Karim had been invited to serve the now sixty-eight-year-old queen during her Jubilee year; he would quickly, forcefully charm his way into her affections. Karim, then just twenty-four, would represent the best of empire to Victoria; he spoke to her of the rich traditions in India, the "jewel in her crown," describing his country's curious culture and history. He also taught her his language and cooked her delicious curries.

It would be an excellent way to mark her Jubilee, she decided:

employ some Indian servants at her residences. After all, she had been Empress of India for more than a decade, and she would need assistance with the bevy of Indian royals who would be arriving to celebrate the Jubilee. Karim, a jail clerk from Agra, was thrilled by the invitation and spent months cramming on court etiquette. He arrived at Windsor three days before the Jubilee began, along with the plump and pleasant Mohammed Buksh, their trunks neatly packed with colorful silk tunics. When the two nervous men met Victoria, they kissed her feet. She described Karim as "much lighter" than Buksh, "tall & with a fine serious countenance," and added that his father was a "native doctor at Agra."

These well-mannered, respectful men perfectly matched what Victoria wanted in her aides; discretion, devotion, and cheer. Their progress was rapid. A few days after they arrived, she wrote, "The Indians always wait now, & do so, so well & quietly." Karim engaged her in long conversations about his exotic homeland. He charmed her, and his duties broadened. And yet he had never intended to come to serve as a mere table servant, he told her. He was ambitious and wanted more. Victoria was readily persuaded to promote him, writing in her journal in August: "It was a mistake to bring him over as a servant to wait at table, a thing he had never done, having been a clerk or *munshi* in his own country, and being of rather a different class to the others." That month, Karim began teaching her Hindustani. This, she wrote, "interests & amuses me very much." By December, she was trying to speak a little of it to visiting Indian royals. (Henry Ponsonby wrote archly to his wife: "She has given me a Hindu vocabulary to study.") When Karim went on leave to India, she missed him, writing that he was "very handy and useful in many ways."

Leaping several rungs of the court ladder at once, the proud Karim was made the queen's official Munshi, or clerk, in 1888. All photographs taken of him serving her meals were destroyed. It was only five years since Brown had died, and Karim's rapid elevation infuriated the royal household. He lacked Brown's integrity and long record of service, and he was far more adept at manipulating his mistress while gaining favors for himself and his family. Victoria gave him a vast tract of land in Agra as well as a furnished bungalow at Windsor and cottages at Osborne and Balmoral. Karim also procured promotions and invitations to prestigious functions for his father and brother in India. He was decorated with the high honor of the Companion of the Most Eminent Order of the Indian Empire, usually awarded to those whose work was of national importance. Puffed up by his success, Karim made increasingly outrageous requests. He asked, for example, for "enormous quantities" of narcotic drugs, including morphine and laudanum, to be sent to his father. It was an amount of poison Victoria's doctor Sir James Reid estimated to be sufficient to kill fifteen thousand men. An emissary was dispatched to explain Reid's refusal to the Munshi.

Partly due to the fact that her charge was far from home, Victoria fretted over every detail of Karim's care. The fact that she grew so quickly and trustingly attached to him underscores the loneliness of a mother whose children were fully grown and married, and whose closest male companions—Albert, Brown, and Disraeli—had all died. A reluctant Reid was entrusted with the care of the Indian servants, and Victoria sent him lengthy missives about their attire, activities, and health. She worried that the cold climate might have been responsible for Karim's battles with scabies and a carbuncle. When Karim lay ill in his room, Victoria visited him frequently throughout the day and sat stroking his hand. The increasingly suspicious Reid—who is the most detailed, if jaundiced, documenter of this relationship—noted the hours Victoria spent "in his room taking Hindustani lessons, signing her boxes, examining his neck, smoothing his pillows, etc."

The queen had rapidly and unilaterally ushered unknown Muslim staff into the upper echelons of her monarchy. The case of Abdul Karim highlights her loyalty, her abhorrence of racism, and her kindness, as well as her susceptibility to charm and her blinding need for intimacy. As the second intimate companion of the queen who had shot up from a lower class, Karim was soon seen as John Brown's successor. But Victoria was forty-four years older than Karim, and far more maternal toward him. She also believed in him, and she took his word when it should have been doubted. It would not be long before, once again, her sanity would be questioned.

CHAPTER 28

The "Poor Munshi"

The Queen seems off her head.

—SIR JAMES REID

Things have come to such a pass that the police have been consulted. . . . But it is of no use, for the Queen says that it is "race prejudice" & that we are all jealous of the poor Munshi (!).

—FRITZ PONSONBY

With one deliberate sweep of her arm, Victoria pushed all the trinkets, photos, inkstands, and papers on her desk onto the carpet. She drew herself up and exhaled loudly. All she had wanted was to take her Munshi with her to southern France—after all, he had traveled with them to Italy before—and now her household had staged a revolt. Either the Munshi went, the gentlemen told her, or they did. They refused to be in a situation where he would eat with the household. It was 1897, ten years after Karim had joined the court on the eve of Victoria's Golden Jubilee; in the intervening decade, Victoria had drawn closer and closer to her Indian aide, and tensions were boiling. Dr. Reid even made an ally of the Prince of Wales, speaking to Bertie about "the crisis which the Queen's treatment of, and relations with," the Munshi was bringing on. Victoria's particular brand of stubborn loyalty was something she'd possessed since childhood. Now in her seventies, she would not be dictated to. What seemed to escape her was that Karim was the one who was bullying her, not the men of the household. She was constantly fretting that he be happy and not leave her. Lord Salisbury attributed this attachment to Victoria's craving for some kind of excitement, which was all too rare in the life of an elderly queen. She won, and Karim came to France for the spring holiday.

By the early 1890s, Karim had become a fixture at court. In 1893, he went to India on leave for six months and brought his wife back with him to England. Two other "wives," whom Karim called "aunts," followed, along with other relatives. (Dr. Reid noted that each time he went to tend to an ill "Mrs. Abdul Karim," a different tongue was presented to him.) Karim's sexual promiscuity resulted in his experiencing recurring bouts of venereal disease, which Dr. Reid seemed to take some pleasure in reporting to the queen. Karim had gonorrhea, he told Her Majesty solemnly at least twice, recording how taken aback Victoria was. Albert would have shuddered, but Victoria tolerated it.

The Munshi was not popular at court. Victoria saw him as vulnerable and proud; those around her saw him as pretentious and affected. Ponsonby thought him a fat fool. Bertie loathed him but was not brave enough to confront his mother, and conferred with Dr. Reid instead. Dr. Reid distrusted him and thought he was exploiting the queen's kindness. In 1894, while sitting in his room in Italy, accompanying the queen on her Continental vacation, Dr. Reid compiled a list of the things that annoyed him most about Karim, who had also joined their traveling group. The list included Karim's complaints about the position of his railway carriage, his desire (backed by the queen) to ride with men of the household, the expense of his trip to Rome, the fact that he commandeered a bathroom meant for the queen's maids, and his complaints that the Italian newspapers "took too little notice of him," which the queen ensured was passed on to newspaper editors so they might report on him more.

Karim continually fought to be recognized as a member of the royal household and to be included among the gentry, much to the horror of Victoria's entourage. John Brown had had a strong disregard for status, and was more of a leveler than a self-promoter, but Karim longed to climb the hierarchy. In 1889, when he found himself seated alongside servants at a gala performance at Sandringham, he rose from his seat and walked out. The queen—true to her pattern of placating him when he was upset—assured him this would not happen again. When Victoria's son Arthur saw Karim mingling with gentry at the Braemar races, he complained to Ponsonby. In 1894, Karim stormed out of the wedding of two of Victoria's grandchildren in Coburg when he noticed he was standing beside some grooms. Karim immediately wrote a letter to the queen so harsh that it made Victoria burst into tears. She capitulated to his demands, and from that moment, the young clerk from Agra was driven about Prince Albert's hometown in a royal carriage, with a footman perched on the box. He was also invited to all state concerts, but, as Dr. Reid wrote, "everyone avoided him." The court circle had become genuinely concerned about the manipulative Karim's hold over the queen, and about what she might compromise, given her need for companionship.

Despite the internal court tensions, and the skepticism about the new and vain object of her affections, these years contained a certain contentment for the septuagenarian Victoria. She returned from her travels full of animated chatter. She roared at the funny anecdotes told by her ladies-in-waiting, with whom she increasingly dined alone (instead of with the entire royal household, plus politicians and dignitaries). Unlike the mournful years following Albert's death, she was unfailingly uplifted by the beauty of her surroundings: "The lights so lovely on the purple hills, golden birches, interspersed with still perfectly green trees." She fluttered enthusiastically about the tableaux vivants performed for her entertainment, wherein the members of the royal household would dress in the costumes of historical or theatrical characters and pose silently as curtains were drawn back to reveal a detailed, frozen scene. The tableaux were prepared in high secrecy, with many hours of rehearsing and posing for photographs. Victoria loved them, and dozens of tableaux were created, in the images of the likes of Queen Elizabeth and Raleigh, the Queen of Sheba, *Carmen,* and *The Winter's Tale*. Karim and Mohammed were eager participants in this elaborately styled performance art, dressing up and posing alongside Victoria's children and companions.

The first chink in the Munshi's persona appeared in 1894 when it became clear he had exaggerated his status. Karim had claimed his father was the surgeon general of the British army in India, but when Dr. Reid discovered that he was just an unqualified hospital assistant, he became determined to expose him. In 1894, after lengthy investigations, four men of the royal household, including Dr. Reid, produced a report declaring Karim to be of low birth and socially fraudulent. In response, Victoria launched an onslaught against what she correctly saw as class snobbery: "To make out that the poor good Munshi is so low is really outrageous & in a country like England quite out of place. . . . She has known 2 Archbishops who were sons respectively of a Butcher & a Grocer." She was "so sorry," she wrote, for "the poor Munshi's sensitive feelings." Dr. Reid was instructed to cease his investigations, and further evidence that the Munshi's father was just an apothecary was denied and ignored.

With good reason, Victoria suspected that part of the horror and suspicion with which Karim was regarded was the result of racism. (One of the complaints Dr. Reid repeated in his report, for example, was about the Munshi's wife and mother-in-law: "More degraded and dirty than the lowest labourers in England; spitting all over the carpets. Performing functions in sitting rooms, etc.") It was crucial to stamp out prejudice, decided the queen, who herself was remarkably free of it. She forbade people to use the term "black men"; even Lord Salisbury got in trouble for it. Priests had assured her that Muslims, even though non-Christian, could contain the spirit of Christ, and she instructed those around her accordingly. For all of Victoria's conservatism about women's rights, she was remarkably progressive in these other ways. But Karim himself exhibited much of the prejudice she hated, and of which she saw him as a victim. He acted superior to his fellow countrymen, and on the trip to Italy in 1894, he refused "to allow other Indians in any part of the same railway carriage as himself."

Attacks on the Munshi only caused the queen to pull him closer. The astute Henry Ponsonby watched with despair as he clambered ever higher in the queen's affections, writing: "The advance of the Black Brigade [Karim] is a serious nuisance. I was afraid that opposition would intensify her desire to advance further. Progression by antagonism." Karim was given John Brown's old room, and his portrait was painted against a background of gold. In October 1889, Victoria had even taken him up to the remote cottage called Glassalt Shiel in Balmoral, despite having sworn she would never spend a night there again after Brown died.

In June of 1889, when one of Victoria's jeweled brooches went missing, she accused her dresser of failing to pin it on her shawl. The dresser insisted she had indeed pinned it, but no search turned the brooch up. A few weeks later, Mahomet, the other Indian servant who had been hired at the time of the Jubilee, revealed that it had been stolen and sold by Karim's brother-in-law Hourmet Ali to a local Windsor jeweler. The queen was furious when shown the evidence by one of her dressers, Mrs. Tuck. But she was not angry with Ali—she was angry with Mrs. Tuck and the jeweler, yelling, "That is what you English call justice!" After Karim told her Ali was only following an Indian custom to pick up and pocket lost items without saying anything, Victoria instructed all involved to remain silent, insisting she believed in Ali's honesty. Dr. Reid wrote with a sigh: "So the theft, though proved absolutely, was ignored and even made a virtue of for the sake no doubt of [Karim] about whom the Queen seems off her head."

The queen chose to ignore all evidence against the Munshi for as long as she could. In April 1897, Henry Ponsonby wrote:

> We have been having a good deal of trouble lately about the Munshi here, and although we have tried our best, we cannot get the Queen to realize how very dangerous it is for her to allow this man to see every confidential paper relating to India. The Queen insists on bringing the Munshi forward as much as she can, & if it were not for our protest, I don't know where She would stop. Fortunately he happens to be a thoroughly stupid and uneducated man, & his one idea in life seems to be to do nothing & to eat as much as he can.

Most of Karim's social elbowing was harmless. What was of greater concern to the men of the household was how the Munshi gradually inveigled his way into handling—and, increasingly, shaping—the queen's correspondence regarding his country. Karim was bent on persuading the queen to address the plight of Muslim minorities in India, including their representation on local councils. Victoria automatically began to pass to Karim any Indian petitions that she thought required only a polite refusal, allowing him to respond.

The real problem, Ponsonby continued, was that while Karim himself was dim, he had a clever friend, Rafiuddin Ahmed, who was involved with the Muslim Patriotic League in London. Karim had previously urged Victoria to help promote Ahmed's career at the bar, which she had dutifully done. At one point, the queen even suggested he be sent to the embassy at Constantinople to ensure a Muslim diplomatic presence. This request was refused by the prime minister, Lord Salisbury, who told her he would have leapt at the opportunity were it not for the prejudice other people harbored. There were broad suspicions that Ahmed had been leaking state secrets to English enemies in Afghanistan—then controlled by Britain—and extracting crucial information from the Munshi, who was by now reading "the Viceroy's letters, & any letters of importance that come from India." When the Munshi traveled with Victoria to Europe that summer of 1898, against the wishes of the court, he foolishly invited Ahmed to come too. Ahmed was promptly kicked out by Arthur Bigge, who had succeeded Sir Henry Ponsonby as the queen's private secretary after Ponsonby died in 1895. It was then, as the court settled into the Hotel Excelsior Regina looking out over the shimmering Mediterranean in Nice, that the tensions finally erupted.

Victoria's doctor steeled himself for a prolonged, unpleasant confrontation with his queen. He felt he had little choice; it was not just that this Indian man was irritating and controlling, but he was a potential threat to Britain's security. What was at stake now, Dr. Reid declared boldly to a solemn Victoria, was the reputation of the throne. The chief of police in London had told Dr. Reid that the Munshi was embroiled with the Muslim Patriotic League. Dr. Reid, spurred by a mixture of legitimate grievances and snobbish gossip, made sure the queen knew that he had "been questioned as to her sanity." Victoria burst into tears. She knew what people said about her, and admitted to Dr. Reid "she had been foolish in acceding to his constant demands for advancement but yet trying to shield him." Over the next few days, Victoria veered between repentance and rage.

It was finally time to confront the "scoundrel" Karim. While other members of the court were walking along the curved beach below, Dr. Reid wheeled on him, telling him he knew he was "an impostor" from a low class, who was uneducated, inexperienced as a secretary, and had "a double face, one which you show to the Queen, and another when you leave her room." He also accused Karim of cheating the queen of money. Karim had claimed receipts were not required for any expenses in India and so should not be required of him in Britain; as his expenses mounted, suspicions grew. By the time the group left France weeks later, Karim was subdued. An exhausted Victoria told her gentlemen to stop talking "about this painful subject." She continued to defend her "poor M." and repeatedly said that the Indians who disliked him did so because they were Hindus and he was Muslim. Victoria continued to fight back for the next two years, trying to clear the Munshi's name as well as the name of his friend Ahmed.

Part of Victoria's attachment to her Indian attendants arose from her own need for gentle physical care. She was then well into her seventies, and the complications caused by pregnancy, labor, and weight gain had made walking hellish and standing for any length of time impossible. Just as Albert had done when she was convalescing from childbirth, she wanted to be lifted carefully and tenderly from bed to chair, and chair to carriage. The Indians, she wrote, were "so clever" when they lifted her, and "they never pinch me." What her court saw, but refused to recognize, was the value of the succor a quiet, attentive man brought to an aging queen.

In 1895, grief came again to the court. Beatrice's husband, the beloved Liko, asked if he could serve in the Ashanti mission in Africa, wherein Britain would gain control of the gold-rich lands now known as Ghana. Liko's relationship with Beatrice had cooled, and he had become close to her beautiful sister Louise. An artistic, intelligent woman, Louise was a talented sculptor whose husband was almost certainly gay; she conducted affairs outside her marriage and had a decades-long liaison with a mentor, the sculptor Joseph Edgar Boehm. When Liko and Beatrice suspected that Louise was having an affair with the queen's new secretary, Arthur Bigge, Louise accused them of a smear campaign. Lord Lorne was forced to come to her defense as the rows in the royal family grew ugly. Liko escaped to war, with Victoria's reluctant permission.

A few weeks later, Liko contracted malaria, and he died on a transport ship en route to Ghana on January 20, 1896, before even witnessing battle. Victoria was wretched. Her favorite child was now bowed with her own grief, the two black-clad women paired in misfortune. Beatrice was then made even more miserable when a grieving Louise told her she had been "Liko's confidante and Beatrice meant nothing to him, indicated by a *shrug* of the *shoulders*!" Biographer Lucinda Hawksley concludes that "the likelihood of Liko having found Louise a more sympathetic confidante (in the true meaning of the word) than Beatrice was very high." Beatrice, known as "the shy princess," would live out the last part of her life as she had the first: devoted to her mother, and to the preservation—and sanitization—of her mother's words. Her life's work would become the rewriting and editing of her mother's diaries, in one of the greatest acts of censorship in history.

Dr. Reid did not give up in his mission to discredit Karim, and in 1897, he finally had some success. Earlier that year, in February, Dr. Reid had spoken with the queen "about the Munshi having a relapse of venereal disease." When told that Karim's gonorrhea had flared up again in December, the queen was "greatly taken aback." But it was Karim's self-serving and unseemly quest for publicity that finally gave the queen pause. A photo published in the *Daily Graphic* on October 16, 1897, showed the rounding queen, dressed in a white shawl and black feathered hat, signing papers as a portly Karim stood next to her, looking at the camera with a self-satisfied, challenging air. The caption was "The Queen's Life in the Highlands, Her Majesty receiving a lesson in Hindustani from the Munshi Hafiz Abdul Karim C.I.E." The photographer told Dr. Reid that this photograph—an embarrassing breach of household protocol—was published at Karim's insistence. When Dr. Reid told the queen, she wrote him a fourteen-page letter, blaming herself for allowing Karim to do it:

> I am terribly annoyed. . . . I don't know what to do. . . . I feel continually aggrieved at my Gentlemen wishing to spy upon and interfere with one of my people whom I have no personal reason or proof of doubting and I am greatly distressed at what has happened.

She begged Dr. Reid to try to put an end to the story and avoid scandal: "My peace of mind is terribly upset. I fear I have made great blunders in this business. . . . I can't read this through and would beg you to burn it as well as my letter this morning." But Karim remained.

When he later became king, in 1901, Bertie wanted to eradicate all traces of the friendship between his mother and an Indian clerk, and he had all the Munshi's papers burned in a large bonfire. Victoria had directed that Karim was to have a place in her funeral procession, but shortly after the funeral, Bertie ordered the Munshi and his wife to leave for India immediately. He sent detectives to India to monitor Karim in case he had smuggled confidential papers out of England. The Munshi returned to Agra, grew fatter on the land the queen had procured for him, and died in 1909, aged only forty-six. Karim never spoke ill of the royal family. His name will forever be conjoined with that of his doting, credulous queen.

One morning in 1896, Gladstone woke with a guilty start. He had been dreaming he was having breakfast with Victoria. They appeared to have had a sexual encounter, which involved some fumbling and confusion about "the how and where of access." This dream horrified him—it was of course unimaginable that he and the queen would ever have been so intimate. There would be a faint moment of rapprochement, though, the next year. In 1897, thanks to Victoria's daughter Louise, Gladstone and his wife, Catherine, saw Victoria in a hotel in Cannes. For the first time, Victoria and Gladstone, both half-blind, elderly, and walking with difficulty, shook hands. The queen pronounced them both "much aged." The two ironclads spoke for a few minutes, after which Gladstone decided "the Queen's peculiar faculty and habit of conversation had disappeared." He was eighty-seven years old and struggling with facial neuralgia, cheek cancer, and catarrh, which had prompted a retreat from any political activity. The last speech he gave was on September 24, 1896—on renewed atrocities by the Turks in Bulgaria. While preparing for her Diamond Jubilee in 1897, Victoria did not ask Gladstone to take any part in it.

In the early morning hours of May 19, 1898, four years after leaving office, Gladstone died. The cause of death was recorded as "syncope senility"; his heart had stopped beating. Even the solemnity of his death did not prevent Victoria being churlish. She was reluctant to write to Catherine Gladstone because she had simply not liked the man: "How can I say I am sorry when I am not?" In a letter to Vicky, she explained her abiding disrespect: "I cannot say that I think he was 'a great Englishman.' He was a clever man, full of talent, but he never tried to keep up the honor and prestige of Gt Britain. He gave away the Transvaal & he abandoned Gordon, he destroyed the Irish church & he tried to separate England from Ireland & he set class against class. The harm he did cannot be easily undone. . . . But he was a good & vy religious man." Gladstone's death was, very oddly, not noted in the Court Circular. Victoria later told the prime minister, Lord Salisbury, that this had been "entirely an oversight."

A quarter of a million people came to gaze at Gladstone's body lying in state in Westminster Abbey before his funeral on May 28. Bertie, who had always had a friendly relationship with Gladstone, acted as pallbearer at the funeral, as did his only surviving son, the future George V. When she heard of Bertie's intention to carry her former foe's coffin, Victoria telegraphed him to ask why: Whose advice had he followed and what was the precedent? The Prince of Wales wrote back bluntly that he was not aware of a precedent and had not acted on advice. In a subsequent telegram to Catherine Gladstone, the highest praise Victoria could summon for Gladstone, the man now described as the colossus of the Victorian age, was that he was "one of the most distinguished statesmen of my reign." The queen would not be commissioning a rash of statues of the Grand Old Man in the towns of Britain. Prime ministers, children, friends, and relatives continued to die around Victoria as she pressed on: some of her subjects were beginning to think her immortal.

CHAPTER 29

The Diamond Empire

No-one ever, I believe, has met with such an ovation as was given to me. . . . The cheering was quite deafening, and every face seemed to be filled with real joy.

—QUEEN VICTORIA, JUNE 22, 1897

There is no one depressed in *this* house; we are not interested in the possibilities of defeat; they do not exist.

—QUEEN VICTORIA, 1900

A reign that spanned six decades, Oscar Wilde declared, should be celebrated with aplomb. For the occasion of Victoria's Diamond Jubilee, the dramatist decided to throw a marvelous party for the local village children in Berneval-sur-Mer in France, where he had gone following his release from English prison on charges of gross indecency. Sporting a bright turquoise shirt, he ladled out "strawberries and cream, apricots, chocolates, cakes and sirop de grenadine . . . a huge iced cake with *Jubilee de la Reine Victoire* in pink sugar, just rosette with green, and a wreath of red roses around it all." He gave the children musical instruments as presents and tried to arrange them into an orchestra playing Britain's national anthem. Wilde conducted as horns blasted and accordions swung.

More champagne was imported in 1897, the year of Victoria's Diamond Jubilee, than in any year before in British history. It was a celebration of imperial might, as well as the core contradiction of Victorianism: massive change and expansion coupled with an apparently unchanged monarch. Victoria was celebrated as the pivot point of the empire, almost the very axis of the earth. The somberly dressed seventy-eight-year-old woman had now reached near-mythical status. Remote tribes in Papua New Guinea worshipped her, stern statues of her studded cities across the globe, and people claimed to spy her profile in American mountain ranges. In W. T. Stead's journal the *Review of Reviews,* her image was placed next to Abraham Lincoln's: "The high water mark of realized success in the Evolution of Humanity," the journal declared, could be seen in "the production of the supreme American man in the person of Abraham Lincoln and the supreme English woman in the person of Queen Victoria."

When her chair was wheeled out onto the Buckingham Palace balcony on the day of her Diamond Jubilee, a voice heard amid the noise yelled, "Go it, old girl!" Victoria, at seventy-eight, was too crippled to step out of her carriage; an open-air service was held outside St. Paul's Cathedral so that she did not need to. Victoria believed her six decades of work gave her the right to demand that she not have to leave her carriage, that she would not be compelled to pay for the celebration, and that no pompous state ceremonial was necessary. She did not want to host a clutch of royals, at great expense and inconvenience, for the second time in a decade, and she therefore ordered that no reigning kings or queens be invited. This included her first grandson, Kaiser Wilhelm II, who was furious. The focus of this Jubilee, instead of visiting monarchs and aristocrats, became empire—a territory that now spanned a quarter of the globe.

Many subjects believed their queen now had some mystical power to control the skies: the sun shone brilliantly as her carriage rolled

along the streets on the day of the Jubilee. When an enormous bal-
loon marked VICTORIA floated up through the trees, a small girl
stopped to stare: "Look! There's Queen Victoria going to Heaven!"
Victoria sat under her black lace parasol, overwhelmed and weeping.
Bertie's wife, Alix, tenderly patted her hand. The author Edmund
Gosse explained the lion's roar of the crowd as the result of "a latent
magnetism passing between the Queen and her people, over the
heads of her official interpreters. It was as though the Queen spoke to
her subjects face to face, as if her very presence hypnotized them."
She never failed to be affected by the curtain of sound that swept the
crowds before her carriage. The bond between Victoria and her subjects was stronger than ever. Life expectancy in those years was forty-
six, and only one in twenty British people was over sixty-five. Almost
everyone in the crowd would have known only Victoria as their sovereign.

The queen's peers were growing older too. Tennyson had passed
away five years before the Diamond Jubilee, at the stately age of
eighty-three. Charles Dickens had died after a stroke in 1870, aged
fifty-eight. Charles Darwin's heart had failed in 1882, when he was
seventy-three. George Eliot—or Mary Ann Evans—published *Mid-
dlemarch* eight years before she died in 1880 at age sixty-one. General
Tom Thumb had lasted only to forty-five. But the formidable
seventy-seven-year-old Florence Nightingale, who had been bedridden for thirty years with what is most likely to have been chronic
brucellosis, stemming from the fever she contracted in the Crimea,
was still conducting her prodigious work on sanitation, famine, and
hospital planning while propped up on pillows in bed. Nightingale
arranged for some illuminations to hang from her balcony in London
for the Jubilee: a VR in lights, with red calico.

Victoria was now aging and increasingly blind. Yet she still had a
certain grace. Many who encountered her gushed about her theatrical sense of timing, her gracious movement, her smile, her silvery
voice. When writer Arthur Benson met her two years before she died,
he was startled by her voice: "It was so slow and sweet—some ex-

traordinary *simplicity* about it—much higher than I imagined it & with nothing cracked or imperious or . . . wobbly. It was like the voice of a very young tranquil woman." There are very few photographs of the queen smiling, which is unfortunate: only the stern profile has been preserved. Part of the reason is that for many years, long exposures were needed to take photographs. As Vicky once wrote to her, "my own dear Mama's face has a charm that . . . no photograph can reproduce." But Victoria did publish a "very like" photo of her beaming at her Jubilee, in which you can see how a smile transformed her face. This she did despite the objections of her daughters Helena and Beatrice, who did not think it appropriate for the queen to smile so broadly.

Mark Twain sat in one of the temporary wooden stands on the Strand to watch the Jubilee procession. Troops from Australia, India, Africa, Canada, New Zealand, and the West Indies made their way around London, looping from Buckingham Palace to St. Paul's Cathedral. Twain, who was then living in Europe and had been commissioned to report on the Jubilee for the *San Francisco Examiner,* was dazzled. He wrote: "British history is two thousand years old, and yet in a good many ways the world has moved further ahead since the Queen was born than it moved in all the rest of the two thousand years put together. . . . She has seen more things invented than any other monarch that ever lived." Since Victoria ascended to the throne in 1837, the lives of people in her country and around the world had been transformed by the invention of the railway, steamship, telegraph, telephone, sewing machine, electric light, typewriter, camera, and more.

Victoria had reigned longer than any British monarch before her, and she was the head of the largest empire in history. They were cheering, Twain wrote, "the might of the British name," for "sixty years of progress and accumulation, moral, material and political." From 1558 to 1603, Queen Elizabeth ruled a land of a hundred thousand square miles and fewer than five million people, but by the late

1800s, Victoria oversaw one-fourth of the inhabitable part of the world containing four hundred million people. Over her lifetime, the number of people on the planet quintupled. Victoria witnessed the expansion of suffrage, the creation of cheap newspapers, and the development of copyright, anesthetics, and modern sanitation. Two hundred crimes previously subject to capital punishment were removed from the statute books. Citizens had won the right to unionize and seen a cut in daily working hours from twelve to eight. There had been a profound push toward equality. In the years she was queen, Victoria saw "woman freed from the oppression of many burdensome and unjust laws; colleges established for her," as Twain wrote, "in some regions rights accorded to her which lift her to near to political equality with man, and a hundred bread-winning occupations found for her where hardly one existed before—among them medicine, the law, and professional nursing."

At the time of Victoria's birth, women were forced to play the role of "angels of the house": they were seen as guardians of morality, which had effectively trapped them in their homes. By the end of the nineteenth century, a new generation tried to hack through old shibboleths. Many women were now living alone, or with female roommates, in a shift dubbed "the revolt of the daughters." Married women, too, had gradually won some rights over their incomes, children, and bodies. In a crucial 1891 case, *Regina v. Jackson,* a husband—Mr. Jackson—had kidnapped his wife and detained her in his house with guards. He brought her to court for the "restitution of conjugal rights," and lost. The judge held that he had no such right. This was hailed as a momentous decision that ended a husband's right to control the body of his wife. (Just two years prior, a judge in *Regina v. Clarence* had held that a man had the right to rape his wife, even when suffering from gonorrhea. There was no concept of "marital rape" in England and Wales until 1991.) *Regina v. Jackson* built on the Married Women's Property Acts of 1870 and 1882, which stated that a wife could control her own earnings and assets (and that a wife was a separate legal entity from her husband), and the 1886 Infant

Custody Act, which introduced the idea that the children's welfare must be considered when awarding custody.

Slowly, women gained toeholds in public life. In 1894, the new passage of the Local Government Act meant that all women who owned property could vote in local elections, become poor-law guardians (who managed local welfare for the unemployed, elderly, and vulnerable), and act on school boards. In 1897, as the country prepared for another round of Jubilee celebrations and troops gathered in Africa, the National Union of Women's Suffrage Societies was formed, linking a host of smaller groups under the leadership of the redoubtable Millicent Garrett Fawcett. For the first time, a bill to give women the vote passed its second reading in the House of Commons. Every inch of progress would be hard and bitterly fought, but by the time of the Jubilee, the small advances for women were touted as a triumph of the British Empire.

Women, men, young, old, British or foreign, the entire Diamond Jubilee spectacle was a crowing of empire; newspapers boasted of British achievement, all of it embodied in a tiny, squat, steadfast figure clad in black. Britain had won wars against Russia, and in India, Afghanistan, Ethiopia, Ashanti, Burma, Canada, New Zealand, and Egypt. Signs of progress were cited repeatedly: the grain tariffs had been repealed, the poor laws amended, and food was cheaper, housing better, wages higher. Members of Parliament no longer dressed in the old-fashioned outfits of silk stockings and pantaloons (as if "for a garden party"), and no one took snuff anymore while addressing the House of Commons. (Members of the American Congress did not give up their communal snuffbox until the mid-1930s.)

The cost of empire, though, was great. Millions of Chinese died in the Opium Wars between 1839 and 1842, again in 1856–60, and again in the Taiping Rebellion of 1850–64 that General Gordon had helped quash. Mass deaths of indigenous people in Canada, Argentina, Uruguay, Paraguay, Australia, New Zealand, and the Pacific Islands occurred under Victoria's rule. Native people were trotted before her as spectacle and trophy. Victoria marveled at their strangeness but, like most, did not consider what British occupation of their lands had meant for them. The assumption of many in England was that colonization meant only progress, not subjugation. There had been devastating famines in India and bloody wars in Afghanistan, and a scramble for the wealth of Africa that had seen the rights of local people brutally trampled. The spoils of empire sparkled on Victoria's neck and wrists, hung on her walls, and scented her palace kitchens. The worst war was still to come, though, a barbaric war that would mark the beginning of the decline of the imperial expansion Victoria had championed.

Indian servants now carried the frail queen-empress from room to room. A life of sycophancy and lack of questioning meant that her every desire was indulged, and yet she still yearned for what she could not command: love and companionship. As she limped through the final decades of her life, most days were spent marking what had already passed. Yet she also longed for longevity; every New Year she prayed that she might be spared for another year, that her faculties would be left intact, especially what was remaining of her eyesight, and that she would be able to lead her country.

In Europe, the next generation of leaders was rising as dark currents of nationalism began to swell again and bulge against national borders. Boys who read about the great queen's Diamond Jubilee would nurture fantasies of their own great nations. Adolf Hitler was eight that year, and toying with becoming a priest. Benito Mussolini was thirteen, rebelling against the monks who taught him, bullying fellow students, and amusing himself by hitting his only friend repeatedly over the head with a brick. Josef Stalin was eighteen, training with Russian Orthodox priests—and, like Wilhelm, had a deformed left arm that he tried to mask in portraits. The British and American opponents of these megalomaniacal future leaders were also training in politics and war. Franklin D. Roosevelt was fifteen when Victoria celebrated her Jubilee, a good student at an Episcopal boarding school, preparing to study at Harvard. Winston Churchill was twenty-two, and veering from fighting wars to reporting on them. Neville Chamberlain was a successful ship manufacturer at twenty-eight. In America, the progressive reformer Teddy Roosevelt, who was thirty-eight, had just been made assistant secretary of the navy; a few years later, in 1901, the cowboy-soldier would become vice president of the United States. But one person they all knew, and whose reach, lands, and wealth they envied, was the British queen.

It is difficult to imagine that Victoria knew nothing of the ugly, brutal results of the scramble for Africa in the late nineteenth century. In these years, Belgium, Italy, Portugal, Spain, Germany, Britain, and France all greedily grabbed large tracts of Africa in pursuit of mineral wealth. Europeans first reached the southernmost part of Africa in 1488, when the Portuguese explorer Bartolomeu Dias sailed around the Cape of Good Hope. But it was not until 1652 that Dutch, German, and French Huguenot settlers established themselves in South Africa permanently—the ancestors of the Boers, or Afrikaners. In 1795 the British began to arrive. The first great rupture with Britain occurred in the early 1830s when the British abolished slavery, which the Boers viewed as important to their economy and in keeping with their sense of racial hierarchy. Many Boers migrated north in "the Great Trek" during the 1830s and 1840s to be free from British rule, and, after a string of bloody battles with the native Zulus, settled in the Transvaal (also known as South African Republic) and the Orange Free State. What we now know as South Africa was then comprised of four entities: the Orange Free State and the Transvaal, both Boer republics; and the two British colonies, Cape Colony and Natal.

Gems and gold would tear the fragile peace apart. When diamonds were discovered in Kimberley, a town in the Northern Cape, in 1869, the British dropped their vague acceptance of Boer control of wealthy African regions. Britain began to push for a South African federation in which they would be dominant, pointing to the number of British subjects who had settled in the region. Migrants streamed to the southern tip of the continent to pan for gold, and new cities mushroomed across remote plains.

When vast gold deposits were discovered in the Transvaal in 1873, President Thomas François Burgers encouraged foreigners—Uitlanders—to settle in his near-bankrupt state, even allocating them two seats in the local parliament. But in 1877, the British annexed the Transvaal, with the support of Disraeli (despite Britain's having formally recognized its independence in 1852). Britain had just annexed large expanses of land across the globe, in Fiji, Malaya, and the West African Gold Coast, claiming it was forced to do so because of the dysfunction of indigenous governments. The Transvaal, though, was the final refuge of the Boers. Three years later, in 1880, they rose to fight for it, with some success. The defeated British agreed to keep the republic under their suzerainty, meaning Britain would have some control but the Transvaal would be internally autonomous. Victoria saw this as a humiliating concession and blamed Gladstone for carelessly losing this lucrative land.

From 1870 to 1914, Europe went from having control of 10 percent of Africa to 90. During these decades of plundering and colonization, many millions of Africans died; one of the most egregious and violent offenders was Victoria's cousin. The Belgian king, Leopold II, the eldest son of her uncle Leopold, was responsible for some of the greatest human rights abuses of the nineteenth century. He ascended the throne in 1865, four years after Albert died, and took control of the Congo as a private citizen. He exploited the ivory and rubber trades there, forcing local populations to work for him. Those who did not meet his deadlines were maimed or killed. The Belgian government estimated that half of the Congo's population of twenty million died under his rule before they forced Leopold II to hand control of the lands over to the state.

King Leopold II was creepy and frightfully ugly, with a particularly large nose. In 1885, he was named in a court case as having paid £800 a month for a regular supply of English virgins to be sent to

Belgium; he especially liked girls aged ten to fifteen (Bertie had also been named as a client of the English brothel that King Leopold II had connections with). His cousin Queen Victoria continued to receive him—perhaps out of respect for his father. Marie Mallet, one of Victoria's ladies of the bedchamber, found him repulsive. In 1897, she recalled a visit from Leopold II to Balmoral: "He can only shake hands with two fingers as his nails are so long that he dares not run the risk of injuring them. He is an unctuous old monster, very wicked, I believe. We imagine he thinks a visit to the Queen gives him a fresh coat of whitewash, otherwise why does he travel five hundred miles in order to partake of lunch." When he visited Victoria, he complained of the Belgian parliament's move toward universal suffrage, which she agreed was "greatly to be deprecated." He also spoke to her about the Congo, though she does not say what about.

Leopold II made a fortune from the Congo. He taxed locals so harshly that many starved; local cannibalistic mercenaries massacred those who did not pay. The shocking human rights abuses were exposed by the British consul, Sir Roger Casement, in 1904, and later satirized by Mark Twain.*

During Victoria's Golden Jubilee, a cancer was growing on the throat of her son-in-law Fritz. Now, after her Diamond Jubilee, Victoria would discover a cancer was probably also spreading across the chest of his widow, her beloved daughter Vicky. Vicky had been afflicted with a host of odd ailments for decades: nerve pain, arthritis, colic, back pain, rashes, fevers, and swollen eyes. (Some continue to speculate that both she and her mother suffered from the amorphously defined porphyria that had felled King George III. This poorly understood disorder, whose symptoms range from migraine

---

* Leopold II's habits never changed. At age sixty-seven, he impregnated a teenage prostitute, whom he installed in a villa and gave a title. He married her just days before he died in 1909. Belgians booed his funeral procession.

to madness, is so nebulous that it became a catchall diagnosis for anyone, especially those of royal or Hanoverian stock, who was suffering from a variety of maladies.) But in 1898, Vicky received a far grimmer diagnosis: breast cancer. She would outlive her mother by only five months.

All seven of Victoria's surviving children had been present to mark her sixty years' reign, as well as the two widowed spouses of Alice and Leopold (Prince Louis of Hesse and Princess Helena of Waldeck and Pyrmont). There had been much loss in the decade since her last Jubilee. A graying fifty-five-year-old Bertie was still grieving the loss of Eddy, his eldest son, and had been embarrassed by another scandal in 1891 when he was called to testify in a court case because a friend had cheated at cards. Now fifty-two and suffering poor health, Affie was bored at Coburg, trying to distract himself from money and marriage troubles with drink. Helena, the daughter whom Victoria neither favored nor bothered as much as the rest, was now forty-one, had four children (she had also lost two babies; one was stillborn and another died when just a few days old), and had immersed herself in charity work. Her husband, Prince Christian of Schleswig-Holstein-Sonderburg-Augustenburg, had unfortunately lost an eye when his brother-in-law Arthur shot him accidentally when out hunting. Arthur was happily married with three children. Beatrice was forty, widowed, and had four children. The family beauty, Louise, who had settled into companionate affection with her husband, Lord Lorne, hosted a fancy dress ball at Devonshire House on the night of the Jubilee, at which guests were invited to dress up in a historical costume predating 1820 (Victoria was born in 1819). Bertie dressed as the Grand Prior of the Order of Saint John of Jerusalem, while Alix came as the pretty, poetic French queen Marguerite de Valois.

In February 1899, less than two years after the Diamond Jubilee, Alfred's only son, also named Alfred, died of what was pronounced to be tuberculosis. (Alfred junior, mad with rage over a fight with his

mother about a commoner he wanted to marry, had in fact shot himself during his parents' wedding anniversary celebration and survived only two more weeks.) To Victoria's annoyance, he was buried
on the tenth of February, her own sacred wedding anniversary. (She
would never abandon her fixation on anniversaries, whether dark or
bright.) Alfred senior—"Affie," then the Duke of Saxe-Coburg—
died of throat cancer the following year, just days shy of his fifty-sixth
birthday; he was the third of Victoria's children to die in her lifetime.
On hearing the news, she cried out: "My 3rd Grown up child, besides
3 very dear sons-in-law. It is hard at 81!" She knew the horror of losing his own son had weakened him. It felt as if the year was full of
"nothing but sadness & horrors of one kind & another."

As Victoria was trundled around the gardens in her pony chair,
the memories of the beautiful, clever young Affie pressed in on her
vividly, and painfully. He had so resembled and pleased Albert, yet in
moving to his father's homeland in his adult years he had become
miserable and loveless. Time wrinkled, and Victoria was hurled back
to those golden hours when Affie and his siblings sat on Albert's back,
riding him like a horse, chortling when they toppled off, on so many
happy days at Osborne and Balmoral. Now all was shadow. The day
after Affie's funeral in 1900, the Boers derailed another train and captured British prisoners. Just a few weeks later, one of Victoria's grandsons would die fighting in Africa.

On October 11, 1899, the Second Anglo-Boer War broke out. Few
things concentrated Victoria's mind as much as military conflict. She
bade many of the troops farewell in person, and recorded details of
the battles in her journal with a palpable anxiety. She was now eighty
years old, but she maintained a keen interest in her army and continued to argue for more resources and men. While she did not see herself as a natural imperialist—writing of China, for example, that the
world at large should not have the impression that we will not let
anyone but ourselves have anything—she was eventually persuaded

of the case for war in Africa. She believed that Britain should protect its subjects and territory. Her caveats were that the poor not be disproportionately burdened by a war tax and that the horses sent to fight be well treated.

The case made for war was straightforward enough. The public was told they needed to protect the oppressed Uitlanders in the Transvaal, most of whom were British citizens, against a tyrannical President Paul Kruger and his Afrikaner government. But several countries were also vying for control of the vast deposits of gold discovered in the Witwatersrand of Transvaal in 1886. Sir Arthur Conan Doyle, the creator of Sherlock Holmes, went to South Africa as a volunteer doctor and said the war was simply a fight over "one of the great treasure chests of the world."

In March 1899, the beleaguered Uitlanders sent a petition with over twenty-one thousand signatures to Victoria, making a direct appeal for protection and warning her that the Boers were preparing for war. They complained of the lack of a free press, the expulsion of British subjects at the will of the president, and overtaxation; they had few rights and were not allowed to meet. The police, explained Henry Ponsonby's replacement, Arthur Bigge, "are entirely composed of Boers, and behave in the most arbitrary and indeed oppressive manner, and are responsible for the murder of one British subject." Arthur Balfour advised Victoria that "without the threat of force, immediate or remote, it is certain that nothing will be done." On October 10, 1899, the South African republics sent a forty-eight-hour ultimatum insisting the British evacuate their troops from Natal and the Cape. When they failed to budge, the Boers invaded British colonies and surrounded the crucial towns of Mafeking, Kimberley, and Ladysmith.

Victoria devoured the reports that came throughout the fall of 1899, sickened by the details. The initial defeats were crushing. She recorded the context of all her discussions, dissected the frequent telegrams she received from commanders at the front, visited the wounded, studied the faces of soldiers' wives for worry, and personally replaced the bugle of a fourteen-year-old boy who had been shot on the field. She argued vehemently, as she had during all conflicts she supported, for more troops to be sent. The siege of Ladysmith, between November 1899 and February 1900, preoccupied her for months. But her accounts of what she was told make it clear that Victoria was receiving spin and lies about the war effort, doubtless in part to lift her spirits, as well as to impress upon her the stoicism of her commanders. She was regularly told the men had done their best when they were lying dead in fields; she was told that they didn't mind the bother of the war and were jolly well glad to be there and fight.

Even at eighty, Victoria demanded her full rights as monarch. When the Cabinet decided to replace commander in chief Lord Wolseley with Lord Roberts, she made it known she was "deeply aggrieved" she had not been told and her advice not sought. Roberts proved to be an effusive, regular correspondent to the queen, although she often upbraided him about the progress of the war. She constantly made her opinions on the conduct of the war known. She knitted too: scarves, comforters, and caps, to be sent directly to her "dear brave soldiers." When these hotly desirable items were snapped up by her officers, she sent a hundred thousand tins of chocolate decorated with her portrait to her men on New Year's. One tin, lodged in a haversack, deflected a bullet, saving a man's life. An attempt was made to collect the images of every man killed in battle so that Victoria could place them in an album; she wrote to the mothers and widows of those lost. She also visited the wounded; though she had to be lifted from carriage to chair, she was determined to attend hospitals and reviews because she knew what her presence would mean to the men.

Morale was one of the queen's primary concerns. When the temporary head of the Foreign Office, Arthur Balfour, came to see her at Windsor with dismal news of a terrible defeat in December 1899, she said plainly, "Please understand that there is no one depressed in *this* house; we are not interested in the possibilities of defeat; they do not exist." Morale was also the reason why, throughout the war, Victoria resisted persistent calls for an inquiry into the conduct of the Boer War. She correctly predicted that such an inquiry could lower morale, but delaying it had the far worse side effect of covering up, and allowing to continue, the British errors and abuses that had been occurring in South Africa. She wrote:

> The Queen must urge on Mr. Balfour very strongly the necessity of resisting these unpatriotic and unjust criticisms of our Generals and of the conduct of the war. If the Government are firm and courageous the country will support them.... You must all show a firm front, and not let it be for a moment supposed that we vacillate in the least. An enquiry after the war itself is over can be held out, but not now. No doubt the War Office is greatly at fault, but it is the whole system which must be changed, and that cannot be just now.

Victoria worried that any problems might be reported back to the Boers and others, smearing Britain's reputation when what they needed was cohesion and strong spirits. She was so grateful for Irish commandos fighting in the war effort that she canceled a vacation to the Continent and went to Ireland instead, her first trip there in thirty-nine years. She was also acutely conscious of race relations within the British military. The fact that Indian soldiers were "auxiliaries" mostly working at the rear of the other forces mystified and angered her. In February 1900, she pleaded with Salisbury: "Why will you not call the whole force out? It could be done.... Not only have Boers invaded Zululand, but employed natives to fight against us. Surely this justifies our using Indians."

She passed her days scouring telegrams. Lord Kitchener was sending depressing missives about the opposition to British troops in South Africa, arguing that the initial defeats the British suffered boosted the number of Boer recruits significantly. As they waited for months to see the besieged township of Ladysmith won, Victoria urged Salisbury to send more men, arguing that the government had failed to invest in increasing the numbers of armed troops since the 1870s despite her urging. She was "horrified" at the "terrible" casualties reported and insisted no movement be made without more troops. She asked: "Would it be possible to warn the young officers not to expose themselves more than is absolutely necessary?" What she did not then know was that the conflict was marked by many deaths resulting from "friendly fire"; this would have devastated her. Victoria's last entry about the war in 1900, on December 31, was glum: "The news from South Africa was not very good. A post of our troops has been rushed by the enemy, and a gun was taken. We have, however, reoccupied the post."

There was growing unease in Britain about the war. Anger grew in Europe and Ireland about what was seen as Britain's unnecessary intervention. In 1900, a fifteen-year-old Italian protester tried to kill Bertie and Alix on a train in Brussels. (They were unharmed.) Then, one of Victoria's most adored grandsons, the cricket-loving Prince Christian Victor, the eldest son of Helena, died of enteric fever while fighting in the war. He was thirty-three and had fought as an officer in several campaigns in Africa. Victoria, already bent with the grief of the defeats, was now shattered. Christian was buried in Pretoria, near his comrades, according to his wishes. Back in Scotland, his grandmother the queen lost interest in food, was unable to sleep, and grew listless. When Dr. Reid saw her on October 29, 1900, she cried almost constantly and was "most depressed." Her journal was littered with the deaths of relatives and friends and the tragedy of this terrible war; it had all become unbearable.

She was slowly growing feebler. For years Victoria had been told to eat less, and her girth had attested to her robust appetites and inability, at times, even to walk for exercise. But by November 10, 1900, she had grown "emaciated" and had lost interest in food. Dr. Reid, on whom Victoria was now dependent, tried to get her to sleep with the opium-based Dover's Powder. Dr. Reid wrote to Bertie to tell him his mother was deteriorating, and he advised against the queen's traveling. Most of those close to Victoria were unaware of the seriousness of her condition, though, and Bertie was no exception. The man who stood to inherit the throne reminded the doctor: "The Queen has much extraordinary vitality and pluck." But by December, in Osborne, the queen stayed in her room, only sipping broth and milk.

As Victoria lay ill and wretched in her bed, the reformer Emily Hobhouse was carefully packing trunks with food and medicine for the women and children locked up in British concentration camps in South Africa. In 1900, in an attempt to combat the Boers' guerrilla warfare tactics, the British had begun systematically burning the homes of Boers in the Orange Free State and the Transvaal, in what was known as "scorched earth policy." The numbers in these camps, where whites were kept separate from blacks, began to swell. Hobhouse—whom Kitchener would call "that bloody woman"— had worked as a welfare campaigner and was determined to bring medical supplies to the encamped. A striking forty-year-old woman with intense brown eyes, Hobhouse sailed for South Africa in January 1901. She was horrified by the death and squalor in tent camps she described as "a living grave." There was little food, medicine, or hygiene, and the camps were teeming with typhoid and blackwater fever. By 1902, twenty-eight thousand whites and fourteen thousand black Africans had died in these horrific grounds, almost double the number of British men who died fighting.

The queen had no idea of the atrocities occurring at British hands in these camps; the details only emerged, to great controversy, after her death. She would have been mortified. (Even her directive about horses had proven useless; hundreds of thousands were slaughtered.) She had disapproved of "hysterical" women sailing to South Africa, "often without imperative reasons," and believed they were a nuisance to the soldiers and officers there. (Lord Roberts prevented women from entering the Orange State unless they had a wounded son or husband, to please the queen.) The historian Jenny de Rueck says the barbaric South African concentration camps "arguably laid down a template for civilian suffering that subsequently the Herero of German South West Africa, the Jews of Europe, the Russians under Stalin, the Cambodians under Pol Pot and most recently the civilians in Rwanda and in all parts of the former Yugoslavia have endured." Gladstone had died the year before the war began; it's certain that he would have been incensed to discover this abuse too.

The likes of Conan Doyle trumpeted the glories of the war, of fighting alongside "ghillies from the Sutherland deer forests, bushmen from the back blocks of Australia, hard men from Ontario, dandy sportsmen from India and Ceylon, the horsemen of New Zealand." He crowed that "on the plains of South Africa, the blood brotherhood of the Empire was sealed." But the seamier side of the war was also being reported, with journalists' dispatches daily slicing through government propaganda. The publisher W. T. Stead sensationally accused British troops of raping women. An illustrious group fought or reported from South Africa: Mahatma Gandhi—who sympathized with the Boers but supported the empire—organized the Indian Ambulance Corps. Lord Baden-Powell commanded a garrison during a 217-day siege on Mafeking. The British poet Rudyard Kipling, the future British prime minister Winston Churchill, and the Australian writer Banjo Paterson all worked as war correspondents. (Paterson described Churchill as "the most curious combination of ability and swagger," adding sharply: "Persons burdened with inferiority complexes might sit up and take notice.") This was the first war the British had fought against Europeans—or those descended from Europeans—since the Crimean War in 1853.

It was also the last of the great imperialist, expansionist wars, when the empire stretched tight over land that rejected its rule. The brutal behavior of the soldiers left a scar on South Africans for generations. Crucially, the nexus between war and glory, between empire and military display, was severed. Perhaps more troublingly for the political class, the British argument that the empire represented the best of democracy was revealed as false—the Boer War had shown the rights of local people being trampled on for economic gain, and the lives of women and children in the camps lost through neglect and inhumanity.

By the end of 1900, the morality of the war was sharply in question. As Stanton Coit, the editor of *Ethical World,* wrote: "Never in this generation has there been among Englishmen of all classes so much self-searching, such self-doubt, as now." Before the war had ended, Victoria's world began to shrink and tremble, and the stout talisman grew thin and frail. As the nineteenth century turned to the twentieth, the empire was dimming, and so was its great queen.

Victoria had been ailing for some time. She grew distracted and melancholy. Cataracts blurred her vision. She struggled to sleep, yet she became unusually placid and was unruffled by the things that once irritated her. In early December 1900, she was "full of morbid ideas of imaginary pains." Dr. Reid settled her with opiates. On December 7, he described her as "nervous, complaining and childish." She traveled to Osborne for Christmas and drank milk and egg flips, but she skipped most meals and went to bed early. On Christmas Day, Lady Churchill, who had been in Victoria's court for half a century, died in her bed at Osborne. The news was broken gently to an ailing Victoria. "The loss to me," read her diary entry, "is not to be told."

On New Year's Day 1901, as Australia was officially declared a federation, Victoria wrote in her journal: "Another year begins & I am feeling so weak & unwell that I enter upon it badly." Dr. Reid sought a second opinion, which confirmed there had been many weeks of "cerebral degeneration." On January 16, after two decades of service, Reid saw Victoria in bed for the first time. She was drowsy and thin, lying curled up on her right side. He "was struck by how small she appeared." Uncharacteristically, nothing annoyed her. The next day, she was moved to her smaller bed, and a screen was placed around her so the men could not see her. When the princesses came to visit her, filing solemnly past her bed, she did not recognize them. The next night, Alix and Bertie sat up all night at her side, talking

The royal couple were instantly enchanted by Balmoral Castle when they first saw it in 1848. Victoria wrote that it "seemed to breathe freedom & peace making one forget the world & its sad turmoil."

Albert thrilled to the solitude of the Highlands, telling his stepmother, "One rarely sees a human face; where the snow already covers the mountain tops, and the wild deer come creeping stealthily around the house. I, naughty man, have also been creeping stealthily after the harmless stags." Victoria waited anxiously for the news of her husband's haul.

THE DEATH OF ALBERT

A progressive thinker and polymath with a fierce work ethic, Albert played a crucial role in the creation of the modern monarchy nonpartisan, constitutional, and respectable. Even though he was just out of his thirties, Albert's punishing workload, melancholy, and poor health made him seem like a much older man.

The memorial portrait of Albert captured him as a young man, dressed like a Christian knight, his life's battle at an end. Victoria inscribed it: "I have fought a good fight, I have finished my course."

In 1862, just a few weeks after the death of her father, Princess Louise, a gifted artist, drew this image of Victoria dreaming of being reunited with Albert. The date was February 10, their anniversary.

In the period after Albert's death, Queen Victoria recreated sober mourning scenes for photographs, gathering her black-clad daughters around his bust. "The whole house," wrote one lady-in-waiting, "seems like Pompeii."

Her children dubbed him "the Queen's stallion," but Victoria proudly called John Brown her best friend, telling him: "No one loves you more than I do." Strong, strapping, and irreverent, Brown was the only man who could persuade Victoria to do something she did not want to do.

Victoria's flamboyant Tory prime minister Benjamin Disraeli made an art form of charm. He entertained and flattered Victoria, calling her his "Faery Queen."

The cerebral William Gladstone was made prime minister four times. He was adored by the British public but was utterly incapable of winning Victoria's favor. He said that "the Queen alone is enough to kill any man."

Victoria died in the arms of her grandson Kaiser Wilhelm II. Just fourteen years later he would be at war with England.

When Beatrice, Victoria's youngest child, married Henry of Battenberg, her mother did not talk to her for seven months. When the dashing Henry died on a ship off the coast of Africa, the two women became companions again.

Bertie, the future King Edward VII, was fond of gambling, horseracing, and brothels. Even as she grew old, Victoria was loath to hand over any official duties to her oldest son.

Abdul Karim, known as "the Munshi," inveigled his way into Victoria's affections as her servant and then as a clerk. Her family disliked and distrusted him.

Even at the age of eighty, Victoria demanded her full rights as monarch. She devoured reports of the Boer War, which broke out in 1899.

There are very few photographs of Victoria smiling, although she had a keen sense of humor. This was taken at her Golden Jubilee in 1887; her daughters thought it an inappropriate image for a monarch.

Scottish doctor James Reid attended Victoria conscientiously for the last decades of her life. She entrusted him with her instructions for burial, and with them the deepest secrets of her life. His immaculately preserved notebooks provide remarkable insights into the heart of a queen.

When Queen Victoria died in 1901, the streets were packed with dense crowds, and were peculiarly silent. Author Henry James said, "We all felt quite motherless."

gently to her. While planning her death, Victoria had been afraid that Bertie might try to override her instructions, and so on January 18 she had told Reid she did not wish to see him. But in her final moments, she was tender, asking her eldest son to "kiss her face." Her doctor watched her become more childlike, and he worried.

The last two decades had been physically torturous for Victoria. When she was properly examined for the first time, on her deathbed, her doctor found that Victoria had a prolapsed uterus and a ventral hernia—sources of significant pain and discomfort—both of which were most likely to have been caused by difficult labors and exacerbated by her subsequent weight gain. Perhaps it is unseemly, too personal to some, to reveal the ailments of a queen. But these conditions also explain some of Victoria's chronic pain and difficulty of movement. She struggled to walk unsupported from 1883, after her fall and the death of John Brown. Other pains she concealed and bore privately. This vulnerability made Victoria especially grateful to those who physically bore her up—John Brown and later her Indian servants. She was extremely sensitive about who might touch her body after she died— she stipulated that it must only be Dr. Reid and female attendants.

Her doctor quietly took charge. Knowing "the princesses would disapprove," Reid secretly sent a telegram to Kaiser Wilhelm, who had asked him to keep him informed about the queen's health. The telegram read: "Disquieting symptoms have developed which cause considerable anxiety. This is private. Reid." The princesses—especially Helena—had not wanted Bertie to come, either, and they made sure he was sent falsely optimistic notes. At Dr. Reid's insistence, Helena relented and Bertie was sent for on January 19. That afternoon, the first official and public bulletin was issued: "The Queen is suffering from great physical prostration accompanied by symptoms that cause anxiety." Arthur began the journey to England from Berlin, accompanied by Kaiser Wilhelm. Beatrice and Helena panicked and vowed to do whatever it took to stop their controversial nephew from stepping on English soil, firing off a telegram to Arthur. Dr. Reid's curious softness toward Wilhelm is best explained by his instinctive recognition of the tenderness that an otherwise cruel, hubristic man was capable of. Pugnacious and belligerent, Wilhelm not only mistreated his own mother but freely crossed his formidable grandmother, too, even, most recently, infuriating her by expressing his support for the Boers. But he also had a deep respect and affection for Victoria, loving her more than he did his own mother.

At 6 P.M. on January 21, Victoria revived and asked Reid if she was better. She then focused on him, worrying that he might be tired and need help. She then remarked there had been "much better news from South Africa today." Lying in her bed, ailing and frail, she asked Reid to stand next to her, and stared directly into his eyes. She was not, she told him firmly, ready to die. "I should like to live a little longer, as I have still a few things to settle. I have arranged most things, but there are still some left, and I want to live a little longer." Her hunger to live was strong, and starkly different from her husband's passivity four decades earlier. Reid reported: "She appealed to me in this pathetic way with great trust as if she thought I could make her live."

Downstairs at Osborne, Bertie, Helena, and Beatrice were still hoping to stave off Wilhelm's visit. Bertie decided to go to London and tell Wilhelm he could not see the queen at the moment, and that not even he had seen her, which was true. Upstairs, Reid and the maids lifted Victoria onto a smaller bed. Instructions she had created in 1875 had stipulated that "no one but John Brown" should watch over her when she died, with her female attendants. With Brown gone, that task fell to Reid.

Victoria was too blind to see who was standing around her in the small green room she had shared with Albert. Poor Vicky, then sixty, was holed up in her apartment in Prussia as cancer crawled across her organs. Sometimes, she wrote to her mother wretchedly, they could hear her cries of pain on the streets below. She could not eat or sleep; the pain was like "ever so many razors driven into my back." But three of Victoria's daughters stood there through the night—Helena, Louise, and Beatrice—as well as Bertie, Alix, Wilhelm, and Dr. Reid and the nurses and maids. Dr. Reid took pity on Wilhelm and allowed him to see Victoria for five minutes on his own. A bishop and the local vicar stood at the foot of her bed reciting Bible verses and praying. Victoria clung to life, grimly. Reid wrote to his wife: "I can't help admiring her determination not to give up the struggle while she can." The prayers went on for hours, until the men grew hoarse. They were asked to stop until it was clear Victoria was close to death. She lay impassive, stubborn, breathing.

At four o'clock on the afternoon of January 22, 1901, a blunt bulletin was issued from Osborne House: "The Queen is slowly sinking." Dr. Reid stationed himself beside her, and Wilhelm stood opposite, like two sentinels of grief, as the others drifted in and out of the room. At five o'clock, the two men dropped to their knees on either side of the bed, and each placed an arm behind her back, propping her up in a semi-upright position. Bertie sat silently at the end of the bed. Louise kneeled next to Dr. Reid. With a final, quiet breath, Victoria died in the arms of her doctor and her grandson. Wilhelm, who would be at war with England in just fourteen years, silently squeezed Reid's hand with gratitude and emotion. But it was Bertie who closed his mother's eyes, sealing the light out.

CHAPTER 30

The End of the Victorian Age:
"The Streets Were Indeed
a Strange Sight"

England's Queen is dead! The words sound as heavily as though one should say, "The sun is no longer in the sky!"

—MARIE CORELLI

It is like a roof being off a house to think of an England Queenless.

—ARTHUR BENSON

A profound, eerie silence hung over London on February 1, 1901. A great crowd stood crammed on streets and corners, standing at windows, and sitting on roofs, craning to catch a glimpse of the polished oak box. The sad silence was broken only by the rattling gun carriage bearing Queen Victoria's coffin. The novelist Maurice Baring said, "London was like a dead city. . . . One went about feeling as if one had cheated at cards." As the steam train carrying Victoria's coffin had rumbled along the track north from Portsmouth to London, thousands had knelt quietly in damp fields and bowed their heads. A crowd lining the rail lines at Battersea Park had silently raised their hats and sighed. Most of them had known no monarch other than the tiny eighty-one-year-old who ruled Britannia for sixty-three years, seven months, and two days.

The white-draped coffin had been placed on a gun carriage and was making its journey from Victoria Station to Paddington before going to Windsor. The pavements were thick with crowds of people dressed in black standing red-eyed in the cold February air. Flower girls in rags of crêpe pressed past people's elbows. The women's rights campaigner Josephine Butler felt as though she had lost a "dear friend": "Everybody is crying, & people's blinds are drawn down. It is a real, personal grief." Henry James stared out of a window at Buckingham Gate and marveled at the "incredibly and immeasurably vast" crowd: "We all felt, publicly, at first, quite motherless." Diarist Lady Monkswell, watching from a shop nearby, cried and trembled when she saw the coffin. "The streets were indeed a strange sight," she said, "thronged with chiefly decent, respectable & middle-aged people, every one in mourning. . . . I silently bid her farewell. The people stood uncovered & silent."

Britons found Victoria's death oddly unnerving—as though the cornerstone of a building had slipped and they were all walking, tilted, on a new earth. Grief was mingled with alarm. Some, who stood mute and cold, craning for a glimpse of the passing coffin, were heard muttering, "God help us." Arthur Benson puzzled at the peculiarly personal grief: people wept openly in public, and even republicans who wanted an end to the monarchy found they were affected. Florence Nightingale ensured her entire house was in full mourning, wanting to do something "to show that one cares." One woman, who went to Hyde Park to watch the procession pass by, wrote: "Intense crowd, never saw anything like it, all silent." The passing of the previous monarch, William IV, by contrast, had barely been noted; no one cried at his funeral.

After an initial ruckus outside Osborne, where press reporters ran along the road screaming, "The Queen is dead!" a hush had quickly fallen over England. Henry James described the ensuing mood as "strange and indescribable": people spoke in whispers, as though scared of something. He was surprised at the reaction, because her death was not sudden or unusual: it was "a simple running down of the old used up watch," the death of an old widow who had thrown "her good fat weight into the scales of general decency." Yet in the following days, the American-born writer felt unexpectedly distressed. He, like so many, mourned the "safe and motherly old middle-class Queen, who held the nation warm under the fold of her big, hideous Scotch-plaid shawl." Victoria had become a kind of talisman of decorum and stability, a shield against upsetting turmoil. And now, her apotheosis was complete. *The Times* wrote that they had lost not just a mother but also a "personal benefactress" they had come almost to worship. The *New York Post* described her power as "mythic glory."

Victoria had wanted a funeral done "with *respect*—but *simply*." Having observed the military funerals held for Prince Leopold and then Beatrice's husband, Liko, she had decided she would also like one. No pomp, just officers in uniform and Highland pipers in kilts, and Beethoven. She insisted her coffin should be "always carried by soldiers or my servants & not by undertakers." She also asked that the gun carriage be muffled so it would not make as much noise as usual. At the center of the booming of guns, waving of plumes, and a fleet of escorting ships lay the still body of the queen. She had her deepest secret packed carefully beside her, concealed by layers of gauze and flowers, then charcoal lining, and a polished wood coffin. Only four people knew what was there: her doctor and three of her ladies. This secret would stay buried with her for a century.

On December 9, 1897, three years before she died, Victoria dictated the confidential, private instructions for her burial, which she said should always be carried by the most senior person traveling with her, and opened only upon her death. These instructions are contained in Dr. Reid's archives, held by his family at Trenton. In them she included a long list of objects she wanted placed in her coffin. On her hands she wanted five rings from Albert as well as rings from Feodora; her mother, Victoire; Louise; and Beatrice. She also wanted a plain, simple gold wedding ring that had belonged to the mother of John Brown, whom she described in effusive terms. Brown had worn the ring for a short time, she said, but Victoria had worn it constantly since his death and wished to be buried with it on her hand. Which finger was not specified.

The queen also requested that framed photographs of Albert and all her children and grandchildren be put in her coffin. She also wanted, as she explained in detail, a colored photograph of John Brown in profile, to be placed in a leather case with some locks of his hair, along with other photographs of him (which she had often carefully carried in her pocket), and placed in her hand. She also asked for the cast of Albert's hand, which she had always kept close to her, to be put in her coffin. As well, she wanted one of Albert's handkerchiefs and cloaks, a shawl made by Alice, and, she wrote, a pocket handkerchief of Brown, whom she praised for his faithfulness and singular devotion, to be placed not near but on her.

The royal family, who would soon set about destroying all record of the broad-shouldered Scot, was shielded from this sight. Dr. Reid was instructed to wrap her hand in gauze after placing Brown's hair in it, then flowers were discreetly arranged over the gauze. Even in death, Brown was with his queen, as well as Albert and her children: his mother's wedding ring on her finger, his portrait and hair in her hand, his handkerchief covering her body.

The gentle, meticulous Dr. Reid carefully arranged the contents of the queen's coffin with her ladies. Her body was measured, prepared, and slid into a silk dressing gown with the Order of the Garter draped across her chest. Her hair was cut off, and white flowers were strewn along the base of the veil that framed her face. Dr. Reid's wife, Susan, said she looked beautiful, "like a marble statue." On January 22, Bertie, the kaiser, Dr. Reid, and some others lifted her body into the coffin before the charcoal was packed in and the lid screwed down. Then the long trip to Windsor began.

The world shuddered at the news of the queen's death. Thousands of telegrams flew to Osborne. In London, actors walked off stages halfway through plays. Traffic stopped. In New York, the stock market closed for a day. In New Guinea, tribes remembered the divine, holy Mother who had loomed over them. In South Africa, Australia, Canada, and India and the farthest reaches of the vast English Empire, people stopped and prayed. Victoria had become an archetypal, maternal deity, cutting across boundaries of culture and religion. Muslims in London prayed for "the Sovereign of the greatest number of The True Believers in the world." The Indian viceroy, Lord Curzon, said the Indians thought of her almost as a saint. A Bengali aristocrat, Maharaja Bahadur Sir Jotindra Mohun Tagore, said she was like "the Great Universal Mother, who is worshipped as the Adya-Sakti of our [Hindu] mythology." In Persia, she was "the good angel who saved us from destruction."

Victoria had, in a way she did not anticipate, changed everything for women. She stirred something that was difficult to name, a longing, or a stiffening of the spine; she was a visible sign of a woman who adored her family, and yet had full rights and an independent income. H. G. Wells believed that at the moment the crown was placed on her head, there was a "stir of emancipation." His mother had followed Victoria's life—every word, joy, or hurt—with a "passionate loyalty":

> The Queen, also a small woman, was in fact my mother's compensatory personality, her imaginative consolation for all the restrictions and hardships that her sex, her diminutive size, her motherhood and all the endless difficulties of life,

imposed upon her. The dear Queen could command her husband as a subject and wilt the tremendous Mr. Gladstone with awe. How would it feel to be in that position? One would say this. One would do that. I have no doubt about my mother's reveries. In her latter years in a black bonnet and a black silk dress she became curiously suggestive of the supreme widow.

A good queen softened men, said the brilliant campaigner Josephine Butler: "It melts away some of their roughness & contempt of women." Even the suffragettes, whose cause the queen had dismissed, cited her example and influence. Emily Davison, who became the first martyr of the suffragette movement in 1913 when she was fatally injured under the hooves of the king's horse at the Derby, wrote a letter to *The Times* arguing that Victoria demonstrated there should be no such thing as "women's work": Victoria had read every document, made her own decisions, and was in no way a "mere figurehead." Without having ever read the queen's diary or studied her correspondence, Davison was right.

And her effect on women spanned the globe. A female Japanese magazine editor congratulated her on "awakening even in these distant parts the ambition to become empress over self." When the American civil rights leader Susan B. Anthony met Queen Victoria in 1899 at a reception in Windsor, she said she felt a "thrill . . . when looking in her wonderful face." Amelia Bloomer claimed, "If it is right for Victoria to sit on the throne in England it is right for any American Woman to occupy the Presidential Chair at Washington." Victoria's vantage point made clever women jealous. "I wonder," wrote the American author Sara Jane Lippincott—known as Grace Greenwood—in 1883, "if her Majesty has ever realized her blessed privilege in being able to converse freely with 'the first men of the age'; to avow her interest in politics . . . without fearing to be set down as a 'strong-minded female out of her sphere.'" But Victoria was so

busy making herself small so Albert would feel big, she did not realize how little she had to fight for.

Because of all this, Victoria's work gave a steady, rarely articulated
impetus to the suffragette campaign. At the time of her death, *Reyn
old's News* wrote that her life had "taught us the power we are will-
fully allowing to go to waste in the womanhood of the nation ...
there are many thousands of possible Victorias in the kingdom. No
longer can it be argued ... women are unfitted for public duties." She
was a symbol of female strength and intelligence. But perhaps her
singularity was what made her more palatable during an era of persistent inequality. She was one woman ruling; she was not, to most, a
sign that more would follow. She inherited power; she did not have
to fight for it or claw it away from men. It was placed gently upon her
head, like a divine burden.

There can be no doubt, though, that the women Victoria championed were mostly white and Western. She was furious if she heard
tales of a woman being groped on a train in England, or of someone
like Lady Florence Dixie being attacked near Windsor. But during
her reign, countless women in India, Afghanistan, and Africa were
raped, killed, and widowed in the series of "little wars" that expanded
the boundaries of the British Empire. Millions starved.* The incongruity of empire weighed on her—her strongest impulse was the
greatness of Britain, but she was distressed to hear of the cost at which
that greatness was achieved. The worst atrocities of the century were
occurring in British concentration camps in South Africa as Victoria
lay dying.

---

* A bedridden Florence Nightingale was working on India, where almost 29 million people died of starvation under British rule as the result of an interminable
round of famine. Nightingale spent many years trying to force the British government to alleviate the poverty there, campaigning for improved irrigation and
reform of land tenure. (Bostridge, *Florence Nightingale,* 473.) She was deeply disappointed when, even after the famine of 1877, in which 4 million died in Bombay and Madras alone, the schemes she supported were not adopted.

———

On February 4, 1901, the body of Queen Victoria was lowered into the mausoleum at Frogmore next to Albert. As her family closed the doors to the marbled grave, the sleet falling outside turned to snow, which brought stillness, silence, and the white funeral Victoria had always dreamed of. Her coffin was draped with white, the horses drawing her coffin were white, and the marble of her grave was white. The drapes everywhere were to be white and gold, and she ordered that no black should be seen anywhere. Victoria was adamant that death should not be associated with darkness, but light. Tennyson had given her this idea, saying to her that death was already dreadful enough, so why should it be "clothed with everything to make it worse?"

She was not to be a queen of scarlet, green, or rose: she had long abandoned plumage, and pretensions to her own beauty, and sought instead to surround herself with beautiful people. Her plain, undecorated demeanor prompted a shepherd boy to ask: "Why don't she put on clothes so that folks might know her?" Victoria was a queen of black or white who ruled as emphatically as she loved. And in death, the widow became a bride again. She asked to be buried in white silk and cashmere, with a cape and veil over her face. Victoria had lived almost as twice as long as her husband, and had ruled on her own for twice as long as they spent ruling together.

When speaking of her greatest desires, the word Victoria repeated throughout her life was "simple." She wanted a simple life. She eschewed corsets, and was primarily concerned with comfort. (She had rolled her eyes at the "new fashion of very tight gowns" in 1867.) The queen was happiest at Glassalt Shiel, a tiny, isolated Scottish cottage in the "lovely wild & haunting country" of the Highlands, away from mansions and castles, manifold eyes and demands. As G. K. Chesterton wrote not long after her death, her "defiant humility" sat at the heart of the empire: "No one could deny that she stood, for the humblest, the shortest and the most indestructible of human gospels, that when all troubles and trouble mongers have had their say, our work can be done till sunset, our life can be lived till death." That was true. But though her humility was defiant, her defiance was not humble.

Victoria did not want to die. Perhaps the greatest contradiction of her character was her belief that she yearned for death; in truth, she clung tenaciously to life. Whenever in danger, she instinctively reared back; when her carriage overturned in Scotland, or old age weighed heavily, she cried out for more time. Just three years before she died, she wrote in her journal: "My great lameness, etc., makes me feel how age is creeping on. Seventy-eight is a good age, but I pray yet to be spared a little longer for the sake of my country and dear ones."

She never stopped working. In the last few months of her life, Victoria complained that while she liked to take a nap after lunch to combat her nighttime insomnia, it "loses time." Three days before she died, although fluid was filling her joints and she was struggling to talk, she spoke to Dr. Reid about South Africa and worried about the war. A woman who had spent most of her life praying to be with her Albert in heaven was still begging her doctor for more time on earth. There were more things to sort out, more disasters to prevent, more wars to fight, more soldiers to protect.

There was always more. Victoria believed that her greatest work—to improve herself, as Albert had bidden her—was not yet complete. "I die," she wrote in instructions to Bertie and Beatrice about her funeral, "in peace with all fully aware of my many faults." Those encircling her bedside knew of her faults: her capriciousness, her temper, her domineering way with her children, her sharp eye, her tendency to self-pity, her unchecked selfishness, her conviction that she was always right. But they also knew of her kindness, her loyalty, her humor, her devotion to her work, her faith, her lack of pretension or prejudice, and her resilience. As Laurence Housman wrote, "The most dramatic thing about Queen Victoria was her duration: in the moving age, to which she gave her name, she remained static." It was why, in her lifetime, she went from a teenager to a totem of empire.

Victoria's heart beat strongly to her last breath, something Dr. Reid made a particular point of noting. This is the greatest clue to understanding the woman who helped shape the modern world, and to dispelling myths about her supposed passivity, her reliance on men and distaste for power. She may have complained often, but she persisted. She grieved for decades, but as generations of statesmen witnessed, she also fought without flinching. Her unbending, steadfast presence shaped a century as she grasped the mantle of power when other women had none. To fly over London today and see her magisterial marble figure looming above the streets is to marvel at how a reclusive, widowed mother of nine achieved unparalleled greatness. The answer is simple: Victoria endured.

Acknowledgments

The writing of this book has spanned continents and years, and the debts of gratitude rival the miles flown. First of all, I am very grateful to Her Majesty, Queen Elizabeth II, for her gracious permission to study the Royal Archives of Britain without restriction and to quote material subject to copyright. The senior archivist, Miss Pamela Clark, was particularly helpful in sharing some of her vast knowledge of these archives. I should also note that on September 9, 2015, as I was doing the final edits on this book, Her Majesty finally surpassed her great-great-grandmother Victoria's record to become Britain's longest-serving monarch.

I have worked in dozens of libraries—and nearby cafés—while working on the life of Victoria: the New York Public Library, the New

York Society Library, Penn University Library, the State Library of New South Wales, the Mitchell Library, the National Library of Australia, the National Library of Scotland, the British Library, the London Library, and Manly Library. I must thank in particular Patrick Fletcher from the New York Society Library; Anna Sander, the Lonsdale Curator of Archives and Manuscripts from Balliol College, Oxford; Dr. Ben Arnold, the assistant admissions officer for the Bodleian Library, Oxford; and Michael Hunt, the curator at Osborne House.

Quentin Bryce, the former governor-general of Australia, provided singular support during her time in office, as she did for so many women. Without her championing, and that of Stephen Brady, then Dame Quentin's official secretary, I would not have been able to procure permission to study in the Royal Archives. For this I will always be deeply grateful. Lady Michaela and Lord Alexander Reid from Lanton Tower, Scotland, generously allowed me unfettered access to the diaries and journals of Dr. James Reid as well as their family scrapbooks, which were fascinating.

My research assistant, Catherine Pope, did excellent work on the long march of Victoria, and her diligence, wit, patience, and keen eye were critical, and hugely appreciated (especially her assistance with the cast of characters). Other valuable assistance came from Jo Seto, Libby Effeney, Sam Register, Lucy Kippist, Madeline Laws, and Cecilia Mackay. Those who read my manuscript and offered important insights include John Barrington Paul, Avery Rome, and Professor Sean Brawley from Macquarie University. Evan Camfield was a ballast in a sea of grammatical imperfections, made some crucial corrections, and has been as cheering as the rest of the team at Random House, whom I have been lucky to work with. Yvonne Ward from La Trobe University generously lent me her files from Germany and Windsor. Carolyn Foley and Geoffrey Robertson provided sage and timely advice, as did Robert Newlinds, who also assisted with some exemplary footnote research.

I am also grateful for my brilliant friends, all of whom helped in myriad ways: most especially Martha Sear, Jill Davison, Annabel

Crabb, Damien Drew, Cathie Forster, Josie Grech, James Hooke, Kerri Ambler, Sarah Macdonald, Ali Benton, Ian Leuchars, John Harwood, Briony Scott, Leigh Sales, Mia Freedman, Judith Whelan, Emma Alberici, Richard Scruby, Morgan Mellish, Ellie Wainwright, Bernard Zuel, John Cleary, Pete Baker, Jonathan Darman, Sterling Brain, Elizabeth Hawke, Kimberley Lipschus, Lisa Wilkinson, Jacqui Maley, Kendall Hill, Jo Dalton, and Sacha Molitorisz. And of course my NYC crew: Katie Maclennan, Kerri Kimball, Lisa Hepner, Mary Morgan, Laura Weinbaum, Bonnie Siegler, and Andrew Sherman.

My colleagues at the ABC understood and enabled my mad urge to write, particularly Tony Hill, Steve Cannane, Gaven Morris, and Mark Scott, as well as the Drum team (Bonnie Symons Brown, Tanya Nolan, Annie White, as well as Emily, Jade, Lily, Mike, and Bennett). Many others helped in ways too numerous to mention: Pat Irving, Annabel Andrews, Ian Macgill, Norman Swan, Walter Shapiro, Meryl Gordon, Darren Saunders, Naama Carlin, Niall Tangney, Jane and Bob Maclennan, and Alex Ellinghausen (for snapping my author shots at midnight during the election campaign). My high school teacher Cate Vacchini taught me that history is more than dates and po-faced portraits, but trenches and pamphlets, propaganda and literature, blackouts and silk stockings as well. And that human hands wrought brutal destruction and exquisite beauty at exactly the same time. I would wish a teacher like her for all children.

Some I must single out for special thanks: the loyal Tim Dick for reading drafts and, with the wonderful Cath Keenan, never failing to take me to the line of hilarity with the rest of the beloved Yum Cha crew; Vanessa Whittaker for camaraderie and her infinite store of droll insights; James Woodford for understanding, goodness, and an uncanny ability to sift chaff from grain; Caitlin McGee for being the kindest, gentlest person I know; Jo Chichester for being hilarious and cool and steadfast, sticking by my side like the best kind of glue; the blazing Lisa Whitby for plucking me from flotsam, believing in me, and plugging ideas to electricity; Peter Fitzsimons, my honorary third brother and the hare to my tortoise in a race in which the hare never sleeps, for egging me on; the singular Maureen Dowd for an uncommon friendship and a thousand NYC adventures; Jonathan Swan for unswerving, unnuanced support; Jo Fox for housing me so magnificently in Notting Hill for many months and ensuring that my writing bouts were punctuated with music festivals and muddy boots; Jacqui Jones, sage and strumpet, for laughter, loyalty, phosphorescence, and endless capacity for conversations about everything, every day, during our decades-long hunt for the horns of Elfland. You are the best.

There are five people who have been pivotal to the conception and execution of this book. Jon Meacham, my brilliant former editor at *Newsweek*, must shoulder much of the blame for my decision to write the life of Victoria. His keen eye and insight were crucial in the early stages. Evan Thomas first lured me to New York to work and has taught me more than he knows. My inimitable agent, Binky Urban, has been an unflagging support from the moment Victoria's name was mentioned. I have also been extremely lucky to have Anna Pitoniak and Kate Medina from Random House as my editors. Anna provided a calm, steady eye and unceasing encouragement, and made many valuable suggestions. Kate was always incisive, thoughtful, and enthusiastic, and immediately, instinctively understood what the book was about.

Which was, in part, to tell the girls I know—especially Ava, Anna, Frances, Evelyn, Sophie, Mary, Grace, Ariel, Rose, Sybilla, and my own daughter, Poppy—that an eighteen-year-old woman ran an empire. You all will reinvent and rule the world.

Finally, my wonderful parents, Judy and Bruce, have always told me to do what I love. Their support has been unstinting and immeasurable. As has that of my steadfast, funny brothers, Mike and Steve; my grace-full sisters-in-law, Kerryn and Annemaree; and my much-loved nieces and nephews: Laura, Cate, Luke, Elijah, and Oscar. My children, Poppy and Sam, are my twin north stars. You have taught me love and made me laugh so hard. This book is for you.

Notes

Abbreviations
QVJ: Queen Victoria's Journal
RA: Royal Archives
CL: *The Collected Letters of Thomas and Jane Welsh Carlyle*

General note: All passages that discuss what Victoria was thinking, feeling, or wearing are based directly on journal entries, letters, and other contemporaneous evidence referenced below.

Epigraphs

vii **"belong to any conceivable category"**: Arthur Ponsonby, *Henry Ponsonby*, 70.

vii **"We are all on the look-out"**: Wyndham, *Correspondence of Sarah Spencer*, July 1844, 348.

Introduction

xxxix **"One feels that the Queen"**: Dyson and Tennyson, *Dear and Honoured Lady*, 76.

xxxix   **"Such a little vixen"**: Rev. Archer Clive, quoted in Clive, *Mrs. Archer Clive,* 87. The full quote reads: "I followed the crowd and found myself *en face* a picture of Prince Albert well enough painted. If he resembles it he is good-natured but decidedly soft and weak, and that won't do for such a little vixen as he is to marry."

xxxix   **"the fair white rose of perfect womanhood"**: A Lady of the Court, *Victoria's Golden Reign,* 2.

xlii   **"I have now received from the Librarian"**: Beatrice to Bertie [George VI], May 10, 1943, Braubridge ark, Sussex, RA, AEC/GG/012/FF2/13.

xliii   **"I know that the Prince and the Queen"**: Morshead to Lascelles, May 14, 1943, RA, AEC/GG/012/FF2/14.

xliii   **Beatrice made her mother tamer**: Benson wrote in his diary that Esher had told him that Beatrice was "engaged in copying from the [Queen's] Diary what she thinks of *public* interest"—which Benson took to mean "the dullest part." Benson Diary, July 25, 1903, 35:81–83; Ward, *Censoring Queen Victoria,* 32.

xliii   **"knowledge and particularly sharp or terse opinions"**: Ward, *Censoring Queen Victoria,* 188.

xliv   **"excessively assertive, unfeminine or insulting"**: Ibid., 309.

xliv   **Even worse, men wrote most**: Ibid., 327. They had a particular bias in favor of Lord Melbourne, whom both Benson and Esher "adored." In the first volume there were excerpts from 35 letters from Queen Victoria to Lord Melbourne, and from 139 of his letters in return. In 1837, six of Melbourne's letters were published, versus four of Victoria's. In 1838, three of her letters were included, but twenty of Melbourne's. Ibid., 191.

xliv   **Victoria wrote an average**: Giles St. Aubyn wrote: "If she had been a novelist, her complete works would have run into seven hundred volumes, published at the rate of one per month!" (*Queen Victoria,* 340.) But this is a conservative estimate.

xlvii   **"prison-like"**: On October 21, 1858, Victoria wrote to Vicky: "I have no feeling for Windsor—I admire it, I think it a grand, splendid place— but without a particle of anything which causes me to love it—none, I feel no interest in anything as if it were not my own; and that of course lessens all the enjoyment of one's existence." She repeated six days later: "How you can call Windsor 'dear' I cannot understand. It is prison-like, so large and gloomy—and for me so dull after Balmoral too, it is like jumping from day into night—fine as it is!" Fulford, *Dearest Child,* 140–41.

Chapter One: The Birth of "Pocket Hercules"

1   **"Poor little victory":** Thomas Carlyle to John A. Carlyle, April 12, 1838, carlyleletters.dukeupress.edu/cgi/content/full/10/1/lt-18380412-TC-JAC-01.

3   **"the crown will come to me and my children":** Stockmar, *Memoirs of Baron Stockmar,* 1:77.

4   **His Majesty's ministers waited:** The officials attending the birth of Victoria included the Duke of Wellington, who had defeated Napoleon at Waterloo four years earlier; the Archbishop of Canterbury; and a man Victoria would grow to despise in her teenage years: Captain John Conroy, her father's Irish equerry, or attendant, who became her mother's confidant.

4   **it was in fact the mother's child:** Some have suggested that because Duke Edward did not have hemophilia and Victoria was a carrier, he was not her father. But there is no evidence for this, and roughly a third of hemophilia cases are a result of spontaneous mutation. It should also be noted that Victoria strongly resembled her father's Hanoverian family. See Stephen Pemberton, *The Bleeding Disease: Hemophilia and the Unintended Consequences of Medical Progress* (Baltimore: Johns Hopkins University Press, 2011), 45.

4   **it was one of the factors:** Worsley, *Courtiers,* 190.

5   **"patience and sweetness":** Duke of Kent to Dowager Duchess of Coburg, May 24, 1819, trans. cited by Woodham-Smith, *Queen Victoria,* 30.

5   *"superbe—d'une beauté extraordinaire":* Martin, *The Prince Consort,* 1:2.

5   **scandalous mutiny by Edward's troops:** In 1802 in Gibraltar, Edward narrowly escaped death at the hands of his own troops on Chrismas Eve. He had been sent to try to restore order to the remote British naval outpost on the southernmost tip of Spain; the undisciplined, often drunk troops had quickly come to loathe his severity and sobriety. After his men mutinied—unsuccessfully, partly because they had been drinking—the Duke of Kent executed three and sentenced eight to life transportation to Australia. (Several of the men escaped upon reaching Port Philip, in southeastern Australia. One disappeared into the bush and lived with the native Aborigines for decades.) The duke was summoned to return to England, and he began a long fight to have his name cleared of charges of brutality. A short time later, in 1804, a yellow fever epidemic swept through Gibraltar, killing most of the population. The mutiny had spared the duke from this likely fate, and also spared the infant daughter who would be born fifteen years later.

6   **only twelve were still alive:** Their two youngest sons died after being
     given smallpox inoculations when aged only four and almost two, and
     their youngest daughter, Amelia, was twenty-seven when she died of a
     skin infection that had followed the measles.

7   **they were unable to save her:** Sir Eardley Holland, writing in the *Journal
     of Obstetrics & Gynaecology* (December 1951), surmised: "It seems hardly
     possible to doubt that Charlotte died of post partum haemorrhage." He
     scoffed at rumors that she died because she had not exercised when preg-
     nant or had been starved during her long labor. If Sir Richard Croft
     made any mistakes, it was not using forceps due to "a mistaken sys-
     tem. . . . of midwifery." Quoted in Longford, *Victoria R.I.,* 151.

7   **rare metabolic disorder:** Peters and Wilkinson, "King George III
     and Porphyria," 3–19. See also holeousia.wordpress.com/2013/03/07/
     re-evaluating-the-porphyria-diagnosis-of-king-george-iiis-madness/.
     King George III had a severe brain fever in 1788, in which he talked
     ceaselessly and temporarily lost the ability to think rationally. The veins
     on his face were so swollen that his wife described it as looking like "black
     currant jelly" (Hibbert, *George III: A Personal History,* 261). Yet the fol-
     lowing year, the king unexpectedly recovered and was well for some
     years. He finally relapsed after his youngest daughter, Amelia, died in
     1810 following a bout of the measles.

7   **"unpleasant laughing":** Fulford, *Royal Dukes,* 38.

8   **His relationship with his wife, Princess Caroline:** She was disgusted by
     his indulgent life and described his home as a brothel. He in turn treated
     her appallingly and spent decades trying to shame and destroy her. He
     claimed his wife was not a virgin when he married her, offering up as
     proof her comment that he had a large penis—which is rather a self-
     serving story, but it marks the beginning of his ongoing obsession with
     his wife's sexual behavior. He tried to prove her infidelity in court so he
     could get a divorce, and failed. The proceedings were so humiliating and
     nasty that the public sided with Caroline. The Prince Regent even urged
     Parliament to pass a bill "to deprive her Majesty Queen Caroline Amelia
     Elizabeth of the title, prerogative, rights, privileges and exemptions of
     Queen Consort of this realm and to dissolve the marriage between his
     Majesty and the said Caroline Amelia Elizabeth." The diarist Creevey
     wrote this should be titled "A Bill to declare the Queen a whore." (Char-
     lot, *Victoria the Young Queen,* 27.) The Prince Regent bribed people to
     testify against his furious wife, and in doing so severely damaged the
     standing of the monarchy.

8   **like "wild beasts":** QVJ, January 3, 1840.

8   **Too far down the succession:** King George III's sixth son, the popular, amiable Augustus Frederick, the Duke of Sussex, was not particularly interested in becoming king, and the seventh son, Adolphus, the Duke of Cambridge, a garrulous man who wore thick blond wigs, was also too far down the line of succession to be a real threat, even though he was the first to marry after Charlotte died.

8   **King George III's five surviving daughters:** Of the six daughters, none had children, and only one was married. The eldest girl, Charlotte, who was painfully shy, wed the Prince of Württemberg in 1797. She had only one child, a girl, who was stillborn. The loss of her daughter broke her heart: she treasured the baby clothes she had brought over from England until the end of her life. Her five younger sisters, Augusta, Elizabeth, Mary, Sophia, and Amelia (who died in 1810), were forced to stay with their mother at Windsor, on the grounds that they were required to keep her nerves still after their father, King George III, went mad. They spent the long days sewing, playing music, and drawing, but they grew frantic with boredom. Two had affairs with servants. They were not even permitted to go to the decadent party their eldest brother, the Prince of Wales, threw for himself when he became Regent, featuring a flowing brook, with fish swimming inside it, down the center of an enormous dining table bordered by green moss and flowers. One sister, Princess Elizabeth, complained: "We go on vegetating as we have done for the last twenty years of our lives." Fulford, *Royal Dukes,* 38; Williams, *Becoming Queen,* 47.

9   **a marriage proposal . . . to which she agreed:** The third son in line, a sailor and the future King William IV, who had ten illegitimate children with an actress whom he had dumped by letter in 1811, also successfully proposed, to the dignified and kind Princess Ameliée Adelaide. But she had a series of traumatic pregnancies and births. Her first baby was premature and died within a few hours, she miscarried her second, and her third died at four months. In 1822, she gave birth to stillborn twins.

9   **"the crown will come to me and my children":** Stockmar, *Memoirs of Baron Stockmar,* 1:77.

10   **In response, Edward was tender:** He also wanted her to become pregnant; the prospect of the next brother in line—Ernest, the Duke of Cumberland—seizing the crown was unbearable. Ernest had a scarred face and extreme Tory views; there were relentless but unsubstantiated rumors that he had sexually assaulted a nun, killed his valet, and impregnated his sister. He had also married a glamorous, twice-widowed German princess who was suspected of murdering at least one of her husbands. Frederica became pregnant, but the child was stillborn.

Chapter Two: The Death of a Father

12   **insisted on breastfeeding:** The Duchess of Kent said while "everybody is most astonished," she "would have been desperate to see my little darling on someone else's breast." Her husband took a great interest in the swelling and emptying of his wife's breasts in a practice he called "maternal nutriment" and "an office most interesting in its nature." Stuart, *The Mother of Victoria,* 76.

13   **"for she will be Queen of England":** Longford, *Queen Victoria,* 24.

13   **starved as a result:** Some deaths also occurred from excessive doses. According to the Registrar General's reports, most opium poisoning deaths occurred in young children, especially infants. Between 1863 and 1867, 235 babies under age one had died, as well as fifty-six children between the ages of one and four; 340 children and adults over five had died. Berridge, *Opium and the People,* 100. Note that today opium—or laudanum tincture—is used to treat the withdrawal symptoms of babies born to mothers who are heroin addicts.

13   **"ignorant hireling nurse(s)":** "Protected Cradles," 108.

13   **drew attention away from the real issues:** Berridge, *Opium and the People,* 97.

14   **"rather a pocket Hercules, than a pocket Venus":** Woodham-Smith, *Queen Victoria,* 33.

14   **"a model of strength and beauty combined":** Plowden, *The Young Victoria,* 35.

14   **"pretty little Princess":** Memoirs of Baron Stockmar, 1:78.

14   **Victoria's uncles:** In June, the duke told a friend that his brother the Regent had not announced Victoria's birth to the courts of Europe, despite her high place in the succession line: "The plan is evidently to *keep me down.*" Three days after Victoria was born, the Duchess of Cumberland gave birth to a son, George, who was next in line. He would grow up to be the blind King of Hanover.

15   **thirty or more:** Chesney, *The Anti-Society,* 14.

16   **her most recent British ancestor:** Sophia, the Electress of Hanover, was George I's mother and Victoria's great-great-great-great-grandmother. All four of Victoria's grandparents were German.

17   **"What business has that infant here?":** St. Aubyn, *Queen Victoria,* 11.

18   **"Ei hoeve to regret":** Woodham-Smith, *Queen Victoria,* 46; Longford, *Victoria R.I.,* 20.

18   **"a real thorn in their side":** Van der Kiste, *George III's Children,* 121.

18   **he hated his wife:** Princess Caroline of Brunswick was spoiled, rude, and rebellious. She was disgusted by the indulgent life the Prince Regent led, and said her husband and his courtiers were constantly drunk; she regularly found them passed out on the sofa, wearing boots, snoring. Popular opinion would have agreed with her. The Prince Regent married her because his mistress urged him to find someone who would not supplant her, and who would allow him to pay off some of his large debts. The fact that Parliament usually raised the annual incomes of the royal offspring when they officially married was responsible for much heartbreak.

18   **"fatigue and depression":** Berridge, *Opium and the People,* 31.

18   **extremely potent and addictive:** The 1868 Pharmacy Act limited the sale of the drug to professional pharmacists, who had existed only since the 1840s.

18   **"the vivacity or serenity of one's intellect":** Berridge, *Opium and the People,* 59.

19   **"I wonder which ones?":** Duff writes that when the duke was at Woolbrook, a fortune-teller came to Sidmouth and told him, "This year two members of the Royal Family will die." (Duff, *Edward of Kent,* 281.) Others claim it was at the military review at Hounslow Heath. For example, Stuart, *The Mother of Victoria,* 87.

19   **"too healthy, I fear":** Duff, *Edward of Kent,* 279. A good account of all this can be found in Hibbert, *Queen Victoria: A Personal History,* 14.

19   **The duke said she stood fire:** Fulford, *Royal Dukes,* 203.

20   **"hardly a spot on":** Woodham-Smith, *Queen Victoria,* 43.

20   **"Human help can no longer avail":** Ibid., 44.

20   **"Do not forget me":** Longford, *Queen Victoria,* 25.

20   **His death came as a great shock:** The Duke of Cumberland said, "I never was so struck in my life" as with the news of his older brother's death. (Duke of Cumberland to the Prince Regent, February 4, 1820, Aspinall and Webster, *Letters of George IV,* vol. 2, letter 790.) The court was surprised by the loss of a man Croker called "the strongest of the strong": "Never before ill in all his life, and now to die of a cold when half the kingdom have colds with impunity. It was very bad luck indeed. It reminds me of Aesop's fable of the oak and the reed." Charlot, *Victoria the Young Queen,* 34.

20   **"That Hercules of a man is no more":** Creston, *Youthful Queen Victoria,* 85.

20   **especially among the women:** On February 4, 1820, Princess Augusta wrote to Lady Harcourt from Windsor Castle about how distressed the

Duke of Clarence had been by Edward's death, adding, "In all my own sorrow I cannot yet bear to think of that good, excellent Woman, the Duchess of Kent, and all Her trials; they really are most grievous. She is the most pious, good, resigned little Creature it is possible to describe." William told Princess Adelaide to go see her every day—said she was a great comfort to her—they could talk the same language—"it makes them such real friends and Comforts to each other." It was a great shame the duchess was unable to reciprocate, or nurture, these friendships. It may well have been because she was jealous: when Adelaide gave birth to a daughter, Elizabeth, in 1820, John Conroy wrote, "We are all on the kick and go. Our little woman's nose has been put out of joint." (Charlot, *Victoria the Young Queen,* 40). Elizabeth died three months later.

21   **a happy union:** Even Queen Victoria, when she read her mother's note-books after she died, was taken aback by the devotion her mother felt for her father: "How very, very much she and my beloved father *loved* each other. *Such* love and affection, I hardly knew it was to *that* extent," she wrote. Benson and Esher, *Letters of Queen Victoria,* 3:560.

21   **"symptoms of wanting":** Hibbert, *Queen Victoria: A Personal History,* 17.

Chapter Three: The Lonely, Naughty Princess

22   **"[Victoria] is watched so closely":** Scott, *Journal,* 2:184, May 19, 1828.

22   **"You see there is no *must* about it":** Hibbert, *Queen Victoria: A Personal History,* 18.

22   **Baroness Louise Lehzen:** George IV made Lehzen, who had initially been hired as a governess for Feodora, a Baroness in 1827.

22   **"Conduct Books":** Four of these books still remain in the Royal Archives, as Lynne Vallone discovered, and they contain a record of outbursts entirely absent from her diaries. In her first, dated October 31, 1831, to March 22, 1832, there are dozens of references to being "rather naughty and peevish," "naughty with Mamma," and "very exceedingly naughty." She was also "very ill-behaved and impertinent to Lehzen," and "naughty and vulgar." Vallone, *Becoming Victoria,* 24.

23   **she made up stories:** Ibid., 22.

23   **"sweet-meats in her hand":** Ibid.

24   **"Two storms, one at dressing and one at washing":** Ibid., 43.

24   **"you may not call me Victoria":** Longford, *Oxford Book of Royal Anecdotes,* 358.

24   **"It was a sort of idolatry":** Victoria herself said she had been "too much an Idol in the House," and was "very much indulged by everyone and set

pretty well *all* at defiance." Benson and Esher, *Letters of Queen Victoria,* 1:19.

24 **her childhood as rather melancholy:** Hibbert, *Queen Victoria: A Personal History,* 19.

25 **"did not know what a happy domestic life was":** Fulford, *Dearest Child,* 111–12.

25 **"To have been deprived of all intercourse":** Charlot, *Victoria the Young Queen,* 52.

25 **holly was pinned:** This may have been irritating but it was far better than the iron collars that were placed around the throats of some other girls. Mrs. Sherwood, the author of *The Fairchild Family,* describes being forced to wear a collar, which was linked to a blackboard, strapped across her shoulders: "I was subjected from my sixth to my thirteenth year. It was put on in the morning and seldom taken off till late in the evening: and I generally did all my lessons standing in stocks. . . . I never sat on a chair in my mother's presence. . . . Even before I was twelve I was obliged to translate fifty lines of Virgil every morning, standing in these same stocks with the iron collar pressing on my throat." Creston, *Youthful Queen Victoria,* 148.

25 **Victoria burst into tears:** The Reverend Davys had a different account of Victoria's discovery: one that gives him a more central role. He said he told her, the previous day, "Princess, to-morrow I wish you to give me a chart of the kings and queens of England." In the morning she gave him a chart, which he scanned closely. He said, "It is well done, but it does not go far enough. You have put down 'Uncle King' as reigning, and you have written 'Uncle William' as the heir to the throne, but who should follow him?" Victoria, hesitating, said, "I hardly liked to put down my-self." Davys says he then told the duchess, who wrote to the Bishop of London informing him that Victoria was now aware of her standing. Tappan, *Days of Queen Victoria,* 33.

26 **"but there is more responsibility":** Martin, *The Prince Consort,* 1:13.

26 **the Duchess of Kent was happy:** Duchess of Kent to the Bishops of London and Lincoln, March 13, 1830, ibid., 1:34.

26 **"& even deplored this contingency":** Vallone, *Becoming Victoria,* 45.

26 **Florence drew up a table:** Gill, *Nightingales,* 90.

26 **crafting immaculate compositions:** Eliot was an outstanding student, and was the best pianist in the school. Hughes, *George Eliot,* 24–25.

27 **"The Princess was her only":** Hibbert, *Queen Victoria: A Personal History,* 21, and Vallone, *Becoming Victoria,* 208.

27 **"not created, but nourished":** Baroness Lehzen to the Duchess of Kent,

June 13, 1837, RA M7/48, translated and quoted in Hudson, *A Royal Conflict,* 72.

28   **"model of perfection"**: Ibid., 19. Victoria was not a great admirer of Queen Anne's, either. At fourteen, she reprimanded her uncle Leopold for sending an extract about Queen Anne, writing, "[I] must beg you as you have sent me to show what a Queen *ought not* to be, that you will send me what a Queen *ought to be*." Leopold described her letter as "very clever, sharp" and responded that he would rise to the task in his next letter on December 2, 1834.

28   **"but not weakness"**: Ibid.

28   **"bright pretty girl"**: Charlot, *Victoria the Young Queen,* 52.

28   **"the most charming child"**: Bamford and Wellington, *The Journal of Mrs. Arburthnot,* 2:186, quoted in Hibbert, *Queen Victoria: A Personal History,* 29.

29   **"Girls should be taught"**: *Works of Hannah More,* 2:376–67.

29   **"a submissive temper and a forbearing spirit"**: Ibid., 2:568.

29   **"a hundred walks and rides"**: Princess Victoria to King Leopold, April 26, 1836, Benson and Esher, *Letters of Queen Victoria,* 1:60.

29   **"We shall miss them at breakfast"**: QVJ, July 13, 1833. (Three years later, in 1836, her other cousins Ferdinand and Augustus came to visit, partly to celebrate Ferdinand's marriage to the Queen of Portugal.)

29   **When they left, Victoria drew a picture**: Eliza later died of tuberculosis at age twenty.

30   **"It is such a VERY VERY GREAT HAPPINESS"**: Three years later her other half nephews, the children of Feodora's brother Charles of Leiningen, came to stay and she was effusive again—in contrast to her terse recitals of the day's lessons, etc. When they were just being demonstrative, she was totally thrilled: "Edward was beyond everything funny. He calls me Lisettche, and a number of other odd names. He has not *respect* for me, I fear, at all."

31   **"Lehzen mended the baby"**: Quoted in Vallone, *Becoming Victoria,* 187.

32   **"nearly unlearned laughing"**: Bauer, *Caroline Bauer and the Coburgs,* 296.

32   **"dear little chicken"**: Vallone, *Becoming Victoria,* 14.

32   **"most indispensable qualifications"**: King Leopold to Princess Victoria, May 22, 1832, quoted in ibid., 102.

32   **"intoxicated by greatness"**: King Leopold to Princess Victoria, May 21, 1833, Benson and Esher, *Letters of Queen Victoria,* 1:46.

32   **"which would astonish you"**: Princess Victoria to King Leopold, December 28, 1834, ibid., 1:52.

32   **"nothing but a coat":** Thackeray, "George the Fourth," 108.

33   **"le roi Georges":** Williams, *Becoming Queen,* 173.

33   **"little bit of the future, aged 7":** Creston, *Youthful Queen Victoria,* 117.

33   **"a wonderful dignity and charm of manner":** Hibbert, *Queen Victoria in Her Letters,* 10.

33   **"fondling an unpopular mistress":** Fulford, *Royal Dukes,* 100.

34   **monitored her every move:** John Conroy had also earned the trust of Victoria's aunt Sophia, but years of paperwork went missing when he took control of Princess Sophia's financial affairs. Victoria was later convinced he siphoned off thousands of pounds for his own use (on top of the house Sophia bought him in Kensington in 1826 for four thousand pounds).

34   **"*attached* and *disinterested* friend I have":** QVJ, November 5, 1835.

34   **"obesity of the heart":** Gardiner, *The Victorians,* 4.

Chapter Four: An Impossible, Strange Madness

36   **"The most formidably":** Cecil, *Young Melbourne,* 385.

37   **"All I underwent there":** QVJ, February 26, 1838.

38   **"My *dearest best* Lehzen":** QVJ, October 31 1835.

38   **"He imagined he":** King Leopold to Queen Victoria, March 9, 1854, RA Y79/35.

39   **Charles of Leiningen defined:** Longford, *Victoria R.I.,* 55.

39   **Conroy told the duchess:** It was said Cumberland had already spread lies that the princess was "diseased in her feet" and would not be able to grow properly (Victoria blamed Conroy's daughter Victoire for this rumor). When the Greville memoirs were published in 1875, Victoria said the claim that Conroy was trying to protect her from Cumberland was a lie.

39   **"all Sir John's invention":** Hudson, *A Royal Conflict,* 208.

40   **New cities that had boomed:** Mitchell, *Lord Melbourne,* 182.

40   **slavery was finally abolished:** There were caveats, though—plantation owners were awarded twenty million pounds in government bonds—approximately 40 percent of the national budget—and the slaves were forced to work for free in an apprenticeship period. They were not officially free for five more years, until August 1, 1838.

40   **"since I lost the Duke of Kent":** Creston, *Youthful Queen Victoria,* 147.

40   **left immediately:** Zeigler, *King William IV,* 278.

40   **encouraging military salutes:** The king was furious. From Greville, July 4, 1833: "The King has been (not unnaturally) disgusted at the Duchess of

Kent's progresses with her daughter through the kingdom, and amongst the rest with her sailings at the Isle of Wight, and the continual popping in the shape of salutes to her Royal Highness." They tried to convince the duchess to stop, as "salutes are a matter of general order, both to army and navy." She refused, and subsequently an Order in Council was issued so that the Royal Standard was to be saluted only when the king or queen was on board. Reeve, *Greville Memoirs,* 3:4.

41   **"the most restless, persevering, troublesome devil possible":** Thomas Creevey, November 2, 1833, Gore, *Creevey,* 345.

41   **"one of the most solemn":** Victoria wrote a long, serious journal entry about her confirmation, in which she said she was sorry for her sin, and wanting to improve in obedience and in devotion as the daughter of a fretful woman. She wrote that she had gone there "with the firm determination to become a true Christian, to try and comfort my dear Mamma in all her griefs, trials and anxieties, and to become a dutiful and affectionate daughter to her. Also to be obedient to dear Lehzen, who has done so much for me." (QVJ, July 30, 1835.) Her mother wrote to her with her usual fretfulness: "Providence has singled you out:—much more is required from you, than from other young Ladies of your age.—In making these comparisons, I feel naturally still more anxious for you, my beloved Victoria." (Vallone, *Becoming Victoria,* 147.) The duchess warned her daughter that a great station in life wouldn't bring her happiness, but a "good, virtuous and well-cultivated mind" would.

42   **"unhappily very fat":** Princess Victoria to Princess Feodora, October 30, 1834, Vallone, *Becoming Victoria,* 221.

42   **"unmentionable things":** Longford, *Victoria R.I.,* 30.

42   **was "generally known":** Brumberg, *Body Project,* xviii. Lynne Vallone also believed menstruation occurred at about age fifteen. In an account of Victoria's early years, Vallone traced how each month, in the third week, Victoria grew grumpy, lost her appetite, and became a little sad. In an entry that has since been omitted from the official edit of her journal and letters, as she was traveling across England she complained of the lack of hedges, the excessive number of ditches, and the dense mass of people she believed to be half drunk. Vallone, *Becoming Victoria,* 157. See also Ashdown, *Queen Victoria's Mother.*

42   **"At such times, women":** Quoted in Showalter and Showalter, "Victorian Women and Menstruation," 85.

43   **"very happy to hear":** Williams, *Becoming Queen,* 188.

43   **"wildly about his face":** Longford, *Victoria R.I.,* 55; Woodham-Smith, *Queen Victoria,* 136.

43   **"bent on marrying":** Browning to Mr. and Mrs. William Wentworth Story, June 21, 1861, quoted in Weintraub, *Victoria,* 88.

43   **was sent to India:** Elphinstone's *Dictionary of National Biography* entry reads: "In 1837 Elphinstone left the guards on being appointed governor of Madras by Lord Melbourne. It was said at the time that his appointment was made in order to dispel a rumour that the young Queen Victoria had fallen in love with him." The church episode is mentioned in Longford, *Victoria R.I.,* 62: "At the beginning of February Dr. Clark allowed her to visit St. James's Palace wearing her grey satin *broche* coat trimmed with roses which Aunt Louise had sent from Paris. She looked so bewitching that young Lord Elphinstone sketched her in church; the Duchess secured his banishment to Madras."

43   **see him banished:** These rumors were revived recently by an Australian writer, Roland Perry. In a book titled *The Queen, Her Lover and the Most Notorious Spy in History* (Sydney: Allen & Unwin, 2014), he claimed that Victoria had an affair with Lord Elphinstone when she was fifteen and he was twenty-seven. Perry did not provide any documentation to back his claim, but in correspondence with this author, Perry said he "came to the story via the KGB," which had obtained copies of unexpurgated correspondence between Victoria and her eldest daughter. To understand it, he said, you "need to be in front of the key players in Moscow and St. Petersburg." No actual evidence was detailed for historians to build upon.

43   **Albert and his brother:** King William IV tried to stop them, without luck. The king was keen to marry Victoria to one of the sons of the Protestant Prince of Orange, instead of a Catholic Coburg, but Victoria did not warm to them.

44   **"turned as pale":** Vallone, *Becoming Victoria,* 179.

44   **"I am sorry to say":** Princess Victoria to King Leopold, May 26, 1836, Hibbert, *Queen Victoria in Her Letters,* 18.

44   **"[Albert] is so sensible":** Princess Victoria to King Leopold, June 7, 1836, ibid.

44   **"his daughters were":** QVJ, January 21, 1839.

44   **"*Why* he outraged":** Hudson, *A Royal Conflict,* 20.

44   **written in code:** Conroy Family Collection, Balliol College Archives and Manuscripts, Conroy 2C, John Conroy 3rd Baronet, 3D 9. See Hudson, *A Royal Conflict,* 33.

44   **Victoria's half sister:** Hudson, *A Royal Conflict,* 33, 34. Conroy's belief that his wife, Elizabeth Fisher, was the illegitimate daughter of the duke was revealed in a journal from Conroy's godson, and a deathbed confession from Edward, son of John: "Sir J, was proud and considered it indelicate

to have let Dchss know about his wife's relation to Pss. Victoria. Sir J has often expressed his idea that it was a disgrace to the honour, & as Ly C was sufficiently fond of Gen. Fisher she would never be told that it was true she was not his own child—hence the silence always observed on this subject, of which proof remains." Conroy Family Collection, Conroy 6F papers, Deathbed confession of Edward Conroy. But the evidence is not convincing.

45　**loathsome Duke of Cumberland:** Ward, "Editing Queen Victoria," 202. In March 1904, Benson came across a memo and correspondence to Victoria from Conroy's daughter. Victoria had crossed everything out in the memo. Benson wrote in his diary: "Sir J.C. was a really mischievous, unscrupulous, intriguing man. He established such an ascendancy over the Dss of Kent that he was thought to be her lover. . . . The Queen had a perfect horror of him. The horror of him appears (tho' this is very mysterious) to date from a time when the Duke of Cumberland with characteristic brutality said before her, when she was just a girl, that Conroy was her mother's lover."

45　**"a real Mephisto":** Woodham-Smith, *Queen Victoria,* 55.

45　**"proceed from witchcraft":** Hudson, *A Royal Conflict,* 51.

45　**the man she called a "monster":** The Kensington System backers included Leopold, Lady Flora Hastings, Princess Sophia, Prince Charles of Leiningen, and the Duke of Sussex. Conroy's powerful friends were unaware of his inability to handle money; thousands of pounds went missing on his watch, and there is strong evidence of impropriety (Victoria decided he was a swindler when her mother's and Aunt Sophia's dubious financial records were released).

Chapter Five: "Awful Scenes in the House"

46　**"They plague her":** Williams, *Becoming Queen,* 281.

47　**workers found corks:** Hollingshead, *Underground London,* 71.

48　**"I trust in God":** Ibid., 367.

49　**Charles of Leiningen:** Before he went, Stockmar told Charles not to see "treachery, lies and fraud as the weapons of success." Stockmar said, frankly but cautiously, that while he often agreed with Conroy, his moodiness and tactlessness were so extreme that even if they managed to make him private secretary, "he would, through his own folly, break his own neck in no time at all." Woodham-Smith, *Queen Victoria,* 130.

49   **Leopold to tell Victoria:** Albert, *Queen Victoria's Sister,* 86.

49   **"more conscious of":** Hudson, *A Royal Conflict,* 102.

49   **"They plague her":** Williams, *Becoming Queen,* 281.

49   **pointed out repeatedly:** On Victoria's eighteenth birthday, the Duchess of Kent made a public statement of martyrdom, saying: "I gave up my home, my kindred, and my duties, to devote myself to that duty which was to be the whole object of my future life." Minutes of the Proceedings of the Court of Common Council, no. 13, June 2, 1837. Records Office, Corporation of London, quoted in Hudson, *A Royal Conflict,* 127.

50   **"Felt very miserable & agitated":** QVJ, May 19, 1837.

50   **Ignorant of any other:** First, she asked her mother that the Dean of Chester be her Privy Purse. Her mother said no. Victoria then asked if she could see Lord Melbourne on her own—again the answer was no. Her mother did not even tell her that Lord Melbourne—who was quite unaware of the depths of Victoria's torment—had offered a compromise deal, where they would accept the king's offer, but the duchess would get two-thirds of Victoria's money.

50   **"Victoria has not written":** Williams, *Becoming Queen,* 252. On June 6, Victoria dictated a memo to Lehzen, outlining the recent events. She wrote: "I have objected on the 19th of May [when the king offered her the extra ten thousand pounds a year] as well as always before to allowing John Conroy any interference in my affairs. Whatever he has done, it has been by order of my Mother, as I requested in *her* name, without making me responsible for any of her actions, as Sir John Conroy is *Her* private secretary and neither *my* Servant, nor Adviser, nor *ever was*."

50   **a bright flag bearing one word flapped:** *Morning Post,* May 25, 1837.

51   **women had fainted:** Paterson, *Voices from Dickens' London,* 45.

52   **"entirely took away":** The Liverpool memo is kept in the Royal Archives. See Longford, *Victoria R.I.,* 59.

54   **Gypsies were maligned:** Behlmer, "The Gypsy Problem," 231.

54   **poor people would respond:** In the 1830s, there was a protracted public debate about poverty as the population boomed, along with the numbers of homeless people. In 1834, Prime Minister Lord Melbourne passed the "poor law," which codified a previously uncoordinated system of poor relief into a formal system of workhouses. Intended to counter the cost of looking after the needy during recessions—landowners were taxed personally for those requiring aid in their area—the laws also aimed to reduce the number of poor and make the conditions inside the workhouses so awful that no one would stay for long. They were much like prisons,

intended to cure poverty instead of criminality. Charles Dickens, who lived close to a workhouse, and whose own father had been jailed for debt, wrote in *Oliver Twist* in 1839 that workhouse boards "established the rule, that all poor people should have the alternative (for they would compel nobody, not they), of being starved by a gradual process in the house, or by a quick one out of it. . . . They . . . kindly undertook to divorce poor married people . . . and, instead of compelling a man to support his family, as they had therefore done, took his family away from him and made him a bachelor!" See also Richardson, *Dickens and the Workhouse*.

Historian Philip Ziegler described the poor law as "a well-intentioned piece of legislation which probably contributed more to the sum of human unhappiness than any other single measure of the nineteenth century." (Ziegler, *Melbourne,* 163.) A series of scandals involving inhumane treatment and near-starvation led to a revision of the law a decade later.

54   **Conroy did not:** QVJ, January 19, 1837.

54   **"He was always personally":** QVJ, June 19, 1837.

54   **"oppressed Person":** Stockmar wrote: "The struggle between the Mama and daughter is still going on. She [the duchess] is pressed by Conroy to bring matters to extremities and to force her Daughter to do her will by unkindness and severity." If the truth were to come out, "the Princess must appear *what she is,* an oppressed Person, and everybody I am sure *would fly to her assistance.*" Woodham-Smith, *Queen Victoria,* 137.

54   **"live on outwardly":** Williams, *Becoming Queen,* 281.

54   **she wrote to the Duchess:** Princess Feodora to the Duchess of Northumberland, March 25, 1835. RA, VIC Addl. Mss U/72/15; Vallone, *Becoming Victoria,* 160.

55   **"awful scenes in the house":** Hudson, *A Royal Conflict,* 219.

55   **"I shall not, at all events, *fail*":** Princess Victoria to King Leopold, June 1837, Benson and Esher, *Letters of Queen Victoria*, 1:95.

Chapter Six: Becoming Queen: "I Am Very Young"

59   **"I was never happy until I was eighteen":** Williams, *Becoming Queen,* 288.

59   **"It will touch every":** Arthur Ponsonby, *Queen Victoria,* 13.

61   **"The severe and afflicting":** Tuer and Fagan, *First Year,* 6–7.

62   **"There never was anything like the first impression":** Greville, *The Great World,* 113.

62   **"handsome as any young lady I ever saw"**: Williams, *Becoming Queen*, 265.

62   **"she filled the room"**: Greville, *The Great World*, 113; Arnstein, *Queen Victoria*, 32.

62   **"in every respect is *perfection*"**: Hibbert, *Queen Victoria: A Personal History*, 53.

63   **A cartoon titled**: Williams, *Becoming Queen*, 292.

63   **"mad with loyalty"**: Ibid., 296; Sallie Stevenson to her sisters, July 12, 1837, Boykin, *Victoria, Albert and Mrs. Stevenson*, 74

63   **"Though not a beauty"**: Woodham-Smith, *Queen Victoria*, 140.

63   **shown unattractive gums**: Creevey was not the only one to make unkind remarks about the queen's teeth. While praising her voice, "very good" bust, feet, and large blue eyes, Sallie Stevenson said that the queen's mouth was "her worst feature." It was "generally a little open; her teeth small and short, and she shows her gums when she laughs, which is rather disfiguring." Boykin, *Victoria, Albert and Mrs. Stevenson*, 107–8. Feodora told Victoria to close her mouth when she sat for her portrait, but the Duchess of Kent said, "No, my dear; let it be as nature made it." Weintraub, *Victoria*, 111.

63   **"quite in love with her"**: September 25, 1837, Gore, *Creevey*, 379.

64   **"growing up simple & good"**: Martineau, *The Collected Letters*, 3.

64   **wiping tears from his eyes**: Victoria often noted Melbourne's tears, which seemed easily bid. He cried on a host of occasions, including her coronation, her first appearance at Parliament, when talking about her future, the parliamentary vote to increase the Duchess of Kent's annuity, the "glories" of England, and the honor of the Duke of Wellington.

64   **the red ribbon**: "The red ribbon" was an idiomatic reference to a knighthood in the Most Honourable Order of the Bath. St. Aubyn, *Queen Victoria*, 68.

64   **"Have you ever heard such impudence?"**: Hibbert, *Queen Victoria: A Personal History*, 90.

65   **relished attacks**: The family nursed the perceived wrong to John Conroy for generations, and became openly vindictive. In the front of one family notebook, stuffed with clippings of Lady Flora Hastings and widespread criticism of the queen, a quote from Lord Byron was scrawled. The words were telling:

> . . . and if we do but watch the hour
> There never yet was human power
> That can resist—if unforgiven

The patient search and vigil long
Of him who treasures up a wrong.

Conroy Family Collection, Balliol College Archives, Conroy Papers, 2C
Residue C.

65 **summon her:** Strickland, *Queen Victoria,* 220–21.

65 **"Her emotion was":** Ashton, *Gossip in the First Decade,* 4.

66 **"sweet as a Virginia":** Weintraub, *Victoria,* 111.

66 **"I delight in the business":** Williams, *Becoming Queen,* 291.

66 **"when it is submitted to you":** King Leopold to Queen Victoria, June 27, 1837, Benson and Esher, *The Letters of Queen Victoria,* 1:104.

66 **this approach:** Greville wrote in his diary on August 30, 1837, that the queen "seldom or never" gave an answer on the spot, and blamed Melbourne. But Melbourne believed it was ingrained, telling Greville, "Such is her habit even with him, and that when he talks with her upon any subject upon which an opinion is expected from her, she tells him she will think it over, and let him know her sentiments the next day." Strachey and Fulford, *The Greville Memoirs,* 3:394; Greville, *The Great World,* 133.

66 **"the *greatest pleasure* to":** Williams, *Becoming Queen,* 291.

67 **worked late:** Thomas Creevey wrote on July 29, 1837: "One day at dinner Lady Georgiana Grey sat next to Madame Lützen, a German who has been Vic's governess from her grave, and according to her there never was so perfect a creature. She said that now Vic was at work morning to night; and that, even when her maid was combing out her hair, she was surrounded by official boxes and reading official papers." Note that he prefaced these remarks with the fact that while Victoria was "idolised," the Duchess of Sutherland was not so smitten with the queen after she snubbed her for being half an hour later for dinner. Maxwell, *The Creevey Papers,* 665.

67 **"slight signs of":** Greville, July 30, 1837, Strachey and Fulford, *The Greville Memoirs,* 3:390. He continued: "It is impossible not to suspect that, as she gains confidence, and as her character begins to develop, she will evince a strong will of her own. In all trifling matters connected with her Court and her Palace, she already enacts the part of Queen and Mistress as if it had long been familiar to her."

67 **"I was very glad":** Weintraub, *Victoria,* 110.

67 **"an abiding and":** Arthur Ponsonby, *Queen Victoria,* 10.

67 **"In spite of Mama and you":** Longford, *Queen Victoria,* 76.

68   **"I am so fond":** QVJ, August 22, 1837.

68   **The editors of:** Ward, "Editing Queen Victoria," 269–71.

68   **"passionate fondness":** Healey, *The Queen's House,* 136.

68   **"a man with a capacity":** Woodham-Smith, *Queen Victoria,* 144.

68   **"[Victoria] has great animal":** Greville, *The Great World,* 133.

69   **"So much":** Boykin, *Victoria, Albert and Mrs. Stevenson,* 76.

70   **"Everybody says that":** Williams, *Becoming Queen,* 292; Vallone, *Becoming Victoria,* 199.

70   **"The whole thing went off beautifully":** QVJ, September 28, 1837.

70   **"You have it in your power":** Williams, *Becoming Queen,* 297.

70   **little influence on:** Baron Stockmar to King Leopold, June 24, 1837, RA, Add. A 11/26.

71   **"The Queen should forget":** Longford, *Queen Victoria,* 72.

71   **"*such* a letter":** QVJ, January 15, 1838.

71   **"plaguing":** QVJ, January 16, 1838.

71   **All the letters:** According to Yvonne Ward, when Benson sent the first installment of the manuscript in March 1904 to John Murray for printing, Murray admitted he could not resist spending the night reading through the selections. Murray wrote: "Many of the letters are of the greatest importance. I am struck by some of those from the Queen to her mother. Her position was a most delicate one in regard to the Duchess of Kent both shortly before and after her Coronation, and these letters display much firmness of character and sense of justice." (Murray to Benson, March 22, 1904, John Murray Archives.) But, Ward writes, "within two months, Benson was asking Murray to return those MSS sections as he had just been directed by Esher that 'certain matters' had to be eliminated." (Benson to Murray, May 17, 1904, ibid.) There was no further mention of any letters between Victoria and the Duchess of Kent from 1837, and none published. Ward, "Editing Queen Victoria," 244.

71   **"ill-used" by both:** Pearce, *The Diaries of Charles Greville,* 162 (July 28).

71   **"pining to death":** Hudson, *A Royal Conflict,* 170.

72   **"I have never heard":** Woodham-Smith, *Queen Victoria,* 149.

72   **"The Queen is a new":** November 13, 1837, Wise, *Diary of William Tayler,* 57.

Chapter Seven: The Coronation:
"A Dream out of *The Arabian Nights*"

73   **"I shall ever remember this day"**: QVJ, June 28, 1838.

73   **"Poor little Queen, she"**: Longford, *Victoria R.I.,* 83; St. Aubyn, *Queen Victoria,* 63.

74   **"The coronation day"**: *The Champion and Weekly Herald,* July 1, 1838.

74   something **"very awful"** was going to happen: QVJ, June 27, 1838; Williams, *Becoming Queen,* 274.

74   **twenty-one-gun salute:** On the day of the coronation, there were twenty-one guns at sunrise, twenty-one guns when Queen Victoria left Buckingham Palace, twenty-one guns when she arrived at Westminster Abbey, forty-one guns when the crown was placed on her head, twenty-one guns when she left the Abbey, and twenty-one guns on her return to Buckingham Palace.

74   **"a thing that you can't give a person"**: QVJ, June 28, 1838.

75   the world was **"alive with men"**: "The Queen's Coronation," *Examiner,* July 1, 1838, 403. Attributed to Dickens by the Pilgrim editors, *Letters of Charles Dickens,* 1:408.

75   **"It is as if the population"**: Strachey and Fulford, *The Greville Memoirs,* June 27, 1838, 4:69.

75   **Nelson Lee struck a gong:** Frost, *The Old Showmen,* 327–28.

76   **"Many as there were the day I went"**: Benson and Esher, *Letters of Queen Victoria,* June 1838.

76   **"making more use"**: Strickland, *Queen Victoria,* 320.

76   **insisted that no harsh measures:** Ibid., 320–21.

76   **"There are more drunken women"**: Hensel, *The Mendelssohn Family,* 2:41. "A drunken woman, with bare shoulders and hair hanging down, tried to dance, and when the police attempted to stop her would shriek out nothing but the word 'coronation'; but a humorous neighbor succeeded in removing her by means of familiar jokes and rough boxes on the ear. So far as I have observed, there are more drunken women here than drunken men: it is incredible how much whisky they can swallow."

76   **"Their hearts"** . . . were **"in their voices"**: [Dickens], "The Queen's Coronation," *Examiner,* July 1, 1838, 403.

77   **"One had to pinch"**: Hensel, *The Mendelssohn Family,* 2:42.

77   **"I have never before"**: Martineau, *Harriet Martineau's Autobiography,* 421.

77   **"cast a dancing radiance"**: Ibid., 421.

78   in Victoria's words, **"*completely overcome*"**: QVJ, June 28, 1838.

78   **"very awkward and uncouth"**: Disraeli to Sarah Disraeli, June 28, 1838, Weibe et al., *Letters of Benjamin Disraeli 1860–1864,* 7:466.

78   **"undoubted queen of this realm"**: *The Illustrated London News,* Illustrated London News & Sketch Limited, 1887, 90:704.

78   **"Pray tell me what I am to do"**: *The Greville Memoirs,* June 29, 1838, 4:111.

78   **"dearly beloved Lehzen"**: QVJ, June 28, 1838.

79   **"so small as to appear puny"**: Martineau, *Harriet Martineau's Autobiography,* 125.

79   **Imperial State Crown:** This crown was embedded with an enormous heart-shaped spinel that had been worn by Edward of Woodstock, the Black Prince, before it was placed into the helmet of Henry V at the Battle of Agincourt in 1415. The crown also had a sapphire that was found on a ring on the corpse of Edward the Confessor when his tomb was cracked open in 1163 (this is thought to be the oldest jewel owned by the royal family). Another 16 sapphires, 11 emeralds, 4 rubies, 1,363 brilliant diamonds, 1,273 rose diamonds, 147 table diamonds, 4 drop-shaped pearls, and 273 round pearls completed the crown. It weighed almost a kilogram.

79   **"appalling prospect"**: Rusk, *Reign of Queen Victoria,* 105.

80   **"I am merely a candidate for the hand of Her Majesty"**: *The Times,* June 29, 1838, 8.

81   **"crowded to suffocation"**: *Morning Chronicle,* quoted in Ashton, *Gossip in the First Decade,* 59.

81   **women brought presents:** Frost, *The Old Showmen,* 328.

81   **"Pig-Faced Lady"**: Sanger, *Seventy Years a Showman,* 74.

81   **"very pleasant and agreeable"**: Charles Dickens, "The Queen's Coronation," *Examiner,* July 1, 1838, 403.

81   **"To amuse and interest [the people] seems"**: Pearce, *The Diaries of Charles Greville,* June 29, 1838, 174.

82   **performed "beautifully—every part of it"**: QVJ, June 28, 1838.

82   **"This is *most provoking*"**: QVJ, July 4, 1838.

83   **"has only to show herself"**: Weintraub, *Victoria,* 114.

83   **It was "impossible"**: *The Champion and Weekly Herald,* July 1, 1838.

Chapter Eight: Learning to Rule

84   **"You lead rather an unnatural life"**: Cecil, *Young Melbourne,* 469.

84   **"like a Father"**: QVJ, September 4, 1838.

85   **Gossips whispered:** *The Diaries of Charles Greville,* 4:93. In September,
      Princess Lieven wrote to Lord Grey that "Lord Melbourne is so assidu-
      ous in his attendance on the Queen—as being so constantly and so per-
      petually with her—that I for myself cannot help imagining that she must
      be going to marry him. It is all, however, according to rule, and I find it
      both proper and in his own interest that Lord Melbourne should keep
      himself absolute master of the situation. He will stand before the new
      parliament in the position of one very high placed in Court favor; but will
      this be enough to keep him in office?" Le Strange, *Correspondence of Prin-
      cess Lieven,* 3:244.

85   **"I hope you are amused":** Countess Grey to Creevey, October 10, 1837,
      Maxwell, *The Creevey Papers,* 327, lordbyron.cath.lib.vt.edu/monograph
      .php?doc=ThCreev.1903&select=vol2.toc.

85   **not passionate about politics:** Melbourne's view was that a passage of one
      bill a year was enough: the English Municipal Bill in 1835, the Irish tithe
      bill in 1837, and the Irish Poor Law. See Mitchell, *Lord Melbourne,* 162.

86   **"That beautiful pale face":** Clarke, *Shelley and Byron,* 51.

87   **Caroline was shattered:** Caroline refused to accept Byron's retreat, turn-
      ing up at his house unannounced and usually dressed as a page, swaddled
      in an enormous coat. She would sneak into his rooms to try to catch him
      with another lover, or simply to scrawl "Remember me" across a book he
      had left lying open. The book was Beckford's *Vathek.* He wrote, in return:

> Remember thee! Remember thee!
> Till Lethe quench life's burning streams
> Remorse and shame shall cling to thee
> And haunt thee like a feverish dream
> Remember thee! Aye, doubt it not,
> Thy husband too shall think of thee,
> By neither shalt thou be forgot,
> Thou false to him, thou fiend to me!

Byron by now loathed her and declared she had no redeemable quality.
She was, he said in his dramatic fashion, an "adder in my path." The final
dramatic incident came at a ball held by Lady Heathcote in July 1813.
Jealous that Byron was talking to another woman, Caroline created a
scene: after she brandished a knife, a skirmish ensued, and she cut herself
with broken glass before being dragged out.

87   **not a prized virtue:** Ziegler, *Melbourne,* 16.

87   **"a remarkable woman, a devoted mother":** Mitchell, *Lord Melbourne,* 5.

87   **"the practice was too common":** Cecil, *The Young Melbourne,* 9.

87   **"threw buckets of ordure":** Mitchell, *Lord Melbourne,* 74.

88   **he paid an annuity:** After Melbourne died, the payments were taken over by his estate, according to Mitchell, *Lord Melbourne,* 217. Lady Branden's husband alleged that Melbourne had seduced his wife, though the evidence produced was thin, and the case was dismissed; it appears Lord Melbourne transferred a decent sum of money to Lord Branden as a result. He then cooled toward Lady Branden, who lost her husband, her honor, as well as her powerful lover, and was reduced to alternately begging and remonstrating in letters to Lord Melbourne, who told her sharply that he would never marry her. Men could continue in society as before, after having been accused of immorality and adultery; the women fell far further, and were often banished and banned from seeing their children.

88   **"I don't think you should give a woman":** QVJ, July 19, 1839.

88   **his experiences at Eton:** Melbourne told Victoria, "I don't think he flogged me enough, it would have been better if he had flogged me more." Esher, *Girlhood of Queen Victoria,* 2:30.

88   **"had always an amazing":** QVJ, October 15, 1838.

89   **consent from an orphan girl:** When she had children of her own, Churchill wrote to Lord Melbourne jokingly about what he had done to her, saying how he made her laugh, and asking if he thought her ten-month-old baby was too young to whip. She wrote: "A propos of children I have not forgotten your *practical* lessons upon whipping and follow up the system with great success upon Caroline at least, for William is too young, don't you think so? He is only 10 months. I remember as though it was yesterday the *execution,* then being thrown into a corner of a large couch there was at Brocket you used then to leave the room and I remember your coming back one day and saying "well cocky does it smart still?" at which of course I could not help laughing instead of crying. Does the Queen whip the royal princes I should like to know?" From the Panshanger MSS, quoted in Mitchell, *Lord Melbourne,* 214.

89   **"He is certainly a queer fellow":** Pearce, *The Diaries of Lord Greville,* 131.

89   **he embodied governments of the past:** Ziegler, *Melbourne,* 203: Melbourne told Victoria "all government has to do is prevent and punish crime, and to preserve contracts." Ziegler writes: "The concept that each government would arrive in office brandishing an imposing array of new laws which it proposed to implement evolved slowly over the nineteenth century. The eighteenth-century idea of government was rather that it should concern itself only with defence, foreign policy and the administration of the country. New laws were only needed to meet specific crises.

In subscribing to this view Melbourne spoke for the majority of political leaders, Whig or Tory. Russell and Peel were the men of the future: Melbourne, Holland, Lansdowne, Palmerston, for the Whigs; Wellington, Aberdeen, Lyndhurst for the Tories; reflected the traditional wisdom of the past."

90   "nothing at all": Cecil, *The Young Melbourne,* 216.

90   "the degree of repression": Ziegler, *Melbourne,* 72.

90   "*very* important &": QVJ, July 18, 1837. Similarly, on August 8: "Talked over many things which were of great and painful interest to me; things gone by, and past, I mean. Lord Melbourne is so kind, so feeling, and entered quite into my feelings." On July 17, she had written that he was her friend: "I know it."

90   "sensitive and susceptible temperament": Longford, *Victoria R.I.,* 66.

90   "for a long time": QVJ, February 6, 1839.

90   "Which is very true": Cecil, *The Young Melbourne,* 413.

91   "he looks loving": Quoted in ibid., 394.

91   "die with laughing": QVJ, December 23, 1837.

92   "did not like any of the Poor": Lord Melbourne to John Russell, October 24, 1837, from Mitchell, *Lord Melbourne,* 282n.

92   used "we" in referring: QVJ, May 25, 1838.

92   **Melbourne was naturally conservative:** Many of Melbourne's private views were conservative, and he associated frequently with Tories. Victoria developed a fierce loyalty for the Whig party, in other words, without realizing what Whigs really were. Whig orthodoxy then was liberty, low taxation, enclosure of land, antidespotism, and democracy. See Cecil, *The Young Melbourne,* 7.

92   "nasty wretch": QVJ, January 27, 1840; Cecil, *The Young Melbourne,* 336.

92   "It is a fact that the": Longford, *Victoria R.I.,* 70.

92   "With the young foolish Queen": Mitchell, *Lord Melbourne,* 240.

93   "I felt how unfit I was": QVJ, December 15, 1838.

93   "By God, I am at it": February 19, 1840, Greville, *The Great World,* 180.

93   "cross and low" ... "incredible weight for my size": Woodham-Smith, *Queen Victoria,* 163.

93   "full with a fine bust": Longford, *Queen Victoria,* 88.

93   "perhaps rather more appearance": Woodham-Smith, *Queen Victoria,* 162.

94   "I told Lord Melbourne": Cecil, *The Young Melbourne,* 424.

94   "just like the nurse": Rhodes James, *Albert, Prince Consort,* 64.

Chapter Nine: A Scandal in the Palace

96   **"[Melbourne] has a young and inexperienced":** September 16, 1838, Parry, *Correspondence of Lord Aberdeen,* 1:113.

96   **"They wished to treat me like a girl":** May 10, 1839, Pearce, *The Diaries of Charles Greville,* 181.

96   **"Those two abominable women":** QVJ, June 21, 1839.

97   **she was an "odious" spy:** QVJ, April 25, 1838.

97   **"awkward business":** QVJ, February 2, 1839.

97   **Melbourne had told her:** QVJ, January 18, 1839.

98   **"loathe one's own sex":** QVJ, February 2, 1839.

98   **"perhaps the most incompetent":** Pearsall, *The Worm in the Bud,* 5.

98   **any other conditions:** In *The Court Doctor Dissected,* 1839, John Fisher Murray, MD, strongly condemned James Clark's lack of medical insight, listing a dozen other ailments that produced pregnancy-like symptoms, such as abdominal tumors, hepatic diseases, digestive organ problems, splenic disease, mesenteric aneurismal disease of the abdominal arteries, dropsy, or umbilical hernia.

98   **a "coarse" Dr. Clark:** On March 13, Lady Flora told her mother James Clark had been irritated by her denial, and "became violent and coarse, and even attempted to browbeat me." *The Times,* September 16, 1839, 3.

99   **"most rigid examination":** Ibid.

99   **"no grounds for believing":** Ibid.

99   **"I must respectfully observe":** Martin, *Enter Rumour,* 41.

99   **might still be pregnant:** Victoria wrote to her mother: "Sir C. Clarke had said that though she is a virgin still that it might be possible and one could not tell if such things could not happen. That there was an enlargement in the womb like a child." Longford, *Victoria R.I.,* 99.

100   **sacked Dr. Clark:** Martin, *Enter Rumour,* 48–49: Lady Sophia wrote to her family that at least one of his aristocratic patients had dismissed him because of what he had done, and that "many medical men have refused to meet him in consultation, as they, and Sir Henry Halford among them, say he has cast an odium on the profession." In QVJ, April 8, 1839, Victoria recorded that Clark had suffered a good deal from the whole affair, and had lost a good many patients, "and that the country papers abused him so."

100   **"It is inconceivable how Melbourne":** Woodham-Smith, *Queen Victoria,* 167.

100   **"This made me laugh excessively":** QVJ, March 18, 1839.

100   **the ugliest woman:** QVJ, January 14, 1839.

100   **"To a female sovereign":** Published in *The Times,* September 16, 1839, 3.

100   **without a word:** Melbourne did respond to the letter, and was rather harsh. He was critical of the "tone and substance" of her letter, but said the queen would do all she could to "soothe the feelings" of Lady Flora and her family.

101   **"so unprecedented and objectionable":** Published in *The Times,* September 16, 1839, 3. In June, the Marquess of Hastings wrote to Lord Melbourne demanding an apology for the tone the PM took in this letter to his mother.

101   **"I blush to send you":** *The Times,* August 12, 1839, 5.

102   **"wicked foolish old woman":** QVJ, April 16, 1839.

102   **"The state of agony":** QVJ, May 7, 1839.

102   **"It was some minutes before":** Ibid.

103   **"The Queen ventures to maintain":** Hibbert, *Queen Victoria: A Personal History,* 93.

104   **"The Queen didn't like his manner":** Benson and Esher, *The Letters of Queen Victoria,* 1:200.

104   **"I said I could *not* give up":** Ibid., 1:208.

104   **plenty of Tory relatives:** Martin, *Enter Rumour,* 62. Lady Harriet Clive was the only Tory among the queen's ladies.

105   **[Peel had] behaved very ill:** QVJ, May 9, 1839.

105   **"Do not fear that I was calm":** Woodham-Smith, *Queen Victoria,* 174.

105   **In a chilly letter:** Peel Papers, vol. 123, letter dated May 10, 1839, British Library Archives, Add. 40, 303, Extract: 40303.

106   **"very much put out":** QVJ, May 30, 1839.

106   **"Tories are capable of every villainy":** Ziegler, *Melbourne,* 299.

106   **"I was very hot about it":** October 30, 1897, Sir Arthur Bigge, in Longford, *Victoria R.I.,* 114.

107   **"bilious attack":** QVJ, June 9, 1839.

107   **"exceedingly rude":** QVJ, April 5, 1839.

107   **"It does not occur to her":** Lady Flora never accused Victoria of malice, but wrote to her mother that the queen was "capable of kindliness of feeling occasionally, but self . . . has been so sedulously cultivated within the last year & half that it does it does not occur to her to feel for another—& in the present instance, be it childishness or be it want of that keen sense of female honor which ones wishes to see, I do not believe she understands that I can have been injured by a rumor which has been proved false." Martin, *Enter Rumour,* 50.

107   **"I found poor Ly. Flora":** QVJ, June 27, 1839. In an account of this meet-

ing, Lady Flora's sister, Lady Sophia, wrote to her mother that: "I begin to think [Victoria] a positive Goose & a Fool—I believe She now pays attention from fear for the expression of interest & indignation is still so great in London that they dread the effect of any want of respect & attention." Martin, *Enter Rumour,* 67.

108   **all she could think:** QVJ, July 6, 1839: Lord Melbourne was uncharitable to the last. Told on June 29 that a motionless Lady Flora was in a "most Christian state of mind," he retorted: "It's easy to say that. I daresay she would like to do mischief again." Victoria added: "which, were she to recover, I fear she would; but, I said to Lord M. I thought people must repent at last." Victoria believed she had repented, but this did not prevent her from seeing the ailing as an inconvenience. (QVJ, July 1, 1839.) As she told Lord M. over dinner, it was awkward having someone dying in the house, because she could not go out, or ask people for dinner. (QVJ, July 3, 1839.)

108   **"& only just raised her hands":** QVJ, July 5, 1839.

108   **a protester wrote:** Martin, *Enter Rumour,* 69.

108   **But the autopsy:** *The Champion and Weekly Herald,* July 14, 1839.

108   **"the uterus and its appendages":** "The Post-Mortem Examination of the Lady Flora Hastings" was published in full in the *Morning Post,* July 9, 1839, 5. It was signed by five doctors. It read:

> There was great emaciation of the whole person.
>
> In the chest: the heart and lungs were in a perfectly healthy state; but there were extensive adhesions of the pleura (or membrane) covering the right lung, to that which lines the ribs—evidently of long standing.
>
> In the abdomen: there were universal adhesions of the peritoneum (or membrane which lines the cavity and covers the viscera), so that it could not be said that there was a single organ which was not, at every point on its surface, intimately connected with the parts in its vicinity. The liver was very much enlarged, extending downwards as low as the pelvis, and upwards so as very materially to diminish the capacity of the right cavity of the chest. The gall bladder contained a small quantity of bile. The liver was of a very pale color, but its structure was not materially different from what exists in the healthy state. The stomach and intestines were distended with air; their coats, especially the muscular, were very much attenuated. The spleen and pancreas were free from disease. Some of the mesenteric glands were enlarged. There were a few

small deposits of unorganized yellow matter, apparently in the substance of the adhesions.

The uterus and its appendages presented the usual appearances of the healthy virgin state.

From the character of the adhesions it was plain that they could be referred only to inflammation at some former and distant period of time. The effect of them must have been to interrupt the passage of the contents of the stomach and intestines, and in various ways to interfere with the due performance of their functions.

108   **"her own country":** QVJ, April 20, 1839.

109   **were later destroyed:** Hibbert, *Queen Victoria in Her Letters,* 5.

109   **"precocious knowledge":** To M. V. Brett, March 13, 1904, Brett, *Journals and Letters,* 1:49.

109   **"What is the good":** Martin, *Enter Rumour,* 73.

109   **overwhelming urge to roll:** Longford, *Victoria R.I.,* 124.

109   **she was often directly blamed:** See the *Spectator* coverage. Quoted in the *Morning Post,* July 22, 1839, 3. (The *Leamington Spa Courier* wrote that "the continuance in office of Sir J. Clark gives some color to the rumor that her Majesty, and not the physician, was the original author of the slander." Martin, *Enter Rumour,* 57.)

109   **accused the court of murder:** *The Era* said the mental distress and physical neglect killed her—and it was MURDER, they wrote in capital letters. A letter writer also called it murder, in the *Morning Post,* July 22, 1839, 3. The *Morning Post* ran a long, vehement campaign against the queen and her court. The *Examiner* (quoted in the *Caledonian Mercury,* July 18, 1839) said Lady Flora had been "destroyed in the flower of her days by the slanders and insults of Court minions, sufficiently profligate and unprincipled to aim at Royal favor by this work of death, and sufficiently fortunate, so far as yet appears, to have attained their object by this cruel and fatal means!" The *Examiner* continued: "Here is in direct terms the wicked charge, that the Queen's favor was to be gained by effecting the death of Lady Flora Hastings, and that the Royal favor has actually been obtained by such means." It was a shocking allegation.

109   **"For myself I feel this trial":** Martin, *Enter Rumour,* 54–55.

110   **"Forgive my poor Child?":** Ibid., 67–68.

110   **"The whole ceremony":** *The Times,* July 20, 1839, 6.

110   **"Her memory is embalmed":** *The Corsair,* August 31, 1839, 5

110   **"At her accession, I was agreeably":** Martineau, *Harriet Martineau's Autobiography,* 418.

Chapter Ten: Virago in Love

115 **"I told Albert that he had come":** Quoted in Hudson, *A Royal Conflict,* 183.

115 **"Queen Victoria, even when she was most infatuatedly":** Shaw, November 21, 1908, *Collected Letters,* 2:817, cited in Weintraub, "Exasperated Admiration," 128.

116 **a "virago queen":** Aronson, *Heart of a Queen,* 53.

117 **"enjoy two or three years more":** Victoria would later deeply regret this delay, writing that she could not now "think without indignation against herself, of her wish to keep the Prince waiting for probably three or four years, at the risk of ruining all his prospects for life, until she might feel inclined to marry! . . . The only excuse the Queen can make for herself is in the fact that the sudden change from the secluded life at Kensington to the independence of her position as Queen Regnant at the age of eighteen, put all ideas of marriage out of her mind, which she now most bitterly repents." Quoted in Woodham-Smith, *Queen Victoria,* 243.

117 **"May I pray you to think":** Jagow, *Letters of the Prince Consort,* 14.

117 **she "may not have the *feeling*":** Benson and Esher, *Letters of Queen Victoria,* 1:177–78.

118 **"thinks seriously of making an offer":** The (Portsmouth) *New Hampshire Journal of Literature and Politics,* August 5, 1837, documented a report in the *Salem Register,* from Massachusetts, which read:

> A mischievous rumor is in circulation that our widower President thinks seriously of making an offer to the young and beautiful Queen of the British Empire. We at first supposed that the British Constitution and Laws presented an insuperable barrier to such a connection—but by the following paragraph from the Boston Daily Advertiser, the young Queen is at liberty to marry whom she chooses *except a Papist.* Although Martin has been almost "every thing by turns and nothing long," yet we believe he was never a professed Catholic—we therefore see no reason why he should not *offer,* or why he may not stand as good a chance as the namby-pamby princes and kinglings of Europe.

118 **"assured him he need have no fear":** QVJ, April 18, 1839.

118 **"*not* NECESSARY":** QVJ, June 24, 1839.

118 **she hoped he would not remarry:** QVJ, October 14, 1839.

119 **"Oh! But you would have":** QVJ, April 18, 1839.

119 **he would not stand idly by:** Jagow, *Letters of the Prince Consort,* 32.

119 **"Cousin Victoria is always friendly":** Stewart, *Albert: A Life,* 26.

119 **"If after waiting, perhaps for three years"**: Martin, *The Prince Consort,* 1:7.

119 **his greyhound stole food:** Victoria and Albert shared a love of dogs. Victoria's favorite breed was the goofy, affectionate cocker spaniel; Albert's was the cool, sleek greyhound. He told Victoria in a letter dated December 31, 1839, that his favorite, Eos, was "very friendly if there is plumcake in the room, very much put out when she has to jump over the stick, keen on hunting, sleepy after it, always proud, and contemptuous of other dogs." (Jagow, *Letters of the Prince Consort,* 47.) Albert brought Eos to England with him, and while he was there, he chose a tan-colored greyhound pup for Victoria.

119 **"for a woman cannot stand alone"**: QVJ, October 14, 1839.

121 **"He seems *perfection"*:** Quoted in Grey, *The Early Years,* 188. She also wrote to Stockmar, the Duke of Sussex, and Queen Adelaide.

121 **"Never. The Duchess of Kent never knew"**: Stuart, *The Mother of Victoria,* 246.

122 a **"great plague"**: QVJ, November 17, 1839.

122 **"The Queen sent for me alone"**: Hibbert, *Queen Victoria: A Personal History,* 110.

122 ***"Liebe Kleine, Ich habe"*:** Longford, *Victoria R.I.,* 135.

123 **"I said to Albert we should be very very intimate"**: QVJ, November 13, 1939.

123 **"often at a loss to believe"**: Jagow, *Letters of the Prince Consort,* 23.

123 **"Oh, the future!"**: November 11, 1839, ibid., 25.

123 **"decisive for the welfare"**: Ibid., 24.

123 **"elasticity of the brain" . . . "great men"**: Rhodes James, *Albert, Prince Consort,* 58.

123 **poor German duchy:** Albert, just three months Victoria's junior, came from Coburg, a small state with half a million inhabitants and a royal house that had become a European dynasty in the early part of the nineteenth century. Jagow describes Leopold, Duke Ernst I's younger brother, as Coburg's "spiritual leader."

123 **"but she has acquired"**: Vallone, *Becoming Victoria,* 31.

124 **His words and ideas:** QVJ, October 26, 1839.

124 **She confessed twice:** QVJ, November 15, 1839.

124 **"with nothing under them"**: QVJ, November 1, 1839.

124 **"looked about him, like a squirrel"**: Bolitho, *A Biographer's Notebook,* 114.

125 **"most unbecoming in a Saxon knight"**: Ibid., 19.

125 **"superb, an extraordinary beauty"**: Stewart, *Albert: A Life,* 8.

125 **blatantly unfaithful:** Rhodes James, *Albert, Prince Consort,* 20–21.

125　**the night she left:** In a letter dated September 21, 1824, she wrote: "Parting from my children was the worst thing of all. They have whooping cough, and they said, 'Mama is crying because she has to go away when we are ill.'" Sotnick, *The Coburg Conspiracy,* 147.

125　**disguising herself as a peasant:** This is a story told by German philologist Max Müller, quoted in Weintraub, *Victoria,* 28.

125　**intercepted the letters:** Sotnick, *The Coburg Conspiracy,* 150.

125　**Duke Ernst was not his father:** For analysis of the issue of Albert's possible illegitimacy, see Rhodes James, *Albert, Prince Consort;* Bolitho, *A Biographer's Notebook,* 102–22. Sotnick outlines the counterargument in *The Coburg Conspiracy.* In short, Sotnick says he was illegitimate; Rhodes James and Bolitho say he wasn't. The salient points are that the rumors about Baron von Meyern, the court chamberlain, began only after she had an affair with Lieutenant von Hanstein, whom she later married. David Duff also argues that Albert was conceived when Leopold visited Coburg at the end of 1818. Duff, *Albert and Victoria,* 28–32, 66. Again, the evidence is circumstantial.

126　**"shameless little sinner":** Ibid., 148.

126　**"there was not even a hint in the documents":** Bolitho, *A Biographer's Notebook,* 103.

126　**they dug up her coffin:** Ponsonby, *The Lost Duchess,* 163.

126　**"with tenderness and sorrow":** Quoted in Jagow, *Letters of the Prince Consort,* 4, attributed to Grey, *The Early Years,* 8.

127　**"an awful moment":** Benson and Esher, *The Letters of Queen Victoria,* 1:248.

128　**"I did a much more nervous thing":** November 26, 1839, Greville, *The Great World,* 175–76.

128　**"A gilded puppet":** Quoted in the *Caledonian Mercury,* November 28, 1839.

129　**aristocratic families often encouraged it:** See Kuper, *Incest and Influence,* 23.

129　**"at least three times as frequent":** Ibid., 18.

129　**about 10 percent of marriages:** Ibid.

129　**"When Benjamin Bunny grew up":** Ibid., 23.

130　**"perpetual self-fertilisation":** Darwin, *Fertilisation of Orchids,* 361.

130　**he had married his own cousin:** Kuper, *Incest and Influence,* 94. Darwin was fascinated by the consequences of in-breeding. Between 1868 and 1877 he published three monographs on cross-fertilization in animals and plants. In the first of these, *The Variation of Animals and Plants Under Domestication,* he proposed that "the existence of a great law of nature is almost proved; namely, that the crossing of animals and plants which are not closely related to each other is highly beneficial or even necessary, and that inter-breeding prolonged during many generations is highly injurious." Darwin thought this was probably true of human beings as well, although he was reluctant at first to press the issue, "as it is surrounded by natural prejudices." In any case, he was bound to consider the implications for his own family. His scientific project and his personal concerns— his own marriage, his illness, and the poor health of his children—could hardly be separated.

130   **Florence Nightingale had raised:** Nightingale, *Cassandra: An Essay,* 47.

130   **the medical establishment was unanimous:** For a wonderful analysis of consanguinity in the nineteenth century, please see Anderson, "Cousin Marriage in Victorian England," and Kuper, *Incest and Influence.*

131   **"starving, cringing, swaggering" people:** Evans, "The Victorians: Empire and Race."

131   **great revival of interest in German philosophy:** Ramsden, *Don't Mention the War,* 32.

132   **"for those nice Tories have cut off half my income":** Jagow, *Letters of the Prince Consort,* 59.

132   **"As long as I live, I will never":** Cecil, *The Young Melbourne,* 478.

132   **"Poor dear Albert":** QVJ, February 2, 1840, from Longford, *Victoria R.I.,* 137. The bill for his naturalization went through without mentioning it—but she was able to declare precedence by royal prerogative later.

132   **"I am usually (alas!) of a rather cold nature":** Prince Albert to Queen Victoria, Gotha, December 28, 1839, Jagow, *Letters of the Prince Consort,* 45.

132   **wrote his fiancée many letters:** On November 15, he wrote to the queen from Calais, still ill from the sea crossing, calling her again "Dearest, deeply loved Victoria." He had not stopped thinking of her since he left Windsor, he wrote, "and your image fills my whole soul. Even in my dreams I never imagined that I should find so much love on earth. How that moment shines for me when I was close to you, with your hand in mine!" (Jagow, *Letters of the Prince Consort,* 26.) Two days later, he wrote, "I kiss you a thousand times." (Ibid., 27.) And from Wiesbaden on November 21, 1839: "I can only imagine you on the 14th in your little sitting room feeling rather lonely; we were so happy sitting there on the little sofa. How I would like to be there by magic to cheer your loneliness. I have these days been distracted by fresh places, fresh conditions, memories, people, events, and yet none of them can smother the painful feeling of separation." (Ibid., 28.)

133   **"Dearly beloved Victoria—I long to talk to you":** Rhodes James, *Albert, Prince Consort,* 85.

133 **especially regarding the men:** Jagow, *Letters of the Prince Consort,* 31–32.

133 **"I know personally nothing":** December 15, 1839, Ibid., 40.

133 **Albert campaigned for weeks:** Jagow, *Letters of the Prince Consort,* 42.

133 **more important to please Albert:** Ibid., 48.

134 **"With burning love for you":** January 6, 1840, ibid., 50.

135 **"I hope Lord Melbourne does not think":** January 13, 1840, ibid., 51.

136 **Melbourne "saw no objection to":** QVJ, January 14, 1840.

136 **"From the Tories, dear Lord":** QVJ, January 1, 1840.

Chapter Eleven: The Bride: "I Never, Never Spent Such an Evening"

137 **"You forget, my dearest Love":** January 31, 1840, Buckingham Palace, Benson and Esher, *The Letters of Queen Victoria,* 268–69.

138 **Would his eye turn:** Victoria brought this subject up with Melbourne at least twice in the weeks before the wedding. First, QVJ, January 19, 1840: They "talked of Albert's dislike for Ladies," and Lord M. said: "It's very well if that holds, but it doesn't always." Victoria "scolded him." Second, on January 23: "I said to Lord M. I had told Stockmar what Lord M. had said to me here and at Windsor, about those very high principles like A.'s not *holding* often, upon which Stockmar said, generally speaking that was true, but that he didn't think that would be A.'s case."

138 **"if ye say, Preserve the queen!":** From the poem "Crowned and Wedded," printed five days after the royal wedding.

139 **"I am sure none of your friends":** QVJ, February 7, 1840.

139 **"seeing his *dear dear* face":** QVJ, February 8, 1840.

139 **"Dear Albert, you have not at all understood":** January 31, 1840, Buckingham Palace, Benson and Esher, *The Letters of Queen Victoria,* 1:268–69.

140 **remove the word "obey":** Warner, *Queen Victoria's Sketchbook,* 92.

140 **"Everything [is] always made":** QVJ, December 5, 1839.

141 **"foolish nonsense":** QVJ, January 7, 1840.

141 **"I declared laughing":** Ibid.

141 **"Dearest,—how are you today":** Benson and Esher, *The Letters of Queen Victoria,* 1:273

142 **"like a pure virgin":** Strickland, *Queen Victoria,* 209.

142 **"a hurried glance around":** *The Times,* February 10, 1840, 5.

142 **"vast numbers":** *The Observer,* February 10, 1840, 3.

142 **"We are all going stark staring mad":** *The Satirist,* February 9, 1840, quoted in Plunkett, *Queen Victoria: First Media Monarch,* 135.

142 **"Poor little thing":** Thomas Carlyle to Margaret A. Carlyle, February 11,

1840. doi:10.1215/lt-18400211-TC-MAC-01; CL 12:40–42, carlyleletters .dukeupress.edu.

143 **"as the King of England":** Williams, *Becoming Queen,* 339.

143 **"Society is unhinged":** Forster, *Life of Charles Dickens,* 1:145.

143 **"On Tuesday we sallied down":** House and Storey, *Letters of Charles Dickens,* 2:25–27.

144 **"remarkably agreeable looking":** February 14, 1840, to Parthenope Nightingale, McDonald, *Nightingale on Society and Politics,* 5:411.

144 **"perfectly composed and spoke distinctly":** McDonald, *Florence Nightingale's European Travels,* 623.

144 **"I did not shed one tear":** QVJ, February 10, 1840.

145 **"There never was":** Longford, *Queen Victoria,* 143.

145 **"SO *delightful*":** QVJ, February 10, 1840.

145 **"The Ceremony was very imposing":** Ibid.

146 **"*of course* in *one* bed":** Ibid.

146 **"I NEVER, NEVER spent such an evening!":** Ibid.

147 **women's animal nature:** Female sexual desire was believed to be particularly dangerous: women were more easily overwhelmed by the power of their sexual passion, it was said, because they were closer to nature and thus more volatile and irrational than men. According to one doctor in 1887, "When they are touched and excited, a time arrived when, though not intending to sin, they lost all physical control over themselves." Groneman, "Nymphomania," 353.

147 **candidates for nymphomania:** Ibid., 340.

148 **specifically excluded women:** Even women who considered themselves open-minded had difficulty with the idea of women doctors. Men had been so effective in establishing themselves as moral and scientific authorities that any woman who sought to place herself in that role was considered mannish or of indeterminate sex. Florence Nightingale was celebrated as a nurse, and therefore acceptable as a nurturer; but Dr. Mary Walker, who treated many patients during the U.S. Civil War, was a byword for freakishness. One exception was Elizabeth Blackwell, who had qualified in America, so was able to practice as a doctor in the United Kingdom.

148 **never consummated:** "It is far from seldom that I meet with cases in which the hymen has never been ruptured." "Ignorance and False Ideas About Sexual Congress" (1865) in Acton, *Functions and Disorders,* 89.

148 **his 1857 declaration:** Tosh, *A Man's Place,* 44.

148 **women tried to avoid:** Mason, *The Making of Victorian Sexuality,* 203. Mason writes that many women were scared of sexual pleasure in the

nineteenth century because they linked orgasms to falling pregnant. Many GPs would have read Copland, who wrote, "It is generally understood by females of all ranks in society, that indifference during intercourse, or suppression of the orgasm will prevent impregnation, and, although they are sometimes deceived in this respect, yet their inference is correct in the majority." Copland, *A Dictionary of Practical Medicine,* 374.

148 **"The majority of women":** Tait, *Diseases of Women,* 36, 41, quoted in Jalland and Hooper, *Women from Birth to Death,* 222.

148 **sex was a chore:** Historian Edward Shorter wrote, "The overwhelming body of evidence suggests that, for married women in the past, sex was a burden to be dutifully, resentfully borne throughout life rather than a source of joy." *A History of Women's Bodies,* 13.

148 **"She had a very low-necked dress":** August 22, 1840, Bolitho, *The Prince Consort,* 24.

149 **"pay more attention to the ladies":** Rhodes James, *Albert, Prince Consort,* 57.

149 **This was partly true:** Stockmar, *Memoirs of Baron Stockmar,* 2:7.

149 **male company:** In 1838, Albert told his childhood friend Prince Wilhelm zu Löwenstein-Wertheim-Freudenberg that "I believe the pleasant days which we spent together [at the university], partly in useful occupation, partly in cheerful intercourse, will ever appear to me as the happiest of my life. In spite of our unrestrained intimacy [*Ungenirheit*] and our many practical jokes, the utmost harmony always existed between us. How pleasant were our winter concerts—our theatrical attempts—our walks to the Venusberg—the swimming school—the fencing ground—! I dare not think back upon all those things." Grey, *The Early Years,* 154.

149 **only women he spoke to:** Extract from Lady Clarendon's Journal, July 21, 1841: "I sat by Prince Albert at dinner today, but could not get on with him. He was civil and good-natured, but did not converse. I believe he does with men, but he appears never to do so with women, except Royalties. He seemed to get on very well with the Queen of the Belgians, who sat the other side of him." Maxwell, *Life and Letters of Clarendon,* 1:221.

149 **"a marked distaste to the opposite sex":** Strachey, *Queen Victoria,* 136.

149 **point to the male friendships:** Some have argued that it is also possible that Albert formed romantic attachments while at Bonn University in the 1830s, although this is mere suggestion, without evidence. The prevalence of homoerotic liaisons at universities at this time has been well documented, especially in England. Ronald Pearsall argues that for many of the upper classes, "Homosexual experiences were the rule rather than the

exception." (Pearsall, *The Worm in the Bud,* 452.) By 1895, the editor William Stead recognized this when he wrote in his *Review of Reviews* after the Oscar Wilde case: "Should everyone found guilty of Oscar Wilde's crime be imprisoned, there would be a very surprising emigration from Eton, Harrow, Rugby and Winchester to the jails of Pentonville and Holloway. Until then, boys are free to pick up tendencies and habits in public schools for which they may be sentenced to hard labor later on." (Ibid., 456.)

149   **attachment to his tutor:** See Gillian Gill's analysis of this in *We Two.* Edward Benson, who collated Victoria's letters in the 1930s, described Albert's affection for Herr Florschütz as "a disordered unnatural fancy." (*Queen Victoria,* 190.) Forty years later, in 1972, David Duff said Albert had "strange and unnatural feelings" for his tutor that had to be "sternly repressed." Again, no evidence was given for this. In 1991, Monica Charlot wrote that Albert "undoubtedly attracted" Florschütz, and said if Duff was right, it would "scarcely be abnormal, given the traumatic effect of his mother's departure and the fact that Florschütz was to supervise the boys' studies for some fifteen years." Charlot does not, however, suggest a homosexual relationship. (Charlot, *Victoria the Young Queen,* 154.)

150   **the categorization of homosexuality:** The word "homosexual" was first used in English in Charles Gilbert Chaddock's 1895 translation of Richard von Krafft-Ebing's *Psychopathia Sexualis,* a study of sexual practices. The country that has been credited with "the invention of homosexuality" was Germany, partly because the politicians felt the need to curb same-sex affection with anti-sodomy laws in the mid-1800s. Beachy, "The German Invention of Homosexuality."

150   **"of Albert's not caring greatly":** QVJ, October 22, 1839.

150   **"I shan't forgive you that":** QVJ, November 4, 1839.

151   **"a great dislike to being in [the] charge of women":** Grey, *The Early Years,* 42.

Chapter Twelve: Only the Husband, and Not the Master

152   **"[Acknowledging] one important truth":** Quoted in Homans and Munich, *Remaking Queen Victoria,* 3.

152   **"In my home life I am very happy":** Prince Albert to Prince Wilhelm zu Löwenstein-Wertheim-Freudenberg, May 1840, quoted in Jagow, *Letters of the Prince Consort,* 69.

153 **"I was not the least frightened":** QVJ, June 10, 1840.

153 **"a little air":** Albert wrote to his grandmother from Buckingham Palace, June 11, 1840, Jagow, *Letters of the Prince Consort,* 70.

153 **"triumphal procession":** QVJ, June 10, 1840.

154 **"you have shown *great fortitude*":** King Leopold to Queen Victoria, Laeken, June 13, 1840, Benson and Esher, *The Letters of Queen Victoria,* 1:286.

154 **"communications of an important nature":** This letter, dated April 3, 1840, was addressed to his workplace, the pub the Hog in the Pound, and read, "Young England—Sir—You are requested to attend tonight, as there is an extraordinary meeting to be holden, in consequence of having received some communications of an important nature from Hanover. You must attend; and if your master will not give you leave, you must come in defiance of him. A. W. Smith, secretary." Murphy, *Shooting Victoria,* 40.

154 **Ernestus Rex:** Jerrold, *Married Life of Victoria,* 84.

154 **they were merely a ruse:** Murphy, *Shooting Victoria,* 38–40.

155 **"Oh, I know to the contrary":** *The Times,* June 12, 1840, 6.

155 **"one should think that your being a lady would":** King Leopold to Queen Victoria, June 13, 1840, Benson and Esher, *The Letters of Queen Victoria,* 1:286.

155 **ruled by a woman:** *The Times,* June 12, 1840, 6.

155 **Oxford was charged with high treason:** In Melbourne, Oxford created a respectable life as a successful painter (under the name of John Freeman), churchwarden, investigative journalist, author, stepfather, and husband of a younger widow. When his book on the city of Melbourne was published, he hoped Victoria might somehow come to read it: "I should like a certain illustrious lady to know that one who was a foolish boy half a century ago is now a respectable, & respected, member of society." He died a year before Victoria did, though, and his story was never published in England. Murphy, *Shooting Victoria,* 510.

155 **strange, contagious "erotomania":** Turner, "Erotomania and Queen Victoria," 226.

155 **"I am very angry":** Miller, *Elizabeth Barrett to Miss Mitford,* 121.

156 **Victoria sent him a handwritten note:** Dekkers, *Dearest Pet: On Bestiality,* 84.

156 **Conservative estimates:** Loudon, *Death in Childbirth.* A graph on p. 14 shows this figure was consistent from 1851 to 1890, when it rose slightly before dropping to four in one thousand births in 1900.

157 excessive "mental emotion": Branca, *Silent Sisterhood,* 86–88. From 1847 to 1876, five women per one thousand live births died, and puerperal fever caused between a third and a half of these deaths. Doctors prescribed opium, champagne, and brandy and soda. Flanders, *The Victorian House,* 20.

157 "nasty girl": Charlot, *Victoria the Young Queen,* 192.

157 "unbounded happiness": Queen Victoria to Vicky, March 24, 1858, Fulford, *Dearest Child,* 77.

157 "Don't correct yourself": Wyndham, *Correspondence of Sarah Spencer,* 306.

157 Victoria soon declared in her journal: Martin, *The Prince Consort,* 1:99–100.

157 "a nurse or man midwife": Woodham-Smith, *Queen Victoria,* 211.

158 "very active; out walking": Wyndham, *Correspondence of Sarah Spencer,* 299.

158 still labored in petticoats, gowns, and chemises: Flanders, *The Victorian House,* 17.

158 "simple tastes and pleasures": July 1841, Wyndham, *Correspondence of Sarah Spencer,* 311.

159 "She is far too open": Memorandum from Mr. Anson on comments made by Lord Melbourne, Windsor Castle, January 15, 1841, Benson and Esher, *The Letters of Queen Victoria,* 1:322. While Victoria was fluent in French and German, and wrote and understood Italian, "the rest of her education she owes to her own natural shrewdness and quickness, and this perhaps has not been the proper education for one who was to wear the Crown of England."

159 "God knows how great": QVJ, February 28, 1840.

159 "a quiet, happy but an inglorious": Unpublished letter from Yvonne Ward collection, Prince Ernest to King Leopold, February 1, 1840, Staatsarchiv Coburg, 567/WE22: 66.

159 sought the title of King Consort: Charlot, *Victoria the Young Queen,* 171–72; Benson and Esher, *The Letters of Queen Victoria,* 1:199; Martin, *The Prince Consort,* 1:256–57.

160 "In my home life I am very happy": Grey, *The Early Years,* 256.

160 "fill up every gap, which, as a woman": Cited in Martin, *The Prince Consort,* 1:74.

161 "her intellect is not for invention": Ruskin, *Sesame and Lilies,* 84, on the "Angel in the House."

161 "Some, at least, of these faculties": Darwin, *Evolutionary Writings,* 303.

161 **"It is quite possible"**: Ellis, *The Wives of England*, 24–25.

161 **that she satisfied herself**: November 23, 1841. Stockmar wrote to Lord Melbourne: "I expressed [to Peel] my delight at seeing the Queen so happy, and added a hope that more and more she would seek and find her real happiness in her domestic relations only." Charlot, *Victoria the Young Queen*, 208.

162 **"She said it proceeded entirely"**: May 28, 1840, "Minutes of Conversations with Lord Melbourne and Baron Stockmar," Benson and Esher, *The Letters of Queen Victoria*, 1:282–83.

162 **Stockmar also suggested**: As recorded by Anson, ibid., 1:283.

163 **signed instantly**: Charlot, *Victoria the Young Queen*, 190.

163 **"Mme. De Lehzen's pale face"**: October 1838, Wyndham, *Correspondence of Sarah Spencer*, 282–83.

164 **"rewards me sufficiently"**: Jagow, *Letters of the Prince Consort*, 69. Also note that women were allowed to attend these meetings but could not speak or become full members. Tyrell, "Women's Mission."

164 **"now all the fashion"**: Woodham-Smith, *Queen Victoria*, 211.

164 **"deeply interesting conversation"**: February 1842, Fox, *Memories of Old Friends*, 289.

164 **"plentifully strewn with thorns"**: Woodham-Smith, *Queen Victoria*, 242.

164 **"Albert had done the correct thing"**: Prince Ernest to King Leopold, February 17, 1840, Staatsarchiv Coburg, 567/WE22: 76. From Ward, "The Womanly Garb," 281.

165 **"I am to be Regent—*alone*"**: Albert to Ernest, July 17, 1840, quoted in Bolitho, *Albert, Prince Consort*, 51.

165 **"She has only twice had the sulks"**: Rhodes James, *Albert, Prince Consort*, 118.

166 **"those of Turco Egypto, as we think of nothing else"**: Queen Victoria to King Leopold, October 16, 1840, Benson and Esher, *The Letters of Queen Victoria*, 1:242–43.

166 **"I wish you could see us here"**: Bolitho, *The Prince Consort*, 31.

167 **"Oh, Madam, it is a Princess"**: Longford, *Queen Victoria*, 153.

167 **"Dearest Albert hardly left me at all"**: Ibid.

167 **Yvonne Ward from La Trobe University**: Ward, "Editing Queen Victoria."

168 **"our dear little child"**: QVJ, December 11, 1840.

168 **"It seems like a dream"**: QVJ, December 20, 1840.

168 **"such a darling"**: QVJ, March 11, 1841.

168 **"This day last year"**: QVJ, December 25, 1840.

168   "quite a little toy": QVJ, February 24, 1841.

169   "The Queen is, like all very young mothers": October 6, 1841, Wyndham, *Correspondence of Sarah Spencer,* 319–20.

169   "The Prince's care and devotion": From a memo written by the queen, recorded by Grey, *The Early Years,* 288–89.

169   "Our young lady flourishes exceedingly": January 5, 1841, Benson and Esher, *The Letters of Queen Victoria,* 1:321.

170   "There is certainly": Ibid., 83.

170   "Wedded life is the only thing": August 22, 1840, Bolitho, *The Prince Consort,* 25.

170   "Your little grand-niece is most flourishing": To King Leopold, December 15, 1840, Benson and Esher, *The Letters of Queen Victoria,* 1:318.

170   large and happy family: Ibid.

171   "I think, dearest Uncle": January 5, 1841, ibid., 321.

171   Some women tried to coat their vaginas with: Aristotle, *History of Animals,* in *The Works of Aristotle,* Smith and Ross, vol. 4, book 7, 583a–b, quoted in Jalland and Hooper, *Women from Birth to Death,* 266.

171   "as large as can be pleasantly introduced": Richard Carlile, *Every Woman's Book,* 25–6, 31–32, 38, 42–43, quoted in Jalland and Hooper, *Women from Birth to Death,* 267.

171   "utterly spoilt" by pregnancy: April 21, 1858, Fulford, *Dearest Child,* 94.

172   "This has been brought about": Woodham-Smith, *Queen Victoria,* 218.

172   "I have my hands very full": November 24, 1840, Bolitho, *The Prince Consort,* 34; Charlot, *Victoria the Young Queen,* 197.

172   head of the house: One of the editors of Victoria's letters, Benson, writes to his co-editor, Esher, that in the year after Bertie was born, "a point of considerable difficulty has turned up. In the documents referring to the formation of the 1855 Govt, there are a good many memoranda signed Victoria R. These are sometimes in the first person singular 'I' and sometimes in the first person plural 'we.' But when they are in the first person singular, the word 'I' always stands for Prince Albert. This will cause great confusion." Esher Papers, 11/5, Benson to Esher, March 4, 1907, quoted in Ward, "Editing Queen Victoria," 217.

172   "The Prince went yesterday": Benson and Esher, *The Letters of Queen Victoria,* 1:371.

173   "perfect happiness": QVJ, February 10, 1841.

Chapter Thirteen: The Palace Intruders

174 **"When a woman is in love":** Bolitho, *Albert the Good,* 86.

175 **"know how they lived at the Palace":** *The Times,* March 17, 1841. *The Blackburn Standard* (December 9, 1840) quotes him saying: "I wanted to know how they lived at the Palace, I was desirous of knowing the habits of the people, and I thought a description would look very well in a book."

175 **"of a most peculiar formation":** *The Times,* December 4, 1840.

176 **three months' hard labor:** *Jackson's Oxford Journal,* December 5, 1840.

176 **notoriously lax:** In July of that year, porters had also discovered a man asleep in the portrait gallery, not far from the queen's bedroom; she had walked through there only a few minutes before. It was Tom Flower, who had tried to gain entrance to the coronation the previous month and had come once more to ask the queen to marry him. He was sent to Tothill Fields Prison.

176 **"youthful folly":** *All the Year Round,* July 5, 1884, 234.

176 **Charles Dickens wrote to the boy's father:** Bondeson, *Queen Victoria's Stalker,* 44. Healey quotes Dickens saying he "strongly doubted the popular belief in the sharpness of his intellect." *The Queen's House,* 150.

176 **"a dull, undersized runt":** Bondeson, *Queen Victoria's Stalker,* 25n; *Examiner,* March 28, 1841. Bondeson adds, "It was later doubted whether it really was Fenimore Cooper who had offered the Boy Jones to emigrate or another American with the same name."

177 **the queen spent £34,000:** Healey, *The Queen's House,* 144.

178 **"the remains of garden stuff":** Woodham-Smith, *Queen Victoria,* 208.

179 **"moral dignity of the Court":** To Baron von Stockmar, Windsor Castle, January 6, 1846, quoted in Jagow, *Letters of the Prince Consort,* 99.

179 **"a very fat lady standing in front":** Healey, *The Queen's House,* 152n.

179 **did not want to wear the appropriate styles:** Wright, *History of Buckingham Palace,* 176.

179 **strict new code of conduct:** Ibid., 174.

179 **the puritanism Albert championed:** One example of the lack of puritanism in the young queen was her admiration and affection for artist George Hayter (when he painted the massive *The Trial of Queen Caroline,* he produced 189 likenesses). She told Lord Melbourne she knew Hayter had not been elected to the Royal Academy because "he had quarreled with his wife, and had separated from her." She still knighted him in 1842. Warner, *Queen Victoria's Sketchbook,* 98.

179 **"extremely strait-laced":** Pearce, *The Diaries of Charles Greville,* September 6, 1841, 203.

179   **did not care "a straw":** Ibid.

180   **did not believe a pregnant Victoria . . . was able to cope:** Memorandum dated May 5, 1841, Benson and Esher, *The Letters of Queen Victoria,* 1:339.

180   **change should come from her:** A document described as "Secret. Memorandum of confidential communications with G. E. Anson, Private Sec. to Prince Albert, May 1841." Peel Papers, vols. 121–23, British Library Archives, Add. 40, 303. Extract: 40301–3.

180   **In a twenty-seven-page:** Memorandum made by Peel, May 28, 1841, ibid.

180   **"natural modesty upon her constitutional views":** "Memorandum of Mr. Anson's last secret interview with Sir R. Peel" (no. 4), May 23, 1841, Benson and Esher, *The Letters of Queen Victoria,* 1:358.

180   **"*elementarily,* as Her Majesty always liked":** Memorandum by Mr. Anson, August 30, 1841, ibid., 1:383.

181   **"Oh! if only it were a dream!":** QVJ, May 10, 1841.

181   **a *"principle":*** Ibid.

181   **"The Queen was the whole day much depressed":** Weintraub, *Uncrowned King,* 120.

181   **"I don't like it":** Woodham-Smith, *Queen Victoria,* 222.

182   **"Why, nobody *likes* going out":** QVJ, May 9, 1841.

182   **"dreadfully affected":** Woodham-Smith, *Queen Victoria,* 223.

182   **Her journal is full of descriptions:** For example, May 5, May 6, May 7, 1841.

182   **drained from the relationship:** Her "dear, kind friend" Melbourne continued to write to her, mostly in a personal vein, but occasionally, inappropriately, advising her on political matters—even on whether she should pay the new income tax. (In volume 1 of the letters [Viscount Melbourne to Queen Victoria, March 21, 1842], Melbourne says Victoria's decision to pay tax is right, but says she doesn't need to.) This infuriated Albert, who told Stockmar to write letters of complaint. (The reformist Peel wanted a 7 percent tax on all incomes over £150, a radical proposition in peacetime.) He continued to write to Victoria even when Stockmar vehemently and repeatedly told him not to. Victoria would repeat this pattern with another, later favorite prime minister, Lord Salisbury, when he lost the office in the 1880s.

183   **"an iceberg with a slight thaw":** Briggs, *The Age of Improvement,* 326.

183   **"more like a dapper shopkeeper":** February 21, 1835, Greville, *The Great World,* 99.

183   **silver plate of a coffin lid:** Briggs, *The Age of Improvement,* 326.

183   **"a dancing master":** September 17, 1841, Pearce, *The Diaries of Charles Greville,* 204.

183 **"present heavy trial":** Benson and Esher, *The Letters of Queen Victoria,*
1:375–76.

184 **"to pick up [her] spirits":** August 24, 1841, September 2, 1841, Ibid.,
1:395–96.

184 **"the Prince was carrying on business":** Memorandum by Mr. Anson, August 30, 1841, quoted in ibid., 383.

184 **"judgment, temper, and discretion":** Ibid., 385.

184 **"corrected one of my old journals":** QVJ, October 1, 1842. While she was
reading her old journal, she scrawled in the margins, "Reading this again,
I cannot forbear remarking what an artificial sort of happiness *mine* was
then, and what a blessing it is I now have in my beloved Husband *real* and
solid happiness, which no Politics, no worldly reverses *can* change; it
could not have lasted long, as it was then, for after all kind and excellent
as Lord M. is, and kind as he was to me, it was but in Society that I had
amusement, and I was only living on that superficial resource, which I
then fancied was happiness! Thank God! for *me* and others, this is
changed, and I *know what* REAL happiness is."

185 **"really became at last, quite foolish":** QVJ, December 17, 1842.

185 **"I know how difficult it is to fight":** Benson and Esher, *The Letters of
Queen Victoria,* 1:460.

185 **happiest and most fulfilling of his life:** Benson and Esher, *The Letters of
Queen Victoria,* 1:392.

185 **welled with tears:** Cecil, *The Young Melbourne,* 532.

185 **"Your Majesty was just setting off":** Lord Melbourne to Queen Victoria,
April 20, 1842, Benson and Esher, *The Letters of Queen Victoria,* 1:494.

185 **died in 1848:** Melbourne isn't mentioned in the journal entry for the day
he died, November 24, 1848; Victoria only learned of it when reading the
papers the next day. She mourned him as a man who was "truly attached"
to her, "and though not a firm Minister, he was a noble, kind-hearted,
generous being." (Queen Victoria to King Leopold, November 27, 1848,
Benson and Esher, *The Letters of Queen Victoria,* 2:204.) As she wrote to
Leopold, though, while she remembered him fondly, "God knows! I
never wish that time back again." November 21, 1848, ibid., 2:203.

185 **"great future danger":** Woodham-Smith, *Queen Victoria,* 216.

186 **"meddled and made mischief":** Ibid., 219.

186 **"always in the Queen's path":** Ibid.

186 **"such a good and humble-minded person":** Boykin, *Victoria, Albert, and
Mrs. Stevenson,* 251.

186 **"the Queen would brook no interference":** Woodham-Smith, *Queen Victoria,* 215.

186   **wet nurses were advised:** Gill, *We Two,* 181.

186   **"spinster gremlin":** Fulford, *The Prince Consort,* 74.

187   **"the Yellow lady":** Ibid., 179. Bennett (*King Without a Crown,* 74) points
       out that words in a letter to Ernest have been wrongly interpreted as
       Albert writing lovingly about Victoria, not nastily about Lehzen, because
       the sentence before it was cut out by Bolitho, *The Prince Consort,* 34. The
       full text reads: "The old hag has conceived a terrible hatred for you and
       takes you for the author of all ill. She said as much to Anson yesterday.
       Yesterday at table she looked most charming, very décolleté, with a bou-
       quet of roses at her breast which seemed as if it was going to fall out."

187   **"sense and information":** Healey, *The Queen's House,* 121.

187   **"much beloved by ... all who frequent the Court":** October 5, 1842,
       Greville, *The Great World,* 205.

187   **"kind and motherly":** Bloomfield, *Court and Diplomatic Life,* 24.

187   **"wretched," "low and depressed":** QVJ, October 27, 1841.

187   **less interested in her work:** In 1840, she had complained to Melbourne
       that the Eastern Question was boring. Longford, *Victoria R.I.,* 149.

187   **a torturous birth:** To his credit, Albert delayed notifying the usual per-
       sons that Victoria was in labor, which meant that several of the dignitar-
       ies, including the Archbishop of Canterbury, arrived late and missed the
       birth; surely Albert was sparing his wife the torture of going through
       excruciating pain while Cabinet ministers sat idly listening. Pearce, *The
       Diaries of Charles Greville,* November 11, 1841, 205.

188   **"I suffered a *whole year*":** Jerrold, *Married Life of Victoria,* 178.

188   **"Bertie and I both suffered":** Fulford, *Dearest Child,* 147.

189   **"so thin, pale and changed":** QVJ, September 4, 1841, October 20, 1841,
       November 2, 1841, October 21, 1842.

189   **so many children died:** There were 154 deaths per 1,000 live births in
       infants under the age of one. Jalland, *Death in the Victorian Family,* 120.

189   **Victoria erupted, upset:** Hibbert, *Queen Victoria: A Personal History,* 152.

189   **"I feel so forlorn":** Woodham-Smith, *Queen Victoria,* 296.

190   **"Lehzen is a crazy, common":** January 16, 1842, quoted in Longford, *Vic-
       toria R.I.,* 160.

190   **"Albert must tell me what he dislikes":** Longford, *Queen Victoria,* 161.

191   **"very different to any":** Memorandum from Victoria to Stockmar,
       January 19/20, 1842, Woodham-Smith, *Queen Victoria,* 231.

191   **"There is often an irritability in me":** Ibid.

191   **"vein of iron":** July 1844: "We are all on the look-out for signs of *illness* in
       the Queen; but this morning she was tripping upstairs to chapel, and the

vein of iron that runs thro' her most extraordinary character enables her to bear up to the last minute, like nobody else." Wyndham, *Correspondence of Sarah Spencer,* 348.

192 **"Felt rather bewildered & low":** QVJ, July 25, 1842.

192 **"It was very painful to me":** Wyndham, *Correspondence of Sarah Spencer,* 331.

192 **"in which she took leave of me":** QVJ, September 30, 1842.

193 **newly married Vicky:** Vicky had married in London on January 25, 1858; this was a visit to her in August of that year. Victoria writes in her journal on August 12, 1858: "As we passed by the station, Lehzen stood there, waving her handkerchief."

194 **popularizing the Christmas tree tradition:** Longford points out (*Victoria R.I.,* 169) that Queen Charlotte had decorated a yew tree at Windsor decades earlier, but Albert was credited with the idea. It became a wildly popular custom.

194 **"good deal preoccupied":** Memorandum by Mr. Anson, Windsor Castle, December 26, 1841, quoted in Benson and Esher, *The Letters of Queen Victoria,* 1:463.

Chapter Fourteen: King to All Intents:
"Like a Vulture into His Prey"

196 **"He is become so identified":** Strachey and Fulford, *The Greville Memoirs,* 5:257.

198 **"it made one impatient to see 'gentlemen'":** QVJ, January 24, 1846.

198 **"tall, handsome man with fair hair and fine features":** For a portrait of Sir Robert Peel see *Illustrated London News,* August 27, 1842, 243.

198 **"very comprehensive & excellent":** QVJ, January 27, 1846. Victoria, who had taken an interest in Peel's speeches as a teenager, read it the next day, and described it as "beautiful, but immeasurably long." QVJ, January 28, 1846.

199 **"to usher in, to give éclat":** House of Commons Debates (*HC Deb*) February 27, 1846, vol. 84, cc249–349. Note that Albert's presence had, before then, been a source of disgruntlement only to Peel's opponents. The press was not interested, and reports of Bentinck's speech failed to mention his excoriation of Albert.

199 **"The Prince merely went":** Martin, *The Prince Consort,* 1:322.

199 **"shows boundless courage":** February 16, 1846, ibid.

200 **"very great sensation":** QVJ, March 16, 1842.

200 **"afraid of catching revolution":** Charlot (*Victoria the Young Queen,* 263) quotes Norman St. John-Stevas, *Walter Bagehot.*

201 **"the removal of impediments":** Parker, *Sir Robert Peel,* 3:223.

201 **"extreme distress":** QVJ, September 28, 1846, quoted in Longford, *Victoria R.I.,* 190.

201 **money raised for the Crimean War a few years later:** Hoppen, *The Mid-Victorian Generation,* 570.

202 **"barbarity of tyrants and the fatuity of idiots":** Quoted in Woodham-Smith, *Queen Victoria,* 411.

202 **disgust at the Irish who murdered those landlords:** QVJ, November 5, 1847.

202 **"It is a constant source of anxiety & annoyance":** Ibid.

202 **She did not visit Ireland until 1849:** After this, the queen made three more visits to Ireland: in 1853, 1861, and 1900.

202 **through puddles and piles of rocks:** All of this is from the *Examiner,* May 14, 1842.

202 **would no longer be suitable for marriage:** Heesom, "The Coal Mines Act of 1842," 75.

202 **only occurred incrementally, against great resistance:** The first effective Factory Act, in 1833, had banned the employment of children under nine in textile mills—except silk and lace mills—and regulated hours of work, to nine a day or forty-eight a week for children under thirteen. Those under thirteen were also required to attend school two hours a day.

203 **and only a quarter of ten- to fourteen-year-olds:** Lavalette, *A Thing of the Past?,* 78. Note that Lavalette argues that working conditions were worse for many children before industrialization, especially those in small-scale and cottage industries, like weavers and knitters.

204 **"observed next morning that she shed tears":** *Odd Fellow,* May 14, 1842.

204 **"childish display of the waste of thousands":** *Northern Star and Leeds General Advertiser,* June 4, 1842.

204 **"the most deserving boy" in each ward be pardoned:** QVJ, August 2, 1845.

204 **it would cripple economic productivity:** In 1844, Peel introduced the Factory Bill that would have cut the hours of children laboring in textile mills to six. Lord Ashley wanted to amend it so that the working hours of all young people, and women, were cut to ten. This amendment was passed, but Peel opposed it and withdrew the bill. (It should be noted that Lord Shaftesbury was named Lord Ashley until 1851, when he became an earl.)

205 **pass the pen to Albert after signing the register:** The fight with the controversial duke was partly due to a fight over some of Victoria's jewels—

they had belonged to Charlotte and should rightfully have gone to the duke, but Victoria would not relinquish them.

205 **"But he was so good & kind & had loved me for myself":** QVJ, June 9, 1842.

205 **"cold public around us, insensible as stone":** Prince Albert to Baron Stockmar, Windsor Castle, February 4, 1844, quoted in Jagow, *Letters of the Prince Consort,* 88.

206 **"the intimate love we bear one another":** QVJ, February 4, 1844.

206 **her eyes filled with tears:** Wyndham, *Correspondence of Sarah Spencer,* 338–39.

206 **"we shall find happiness again":** February 4, 1844, Bolitho, *The Prince Consort,* 69.

206 **devote himself to his family:** Prince Albert to Baron Stockmar, Windsor Castle, February 9, 1844, quoted in Jagow, *Letters of the Prince Consort,* 89.

206 **"agitated with joy and thankfulness":** QVJ, April 12, 1844. The next year, when she went to Germany for the first time, Victoria visited her husband's childhood home in Rosenau and was very moved: "If I were not who I am—*this* would have been my real home, but I shall always consider it my 2nd one." QVJ, August 20, 1845.

207 **"but *where* am I not happy *now?*":** QVJ, August 3, 1843.

207 **"particularly in moments when one is alone":** QVJ, April 27, 1843.

207 **rolled in her bed to the sitting room, then in an armchair:** QVJ, August 6, 1844.

208 **"and flies off with it to his nest":** Stockmar, *Memoirs of Baron Stockmar,* 2:100.

208 **His pigs won first prize at agricultural fairs:** Charlot, *Victoria the Young Queen,* 227.

209 **"boldly and hard":** Queen Victoria to King Leopold, December 12, 1843, Hibbert, *Queen Victoria in Her Letters,* 72.

209 **"cannot understand how any one can suffer from it":** QVJ, February 17, 1843.

209 **"He is King to all intents and purposes":** *The Greville Memoirs,* December 16, 1845, 5:330.

210 **"and that this opinion was duly expressed":** Benson and Esher, *Letters of Queen Victoria,* 1:28.

210 **"who are badly educated, to desperation & violence":** QVJ, April 15, 1845.

210 **"tide of bigotry, and blind fanaticism":** Ibid.

210 **"a kind and true friend":** Queen Victoria, July 1, 1846, quoted in Benson and Esher, *The Letters of Queen Victoria,* 1:100.

210 **in the "simple attire" he had often seen them in:** Peel to Victoria, July 24, 1846, quoted in Parker, *Sir Robert Peel,* 3:452.

211   **his inability to convince his party that it *was* the best:** Greville, *The Greville Memoirs,* 2:325.

211   **"Politics . . . must take only a second place":** QVJ, June 10, 1846.

Chapter Fifteen: Perfect, Awful, Spotless Prosperity

212   **"playing with their human toys":** Jerrold, *Married Life of Victoria,* 94.

212   **"a liberty and a solitude":** Warner, *Queen Victoria's Sketchbook,* 176.

212   **rosy cheeks, and perfectly tailored clothes:** "General Tom Thumb Junior, at Home," *Era,* March 3, 1844.

213   **"tease him a good deal, I should think":** QVJ, March 23, 1844.

214   **during a three-year tour of Britain and Europe:** They stayed in London for four months. Richardson, *The Annals of London,* 267; Barnum, *The Life of P. T. Barnum,* 260; "Court and Aristocracy," *Examiner,* April 6, 1844. On the second visit (the Monday night), Thumb delighted the court with his repertoire:

> His delineation of the Emperor Napoleon elicited great mirth, and this was followed by a representation of the Grecian statues, after which the General danced a hornpipe and sang several of his favorite songs. Her Majesty was pleased to present the General a superb *souvenir,* of mother of pearl, and mounted with gold and precious stones, together with a beautiful gold pencil-case, with the initials of Tom Thumb, and his coat of arms engraved on the emerald surmounting the case.
>
> On his third visit, Thumb sang "Yankee Doodle," and complimented the queen on her taste, evident in the furnishings of the Yellow Drawing Room. [Barnum, *The Life of P. T. Barnum,* 261.]

The *Caledonian Mercury,* on April 25, 1844, reported on Thumb's third visit to Buckingham Palace:

> The Queen asked him to wear the same court dress he had worn for the Queen Dowager. Received in the yellow drawing room with Albert, King and Queen of Belgium, Charles of Leiningen. "He was received by her Majesty with all the familiarity of an old acquaintance." Did imitation of Napoleon in costume, then sang two songs, danced a hornpipe, was there 5:30–7. Much laughter.
>
> Albert asked if he could favor him with a bow, which he did, then "shook hands with the dwarf who, as he made his obeisance to the royal party, paid a compliment to her Majesty on the taste ex-

hibited in the drawing-room, which caused the most hearty laughter at his departure."

Victoria found him "very nice, lively & funny, dancing & singing wonderfully." She was amused that Thumb did not even reach the shoulders of
Vicky, who was then three and a half. QVJ, April 1, 1844, and April 19,
1844.

214 **endowed him with prestige and publicity:** "The Sights of London,"
Morning Post, April 8, 1844.

214 **pulled by pretty ponies:** Bogdan, *Freak Show,* 150–51: "Queen Victoria
saw the little prodigy three times and presented him with gifts which he
ostentatiously displayed when on exhibit. To promote his appearances he
would drive about in an ornate miniature carriage pulled by matching
ponies. The marine-blue, crimson, and white carriage, a gift from Barnum, had been made by the queen's carriage maker."

214 **"God bless you!":** Sanger, *Seventy Years a Showman,* 94.

214 **a wedding dress and a diamond ring:** In *Freak Show* (207), Bogdan writes
of the "The Tallest Couple Alive," whose combined height was claimed
to be fifteen feet eleven inches. Queen Victoria summoned the pair to
Buckingham Palace to give the bride-to-be these gifts before they married on June 17, 1871.

214 **Victoria wrote a letter to his handler expressing her regret:** Sanger was
thrilled; he had first put on his performing costume in the Hyde Park fair
on the day of Victoria's coronation. (He was also, coincidentally, the Lion
Woman's husband.) Sanger, *Seventy Years a Showman,* 70.

215 **wrote Stockmar to her sternly:** Rhodes James, *Albert, Prince Consort,* 131.

215 **by the sea and in the Highlands:** She wanted "a place of one's own, quiet
and retired." Ibid., 140.

216 **"perfect little Paradise":** Ibid., 144.

216 **"the trees seem covered as with feathers":** QVJ, June 9, 1849.

216 **"He is hardly to be kept at home a moment":** QVJ, May 12, 1845.

216 **a form of therapy for him:** QVJ, April 21, 1848.

217 **struggling with depression after Bertie's birth:** QVJ, August 29, 1842.

217 **"who live far away from towns":** Albert writes to Duchess Caroline of
Saxe-Gotha-Altenburg from Windsor Castle, on September 18, 1842,
that "Scotland has made a most favourable impression upon us both. The
country is full of beauty, of a severe and grand character; perfect for sport
of all kinds, and the air remarkably pure and light in comparison with
what we have here. The people are more natural, and marked by that
honesty and sympathy which always distinguishes the inhabitants of

mountainous countries, who live far away from towns." Jagow, *Letters of the Prince Consort*, 81.

217 **"peculiar feelings of admiration & solemnity":** QVJ, September 10, 1848.

217 **"today I shot two red deer":** Quoted in Bolitho, *Albert, Prince Consort*, 104.

218 **chatted with the women for hours:** Greville wrote, "She is running in and out of the house all day, and often goes about alone." September 15, 1849, Strachey and Fulford, *The Greville Memoirs*, 6:186; Greville, *The Great World*, 269.

218 **"so intelligent, modest and well bred":** QVJ, October 3, 1850.

218 **"small house, small rooms, small establishments":** September 15, 1849, Greville, *The Great World*, 269.

218 **"never see, hear or witness these various charms":** Osborne House, October 5, 1849, Wyndham, *Correspondence of Sarah Spencer*, 392–93.

219 **"I hope to conquer my shortcomings":** QVJ, December 31, 1847.

219 **without ever ceasing her work:** Victoria was pregnant or in confinement for almost four of the first five years she was married (forty-four out of sixty months).

219 **"totally unsurmountable disgust":** Ibid., 159.

219 **a heifer in the Balmoral dairy was soon named Princess Alice:** Van der Kiste, *Queen Victoria's Children*, 58. Victoria, writing to Alice, said nursing was "animalistic" and vulgar: "A child can never be as well nursed by a lady of rank & nervous & refined temperament . . . for the less-feeling & the more like an animal the wet nurse is, the better for the child." Ward, "Editing Queen Victoria," 70.

219 **and inappropriate for upper-class women:** She wrote to Vicky: "No lady, and still less a Princess, is fit for her husband or for her position, if she does *that*." Pakula, *Uncommon Woman*, 114.

220 **a persuasive argument in the days before breast pumps existed:** Davidoff and Hall, *Family Fortunes*, 27.

220 **with dubious morals:** A useful summary of middle-class practices can be found in Lynda Nead's *Myths of Sexuality*, 27:

> The ways in which women are supposed to fulfil their role as mother undergoes historical shifts. One of the key changes in attitudes during the nineteenth century concerned the question of wet-nursing. During the eighteenth century, wet-nursing had been usual practice amongst upper-class families; however, at the beginning of the nineteenth century, and particularly during the cholera outbreaks and political crises of the 1840s, the habit came under increasing attack. The moral and physical health of the

working-class women who were engaged as nurses was called into question and doctors described the possibility of moral/physical contamination from nurse (i.e, working class) to child (i.e., middle class) through the feeding. Middle-class women were strongly urged to feed their children themselves; breast-feeding was re-defined as a natural and healthy practice for the responsible middle-class mother, and childcare became a site for the separation and insulation of the middle class from corruption by the class below it.

220 **"more like an animal" suckled them:** Victoria, writing to Alice, said nursing was "animalistic" and vulgar. (Ward, "Editing Queen Victoria," 70. These letters are quoted in Pakula, *Uncommon Woman*, 215.)

220 **Most Englishwomen ... Victoria spent sixteen:** Flanders, *The Victorian House*, 14.

220 **almost double the era average of 5.5 children:** Ibid., 14.

220 **"which God knows receive a shock enough in marriage alone":** Fulford, *Dearest Child*, 77–78. For another discussion, see Chapter 4, "Queen Victoria and the Shadow Side," in Helsinger et al., *The Woman Question*, 1:63–77.

220 **more ... than the average Victorian male:** The Rudyard Kipling verses below are quoted in Flanders, *The Victorian House*, 15: "We asked no social questions—we pumped no hidden shame—We never talked obstetrics when the Little Stranger came." Rudyard Kipling, "The Three Decker," in *Rudyard Kipling's Verse*, 380.

221 **"difficult to uphold in the face of so many women":** Quoted in Bolitho, *Albert, Prince Consort*, 109.

221 **"such a flashing look of gratitude from the Queen!":** February 9, 1844, Wyndham, *Correspondence of Sarah Spencer*, 339–40.

221 **in a large basket delighted her:** QVJ, March 7, 1843: "Went to the nursery, where Albert played delightfully with the children, pulling them about in a basket, one after the other & together, which greatly delighted them. All this is so pleasant here, at Claremont, where the nursery is so close to our rooms, whereas alas! at Buckingham Palace, it is literally a mile off, so that we cannot run in and out as we would like."

221 **"manages them so beautifully and firmly":** Rhodes James, *Albert, Prince Consort*, 231.

222 **"forget their first duties":** Fulford, *Dearest Child*, 205, quoted in Sanders, *Victorian Fatherhood*, 30.

222 **"George III cared very little for his children":** QVJ, January 20, 1848.

222 **"and various intense precautions":** February 3, 1842, Wyndham, *Corre-spondence of Sarah Spencer,* 326. Albert checked the access to the children's apartments: "And the intricate turns and locks and guardroooms, and the various intense precautions, suggesting the most hidden dangers, which I fear are Not altogether imaginary, made one shudder! The most important key is never out of Albert's own keeping, and the very thought must be enough to cloud his fair brow with anxiety. Threatening letters of the most horrid kind (probably written by mad people), aimed directly at *the children,* are frequently received. I had rather no one but our own family knew all this. It had better not be talked about; and hitherto this has been kept from me and all of us here."

222 **important part of parenting:** As Australian scholar Yvonne Ward has demonstrated, Victoria's correspondence with Queen Donna Maria II of Portugal, for example, shows how preoccupied she was with her children. Both women worked and labored throughout crises, wars, assassi-nation attempts, and foreign conflicts. In their letters, omitted from Victoria's edited letters, they discussed the use of wet nurses, cholera, ty-phoid, vaccinations against smallpox, and weaning, as well as their desire that their husbands not be emasculated by their jobs, but be recognized as their masters.

Victoria wrote to Maria on June 2, 1842, "I assure you that I share entirely your opinion, the husband should always be first; I'm doing ev-erything in order that it be thus—and I am always saddened that he must be below me in rank; for it pains me to be Queen and he merely the Prince; but in my heart and in my house he comes first and is the master and head." Victoria to Maria, June 2, 1842, Lisbon Archives, Torre do Tombo, Caixa 7322/CR150-1, quoted in Ward, "Editing Queen Victo-ria," 251.

222 **and showed them off proudly:** QVJ, December 26, 1840: "The Baby was brought down and I showed her to all the ladies. She was awake, & very sweet, & I must say, I am very proud of her."

222 **how many hours she spent with her babies:** Wyndham, *Correspondence of Sarah Spencer,* 391. Anson also noted that the queen "interests herself less and less about politics ... and ... is a good deal occupied with the little Princess Royal." Ward, "Editing Queen Victoria," 88–89.

222 **"as much as possible with their parents":** Martin, *The Prince Consort,* 2:182.

222 **"fear and trembling":** Ibid.

222 **"a great blessing and cheer & brighten up life":** QVJ, February 10, 1852.

222 **as though asleep with his eyes open:** Jerrold, *Married Life of Victoria,* 230.

223 **"a very good child & not at all wanting in intellect":** Ibid., 234.

223 **the queen thought he was stupid:** January 22, 1848. Greville added "the hereditary and unfailing antipathy of our Sovereigns to their Heirs Apparents seems thus early to be taking root, and the Q. does not much like the child." Strachey and Fulford, *The Greville Memoirs,* 6:9; Greville, *The Great World,* 238.

223 **"The intellectual organs are only moderately developed":** Rhodes James, *Albert, Prince Consort,* 238.

223 **"feel the strong pulsations of a nation's heart":** Reverend D. Newell, quoted in Homans and Munich, *Remaking Queen Victoria,* 42.

223 **"the good example it presents":** Queen Victoria to King Leopold, October 29, 1844, Benson and Esher, *The Letters of Queen Victoria,* 2:32.

223 **understood her people with a canny intuition:** When Victoria received glowing reviews for her book *More Leaves from the Journal of Our Life in the Highlands,* published in 1884 and dedicated to John Brown, she said that she was certain she knew "perfectly well what my people like and appreciate and that is 'home life' and simplicity." Fulford, *Beloved Mama,* 160.

224 **"All is well with us":** Jagow, *Letters of the Prince Consort,* 141

Chapter Sixteen: Annus Mirabilis: The Revolutionary Year

225 **"The uncertainty everywhere, as well as for the future":** QVJ, April 3, 1848.

226 **they had been hiding in to try to arrest the king:** Mr. Featherstonhaugh, British Consul at Havre, to Viscount Palmerston, March 3, 1848, Benson and Esher, *The Letters of Queen Victoria,* 2:188.

226 **thousands gathered on the streets to protest:** Alexis de Tocqueville wrote that Paris was sinister and frightening at this time: "There were a hundred thousand armed workmen formed into regiments, without work and dying of hunger, but with heads full of vain theories and chimerical hopes." Tocqueville, *Recollections,* 98.

226 **drank and danced in the palace, raiding the royal closets:** Ward, "1848: Queen Victoria," 180.

226 **concealing his eyes with enormous goggles:** Mr. Featherstonhaugh, British Consul at Havre, to Viscount Palmerston, March 3, 1848, Benson and Esher, *The Letters of Queen Victoria,* 2:187.

227 **Victoria and Albert's second visit to Eu in 1845:** Queen Louise to Queen Victoria, October 7, 1844, ibid., 22–23.

227 **still loved her French family:** Victoria wrote to Baron Stockmar on

March 6, 1848, that she had longed to be on better terms with the French family, which indicates she had forgiven them for the Spanish marriage backflip: "You know my love for the family; you know how I longed to get on better terms with them again.... Little did I dream that this would be the way we should meet again, and see each other all in the most friendly way. That the Duchess de Montpensier, about whom we have been quarrelling for the last year and a half, should be here as a fugitive, and dressed in the clothes I sent her, and should come to thank *me* for *my kindness,* is a reverse of fortune which no novelist would devise, and upon which one could moralise for ever." Martin, *The Prince Consort,* 2:24.

228   **the day after she greeted Louis Philippe and Marie-Amelie:** Queen Victoria to King Leopold, March 7, 1848, Benson and Esher, *The Letters of Queen Victoria,* 2:163.

228   **"What could be more dreadful!":** QVJ, February 29, 1848. Writing about the day of abdication Victoria was most struck by the anxiety of the mother whose children were wrested out of her arms: "Poor Hélène had her children torn from her. What could be more dreadful! Paris was pushed along into a corridor but returned to her whereas poor little Robert got entirely lost for 3 days! However a gentleman had taken care of him & managed to let poor Hélène know, who it seems behaved throughout with wonderful courage."

228   **"and hearing those dreadful cries and shrieks":** QVJ, February 27, 1848.

228   **"like a crushed rose":** QVJ, May 16, 1848.

228   **"people [who] are going on in a disgusting way":** In her journal she called them a "mob of bloodthirsty ruffians," "horrible shrieking mob" (QVJ, February 28, 1848), "infuriated, armed mob," "horrid infuriated mob" (QVJ, February 29, 1848), and "the dreadful rabble" (QVJ, March 5, 1848), and said, "people are going on in a disgusting way" (QVJ, March 1, 1848).

229   **to avoid embarrassing her son, King Edward VII:** Most of the cuts were made because they were too overtly political, or revealed a side of Victoria that would have been too strident or unfeminine for Edwardian eyes. Ward, "Editing Queen Victoria," 309.

229   **"Iniquity from wherein all the mischief comes":** Note also another excision: Victoria said she wished there would be peace in Europe when "this madness is over" in France. The words "in France" were deleted from the final version of the letter, February 6, 1849. Ibid., 241.

229   **"and everybody will admit that":** March 11, 1848, cited in Ward, *Censoring Queen Victoria,* 163.

229 **who burst into tears:** Bolitho, *Albert, Prince Consort,* 100. Victoria also wrote to Leopold on March 11: "Our little riots here are mere nothings, and the feeling here is good." Martin, *The Prince Consort,* 2:8.

229 **protests were scaring her French relations:** QVJ, March 6, 1848.

229 **"one cannot help being more anxious":** QVJ, March 7, 1848.

229 **to advise on foreign policy:** Martin, *The Prince Consort,* 2:158.

229 **the Duke of Coburg and Gotha:** He wrote to his distressed brother Ernest: "Such an outbreak of the people is always something *very dreadful*" and recommended that "the laws for election should be liberal and extended." Victoria's sister Feodora wrote from Stuttgart on April 7, 1849: "I think you can hardly have an idea of the state Germany is in now. The want of respect for all that is called law is dreadful. . . . You have no idea how low Ernest sometimes is; it quite distressed me to see it. I think women can bear up better against the blows of misfortune than men." Martin, *The Prince Consort,* 2:25.

229 **extending military power to quell the local riots:** Bolitho, *Albert, Prince Consort,* 101.

230 **"if only we are spared to one another to share everything":** QVJ, April 3, 1848.

231 **"it is only trifles that irritate my nerves":** Queen Victoria to King Leopold, April 4, 1848, Benson and Esher, *The Letters of Queen Victoria,* 2:166–67.

231 **"her departure was due to personal alarm":** Phipps to the Prince, April 9, 1848, Woodham-Smith, *Queen Victoria,* 288.

231 **special constables on the day of the meeting:** Goodway, *London Chartism, 1838–1848,* 131.

231 **any foreign citizen against whom allegations had been made:** The act was passed in 1848, but not enforced, and was rescinded in 1850. Bloom, *Victoria's Madmen,* 110.

231 **troops were hidden at various points around London:** See Schama, *A History of Britain.*

231 **Lord John Russell lined his windows with parliamentary papers:** Belchem, "The Waterloo of Peace," 255.

232 **The troops were told to fire if necessary:** QVJ, April 6, 1848.

232 **"will have a beneficial effect in other countries":** QVJ, April 10, 1848.

233 **help the working class at a time of distress:** Benson and Esher, *The Letters of Queen Victoria,* 2:224.

233 **"coming in consequence to wrong conclusions":** Quoted in Martin, *The Prince Consort,* 2:75.

233 **Victoria wrote, a little guiltily:** QVJ, April 6, 1848. She wrote: "Albert is

so overwhelmed with business, that he has to get up very early. I am not half grateful enough for the many ways in which he helps me. . . . Took a short drive with Albert in the Barouche, then went about the garden in my pony chair, & Albert played with the 4 children. He is so kind to them & romps with them so delightfully, & manages them so beautifully & yet firmly."

233 **"like a plague":** QVJ, June 10, 1848.

233 **laborers stood on the lawns armed with sticks:** QVJ, June 13, 1848.

234 **a man ran up:** QVJ, June 17, 1848.

234 **Lady Emily Lamb, to whom he was then engaged:** Chambers, *Palmerston: The People's Darling,* 178–79.

235 **argue against Palmerston a decade later:** Woodham-Smith, *Queen Victoria,* 304–5: "There had been a change in accommodation at Windsor and the room entered by Lord Palmerston was normally occupied by a lady not averse from his attentions, whom he was accustomed to visit there." Also, according to Feuchtwanger, *Albert and Victoria,* 89, Albert told Lord Russell that Palmerston should not be allowed to force himself upon the queen, either, which seems either untrue or uncharacteristically rude and indelicate.

235 **"dignified courtesy towards other Sovereigns and their governments":** Martin, *The Prince Consort,* 2:300–301.

235 **failing to update her on the feud between Austria and Sardinia:** September 4, 1848, Bolitho, *Albert, Prince Consort,* 103.

236 **wrestling with their own rebels in Ireland:** QVJ, July 24, 1848. Victoria wrote: "For us to join with this unrecognised Govt & be the 1st to act in concert with them, in helping revolted subjects to throw off their allegiance, while at the same time we are grappling with Rebellion in Ireland, is to dishonour & disgrace the name of England. I expressed myself strongly to Ld Palmerston on this subject."

236 **This was later edited out of their official correspondence:** Ward, "Editing Queen Victoria," 224. Victoria and Albert contested much Palmerston did as foreign minister between 1846 and 1851. Esher cut out many passages of criticism of Palmerston by Victoria, Albert, and Leopold just before printing, "most likely in deference to King Edward." They deleted all references to the Pilgerstein nickname.

236 **Victoria often wrote . . . about how much she despised:** Victoria even blamed Palmerston for the European revolutions, so great was her contempt. In an odd twist of logic, she also considered him responsible for the Spanish marriage fallout that had created a dispute between France

and England: "There can be no doubt that the greatest interests of Europe have been sacrificed to Ld Palmerston's ambition, & headstrong policy. It is very dreadful to contemplate." QVJ, May 7, 1848.

237 **"and this without her knowledge":** Queen Victoria to Viscount Palmerston, February 17, 1850, Benson and Esher, *The Letters of Queen Victoria,* 2:234.

237 **angered Greece, and alienated France:** Martin, *The Prince Consort,* 2:277.

237 **use her constitutional powers to dismiss him:** When Russell read this out in Parliament the following year, the MPs were shocked, and a mortified Palmerston declared he would never work with Russell again. (On March 4, 1851, the queen wrote to Lord Russell reminding him that he too "must keep her constantly informed of what is going on and of the temper of the parties in and out of the Parliament.")

237 **"an unparalleled outrage":** Greville, *The Great World,* 289.

238 **"who has equally duties & obligations":** QVJ, August 6, 1848.

238 **people on the streets of Dublin were crying for food:** Woodham-Smith, *Queen Victoria,* 295.

238 **people in Ireland could be arrested without a warrant:** QVJ, July 21, 1848.

238 **her views were considered strident:** The word "dirtier" was also cut out of the published version of one of her letters when describing the Irish people during her visit to Dublin in 1849: "A more good-humored crowd I never saw, but noisy and excitable beyond belief, talking, jumping, and shrieking instead of cheering. . . . You see *dirtier,* more ragged & wretched people here than I ever saw anywhere else." Queen Victoria to King Leopold, August 6, 1849, Ward, "Editing Queen Victoria," 309.

239 **her sympathy for their tenants waned:** Murphy, *Abject Loyalty,* 66: "However, as the year wore on, the attention of both Victoria and Albert became fixed on the rising number of outrages in Ireland against landlords. In 1846 there were sixty-eight murders in Ireland. In 1847 there were ninety-eight. . . . Unable to comprehend the starvation of faceless masses, Victoria and Albert were able to sympathize with the plight of individual landlords with whom they had often had personal contact."

239 **"the enjoyments of this world":** Bolitho, *Albert, Prince Consort,* xi.

240 **establishment of banks especially for savings:** Martin, *The Prince Consort,* 2:228.

240 **"But there is the rub":** May 13, 1849, quoted in Bolitho, *Albert, Prince Consort,* 113.

240 **putting them in a sorry state:** Ibid., xii.

241 **"British peculiarity seemed to be underlined once again":** Taylor, "The 1848 Revolutions," 146. Such comments were frequently removed or tempered by the editors—Esher in particular, in his enthusiasm for France.

241 **leaders of the Irish independence and Chartist movements:** Ibid., 155.

241 **Victoria was immensely proud of that:** In her closing of Parliament in 1848, on September 5, Victoria said: "My people, on their side, feel too easily the advantages of order and serenity to allow the promoters of pillage and confusion any chance of success in their wicked designs." Martin, *The Prince Consort,* 2:106.

241 **the man who had been his ally in his rise to power:** Queen Victoria to King of the Belgians, July 9, 1850, Benson and Esher, *The Letters of Queen Victoria,* 2:256.

242 **Peel was hugely popular in death:** As Victoria wrote, "From the highest to the lowest grief is shown & felt in a manner, hardly ever before known for a person in his position. All the lower & middle classes realize that they have lost a father & a friend." QVJ, July 3, 1848.

242 **Albert mourned him like a brother, wrote Victoria:** QVJ, October 9, 1849.

242 **Uncle Leopold lost his much-loved second wife, Louise:** QVJ, March 21, 1849.

Chapter Seventeen: What Albert Did: The Great Exhibition of 1851

243 **"We are capable":** QVJ, April 29, 1851.

244 **a fog that made the spectacle seem unreal:** "The Opening," *Preston Guardian,* May 3, 1851.

244 **"beautiful beyond the power of language to describe":** "Royal Inauguration of the Great Exhibition of 1851," *Morning Post,* May 2, 1851, 5.

245 **"a day to live forever":** QVJ, May 1, 1851.

245 **"and I can think of nothing else":** Benson and Esher, *The Letters of Queen Victoria,* 2:318. Victoria writes to Leopold: "I wish you could have witnessed May 1st, 1851, the *greatest* day in our history, the most beautiful, and imposing, and touching spectacle ever seen and the triumph of my beloved Albert. Truly it was astonishing, a fairy scene.... Albert's dearest name is immortalized with this great conception, his own, and my own dear country showed she was worthy of it. The triumph is immense."

245 **described the opening as "quite satisfactory":** Fulford, *The Prince Consort,* 222.

245   **shapes of the continents and the celestial heavens above:** Leapman, *The World for a Shilling,* 152.

245   **pulling the ocean's tides with its heartbeat:** Ibid.

246   **the whole of the Exhibition:** For a fuller description of the displays, see the excellent account contained in Leapman, *The World for a Shilling,* 133.

246   **"had a ludicrous effect":** QVJ, May 19, 1851.

246   **"It must be amusing to wash yourself with yourself":** Cowen, *Relish,* 221.

247   **"a deep hum like the sea heard from the distance":** Shorter, *Charlotte Brontë and Her Circle,* 425–26.

247   **begun in the sixteenth century, as a child:** The tradition of industrial exhibitions began with the Frankfurt fairs in the sixteenth century. Exhibitions began in Paris in 1798 and continued sporadically.

247   **and helping to launch the penny post:** Cole had also vigorously campaigned for the standard gauge railway track, managed South Kensington Museum for two decades, and was responsible for the Royal College of Music and Albert Hall. Rhodes James, *Albert, Prince Consort,* 195.

247   **Albert was then the president:** Cole and Albert had worked together on some smaller Society of the Arts exhibitions that had drawn increasingly large crowds. Ten thousand attended one in 1849; about the same number would visit the Great Exhibition daily.

247   **serious moral and patriotic underpinnings:** It was a time when it was assumed that humanity was beginning to attain a higher kind of enlightenment; as Tennyson put it in *In Memoriam,* mankind must "Move upward, working out the beast / And let the ape and tiger die."

247   **"civilization and the attainment of liberty":** Martin, *The Prince Consort,* 2:246.

247   **"able to direct their further exertions":** Ibid., 2:248.

248   **"a cucumber frame between two chimneys":** Fulford, *The Prince Consort,* 221.

248   **"truly a marvelous piece of art":** Rhodes James, *Albert, Prince Consort,* 199.

248   **"palmed upon the people of this country":** Ibid., 197. Also, as Cecil Woodham-Smith points out, Colonel Sibthorp had vehemently opposed the Public Libraries Act too, because he did not like reading. *Queen Victoria,* 310.

249   **to prevent the Exhibition from taking place:** Martin, *The Prince Consort,* 2:358.

249   **"and to drive myself crazy":** Rhodes James, *Albert, Prince Consort,* 100. See also Woodham-Smith, *Queen Victoria,* 313n17.

249   **"the whole thing would fall to pieces":** Martin, *The Prince Consort,* 2:244.

249 these mechanisms would transform their lives: Cowen, *Relish,* 221.

249 "the greatness of man's mind": QVJ, June 7, 1851.

250 "England's sins and negligences": Ackroyd, *Dickens,* 632.

251 "and I can't bear that": To Lavinia Watson, July 11, 1851, Hartley, *Selected Letters of Dickens,* 234.

251 which he alternately called a "Gigantic Birdcage": Thomas Carlyle to John A. Carlyle, January 12, 1851, The Carlyle Letters Online, doi: 10.1215/lt-18510112-TC-JAC-01; CL 26: 12–14. carlyleletters.dukeupress .edu.

251 a "big Glass Soapbubble": Thomas Carlyle to Joseph Neuberg, July 25, 1851, The Carlyle Letters Online, doi: 10.1215/lt-18510725-TC-JN-01; CL 26: 110–13. carlyleletters.dukeupress.edu.

251 "that ever was built in the world": Thomas Carlyle to Jean Carlyle Aitken, June 10, 1851, The Carlyle Letters Online, doi: 10.1215/lt-18510610 -TC-JCA-01; CL 26: 85–86. carlyleletters.dukeupress.edu.

251 calling it the "Exhibition of *Wind*dustry": Thomas Carlyle to Jean Carlyle Aitken, August 4, 1851, The Carlyle Letters Online, doi: 10.1215/lt -18510804-TC-JCA-01; CL 26: 118–19. He softened slightly once he had been there with his wife, Jane, but he remained grumpy about the ostentation and nuisance. January 29, 1851, doi: 10.1215/lt-18510129-TC -TSS-01; CL 26: 29-31. carlyleletters.dukeupress.edu.

251 called him "something of a prig": Woodward, *The Age of Reform,* 106.

251 advancement of their public image by 1851: QVJ, June 20, 1851.

251 "native and [to] the manner born": *Bristol Mercury,* May 3, 1851.

252 "follow the dictates of that spirit within": McDonald, *Florence Nightingale: An Introduction,* 129.

252 "where no one of the three can be exercised": Nightingale, Florence, *Cassandra,* 25–27. She continued: "We fast mentally, scourge ourselves morally, use the intellectual hair shirt, in order to subdue the perpetual daydreaming, which is so dangerous! We resolve: 'this day, month I will be free from it;' twice a day with prayer and written record of the times when we have indulged in it, we endeavor to combat it. Never, with the slightest success."

253 "in nine cases out of ten": Ibid., 40.

253 "ye women, all ye that sleep, awake!": Nightingale, *Cassandra.*

253 Queen Victoria's was Albert: To Florence Nightingale the opening of the Great Exhibition was like "the opening of a new era in the world." She praised Albert for the two great ideas she saw contained in it (most men, she wrote, had "but half a one"): "the greatness of *work,* and not of rank or wealth or blood; the other, the unity of human race. It was the first

time that workingmen and a Queen ever walked in procession together, that a Queen's husband ever appeared as a working man. . . . Idea the second, unity of human race: we have forever done with thanking God that we are not as other men are." McDonald, *Nightingale on Society and Politics,* 5:187.

253 **"grows daily fonder and fonder of politics":** Benson and Esher, *The Letters of Queen Victoria,* 2:438.

254 **"Alice & Affie have witnessed such an event":** QVJ, June 27, 1850.

255 **and the cane was withdrawn from sale:** A small article published in *The New York Times* in 1899 reported: "The cane with which Robert Pate, a retired Lieutenant, attacked the Queen in 1850, inflicting a wound upon her Majesty the scar of which she still carries, was advertised to be sold by auction this week, but the owner received an official communication from Osborne, Isle of Wight, in consequence of which he withdrew the cane for sale. Pate, who was sentenced to transportation for seven years for his assault upon her Majesty, died in 1895." "The Cane That Wounded Royalty," *The New York Times,* January 15, 1899.

255 **"soothing, quieting and delightful beyond measure":** QVJ, April 22, 1853.

255 **returned a surplus of almost £200,000:** Rhodes James, *Albert, Prince Consort,* 110.

256 **"imprudently heaping up a pile of combustibles":** Albert to Queen Victoria, Osborne, May 9, 1853, RA, VIC/MAIN/Z/140 9 to 18.

257 **"beautiful strain of music":** Rappaport, *Magnificent Obsession,* 14.

257 **"untiring love, tenderness & care":** QVJ, April 22, 1853.

257 **"when I have business elsewhere":** Woodham-Smith, *Queen Victoria,* 329.

Chapter Eighteen: The Crimea: "This Unsatisfactory War"

258 **"This unsatisfactory war":** Dyson and Tennyson, *Dear and Honoured Lady,* 39.

258 **"with such courage and good humor":** Queen Victoria to King Leopold, October 13, 1854, Benson and Esher, *The Letters of Queen Victoria,* 3:63.

259 **"one feels wretched at being a woman":** QVJ, February 13, 1854.

259 **the worry of staying behind:** Chesney, *Crimean War Reader,* 29.

259 **"I shall *never* forget the touching, beautiful sight":** QVJ, February 28, 1854.

259 **when she first mentioned the possibility of conflict:** QVJ, February 9, 1854.

260 **out of a population of about thirty-five million:** Faroqhi et al., *Economic and Social History,* 2:778.

261 **without seeking her consent:** She wrote on October 10: "We were a good deal concerned at finding we were pledged to a very dangerous policy which Ld Aberdeen himself did *not like,* & which I ought previously to have been asked about." Benson and Esher, *The Letters of Queen Victoria,* 3:552.

261 **precariousness of an exclusive alliance with France:** Stockmar, *Memoirs of Baron Stockmar,* 2:475.

261 **offering support to Turkey without having bound it:** Not even the Crown had that power, she pointed out to Lord Clarendon.

261 **unable to slow the momentum to fight:** Queen Victoria to the Earl of Clarendon, October 11, 1853: "It appears to the Queen, moreover, that we have taken on ourselves in conjunction with France all the risks of a European war without having bound Turkey to any conditions with respect to provoking it." Benson and Esher, *The Letters of Queen Victoria,* 2:456.

261 **"It is an anxious state of things":** QVJ, December 20, 1853.

262 **"I told him this would never do":** QVJ, February 25, 1854.

262 **a short, relatively bloodless war:** QVJ, March 24, 1854.

262 **"is a great thing":** Bostridge, *Florence Nightingale,* 203.

262 **"Never such enthusiasm seen among the population":** Chesney, *Crimean War Reader,* 47.

263 **"as a careful nurse would a small baby":** "Campaigning in the Crimea," *The Times,* October 21, 1854, 9.

263 **"the groans of the wounded went through me":** "The Battle of the Alma," *The Times,* October 18, 1854, 8.

263 **"a mass of putridity":** "Turkey: From Our Own Correspondent," *The Times,* October 13, 1854, 8.

264 **who were, wrote the correspondent, "totally useless":** Ibid.

264 **the rest succumbed to disease:** The death rate was not brought down until mid-1855, after a sanitary commission sailed to Scutari from England and undertook substantial changes to the hospital, with large-scale reengineering. Overall, about 650,000 died in the war. Most were Russian—475,000—French deaths numbered 95,000 (75,000 from disease). Roughly half of the British deaths were from cholera, diarrhea, and dysentery, and more than 5,000 died from typhus, malaria, typhoid, frostbite, and scurvy. Ponting, *The Crimean War,* 334.

264 **"What will be said when it is known":** "The Crimea: From Our Own Correspondent," *The Times,* October 12, 1854, 7.

265 **Victoria Theatre donated one night's ticket sales:** Grey, *The Noise of Drums and Trumpets,* 104. *The Times*'s reporter was the Irishman William Howard Russell, the first war correspondent of modern newspapers,

whose candid, wrenching accounts changed the way the public viewed the war.

265 **inefficiency, incompetence, and stupidity:** The great paradox of what became the Florence Nightingale legend was that she was lionized as a tender nurturer bearing aloft a lamp, while her real talent was in her keenly honed analytical skills and ken for organization.

265 **Her trip was quickly arranged:** Having decided she now wanted to take three to four nurses, on that Saturday Nightingale sought the advice of the Secretary at War, a friend, Sidney Herbert, who was out of town. Coincidentally, Sidney Herbert wrote to her on Sunday and asked her if she would lead a group of nurses, provided for by the government, to the Scutari hospital. See Bostridge, *Florence Nightingale,* 205–6. This made it official.

265 **"My whole soul and heart are in the Crimea":** November 14, 1854, Benson and Esher, *The Letters of Queen Victoria,* 3:66.

265 **before they had even cocked a gun at the enemy:** Rappaport writes that about ten thousand British and French soldiers were either dead or out of action due to cholera. *Queen Victoria,* 106.

265 **saw dead bodies bobbing in the Scutari harbor:** "William Howard Russell, the *Times* correspondent, reported seeing dead bodies rising from the bottom of the harbor and bobbing around in the water, 'all buoyant, bolt upright, and hideous in the sun.' " Bostridge, *Florence Nightingale,* 203.

265 **their incompetence revealed to enemies and allies alike:** Russell became famous—Victoria even mentioned him in her diary. In her journal on February 16, 1855, she wrote: "The French however also suffer dreadfully, only they have no "Times" reporter to trumpet it out, which we do, to our eternal shame."

265 **"the misery, the suffering":** QVJ, May 28, 1855.

266 **her "beloved" troops were constantly in her thoughts:** Queen Victoria to Lord Panmure, March 5, 1855, Benson and Esher, *The Letters of Queen Victoria,* 3:143–44.

267 **and downplayed the newspaper reports:** Sir John McNeill said even the lack of preparation had been grossly exaggerated—contradicting evidence Florence Nightingale was to give—and falsely vowed to the queen that her "sick and wounded soldiers were better cared for, than in any other Army." QVJ, July 24, 1855.

267 **"'gladly give up his life to prove his devotion to Yr Majesty'":** Ibid.

267 **The bullets wounded or killed about 240 out of 660:** Rappaport, *No Place for Ladies,* 86.

268 **she lay awake for hours:** QVJ, November 12, 1854.

268   **her empathy and imagination made her wretched:** QVJ, October 28, 1854, and November 9, 1854.

268   **"war never before was so horrible":** Wyndham, *Correspondence of Sarah Spencer,* 414.

269   **"welfare and *success* of her army":** Queen Victoria to the Duke of Newcastle, Secretary for War (commenting on a letter he had sent to Lord Raglan, the British Commander in the Crimea). Benson and Esher, *The Letters of Queen Victoria,* 3:86.

269   **"true orthodox English manner":** Stockmar, *Memoirs of Baron Stockmar,* 2:481.

269   **refused to swear, gamble, or keep a mistress:** Ibid., 485.

269   **over a dispute about a reform bill:** The queen wrote in 1856: "Albert and I agreed that of all the Prime Ministers we have had, Lord Palmerston is the one who gives the least trouble, and is most amenable to reason and most ready to adopt suggestions. The great danger was foreign affairs, but now that these are conducted by an able, sensible and impartial man [Lord Clarendon], and that he [Lord Palmerston] is responsible for the *whole,* everything is quite different." QVJ, August 21, 1856.

269   **"infamous and *now* almost ridiculous":** QVJ, January 9, 1854; QVJ, January 4, 1854; QVJ, January 10, 1854, Benson and Esher, *The Letters of Queen Victoria,* 3:8.

270   **"afraid to do what I should think to be right":** QVJ, January 23, 1854.

270   **"the Eastern Question & their desire for war":** QVJ, January 5, 1854.

270   **defended Albert's role as a key adviser:** Lords Aberdeen and Hardinge led it in the Upper House. Victoria wrote in her diary on February 1: "Ld John has stated our position very strongly & we think it is *very important* for the *future.* On looking into the newspapers, we found that Ld Aberdeen had concluded his speech by an admirable defence of my beloved one, & that Ld Derby had also spoken very strongly on the subject. . . . I read all the speeches to Albert, & felt so happy & proud." Albert's position, though, remained undefined.

270   **the jeering had stopped in the crowds:** QVJ, February 20, 1854.

270   **"various and profound knowledge":** Martin, *The Prince Consort,* 110.

270   **"had to take a back seat":** Esher to Maurice Brett, August 9, 1905, Brett, *Journals and Letters,* 2:97; Ward, "Editing Queen Victoria," 288.

271   **the country house owned by Uncle Leopold:** Weintraub, *Victoria,* 167

271   **"The door immediately swings open":** Strachey, *Queen Victoria,* 161.

271   **"a balance within themselves and with humanity in general":** Albert to Ernest, unpublished, from Yvonne Ward's files.

272   Victoria was now calling Albert her "Lord & Master": QVJ, May 13, 1854.

272   "Few women are so blessed with *such* a Husband": QVJ, February 10, 1854.

272   the wife of the prime minister: QVJ, April 28, 1854: "Sir C. Wood gave me such an account of Lady John Russell's behaviour & *how* she rules & plagues poor Ld John, putting *her* opinion & that of *her family*, before his!"

272   "an exemplary mother & an affectionate true friend": QVJ, November 20, 1853.

272   more intellectually capable than she was: Queen Victoria to Vicky, December 18, 1860, quoted in Fulford, *Dearest Child*, 293.

272   "King, instead of me!": QVJ, June 20, 1855.

273   "will try to put down in a few words, what I mean": QVJ, October 24, 1854.

273   "*no* wife ever loved . . . as I do," she wrote: QVJ, Albert's birthday, August 26, 1854.

273   mustaches were "very popular" among the Guards: QVJ, July 30, 1854.

273   "my general usefulness to the Queen": Martin, *The Prince Consort*, 2:256–57.

274   "This position is a most peculiar and delicate one": Ibid., 260.

274   to Victoria's great satisfaction: QVJ, June 25, 1857.

274   "acts in everything by his inspiration": October 8, 1857, Pearce, *The Diaries of Charles Greville*, 329.

275   mopping the brows of her wounded troops: She also wrote in QVJ, December 8, 1854: "I envy her being able to do so much good & look after the noble brave heroes, whose behaviour is admirable. Dreadfully wounded as many are, there is never a murmur or a complaint!"

275   pleased to hear that many had cried that day: She was also happy to report a letter from her containing a message to Florence Nightingale had been stuck up in every ward. Queen Victoria to King Leopold, Buckingham Palace, May 22, 1855, Benson and Esher, *The Letters of Queen Victoria*, 3:161.

275   "so bright an example to our sex": Queen Victoria to Florence Nightingale, [January] 1856, ibid., 170.

275   to lobby for a royal commission: McDonald, *Nightingale on Society and Politics*, 5:412. In 1861, Victoria also offered Florence an apartment in Kensington Palace, but Florence did not accept it.

275   "clear and comprehensive in her views of everything": QVJ, September 21, 1856.

275	**"and refusing all public demonstrations"**: Albert wrote simply in his diary: "She put before us all the defects of our present military hospital system, and the reforms that are needed. We are much pleased with her; she is extremely modest." Martin, *The Prince Consort,* 3:410.

276	**"and appreciated my sympathy and interest"**: QVJ, September 21, 1856.

276	**care for the wounded in the American Civil War:** The *Atlantic Monthly* wrote in December 1861 that the British nurse's "practical hard work, personal reserve and singular administrative power" had heightened expectations for the treatment of injured soldiers. They wrote that it was "through her, mainly . . . that every nation has already studied with some success the all-important subject of Health in the Camp and in the Hospital. It now lies in the way of American women to take up the office, and, we may trust, to better the instruction." Grant, "New Light on the Lady."

276	**"like a person who wanted to die"**: McDonald, *Nightingale on Society and Politics,* 5:415. The original source cited is notes by Oxford tutor and theologian Benjamin Jowett of conversations with Nightingale in 1879. "[Queen Victoria was] full of interest in great subjects though stupid— the least self-reliant person she had ever known. If left alone ten minutes [she] would send for her husband to entame [begin] the conversation—so superior to all her surroundings. He [Prince Albert] seemed oppressed with his situation, full of intelligence, well up in every subject, yet . . . Had he gained his way there would have been no united Italy or united Germany. He thought that the world could be managed by prizes and exhibitions and good intentions. . . . He was like a person who wanted to die. They used to play with the children in a clumsy sort of way, not knowing what to say to them."

277	**of a sunny week at Osborne:** QVJ, March 17, 1854.

277	**playing with stuffed mice:** Bloomfield, *Court and Diplomatic Life,* 1:126.

277	**hiding quietly in the heather as Albert hunted deer:** Ibid., 125.

277	**"he is really delighted with Vicky"**: Queen Victoria to the King of Belgium, September 22, 1855, Benson and Esher, *The Letters of Queen Victoria,* 3:187.

277	**"but unfortunately has also done great harm"**: Longford, *Victoria R.I.,* 146.

277	**"I may be *too* happy"**: QVJ, May 24, 1853.

278	**after a 349-day siege, Sevastopol had fallen:** Six months before then, Czar Nicholas had died, on March 2, 1855, of pulmonic apoplexy, after an attack of influenza.

278	**"wild & exciting beyond everything"**: QVJ, September 10, 1855.

Chapter Nineteen: Royal Parents and the Dragon of Dissatisfaction

279 **"the pride of sovereignty to the level of petty life":** Bagehot, *The English Constitution,* 38.

279 **bolts, cutlery, metals, or buttons:** In 1840, it was made illegal to enter the sewers, and a reward was given for reporting people doing so. This meant it was then usually done at night, by lantern light.

280 **"sewer-hunters beset":** Mayhew, *Mayhew's London,* 326.

280 **The work was filthy, but surprisingly lucrative:** Mayhew's informants told him they earned about six shillings a day; equivalent to about fifty dollars a day today. Mayhew wrote: "At this rate, the property recovered from the sewers of London would have amounted to no less than £20,000 [today $3.3 million] per annum." Ibid., 333.

280 **to the river in large murky pipes:** The growth in popularity occurred from 1810, and escalated after 1830. In 1848, the Metropolitan Sewers Commission ensured the connection of house drains and cesspools to sewers for the first time. In 1852, 11,200 out of the 16,200 houses in the city were linked to sewers.

280 **turned to black in less than half a century:** In the early 1800s, land under most London homes was honeycombed by cesspools filled with sewage, emptied by hand by night watchmen. Henry Mayhew reported that in poor houses, "many people simply used a convenient corner, or a hole in the floorboards, and excrement lay around in hallways and rooms and on stairways. The stench in these buildings was unbearable to those not used to it." Quoted in Paterson, *Voices from Dickens' London,* 23.

280 **By 1851, there were 306,000:** Picard, *Victorian London,* 50.

280 **increasing acidity and murkiness in the water:** The smell was acute at low tide: the banks were piled with excrement and crawled with bright red worms boys called bloodworms. Ibid., 10.

280 **"harassing fatigues and anxieties of official duties":** *Civil Engineer and Architect's Journal* 15 (1852), 160.

280 **leaking excrement and crawled with rodents:** In the words of one royal courtier, "There are more stinks in royal residences than anywhere else." St. Aubyn, *Queen Victoria,* 328.

280 **"the rat made an awful noise":** QVJ, November 22, 1849.

280 **wearing a belt set with cast-iron rats:** Black also provided rats for rat-baiting competitions, where a crowd of rats was placed in a pit and bets were held as to how quickly a terrier could kill them all. This was a popular mid-Victorian pastime.

280 **they grew sick from "the fearful smell!":** QVJ, June 28, 1858. Sanitation was one of Albert's myriad passions, though, and he was constantly experimenting with various sewage fertilization schemes on his properties, as part of his research into methods of improving the living conditions of the working class.

280 **without having to hold handkerchiefs over their noses:** But, wrote *The Times,* "that hot fortnight did for the sanitary administration of the metropolis what the Bengal mutinies did for the administration of India." *The Times,* July 21, 1858, 9.

281 **water temperature was at a record high:** Testimony from a civil engineer, *The Times,* July 14, 1858, 5.

281 **to avoid prolonged exposure to the fumes:** In one case, on June 23, 1858, the judge in the Court of Exchequer said he would quickly sum up because of the stench. A juror agreed he was made ill by it and the judge responded: "I deem it my public duty to notice the condition of the river and its effect on all around me. It is impossible to conceal from one's-self the fact that we are not sitting to try a most important case in the middle of a stinking nuisance." (*The Times,* June 24, 1858, 11.) *The Times* campaigned for months to goad the authorities to clean the river, advising their readers to have a tumbler of sherry and ice to steel themselves, then walk to the Thames at low tide: "There you shall see in the brief space of half an hour and two or three miles a hundred sewers disgorging solid filth, a hundred chimneys vomiting smoke, and strange, indescribable, sickening vapors; a hundred broad acres of unnatural, slimy, chymical compost, a hundred pair of paddlewheels stirring up the mud. The water—the liquid rather—is inky black. Naked imps, issuing from dark arches or dropping from coal barges, play in mud and water like the monster brood of the Nile. . . . We believe this to be the uncleanest, foulest river in the known world." *The Times,* June 17, 1858, 8.

281 **"most head-and-stomach distracting nature":** Quoted in Picard, *Victorian London,* 51–52. This account of the impact on the Thames is highly worth reading.

281 **The stench was no respecter:** There were lengthy delays and many arguments about money, responsibility, and solutions before Joseph Bazalgette, civil engineer of the Metropolitan Board of Works, was permitted to embark on his plan of diverting sewage from the Thames by building intercepting super-sewers running north and south along the edge of the river, which carried the effluent to plants outside the city. (Paterson, *Voices from Dickens' London,* 31.) In 1858, Parliament granted him three

million pounds. His scheme began in increments as embankments were built alongside; under the streets, 165 miles of main sewers were connected to 1,100 miles of local sewers to carry the sludge away from the center of the city. It was fully functioning by the mid-1870s.

281 **"Can I have no more fun in bed?":** Duff, in *Albert and Victoria,* 225, calls this "private information." He wrote, "It has been passed down that he [Sir James Clark] revealed, to members of his own profession, the Queen's reply to his advice that she should have no more children. The reply was 'Oh, Sir James, can I have no more fun in bed?'"

281 **"hardly able to do what is expected of her":** Letter dated March 3, 1857. Bolitho, *The Prince Consort,* 170. The month before Beatrice was born, Albert wrote to Viscount Palmerston saying Victoria's health was bad and she needed to go to Windsor: "The Queen feels herself physically quite unable to go through the anxiety of a Ministerial crisis." Benson and Esher, *The Letters of Queen Victoria,* 3:290.

281 **"I have felt better":** QVJ, April 29, 1857. "Afterwards," she wrote, "there was a small Party & a very pretty, gay little Dance, in the Saloon. . . . Was surprised at myself,—at being so strong, that I was able to dance all the evening, after such a tiring Levee, & only 2 months after the birth of my 9th child! I am indeed truly thankful."

281 **"which I so much wished for!":** QVJ, April 29, 1857.

282 **"A greater duck":** QVJ, December 18, 1857.

282 **"the most amusing baby we have had":** Prince Albert to Baron Stockmar, April 2, 1858, Martin, *The Prince Consort,* 4:177.

282 **"If only she could remain, just as she is":** QVJ, April 14, 1858. Then on January 23, 1859, she tried to draw her youngest: "Drew little Beatrice, who is the greatest love imaginable, so round & plump, & so lively."

282 **five Indian soldiers to one British:** In 1856, there were 233,000 Indians to 45,000 Britons (Charlot, *Victoria the Young Queen,* 370). The sepoys were also angered by some cuts in pay, and an insistence that the Bengal army must serve overseas, which would make a high-caste person's position perilous.

283 **Victoria tried to goad the Cabinet into action:** Queen Victoria to the Viscount Canning, December 2, 1858, Benson and Esher, *The Letters of Queen Victoria,* 3:389.

283 **delaying the Chinese War by a year:** The Chinese War was concluded on June 26, 1858. The Treaty of Tien-tsin further opened up China to British trade and diplomacy.

283 **children's shoes with the feet still in them:** Victoria was horrified, writing

in her journal on September 18, 1857: "After our breakfast with Jane C.,
reading newspapers with awful details of the fearful massacre at Cawnpore. 88 officers, 70 ladies & children, 120 women & children, & 400 residents perished! The courtyard with 2 inches of blood, tresses of hair &
clothes of the poor ladies left,—*all* that was found!" She was later further
distressed, on behalf of the dignity of the women, that the details of their
torture became public. QVJ, December 14, 1857.

284   **"the agonies gone thro' of the massacres":** Queen Victoria to Lady Canning, September 8 1857, cited in Surtees, *Charlotte Canning,* 238. Victoria
did write later, on October 22, 1857 (p. 243), to ask: "What I wish to know
is whether there is any *reliable evidence* of eye witnesses—of horrors, like
people having to eat their children's flesh & other unspeakable & dreadful
atrocities which I could not write?"

284   **while they watched hundreds of rebels hanged:** St. Aubyn, *Queen Victoria,* 306.

284   **chastised his troops for this behavior:** Lord Canning wrote to Victoria:
"One of the greatest difficulties which lie ahead—and Lord Canning
grieves to say so to your Majesty—will be the violent rancor of a very large
proportion of the English community against every native Indian of every
class. There is a rabid and indiscriminate vindictiveness abroad. . . . Not
one man in ten seems to think that the hanging and shooting of forty or
fifty thousand mutineers, besides other Rebels, can be otherwise than prac-
ticable and right." Viscount Canning to Queen Victoria, Calcutta, September 25, 1857, Benson and Esher, *The Letters of Queen Victoria,* 3:318–19.

284   **"see them happy, contented and flourishing":** St. Aubyn, *Queen Victoria,*
307. The queen also wrote in her journal at this time—November 1,
1857—that she spoke "very strongly" to Lord Palmerston "about the bad
vindictive spirit, exhibited by many people here & by some of the Press
&c—, & of the absolute necessity for showing our desire to be kind to the
peaceable inhabitants; also that the death penalty should not be enforced
indiscriminately on all the mutineers, for there must be a wide difference
between those who had committed murders & atrocities, or fought
against us, & those who had merely left their muskets & knapsacks behind, & these I fear, have also been hung."

284   **which had governed most of India since 1601:** It was established on December 31, 1600.

284   **education and ability, not class or creed:** Her statement read: "Firmly
relying on the truth of Christianity, and acknowledging with gratitude
the solace of our religion, we disclaim alike the right and the desire to

impose our convictions on any of our subjects. It is our Royal will and pleasure that no one shall in any wise suffer for his opinions or be disquieted by reason of his religious faith or observance." Martin, *The Prince Consort,* 4:335–36.

284 **complained of Indians behaving "like animals":** QVJ, April 16, 1859.

285 **"It is not *every* day":** Queen Victoria to the Earl of Clarendon, October 25, 1857, Benson and Esher, *The Letters of Queen Victoria,* 3:321.

285 **"I could hardly command myself":** QVJ, January 25, 1858.

285 **"how long it may be before we see her again!":** QVJ, February 2, 1858.

285 **The thought of separation was "especially painful":** Martin, *The Prince Consort,* 4:132.

285 **She felt she owed her father more than anyone:** Vicky to Prince Albert, Charlot, *Victoria the Young Queen,* 386.

286 **"what a void you have left in my heart":** Martin, *The Prince Consort,* 4:146.

286 **"and therefore shall miss her sadly":** Queen Victoria to King Leopold, January 12, 1858, Benson and Esher, *The Letters of Queen Victoria,* 3:333.

286 **with Austria ruling the north:** When the European map was redrawn at the Congress of Vienna, held at the end of the Napoleonic Wars in 1814, Austria was given the Kingdom of Lombardy-Venetia.

286 **would ignite a full-blown European war:** The French had also been furious when it was revealed that the Italian conspirators who had made an attempt on their emperor's life had sought asylum in England, where they had hatched revolutionary plans and made grenades.

287 **played a crucial part in staying Britain's hand:** This amounted to an agreement between France and Austria for a confederation of Italian states, which almost entirely ignored the desires of the Italians for self-rule, and annexed Nice and Savoy to France.

287 **Victoria and Albert were now at the height of their powers:** August 28, 1905, Brett, *Journals and Letters,* 2:103–6. See Ward, "Editing Queen Victoria," 221.

288 **"would have become very strained":** Esher continued in a private letter to his son, "Also there were signs of incipient trouble between him and the P. of Wales, young as the Prince was so that perhaps his early death was no great misfortune. Probably his mission was fulfilled and his work done, in the training which he gave the Queen. He lived long enough to sow the seed but not to see the ear ripen. Perhaps it was as well." Esher to Maurice Brett, August 18, 1905, Brett, *Journals and Letters.* Quoted in Ward, "Editing Queen Victoria," 229.

288   **she called it "horrid news"**: Queen Victoria to Vicky, May 26, 1858, Ful-
       ford, *Dearest Child,* 108.

288   **"our poor nature becomes so very animal and unecstatic"**: Queen Victoria
       to Vicky, June 15, 1858, ibid., 115. The full passage: "I think much more of
       our being like a cow or a dog at such moments; when our poor nature
       becomes so very animal and unecstatic—but for you, dear, if you are sen-
       sible and reasonable and not in ecstasy nor spending your day with nurses
       and wet nurses, which is the ruin of many a refined and intellectual young
       lady, without adding to her real maternal duties, a child will be a great
       resource. Above all, dear girl, do remember never to lose the modesty of a
       young girl towards others (without being prude); though you are married
       don't become a matron to whom everything can be said and who minds
       saying nothing herself—I remained to a particular degree (indeed feel so
       now) and often feel shocked at the confidences of other married ladies. I
       fear abroad they are very indelicate about such things." It was only in let-
       ters to Vicky that Victoria complained so robustly. See also ibid., 77–78, 94.

288   **"relieved from a great weight"**: QVJ, January 27, 1859.

288   **"very severe"**: QVJ, January 29, 1859.

288   **Albert advised rest**: Prince Albert to Vicky, March 16, 1859, Martin, *The
       Prince Consort,* 4:333.

289   **hung weakly from its socket, paralyzed**: QVJ, May 21, 1859.

289   **"fine fat child, with a beautiful white soft skin"**: QVJ, September 25,
       1860.

289   **"the best children I ever saw"**: She now understood, she wrote, the "over-
       flowing tenderness" her mother used to feel for her children. QVJ, Au-
       gust 16, 1861.

289   **the queen grew slender and content**: Wyndham, *Correspondence of Sarah
       Spencer,* 419.

289   **"so peaceable & happy in this little cottage"**: QVJ, August 30, 1849.

290   **fancy black satin dress adorned with white ribbons and orange flowers**:
       QVJ, October 9, 1861.

290   **"particularly well, cheerful and active"**: Prince Albert to Baron Stock-
       mar, October 11, 1859, Martin, *The Prince Consort,* 4:411.

290   **"Oh! if only the time did not fly so fast!"**: QVJ, October 13, 1857.

290   **"We danced in the New Year"**: Martin, *The Prince Consort,* 4:424.

290   **"we are like 2 sisters!"**: QVJ, June 1, 1859.

290   **they had both married and borne children**: Victoria wrote to Vicky: "A
       married daughter, be she ever so young, is at once, on a par with her
       mother." Queen Victoria to Vicky, April 21, 1959, Fulford, *Dearest Child,*
       184.

291 **as fulfillment of his "sacred duty":** Prince Albert to Baron Stockmar, February 15, 1858, Martin, *The Prince Consort,* 4:153.

291 **"I might almost say, spasm of the soul":** Albert wrote, "I explain this hard-to-be-comprehended mental phenomenon thus. The identity of the individual is, so to speak, interrupted; and a kind of Dualism springs up by reason of this, that the *I which has been,* with all its impressions, re-membrances, experiences, feelings, which were also those of youth, is at-tached to a particular spot, with its local and personal associations, and appears to what may be called *the new I* like a vestment of the soul which has been lost, from which nevertheless *the new I* cannot disconnect itself, because its identity is in fact continuous. Hence, the painful struggle, I might almost say, spasm of the soul." Prince Albert to Vicky, March 10, 1858, Martin, *The Prince Consort,* 4:178.

291 **"dependent on herself!":** Queen Victoria to King Leopold, February 9, 1858, Benson and Esher, *The Letters of Queen Victoria,* 3:334.

291 **"how do your poor maids bear this hurry scurry?":** Queen Victoria to Vicky, February 6, 1858, Fulford, *Dearest Child,* 32–33. Victoria also reg-ularly admonished her daughter for not writing frequently enough, or providing enough detail, including about cold sponging and the temper-ature of her rooms, even though Albert scolded her for being demanding. When Vicky failed to provide sufficient information about her health in telegrams, Victoria stomped her foot in print: "You don't say whether your cold is better or not, but merely: 'I am still unwell' and—'I am pretty well.' Were you feverishly unwell with it or not? . . . Accustomed as I was to know everything about you from hour to hour, I get terribly fidgeted at not knowing what really is the matter." Queen Victoria to Vicky, Feb-ruary 20, 1858, Fulford, *Dearest Child,* 54.

291 **an oppressive zealousness and control:** Victoria also suggested beginning her letters with headings, and asked for Vicky's ladies to provide a list of her daughter's outfits, a full account of all public and private presents she received and a sketch of how Vicky arranged her furniture.

292 **"I watch over you as if I were there":** Queen Victoria to Vicky, December 11, 1858, Fulford, *Dearest Child,* 151.

292 **"few people have good teeth abroad":** June 30, 1858, ibid., 120.

292 **"you know how that fattens":** Queen Victoria to Vicky, April 14 1858, ibid., 90.

292 **"overdid the passion for the nursery":** She warned her against losing time "if you overdid the passion for the nursery. NO lady, and less still a Prin-cess, is fit for her husband or her position, if she does that. I know, dear, that you will feel and guard against this; but I only just wish to remind

you and warn you, as with your great passion for little children (which are mere little plants for the first six months) it would be very natural for you to be carried away by your pleasure at having a child." (Queen Victoria to Vicky, November 17, 1858, ibid.,144.) Victoria told Vicky, in a letter written on March 16, that she only really liked babies over the age of three to four months, "when they really become very lovely." (Ibid., 167.) It was newborns that she disliked, writing again, on May 2, 1859, that she only cared for them when they became "a little human; an ugly baby is a very nasty object—and the prettiest is frightful when undressed—till about four months; in short as long as they have their big body and little limbs and that terrible froglike action. But from four months, they become prettier and prettier. And I repeat it—your child would delight me at any age." (Ibid., 191.)

292   **put to bed only about four times a year:** Queen Victoria to Vicky, May 14, 1859, ibid., 193.

292   **given how harsh a disciplinarian she had been:** Victoria had strictly disciplined Vicky as a child, and now credited her approach with having produced a woman with a sterling character. She regularly reminded her daughter what a great trial she had been as a child: "A more insubordinate and unequal-tempered child and girl I think I never saw! . . . The trouble you gave us all—was indeed very great. Comparatively speaking, we have none whatever with the others. You and Bertie (in very different ways) were indeed great difficulties. . . . I am very curious to know whether I shall find still some of the old tricks of former times in you? The standing on one leg, the violent laughing—the cramming in eating, the waddling in walking." Queen Victoria to Vicky, July 28, 1858, ibid., 124–25.

292   **their belief that Albert was a demigod:** Vicky to Queen Victoria, February 15, 1858, ibid., 46.

292   **"very violent feelings of affection":** Queen Victoria to Vicky, June 9, 1858, ibid., 69.

292   **"when he is away I feel quite paralysed":** Queen Victoria to Vicky, June 9, 1858, ibid., 112.

293   **"those immense features and total want of chin":** Queen Victoria to Vicky, November 27, 1858, ibid., 147.

293   **his large mouth, and his new hairstyle:** Seven months later, Victoria bemoaned the fact that his mouth and nose were continuing to grow, with a hanging "Coburg nose" just like his mother's and an absent chin. Queen Victoria to Vicky, June 29, 1859, ibid., 198.

293   **"to have no head and all face":** Queen Victoria to Vicky, September 2,

1859, ibid., 208. Victoria continued in another letter, April 7, 1860: "He is not at all in good looks; his nose and mouth are too enormous and as he pastes his hair down to his head, and wears his clothes frightfully—he really is anything but good looking. That coiffure is really too hideous with his small head and enormous features."

293   **"and not an engaging child though amusing"**: Queen Victoria to Vicky, November 24, 1858, ibid., 146.

293   **"so very large and long that it spoils her looks"**: Queen Victoria to Vicky, April 9, 1859, ibid., 175.

293   **"are all so amusing and communicative"**: Queen Victoria to Vicky, December 4, 1858, ibid., 149.

293   **defending him was a vain exercise:** When a mother is so honest about her dislike of her son, some will likely recoil. Vicky urged her mother to forgive Bertie and be patient, arguing that he was capable of being kind and nice, and anxious to please his mother. ("His heart is very capable of affection, of warmth of feeling, and I am sure that it will come out with time and by degrees. He loves his home and feels happy here and those feelings must be nurtured, cultivated for if once lost they will not come again easily." Vicky to Queen Victoria, April 4, 1861, ibid., 318.) It would be awful, she wrote, if there were an estrangement. But Victoria would not budge. The onus was on Bertie, she insisted, to be "more tender and affectionate," and to take an interest in what interested his parents. (Queen Victoria to Vicky, April 10, 1861, ibid., 320.) Vicky's heart sank while reading it.

293   **"pride of sovereignty to the level of petty life"**: Bagehot, *The English Constitution,* 38.

293   **one in four wives and two in three widows worked:** This census simultaneously recognized women as dependents of men and as independent workers. " 'Women . . . in certain branches of business at home render important services; such as the wives of farmers, of small shopkeepers, innkeepers, shoemakers, butchers' and were listed in those categories." Hall, *White, Male and Middle Class,* 176. The census also for the first time listed as an occupation "Wife, mother and mistress of an English family."

293   **ranks of working women swelled rapidly and became respectable:** See Schama, *A History of Britain,* 144.

294   **what her daughters might go through:** Queen Victoria to Vicky, April 20, 1859, Fulford, *Dearest Child,* 182.

294   **"That always sticks in my throat":** Queen Victoria to Vicky, May 16, 1860, ibid., 254.

295 **"men who ... forget their first duties"**: Queen Victoria to Vicky, August 10, 1859, ibid., 205.

295 **"you would find that the greatest help of all"**: Woodham-Smith, *Queen Victoria,* 331.

295 **"friendly terms with people you have just been scolding"**: October 1, 1856, quoted in Rhodes James, *Albert, Prince Consort,* 244.

296 **especially with the strong-willed, self-certain Bertie:** September 17, 1855, Strachey and Fulford, *The Greville Memoirs,* 7:157; Pearce, *The Diaries of Charles Greville,* 317.

296 **"a clever, honest & well intentioned boy"**: QVJ, April 7, 1859.

296 **"so like his precious father"**: Benson and Esher, *The Letters of Queen Victoria,* 3:541; QVJ, July 21, 1859.

296 **"refreshing and cheering to one's heart"**: Queen Victoria to Vicky, May 2, 1859, Fulford, *Dearest Child,* 190.

296 **she called him a "hard-hearted and a great tyrant"**: Queen Victoria to Vicky, July 21, 1858, ibid., 124.

296 **"It is too wretched"**: Queen Victoria to Vicky, September 27 (then October 1), 1858, ibid., 134.

296 **tame wild horses almost instantly into submission:** QVJ, January 13, 1858.

297 **declared his intention to marry Vicky:** QVJ, September 20, 1858.

297 **wanted to escape to Australia with the children:** Queen Victoria to Vicky, undated, c. April 18, 1859, Fulford, *Dearest Child,* 180.

297 **he would protect them as he had done before:** QVJ, December 31, 1860.

297 **"fearful possibility of what I will not mention"**: Queen Victoria to King Leopold, May 25, 1859, Benson and Esher, *The Letters of Queen Victoria,* 3:334.

297 **the Duchess of Kent died:** Victoire had also been struggling with erysipelas, an intense skin infection, for years.

297 **"My childhood, all seems to crowd in upon me"**: QVJ, March 16, 1859.

297 **"*She* is gone!"**: Queen Victoria to King Leopold, March 16, 1861, Benson and Esher, *The Letters of Queen Victoria,* 3:555.

298 **"sweet innocent little voice & prattle"**: QVJ, April 7, 1861.

298 **She could not bear loud conversation or crowds:** Queen Victoria to King Leopold, Windsor Castle, March 26, 1861, Benson and Esher, *The Letters of Queen Victoria,* 3:556.

298 **"I know what the consequences may be"**: Bolitho, *The Prince Consort,* 213.

298 **"controlling her feelings"**: Quoted in Longford, *Victoria R.I.,* 292. The date she provides is October 22, 1861.

298 **"your great difficulty in life"**: Richardson, *Victoria and Albert,* 214.

299 **"& never let me survive!":** QVJ, May 24, 1861.

299 **"tremble so now for all those dear to me!":** QVJ, December 7, 1857.

299 **"mucous membranes in a state of constant irritation":** Prince Albert to Baron Stockmar, May 28, 1859, Martin, *The Prince Consort,* 4:449–50.

299 **Victoria blamed it on overwork:** Fulford, *Dearest Child,* 174.

300 **"he's so completely overpowered by everything":** Queen Victoria to Vicky, February 16, 1861, ibid., 308.

300 **"born to suffer":** Queen Victoria to Vicky, February 21, 1861, ibid., 310. At least one close observer thought the queen too needy to nurse her husband. Stockmar, who was a doctor as well as a trusted adviser, grew anxious and attributed one bout of gastric attack to sudden changes in temperature—and "worries of both body and mind to which you are daily exposed." He wrote pointedly: "All round you there is a want of thoughtful care for the repose, the tending and the nursing which are so necessary for the sick and convalescent." Baron Stockmar to Prince Albert, November 8, 1859, Martin, *The Prince Consort,* 4:414.

300 **"If anything serious should ever happen to him, he will die":** From Woodham-Smith, *Queen Victoria,* 402—the note she provides is *Memoirs of Ernest II,* 4:55.

300 **"he had been here for the last time in his life":** *Memoirs of Ernest II,* 4:55.

300 **Life . . . was an interminable treadmill:** Bolitho, *The Prince Consort,* 217.

300 **"to understand the truth of this more and more":** Prince Albert to Ernest, November 14, 1856, ibid., 166.

300 **"I feel so lost without him":** Queen Victoria to King Leopold, September 15, 1859, Martin, *The Prince Consort,* 4:409.

301 **"& the Tattoo from the Barracks":** QVJ, June 22, 1860.

Chapter Twenty: "There Is No One to Call Me Victoria Now"

305 **"I tremble for the Queen":** Strafford, *Diary of Henry Greville,* 3:417.

306 **mixing freely with unmarried men:** For a fascinating discussion of this decade, see Mason, *The Making of Victorian Sexuality,* 119–25.

306 **"But so it is, in the year 1861":** Grey, *Passages in the Life,* 3:304.

306 **"Some were no doubt American":** QVJ, August 28, 1868.

306 **"Curragh—N.C. 3rd time":** Ridley, *Bertie,* 54.

307 **"a pistol packed at the bottom of a trunk":** From King, *Twilight of Splendor,* 135.

307 **"at the Curragh Camp near Dublin":** Costello, *A Most Delightful Station,* 98.

307   **the queen sighed, that was so much worse:** Queen Victoria to Vicky, April 27, 1859, Fulford, *Dearest Child,* 187.

307   **"whispering sweet nothings":** *New York Herald,* September 19, 1860; Charlot, *Victoria the Young Queen,* 404.

308   **"liking they have for my unworthy self":** Queen Victoria to Vicky, Windsor Castle, November 10, 1860, Fulford, *Dearest Child,* 279.

308   **"sunk into vice and debauchery":** Woodham-Smith, *Queen Victoria,* 416.

309   **"capable of enthusiasm about anything in the world":** Queen Victoria to Vicky, October 1, 1861, Fulford, *Dearest Child,* 353.

309   **The union would not be a "triumph of Denmark":** Bolitho, *The Prince Consort,* 215.

309   **"in his hastiness & over-love of business":** Queen Victoria to Vicky, October 1, 1861, Fulford, *Dearest Child,* 354.

310   **"many a storm" had "swept over":** Albert wrote to Baron Stockmar on their twenty-first anniversary: "How many a storm has swept over it, and still it continues green and fresh, and throws out vigorous roots, from which I can, with gratitude to God, acknowledge that much good will yet be engendered for the world!" Martin, *The Prince Consort,* 5:292.

310   **the only one he could talk to unreservedly:** QVJ, July 9, 1863.

310   **he was "never very robust":** QVJ, October 9, 1862.

310   **"he needed protection":** *Memoirs of Ernest II,* 18–19.

310   **work, write, and get warm:** Prince Albert to Vicky, September 1, 1858, Martin, *The Prince Consort,* 4:253. He told Vicky that his bout of illness in December 1860 was cholera. Victoria was, as usual, sheltered from this information.

311   **"I should be quite ready to die tomorrow":** Ibid., 5:344. He continued: "I am sure, if I had a severe illness, I should give up at once, I should not struggle for life. I have no tenacity of life."

311   **She had never seen him "so low":** Queen Victoria to Vicky, November 27, 1861, Fulford, *Dearest Child,* 369–70.

311   **as though cold water were being poured down his spine:** Martin, *The Prince Consort,* 5:353. (This is a fuller version than the account given in Victoria's diary for that day.)

311   **"They are such ruffians!":** Queen Victoria to Vicky, November 30, 1861, Fulford, *Dearest Child,* 370.

312   **Victoria agreed:** Martin, *The Prince Consort,* 5:349.

312   **"and a suitable apology":** Queen Victoria to Earl Russell, December 1, 1861, Benson and Esher, *The Letters of Queen Victoria,* 3:598.

313   **"terribly nervous and distressed":** QVJ, December 2, 1861.

313   **"not fit to attend a sick cat":** Fulford, *The Prince Consort,* 269.

313   **"Sometimes he has such a strange wild look":** Martin, *The Prince Consort,* 5:356. The word "wild" was cut out of Victoria's journal account.

313   **"I'm so silly":** For an excellent account of the death of Albert, his funeral, and the mourning that followed, see Helen Rappaport's *Magnificent Obsession.* This quote is from p. 61.

314   **how awful it was to be deprived of her husband:** QVJ, December 7, 1861.

314   **His eyes brimmed with tears as Alice played for him:** Beatrice cut some of the more intimate descriptions of Albert's death out of her mother's journal. We can see this by comparing Theodore Martin's official *Life of the Prince Consort*—which relied on Victoria's original diaries—to the version left in Victoria's diaries. For example, Beatrice deleted the reference to Albert feeling like water was being poured down his back; descriptions of his panting, choking on tea, and crying as he listened to Alice playing chorales, and stroking Victoria's face and calling her endearments, as well as Victoria kissing him. She also cut out Victoria's remarks to Albert that he was sick through overwork: "It is too much: You must speak to the Ministers!" (Victoria said it was also his fault for taking on projects by his own volition, answering: "It is not that alone; it is your own concerns." Longford, *Victoria R.I.,* 296.) Beatrice also removed Albert's saying to Victoria that as he lay in the Blue Room he heard the birds and thought of those he had heard in the Rosenau in his childhood: a troubling sign. (Martin, *The Prince Consort,* 5:357.) On December 7, for example, Victoria's original diary read: "But I seem to live in a dreadful dream. Later in the day, my angel lay in bed, and I sat by him, watching. The tears fell fast, as I thought of the days of anxiety, even if not of alarm, which were in store for us, of the utter shipwreck of our plans." Beatrice changed these sentences to: "But I seem to be living in a dreadful dream.—Albert lay late on the bed in the bedroom & I sat by him watching him often repressing my tears with difficulty."

On December 8, Victoria's journal read: "He was so pleased to see me—stroked my face, and smiled, and called me 'liebe Frauchen' (dear little wife). . . . Precious love! His tenderness this evening, when he held my hands, and stroked my face, touched me so much—made me so grateful." (Martin, *The Prince Consort,* 5:359.) Beatrice changed it to "Went in to see dearest Albert, who was so pleased to see me, stroking my face & smiling." On December 9, Beatrice deleted the words "He was so kind, calling me 'gutes Weibchen' (good little wife) and liking me to hold his dear hand." (Ibid., 359.)

314   **cupping them in his before bending to pray:** Longford, *Victoria R.I.,* 298.

314   **"Prepare to meet Thy God, O Israel!":** Queen Victoria to Vicky, October
        7, 1861, Fulford, *Dearest Child,* 356.

314   **he told his daughter Alice he was dying:** Alice was the one Albert con-
        fided in, not Victoria, when he realized he was facing death. When Alice
        said she had told Vicky he was "very ill," he corrected her: "You should
        have told her I am dying, yes I am dying." Rappaport, *Magnificent Obsess-
        sion,* 69; Strafford, *Henry Greville,* 3:420.

315   **"as if I should go mad!":** Longford, *Victoria R.I.,* 299.

315   **"there was no reason to anticipate anything worse":** Victoria could not
        bring herself to describe the events of Albert's death until February 1872,
        when she wrote an account from notes she made at the time.

316   **"and not taking notice of me":** Martin, *The Prince Consort,* 5:363.

316   **Albert never recognized the face of his son by his bed:** Maxwell, *Life and
        Letters of Clarendon,* 2:255. Sir G. C. Lewis to Lord Clarendon, December
        19, 1861: "Granville told me that the prince never recognized the Prince
        of Wales, so that he must have passed the last day in a state of uncon-
        sciousness."

316   **"But that was nothing to this":** Rappaport, *Magnificent Obsession,* 81. See
        also the account of Lady Geraldine Somerset, whose diaries are held in
        the Royal Archives.

317   **"and to give one kiss to his little wife":** This was from a telling of the
        story by Lady Winchester, December 25, 1861, Rappaport, *Magnificent
        Obsession,* 81.

318   **"Papa is gone on a visit to Grandmama":** Ibid., 83.

318   **his stomach problems and his toothaches:** Ibid., 249–60. Rappaport ar-
        gues, as many others have, that the stress caused by the queen's postna-
        tal depression and cavernous grief for her mother "would have made
        matters worse." There is doubtless some truth to this; the emotional
        strain of supporting an anxious, melancholic, and needy wife would
        have been substantial. It is astonishing, though, how many people im-
        plicitly, and occasionally directly, blame Victoria for the death of her
        husband because she had struggled with depression, motherhood, and
        grief.

318   **"the most important man in the country":** *Daily Telegraph,* December 16,
        1861, ibid., 94.

318   **admired Albert's "motives, sagacity and tact":** Maxwell, *Life and Letters
        of Clarendon,* 2:250.

318   **"far greater importance than the public dream of":** Lord Clarendon to
        Sir George Lewis, December 14, 1861, ibid., 251.

319   "like parting with her heart and soul": Villiers, *A Vanished Victorian,* 309.

319   "as if it were their own private sorrow": QVJ, January 21, 1862.

319   "talk as if the Queen was one of themselves": Rappaport, *Magnificent Obsession,* 116, cites Wolffe, *Great Deaths,* 195. Letters poured in from other countries: even President Abraham Lincoln sent a letter offering sympathy for her "irreparable bereavement with an unaffected sorrow," signing himself "Your Good Friend." Rappaport, *Magnificent Obsession,* 135.

319   "Oh! I want my mother!": Rappaport, *Magnificent Obsession,* 91.

320   a life that might contain happiness now: *The Times,* December 24, 1861, 6; Jerrold, *The Widowhood of Queen Victoria,* 11.

320   Lady Augusta Bruce: Lady Augusta Bruce was the sister of Bertie's governor, General the Hon. Robert Bruce. Lady Augusta later married the Very Reverend Arthur Stanley, Dean of Westminster.

320   "The whole house seems like Pompeii": Baillie and Bolitho, *Letters of Lady Augusta Stanley,* 251.

Chapter Twenty-One: "The Whole House Seems Like Pompeii"

321   "I have, since he left me": Queen Victoria to Vicky, April 29, 1863, Fulford, *Dearest Mama,* 205–6.

322   "belief in the *Life presence* of the Dead": Quoted in Dyson and Tennyson, *Dear and Honoured Lady,* 69. Victoria's belief in future reunion was commonly held in the 1860s and 1870s. Wolffe, *Great Deaths,* 205.

322   *"Where all things round me breathed of him"*: Queen Victoria's Album Consolativum 1862–1886, British Library Archives, Add. 62089–62090, 30.

322   his eyes welling: QVJ, April 14, 1862.

322   "The Queen is not stout": May 9, 1863, Dyson and Tennyson, *Dear and Honoured Lady,* 78.

323   "the Queen is a woman to live and die for": Ibid., 76. The full quote reads: "The Queen's face is beautiful. Not the least like her portraits but small and childlike, full of intelligence and ineffably sweet and of a sad sympathy. A. was delighted with the breadth and freedom and penetration of her mind. One felt that no false thing could stand before her. We talked of all things in heaven and earth it seemed to me. I never met a Lady with whom I could talk so easily and never felt too little shy with any stranger after the first few minutes. She laughed heartily at many things that were said but shades of pain and sadness passed over a face

that seemed sometimes all one smile. . . . One feels that the Queen is a woman to live and die for."

323 **"a Father who strangled you":** QVJ, May 8, 1863.

323 **Tennyson be appointed poet laureate:** The Prince Consort was taken with Tennyson's retelling of the legends of the Arthurian Knights, *Idylls of the King*. The night before a letter arrived offering him the position, Tennyson dreamed that Albert had kissed him on the cheek. Six years later, Albert had dropped in unexpectedly on the Tennysons' property on the Isle of Wight—to the horror of his wife, Emily, as the house was cluttered and in disarray; they were preparing for a sale of furniture and paintings. Albert chatted comfortably with the poet for some time as one of his gentlemen gathered cowslips outside, to be made into tea for the royal couple later.

323 **"hideous dream":** QVJ, February 1, 1862.

324 **had known all their names:** QVJ, January 27, 1862.

324 **"*nothing* from my beloved one":** QVJ, May 24, 1863.

324 **cause a "national calamity":** Lord Clarendon to Sir George Lewis, December 14, 1861, Maxwell, *Life and Letters of Clarendon,* 2:251.

324 **initial stages of her grief:** Charles Phipps wrote to Palmerston: "The Queen, though in an agony of grief, is perfectly collected, and shows a self control that is quite extraordinary. Alas! She has not realized her loss—and when the full consciousness comes upon her—I tremble—but only for the depth of her grief. What will happen—where can She look for that support and assistance upon which She has leaned in the greatest and the least questions of her life?" Quoted in Rhodes James, *Albert, Prince Consort,* 273.

324 **"dignify a hero":** McDonald, *Nightingale on Society and Politics,* 5:418.

324 **not to submit to her pain:** Lord Clarendon to Duchess of Manchester, December 17, 1861: "She seems to remember how much he disapproved and warned her against such extravagant grief as she manifested at her mother's death. If she can support herself in this frame of mind, it is all one can hope for; but as yet it is, of course, early days for believing that her nervous system may not give way." Maxwell, *Life and Letters of Clarendon,* 2:253.

324 **"I could go mad from the desire":** Bolitho, *Albert, Prince Consort,* 229.

325 **"showed embarrassing emotion":** From Lady Clarendon's journal, February 3, 1862, ibid., 258. Lady Clarendon also claimed Victoria said "she knew she would go mad with worry," and that "three times at Balmoral she had thought she was going mad." Bolitho, *The Reign of Queen Victoria,* 187.

325 **deaths of various relatives and dignitaries:** See Rappaport, *Magnificent Obsession,* 37. Victoria had carefully mourned her aunt Louise in 1850, the King of Hanover in 1851, the Duke of Wellington in 1852, Czar Nicholas in 1855, her half brother Prince Charles of Leiningen in 1856, her cousin the Duchess of Nemours in 1857, her brother-in-law the Prince of Hohenlohe-Langenburg in April 1860, Albert's stepmother, Marie of Saxe-Coburg and Gotha, in September 1860, and Friedrich Wilhelm IV, the old king of Prussia, in January 1861.

325 **had always appealed to her:** She wrote to Vicky on July 6, 1859: "You must promise me that if I should die your child or children and those around you should mourn; this really must be, for I have such strong feelings on the subject." Fulford, *Dearest Child,* 199–200. In 1863, she wrote to *The Times* concerning a rumor she might stop wearing her widow's weeds: "This idea cannot be too explicitly contradicted." Rappaport, *Queen Victoria,* 407.

326 **"habits entertained by both of us":** April 11, 1862, McClintock, *The Queen Thanks Sir Howard,* 50.

326 **"noise, excitement, etc":** Ibid., 49.

326 **frivolous, gossipy, and shallow:** Victoria told General Bruce that Bertie should face "in a proper spirit, the cureless melancholy of his poor home." Rappaport, *Magnificent Obsession,* 154; Sir George Aston, *The Duke of Connaught and Strathearn,* 47–48.

326 **"Day is turned into night":** Bloomfield, *Court and Diplomatic Life,* 2:150.

326 **"crown of righteousness":** QVJ, January 19, 1863.

326 **"more disposed to do good":** Bolitho, *The Prince Consort,* 161.

327 **"All alone!"** Longford, *Victoria R.I.,* 308.

327 **she would "succumb":** Bolitho, *The Prince Consort,* 219–20.

327 **"which she had to sign, etc.":** Maxwell, *Life and Letters of Clarendon,* 261.

327 **through sheer madness:** Villiers, *A Vanished Victorian,* 317.

327 **the impact this would have:** Ibid., 318.

327 **went through to August:** Maxwell, *Life and Letters of Clarendon,* 261–62.

328 **"less a national loss":** Rappaport, *Magnificent Obsession,* 76.

328 **"We have buried our sovereign":** Wiebe et al., *Letters of Benjamin Disraeli,* 165.

328 **she might abdicate:** Lord Howden to Lord Clarendon, June 4, 1864: "The French papers talk of the abdication of Queen Victoria. I am beginning to think there may be something in it. I have always thought that, with the turn her mind took from the beginning of her widowhood, she would have done well, for her own interest, happiness and *reputation,* to

have abdicated on the day her son came of age. She would *then* have left a great name and a great regret." Maxwell, *Life and Letters of Clarendon,* 2:292–93.

328 **blamed for his father's death:** Florence Nightingale, December 22, 1861: "One of the causes which brought in Albert's illness, and about which he talked when delirious, was the shortcoming of the Prince of Wales." McDonald, *Nightingale on Society and Politics,* 5:419.

328 **complained about his "ugly" legs:** Note that Vicky was similarly frank about her own children, once writing about her son Henry, upon his getting a uniform on his tenth birthday: "His poor ugly face will look worse than ever, and he has grown if possible much plainer still since last year." Vicky to Queen Victoria, August 7, 1872, Fulford, *Darling Child,* 57.

328 **She prayed that she would outlive him:** See ibid., 231.

328 **"unconquerable aversion" to her son:** Villiers, *A Vanished Victorian,* 313.

328 **state of "enforced idleness":** The Hon. Emily Eden wrote to the Earl of Clarendon in 1863: "I see what Princess Louise means about the 'enforced idleness' of the Prince of Wales, which may lead to evil. The Prince Consort would have devised some work for him—made him Regent of Scotland or a clerk in the Audit Office or bailiff of the home farm—something distinguished that would have kept him out of harm." Maxwell, *Life and Letters of Clarendon,* 2:284.

328 **"indeed of all her counsels":** Rappaport, *Magnificent Obsession,* 131.

328 **"trembling and *alone*":** Letter to King Leopold, June 16, 1863, Buckle, *The Letters of Queen Victoria Between 1862 and 1878,* 1:91.

329 **distressed her children:** QVJ, November 1, 1862.

329 **"able to talk more myself":** QVJ, April 28, 1863.

329 **would have wished her to promote:** Leopold had encouraged this view, writing to her to tell her it was "justifiable" to think "the departed continue to take an interest in what is doing in the plans they left, and that to see what they had wisely planned destroyed or neglected becomes a *source of trouble and pain to them.*" King Leopold to Queen Victoria, January 16, 1862, Buckle, *The Letters of Queen Victoria Between 1862 and 1878,* 1:11.

329 **"vain show of a drawing room":** McDonald, *Nightingale on Society and Politics,* 5:419–20.

330 **could live in one of her homes:** Queen Victoria to King Leopold, Balmoral, May 18, 1863, Buckle, *The Letters of Queen Victoria Between 1862 and 1878,* 1:85.

330 **were both "much moved":** QVJ, September 8, 1862.

330 **what she lacked was peers:** Lady Lyttelton said, a few days after Albert

had died, that Victoria "has *no* friend to turn to." Wyndham, *Correspondence of Sarah Spencer,* 422.

330   **"terrible height":** QVJ, August 7, 1883.

331   **Victoria wanted to sob:** "It breaks my heart to think of the poor Children without a Father, whom they so badly need,—the difficulties of their education & position, & I so utterly helpless." QVJ, May 11, 1862.

331   **"what I suffered in the Chapel":** QVJ, March 10, 1863.

332   **taboo subject at family dinners:** Ridley, *Bertie,* 95–97.

332   **"hardly possible to live without it":** To Lady Mallet, December 30, 1861, Rappaport, *Magnificent Obsession,* 120; S. Jackman and H. Haasse, *A Stranger in the Hague,* 227.

332   **"*without* her *previous sanction* being obtained":** To Viscount Palmerston, August 11, 1863, Buckle, *The Letters of Queen Victoria Between 1862 and 1878,* 1:102.

332   **"my duty shall be done fearlessly":** Fulford, *Dearest Mama,* 205–6.

333   **undermined their authority and influence:** Hansard, House of Lords Debates, May 26, 1864, vol. 175, ccc 616–17. He described it as a "difficulty of the greatest magnitude which has materially affected the influence of this country with Foreign Powers."

333   **"it is too dreadful":** QVJ, May 27, 1864.

333   **"many a false step":** QVJ, March 6, 1864; QVJ, June 1, 1864.

333   **ceded to Prussia and Austria:** Victoria wrote to the King of Prussia on May 28, 1864, urging him to moderate his demands and agree to concessions Denmark would favor. Buckle, *The Letters of Queen Victoria Between 1862 and 1878,* 1:203.

333   **appeared again just a few days later:** This is reported in *Trewman's Exeter Flying Post or Plymouth and Cornish Advertiser,* March 30, 1864. Some believe this story to be apocryphal, but if so, it remains, as Tisdall suggests, a sign of "how the wind was blowing in London." Tisdall, *Queen Victoria's John Brown,* 87.

334   **"I thought you were all *killed*!":** QVJ, October 7, 1863.

334   **thumb that would remain crooked:** QVJ, November 6, 1864.

334   **subliminal will to live:** QVJ, October 10, 1863.

334   **long hours of prayer:** See her letter to King Leopold, February 25, 1864, Buckle, *The Letters of Queen Victoria Between 1862 and 1878,* 168.

334   **Victoria grew calmer:** On October 23, 1863, for example, she wrote in her journal, "The beauty of the day & scenery were indescribable, & though I can no longer find any *real* joy in anything, such splendid works of God's own hand, such peace & stillness, do me good."

334   **"so hard for me at first":** QVJ, December 14, 1864.

Chapter Twenty-Two: Resuscitating the
Widow of Windsor

336 **"suits best *our sad sisterhood*"**: Queen Victoria to Lady Waterpark, September 21, 1864, British Library Manuscripts, Add. 60750, Extract 60750, Lady Waterpark, vol. 1.

336 **"An English lady in mourning"**: Shaw, *Collected Letters, 1898–1910,* 817.

336 **fallen into the single shaft:** Shortly after this disaster, Parliament passed a law to ensure no mine could again have just a single shaft; there would need to be two ways in and two ways out.

336 **"her heart bled for them":** January 23, 1862, Lady Cavendish's Diary, ladylucycavendish.blogspot.com/2006/11/23jan1862-200-hartley-colliers-found.html.

336 **lost their husbands in the Hartley disaster:** QVJ, December 18, 1862.

337 **idea of being united with him someday:** Walter Walsh, *The Religious Life of Queen Victoria,* 116.

337 **"any other in high position":** e.g., QVJ, April 29, 1865.

337 **"except in the sense of duty":** This was done after first checking that her health was good, she was able to walk and ride, and that she was prepared to represent the queen at social functions. Queen Victoria to Fanny Howard, September 14, 1863, British Library Manuscripts, Add. 60750, Extract 60750, Lady Waterpark, vol. 1.

337 **"inexpressibly sad and dreadful":** Rappaport, *Magnificent Obsession,* 151.

337 **"utterly broken-hearted" queen:** Queen Victoria to Mrs. Lincoln, April 29, 1865, Buckle, *The Letters of Queen Victoria Between 1862 and 1878,* 1:266.

337 **but only one in seven men:** Jalland, *Death in the Victorian Family,* 230. According to one estimate, about 19 percent of marriages in the 1860s would have ended by one spouse's death, and about 47 percent within twenty-five years.

337 **"a form of social exile":** Ibid., 231.

338 **"whether she likes it or not":** Quoted in Houston, *Royalties,* 148. Also Jay, "Mrs. Brown," 194.

339 **three doctors:** Sir James Clark, Dr. Jenner, and Dr. Watson.

339 **"becomes weaker and weaker":** Queen Victoria to Earl Russell, December 8, 1864, Buckle, *The Letters of Queen Victoria Between 1862 and 1878,* 1:244–45. She confided to Leopold that her nerves were getting worse in August 1865, and only complete quiet made her better. (Queen Victoria to King Leopold, August 31, 1865, ibid., 1:274.) Some said the queen showed signs of anxiety *before* Albert died. Lady Lucy Cavendish wrote on February 5, 1864: "One can't blame the Queen for shrinking from

doing it this one year more: even with the Prince by her side, her nervousness used to be nearly overpowering." ladylucycavendish .blogspot.com/2009/01/05feb1864-parliament-opens-without.html.

339 **"some complete breakdown":** Queen Victoria to Earl Russell, May 25, 1866, Buckle, *The Letters of Queen Victoria Between 1862 and 1878,* 1:329.

339 **likely to die soon:** Letter to King Leopold, June 16, 1863, ibid., 91.

339 **severe form of agitation:** Even at smaller occasions, like the christening of Alix and Bertie's first baby, Albert Victor, Victoria wrote: "Feeling every eye fixed on me was dreadful." QVJ, March 10, 1864.

340 **"in whom I have confidence":** QVJ, October 26, 1864.

340 **"so cheerful and attentive":** Letter to King Leopold, February 24, 1865, Buckle, *The Letters of Queen Victoria Between 1862 and 1878,* 1:255.

340 **a "very severe trial" for her:** Sir Charles Phipps to Earl Russell, Osborne, December 20, 1865, ibid., 1:289. Victoria needed to go in part to secure financial support for her children—Helena was marrying a poor prince, Christian of Schleswig-Holstein, and Alfred was almost eighteen.

340 **"violent nervous shock" of the effort:** Queen Victoria to Earl Russell, February 7, 1866, ibid., 1:299.

340 **it was "not usual" practice:** QVJ, March 11, 1866.

341 **Second Reform Bill:** The 1867 Reform Act added 938,000 voters to an electorate of 1,057,000 in England and Wales. Woodward, *The Age of Reform,* 187.

341 **"for those beneath them":** QVJ, July 24, 1867.

341 **just as Palmerston had been:** Queen Victoria to Lord Stanley, December 11, 1867, Buckle, *The Letters of Queen Victoria Between 1862 and 1878,* 1:472. See also letter dated December 16, 1867, ibid., 1:476.

341 **asked the British government to pay if she did:** For example, in 1869, when asked to host the Viceroy of Egypt, Victoria argued she had too much work, no husband, was ill, and could not be expected to entertain as often as she had done previously. Letter to Gladstone, May 31, 1869, ibid., 1:601.

341 **"The word *distasteful* is hardly applicable":** Queen Victoria to the Earl of Derby, July 4, 1867, ibid., 1:443.

342 **"He can only offer devotion":** Disraeli to Queen Victoria, February 26, 1868, ibid., 1:505.

342 **"top of the greasy pole":** Monypenny and Buckle, *Life of Benjamin Disraeli,* 4:600.

343 **"a very radiant face":** Bradford, *Disraeli,* 278.

343 **she had never had such letters before:** Maxwell, *Life and Letters of Clarendon,* 2:346.

343   **lasted only ten months:** In these months, he passed important anti-corruption laws and outlawed public executions.

343   **he could not understand how:** Mrs. Gladstone told her husband in 1867: "Do pet the Queen, and for once believe you can, you dear old thing." Magnus, *Gladstone: A Biography,* 160.

344   **"I might even say tenderness towards her":** Longford, *Victoria R.I.,* 362.

344   **"to pacify Ireland":** Morley, *The Life of Gladstone,* 2:252.

344   **"emphatic verdict of the nation":** Buckle, *The Letters of Queen Victoria Between 1862 and 1878,* 1:572.

344   **"dangerous if not disastrous":** Ibid., 1:603.

345   **Bertie's "immoral example":** Williams, *The Contentious Crown,* 39.

345   **"Prince of Wales is not respected":** Shannon, *Gladstone: Heroic Minister,* 92.

345   **Victoria felt trapped:** QVJ, December 20, 1867.

345   **he could not breathe:** QVJ, June 26, 1868.

346   **"affecting all classes of the people":** *The Sydney Morning Herald,* March 13, 1868, 5. (Victoria did not find out until April 25.)

346   **"The great questions of the time":** Steinberg, *Bismarck: A Life,* 181

346   **became known as the Seven Weeks' War:** This was also known as Italy's Third Independence War. Victoria unsuccessfully pleaded with the king of Prussia to avoid it.

346   **unified in a North German Confederation:** Bismarck didn't want France or Russia to intervene, so pushed King Wilhelm I of Prussia to make peace with Austria quickly. The Peace of Prague on August 23, 1866, led to the North German Confederation.

346   **"a most useful ally to England":** Queen Victoria to Lord Stanley, August 7, 1866, Buckle, *The Letters of Queen Victoria Between 1862 and 1878,* 1:364.

346   **thought his aggressive conduct "monstrous":** QVJ, April 4, 1866.

347   **rumors endure about Lorne's sexuality:** Sandwell, "Dreaming of the Princess," 47.

347   **quietly sent out for adoption:** Hawksley, *The Mystery of Princess Louise.*

347   **"chief object in life":** QVJ, February 4, 1868.

347   **kissed him good night religiously:** QVJ, February 10, 1868.

347   **"in constant anxiety about him":** QVJ, June 7, 1860.

348   **the loss of her surrogate father:** QVJ, December 10, 1865.

348   **it is only in recent years (since the mid-1980s):** Maercker and Lalor, "Diagnostic and Clinical Considerations."

349   **deep, consuming mourning:** Consider the criteria for PCBD: persistent yearning, intense sorrow and emotional pain, and preoccupation with the

deceased and circumstances of the death. These further symptoms must be experienced for more than a year: disbelief or emotional numbness over the loss, difficulty with positive reminiscing about the deceased, bitterness, anger, maladaptive appraisals about oneself in relation to the deceased or the death (e.g., self-blame), and excessive avoidance of reminders of the loss. Other symptoms include a desire to die in order to be with the deceased, difficulty trusting other individuals since the death, feeling alone or detached from other individuals since the death, feeling that life is meaningless or empty without the deceased, the belief that one cannot function without the deceased, confusion about one's role in life, a diminished sense of one's identity (e.g., feeling that a part of oneself died with the deceased), and a difficulty or reluctance in pursuing interests since the loss or in planning for the future. Physical complaints include pain and fatigue. *Diagnostic and Statistical Manual of Mental Disorders,* 5th ed., Appendix, Conditions for Further Study, Persistent Complex Bereavement Disorder, 7–8.

349 **death was sudden and unexpected:** Jalland, *Death in the Victorian Family,* 321.

349 **Victoria was ripe to grieve:** Shear et al., "Complicated Grief," 105. See also Prigerson et al., "Prolonged Grief Disorder," e1000121.

349 **what people thought appropriate:** As Patricia Jalland found, "Chronic and obsessive grief was very rare amongst these nineteenth-century families, probably more so than today. . . . The image of Queen Victoria as the eternal widow of Windsor has been so pervasive that she has sometimes been seen as representative, rather than the reverse." Jalland, *Death in the Victorian Family,* 318.

349 **she would be happy again:** Almost two years after Albert had died, Victoria told Major Elphinstone she was soothed by sympathy and found it in "some" of her children: "Major Elphinstone hopes for less depression of spirits but she feels this can never never be; on the contrary as time goes on and others feel less, her deep settled melancholy—her ever increasing helplessness and loneliness are more keenly and acutely felt. The struggle gets daily worse, the want hourly more felt, her shaken health and shattered nerves less able to bear the trials and work and sorrow and above all the desolation." McClintock, *The Queen Thanks Sir Howard,* 51.

349 **"That is what I call twaddle":** Bell, *Randall Davidson,* 1:83.

349 **wanted to live for her family and friends:** Queen Victoria to Lady Waterpark, Osborne, February 10, 1867, British Library Manuscripts, Add. 60750, Extract 60750, Lady Waterpark, 1:271.

Chapter Twenty-Three: The Queen's Stallion

351   **"though coarsely made"**: Wilfrid Scawen Blunt's diary, quoted in Lambert, *Unquiet Souls,* 41.

351   **"God knows, how much I want to be taken care of"**: Queen Victoria to Vicky, April 5, 1865, Fulford, *Your Dear Letter,* 21.

351   **tracks too rocky, roads too wet:** "My dear pony went beautifully, like a cat & the way Brown carried me over & along the stones admirable." (QVJ, August 24, 1860.) She described him as "so thoughtful & full of initiative, making an admirable guide & servant." (QVJ, August 28, 1860.) Then, "Brown with his strong, powerful arm, helped me along wonderfully." (QVJ, September 20, 1859.) The next day, on a trip to Craig Gewish, on the ascent, "One had heather up to one's knees, holes, slippery ground & stones 2 or 3 ft. high to get over. I tried my best, but could never have got on, without Brown's help. . . . The going down was a wonderful but very amusing affair, for the Children did nothing but slip & roll, laughing at every step. It is quite a perpendicular descent & so slippery, that Brown, in trying to keep me up, came down his whole length." Then: "The descent was far easier, but the path was very rough in parts & I had recourse to Brown's strong arm to steady me." (QVJ, October 28, 1874.)

352   **"so very good humored & willing"**: QVJ, October 3, 1850.

352   **who sang duets for her:** QVJ, June 24, 1871.

352   **her old loyal governess, Lehzen:** QVJ, September 12, 1870.

352   **loss of her sister Feodora was "irreparable"**: QVJ, September 23, 1872. See also QVJ, December 31, 1872.

353   **queenly duty up in Scotland:** Kuhn, *Henry and Mary Ponsonby,* 97.

353   **or manage a ministerial crisis:** In 1866, when Lord Russell was due to resign, Victoria was in Scotland. Lady Frederick Cavendish wrote in her diaries that "the Queen is seriously to blame for staying at Balmoral," as nothing could be settled without her being there. (June 22, 1866, Cavendish, *The Diary of Lady Frederick Cavendish,* 10.) Three days later she said Victoria's "poor terrible fault" in staying in Scotland had "given rise to universal complaint, and much foul-mouthed gossip." (June 25, 1866, ibid.)

353   **"The Queen will talk as if she were Mrs. Jones"**: Arthur Ponsonby, *Henry Ponsonby,* 71.

353   **"so roughly as he does to the Queen"**: Ibid., 126.

353   **"canna ye hold yer head still!"**: Cullen, *The Empress Brown,* 10. He cites as a reference Tisdall, *Queen Victoria's John Brown.* This was printed in the United States as *Queen Victoria's Mr. Brown* in 1938. Note that Victo-

ria wrote to Leopold in 1861 that Brown "takes the most wonderful care of me, combining the offices of groom, footman, page, and maid, I might almost say, as he is so handy about cloaks and shawls." Cullen, *The Empress Brown,* 49.

353 **Brown treated Victoria "like a small child":** Cullen, *The Empress Brown,* 12.

353 **"was the plainspoken reply":** Queen Victoria to Vicky, September 26, 1859, Fulford, *Dearest Child,* 211.

354 **"poor man":** Cullen, *The Empress Brown,* 170, citing Bolitho, *The Reign of Queen Victoria.*

354 **"The Queen says sartenly not":** Arthur Ponsonby, *Henry Ponsonby,* 126. "In conveying messages he never had recourse to any softening civilities. When the Mayor of Portsmouth came to ask the Queen to go to a Volunteer review, the Private Secretary sent in the request to her and hoped to get the reply privately that he might convey it civilly to the Mayor. As they both sat in the Equerry's room waiting, Brown put his head in and only said, 'The Queen says sartenly not.' So there was an end of the matter and the Mayor went away much crestfallen."

355 **particularly grew to loathe Brown:** On one instance, Brown hit and yelled at Leopold and punished him cruelly, isolating him and removing his dog. Ridley, *Bertie,* 135; Downer, *Queen's Knight,* 178–84.

355 **"following me about everywhere":** Cullen, *The Empress Brown,* 123.

355 **"a sort of strange presentiment":** Queen Victoria to Vicky, November 13, 1861, Fulford, *Dearest Child,* 365–66.

355 **"Rasputin in a kilt":** Cullen, *Empress Brown,* 12, 26.

355 **visited her grandmother Victoria with her mother, Alice:** Ibid., 12.

356 **"how great an imprudence has been committed":** Ibid., 91.

356 **"and John Brown was her medium":** Williams, *The Contentious Crown,* 34.

356 **"the effect on her mind might be dangerous":** July 6, 1867, Vincent, *Disraeli, Derby and the Conservative Party,* 313.

357 **consider this comfort a gift from God:** Longford, *Victoria R.I.,* 326.

357 **ever given or witnessed birth:** The first suggestions of a marriage and possible son were in the *Lausanne Gazette* in 1866, and in *Tinsley's Magazine* and *The Tomahawk* in 1867.

358 **"'every conjugal privilege'":** Lambert, *Unquiet Souls,* 41. Lambert also mentions on p. 42 that Blunt also wrote about a Lord Rowton, who, as Montagu Corry, had for many years been Disraeli's private secretary and a frequent visitor to royal establishments: "Of the Queen he has talked much and I was surprised to find him attaching a sexual import to her

affection for John Brown. He mentioned in that connection the statue she had had made of Brown by Boehm, which is precisely what XX [Blunt's usual code for Catherine Walters] told me as having been related to her by Boehm himself. So I fancy it must be true." (Wilfrid Scawen Blunt diaries, January 28, 1902, cited in ibid., 42.) Lambert adds a footnote: "It is in the nature of these speculations that evidence is very hard to obtain. The only other independent corroboration I have been able to acquire is from a university professor who, working in the Windsor Castle archives, was by error brought a pile of letters between Queen Victoria and her ghillie. From them he deduced that the affair was far from platonic."

358   **diaries of the prominent and powerful:** Lewis Harcourt wrote: "Lady Ponsonby told the H. S. [Home Secretary] a few days ago that Miss Macleod declares that her brother Norman Macleod confessed to her on his deathbed that he had married the Queen to John Brown and added that he had always bitterly repented it. Miss Macleod would have had no object in *inventing* such a story so that one is almost inclined to believe it, improbable and disgraceful as it sounds." Lord Harcourt diaries, February 17, 1885, Bodleian Special Collections, MS Harcourt dep. 365.

359   **"No, it is here":** Sir James Reid's personal diary, Reid Family Archives, Lanton Tower, Lanton.

359   **exactly what "it" might be:** Lady Reid believes "it" was the bruise Victoria acquired during her fall. Correspondence with Michaela Reid, April 3, 2016.

359   **"accidentally seen something":** Longford, *Queen Victoria,* 62.

360   **"very compromising":** Sir James Reid, notebooks, vol. 25 (1904–5), Reid Family Archives, Lanton Tower, Lanton. A letter written by Lord Knolly to Sir James, on May 9, 1905, plain white paper with a red Buckingham Palace embossed up the top, was pasted in a scrapbook. It read:

> My dear Reid.
>   I have submitted your letter of yesterday to the King.
>   He appreciates very much the tact, judgment and diplomatic skill which you have shown in regard to the recovery of the letters, & he would be glad to see you with them at 6:30 on Thursday next.

Sir James made a note in blue ink, pasted in alongside this:

> May 11th—at 6:30 went to Buckingham Palace & had an audience of the King's & delivered over to him the tin box with over 300 let-

ters of the late Queen to Dr Profeit (about J.B.) which, after six months negotiations, I had got from George Profeit—many of them most compromising—Thanked by the King—Saw also Lord Knolly.

360   **less defiant if they were full-blown lovers:** Note that Henry Ponsonby did not believe that Brown was anything more than a servant.

361   **rubies as well as diamonds:** Cullen, *The Empress Brown,* 123.

362   **convinced France to attack:** Europe had rumbled with France's dissatisfaction after the settling of spoils following the 1866 war with Prussia.

362   **"absolute necessity":** July 16, 1870, Buckle, *The Letters of Queen Victoria,* 1:37.

362   **"preaching neutrality and prudence would be useless":** Fulford, *Your Dear Letter,* 322.

362   **Her heart, though, was with Germany:** Victoria agreed with Vicky that the Germans were superior not just physically, but "morally" too. QVJ, February 16, 1871.

362   **captured along with 104,000 of his men:** Howard, *The Franco-Prussian War,* 223.

363   **staged a coup on September 4, 1870:** Victoria protested that the French were "ungrateful" to not have even once raised their voice in favor of the "unfortunate Emperor." QVJ, September 5, 1870.

363   **"À la guillotine!":** QVJ, September 23, 1870.

363   **"apparent want of sympathy with the landlords.":** Buckle, *The Letters of Queen Victoria Between 1862 and 1878,* 2:7.

363   **"I pray earnestly it may":** QVJ, June 11, 1870.

364   **"so innocently in a Scottish retreat":** Arthur Ponsonby, *Henry Ponsonby,* 124.

364   **was the subject of much chatter:** Vincent, *Disraeli, Derby and the Conservative Party,* 198.

365   **"next at Lord Penzance's Court":** Ridley, *Bertie,* 129.

365   **"touchy, vague and willful":** Hibbert, *Queen Victoria in Her Letters and Journals,* 210.

365   **"excessively plain":** Letter to Vicki, December 1, 1872, Fulford, *Darling Child,* 70.

365   **for looking older than her twenty-four years:** Fulford, *Darling Child,* 44.

365   **foolish to not take her advice, she thought:** She told Vicky "gratitude to parents, respect for age and authority are not what they should be in these days!" Ibid., 47.

365   **parted his hair down the middle:** Ibid., 25.

366   **"and I could not live without her":** April 16, 1873, ibid., 86.

366   **"anxiety for my own children and of no great interest":** May 8, 1872, ibid., 40.

366   **most attuned to her needs . . . were praised:** See ibid., 39.

366   **thought of losing another daughter:** QVJ, October 16, 1870.

366   **"especially a daughter's marriage":** September 14, 1873, Fulford, *Darling Child,* 108. When Louise became engaged, Victoria was also occupied with the thought of some purity of blood in the family, writing: "When the Royal family is so large, and our children have (alas!) such swarms of children, to connect some few of them with the great families of the land—is an immense strength to the Monarchy and a great link between the Royal Family and the country. . . . Besides which, a new infusion of blood is an absolute necessity—as the race will else degenerate bodily and physically." Fulford, *Your Dear Letter,* 306.

366   **"I am very tired":** July 3, 1873, Fulford, *Darling Child,* 99.

366   **"utter degeneration of everything":** QVJ, March 4, 1869.

366   **"to imagine a politer little woman":** Fawcett, *Life of Queen Victoria,* 225.

367   **her seclusion was damaging the monarchy:** Arthur Ponsonby, *Henry Ponsonby,* 71.

367   **"sink to nothing at all":** Ibid., 21.

367   **they could do very well without her:** March 15, 1869, Vincent, *Disraeli, Derby and the Conservative Party,* 340.

367   **the public grief was extraordinary:** Even when he was thought to be dying, *Reynolds Newspaper* prematurely published an obituary that slammed Bertie's life as "an incessant round of frivolous amusement." *Reynolds Newspaper,* December 10, 1871, 4–5. Cited in Williams, *The Contentious Crown,* 74.

367   **waiting for bulletins:** *The Times,* December 9, 1871, 9.

367   **"a foundation stone laid or a bazaar opened":** *Graphic,* December 9, 1871.

368   **"enable him to lead a new life":** Queen Victoria to Vicky, December 20, 1871, Fulford, *Darling Child,* 20.

368   **"cold, dreary and dingy":** QVJ, February 27, 1872.

368   **"*The Times* declared gravely":** *The Times,* February 28, 1872, 5.

368   **"They want the gilding for their money":** Arthur Ponsonby, *Henry Ponsonby,* 72.

368   **"saw him spring round and suspected him":** Queen Victoria to Vicky, March 4, 1872, Fulford, *Darling Child,* 33.

368   **the sole recipient of this medal:** Cullen, *The Empress Brown,* 158.

368   **his broad chest with satisfaction:** Queen Victoria to Vicky, March 13, 1872, Fulford, *Darling Child,* 34.

368   **rode for miles over the Highlands:** "Hearing the Queen was going out and seeing John Brown with a basket, one of the Maids of Honour asked if it was tea he was taking out. 'Well no,' he replied, 'she don't much like tea. We tak oot biscuits and sperruts.'" Arthur Ponsonby, *Henry Ponsonby,* 126.

369   **convinced that her nerves ... would never recover:** Queen Victoria to Vicky, November 3, 1874, Fulford, *Darling Child,* 160.

369   **"require too much is quite fearful":** Ibid., 209.

369   **Loch Muick in the Highlands:** She hid away in the Glassalt Shiel, Loch Muick, e.g., November 21, 1877: "The absence of all interruptions makes it the only place in the world where I can have complete rest." Ibid., 269.

369   **"a strange & marvellous manner":** QVJ, December 19, 1876.

369   **"as though I were again living with her":** September 3, 1873, Fulford, *Darling Child,* 106–7.

369   **"Alone, alone, as it will ever be":** QVJ, May 24, 1871.

370   **"No one loves you more":** Cullen, *The Empress Brown,* 216. After Brown's death, Victoria copied out an extract from a diary or journal entry from 1866, and this was found among Hugh Brown's things when he died. "Often my beloved John would say: 'You haven't a more devoted servant than Brown'—and oh! *How* I felt that! Often & often I told him no one loved him more than I did or had a better friend than me: & he answered 'Nor you—than me. No one loves you more.'"

370   **"fight and make the Queen do what she did not wish":** Arthur Ponsonby, *Henry Ponsonby,* 128.

370   **"that would have killed her at once":** Cullen, *The Empress Brown,* 131.

370   **"(especially in the Higher Classes)":** Longford, *Victoria R.I.,* 354.

370   **"From his best friend V.R.I.":** Cited in ibid., 456.

Chapter Twenty-Four: The Faery Queen Awakes

371   **"'I don't know what you mean by your way'":** Carroll, *Through the Looking-Glass,* 16.

371   **"What nerve! What muscle! What energy!":** Monypenny and Buckle, *Life of Benjamin Disraeli,* 6:503.

371   **an "immense number of little frogs":** QVJ, June 28, 1875.

372   **found the sight of the frogs "quite dreadful":** QVJ, June 28, 1875, then July 2, 1875.

372   **rolling around the feet of Turkish militia:** Brown, "Henry James and Ivan Turgenev," 112.

372   **handwritten copies were passed around instead:** Whitehead, "The Bulgarian Horrors," 232. See also Tedford, "The Attitudes of Henry James

and Ivan Turgenev." Note that novelist Henry James translated it from a French version for *The Nation* in October 1876, even though he did not "share the Russian eagerness for war." Goldsworthy, *Inventing Ruritaniu,* 29.

372   **locked inside churches and burned alive:** See, for example, *Daily News,* July 13, 1876.

372   **"like balls from one Turk to another":** Ibid., July 1, 1876.

372   **"coffee house babble":** Hansard, House of Commons, August 11, 1876, vol. 2341, col. 203.

373   **press the politicians to properly investigate:** *Daily News,* June 23, 1876.

373   **fate of Christian subjects in Turkish lands:** Matthew, *Gladstone: 1809–1898,* 266.

373   **Gladstone ... was enraged:** QVJ, March 13, 1873.

374   **"fuel to the flame":** QVJ, September 8, 1876.

374   **"two old bagpipes":** Matthew, *Gladstone: 1809–1898,* 325.

374   **Charles Darwin contributed fifty pounds to a relief fund:** Patton, *Science, Politics and Business,* 127.

374   **"only pierced with a bayonet":** *Spectator,* July 23, 1876, 10.

374   **"Sonnet on the Massacre of the Christians in Bulgaria":** Varty, *Collected Poems of Oscar Wilde,* xvii.

374   **"mischief maker and firebrand":** September 26, 1876, Leonard, *The Great Rivalry,* 169.

375   **"an affront to British prestige":** Taylor, *The Struggle for Mastery,* 234.

376   **"lead a Conservative party to victory":** Monypenny and Buckle, *Life of Benjamin Disraeli,* 5:169–70, 172.

376   **"how unpopular he is!":** February 14, 1874, Fulford, *Darling Child,* 129.

376   **"and so wonderfully unsympathetic":** February 17, 1872, Fulford, *Dearest Child,* 29.

376   **juicy tidbits of gossip:** Mary Ponsonby liked Gladstone's politics but preferred Disraeli's company.

376   **"I treat her like a woman":** Longford, *Victoria R.I.,* 402.

376   **"he will never understand a man, still less a woman":** Rhodes James, *Rosebery,* 112.

377   **"I thought I was the cleverest woman":** Quoted in Leonard, *The Great Rivalry,* 203. See also Cornwallis-West, *Lady Randolph Churchill,* 97.

377   **"and putting his head on one side":** Rhodes James, *Rosebery,* 64.

377   **"glided about the room like a bird":** Longford, *Victoria R.I.,* 400.

377   **a genuine, deep affection for Victoria:** QVJ, March 13, 1873.

377   **"the only person in this world left to me that I do love":** St. Aubyn, *Queen Victoria,* 427.

377 **"fond of backstairs intrigue":** Blake, *Disraeli,* 50.

377 **intellectual equals, unlike Albert:** Disraeli told Matthew Arnold, "Everyone likes flattery, and when it comes to royalty you should lay it on with a trowel." St. Aubyn, *Queen Victoria,* 427.

377 **"male society is not much to my taste":** October 1874 to Lady Bradford, Buckle, *The Life of Benjamin Disraeli,* 5:348.

378 **punishable by death as recently as 1861:** Kuhn, "Sexual Ambiguity," 16.

378 **Disraeli might have been "what today we might call gay":** Kuhn, *The Politics of Pleasure,* 11.

378 **"I rejoice . . . at every Russian defeat":** Fulford, *Darling Child,* 253.

378 **prodding his Cabinet with the queen's staunchness:** Longford, *Victoria R.I.,* 411.

378 **he will "bite, now that he is roused":** February 20, 1878, Fulford, *Darling Child,* 283.

378 **whip the Russians herself:** In the middle of the melee was a new member of the royal family, Marie, who was, awkwardly, a Russian. The daughter of the Russian czar had married the raffish Affie on January 23, 1874. Victoria quickly grew very fond of Marie, praising her even temper and good humor, even though she was puzzled that anyone could genuinely love her reserved, sometimes rude son. Victoria loved people who made her laugh. She was sympathetic toward her daughter-in-law in those years, who was caught in Britain while the queen and prime minister railed against her country. But Marie was resilient and impressive, and her origins were ignored.

379 **"kiss the feet of the great barbarians":** Chapter 8 of Strachey, *Queen Victoria.*

379 **"I would gladly throw all up and retire into quiet":** February 15, 1878, Fulford, *Darling Child,* 282.

379 **"the Faery writes every day and telegraphs every hour":** Disraeli appears to have started using the term "Faery" after he became prime minister for the first time. Monypenny and Buckle, *Life of Benjamin Disraeli,* 6:150.

380 ***"Der alte Jude, das ist der Mann":*** Ibid., 6:311.

380 **"I can never forget it":** Longford, *Victoria R.I.,* 415.

380 **She opened Parliament three times while Disraeli was PM:** St. Aubyn, *Queen Victoria,* 430. The years were 1876, 1877, and 1880.

380 **shaped Tory rhetoric for a century to come:** See Matthew, *Gladstone: 1809–1898,* 267.

380 **"so much quicker than that of Mr. Gladstone":** November 26, 1875, Buckle, *The Letters of Queen Victoria Between 1862 and 1878,* 2:428.

381 **"the angels in the marble":** Leonard, *The Great Rivalry,* 151.

381   **protected from newly enfranchised working-class voters:** Ibid.

381   **labor rights, arguing they were as important as property rights:** Hibbert, *Disraeli,* 296.

382   **new laws . . . for the creation of working-class housing:** Much of this progressive legislation was promoted and inspired by Richard Cross, who was the reforming home secretary in the government from 1874 to 1880. Disraeli was perfectly happy to take credit for these reforms.

382   **"an absolute falsehood":** QVJ, April 2, 1876.

384   **"almost incredible, & most mysterious!":** QVJ, December 14, 1878.

384   **"The good are always taken, the bad remain":** QVJ, December 14, 1878.

384   **"if going through life as smoothly as possible really constitutes happiness":** January 3, 1877, Fulford, *Darling Child,* 236.

384   **whose wasted arm had troubled her so much:** Ibid., 26.

384   **"shaken the elasticity out" of her:** QVJ, May 24, 1879.

384   **she seemed to have shrunk in height:** Gladstone told his wife Victoria weighed eleven stone eight ounces, "which was rather much for her height." St. Aubyn, *Queen Victoria,* 335. See also Bassett, *Gladstone to His Wife.*

384   **the queen at a wedding:** Arthur, whom Vicky described as "universally respected and liked" and a "model Prince" like his father, got engaged in 1878 to a Prussian princess, Louise, the youngest daughter of Fritz Carl. Victoria was grumpy when she heard of the engagement—it had happened more quickly than she had wanted, she did not like the Prussian royal family, and she wished Louise were prettier: her nose and mouth were reportedly ugly and her teeth were bad. March 12, 1878, Fulford, *Darling Child,* 284. (It is striking, looking back at the discussion of potential candidates for matrimony between Victoria and Vicky, how the women were discussed in blunt, almost commercial terms—as though their gums were being inspected like Thoroughbreds'; their physical characteristics were dissected in great detail.) But for the wedding, Victoria wore a long white veil and the Koh-i-Noor diamond, as well as a court train for the first time since Albert died.

385   **privately dismissing her "ugly old face":** August 4, 1875, Fulford, *Darling Child,* 187.

385   **"My dear Grandmama is very tiny":** Ibid., 144.

Chapter Twenty-Five: Enough to Kill Any Man

389   **"The Queen alone is enough to kill any man":** Hardie, *Political Influence,* 73.

389   **Ponsonby ... was shocked by the language she used:** Aronson, *Victoria and Disraeli,* 183.

390   **"I cd not trust him or give him my confidence":** Memorandum by Queen Victoria, April 18, 1880, RA, VIC/MAIN/C/34/65.

390   ***"may submit* to his democratic rule but *not the Queen":* Arthur Ponsonby, *Henry Ponsonby,* 184.

390   **a man who had been the enemy of her government:** Aldous, *The Lion and the Unicorn,* 307.

391   **Victoria grumpily summoned Gladstone to Windsor:** Once the Queen commissioned Gladstone and he kissed her hand, he was formally acknowledged as parliamentary leader of the Liberal Party as well as prime minister.

391   **"perfect courtesy from which she never deviates":** Jenkins, *Gladstone,* 438.

391   **"very strong language":** QVJ, April 23, 1880.

391   **consent to their being made ministers:** QVJ, April 27, 1880.

391   **bring in "democratic leaning":** Letter to Henry Ponsonby, April 8, 1880, quoted in St. Aubyn, *Queen Victoria,* 445.

391   **"All things considered, I was much pleased":** Aldous, *The Lion and the Unicorn,* 310.

392   **he would not be in office long:** Monypenny and Buckle, *Life of Benjamin Disraeli,* 539.

392   **risen to 11.4 percent:** These are trade union statistics, cited in Blake, *Disraeli,* 697.

392   **"the fall of the government over wh. I presided":** Quoted in ibid., 721.

392   **"their wives and families":** Aldous, *The Lion and the Unicorn,* 296.

392   **the mood of fatigue among the electorate:** See Taylor, *The Struggle for Mastery,* 268.

393   **which had been annexed by Britain in 1877:** This was particularly difficult for Victoria to stomach, as in 1881 Transvaal Boers had wiped out a British force at the battle of Majuba Hill. (Longford, *Victoria R.I.,* 440.) She had not wanted to see African natives under the control of Boers—"a most merciless and cruel neighbour, and in fact oppressor, just like the southern slave-owners in *Uncle Tom's Cabin.*" (QVJ, July 30, 1881.)

393   **necessary means of protecting her empire:** She wrote to Disraeli in 1879: "If *we are* to maintain our position as a *first-rate* Power, we must, with our Indian Empire and large Colonies, be *Prepared for attacks* and *wars, somewhere* or *other,* CONTINUALLY." July 28, 1879, Queen Victoria to Lord Beaconsfield, Buckle, *The Letters of Queen Victoria Between 1879 and 1885,* 3:37–38.

393   **"an American stumping orator":** QVJ, December 2, 1879.

393   "a little *personally* elated": Aldous, *The Lion and the Unicorn,* 299.

393   "some magnificent castle in an Italian romance": Aronson, *Victoria and Disraeli,* 184.

393   "She would only ask me to take a message to Albert": Blake, *Disraeli,* 474.

393   "truest kindest friend's" final moments: Disraeli had refused Victoria's offer of a baronetcy a year earlier, but had managed to procure one for Corry, who had become like a son to him, instead. Gladstone compared it to Caligula making his horse a consul. Some have since suggested Corry was Disraeli's lover, and like a wife to him. Kuhn, "Sexual Ambiguity," 16.

393   the most "extraordinary man" . . . had passed: Aldous, *The Lion and the Unicorn,* 319.

394   "All display without reality or genuineness": Shannon, *Gladstone: Heroic Minister,* 275.

394   "his favorite flowers from Osborne": Blake, *Disraeli,* 752.

395   "such want of respect" . . . they "nearly tumbled over one another": QVJ, January 5, 1881.

395   "only a piece of Parliamentary gossip": Hardie writes that this was "an extraordinary lapse" on Disraeli's part: "As early as the reign of Queen Anne, Swift had observed that it was well known 'that Speeches on these occasions are ever digested by the advice of those who are in the chief confidence, and, consequently, that they are the sentiments of Her Majesty's Ministers, as well as his own.'" Hardie, *Political Influence,* 76–77.

395   it was obviously the sovereign's speech: Ibid., 76, 192–93.

395   "things are allowed to go on as they have done of late years": Queen Victoria to Lord Granville, June 5, 1880, Buckle, *The Letters of Queen Victoria Between 1879 and 1885,* 3:108.

396   Her own private struggles: In 1879, Vicky's son Waldemar died of diphtheria. He was only eleven. Vicky was further wounded when Bismarck thoughtlessly gave a soiree on the night of the funeral. Victoria wrote sadly to her daughter: "My heart bleeds and aches for you." "My wonder is," she wrote, "how one lives at all through such terrible trials and shocks as that one and that life is not stopped at once."

397   "with totally different duties and vocations": Rappaport, *Queen Victoria,* 428.

397   not their entering the serious professions or voting: Queen Victoria to Vicky, June 26, 1872, Fulford, *Dearest Child,* 51. She told Vicky women should be "sensibly educated"—and "employed whenever they can be usefully" but not "unsexed and made doctors (except in one branch), lawyers, voters etc. Do that, and you take at once away all their claim to

protection on the part of the male sex."

397 **Victoria described herself, conveniently, as "anomalous":** Ibid., 67.

397 **"men were seldom fit for the work":** Longford, *Victoria R.I.,* 395.

398 **the idea of training women as doctors was "repulsive":** When she found out that her daughter Louise had arranged a secret meeting with the doctor Elizabeth Garrett—the first woman to qualify as a doctor in Britain— just to discuss her studies, Victoria was enraged. Louise, however, said, "It was a great pleasure to find her so enthusiastic in her work. . . . She is one of those who can prove how much women can learn, if they put their whole heart, and soul in what they are about." Hawksley, *The Mystery of Princess Louise,* 114.

398 **"while her husband was walking about in London":** Queen Victoria to Vicky, February 24, 1872, Fulford, *Dearest Child,* 30.

398 **crippled the British defense forces in the Crimea, in India, and in England:** Levine, "Venereal Disease." After witnessing its ravages in the Crimea, in 1862 Florence Nightingale organized a sanitary commission on venereal disease.

398 **admitted to the hospital for syphilis or gonorrhea:** Walkowitz, *City of Dreadful Delight,* 49.

399 **blasted from pulpits and Parliament alike:** Pearsall, *The Worm in the Bud,* 278.

399 **escaped scrutiny and condemnation:** The double standard was glaringly obvious to women like Josephine Butler, one of the greatest social reformers of the Victorian age, who realized, "A moral sin in a woman was spoken of as immensely worse than in a man." (As J. Miller argued in 1859, "A woman falls but once, and society turns upon her as soon as the offence is known. A man falls many times, habitually, confessed by; yet society changes her countenance on him but little, if at all." *Prostitution Considered,* 26.) Butler trekked across England and Europe inspecting brothels, advocating change, and befriending sex workers, often taking them into her home and nursing them.

399 **"under the present complex forms of life":** Wilson, *Eminent Victorians,* 108.

399 **total population of 2.3 million men and women:** Pearsall, *The Worm in the Bud,* 250. "Dr. Acton, one of the less unreliable of the early Victoria specialists, stated that one in thirteen or fourteen of unmarried women of full age was immoral, but this statement contradicts other data." Ibid., 276. Police reports were much lower.

399 **most commonly syphilis:** According to Judith Walkowitz, syphilis was "endemic" during the Victorian era, as well as the Edwardian, and was "most prevalent among men of the upper and middle ranks and among

the casual laboring poor." Walkowitz, *Prostitution and Victorian Society,*
50. Mary Carpenter provides an estimate of circa 10 percent of the population. *Health, Medicine, and Society,* 72.

399 **ravagcd childrcn born to thcm:** In thc first half of 1846, there were fifty
six deaths due to syphilis in London. Thirty were babies under one.
Walkowitz, *Prostitution and Victorian Society,* 49.

399 **kidney failure, poisoning, and mouth sores:** Frith, "Syphilis—Its Early
History."

400 **"irregular indulgence of a natural impulse":** Davidson and Hall, *Sex, Sin
and Suffering,* 121.

400 **"paid me several shillings . . . to go with him":** Wilson, *Eminent Victorians,* 188.

400 **"poisoning the blood of the nation":** Though many of them ended up
leading respectable lives, a woman who made a living from selling her
body, he said, was "nothing better than a paid murderess, committing
crime with impunity." Hemyng wrote that sex workers were "poisoning
the blood of the nation." "The woman was nothing better than a paid
murderess, committing crime with impunity." Bracebridge Hemyng,
"Prostitution in London," in Mayhew, *London Labour,* 4:235.

400 **he was convinced that this was why the queen hated him:** Magnus, in
Gladstone: A Biography, 425–26, writes that Gladstone told his sons in
1897 that if the queen really thought the stories about his relationships
with sex workers were true, then she had been remarkably kind, but continued: "I do not speak lightly, when I state my conviction that the circumstances of my farewell, which I think were altogether without
parallel, had serious causes, beyond the operation of mere political disagreements, which no doubt went for something, but which were insuf-
ficient to explain them. Statements, whether true or false, must have been
carried to her ears, which in her view required (and not merely allowed)
the mode of proceeding which was actually adopted." Magnus argues
that while the queen would have heard some of the "foul stories," "few
responsible persons, even among Gladstone's bitterest enemies, gave
them credence." When Lord Stanmore told Gladstone that the queen
might have been suspicious of his intentions, he answered, "If the Queen
thinks that of me, she is quite right to treat me as she does." St. Aubyn,
Queen Victoria, 446.

400 **Gladstone could listen to a sermon without "rising to reply":** April 19,
1875, Longford, *Victoria R.I.,* 528.

401 **"half a most lovely statue, beautiful beyond measure":** Marlow, *The Oak
and the Ivy,* 68.

401 "a keen appreciation of a pretty face": Isba, *Gladstone and Women,* 115.

401 "There is but one of whom I know": Ibid., 119.

402 his "religio-sexual emotional crises": Jenkins, *Gladstone,* 100.

402 "strange, questionable, or more": Ibid.

402 "required to be limited and purged": Ibid.

402 made their way to Victoria, causing her coldness: Matthew, *Gladstone: 1809–1898,* 425–26.

402 "to pursue and possess every sort of women": Matthew, *Gladstone: 1809–1898,* 630.

403 "underpaying, undervaluing and overworking" of women: Shaw, *Mrs. Warren's Profession,* 181.

403 "to see how much one is loved": Letter of March 6, 1882, Longford, *Victoria R.I.,* 446.

403 key role in establishing women's soccer in Britain: One of her older brothers, the ninth Marquess of Queensberry, called Oscar Wilde a "somdomite" (famously, he couldn't spell the word "sodomite") when he had a relationship with his son Lord Alfred Douglas. Wilde sued for libel, and the resulting court case—where truth was a defense—led to his bankruptcy and ruination. He was convicted of "gross indecency" for relationships with men. After he left jail, Wilde went to France, where he died in Paris, at the Hotel d'Alsace.

404 and that marriages should be equal: Dixie, *Gloriana,* 129–30.

404 doubt was cast on the veracity of her claims: *Pall Mall Gazette,* March 19, 1883. See also *Aberdeen Weekly Journal,* March 19, 1883.

404 "I know not how to bear it, or how to believe it possible": Cullen, *The Empress Brown,* 201.

405 "Fancy the Queen on a tricycle": Ibid., 204.

405 "depriving of all she so needs": Queen Victoria to Viscount (later Earl of) Cranbrook, Windsor, March 30, 1883. Grosvenor, "Dear John." Victoria wrote on this at length: "Perhaps never in history was there so strong and true an attachment, so warm and loving a friendship between the sovereign and servant [the phrase "between the sovereign and servant," added above the text, is believed to have been included later] as existed between her and dear faithful Brown. Strength of character, as well as power of frame—the most fearless uprightness, kindness, sense of justice, honesty, independence and unselfishness, combined with a warm tender heart, retaining the homely simplicity of his early life, made him one of the most remarkable men who could be known—and the Queen feels that life for the second time is become most trying and sad to bear depriving of all she so needs."

405   **with the little time he had left to live:** QVJ, August 7, 1883.

405   **"so womanly, and so lonely":** Lord Hallam Tennyson to Victoria, Isle of Wight, October 22, 1892, RA, VIC/MAIN/R/44/ 14. Lord Tennyson's son wrote to Victoria in response to a letter the queen had sent him about his father's death. He told Victoria, "May I venture to add that at the end of the interview he said to me 'I had tears in my eyes when I parted with the Queen, for she is so womanly, and so lonely.'" (This could also be "lovely"; the word is hard to read, but the "n" is very close to the other "n"s in Lord Tennyson's writing.)

406   **it had only five for Disraeli:** Cullen, *The Empress Brown,* 204.

406   **"painful for the Queen":** Henry Ponsonby to Queen Victoria, February 28, 1884, RA, VIC/ADDA12/902.

406   **That is what she wanted the world to understand:** Queen Victoria to Henry Ponsonby, February 23, 1884, RA, Add. A/12/899. See also Kuhn, *Henry and Mary Ponsonby,* 220–21.

407   **a tame life in the wild Highlands:** These books also had a political purpose too, effectively silencing those who accused her of being too interfering and biased politically: why, she was just a royal dame wandering through the hills of Scotland.

407   **"It was very exhilarating":** "Kenward Philip," *John Brown's Legs or Leaves from a Journal in the Lowlands,* dedicated to "the Memory of those extraordinary Legs, poor bruised and scratched darlings." From Longford, *Victoria R.I.,* 460.

407   **not be "worthy of such confidences":** Bell, *Randall Davidson,* 94.

408   **"'No one loves you more'":** Cullen, *The Empress Brown,* 216.

408   **"does become sadder and sadder and harder":** Queen Victoria to Vicky, January 2, 1884, Fulford, *Beloved Mama,* 155.

408   **"succession of trials and sufferings":** Queen Victoria to Vicky, March 26, 1884, ibid., 162.

408   **Childhood games could be fatal:** Kerr, "The Fortunes of Haemophiliacs," 359–60.

409   **who ensured she was always near her son:** Bennett, *Queen Victoria's Children,* 124.

409   **Leopold should not engage in strenuous exertion:** Footnote 66 in Kerr, "The Fortunes of Haemophiliacs," cites "Editorial: Prince Leopold," *British Medical Journal* 1 (1868): 148.

409   **the blood of hemophiliacs took longer to clot:** Potts and Potts, *Queen Victoria's Gene,* 51.

409   **avoidance of violent boyhood games, and rest:** Walker, "On Haemo-

philia," 605–7.

409 **he wanted to either "live or die hard":** Rushton, "Leopold: The 'Bleeder Prince,'" 487.

409 **longevity and the ability to earn an income:** Kerr, "The Fortunes of Haemophiliacs," 367.

409 **"so dreadful an entail of disease":** Legg, *A Treatise on Haemophilia.*

409 **Victoria knew ... but she allowed it:** Rushton, "Leopold: The 'Bleeder Prince,'" 486.

410 **"on the most important day of his life":** Potts and Potts, *Queen Victoria's Gene,* 48.

Chapter Twenty-Six: "Two Ironclads Colliding": The Queen and Mr. Gladstone

411 **"One could do business with her!":** Vovk, *Imperial Requiem,* 61.

413 **without executing it himself:** Jenkins, *Gladstone,* 511.

413 **"We are pianos":** Longford, *Victoria R.I.,* 467.

413 **"Tell the inhabitants":** Zetland, *Lord Cromer,* 110.

413 **"but it is my nature, and I cannot help it":** Gordon, *The Journals,* 59.

413 **"acts even upon the sanest men like strong drink":** By September he was calling him "quite mad." Jenkins, *Gladstone,* 212.

414 **"most extraordinary man":** Queen Victoria to Vicky, Windsor Castle, February 20, 1884, Fulford, *Beloved Mama,* 159.

414 **to ensure that the soldiers stayed in the Sudan:** She also instructed him to burn her "so very confidential" letter. She placed similar demands on his wife, Lady Wolseley. "THREATEN to resign if he does *not* receive strong support. *It must never appear* or Lord Wolseley *ever let out* the hint I give *you*. But I really think they *must be frightened*." May 28, 1885, Buckle, *The Letters of Queen Victoria Between 1879 and 1885,* 3:619.

414 **"till the pistol is pointed at their breast":** Queen Victoria to Vicky, February 27, 1884, Fulford, *Beloved Mama,* 160.

414 **"If anything befalls him the result will be awful":** Cited in Hibbert, *Queen Victoria: A Personal History,* 371.

414 **This was to her a deeply personal humiliation:** Victoria wrote to Vicky on February 7, 1885, upon hearing Gordon had been captured, calling Gladstone an "old sinner" and crying: "We are just too late as we always are and it is I, who have, as the head of the nation, to bear the humiliation." Fulford, *Beloved Mama,* 182.

414 **"will be forever branded with the blood of Gordon that heroic man":**

Queen Victoria to Vicky, Osborne, February 11, 1885, ibid., 182.

415   **"upon the express application of General Gordon":** Jenkins, *Gladstone,* 514.

415   his hands mottled with a rash: Matthew, *Gladstone: 1809–1898,* 400.

416   **"And now, gentlemen, to business":** Seaman, *Victorian England,* 447.

416   **he called Victoria's views "quite worthless":** Jenkins, *Gladstone,* 501.

416   **"insisting on their meeting":** Kuhn, *Henry and Mary Ponsonby,* 205.

416   **"all I care to live for now":** Longford, *Victoria R.I.,* 372.

416   **"squelching in too many imperial quagmires":** In South and North Africa and in Central Asia. Jenkins, *Gladstone,* 501.

417   **"Pleasure has for ever died out of my life":** June 20, 1884, Fulford, *Beloved Mama,* 168.

418   **"it is greatly valued but how rarely it lasts":** Queen Victoria to Vicky, January 15, 1879, Fulford, *Beloved Mama,* 34.

418   **it is remarkable that the biddable Beatrice did not:** Dyhouse, *Feminism and the Family,* 27.

418   **"very sweet, pure & calm":** QVJ, July 23, 1885. She was more moved than she had been at any of the other eight of her children's weddings, she said, "but full of confidence."

418   **hugged her hard, crying:** Ibid.

419   **"like a schoolgirl set free from school":** Lady Geraldine Somerset, quoted in Hibbert, *Queen Victoria: A Personal History,* 373.

420   **"not excepting Disraeli":** Roberts, *Salisbury,* 795.

420   **"their polished manners and deference":** Ibid., 793.

420   **"especially the middle class of her subjects":** Longford, *Victoria R.I.,* 567.

420   **in a report called** *The Bitter Cry of Outcast London:* Ibid., 461.

421   **if an inquiry would be conducted into it:** October 30, 1883, Buckle, *The Letters of Queen Victoria Between 1879 and 1885,* 3:451–52.

421   **"I am terrified for the country":** Queen Victoria to Mr. Goschen, January 27, 1886, RA, VIC/MAIN/C/37/158.

421   **"Lord Salisbury for the Country—the World—and** *me!***":** Memorandum by Queen Victoria, January 28, 1886, RA, VIC/MAIN/C/37/163.

422   **discourage Gladstone from standing in the upcoming election:** Queen Victoria to Lord Tennyson, Osborne, July 12, 1885, Dyson and Tennyson, *Dear and Honoured Lady,* 120.

422   **Tennyson protested he had little influence over him:** Lord Tennyson to Queen Victoria, Freshwater, Isle of Wight, July 20, 1885, ibid., 121.

422   **a view for which she chastised him:** Queen Victoria to Mr. Goschen, Osborne, January 31, 1886, RA, VIC/MAIN/C/37/204.

422 **"put an end to the nervous excitement"**: Memorandum by General Sir Henry Ponsonby to Queen Victoria, Osborne, January 29, 1886, RA, VIC/MAIN/C/37/176.

422 **"she left him free to accept or not"**: Memorandum by Henry Ponsonby, St. James Palace, London, January 30, 1886, RA, VIC/MAIN/C/37/199.

422 **which he considered a "great sacrifice"**: Sir Henry Ponsonby to Queen Victoria, St. James, February 3, 1886, RA, VIC/MAIN/C/37/228.

423 **not for her own sake, but "for the country's"**: Telegram from Queen Victoria to Henry Ponsonby, March 2, 1886, RA, VIC/MAIN/C/37/239b.

423 **Or was this just a diplomatic paving of the way toward implementation**: Memorandum from Lord Goschen to Queen Victoria, January 29, 1886, RA, VIC/MAIN/C/37/192.

423 **his greatest, most farsighted, and yet most self-destructive quest**: As early as 1845, he wrote to his wife: "Ireland, Ireland! that cloud in the west, that coming storm." Jenkins, *Gladstone,* 276.

423 **when he disestablished the Church of Ireland in 1869**: He had also, crucially, introduced secret voting in Ireland.

423 **The bulk of Irish farmers**: Samuel Clark, *Social Origins of the Irish Land War* (Princeton, N.J.: Princeton University Press, 1979), 120.

424 **Gladstone was "always excusing the Irish"**: Longford, *Victoria R.I.,* 446.

424 **the opposition to his "dreadful" bill**: QVJ, July 9, 1880.

424 **The queen advocated martial law**: The violence was so bad, especially against landlords, that it might even, she wrote, "become necessary to propose martial law." (QVJ, December 11, 1880.) She also encouraged the Chief Secretary to Ireland, Forster, to threaten to resign if he was not given enough resources to stomp out the "lawlessness and terrorism." (QVJ, December 16, 1880.) Four months later, Gladstone introduced a Coercion Act that temporarily suspended habeas corpus, so those suspected of criminal activity could be arrested without trial. While expanding police powers, Gladstone also introduced laws to clear poor farmers of rent arrears.

424 **protect the empire and defeat the Home Rule bill**: Kuhn, *Henry and Mary Ponsonby,* 208–9.

424 **write a memorandum on his precise intentions**: Queen Victoria to William Gladstone, Osborne, February 4, 1886, RA, VIC/MAIN/C/37/240.

424 **Gladstone's letter . . . did not placate her**: QVJ, February 3, 1886.

424 **"the Empire is in danger of disintegration and serious disturbance"**: QVJ, May 6, 1886.

424 **"those who may have the honor to be Your Majesty's advisers"**: Letter

from Gladstone, May 8, 1886, excerpted in QVJ, May 8, 1886.

425   **"This, if I understand it":** Matthew, *Gladstone: 1809–1898,* 508.

425   **"I cannot help feeling very thankful":** QVJ, July 20, 1886.

425   **"sacrificing himself for Ireland":** QVJ, February 1, 1886.

425   **"One prayer absorbs all others":** Matthew, *Gladstone: 1809–1898,* 558.

426   **"who was in some things an excellent woman of business":** Arthur Ponsonby, *Henry Ponsonby,* 80–81.

426   **it was just surprising to see it done at all:** Samuel Johnson, who, when a friend told him he had heard a woman preach at a Quakers' meeting, said, "Sir, a woman's preaching is like a dog's walking on his hinder legs. It is not done well; but you are surprised to find it done at all." July 31, 1768, Boswell, *The Life of Samuel Johnson,* 405.

427   **wrote Sir Edmund Gosse in 1901:** Gosse, "The Character of Queen Victoria," 333. He continued: "She regarded herself, professionally, as the pivot round which the whole machine of state revolves. This sense, this perhaps even chimerical conviction of her own indispensability, greatly helped to keep her on her lofty plane of daily, untiring duty. And gradually she hypnotized the public imagination." Ibid., 337.

427   **"She knows what she is talking about":** Creston, *The Youthful Queen Victoria,* 5.

427   **"not always yield at once to the opinion of a single Minister":** Brett, *Journals and Letters,* 1:74: "The Queen has several times this session remonstrated with her Ministers, and I must confess that on every occasion I think her interference has been justified. She always gives way before the authority of the cabinet but she will not always yield at once to the opinion of a single Minister. Mr. Gladstone is indignant with her and asserts that he would never be surprised to see her turn the Government out after the manner of her uncles."

427   **"she will become one combatant among many":** Bagehot, *The English Constitution,* 48.

427   **"the right to encourage; and the right to warn":** Ibid., 60.

427   **But it was not until after Bertie ascended the throne:** It could also be argued that Bagehot's formulation took hold during the reign of King George V. See Heffer, *Power and Place,* 463.

428   **"the seasonable addition of nice and pretty events":** Bagehot, *The English Constitution,* 37.

428   **"those still so imperfectly educated as to need a symbol":** Ibid., 41.

428   **provided the monarch was unprejudiced:** Ibid., 54.

428   **But who would be the judge of the monarch's discernment?:** Ibid., 65.

428   "show itself in *well-considered inaction*": Ibid., 57.

428   to form a separate group of Liberal Unionists: Hardie, *Political Influence*, 91–92.

429   "but whether it is wise ... must depend on circumstances": Longford, *Victoria R.I.*, 516.

429   "permanent Premier": Martin, *The Prince Consort*, 2:445.

429   Henry Ponsonby tacked in the other direction: Aronson, *Victoria and Disraeli*, 192.

430   view his queen as "somewhat unmannerly": Ibid., 565.

430   "had I the power, to break through": Jenkins, *Gladstone*, 468–69.

430   "I am convinced, from a hundred tokens": Jenkins, *Dilke: A Victorian Tragedy*.

431   she told him to be "very cautious," in 1883: Buckle, *The Letters of Queen Victoria Between the Years 1879 and 1885*, 3:241.

431   to be "very guarded in his language": Ibid., 395.

431   "She feels, as he [Gladstone] puts it, aggrieved": Bahlmann, *The Diary of Hamilton*, 486–87.

432   "finger in between two ironclads colliding": Kuhn, *Henry and Mary Ponsonby*, 202.

432   "the elevation of her own nature": Gladstone to Samuel Smith, April 11, 1892, quoted in Bell and Offen, *Women, the Family, and Freedom*, 2:224.

Chapter Twenty-Seven: The Monarch in a Bonnet

433   The symbol that unites this vast Empire: Arthur Ponsonby, *Henry Ponsonby*, 79.

434   she was the Queen who wore a bonnet, not a crown: Ibid.

434   "masses and millions of people": Williams, *Becoming Queen*, 343.

434   "You done it well! You done it well!": Housman, *The Unexpected Years*, 220.

434   "in no way wore them around her person": *Illustrated London News*, June 25, 1887.

435   "to make bejeweled bonnets their wear at garden-parties": Ibid., July 9, 1887, 38.

435   ten thousand little balloons, and forty-two thousand other toys: Pearce et al., "Queen Victoria's Golden Jubilee," 597.

435   "bonfires were lighted and kept blazing until daybreak": Rusk, *Reign of Queen Victoria*, 304.

435   the skies were still light with the midnight summer sun: *Illustrated Lon-*

don News, July 2, 1887.

436 "have been appreciated by my people": Ibid.

436 gave the bulk of the money to establish the Queen's Jubilee Nursing Institute: See qni.org.uk/about_qni/our_history.

436 "risk of admitting American women of light character": December 11, 1887, quoted in Longford, *Victoria R.I.,* 497.

437 "Will the Prince of Wales . . . ever reign over us?": Quoted in Ridley, *Bertie,* 248.

439 he would never forgive her: John Röhl, emeritus history professor at the University of Sussex, also believes Wilhelm had an erotic obsession with his mother when he was a boy, expressed in sexual dreams that made him hate her when she failed to respond to his longing, or inappropriate comments. See independent.co.uk/news/uk/home-news/kaiser-wilhelm-iis -unnatural-love-for-his-mother-led-to-a-hatred-of-britain-8943556.html.

439 "plunge Germany into war without foreseeing or wishing it": Corti, *The English Empress,* 259.

439 switched to support their brother: Pakula, *An Uncommon Woman,* 471.

440 "It does seem an impossible dream": Ramm, *Beloved and Darling Child,* 64.

440 that might mean a disastrous foreign policy: Corti, *The English Empress,* 266.

440 "must not allow themselves to be led by a woman": Pakula, *An Uncommon Woman,* 470.

441 "One could do business with her!": Vovk, *Imperial Requiem,* 61.

441 "Grandmama behaved quite sensibly at Charlottenburg": Victoria wrote in her diary on April 25, 1888: "I appealed to Pce Bismarck to stand by poor Vicky, & he assured me he would, that hers was a hard fate."

441 "high time the old lady died": Pakula, *An Uncommon Woman,* 483.

441 He was, by then, a "perfect skeleton": Corti, *The English Empress,* 280.

441 "What is happening to me?": Ibid., 301.

442 and the unification of his homeland: Pakula, *An Uncommon Woman,* 439.

442 "How am I to bear it? You did, and I will do": Hibbert, *Queen Victoria: A Personal History,* 388.

442 "after which they may be cast aside": Pakula, *An Uncommon Woman,* 441.

443 "it is enough to make one quite giddy": Emperor William II to Sir Edward Malet, June 14, 1889, Buckle, *The Letters of Queen Victoria Between 1879 and 1885,* 3:504.

443 he tried to counter it where he could: Statement of the Empress Frederick, 1888, in Corti, *The English Empress,* 293.

443 The father would certainly have fought what the son fostered: Pakula,

An Uncommon Woman, 457.

443 **"on account of the number of votes":** Kronberg Letters, July 6, 1892, cited in Longford, *Victoria R.I.,* 518.

444 **"an old, wild incomprehensible man of eighty-two and a half":** Jackson, *Harcourt and Son,* 213

444 **"a feeble expression about the mouth, & the voice altered":** QVJ, August 15, 1892.

445 **"but she knows he would not accept it":** Windsor Castle, March 3, 1894, Buckle, *The Letters of Queen Victoria Between 1886 and 1901,* 2:372–73.

445 **"I could neither love nor like it":** Magnus, *Gladstone: A Biography,* 425–26.

445 **"I kissed her when she left":** QVJ, March 3, 1894.

445 **"settling a tradesman's bill":** March 10, 1894, Matthew, *Gladstone: 1809– 1898,* 610.

446 **"I have not been able to fathom, and probably never shall":** Ibid.

446 **her descendants thronged the courts of the Continent:** When the Duke and Duchess of York had a baby, who would become Edward VIII (and then Duke of Windsor), there were, for the first time, Victoria thought, "three direct heirs as well as the Sovereign alive." Other European matches included those of Princess Sophie of Prussia (daughter of Vicky), who married King Constantine I of Greece; Princess Maud (daughter of Bertie), who married Prince Carl of Denmark; Princess Marie (daughter of Alfred), who married Ferdinand of Romania; Princess Margaret of Connaught (daughter of Arthur), who married Prince Gustaf Adolf of Sweden; and Princess Victoria Eugenie (daughter of Beatrice), who married King Alfonso XIII of Spain.

447 **would later die in the Russian Revolution:** In 1917, she and her husband— Nicholas II—were imprisoned, then executed in the basement of their prison. Alix, who had stirred the anger of the starving peasants with her curious attachment to Rasputin, the hermit who cared for her hemophiliac son, was making the sign of the cross as she turned from the gunfire. In 2000, the Greek Orthodox Church canonized her.

448 **"native doctor at Agra":** QVJ, June 23, 1887.

448 **"Indians always wait now, & do so, so well & quietly":** QVJ, June 28, 1887.

448 **"and being of rather a different class to the others":** QVJ, August 11, 1888.

448 **"interests & amuses me very much":** QVJ, August 30, 1887.

448 **"very handy and useful in many ways":** QVJ, November 2, 1888.

449 **Karim made increasingly outrageous requests:** When Victoria instituted the Most Exalted Star of India and the Most Eminent Order of the British Empire she insisted that they carry no Christian symbols so that they

would be acceptable to her Hindu and Muslim subjects.

449 **estimated to be sufficient to kill fifteen thousand men:** Reid, *Ask Sir James*, 137.

449 **"examining his neck, smoothing his pillows, etc":** Ibid., 133.

Chapter Twenty-Eight: The "Poor Munshi"

451 **"The Queen seems off her head":** Reid, *Ask Sir James*, 132.

451 **"we are all jealous of the poor Munshi":** Fritz Ponsonby—Henry's son, and now a junior equerry in the household—about Karim Abdul, April 27, 1897, Longford, 539.

452 **the Munshi was bringing on:** Reid, *Ask Sir James*, 143.

452 **craving for some kind of excitement:** Ibid., 154.

453 **so they might report on him more:** Ibid., 139.

453 **"everyone avoided him":** Ibid., 140.

453 **"interspersed with still perfectly green trees":** QVJ, October 23, 1891.

454 **Queen of Sheba,** *Carmen,* **and** *The Winter's Tale:* January 6, 1888, Balliol College, Marie Mallet Archives, Lady in Waiting, Mallet V 1-11, Envelope marked "Mallet V i. First Waiting as Maid of Honor, 1887, Letters to her Mother."

454 **"who were sons respectively of a Butcher & a Grocer":** Arthur Ponsonby, *Henry Ponsonby,* 131.

454 **"Performing functions in sitting rooms, etc.":** Reid, *Ask Sir James,* 139.

455 **could contain the spirit of Christ:** Longford, *Victoria R.I.,* 509.

455 **"to allow other Indians in any part of the same railway carriage as himself":** Reid, *Ask Sir James,* 139.

455 **"Progression by antagonism":** Ibid., 138.

455 **"about whom the Queen seems off her head":** Ibid., 132.

456 **she thought required only a polite refusal:** Longford, *Victoria R.I.,* 508.

456 **"any letters of importance that come from India":** Letter from Fritz Ponsonby about Karim Abdul, April 27, 1897.

457 **"been questioned as to her sanity":** Reid, *Ask Sir James,* 144.

457 **should not be required of him in Britain:** Ibid., 146.

457 **"about this painful subject":** Ibid.

458 **"they never pinch me":** King, *Twilight of Splendor,* 201.

458 **"the likelihood of Liko ... was very high":** Hawksley, *The Mystery of Princess Louise,* 269.

459 **"greatly taken aback":** Reid, *Ask Sir James,* 153.

460 **"beg you to burn it as well as my letter this morning":** Ibid., 152.

460 **"the how and where of access"**: Matthew (*Gladstone: 1809–1898,* 610) argues that this dream, in 1896, "may have had a sexual dimension, for he
records having a 'small perturbation as to the how and where of access.'
'Reserved for acccess' was the phrase he had used in 1839 to describe his
virginity on marriage (see 14 June 39)." (At the end of that year, 1896, he
also made a private statement—called the *Declaration*—addressing "ru-
mours which I believe were at one time afloat" for a time when he would
not be present to defend himself. He declared before the sight and judgment seat of God "that at no period of my life have I been guilty of the act
which is known as that of infidelity to the marriage bed." The full declaration, dated December 7, 1896, read:

> With reference to rumours which I believe were at one time afloat,
> although I know not with what degree of currency: and also with
> reference to the times when I shall not be here to answer for myself;
> I desire to record my solemn declaration and assurance, as in the
> sight of God and before His judgment seat, that at no period in my
> life have I been guilty of the act which is known as that of infidelity
> to the marriage bed. I limit myself to this negation, and I share it
> with my dear Son Stephen, both as the eldest surviving of our sons,
> and as my pastor. It will be for him to retain or use it, confidentially
> unless necessity should require more, which is unlikely: and in any
> case making it known to his brothers.

Chapter Twenty-Nine: The Diamond Empire

462 **"they do not exist"**: Cecil, *Life of Robert, Marquis of Salisbury,* 3:191.
462 **should be celebrated with aplomb**: On November 23, 1896, Victoria
wrote in her journal: "Today is the day on which I have reigned longer,
by a day, than any English sovereign."
463 **Wilde conducted as horns blasted and accordions swung**: Moyle, *Constance,* 302.
463 **any year before in British history**: Morris, *Heaven's Command,* 534.
463 **"in the person of Queen Victoria"**: Homans and Munich, *Remaking
Queen Victoria,* 49.
463 **"Go it, old girl!"**: Longford, *Victoria R.I.,* 548.
464 **"Look! There's Queen Victoria going to Heaven!"**: Arnstein, "Queen
Victoria's Diamond Jubilee," 594.
464 **"as if her very presence hypnotized them"**: Gosse, "The Character of

Queen Victoria," 310. Note not all were hypnotized. Thomas Hardy escaped to Switzerland to avoid the crowds. (Tomalin, *Thomas Hardy,* 269.) There were even reports of a scandalous ribaldry. In Camden, a wag suggested at a parish meeting that as "Her Gracious Majesty has been very useful to this country for many years, so what we should want to be putting up to her memory is something that will go on being useful to us here. Now what we in Camden most wants, say, is a public urinal." Shouts of laughter erupted until the rector asked for the next suggestion. (Housman, *The Unexpected Years,* 219.)

464   **a VR in lights, with red calico:** McDonald, *Nightingale on Society and Politics,* 5:427.

465   **"a very young tranquil woman":** This is from an unpublished diary entry for May 24, 1899, quoted in Arnstein, "Queen Victoria's Diamond Jubilee," 20. He credits this citation to Yvonne M. Ward of La Trobe University. Most, Arnstein thinks, detected no trace of a German accent—others differ.

465   **"My own dear Mama's face has a charm":** Fulford, *Your Dear Letter,* 315

465   **appropriate for the queen to smile so broadly:** Ward, "Editing Queen Victoria," 266–7. Sir Edmund Gosse wrote of Queen Victoria in 1901: "Of her personal attributes, her smile was perhaps the most notable. It played a very large part in the economy of her power, and something of the skill of her dramatic instinct passed into its exercise. No smile was the least like it, and no shadow of it is preserved for posterity in any one of her published likenesses. In particular, under the evil spell of the photographic camera it disappeared altogether, and those who never saw it can have little idea of the marvelous way in which it brightened and exhilarated the lines of the Queen's features in advancing years." Gosse, "The Character of Queen Victoria," 315.

466   **crimes previously subject to capital punishment were removed from the statute books:** Arnstein, "Queen Victoria's Diamond Jubilee," 199.

467   **while addressing the House of Commons:** *Illustrated London News,* June 21, 1897.

468   **hitting his only friend repeatedly over the head with a brick:** Neville, *Mussolini,* 19.

470   **blamed Gladstone for carelessly losing this lucrative land:** Lee, *Queen Victoria,* 523. Victoria also met with the diamond magnate Cecil Rhodes without any apparent understanding of what his trade entailed. She listened, rapt, as he described the mines and the preparation of the stones, while he in turn was reportedly taken aback that she knew so much about

South Africa.

471 **though she does not say what about:** QVJ, March 18, 1891.

472 **a friend had cheated at cards:** When Bertie was playing baccarat with friends at a country house in 1891, one of the group, Sir William Cumming, was found cheating. Bertie was called as a witness in the resulting trial. For the Prince of Wales to have been involved in such a dishonorable event was considered disgraceful, but Victoria remained loyal.

473 **"Nothing but sadness & horrors":** QVJ, July 31, 1900.

473 **"not let anyone but ourselves have anything":** March 27, 1898, Buckle, *The Letters of Queen Victoria Between 1886 and 1901,* 3:238–39.

474 **"responsible for the murder of one British subject":** Sir Arthur Bigge to Queen Victoria, Buckle, *The Letters of Queen Victoria Between 1886 and 1901,* 3:362.

474 **"it is certain that nothing will be done":** Balfour was running the Foreign Office during Lord Salisbury's illness. His official title was First Lord of the Treasury.

475 **she had not been told and her advice not sought:** Pakenham, *The Boer War,* 245.

475 **her "dear brave soldiers":** Jerrold, *The Widowhood of Queen Victoria,* 439.

475 **"they do not exist":** Cecil, *Life of Robert, Marquis of Salisbury,* 3:191.

476 **"and that cannot be just now":** Queen Victoria to Mr. Balfour, February 4, 1900; Parkhouse, *Memorializing the Anglo-Boer War,* 555.

476 **"Surely this justifies our using Indians":** Queen Victoria to the Marquess of Salisbury, February 11, 1900, Buckle, *The Letters of Queen Victoria Between 1886 and 1901,* 3:485.

477 **"expose themselves more than is absolutely necessary":** Queen Victoria to the Marquess of Lansdowne, January 30, 1900; Parkhouse, *Memorializing the Anglo-Boer War,* 555.

477 **"We have, however, reoccupied the post":** QVJ, December 31, 1900.

477 **she cried almost constantly and was "most depressed":** Reid, *Ask Sir James,* 197.

478 **"The Queen has much extraordinary vitality and pluck":** Ibid., 198.

478 **"a living grave":** Jenny de Reuck, "Social Suffering and the Politics of Pain: Observations on the Concentration Camps in the Anglo-Boer War 1899–1902," in Sue Kossew and Dianne Schwerdt, editors, *Re-Imagining Africa: New Critical Perspectives* (Huntington, N.Y.: Nova Science Publishers, 2001), 87.

478 **She would have been mortified:** Victoria had taken pride in the decent

way the British treated their captives. Yet when she heard hundreds of prisoners were being maltreated, she wrote: "Treatment of prisoners disgraceful and inhuman." She instructed Lord Lansdowne on June 13, 1900, to complain to Lord Roberts and point out how well the British treated their prisoners. Buckle, *The Letters of Queen Victoria Between 1886 and 1901,* 3:562.

478 **"hysterical . . . imperative reasons":** Mr. Chamberlain to Sir Alfred Milner, April 3, 1900, ibid., 3:520.

478 **unless they had a wounded son or husband, to please the queen:** Lord Roberts to Queen Victoria, April 15, 1900, ibid., 3:528.

478 **"arguably laid down a template":** de Reuck, "Social Suffering and the Politics of Pain," 86.

479 **"the blood brotherhood of the Empire was sealed":** Doyle, *The Great Boer War,* 259–60. See gutenberg.org/files/3069/3069-h/3069-h.htm.

480 **"so much self-searching, such self doubt, as now":** Van Wyk Smith, "The Boers and the Anglo-Boer War," 429–46.

480 **"full of morbid ideas":** Sir James Reid, December 2, 1900, Reid Family Archives, Lanton Tower, London.

480 **"nervous, complaining, and childish":** Ibid., December 7, 1900.

480 **"cerebral degeneration":** Sir James Reid, "Pencil notes of what occurred during the last days of Queen Victoria's life and at her death," January 15, 1901, Reid Family Archives, Lanton Tower, London.

480 **"The loss to me":** St. Aubyn, *Queen Victoria,* 592.

480 **"was struck by how small":** Reid, "Pencil notes of what occurred."

481 **she had told Reid she did not wish to see him:** Reid, *Ask Sir James,* 203. Dr. Reid was so worried about it that at one point in Victoria's final illness, he had decided not to tell her that Bertie was there. In another set of directions that Victoria gave to Reid, she instructed that she wanted only Reid—and other doctors she named, as well as Beatrice, or another one of her younger daughters, or Arthur—to attend her. She explicitly ordered that neither Bertie nor any of her ministers be allowed to override any of her instructions. Sir James Reid, notebooks, vol. 20 (1897–98), Reid Family Archives, Lanton Tower, Lanton.

481 **asking her eldest son to "kiss her face":** Sir James Reid: "Pencil notes of what occurred during the last days of Queen Victoria's life and at her death." January 21, 1901, Reid Family Archives, Lanton Tower, Lanton.

481 **She struggled to walk unsupported from 1883:** Weintraub, *Victoria,* 632.

481 **it must only be Dr. Reid and female attendants:** She wrote in instructions to Bertie and Beatrice about her funeral that she wished

I with my Remains to be touched by no one but my own personal female attendants & *no one* but them—assisted by such persons (or personal attendants) as have been in *constant* & *close personal* attendance on me during my life since.

I desire that my remains should be *watched* over, by those my faithful attendants, & that they *only* should assist in placing me in my Coffin. I desire in having my Personal attendants to include in these my Indian Attendants so far as they are not precluded by their Religion from assisting in those last duties.—Their gentleness & care of me are beyond all praise now that I am so lame & require so much help.

October 25, 1897. RA, VIC/MAIN/F/23/1-9a.

481   **"This is private. Reid":** Reid, *Ask Sir James,* 203.
481   **The princesses—especially Helena:** Ibid., 204.
482   **loving her more than he did his own mother:** Ibid., 196.
482   **"as if she thought I could make her live":** Ibid., 206.
482   **"ever so many razors driven into my back":** Packard, *Victoria's Daughters,* 309.
483   **"not to give up the struggle while she can":** Reid, *Ask Sir James,* 211.
483   **"The Queen is slowly sinking":** January 22, 1901, 4 P.M. Signed by James Reid, MD, Douglas Powell, MD, Norman Barlow, MD. RA VIC/MAIN/F/23/25.
483   **closed his mother's eyes, sealing the light out:** Reid, who was clearly in charge, is the one who told Bertie to do this. By his account, all the family shook his hands by the bedside, and afterward Bertie thanked him for all he had done for the queen. Reid, *Ask Sir James,* 212.

Chapter Thirty: The End of the Victorian Age: "The Streets Were Indeed a Strange Sight"

484   **"'The sun is no longer in the sky!'":** Corelli, *The Passing of a Great Queen,* 3.
484   **"It is like a roof being off a house to think of an England Queenless":** January 19, 1901, Benson Diary, Magdalene College Library, Cambridge, vol. 5, 1900–1901, 130.
484   **"One went about feeling as if one had cheated at cards":** Baring, *The Puppet Show of Memory,* 215–16.
484   **silently raised their hats and sighed:** Housman, *The Unexpected Years,* 221.

485 **in rags of crêpe:** A comment made by Beatrice Webb, cited in Wolffe, *Great Deaths,* 242.

485 **"It is a real, personal grief":** "I am sure our hearts are all *one* today in thinking of our dear, dear Mother Queen, the mother of her people, dutiful faithful, courageous. One feels as if one had lost a dear friend. Everybody is crying, & people's blinds are drawn down. It is a real, personal grief. They cannot understand, I am sure, on the Continent, the sorrow we feel, but how wonderful is this electric thrill of love & sorrow through her whole Empire." Jordan, *Josephine Butler,* 285.

485 **"We all felt, publicly, at first, quite motherless":** Edel, *Henry James: Selected Letters,* 328–29.

485 **do something "to show that one cares":** Bostridge, *Florence Nightingale,* 518.

485 **"Intense crowd, never saw anything like it, all silent":** Nicholson, *A Victorian Household,* 184.

485 **a hush had quickly fallen over England:** Corelli, *The Passing of a Great Queen,* 46–48.

486 **"with *respect*—but *simply*":** January 26, 1897, Instructions for Burial, RA, VIC/MAIN/F/23/1-9a, 12–16, 18–37.

486 **"not by undertakers":** January 26, 1897, Memorandum by Queen Victoria, RA, VIC/MAIN/F/23/1-9a, 12–16, 18–37.

486 **and opened only upon her death:** Sir James Reid, notebooks, vol. 2 (1881–83), Reid Family Archives, Lanton Tower, Lanton.

487 **discreetly arranged over the gauze:** These instructions were kept in her maid's pocket, at all times, and now are in the archives of Sir James Reid, the doctor who was with Victoria when she died.

487 **arranged the contents of the queen's coffin with her ladies:** Reid carefully recorded the details of her death. Lady Reid said Victoria's last words to him were, "I will do anything you like." Susan Reid to Mary, i.c., Mrs. John F. Reid, January 26, 1901, Reid Family Archives, Lanton Tower, Lanton.

487 **"like a marble statue":** Susan Reid to Mrs. Reid, January 25, 1901, Reid Family Archives, Lanton Tower, Lanton.

488 **the stock market closed for a day:** RA, VIC/MAIN/F/23/32: clipping from *The Times,* February 2, 1901: "Today the financial and commercial exchanges of New York will be closed as a mark of respect and sympathy . . . [a] pause in the busy life of New York."

488 **"the greatest number of The True Believers in the world":** Wolffe, *Great Deaths,* 229.

488 **said the Indians thought of her almost as a saint:** Ibid.

488   **"who is worshipped as the Adya-Sakti of our [Hindu] mythology"**: Ibid., 230.

488   **"the good angel who saved us from destruction"**: Ibid., 231.

489   **"became curiously suggestive of the supreme widow"**: Wells, *Experiment in Autobiography,* 27.

489   **"some of their roughness & contempt of women"**: Jordan, *Josephine Butler,* 285.

489   **"ambition to become empress over self"**: Quoted in Longford, *Victoria R.I.,* 504.

489   **"any American Woman to occupy the Presidential Chair at Washington"**: Quoted in Rappaport, *Queen Victoria,* 426.

489   **"'strong-minded female out of her sphere'"**: Greenwood, *Queen Victoria,* 390–91.

490   **"women are unfitted for public duties"**: *Reynolds Newspaper,* January 27, 1901. Cited in Rappaport, *Queen Victoria,* 430; Williams, *The Contentious Crown,* 145.

491   **no black should be seen anywhere**: October 25, 1897, RA, VIC/MAIN/ F/23/1-9a.

491   **"clothed with everything to make it worse?"**: QVJ, March 6, 1873.

491   **"Why don't she put on clothes so that folks might know her?"**: Craig, "The Crowned Republic?," 173.

491   **"lovely wild & haunting country"**: QVJ, September 26, 1848.

492   **"our life can be lived till death"**: G. K. Chesterton, "Queen Victoria," 234.

492   **"for the sake of my country and dear ones"**: May 24, 1897, Duff, *Queen Victoria's Highland Journals,* 223.

492   **"in peace with all fully aware of my many faults"**: October 25, 1897, RA, VIC/MAIN/F/23/1-9a.

492   **"to which she gave her name, she remained static"**: Housman, *The Unexpected Years,* 370.

493   **something Dr. Reid made a particular point:** Dr. Reid jotted down that as the queen faded, her heart was strong and steady to the end despite physical weakness and "cerebral exhaustion." Despite the odd lapse, her mind was not clouded, Dr. Reid said, citing as evidence the fact that she could still recognize several members of her family until minutes before her death. Sir James Reid, Medical Report, January 23, 1901, Reid Family Archives, Lanton Tower, Lanton.

Bibliography

Primary Sources

In the writing of this book, I have drawn upon material from manuscript collections, archives, and libraries in England, America, Germany, and Australia. In the Royal Archives, Windsor Castle, Berkshire, England, I read letters to and from Victoria and her husband, children, prime ministers, secretaries, ministers, friends, and members of the royal household. I walked repeatedly through the rooms she lived in at Osborne House on the Isle of Wight, as well as at Windsor Castle, Buckingham Palace, and Balmoral Castle in Scotland. Osborne House is virtually unchanged from the moment Victoria died, and is still crammed with mementoes, with sculptures of baby's limbs, snippets of children's hair, paintings commissioned by a young, wealthy husband and wife.

Victoria has left many millions of words behind. Happily for the researcher, her journals are now available online. A century ago, the Herculean task of editing her letters was carried out by Arthur Christopher Benson and Viscount Esher, followed by George Earle Buckle. Her letters to her eldest daughter are kept at Friedrichshof, near Frankfurt in Germany, and managed by the Kurhessische Hausstiftung, the family foundation of the House of Hesse. Roger Fulford spent the years between 1964 and 1981 editing them; Agatha Ramm produced the final volume in 1991.

Other material was drawn from collections including the following:

Aberdeen Papers, British Library Manuscripts Collection, St. Pancras, London

Althorp Papers, Correspondence with Sir Henry Ponsonby, Private Secretary to Queen Victoria, many on behalf of the Queen, British Library

Ayrton papers, British Library

Arthur Benson Diary, Magdalene College Library, Cambridge England.

British Library Newspaper Collections, Colindale Avenue, London, England

Diaries of Lady Katherine Clarendon, Clarendon Papers, MSS Eng. E. 2122-5, Bodleian Library Special Collection

Conroy Family Collection Papers, Balliol College, Oxford

Lord Cross papers, British Library

Benjamin Disraeli correspondence with Queen Victoria, Western Manuscripts, MSS Disraeli, NRA 842 Disraeli, Bodleian Library Special Collection

Empress Frederick Letters, Kurhessische Hausstiftung, Schloss Fasanerie, Eichenzell, Germany

Ernest II, Duke of Saxe-Coburg, Staatsarchiv Coburg, Germany

Gladstone Papers, including correspondence with Queen Victoria and her private secretaries 1845–94, British Library

Sir William Harcourt, Correspondence with Queen Victoria 1880–81, MS Harcourt dep. 365; and 1882–83, MS Harcourt dep. 2 Bodleian Library Special Collection

Archives of Princess Dorothea von Lieven, British Library Manuscript Collections

Princess Dorothea von Lieven letters to Marie Mallet Repository, Balliol College, Oxford

Marie Mallet Archives, Lady in Waiting, Balliol College, Oxford

Morier Family Papers, K1/4/4, 1866–72, Queen Victoria's letters to General Peel, Balliol College, Oxford

Nightingale Papers Vol XII, Add. MSS 45750, British Library

Peel Papers, British Library

Queen Victoria Collection, Kensington Palace, London, England

Queen Victoria's "Album Consolativum," British Library

James Reid Papers, Reid Family Archives, Lanton Tower, Lanton, Scotland

Yvonne Ward, PhD dissertation, "Editing Queen Victoria: How Men of Letters Constructed the Young Queen," Borchardt Library at La Trobe University in Bundoora, Australia

Lady Waterpark's diary as Lady in Waiting to Queen Victoria, 1865–1891, British Library

Women's Suffrage file, Add. 74952, Jubilee appeal: 1897, British Library

Journals and Articles

Anderson, Nancy Fix. "Cousin Marriage in Victorian England." *Journal of Family History* 11, no. 2 (September 1986): 285–301.

Arnstein, Walter L. "Queen Victoria's Diamond Jubilee." *The American Scholar* 66, no. 4 (Autumn 1997): 591–97.

Baker, Kenneth. "George IV: A Sketch." *History Today* 55 (2005). historytoday.com/kenneth-baker/george-iv-sketch.

Beachy, Robert. "The German Invention of Homosexuality." *The Journal of Modern History* 82, no. 4, Science and the Making of Modern Culture (December 2010): 801–38.

Behlmer, George K. "The Gypsy Problem in Victorian England." *Victorian Studies* 28, no. 2 (1985): 231–53.

Berridge, Virginia. "Queen Victoria's Cannabis Use: Or, How History Does and Does Not Get Used in Drug Policy Making." *Addiction Research and Theory* 11 (2003): 213–15.

Brown, Catherine. "Henry James and Ivan Turgenev: Cosmopolitanism and Croquet." *Literary Imagination* 15, no. 1 (2013): 109–23. doi:10.1093/litimag/imt014.

Brumberg, Joan Jacobs. "Chlorotic Girls, 1870–1920: A Historical Perspective on Female Adolescence." *Child Development* 53 (1982): 1468–77. doi:10.2307/1130073.

Craig, David M. "The Crowned Republic? Monarchy and Anti-Monarchy in Britain, 1760–1901." *The Historical Journal* 46, no. 1 (March 2003): 167–85. doi:10.1017/S0018246X02002893.

DeLuca, Geraldine. "Lives and Half-Lives: Biographies of Women for Young Adults." *Children's Literature in Education* 17, no. 4 (1986): 241–52.

Demos, John, and Virginia Demos. "Adolescence in Historical Perspective." *Journal of Marriage and Family* 31 (1969): 632–38. doi:10.2307/349302.

Evans, Richard J. "The Victorians: Empire and Race." Lecture delivered at Gresham College, April 11, 2011. gresham.ac.uk/lectures-and-events/the-victorians-empire-and-race.

Frith, John. "Syphilis—Its Early History and Treatment Until Penicillin and the Debate on Its Origins." *Journal of Military and Medical Health* 20, no. 4 (December 2012): 49–58. search.informit.com.au/documentSummary;dn -395151977487523;res-IELHEA.

Gosse, Edmund. "The Character of Queen Victoria." *Quarterly Review* 193 (January–April 1901): 301–37.

Grant, Susan-Mary. "New Light on the Lady with the Lamp." *History Today* 52, no. 9 (September 2002): 11–17.

Groneman, Carol. "Nymphomania: The Historical Construction of Female Sexuality." *Signs* 19, no. 2 (1994): 337–67.

Grosvenor, Bendor. "Dear John." *History Today* 55, no. 1 (January 2005).

Heesom, Alan. "The Coal Mines Act of 1842, Social Reform, and Social Control." *The Historical Journal* 24, no. 1 (March 1981): 69–88. doi: http://dx.doi .org/10.1017/S0018246X00008037.

Jay, Elisabeth. "'Mrs. Brown' by Windsor's Other Widow." *Women's Writing* 6, no. 2 (1999): 191–200. doi: 10.1080/09699089900200066.

Kerr, C. B. "The Fortunes of Haemophiliacs in the Nineteenth Century." *Medical History* 7, no. 4 (October 1963): 359–70. doi: 10.1017/S0025727300028829.

King, Kathryn R., and William W. Morgan. "Hardy and the Boer War: The Public Poet in Spite of Himself." *Victorian Poetry* 17, nos. 1 and 2 (Spring–Summer 1979): 66–83.

Kuhn, William. "Sexual Ambiguity in the Life of Disraeli." *Gay and Lesbian Review Worldwide* 13, no. 4 (2006): 16–18.

Larsson, S. Anders. "Life Expectancy of Swedish Haemophiliacs." *Journal of Haematology* 59 (1985): 593–602. doi: 10.1111/j.1365-2141.1985.tb07353.x.

Levine, Philippa. "Venereal Disease, Prostitution, and the Politics of Empire: The Case of British India." *Journal of the History of Sexuality* 4, no. 4 (1994): 579–602.

Linton, E. Lynn. "The Judicial Shock to Marriage." *The Nineteenth Century* 29 (May 1891): 691–700.

Maercker, Andreas, and John Lalor. "Diagnostic and Clinical Considerations in Prolonged Grief Disorder." *Dialogues in Clinical Neuroscience* 14, no. 2 (June 2012): 167–76.

Morton, Tom. "Jewel in the Crown." *Frieze* no. 66 (April 2002).

"Notes of the Month." *Civil Engineer and Architect's Journal* 15 (1852): 159–60.

Pearce, Brian Louis, et al. "Queen Victoria's Golden Jubilee 1887." *Journal of the Royal Society of Arts* 135 (July 1987): 573–97.

Peters, Timothy J., and D. Wilkinson. "King George III and Porphyria: A Clinical Re-Examination of the Historical Evidence." *History of Psychiatry* 21, no. 1 (2010): 3–19.

Plunkett, John. "Of Hype and Type: The Media Making of Queen Victoria 1837–1845." *Critical Survey* 13, no. 2 (Summer 2001): 7–25.

Prigerson, Holly G., et al. "Prolonged Grief Disorder: Psychometric Validation of Criteria Proposed for DSM-V and ICD-11." *PLoS Medicine* 6, no. 8 (August 2009): e1000121. doi: 10.1371/journal.pmed.1000121.

"Protected Cradles." *Household Words,* 2:31 (October 26, 1850): 108–12.

Raven, Thomas F. "The Hæmorrhagic Diathesis." *The British Medical Journal* 1 (November 8, 1884): 686. archive.org/details/britishmedicaljo11884brit.

Reid, Michaela. "Sir James Reid, Bt: Royal Apothecary." *Journal of the Royal Society of Medicine* 94, no. 4 (April 2001), 194–95.

Rushton, Alan R. "Leopold: The 'Bleeder Prince' and Public Knowledge About Hemophilia in Victorian Britain." *Journal of the History of Medicine and Allied Sciences* 67, no. 3 (July 2012): 457–90. doi:10.1093/jhmas/jrr029.

Shaw, George Bernard. "The Ugliest Statue in London." *Arts Gazette* (May 31, 1919).

Shear, M. Katherine, et al. "Complicated Grief and Related Bereavement Issues for DSM-5." *Depression and Anxiety* 28, no. 2 (February 2011): 103–17. doi: 10.1002/da.20780.

Showalter, Elaine, and English Showalter. "Victorian Women and Menstruation." *Victorian Studies* 14, no. 1 (September 1970): 83–89.

St. John, Ian. "Queen Victoria as a Politician." *The Historian* 80 (December 1, 2003).

Tait, Robert Lawson. "Note on the Influence of Removal of the Uterus and Its Appendages on the Sexual Appetite." *The British Gynæcological Journal* 4 (1888): 310–17.

Taylor, Miles. "The 1848 Revolutions and the British Empire." *Past and Present* 166, no. 1 (2000): 146–180. doi:10.1093/past/166.1.146.

Tedford, Barbara Wilkie. "The Attitudes of Henry James and Ivan Turgenev Toward the Russo-Turkish War." *Henry James Review* 1, no. 3 (Spring 1980): 257–61. doi: 10.1353/hjr.2010.0139.

Turner, Trevor. "Erotomania and Queen Victoria: Or Love Among the Assassins?" *BJPsych Bulletin* 14 (1990): 224–27. doi: 10.1192/pb.14.4.224.

Tyrell, Alex. "Women's Mission and Pressure Group Politics in Britain 1825–60." *Bulletin of the John Rylands University Library of Manchester* 63, no. 1 (Autumn 1980): 194–230.

Van Wyk Smith, Malvern. "The Boers and the Anglo-Boer War (1899–1902) in the Twentieth-Century Moral Imaginary." *Victorian Literature and Culture* 31, no. 2 (September 2003): 429–46. doi: 10.17/S1060150303000226.

Walker, John West. "On Haemophilia." *The British Medical Journal* 1 (1872): 605–60.

Ward, Yvonne M. "The Womanly Garb of Queen Victoria's Early Mother-
    hood, 1840–42." *Women's History Review* 8, no. 2 (1999): 277–94. doi:10
    .1080/09612029900200211.
Weintraub, Stanley. "Exasperated Admiration: Bernard Shaw on Queen Vic-
    toria." *Victorian Poetry* 25, nos. 3–4 (Autumn–Winter 1987): 115–32.

Books

Ackroyd, Peter. *Dickens*. London: Sinclair-Stevenson, 1990.
Acton, William. *The Functions and Disorders of the Reproductive Organs in Child-
    hood, Youth, Adult Age, and Advanced Life: Considered in Their Physiological,
    Social, and Moral Relations*. London: Churchill, 1857.
Albert, Harold A. *Queen Victoria's Sister: The Life and Letters of Princess Feo-
    dora*. London: Robert Hale, 1967.
Albert, Prince Consort. *The Principal Speeches and Addresses of His Royal High-
    ness the Prince Consort*. London: John Murray, 1862.
Aldous, Richard. *The Lion and the Unicorn: Gladstone vs Disraeli*. London: Pim-
    lico, 2007.
Altick, Richard D. *Victorian People and Ideas*. New York: W. W. Norton, 1973.
Anderson, William James. *The Life of F.M., H.R.H. Edward, Duke of Kent: Il-
    lustrated by His Correspondence with the De Salaberry Family, Never Before
    Published, Extending from 1791 to 1814*. Ottawa, Ont.: Hunter, Rose, 1870.
Arnstein, Walter L. *Queen Victoria*. New York: Macmillan, 2003.
Aronson, Theo. *Heart of a Queen: Queen Victoria's Romantic Attachments*. Lon-
    don: Thistle, 2014.
———. *Victoria and Disraeli: The Making of a Romantic Partnership*. New York:
    Macmillan, 1977.
Ashdown, Dulcie. *Queen Victoria's Mother*. London: Hale, 1974.
Ashton, John. *Gossip in the First Decade of Victoria's Reign*. London: Hurst and
    Blackett, 1903.
Aspinall, A[rthur]., ed., *The Letters of King George IV, 1812–1830*. 3 vols. Cam-
    bridge: Cambridge University Press, 1938.
Aston, George, Sir. *His Royal Highness, the Duke of Connaught and Strathearn: A
    Life and Intimate Study*. London: G. G. Harrap, 1929.
Bagehot, Walter. *The English Constitution*. London: Kegan Paul, Trench, 1888.
Bahlman, Dudley W. R., ed. *The Diary of Sir Edward Walter Hamilton 1880–
    1885*. 2 vols. Oxford: Clarendon Press, 1972.
Baillie, Albert Victor, and Hector Bolitho, eds. *Letters of Lady Augusta Stanley,
    a Young Lady at Court, 1849–1863*. London: G. Howe, 1927.

Bamford, Francis, and the Duke of Wellington, eds. *The Journal of Mrs Arbuthnot.* 2 vols. London: Macmillan, 1950.

Baring, Maurice. *The Puppet Show of Memory.* Boston: Little, Brown, 1922.

Barnum, P. T. *The Life of P. T. Barnum: Written by Himself.* London: Sampson Low, 1855.

Bartley, Paula. *Prostitution: Prevention and Reform in England, 1860–1914.* London: Routledge, 2000.

Bassett, A. Tilney, ed. *Gladstone to His Wife.* London: Methuen, 1936.

Basu, Shrabani. *Victoria and Abdul: The True Story of the Queen's Closest Confidant.* Stroud, U.K.: History Press, 2011.

Bauer, Karoline. *Caroline Bauer and the Coburgs.* Edited and translated by Charles Nisbet. London: Vizetelly, 1887.

Belchem, John. "The Waterloo of Peace and Order: The United Kingdom and the Revolutions of 1848." In *Europe in 1848: Revolution and Reform,* edited by Dieter Dowe et al., translated by David Higgins, 242–57. New York: Berghahn Books, 2001.

Bell, G.K.A. *Randall Davidson, Archbishop of Canterbury.* London: Oxford University Press, 1935.

Bell, Susan Groag, and Karen M. Offen, eds. *Women, the Family, and Freedom: The Debate in Documents.* Vol. 2, 1880–1950. Stanford, Calif.: Stanford University Press, 1983.

Bennett, Daphne. *King Without a Crown: Albert, Prince Consort of England, 1819–61.* London: Pimlico, 1983.

———. *Queen Victoria's Children.* London: Victor Gollancz, 1980.

Benson, Arthur Christopher, and Viscount Esher, eds. *The Letters of Queen Victoria: A Selection from Her Majesty's Correspondence Between the Years 1837 and 1861.* 3 vols. London: John Murray, 1907.

Benson, Edward F. *Queen Victoria.* London: Longmans, Green, 1935.

Benson, Elaine. *Unmentionables: A Brief History of Underwear.* New York: Simon and Schuster, 1996.

Berridge, Virginia. *Opium and the People: Opiate Use and Drug Control Policy in Nineteenth and Early Twentieth Century England.* Rev. ed. London: Free Association Books, 1999.

Best, Geoffrey. *Mid-Victorian Britain 1851–75.* London: Fontana, 1985.

Blake, Robert. "Constitutional Monarch: The Prerogative Powers." In *The Law, Politics, and the Constitution: Essays in Honour of Geoffrey Marshall,* edited by David Butler, Robert Summers, and Vernon Bogdanor. Oxford: Oxford University Press, 1999.

———. *Disraeli.* London: Methuen, 1966.

Bloom, Clive. *Victoria's Madmen: Revolution and Alienation.* Basingstoke, U.K.: Macmillan, 2013.

Bloomfield, Georgiana. *Reminiscences of Court and Diplomatic Life.* London: Kegan Paul, Trench, 1883.

Blyth, John. *Caro: The Fatal Passion, the Life of Lady Caroline Lamb.* London: Rupert Hart-Davis, 1972.

Bogdan, Robert. *Freak Show: Presenting Human Oddities for Amusement and Profit.* Chicago: University of Chicago Press, 1990.

Bolitho, Hector. *Albert the Good and the Victorian Reign.* New York: D. Appleton, 1932.

———. *Albert: Prince Consort.* Rev. ed. London: David Bruce and Watson, 1970.

———. *A Biographer's Notebook.* London: Longmans, Green, 1950.

———, ed. *Further Letters of Queen Victoria, from the Archives of the House of Brandenburg-Prussia.* Translated by Mrs. J. Pudney and Lord Sudley. London: Thornton Butterworth, 1938.

———, ed. *The Prince Consort and His Brother: Two Hundred New Letters.* London: Cobden-Sanderson, 1933; New York: Appleton-Century, 1934.

Bolitho, Hector. *The Reign of Queen Victoria.* London: Collins, 1949.

Bondeson, Jan. *Queen Victoria's Stalker: The Strange Story of the Boy Jones.* Stroud, U.K.: Amberley, 2010.

Bostridge, Mark. *Florence Nightingale: The Making of an Icon.* New York: Farrar, Straus and Giroux, 2008.

Boswell, James. *The Life of Samuel Johnson.* London: G. Cowie, 1824.

Boykin, Edward, ed. *Victoria, Albert, and Mrs. Stevenson.* London: Rinehart, 1957.

Bradford, Sarah. *Disraeli.* London: Phoenix, 1982.

Branca, Patricia. *Silent Sisterhood: Middle-Class Women in the Victorian Home.* London: Routledge, 1975.

Brett, Maurice V., ed. *Journals and Letters of Reginald Viscount Esher.* 4 vols. London: Ivor Nicholson and Watson, 1934–1938.

Briggs, Asa. *The Age of Improvement, 1763–1867.* London: Longman, 1993.

———. *Victorian People: A Reassessment of Persons and Themes 1851–1867.* New York: Harper and Row, 1963.

Brumberg, Joan Jacobs. *The Body Project: An Intimate History of American Girls.* New York: Random House, 1997.

Bryson, Bill. *At Home: A Short History of Private Life.* London: Black Swan, 2011.

Buckle, George Earle, ed. *The Letters of Queen Victoria: A Selection from Her*

Majesty's Correspondence and Journal Between the Years 1862 and 1878. 2nd ser. 2 vols. London: John Murray, 1926–28 [1862–78].

———, ed. *The Letters of Queen Victoria: A Selection from Her Majesty's Correspondence and Journal Between the Years 1862 and 1885.* 2nd ser. London: John Murray, 1928 [1879–85].

———, ed. *The Letters of Queen Victoria: A Selection from Her Majesty's Correspondence and Journal Between the Years 1886 and 1901.* 3rd ser. 3 vols. London: John Murray, 1930–32.

Caine, Barbara. *Victorian Feminists.* Oxford: Oxford University Press, 1992.

Carlyle, Thomas. *The Collected Letters of Thomas and Jane Welsh Carlyle.* Edited by Brent E. Kinser. Durham, N.C.: Duke University Press, 1970–2016. http://carlyleletters.dukeupress.edu.

Carpenter, Mary Wilson. *Health, Medicine, and Society in Victorian England.* Victorian Life and Times. Santa Barbara, Calif.: Praeger, 2009.

Carroll, Lewis. *Through the Looking-Glass.*

Cavendish, Lady Lucy Caroline Lyttelton. *The Diary of Lady Frederick Cavendish.* Edited by John Bailey. Vol. 2. New York: Frederick A. Stokes, 1927.

Cecil, David. *The Young Melbourne and Lord M.* London: Phoenix Press, 2001.

Cecil, Lady Gwendolen. *Life of Robert, Marquis of Salisbury.* 4 vols. London: Hodder and Stoughton, 1921.

Chambers, James. *Palmerston: The People's Darling.* London: John Murray, 2005.

Charlot, Monica. *Victoria the Young Queen.* Oxford: Basil Blackwell, 1991.

Chesney, Kellow. *The Anti-Society: An Account of the Victorian Underworld.* Boston: Gambit, 1970.

———. *Crimean War Reader.* London: Frederick Muller, 1960.

Chesterton, G. K. "Queen Victoria." In *Varied Types,* 225–34. New York: Dodd, Mead, 1903. Reprint, Rockville, Md.: Wildside Press: 2005. [chapter in a book]

———. *What's Wrong with the World.* New York: Dodd, Mead, 1910.

Clarke, Isabel C. *Shelley and Byron: A Tragic Friendship.* London: Hutchinson, [1934].

Clarke, J. F. *Autobiographical Recollections of the Medical Profession.* London: J. and A. Churchill, 1876.

Clive, Mary, ed. *Caroline Clive: From the Diary and Family Papers of Mrs. Archer Clive, 1801–1873.* London: Bodley Head, 1949.

Colley, Linda. *Britons: Forging the Nation 1707–1837.* London: Vintage, 1996.

Connell, Brian. *Regina vs. Palmerston: The Private Correspondence Between Queen Victoria and Her Foreign and Prime Minister, 1837–1865.* New York: Doubleday, 1961.

Copland, James. *A Dictionary of Practical Medicine.* New York: Harper and Brothers, 1845.

Corelli, Marie. *The Passing of a Great Queen: A Tribute to the Noble Life of Victoria Regina.* New York: Dodd, Mead, 1901.

Cornwallis-West, Mrs. George. *The Reminiscences of Lady Randolph Churchill.* London: Edward Arnold, 1908.

Corti, Egon Caesar. *The English Empress: A Study in the Relations Between Queen Victoria and Her Eldest Daughter, Empress Frederick of Germany.* Translated by E. M. Hodgson. London: Cassell, 1957.

Costello, Con. *A Most Delightful Station: The British Army on the Curragh of Kildare, Ireland, 1855–1922.* Cork, Ire.: Collins Press, 1996.

Cowen, Ruth. *Relish: The Extraordinary Life of Alexis Soyer, Victorian Celebrity Chef.* London: Weidenfeld and Nicolson, 2006.

Creston, Dormer. *The Youthful Queen Victoria: A Discursive Narrative.* London: Macmillan, 1952.

Cullen, Tom A. *The Empress Brown: The Story of a Royal Friendship.* London: Bodley Head, 1969.

Darby, Elisabeth, and Nicola Smith. *The Cult of the Prince Consort.* New Haven, Conn.: Yale University Press, 1983.

Darwin, Charles R. *Evolutionary Writings.* Edited by James A. Secord. Oxford: Oxford University Press, 2010.

———. *Fertilisation of Orchids.* London: John Murray, 1862.

Davenport-Hines, Richard. *Sex, Death, and Punishment: Attitudes to Sex and Sexuality in Britain Since the Renaissance.* London: Collins, 1990.

Davidoff, Leonore, and Catherine Hall. *Family Fortunes: Men and Women of the English Middle Class, 1780–1850.* Rev. ed. London: Routledge, 2002.

Davidson, Roger, and Lesley A. Hall, eds. *Sex, Sin and Suffering: Venereal Disease and European Society Since 1870.* London: Routledge, 2001.

Dekkers, Midas. *Dearest Pet: On Bestiality.* London: Verso, 2000.

Dennison, Matthew. *The Last Princess: The Devoted Life of Queen Victoria's Youngest Daughter.* London: Phoenix, 2007.

Diamond, Michael. *Victorian Sensation.* London: Anthem Press, 2003.

Disraeli, Benjamin. *Benjamin Disraeli Letters: 1860–1864.* Edited by M. G. Wiebe et al. Toronto: University of Toronto Press, 2009.

Dixie, Lady Florence. *Gloriana; Or, The Revolution of 1900.* London: Henry and Company, 1890.

Douglass, Paul. *Lady Caroline Lamb: A Biography.* New York: Macmillan, 2004.

Downer, Martyn. *The Queen's Knight: The Extraordinary Life of Queen Victoria's Most Trusted Confidant.* London: Corgi, 2008.

Doyle, Arthur Conan. *The Great Boer War.* London: Smith, Elder, 1900. gutenberg.org/files/3069/3069-h/3069-h.htm.

Duff, David. *Albert and Victoria.* London: Frederick Muller, 1972.

———. *Edward of Kent: The Life Story of Queen Victoria's Father.* London: Frederick Muller, 1973.

———. *The Shy Princess: The Life of Her Royal Highness Princess Beatrice, the Youngest Daughter and Constant Companion of Queen Victoria.* London: Evans Brothers, 1958.

Duff, David, and Victoria, Queen of Great Britain. *Queen Victoria's Highland Journals.* Rev. ed. Exeter, U.K.: Webb and Bower, 1980.

Duff, Ethel M. *The Life Story of H.R.H. the Duke of Cambridge.* London: Stanley Paul, 1938.

Dyhouse, Carol. *Feminism and the Family in England, 1880–1939.* New York: Basil Blackwell, 1989.

Dyson, Hope, and Charles Tennyson, eds. *Dear and Honoured Lady: The Correspondence Between Queen Victoria and Alfred Tennyson.* London: Macmillan, 1969.

Ellis, Sarah Stickney. *The Wives of England: Their Relative Duties, Domestic Influence, and Social Obligations.* New York: D. Appleton, 1843.

Erickson, Carolly. *Her Little Majesty: The Life of Queen Victoria.* New York: Simon and Schuster, 1997.

Ernest II. *Memoirs of Ernest II, Duke of Saxe-Coburg-Gotha.* 4 vols. London: Remington, 1888.

Erskine, Mrs. Steuart, ed. *Twenty Years at Court: From the Correspondence of the Hon. Eleanor Stanley, Maid of Honour to Her Late Majesty Queen Victoria, 1842–1862.* London: Nisbet, 1916.

Esher, Reginald Baliol Brett, Viscount, ed. *The Girlhood of Queen Victoria: A Selection from Her Majesty's Diaries Between the Years 1832 and 1840.* 2 vols. London: John Murray, 1912.

Faroqhi, Suraiya et al. *An Economic and Social History of the Ottoman Empire: 1300–1914,* vol. 2, *1600–1914.* Cambridge: Cambridge University Press, 1997.

Farwell, Byron. *Queen Victoria's Little Wars.* New York: Harper, 1972.

Fawcett, Millicent Garrett. *Life of Her Majesty Queen Victoria.* Boston: Roberts Brothers, [1895].

Feuchtwanger, E. J. *Albert and Victoria: The Rise and Fall of the House of Saxe-Coburg-Gotha.* London: Hambledon Continuum, 2006.

Fildes, Valerie. *Wet Nursing: A History from Antiquity to the Present.* Oxford: Basil Blackwell, 1988.

Fisher, Trevor. *Prostitution and the Victorians.* New York: St. Martin's, 1997.

Flanders, Judith. *The Victorian House: Domestic Life from Childbirth to Death-bed.* London: Harper, 2004.

Forster, John. *The Life of Charles Dickens.* 2 vols. (London: Chapman and Hall, 1904

Fox, Caroline. *Memories of Old Friends: Being Extracts from the Journals and Letters.* Edited by Horace N. Pym. London: Smith, Elder, 1882.

Frost, Thomas. *The Old Showmen, and the Old London Fairs.* London: Tinsley Brothers, 1874.

Fulford, Roger. *George the Fourth.* Rev. and enl. ed. London: Gerald Duckworth, 1949.

———. *The Prince Consort.* London: Macmillan, 1949.

———. *Royal Dukes: The Father and Uncles of Queen Victoria.* New and rev. ed. London: Fontana, 1973.

———, ed. *Dearest Child: Letters Between Queen Victoria and the Princess Royal 1858–61.* London: Evans Brothers, 1964.

———, ed. *Dearest Mama: Letters Between Queen Victoria and the Crown Princess of Prussia 1861–1864.* London: Evans Brothers, 1968.

———, ed. *Your Dear Letter: Private Correspondence of Queen Victoria and the Crown Princess of Prussia 1865–1871.* New York: Scribner, 1971.

———, ed. *Darling Child: Private Correspondence of Queen Victoria and the Crown Princess of Prussia, 1871–1878.* London: Evans Brothers, 1976.

———, ed. *Beloved Mama: Private Correspondence of Queen Victoria and the German Crown Princess, 1878–85.* London: Evans Brothers, 1981.

Gardiner, John. *The Victorians: An Age in Retrospect.* London: Hambledon and London, 2002.

Gardiner, Juliet. *Queen Victoria.* London: Collins and Brown, 1997.

Gill, Gillian. *Nightingales: Florence and Her Family.* London: Sceptre, 2004.

———. *We Two: Victoria and Albert: Rulers, Partners, Rivals.* New York: Ballantine, 2010.

Gillen, Mollie. *The Prince and His Lady: The Love Story of the Duke of Kent and Madame de St. Laurent.* London: Sidgwick and Jackson, 1970.

Goldsworthy, Vesna. *Inventing Ruritania: The Imperialism of the Imagination.* New Haven, Conn.: Yale University Press, 1998.

Goodway, David. *London Chartism, 1838–1848.* Cambridge: Cambridge University Press, 2002.

Gordon, Charles George. *The Journals of Major-Gen. C. G. Gordon, C. B., at Khartoum.* London: K. Paul, Trench, 1885.

Gore, John, ed. *Creevey.* Rev. ed. London: John Murray, 1948.

———, ed. *Creevey's Life and Times: A Further Selection from the Correspondence of Thomas Creevey, Born 1768—Died 1838.* London: John Murray, 1934.

Gorham, Deborah. *The Victorian Girl and the Feminine Ideal.* Canberra: Croom Helm, 1982.

Greenwood, Grace [Sara Jane Lippincott]. *Queen Victoria: Her Girlhood and Womanhood.* New York: John R. Anderson and Henry S. Allen, 1883.

Greville, Charles. *The Great World: Portraits and Scenes from Greville's Memoirs, 1814–1860.* Edited by Louis Kronenberger. Garden City, N.Y.: Doubleday, 1963.

———. *The Greville Memoirs.* Rev. ed. Edited by Roger Fulford. London: Batsford, 1963.

———. *The Greville Memoirs.* (second part): *A Journal of the Reign of Queen Victoria from 1837 to 1852.* Edited by Henry Reeve. 3 vols. London: Longmans, Green, 1885.

———. *The Greville Memoirs: A Journal of the Reigns of King George IV and King William IV.* Edited by Henry Reeve. 2 vols. New York: D. Appleton, 1896. Reprint, London: Forgotten Books, 2013.

———. *The Greville Memoirs: A Journal of the Reigns of King George IV and King William IV and Queen Victoria.* Edited by Henry Reeve. 8 vols. London: Longmans, Green, 1888.

Grey, Charles. *The Early Years of His Royal Highness the Prince Consort.* New York: Harper and Brothers, 1867. Reprint, London: Forgotten Books, 2013.

Grey, Elizabeth. *Caroline: Passages in the Life of a Fast Young Lady.* 3 vols. London: Hurst and Blackett, 1862.

———. *The Noise of Drums and Trumpets: W. H. Russell Reports from the Crimea.* London: Longman, 1971.

Guedalla, Philip, ed. *The Queen and Mr. Gladstone.* 2 vols. London: Hodder and Stoughton, 1933.

Hall, Catherine. *White, Male and Middle-Class: Explorations in Feminism and History.* Cambridge, U.K.: Polity Press, 1992.

Halliday, Stephen. *The Great Stink of London: Sir Joseph Bazalgette and the Cleansing of the Victorian Capital.* Stroud, U.K.: Sutton, 1999.

Handford, Thomas. *Queen Victoria: Her Glorious Life and Illustrious Reign.* Atlanta: Franklin, 1901.

Hardie, Frank. *The Political Influence of Queen Victoria.* 2nd ed. London: Routledge, 1963.

Hardyment, Christina. *Dream Babies: Child Care from Locke to Spock.* London: Jonathan Cape, 1983.

Harrison, J.F.C. *Early Victorian Britain, 1832–51.* London: Fontana, 1988.

Hartley, Jenny, ed. *The Selected Letters of Charles Dickens.* Oxford: Oxford University Press, 2012.

Hastings, Flora, *Poems by the Lady Flora Hastings.* Edinburgh: William Blackwood and Sons, 1842.

Hawksley, Lucinda. *The Mystery of Princess Louise: Queen Victoria's Rebellious Daughter.* London: Chatto and Windus, 2013.

Healey, Edna. *The Queen's House: A Social History of Buckingham Palace.* London: Michael Joseph in association with the Royal Collection, 1997.

Heffer, Simon. *Power and Place: The Political Consequences of King Edward VII.* London: Weidenfeld and Nicolson, 1998.

Helsinger, Elizabeth K., Robin Lauterbach Sheets, and William Veeder, eds. *The Woman Question: Defining Voices, 1837–1883.* Vol. 1, *The Woman Question: Society and Literature in Britain and America, 1837–1883.* New York: Garland, 1983.

Hensel, Sebastian. *The Mendelssohn Family (1729–1847) from Letters and Journals.* 2nd rev. ed. Translated by Carl Klingemann and an American collaborator. 2 vols. London: Sampson Low, 1882.

Hewitt, Margaret. *Wives and Mothers in Victorian Industry.* Westport, Conn.: Greenwood Press, 1975.

Hibbert, Christopher. *Disraeli: A Personal History.* London: Harper Perennial, 2005.

———. *George III: A Personal History.* London: Viking, 1998.

———. *George IV: Regent and King, 1811–1830.* London: Allen Lane, 1973.

———. *Queen Victoria: A Personal History.* London: HarperCollins, 2000.

———. *Queen Victoria in Her Letters and Journals: A Selection.* Stroud, U.K.: Sutton, 1986.

Hilton, Boyd. *A Mad, Bad, and Dangerous People? England, 1783–1846.* Oxford: Oxford University Press, 2006.

Hobhouse, Hermione. *Prince Albert: His Life and Work.* London: Hamish Hamilton, 1983.

Hochschild, Adam. *King Leopold's Ghost: A Story of Greed, Terror, and Heroism in Colonial Africa.* London: Pan, 2002.

Holcombe, Lee. *Victorian Ladies at Work: Middle-Class Working Women in England and Wales, 1850–1914.* Newton Abbot, U.K.: David and Charles, 1973.

Hollingshead, John. *Underground London.* London: Groombridge and Sons, 1862.

Holmes, Richard. *Queen Victoria.* New York: Boussod, Valadon, 1897.

Homans, Margaret. *Royal Representations: Queen Victoria and British Culture, 1837–1876.* Chicago: University of Chicago Press, 1998.

Homans, Margaret, and Adrienne Munich, eds. *Remaking Queen Victoria.* Cambridge: Cambridge University Press, 1997.

Hoppen, K. Theodore. *The Mid-Victorian Generation, 1846–1886.* The New Oxford History of England. Oxford: Clarendon Press; New York: Oxford University Press, 1998.

Horn, Pamela. *The Victorian Town Child.* Stroud, U.K.: Sutton, 1997.

Hough, Richard, ed. *Advice to a Grand-daughter: Letters from Queen Victoria to Princess Victoria of Hesse.* London: Heinemann, 1975.

Houghton, Walter E. *The Victorian Frame of Mind, 1830–1870.* New Haven, Conn.: Yale University Press, 1985.

House, Madeline, and Graham Storey, eds., *The Letters of Charles Dickens,* Pilgrim Edition. 12 vols. Oxford: Clarendon Press; New York: Oxford University Press, 1965–2002.

Housman, Laurence. *The Unexpected Years.* London: Jonathan Cape, 1937.

Houston, Gail Turley. *Royalties: The Queen and Victorian Writers.* Charlottesville: University Press of Virginia, 1999.

Howard, Michael. *The Franco-Prussian War: The German Invasion of France, 1870–1871.* London: Routledge, 2001.

Howell, Philip. *Geographies of Regulation: Policing Prostitution in Nineteenth-Century Britain and the Empire.* Cambridge: Cambridge University Press, 2009.

Hudson, Katherine. *A Royal Conflict: Sir John Conroy and the Young Victoria.* London: Hodder and Stoughton, 1994.

Hughes, Kathryn. *George Eliot: The Last Victorian.* London: Fourth Estate, 1998.

Hunt, Leigh. *The Old Court Suburb: Or, Memorials of Kensington, Regal, Critical and Anecdotical.* London: Hurst and Blackett, 1855.

Isba, Anne. *Gladstone and Women.* London: Hambledon Continuum, 2006.

Jackman, Sophie, and Hella S. Haasse, eds. *A Stranger in the Hague: The Letters of Queen Sophie of the Netherlands to Lady Malet, 1842–1877.* Durham, N.C.: Duke University Press, 1989.

Jackson, Patrick. *Harcourt and Son: A Political Biography of Sir William Harcourt, 1827–1904.* Madison, N.J.: Fairleigh Dickinson University Press, 2004.

Jagow, Kurt, ed. *Letters of the Prince Consort, 1831–1861.* Translated by E.T.S. Dugdale. London: John Murray, 1938.

Jalland, Patricia. *Death in the Victorian Family.* Oxford: Oxford University Press, 1996.

Jalland, Patricia, and John Hooper, eds. *Women from Birth to Death: The Female Life Cycle in Britain 1830–1914.* Brighton, U.K.: Harvester, 1986.

James, Henry. *Henry James: Selected Letters.* Edited by Leon Edel. Cambridge, Mass.: Belknap Press of Harvard University Press, 1987.

Jenkins, Elizabeth. *Lady Caroline Lamb*. London: Sphere Books Limited, 1972.

Jenkins, Roy. *Gladstone*. London: Pan, 2002.

———. *Sir Charles Dilke: A Victorian Tragedy*. Rev. ed. London: Collins, 1965.

Jerrold, Clare. *The Married Life of Queen Victoria*. London: G. Bell and Sons, 1913.

———. *The Widowhood of Queen Victoria*. London: Eveleigh Nash, 1916.

Jordan, Jane. *Josephine Butler*. London: John Murray, 2001.

Juste, Théodore, ed. *Memoirs of Leopold I, King of the Belgians*. Translated by Robert Black. 2 vols. London: Sampson Low, Son, and Marston, 1868.

King, Greg. *The Last Empress: The Life and Times of Alexandra Feodorovna, Tsarina of Russia*. New York: Carol, 1994.

———. *Twilight of Splendor: The Court of Queen Victoria During Her Diamond Jubilee Year*. Hoboken, N.J.: John Wiley and Sons, 2007.

Kipling, Rudyard. *Rudyard Kipling's Verse: Inclusive Edition, 1885–1919*. Garden City, N.Y.: Doubleday, Page, 1919. archive.org/stream/rudyard kiplings00compgoog#page/n390/mode/2up.

Kuhn, William M. *Democratic Royalism: The Transformation of the British Monarchy, 1861–1914*. Studies in Modern History. New York: St Martin's, 1996.

———. *Henry and Mary Ponsonby: Life at the Court of Queen Victoria*. London: Duckworth, 2002.

———. *The Politics of Pleasure: A Portrait of Benjamin Disraeli*. London: Free Press, 2006.

Kuper, Adam. *Incest and Influence: The Private Life of Bourgeois England*. Cambridge, Mass.: Harvard University Press, 2009.

Lady of the Court, A. *Victoria's Golden Reign: A Record of Sixty Years as Maid, Mother, and Ruler*. London: Richard Edward King, 1899.

Lamb, Lady Caroline. *Glenarvon*. London: J. M. Dent, 1995.

Lambert, Angela. *Unquiet Souls: The Indian Summer of the British Aristocracy, 1880–1918*. London: Macmillan, 1984.

Lamont-Brown, Raymond. *John Brown: Queen Victoria's Highland Servant*. Stroud, U.K.: Sutton, 2000.

Langland, Elizabeth. *Nobody's Angels: Middle-Class Women and Domestic Ideology in Victorian Culture*. Ithaca, N.Y.: Cornell University Press, 1995.

Lavalette, Michael, ed. *A Thing of the Past?: Child Labour in Britain in the Nineteenth and Twentieth Centuries*. Liverpool: Liverpool University Press, 1999.

Leapman, Michael. *The World for a Shilling: How the Great Exhibition of 1851 Shaped a Nation*. London: Review, 2002.

Lee, Sidney. *Queen Victoria: A Biography*. New York: Macmillan, 1903.

Lee, Stephen. *Aspects of British Political History, 1815–1914*. London: Routledge, 1994.

Legg, J. Wickham. *A Treatise on Haemophilia, Sometimes Called the Hereditary Haemorrhagic Diathesis.* London: H. K. Lewis, 1872.

Leonard, Richard L. *The Great Rivalry: Disraeli and Gladstone.* London: I. B. Tauris, 2013.

Levine, Philippa. *Prostitution, Race, and Politics: Policing Venereal Disease in the British Empire.* New York: Routledge, 2003.

Lieven, Dorothea, Princess. *Correspondence of Princess Lieven and Earl Grey.* Edited and translated by Guy Le Strange. 3 vols. London: R. Bentley, 1890.

Loeb, Lori Anne. *Consuming Angels: Advertising and Victorian Women.* New York: Oxford University Press, 1994.

Longford, Elizabeth, ed. *Louisa, Lady in Waiting: The Personal Diaries and Albums of Louisa, Lady in Waiting to Queen Victoria and Queen Alexandra.* London: Jonathan Cape, 1979.

―――. *The Oxford Book of Royal Anecdotes.* Oxford: Oxford University Press, 1989.

―――. *Queen Victoria: Born to Succeed.* Stroud, U.K.: History Press, 2009.

―――. *Victoria R.I.* London: Pan Books, 1966.

Loudon, Irvine. *Death in Childbirth: An International Study of Maternal Care and Maternal Mortality, 1800–1950.* Oxford: Oxford University Press, 1992.

Lutyens, Mary, ed. *Lady Lytton's Court Diary 1895–1899.* London: Rupert Hart-Davis, 1961.

Lyttelton, Sarah Spencer. *Correspondence of Sarah Spencer, Lady Lyttelton, 1787–1870.* Edited by the Hon. Mrs. Hugh Wyndham. London: John Murray, 1912.

Magnus, Philip. *Gladstone: A Biography.* London: John Murray, 1954.

―――. *King Edward the Seventh.* London: John Murray, 1964.

Mallet, Victor, ed. *Life with Queen Victoria: Marie Mallet's Letters from Court 1887–1901.* London: John Murray, 1868.

Marcus, Steven. *The Other Victorians: A Study of Sexuality and Pornography in Mid-Nineteenth-Century England.* London: Weidenfeld and Nicolson, 1966.

Marlow, Joyce. *The Oak and the Ivy: An Intimate Biography of William and Catherine Gladstone.* New York: Doubleday, 1977.

Marples, Morris. *Wicked Uncles in Love.* London: Michael Joseph, 1972.

Martin, Robert Bernard. *Enter Rumour: Four Early Victorian Scandals.* London: Faber and Faber, 1962.

Martin, Theodore. *The Life of His Royal Highness the Prince Consort.* 5 vols. London: Smith, Elder, 1875–80.

Martineau, Harriet. *The Collected Letters of Harriet Martineau.* Edited by Deborah Anna Logan. 5 vols. London: Pickering and Chatto, 2007.

————. *Harriet Martineau's Autobiography*. Edited by Maria Weston Chapman. Boston: James R. Osgood, 1877.

————. *A History of the Thirty Years' Peace, A.D. 1816–1846*. 4 vols. London: George Bell and Sons, 1877.

Mason, Michael. *The Making of Victorian Sexuality*. Oxford: Oxford University Press, 1995.

Matson, John. *Dear Osborne: Queen Victoria's Family Life in the Isle of Wight*. London: Hamish Hamilton, 1978.

Matthew, H.C.G. *Gladstone: 1809–1898*. Oxford: Oxford University Press, 1997.

Matthew, H.C.G., and K. D. Reynolds. "Victoria (1819–1901)." In *Oxford Dictionary of National Biography*. Oxford University Press, 2004; online ed., May 2012. doi:10.1093/ref:odnb/36652.

Maxwell, Herbert. *The Creevey Papers: A Selection from the Correspondence and Diaries*. 2 vols. London: John Murray, 1905.

————. *Life and Letters of George William Frederick, Fourth Earl of Clarendon, K.G., G.C.B.* 2 vols. London: Edward Arnold, 1913.

Mayhew, Henry. *London Labour and the London Poor*. Selected by Victor Neuburg. London: Penguin, 1985.

————. *Mayhew's London, Being Selections from "London Labour and the London Poor" by Henry Matthew*. Edited by Peter Quennell. London: Pilot Press, [1949].

McClintock, Mary Howard. *The Queen Thanks Sir Howard: The Life of Major-General Sir Howard Elphinstone, V.C., K.C.B., C.M.G., by His Daughter, Mary Howard McClintock*. London: John Murray, 1945.

McDonald, Lynn, ed. *Florence Nightingale: An Introduction to Her Life and Family*. Vol. 1 of *The Collected Works of Florence Nightingale*. Waterloo, Ont.: Wilfrid Laurier University Press, 2001. Baltimore: Project MUSE, 2012, 2013.

————, ed. *Florence Nightingale on Society and Politics, Philosophy, Science, Education and Literature*. Vol. 5 of *The Collected Works of Florence Nightingale*. Waterloo, Ont.: Wilfrid Laurier University Press, 2003.

————, ed. *Florence Nightingale's European Travels*. Vol. 7 of *The Collected Works of Florence Nightingale*. Waterloo, Ont.: Wilfred Laurier University Press, 2004.

McHugh, Paul. *Prostitution and Victorian Social Reform*. London: Croom Helm, 1980.

Miller, Betty. *Elizabeth Barrett to Miss Mitford: The Unpublished Letters of Elizabeth Barrett Browning to Mary Russell Mitford*. London: John Murray, 1954.

Miller, J. *Prostitution Considered in Relation to Its Cause and Cure*. Edinburgh: Sutherland and Knox, 1859.

Mitchell, Leslie George. *Lord Melbourne, 1779–1848*. Oxford: Oxford University Press, 1997.

Mitchell, Sally. *Daily Life in Victorian England*. Westport, Conn.: Greenwood Press, 1996.

Monypenny, William F., and George Earle Buckle. *The Life of Benjamin Disraeli, Earl of Beaconsfield*. 6 vols. London: J. Murray, 1910–20.

More, Hannah, *The Works of Hannah More*. 2 vols. New York: Harper and Brothers, 1840.

Morley, John. *The Life of William Ewart Gladstone*. 3 vols. New York: Macmillan, 1904.

Morris, Jan. *Farewell the Trumpets: An Imperial Retreat*. New York: Penguin, 1978.

———. *Heaven's Command: An Imperial Progress*. London: Faber and Faber, 2003.

———. *Pax Britannica: The Climax of an Empire*. New York: Penguin, 1968.

Morris, R. J., and Richard Rodger, eds. *The Victorian City: A Reader in British Urban History, 1820–1914*. London: Longman, 1993.

Moyle, Franny. *Constance: The Tragic and Scandalous Life of Mrs. Oscar Wilde*. London: John Murray, 2012.

Murphy, James H. *Abject Loyalty: Nationalism and Monarchy in Ireland During the Reign of Queen Victoria*. Washington, D.C.: Catholic University of America Press, 2001.

Murphy, Paul Thomas. *Shooting Victoria: Madness, Mayhem, and the Rebirth of the British Monarchy*. London: Head of Zeus, 2013.

Murray, John Fisher. *The Court Doctor Dissected*. London: William Edward Painter, 1839.

Nead, Lynda. *Myths of Sexuality: Representations of Women in Victorian Britain*. Oxford: Basil Blackwell, 1988.

Neale, Erskine. *Life of H.R.H. Edward, Duke of Kent: Father of Queen Victoria*. London: Richard Bentley, 1850.

Nelson, Michael. *Queen Victoria and the Discovery of the Riviera*. London: I. B. Tauris, 2001.

Neville, Peter. *Mussolini*. 2nd ed. London: Routledge, 2014.

Nicholson, Shirley. *A Victorian Household*. London: Barrie and Jenkins, 1988.

Nightingale, Florence. *Cassandra: An Essay*. Introduction by Myra Stark. Old Westbury, N.Y.: Feminist Press, 1979.

Normington, Susan. *Lady Caroline Lamb: This Infernal Woman*. London: House of Stratus, 2002.

Packard, Jerrold M. *Victoria's Daughters.* New York: St. Martin's, 1998.

Pakenham, Thomas. *The Boer War.* London: Weidenfeld and Nicolson, 1979.

Pakula, Hannah. *An Uncommon Woman: The Empress Frederick, Daughter of Queen Victoria, Wife of the Crown Prince of Prussia, Mother of Kaiser Wilhelm.* London: Phoenix, 2006.

Parker, Charles Stuart, ed. *Sir Robert Peel: From His Private Papers.* 3 vols. London: John Murray, 1899.

Parkhouse, Valerie B. *Memorializing the Anglo-Boer War of 1899–1902.* Kibworth Beauchamp, U.K.: Troubador, 2015.

Parry, E. J., ed. *The Correspondence of Lord Aberdeen and Princess Lieven.* 2 vols. London: Royal Historical Society, 1938.

Paterson, Michael. *Voices from Dickens' London.* Cincinnati: David and Charles, 2006.

Patton, Mark. *Science, Politics and Business in the Work of Sir John Lubbock: A Man of Universal Mind.* Farnham, U.K.: Ashgate, 2007.

Paxman, Jeremy. *The Victorians: Britain Through the Paintings of the Age.* London: BBC Books, 2009.

Pearce, Edward, and Deanna Pearce, eds. *The Diaries of Charles Greville.* London: Pimlico, 2011.

Pearsall, Ronald. *The Worm in the Bud: The World of Victorian Sexuality.* Stroud, U.K.: Sutton, 2003.

Perkin, Harold. *The Origins of Modern English Society.* 2nd ed. London: Routledge, 2002.

Picard, Liza. *Victorian London: The Life of a City 1840–1870.* London: Weidenfeld and Nicolson, 2005.

Pilbeam, Pamela. *Madame Tussaud and the History of Waxworks.* London: Hambledon and London, 2003.

Plowden, Alison. *The Young Victoria.* Stroud, U.K.: History Press, 1981.

Plunkett, John. *Queen Victoria: First Media Monarch.* Oxford: Oxford University Press, 2003.

Ponsonby, Arthur. *Henry Ponsonby, Queen Victoria's Private Secretary, His Life from His Letters.* London: Macmillan, 1943.

———. *Queen Victoria.* Great Lives. London: Duckworth, 1933.

Ponsonby, D. A. *The Lost Duchess: The Story of the Prince Consort's Mother.* London: Chapman and Hall, 1958.

Ponsonby, Frederick, ed. *Letters of the Empress Frederick.* London: Macmillan, 1928.

———. *Sidelights on Queen Victoria.* New York: Sears Publishing, 1930.

Ponting, Clive. *The Crimean War.* London: Chatto and Windus, 2004.

Pope-Hennessy, Una. *Charles Dickens 1812–1870.* London: The Reprint Society, 1947.

Porter, Roy. *London: A Social History.* London: Penguin, 2000.

Potts, D. M., and W.T.W. Potts. *Queen Victoria's Gene.* Stroud, U.K.: Sutton, 1995.

Pudney, John. *The Smallest Room: A Discreet Survey Through the Ages.* London: Michael Joseph, 1954.

Quennell, Peter, ed. *The Private Letters of Princess Lieven to Prince Metternich, 1820–1826.* New York: E. P. Dutton, 1938.

Ramm, Agatha, ed. *Beloved and Darling Child: Last Letters Between Queen Victoria and Her Eldest Daughter, 1886–1901.* Stroud, U.K.: Sutton, 1998.

Ramsden, John. *Don't Mention the War: The British and the Germans Since 1890.* London: Abacus, 2007.

Rappaport, Helen. *Magnificent Obsession: Victoria, Albert and the Death That Changed the Monarchy.* London: Windmill Books, 2012.

———. *No Place for Ladies: The Untold Story of Women in the Crimean War.* London: Arum, 2007.

———. *Queen Victoria: A Biographical Companion.* Santa Barbara, Calif.: ABC-CLIO, 2003.

Reid, Michaela. *Ask Sir James: The Life of Sir James Reid, Personal Physician to Queen Victoria and Physician-in-Ordinary to Three Monarchs.* London: Hodder and Stoughton, 1987.

Reynolds, Helen. *A Fashionable History of Underwear.* Oxford: Heinemann Library, 2003.

Rhodes James, Robert. *Albert, Prince Consort: A Biography.* London: Hamish Hamilton, 1983.

———. *Rosebery.* London: Phoenix, 1995.

Richardson, Joanna. *Victoria and Albert: A Study of a Marriage.* London: J. M. Dent and Sons, 1977.

Richardson, John. *The Annals of London: A Year-by-Year Record of a Thousand Years of History.* London: Cassell, 2001.

Richardson, Ruth. *Dickens and the Workhouse: Oliver Twist and the London Poor.* Oxford: Oxford University Press, 2012.

Ridley, Jane. *Bertie: A Life of Edward VII.* London: Chatto and Windus, 2012.

Roberts, Andrew. *Salisbury: Victorian Titan.* London: Phoenix, 2006.

Robinson, Lionel G. *Letters of Dorothea, Princess Lieven, During Her Residence in London, 1812–1834.* London: Longmans, Green, 1902.

Rowbotham, Judith. *Good Girls Make Good Wives: Guidance for Girls in Victorian Fiction.* Oxford: Blackwell, 1989.

Rowse, A. L. *Windsor Castle in the History of the Nation.* London: Weidenfeld and Nicolson, 1974.

Rusk, John. *The Beautiful Life and Illustrious Reign of Queen Victoria.* Boston: James H. Earle, 1901.

Ruskin, John. *Sesame and Lilies: Two Lectures Delivered at Manchester in 1864.* London: Smith, Elder, 1865.

Sanders, Valerie. *The Tragi-Comedy of Victorian Fatherhood.* Cambridge: Cambridge University Press, 2009.

Sandwell, Ruth. W. "Dreaming of the Princess: Love, Subversion, and the Rituals of Empire in British Columbia, 1882." In *Majesty in Canada: Essays on the Role of Royalty,* edited by Colin Coates, 44–67. Toronto: Dundurn Group, 2006.

Sanger, George. *Seventy Years a Showman.* London: MacGibbon and Kee, 1966.

Schama, Simon. *A History of Britain: The Fate of Empire, 1776–2000.* London: Hyperion, 2002.

Schlicke, Paul. *Dickens and Popular Entertainment.* London: Unwin Hyman, 1988.

Scott, Sir Walter. *Journal.* 2 vols. Edinburgh: David Douglas, 1828.

Seaman, L.C.B. *Victorian England: Aspects of English and Imperial History, 1837–1901.* London: Routledge, 2002.

Shannon, Richard. *Gladstone: Heroic Minister, 1865–1898.* Vol. 2 of *Gladstone.* London: Allen Lane, 1999.

Shaw, George Bernard. *Collected Letters.* Edited by Dan H. Laurence. Vol. 2, *1898–1910.* London: Reinhardt, 1972. capitadiscovery.co.uk/sussex-ac/items/85550.

———. *Mrs. Warren's Profession.* Rockville, Md.: Wildside Press, 2009.

Shoemaker, Robert. *Gender in English Society, 1650–1850: The Emergence of Separate Spheres?* London: Longman, 1998.

Shorter, Clement K. *Charlotte Brontë and Her Circle.* New York: Dodd, Mead, 1896.

Shorter, Edward. *A History of Women's Bodies.* New York: Basic Books, 1982.

Showalter, Elaine. *The Female Malady: Women, Madness, and English Culture, 1830–1980.* London: Virago, 1987.

Siegel, Dina. *The Mazzel Ritual Culture, Customs and Crime in the Diamond Trade.* New York: Springer, 2009.

Smith, Victoria Ruth. "Constructing Victoria: The Representation of Queen Victoria in England, India, and Canada, 1897–1914." Ph.D. diss., Rutgers University, 1998. DAI 1998 59(1): 286-A. DA9823210. Fulltext: ProQuest Dissertations and Theses.

Sotnick, Richard. *The Coburg Conspiracy: Royal Plots and Manoeuvres.* London: Ephesus, 2008.

Spongberg, Mary. *Feminizing Venereal Disease: The Body of the Prostitute in Nineteenth-Century Medical Discourse.* London: Macmillan, 1997.

St. Aubyn, Giles. *Queen Victoria: A Portrait.* London: Sceptre, 1991.

Steinberg, Jonathan. *Bismark: A Life.* New York: Oxford University Press, 2011.

Stewart, Jules. *Albert: A Life.* London: I. B. Tauris, 2012.

Stockmar, Christian Friedrich von. *Memoirs of Baron Stockmar.* [Compiled from His Papers] by His Son Baron E. Stockmar. Edited by F. Max Müller. Translated by G[eorgiana] A[delaide] M[üller]. 2 vols. London: Longmans, Green, 1873.

Stoughton, John. *Windsor: A History and Description of the Castle and the Town.* London: Ward and Co., 1862.

Strachey, Lytton. *Queen Victoria.* New York: Harcourt, Brace, 1921.

Strachey, Lytton, and Roger Fulford, eds. *The Greville Memoirs, 1814–1860.* 8 vols. London: Macmillan, 1938.

Strafford, Alice Byng, ed. *Leaves from the Diary of Henry Greville.* 4 vols. London: Smith, Elder, 1883–1904.

Strickland, Agnes. *Queen Victoria from Her Birth to Her Bridal.* 2 vols. London: Henry Colburn, 1840.

Stuart, Dorothy Margaret. *Dearest Bess: The Life and Times of Lady Elizabeth Foster.* London: Methuen, 1955.

———. *The Mother of Victoria: A Period Piece.* London: Macmillan, 1941.

Sudley, Lord, ed. and trans. *The Lieven-Palmerston Correspondence, 1828–1856.* London: John Murray, 1943.

Surtees, Virginia. *Charlotte Canning: Lady-in-Waiting to Queen Victoria and Wife of the First Viceroy of India 1817–1861.* London: John Murray, 1975.

Sweet, Matthew. *Inventing the Victorians.* London: Faber and Faber, 2001.

Tait, Lawson. *Diseases of Women.* 2nd ed. New York: W. Wood, 1879.

Tappan, Eva March. *In the Days of Queen Victoria.* Boston: Lee and Shepard, 1903.

Taylor, A.J.P. *The Struggle for Mastery in Europe 1848–1918.* Oxford: Clarendon Press, 1954.

Thackeray, William Makepeace. "George the Fourth." In *The Four Georges.* Vol. 27 of *The Works of William Makepeace Thackeray.* New York: Harper and Brothers, 1898.

Thompson, Dorothy. *Queen Victoria: The Woman, the Monarchy, and the People.* New York: Pantheon, 1990.

Thompson, E.P. *The Making of the English Working Class.* New York: Vintage, 1966.

Thompson, F.M.L. *The Rise of Respectable Society: A Social History of Victorian Britain, 1830–1900.* London: Fontana, 1988.

Tisdall, E.E.P. *Queen Victoria's John Brown: The Life Story of the Most Remarkable Royal Servant in British History.* London: Stanley Paul, 1938.

Tisdall, E.E.P. *Queen Victoria's Private Life, 1837–1901.* London: Jarrolds, 1961.

Tocqueville, Alexis de. *Recollections: The French Revolution of 1848.* Edited by J. P. Mayer and A. P. Kerr. Translated by George Lawrence. New York: Doubleday, 1970.

Tomalin, Claire. *Charles Dickens: A Life.* London: Viking, 2011.

———. *Thomas Hardy: The Time-Torn Man.* London: Viking, 2006.

Tosh, John. *A Man's Place: Masculinity and the Middle-Class Home in Victorian England.* New Haven, Conn.: Yale University Press, 1999.

Tuer, Andrew White, and Charles E. Fagan. *The First Year of a Silken Reign.* London: Field and Tuer, 1887.

Uglow, Jennifer S. *Elizabeth Gaskell: A Habit of Stories.* London: Faber and Faber, 1994.

Ulrich, Melanie Renee. "Victoria's Feminist Legacy: How Nineteenth-Century Women Imagined the Queen." Ph.D. diss., University of Texas, Austin, 2005. hdl.handle.net/2152/1745. DAI 2006 66(8): 2942-A. DA3184538. Fulltext: ProQuest Dissertations and Theses.

Vallone, Lynne. *Becoming Victoria.* New Haven, Conn.: Yale University Press, 2001.

———. *Disciplines of Virtue: Girls' Culture in the Eighteenth and Nineteenth Centuries.* New Haven, Conn.: Yale University Press, 1995.

Vanden Bossche, Chris R. "Moving Out: Adolescence." In *A Companion to Victorian Literature and Culture.* Edited by Herbert F. Tucker. Oxford: Blackwell, 1999.

Van der Kiste, John. *Queen Victoria's Children.* Stroud, U.K.: History Press, 2013.

———. *Sons, Servants & Statesmen: The Men in Queen Victoria's Life.* Stroud, U.K.: Sutton, 2006.

Villiers, George. *A Vanished Victorian, Being the Life of George Villiers, Fourth Earl of Clarendon, 1800–1870.* London: Eyre and Spottiswoode, 1938.

Vincent, John, ed. *Disraeli, Derby and the Conservative Party: Journals and Memoirs of Edward Henry, Lord Stanley [Derby], 1849–1969.* Brighton, U.K.: Harvester Press, 1978.

Vovk, Justin C. *Imperial Requiem: Four Royal Women and the Fall of the Age of Empires.* Bloomington, Ind.: iUniverse Star, 2014.

Wake, Jehanne. *Princess Louise: Queen Victoria's Unconventional Daughter.* London: Collins, 1988.

Walkowitz, Judith R. *City of Dreadful Delight: Narratives of Sexual Danger in Late-Victorian London.* Chicago: University of Chicago Press, 1992.

Walkowitz, Judith. *Prostitution and Victorian Society: Women, Class, and the State.* Cambridge: Cambridge University Press, 1980.

Walsh, Walter. *The Religious Life and Influence of Queen Victoria.* London: Swann Sonnenschein, 1902.

Ward, Yvonne M. *Censoring Queen Victoria: How Two Gentlemen Edited a Queen and Created an Icon.* London: Oneworld, 2014.

————. "Editing Queen Victoria: How Men of Letters Constructed the Young Queen." Ph.D. diss., La Trobe University, 2004. arrow.latrobe.edu .au:8080/vital/access/manager/Repository/latrobe:35628?exact=creator%3A %22Ward%2C+Yvonne.%22.

————. "1848: Queen Victoria and the Cabinet D'Horreurs." In *1848: The Year the World Turned?* Edited by Kay Boardman and Christine Kinealy, 173–88. Newcastle upon Tyne, U.K.: Cambridge Scholars Publishing, 2007.

Warner, Marina. *Queen Victoria's Sketchbook.* London: Macmillan, 1979.

Weinreb, Ben, and Christopher Hibbert, eds. *The London Encyclopaedia.* Rev. ed. London: PaperMac, 1993.

Weintraub, Stanley. *Disraeli: A Biography.* New York: Dutton, 1993.

————. *Uncrowned King: The Life of Prince Albert.* New York: Free Press, 1997.

————. *Victoria.* London: John Murray, 1996.

Wells, H. G. *Experiment in Autobiography: Discoveries and Conclusions of a Very Ordinary Brain (Since 1866).* London: V. Gollancz, 1934.

White, Jerry. *London in the Nineteenth Century: "A Human Awful Wonder of God."* London: Jonathan Cape, 2007.

Whitehead, Cameron, "The Bulgarian Horrors: Culture and the International History of the Great Eastern Crisis, 1876–1878." PhD diss., University of British Columbia, 2014. doi:10.14288/1.0167317.

Wilde, Oscar. *Collected Poems of Oscar Wilde.* Edited by Anne Varty Ware. Hertfordshire, U.K.: Wordsworth Editions, 2000.

Williams, Kate. *Becoming Queen.* London: Arrow, 2009.

Williams, Richard. *The Contentious Crown: Public Discussion of the British Monarchy in the Reign of Queen Victoria.* Aldershot, U.K.: Ashgate, 1997.

Wilson, A. N. *Eminent Victorians.* London: BBC Books, 1989.

————. *The Victorians.* New York: W. W. Norton, 2002.

Wise, Dorothy, ed. *Diary of William Tayler, Footman, 1837.* London: The St. Marylebone Society, 1987.

Wise, Sarah. *The Blackest Streets: The Life and Death of a Victorian Slum.* London: Bodley Head, 2008.

Wohl, Anthony. *Endangered Lives: Public Health in Victorian Britain*. London: J. M. Dent, 1983.

——, ed. *The Victorian Family: Structure and Stresses*. London: Croom Helm, 1978.

Wolffe, John. *Great Deaths: Grieving, Religion, and Nationhood in Victorian and Edwardian Britain*. Oxford: Oxford University Press, 2000. prism.talis.com/sussex-ac/items/671687.

Woodham-Smith, Cecil. *The Great Hunger: Ireland 1845–1849*. London: Hamish Hamilton, 1962.

——. *Queen Victoria: Her Life and Times*. London: Cardinal, 1975.

Woods, Robert. *The Demography of Victorian England and Wales*. Cambridge: Cambridge University Press, 2000.

Woodward, Ernest. *The Age of Reform, 1815–1870*. 2nd ed. Oxford: Clarendon Press, 1988.

Worsley, Lucy. *Courtiers: The Secret History of the Georgian Court*. London: Faber and Faber, 2010.

Wright, Marcus Joseph. *Sketch of Edward Augustus, Duke of Kent*. Richmond, Va.: William E. Jones, printer, 1889. hdl.loc.gov/loc.gdc/scd0001.00206909626.

Wright, Patricia. *The Strange History of Buckingham Palace: Patterns of People*. Stroud, U.K.: Wrens Park, 1999.

Zeepvat, Charlotte. *Prince Leopold: The Untold Story of Queen Victoria's Youngest Son*. Stroud, U.K.: Sutton, 1999.

Zetland, Lawrence John Lumley Dundas, Marquis of. *Lord Cromer: Being the Authorized Life of Evelyn Baring, First Earl of Cromer*. London: Hodder and Stoughton, 1932.

Ziegler, Philip. *King William IV*. London: Collins, 1971.

——. *Melbourne: A Biography of William Lamb, 2nd Viscount Melbourne*. London: Collins, 1976.

Illustration Credits

Insert

Sir William Beechey, *Prince Edward, Duke of Kent and Strathearn* (1818). © National Portrait Gallery, London.

Richard Rothwell, *Victoria, Duchess of Kent* (c. 1832). Royal Collection Trust © Her Majesty Queen Elizabeth II, 2016. Photo: Bridgeman Images.

Stephan Poyntz Denning, *Victoria* (1823). Dulwich Picture Gallery, London, UK. Photo: Bridgeman Images.

Henry Tanworth Wells, *Victoria Regina* (1887). Royal Collection Trust © Her Majesty Queen Elizabeth II, 2016. Photo: Bridgeman Images.

Victoria and Albert, 1851. Photo: Bettmann/Getty Images.

Thomas Sully, *Victoria* (1838). Metropolitan Museum of Art, New York. Bequest of Francis T. Sully Darley, 1914. Acc. No. 14.126.1. metmuseum.org.

John Partridge, *Prince Albert* (1840). Royal Collection Trust © Her Majesty Queen Elizabeth II, 2016. Photo: Bridgeman Images.

Queen Victoria, *Prince Albert* (1840), by Royal Collection Trust © Her Majesty Queen Elizabeth II, 2016. Photo: Bridgeman Images.

Franz Xaver Winterhalter, *Victoria* (1859). Royal Collection Trust © Her Majesty Queen Elizabeth II, 2016. Photo: Bridgeman Images.

Princess Victoria as Crown Princess of Prussia (c. 1865). Photo: akg-images.

Victoria with her four eldest children (1854), by Roger Fenton. Royal Collection Trust © Her Majesty Queen Elizabeth II, 2016.

Victoria and Albert with their children outside Osborne House (1854). Royal Collection Trust © Her Majesty Queen Elizabeth II, 2016

Albert Edward, Prince of Wales (1861. Photo: Archive Photos/Getty Images.

Queen Victoria, *Princess Beatrice* (1859). Royal Collection Trust © Her Majesty Queen Elizabeth II, 2016. Photo: Bridgeman Images

Henry Courtney Selous, *The Opening of the Great Exhibition* (1851–52. Private Collection. Photo: Bridgeman Images.

Carl Friedrich Koepke, *Louise, Baroness Lehzen* (c. 1842). Royal Collection Trust © Her Majesty Queen Elizabeth II, 2016. Photo: Bridgeman Images.

After George Dawe, *Leopold I, King of the Belgians* (c. 1844–50). Royal Collection Trust © Her Majesty Queen Elizabeth II, 2016. Photo: Bridgeman Images.

Sir Edwin Henry Landseer, *William Lamb, 2nd Viscount Melbourne* (1836). © National Portrait Gallery, London

Henry Pickersgill, *Sir John Conroy* (1837). Private Collection. Photo: Bridgeman Images.

Alfred, Lord Tennyson (c. 1880). Photo: PVDE / Bridgeman Images.

Franz Xaver Winterhalter, *Sir Robert Peel* (1844) (detail). Royal Collection Trust © Her Majesty Queen Elizabeth II, 2016. Photo: Bridgeman Images.

J. Woods, after Hablot Browne and R. Garland, *Buckingham Palace and Marble Arch* (1837). Royal Collection Trust © Her Majesty Queen Elizabeth II, 2016. Photo: Bridgeman Images.

Joseph Nash, *The Queen Driving Out with Louis-Philippe from the Quadrangle at Windsor Castle, 10 October 1844*. Royal Collection Trust © Her Majesty Queen Elizabeth II, 2016. Photo: Bridgeman Images.

Osborne House illustration from T. Nelson, *English Scenery*, 1889. Private Collection. Photo: Look and Learn / Bridgeman Images.

August Becker, *Balmoral* (1865). Royal Collection Trust © Her Majesty Queen Elizabeth II, 2016. Photo: Bridgeman Images.

Sir Edwin Landseer, *Queen Victoria Landing at Loch Muick* (1850). Royal Collection Trust © Her Majesty Queen Elizabeth II, 2016. Photo: Bridgeman Images.

Queen Victoria, *A Highland Landscape* (1859). Royal Collection Trust © Her Majesty Queen Elizabeth II, 2016. Photo: Bridgeman Images.

Albert in later years (undated photograph). Photo: Bettmann / Getty Images.

Edward Henry Corbould, *Memorial Portrait of the Prince Consort* (1863). Royal Collection Trust © Her Majesty Queen Elizabeth II, 2016. Photo: Bridgeman Images.

Princess Louise, *Queen Victoria Dreaming of Her Reunion with Prince Albert* (1862). Royal Collection Trust © Her Majesty Queen Elizabeth II, 2016. Photo: Bridgeman Images.

Victoria's daughters grouped around a bust of their father (1862), by William Bambridge. Royal Collection Trust © Her Majesty Queen Elizabeth II, 2016.

Victoria on horseback at Balmoral (1863), by George Washington Wilson. Private Collection. Photo: Bridgeman Images.

John Brown with the dogs Corran, Dacho, Rochie and Sharp (1871). Libby Hall Collection, Bishopsgate Institute, London.

Benjamin Disraeli, 1st Earl of Beaconsfield (1878). Photo: Pictures from History/Cornelius Jabez Hughes/Bridgeman Images.

William Ewart Gladstone (c. 1890). Photo: Chris Hellier/Alamy.

Bruno Strassberger, *Kaiser Wilhelm II* (c. 1890s). Historisches Museum der Stadt, Vienna. Photo: Bridgeman Images.

Victoria and Princess Beatrice (c. 1880), by W. & D. Downey. Photo: Granger Collection/Alamy.

Victoria and Edward, Prince of Wales, in Coburg (1895). Photo: adoc-photos.

Victoria and Abdul Karim, "The Munshi" (c. 1894). The Illustrated London News Picture Library, London. Photo: Bridgeman Images.

Heinrich von Angeli, *Victoria* (1899). Royal Collection Trust © Her Majesty Queen Elizabeth II, 2016. Photo: Bridgeman Images.

A Jubilee Portrait of Queen Victoria Laughing (1887). Photo: TopFoto.

Sir James Reid, Physician-in-Ordinary to the Queen (1901). Private collection. Photo: Look and Learn / Illustrated Papers Collection / Bridgeman Images

Victoria's funeral procession passes Wellington Arch (1901). Private collection. Photo: Bridgeman Images.

Index

ABOUT THE AUTHOR

JULIA BAIRD is a journalist, broadcaster, and author based in Sydney, Australia. She is a columnist for the *International New York Times* and *The Sydney Morning Herald,* and host of *The Drum* on ABC TV (Australia). Her writing has appeared in *Newsweek, The New York Times, The Philadelphia Inquirer, The Guardian, The Washington Post, The Monthly,* and *Harper's Bazaar*. She has a Ph.D. in history from the University of Sydney. In 2005, Baird was a fellow at the Joan Shorenstein Center on Media, Politics, and Public Policy at Harvard University, after which she spent several years as deputy editor of *Newsweek* in New York.

Facebook.com/JuliaBairdOnline
@bairdjulia

ABOUT THE TYPE

This book was set in Granjon, a modern recutting of a type-face produced under the direction of George W. Jones (1860–1942), who based Granjon's design upon the letterforms of Claude Garamond (1480–1561). The name was given to the typeface as a tribute to the typographic designer Robert Granjon (1513–89).